BATTLES

of the

AMERICAN REVOLUTION
1775-1781

including

BATTLE MAPS and CHARTS

of the

AMERICAN REVOLUTION

WASHINGTON

on the St Memin Graven in possesion of J.Carson Brevoort Esq.

BATTLES

of the

AMERICAN REVOLUTION

1775-1781

including

BATTLE MAPS and CHARTS

of the

AMERICAN REVOLUTION

by

HENRY B. CARRINGTON

PROMONTORY
◄═PRESS═►
New York

Publisher's Note:

Battles of the American Revolution 1775-1781
was originally published in 1877.
Battle Maps and Charts of the American Revolution
was originally published in 1881.
Both books are combined in this edition with material from the
1881 book printed on the reverse side of each map.

ISBN 0-88394-007-8
LC No. 73-89252

Outline of the Atlantic Coast

THE geographical features of the theatre of war define its critical and strategic elements. General Howe expressed his estimate of the impending struggle when he succ eded Gage, October 10th, 1774, by assuming command "in all the Atlantic Colonies, from Nova Scotia to West Florida, inclusive."

Lord Dartmouth had previously advised that New York be made the base of British operations, at the expense of abandoning Massachusetts; and when Washington assumed command of the American army before Boston, July 3d, 1775, he urged forward the siege and all other operations, with view to the earl est practicable occupation of New York. Reference to the map explains their purpose.

From the usual formation of armies by right, centre and left divisions, there is derived an analogous g ographical separation into right, centre and left zones, or belts, of operation. Thus, from New York as a base, there is developed, as the right zone, New England which could be completely isolated from the *centre* (New Jersey and Pennsylvania) whenever the force at New York had naval control of Hudson river and Long Island sound.

The adequate occupation of Chesapeake bay, by a force from New York, would alike isolate the South from the centre, and prevent inter-support. This was true British policy

A wise counter strategy, devolved upon the American commander the necessity of holding the central zone, so firmly, as to threaten New York, support the other zones, and thwart all efforts, permanently to isolate, and thereby conquer in detail, New England and the South. His location amid the fastnesses of New Jersey, except while at Valley Forge, when Howe held Philadelphia in force, as an advanced base, and the garrison of New York was too feeble for offensive action, enabled him so well to fulfill the best strategic conditions of ultimate success, that New England was abandoned by Clinton, New York imperilled, and Yorktown was captured. Incursions and depredations only irritated the people.

A classification by teachers and pupils, of the events of the war, by their relations to these zones and their effect in separating, or associating the different sections, in opposition to Great Britain, will insure a fair basis for a judgment upon the character of the soldiers of that war.

The substantial unity of the colonies in their assertion of independence, coupled with the fact that, when Boston was evacuated, there remained no effective British garrison upon Colonial soil, requires that the war be considered as one between two independent States, and that the aggressiveness of Great Britain be treated as an invasion, for conquest.

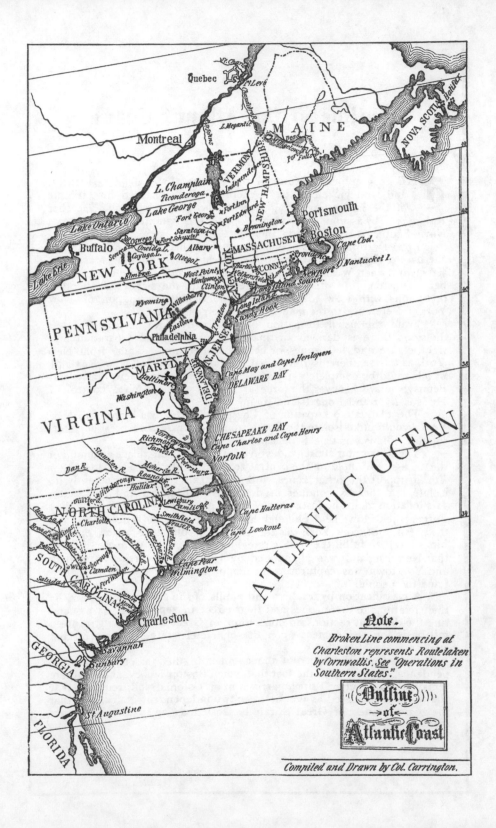

Quebec

Montreal

MAINE

NOVA SCOTIA

L. Champlain
Ticonderoga
Lake George
Fort George
VERMONT
NEW HAMPSHIRE
Portsmouth
Boston
Cape Cod.

Lake Ontario
Buffalo
Oswego
Seneca
Cayuga L.
Oneida L.
Albany
Saratoga
Fort Schuyler
MASSACHUSETTS
Bennington

Lake Erie
NEW YORK
Elmira
Otsego L.
West Point
Montgomery
Clinton
CONN.
Hartford
Wethersfield
New Haven
Providence
Newport
Nantucket I.
Long Island Sound

Wyoming
Wilkesbarre
Long Island
Sandy Hook

PENNSYLVANIA
Easton
Trenton

Philadelphia

MARYLAND
Baltimore
Cape May and Cape Henlopen
DELAWARE BAY

Washington

VIRGINIA
Richmond
York R.
James R.
CHESAPEAKE BAY
Cape Charles and Cape Henry
Norfolk

Dan R.
Staunton R.
Hillsborough
Meherin R.
Roanoke R.
Petersburg
Halifax

Guilford
N. CAROLINA
Lewisburg
Pamlico
Smithfield
Newbern
Neuse R.
Cape Hatteras
Cape Lookout

Charlotte
Catawba R.
King's Mt.
Great Peedee R.
Northampton
Cape Fear

SOUTH CAROLINA
Broad R.
Winnsborough
Camden
Fort Watson
Cape Fear
Wilmington

Saluda R.
Santee
Monk's

Charleston

GEORGIA
Savannah
Bunbury

St Augustine

FLORIDA

ATLANTIC OCEAN

Note.
Broken Line commencing at
Charleston represents Route taken
by Cornwallis. See "Operations in
Southern States".

Outline
of
Atlantic Coast

Compiled and Drawn by Col. Carrington.

CONTENTS.

CONTENTS.

TOPOGRAPHICAL ILLUSTRATIONS.

Summary of Events

The War for American Independence

Had its true policy declared by Gen. NATHANIEL GREENE, then in camp before Boston, during June, 1775. It was this, in brief:

(SEE CARRINGTON'S "BATTLES OF THE AMERICAN REVOLUTION," pp. 80-91.)

1. One General-in-Chief.
2. Enlistments, for the war.
3. Bounties, for families of soldiers in the field.
4. Service, to be general, regardless of place of enlistment.
5. Money loans to be effected, equal to the demands of the war.
6. A Declaration of Independence, with the pledge of all the resources, of each Colony, to its support.

Original Army Organization

GEORGE WASHINGTON
Commander-in-Chief

HORATIO GATES
Adjutant General

Major Generals
(RANKING AS NAMED)

ARTEMAS WARD   CHARLES LEE   PHILIP SCHUYLER
ISRAEL PUTNAM

Brigadier Generals
SETH POMEROY, RICHARD MONTGOMERY, DAVID WOOSTER
WILLIAM HEATH, JOSEPH SPENCER
JOHN THOMAS,   NATHANIEL GREENE.

Declaration of Independence
JULY 4th, 1776

Surrender of Cornwallis
OCTOBER 19th, 1781

Cessation of Hostilities
OFFICIALLY DECLARED, APRIL 18th, 1783

GREETING.

I**T is eminently proper that an effort to give fresh distinctness to facts and principles should be introduced to the public by some outline of the method adopted.**

The author has accepted the reports of commanding officers as to all matters peculiarly within their personal knowledge, unless some serious conflict of opinion, or marked discrepancy in statements of fact, has compelled resort to other authority.

Anecdotes, whether authentic or traditional, as well as incidents affecting the personal habits or life, of officers engaged in the Revolutionary War, are excluded from consideration. So long as military negligence, errors of judgment, or of execution, and incompetency, or the correlative excellencies, can be determined from operations and results, without the introduction of special criticism, it has been more agreeable to the author, and more consonant with the spirit of this undertaking, to submit all issues to that simple test.

The Bibliographical Table, at the end of the volume, embraces the list of authors consulted.

No statements of fact have been made without responsible authority.

No map has been completed without the careful study of those heretofore published, and of many never in print at all, and a personal examination of the battle-fields, or consultation with those who have made such examination.

In the correction of river courses, as in the " Plan of the Battle of Monmouth," reference has been made to modern atlases and actual surveys, geological or otherwise.

The delineation of surface is not designed to furnish a technical *exactness of detail*, but aims to so impress the reader with the objective of the text, that there may be that real recognition of the battle-fields and battle movements which topographical illustration alone can supply.

The inducements which led the author to preface the historical record with simple outlines of military science are elsewhere stated.

While it has appeared best to avoid technical terms as a general rule, there has been ever present, as the prime incentive to the whole work, the assurance that the education of the times, and the dependence of all authority upon the people for its ultimate protection, enforce upon the people the consideration of military principles, as well as of military history. A nation which values a patriotic record, and has the nerve to sustain that record, is never harmed by an intelligent idea of " The principles which underlie the national defence." The dedication of this volume is therefore the key to its mission.

The impulse which started this venture upon the sea of thought has gained fresh breath from the sympathy of scholar and soldier. The words of Bancroft, Woolsey, Day, Evarts, Brinsmade and Crane, and of Generals Sherman, Townsend, and Humphreys, have imparted courage, as well as zest, to both study and execution.

If nothing new has been evolved out of fresh readings of many authors, there will be *this* satisfaction to the citizen or stranger—that the substantial issues of arms which marked the war of American Revolution have been compressed into a single volume; that the topographical illustrations are in harmony with all fair historical narratives of that war, and that they so reconcile the reports of opposing commanders as to give some intelligible idea of the battle-issues themselves.

It would be indeed rude not to thank the British and French authorities, American Legations abroad, and many eminent scholars of both countries, as well as gentlemen in charge of American public libraries, who extended courtesies, facilitated research, and expressed their warm sympathy, during visits in behalf of the enterprise *now floating out of port to meet its destiny*.

It would be a violation of honor not to testify of obligation to one who, long since, visited every battle-field herein discussed, who obtained from survivors of the revolutionary struggle the data which otherwise would have had no record, and who, as the only living link which connects times present with times *a hundred years ago*—has invited the author to share the benefit of his labors, and has made possible much that must have been crude or imperfect but for the generous coöperation of BENSON J. LOSSING.

CHAPTER I.

THE REVOLUTIONARY EPOCH.

THE soldiers of 1775–1781 were not deficient in military skill and ready appliance of the known enginery and principles of war. In spite of modern improvements in gunnery, transportation, and hospital adjustments, and in all that relates to pure Logistics, there has been no substitution of agencies that has involved other principles than those which belonged to those campaigns. Then, as now, every contest was largely determined by the skillful application of the laws which underlie all human success. Even the introduction of steam-propulsion has not suspended the laws of Nature, which laws, for all time, have made sport of those who go upon the sea in ships. The repeated storms which diverted British and French fleets from their projected course, or those which affected the operations on land at times of real crisis, are not without their equally decisive counterparts in all wars of early or later date. It is an instructive fact, in military as in civil life, to illustrate the inability of human foresight to force the future to its feet and then compel its issues. No more then than since did the negligence of a picket-guard, the recklessness of a rash leader, or the waste of a commissary, prove fatal to well-advised movements and blast a fair promise of real fruit. Then, as since, one gallant defense at an unexpected point, one error of guides, one precipitancy of an issue not fully ripe, determined that issue adversely.

Then, as since, injustice to an antagonist, or an undue confidence in attack or defense, brought dismal defeat. Then, as ever, the violation of the claims of humanity, contempt for conscientious opponents and attempts to use force beyond a righteous limit, worked its fatal reaction ; and then, as since, the interference of cabinets, or the substitution of extrinsic for vital issues, worked the discomfiture of wise military plans on either side of the struggle. It is equally true that in the face of the more sharply defined social grades then existing the general spirit of the warfare was honorable to both parties; and the issues between Washington and Howe, or other generals of responsible command, as disclosed in their correspondence, were as courteously discussed as are like issues now.

Even with the modern miracle of journalism, which fastens its imprint upon the minutest word or fact in the career of men and nations, there is as much of license, of hyperbole and partisan abuse, as in those days when the mother country and the colonies engaged in a deadly wrestle. Jealousies of rank, thirst for office, aspersions of character, and suspicions of all who attained success, had their place then, as since; and as a century of time has revived only the more agreeable features of that struggle, it is not to be overlooked that Howe and Clinton and Cornwallis, as well as Washington and his generals, had their heartaches as well as their laurels, and administered their trusts under responsibilities and burdens never surpassed.

The war itself was no sudden rebellion against authority, nor a merely captious and arbitrary assertion of the popular will. It was even then admitted by the noblest of English statesmen that the English government, as so tersely stated by Mr. Bancroft, " made war on the life of her own life."

The era of facts, therefore, which marks this volume, was the fruit of English thought relating back to Magna-Charta.

Humanity made constant progress in the assertion of normal rights, and the passing issues which ripened into American independence only indicated the culmination of those issues to a more substantial vindication. Prerogative of church and state, the centralization of property and authority, the irresponsibility to the people of men who asserted absolutism by virtue of ancestry, or the so-called *divine right*, had involved England in bloody wars, alienated faithful subjects, induced domestic disorders, and made natural, as certain, the separation of the American colonies.

Emancipation from Papal dictation did not bring a corresponding grant of genuine religious liberty to the earnest people.

Human conscience, bound to its Author by intrinsic obligation, which no human authority can long control or evade, asserted its power over the lives and conduct of sober-minded men.

The bonds which confined its expression, and drove devout Christian men and women to secret conclave and worship, became too stringent for those who obeyed God as the Supreme Arbiter of life present and life future.

The presumption that the governed should have a voice in shaping the policy which exercised control, was solved by its positive averment as a principle; and the reluctance of authority to bend its measures to meet this human craving and rightful demand, only quickened the sentiment of resistance to every evasion or defiance of the right. Every domestic struggle which marked the centuries of British growth, had this warp for every woof.

Invisible, but present! despised, but quick with life, the new element was giving robustness and nerve to the British people, and both shape and endurance to the British constitution.

The state itself, as it began to feel the spur of the new impulse, began also to render tribute to the true patriotism which a high moral and religious obligation alone develops.

The interregnum of Cromwell was resplendent with national glory; and the enthusiasm of free men began to testify in clear and significant tones of the greatness of a people, who so freely contributed of life and treasure to dignify and maintain a genuine national liberty.

Ripe statesmen and hereditary officials, alike, saw the drift of human thought; but, as this pulse-beat strengthened, the hatred of innovation, and cultivated doubt of the capacity and nerve of the commons to mingle with and share the control of public affairs prolonged the established contempt for the commons, while intensifying the popular purpose to resist the presumption of caste and undele gated authority.

The exodus of colonists to America, was the combined fruit of this misconception of the rights of the people, and of the latent resistance which rules the life whenever the human soul makes duty its purpose, and conscience its guide.

The Puritans of New England, the Huguenots of South Carolina, and the emigrants to Maryland, alike shared in the impulse to escape from hierarchical control, and work for freedom, self-government, and the best interests of the governed. The emigration to Maryland had its small element which maintained the obligation of conscience to superior, foreign control; but the majority, who were laboring men, and independent of every such obligation, asserted their due share in giving shape to the colony, and thus its birth-hour was accompanied by the same birth-rights which made the New England colonies memorable for all time.

A century, and then a half century more, passed by, while the dynastic element persistently failed to realize the fact, that the colonies were energized by principles which belonged to man by right, and which no physical forms could long restrain.

They were the principles which, in fact, made Great Britain great. The Anglo-Saxon blood was directing the heart-beats, but it had the *oxygen of a higher life*, and a bolder, if not a fiercer, activity. Prompt to meet obligation and render legitimate homage to lawful authority, it brooked no trammels which partook of oppression or injustice; still hopeful, and for a long time confident, that sagacious statesmen would so control and shape dynastic power as to admit of genuine loyalty without the loss of self-respect.

The old French war of 1756, brought home to the colonies some very heavy responsibilities, and these they met with a free expenditure of blood and treasure. But it taught them how much they must cultivate their own resources, and how little could be realized from the throne, in the assurance of a pervasive and lasting peace.

Sacrifices brought only partial equivalents, so that ordinary taxes took the color of enforced tribute. Slowly but surely the procrastination, uncertainty, and prevarications of officials compelled the subjects to repeated demonstrations of their wishes, and of their claim to be represented in the councils of the nation, until the Revolution enforced their will and determined their future.

After the lapse of more than a century, the great English Nation and the American Republic review that period of struggle with equal satisfaction, as the evidence of the superintending control of a Higher Authority, and both nations accept the results of the war and the developments since realized, as the best possible conclusion of the ordeal undergone, and the best pledge to the world of the spirit with which both nations shall aim to dignify national life, while honoring the rights and highest interests of every individual life.

The power and glory of England, are not in her army or navy, or her displays of physical force, so much as in the development of all her people of all classes, in the culture and ripeness which peace and freedom involve. And the American Republic, which dismissed to their farms and merchandise a million men, when their use was needless, while unarmed, is, by the compensations of intelligence and industry, armed to the teeth against all unrighteous intervention or violence.

It is the earnest man of peace, calmly pursuing life's ends, rendering justice and thus deserving justice, who, in the aggregate, makes a state respected ; and thus let the future develop both mother country and its first born, so that the world shall render to each the homage which *every true man* deserves !

CHAPTER II.

LEXINGTON AND CONCORD. THEIR LESSONS.

THE skirmishes of Lexington and Concord were such pulsations of an excited people as not to have a proper place in a strict Battle Record, except as they mark the progress of public sentiment toward the maturing issue of general war.

Raw militia, jealous of the right to bear arms, and thoroughly set in purpose, to vindicate that right and all the franchises of a free people, by the extreme test of *liberty or life*, had faced the disciplined troops of Great Britain, without fear or penalty.

The quickening sentiment which gave nerve to the arm, steadiness to the heart, and force to the blow, was one of those historic expressions of human will, which over-master discipline itself. *It was the method of an inspired madness.* The onset swept back a solid column of trained soldiers, because the moral force of the energizing passion was imperative and supreme. No troops in the world could have resisted that movement. Discipline, training, and courage are exponents of real power; but there must be something more than these to enable any moderate force of armed men to cope with a people already on fire with the conviction, that the representatives of national force are employed to smother the national life. The troops themselves had a hard ordeal to undergo. Sent out to collect or destroy some munitions of war, and not to engage an enemy, they were under a restraint that stripped them of real fitness to meet so startling an issue as one of open resistance and active assault. There was a clear reluctance on their part, to use force until the first hasty delivery of fire opened hostilities.

The ill-judged policy which precipitated these memorable skirmishes was directly in the way of military success. It impaired the confidence of soldiers in their ability to maintain the impending struggle, while at the same time intensifying the fever and strengthening the nerve of the uprising commons.

Lexington and Concord were the exponents of that daring which made the resistance on Breed's Hill possible. The invincibility of discipline was shattered, when the prestige of the army went down before the rifles of farmers. The first tendency was to make those farmers too confident of the *physical strength* of *moral opinions*, and to underrate the value of an organized force. Years of sacrifice and waste, enforced an appreciation of its value; and the failures, flights, and untoward vicissitudes of many battle-fields were made their instructors in the art of war.

The military demonstration of April 19th, 1775, was but supplemental to similar movements for the suppression of the general arming, and for the seizure of guns and powder, which began in 1774.

A battery had been established on Boston Neck as early as August of that year. The citizens had refused to furnish quarters for the royal troops, and when the government, during the month of September, attempted to build public barracks, the mechanics of Boston refused to work at any price, and both artisans and laborers had to be brought from the colony of New York. Under date of August twenty-seventh, 1775, Dr. Joseph Warren wrote as follows : " As yet, we have been preserved from action with the soldiery, and we shall endeavor to avoid it until we see that it is necessary, and a settled plan is fixed on for that purpose."

The Provincial Congress that organized October twenty-sixth adopted a plan for the organization of the militia, with the express understanding that one-fourth of the aggregate force should be in readiness for service at the shortest notice. The " minute men " of the Revolution, were thus called into being.

Artemas Ward and Seth Pomeroy were chosen general officers. A concentration of military stores and arms at Concord and Worcester was formally authorized. Under date of November tenth, General Gage denounced as treasonable the proceedings of that body.

On the ninth day of February, 1776, a second Provincial Congress, " empowered and directed the Committee of Public Safety, to assemble the militia whenever it was required, to resist the execution of certain Acts of Parliament," just then promulged.

The following citizens composed that committee, viz., John Hancock, Joseph Warren, Benjamin Church, Richard Devens, Benjamin White, Joseph Palmer, Abraham Watson, Azor Orne, John Pigeon, William Heath, and Thomas Gardner.

The following "Committee of Supplies," was announced, viz., Elbridge Gerry, David Cheever, Benjamin Lincoln, Moses Gill, and Benjamin Hall.

At the same time, John Thomas and William Heath were added to the list of general officers. That legislative body went so far as to warn the people that it was, " The Christian and social duty of each individual, with a proper sense of dependence on God, to defend those rights which heaven gave them, and no one ought to take from them."

By the first day of January, 1775, the garrison of Boston had been increased to thirty-five hundred men, and mounted three hundred and seventy men as a daily guard-detail, besides a field-officers' guard of one hundred and fifty men on Boston Neck. Three brigades were organized and were officered, respectively, by Generals Lord Percy, Pigott and Jones. In November of 1774, General Gage had advised the British government, that he, " *was confident, that to begin with* an army twenty thousand strong, would in the end save Great Britain blood and treasure."

Meanwhile, the militia drilled openly, rapidly completed company organizations, and made many sacrifices to procure arms, powder and other materials of war. The Home government, in view of the serious aspect of affairs, ordered Generals Howe, Clinton, and Burgoyne to join General Gage, and announced that " ample reinforcements would be sent out, and the most speedy and effectual measures would be taken to put down the rebellion," then pronounced to already exist.

On the eighth of April, the Provincial Congress resolved to take effectual measures to raise an army, and requested the coöperation of Rhode Island, New Hampshire, and Connecticut. On the thirteenth, it voted to raise six companies of artillery, to pay them, and keep them at drill. On the fourteenth, it advised citizens to leave Boston and to remove to the country. On the fifteenth, it solemnly appointed a day for " Public Fasting and Prayer," and adjourned to the tenth day of May.

The Committee of Public Safety at once undertook the task of securing powder, cannon and small arms. A practical embargo was laid upon all trade with Boston. The garrison could obtain supplies only with great difficulty, and, as stated by Gordon, "nothing was wanting but a spark, to set the whole continent in a flame."

As a matter of military policy, the statesmanship of war, the whole drift of the Governor's conduct was not to placate, but to excite the people. It was the precursor of military failure. All demonstrations were those of force, and not those of wisdom, or comity. His purpose to seize the stores then accumulating at Concord had no indorsement of his officers or council, for he advised with neither. It was predicated upon his individual opinion, by which he afterwards sought to justify his conduct, that the show of force in the field and the arrest of leading patriots would extinguish the rebellion.

This rapid and very partial outline of events which immediately preceded the skirmishes of Concord and Lexington, is important in order to disclose the circumstances which so quickly culminated in the siege of Boston, the action on Breed's Hill, and the evacuation of the city. General Gage, as he said, communicated his plan for seizure of the stores at Concord to but one person, and yet it was soon known to Hancock and Adams, so that the colonists took prompt measures to meet the issue. When Lord Percy left Headquarters on the evening of April eighteenth, he passed a group of men, on Boston Common, and heard one man say: "The British troops have marched, but they will miss their aim." "What aim?" inquired Lord Percy, "Why, the cannon at Concord," was the reply.

The detachment, consisting of the Grenadiers of the garrison, the Light Infantry, and Major Pitcairn, of the Marines, all under command of Lieutenant Colonel Smith of the Tenth regiment of infantry, started on the night of the eighteenth, with every reason to believe that their movement was a secret to all but the Governor and themselves. Taking boats up the Charles river as far as Phipps farm, now Lechmere Point, they landed promptly, and pushed for Concord, twenty miles from Boston. The ringing of bells and the firing of small arms soon showed that the country was aroused. A messenger was sent for reinforcements. Sixteen companies of foot, and a detachment of marines, under Lord Percy, was promptly advanced to their support, uniting with them at about two o'clock in the afternoon, on their return from Concord, and making the aggregate of the entire command about eighteen hundred men.

This eventful day closed. The stores at Concord, which had not been removed, were destroyed. The casualties on the British side were seventy-three killed, one hundred and seventy four wounded, twenty six missing. The colonists lost forty-nine killed, thirty-nine wounded, and five missing.

Stedman thus sums up the result. "The events of the day on which blood was first shed, in the contest between Great Britain and her colonies, served to show that if the Americans were unacquainted with military discipline, they were not destitute of either courage or conduct, but knew well how, and dared, to avail themselves of such advantages as they possessed. A kind of military furor had by this time seized the inhabitants of the colonies. They were willing to risk the consequences of opposing in the field, their juvenile ardor to the matured strength of the parent state, and in this resolution they were encouraged to persist, by recollecting the events of the nineteenth of April, by which it appeared, according to their manner of reasoning, that in such a country as America, abounding in dangerous passes and woody defiles, the British troops, with all their valor, discipline and military skill, were not, when opposed to the Americans, so formidable as had been generally apprehended."

The promptness, coolness and moderation of Lord Percy saved the command of Lieutenant Colonel Smith. It was worn out by hard marching, and the fretful kind of warfare which decimated its ranks, and only under the escort of his command were they enabled to reach Boston in safety. It is a historical fact, that Major Pitcairn, whose reputation and character were of a high order, deeply felt the misfortune which so intimately associated his name with the affair at Lexington.

Dr. Dwight says that the expedition to Concord, "was one which in other circumstances would have been merely of little tales of wonder and woe, but it became the preface to the history of a nation, the beginning of an empire, and a theme of disquisition and astonishment to the civilized world."

The issue was joined. The siege of Boston followed. The beginning of the end began to appear in full view of many English statesmen, and thenceforth their disregarded warnings, and their unexampled assurance of sympathy with the American people, were among the most inspiring elements which sustained the struggle and assured the ultimate result.

And now, that the presentation of some of the principles which distinguished the epoch of the American Revolution and gave character as well as strength to the new State, and a brief statement as to the issue at arms which introduced the struggle have been made, the discussion of the art of war is next in order, to be followed by its application to the battle-issues themselves.

CHAPTER III.

MILITARY SCIENCE THE KEY TO MILITARY HISTORY.

IT is a prime factor in the right estimate of any historical epoch, or issue, that the data command confidence; and the value of all conclusions will be determined by the fitness with which cognate principles are applied to the events or characters unfolded.

The integrity of a narrative may indeed be verified through the absolute want of conformity to another version; but the consistency of either with a sound final judgment must depend upon the success of the effort to clear the story of all extrinsic color and stage-effect which the *locus*, or *animus* of the author has cast upon the scenes and actors. To review the battles of the American Revolution and so test their record as to impart lessons of value to the student of military science, is equally an effort to interest the general scholar; and the earnest youth who struggles to attain ripeness for true citizenship by æsthetic culture and faithful brain-work, cannot afford to break away from the examination, as from some cold and barren sphere of thought.

More than this is involved in the present discussion. History is the life-record of man, and its fruitage matures in proportion as experience evolves wisdom for the future. National history is therefore not the exclusive possession of its subject; but stands as a witness to all nations, and it is their right as well as duty to demand a just interpretation of its facts.

Patriotism that is mature and abiding, is linked with charity. Justice is embosomed with love of country. Both elements attach to an abiding record.

We measure a painting by the rules of art, and gauge a freshly invented motor by the principles applied. Thus, also, and in a truly catholic spirit, are *battles* and *battle-direction* to be estimated, and thus alone can there be developed out of human conflict some enduring product for the instruction and benefit of succeeding generations.

While all axiomatic truth is but indifferently served by many who, of necessity bow to its dicta; so a worthy purpose may fail of standard fruition through fault of the agent. The proposed discussion seeks to analyze all accessible data, and thus afford to the general student some basis for sound judgment as to the battle-fields and battle-direction of the war of the American Revolution, while applying to their elucidation those accepted principles of military science which impart value to military action.

The consideration of minor issues and isolated skirmishes is foreign to the purpose; but it is requisite, that the annual campaigns of the struggle shall obtain their legitimate sequence, and hold their intrinsic relations to the ultimate achievement of American Independence.

The swift progress of international courtesy in the direction of closer national affinities imparts signal interest to the investigation; and although an era of universal peace is not already overlapped by the hastening present, it is safe to assert that the time has come when Great Britain and the United States can pleasantly do justice to old-time valor, and welcome, as already assured, a future identity of aspiration and progress.

Other incidents peculiar to this age of general education, force the people themselves to a closer view, and wiser appreciation of military art. Great Britain already depends largely upon her organized militia for national defense. Her regular army, the nucleus for efficient expansion, is but a national police, to watch over her world-wide interests, and assure her subjects that the mother country does not neglect the rights of any who render homage.

The mobilization of Germany and the conscript system of France bear home to every household the consideration of military contingencies and military antecedents. But it is true of the United States, as of Great Britain, that the regular army has but light responsibility for domestic peace. The conservation of resources, attended by education of the masses and the wise development of industrial labor, furnish a basis of resistance to assault from without, that will wear out any antagonist which estimates its means of aggression by the numerical list of bristling bayonets which it holds in position, at the expense of civil growth.

Continental army budgets, and continental military dilation have involved one error ; and the American militia system, notwithstanding its elasticity and its prodigious expenditures of vital force in an extreme hour of national peril, has involved an equally serious error. The responsibility for military direction has been cast upon military experts exclusively ; or the attainment of high positions by the adventurer has developed the idea that any good patriot might, by easy transition, leap to a place of honorable command, and discharge its functions with eminent success.

But the philosophy of war is not exclusively within the province of the military man, and there are governing laws which translate the events of battle history, and impart to them a life and meaning well worthy the sober thought of the citizen and scholar.

Hitherto, the literature of military science has been addressed to experts only, and the world at large has been satisfied with some graphic narrative, regardless of the mental processes which evolved the results and made success possible, or assured defeat. While physics and physiology are deemed indispensable to every sound curriculum of study, the logic of war has been as listlessly and coolly ignored, as if its precepts imposed upon the time of the general scholar, and were utterly foreign to a sound education of the young men of Great Britain and the United States.

In Continental Europe, however, with a little more of theoretical instruction, the physical drill in arms has largely absorbed that industrial labor which is the life-blood of a civilized state, and the individ·uality of the citizen has been merged in the military martinet. *He may be one small cog in the vast complication of adjusted machinery, or one little nerve in the enfolding sheath, but he is not a responsible part of the controlling element that works the machine, or thrills the nerve with its vital force.*

In the United States, where military obligation is feather-light in time of peace, and hardly less in Great Britain, the assumption is ever at hand, that when a crisis shall demand the soldier, there will be found the hero and the victory.

This is trifling with grave issues. It is a very rare, if not an impossible matter in modern times, for a great war to ensue without antecedent deliberation on the part of one or both of the parties in interest. The mighty aggregate of European armies is closely related to intense brain-work, and no advocate more exhaustively anticipates the contingencies of evidence and the scope of past adjudications, than do the adepts in military science review their maps, and speculate upon the very recesses, as well as the resources of the country they purpose to attack.

It is, therefore, possible and becoming, for the educated masses of a free people to learn something of the principles which underlie the national defense. These principles have not been unfolded in due proportion and with that familiarity, which has carried those of natural science into every household. The heads of mechanics and of farmers' sons, have ached from the elaboration of some fresh invention ; and this, the fruit of independence of thought and personal action, rightly fits the demand of the times. But with all this, there is a subtle, unacknowledged sentiment, that the civil functions of the state will be smoothly and fairly performed by those in charge. This is predicated upon the fact that laws are in force, and that those laws are assured of wise and competent sanction. Here begins for military science, its starting point, its genesis. And yet, before its discussion, there is to be established certain ground-work, necessarily ignored by strictly military writers, while integral and fundamental to the general purpose in view.

Military law, while that of force, as is all police law, is founded upon the adaptation of all necessary means to meet an impending crisis, and its methods of application are controlled by that cricis. The wisdom of the statesman is only different in degree from that of the householder, and both aim after a wise constraint of offending elements, and the radication of those that are eminently just and proper.

To meet the demand adequately, wisely, and successfully, to anticipate all counter-action, and thereby assure ultimate results, is the expressive logic for personal action, municipal action, and military action.

The brain-power is banded to various shaftings. The mental processes are different, by virtue of different applications, but the prime activities are the same.

The domain of natural science has its departments and sections. It is so with all physics. And yet, to the great enigma of essential force, the military art, all sciences extend their aid. No laboratory fails of experts in its behalf. All dynamic force pays tribute to its demand. This rests upon a simple necessity. Inasmuch as offenses against society and law, require the sanction of force, so shall all appliances of art and science contribute their full measure so to perfect and apply that force as to secure to the state its integrity and safety.

Military science is, therefore, the art of employing force to vindicate or execute authority. Its offices task all possible energies, involve all possible errors, and meet all possible trials, that betide human experience. The guerilla and bandit may, through wisdom, nerve and commensurate skill become a soldier ; while the scholar, in high command, may drop the sceptre of the state which he is called to uphold, not from want of patriotic zeal, but because he is not wise in a life-and-death struggle.

In the battles of the American Revolution, illustrations of the art of war, in the more scientific, as in the more generally accepted meaning of the term, were numerous and memorable. Independently of the numbers engaged, the vast territory involved, the distances traversed with an ocean to be crossed, the consanguinity of the parties at issue, and the new political principles evoked, that battle history has peculiar value. Not a single principle put under tribute by great captains, before and since that period, failed to have its expression, and not unseldom its masterly application. The philosophy of Frederic and Jomini assert nothing beyond the skill and wisdom therein illustrated.

It is assumed that all truth which bears direct relation to a better understanding of those battles, is of value to the student. History must be placed side by side with the philosophy which interprets that history. Civil codes bear their part in the elucidation, and military science must fill its place, or the judgment will fail to reach the conclusions which convert the antecedent experience of men into safe guides for the resolution of the future. In the proposed brief discussion of military science, the purpose is to set forth only those fundamental laws and relations which will aid the reader in his judgment of the facts, inspire fresh respect for that talent which sustains the commonwealth in an hour of danger, and possibly induce a higher sense of responsibility for a fit preparation to meet all the contingencies which can come to the body politic.

In the discussion of battles and *battle-direction*, including the topographical illustration, the standard authorities of both countries have been summoned to the witness-stand, and are duly accredited.

CHAPTER IV.

APOLOGY FOR THE MILITARY ART.

THE principles of the military art, having their application in the use of force, all normal elements that shape or apply to force, in the direction of establishing or protecting the state, have their appropriate place and relations. Those principles, as already intimated, are not of necessity and exclusively professional, nor are they so much matters of discovery as the direct application of human wisdom to recognized exigencies.

All primitive questions of ethics or morals, and all discussion as to the abstract right to go to war, are merged in the actual, inevitable struggles that do and must occur.

The progress of invention has indeed developed machinery to intensify physical force and multiply its forms of action; but the essential principles have not been created; they are only more fully detected, unfolded and utilized.

The successful man, of whatever calling, must achieve that success through intimacy with the springs and modes of human action, and by use of such skill in the adjustment of plans as to meet or anticipate such action.

Mental philosophy demands as much credit for military success, as for any other success.

Geographical discovery, so called, has always had some antecedent hypothesis of the proper harmony of the physical world, and has thus been impelled to push the conviction to assurance. So with physics, whether of earth or heaven. Even the diversities of the earth's surface and all avenues of inter communication have proved as vital to military as to commercial or political relations. The art of war, in common with other science, applies sound reasoning to all possible contingencies that can come within its sphere of duty.

It shares the limitations of all finite knowledge, and is not closeted with some military bureau, nor stored in any arsenal. It inheres wherever sagacity, observation, quickness, and precision, have their best harmony and material.

Types of mind of equal strength in all those elements will drift with the circumstances of birth, or education—will seek various objectives and exhibit dissimilar manifestations, so that society, in all its civil adjustments and growth, only employs the same faculties which conserve the rights of the state, and vindicate its honor, when peril invokes the aid of sanction and a corresponding physical support. The maxims of English common law which affect civil life, and civil relations, are but accumulated experience, beyond date or memory, indicating how society may so happily and securely subsist, that the rights of the many shall be but the aggregate of individual rights.

These flow from the past, gaining volume and illumination with the centuries: but these are not older nor more consistent with human reason than are the general maxims which inspire a wise self defense, and the consequent, national defense. They flow together, one and indivisible. It is as great an error to predicate of the art of war, that it is abnormal and beyond the field of the scholar, as to treat the whole system of state and municipal politics as of immaterial concern to the individual citizen, in his comparatively passive sphere of trust and dependence.

In proportion as the citizen freely exercises his civil rights, and takes part in their establishment and perpetuation, so does it become his privilege and duty to understand, *why*, *when*, and *how*, he shall respond to their hearty support if assailed. The delegation of certain trusts to the cabinet, the bench, or the bailiff, is predicated upon the idea that these are agents of the people, duly responsible for the trusts in their charge; but the obligation to render all needed physical and moral support to the faithful discharge of the functions of their trust, is imperative in every well ordered state. These functions are performed almost automatically during peace, with but incidental friction, and under light burdens.

But the contingencies of lawlessness and violence and a consequent appeal to force are not to be ignored, because in abeyance, or out of sight.

In the state, as in the household, during wholesome peace, the supremacy of law seems to be most positive when the external display

of sanction is least prominent. *The visible whip stands for its ready use.*
There is no exception in the case of states having large armies; for
there every outlook comprehends a possible struggle, which of itself
precludes the idea of substantial peace.   There is *no rest*, and *peace
means rest from conflict*, with a corresponding devotion of personal
and national resources to permanent good.

While therefore, that sanction which is the reserve force to compel order, may not be paraded in the sight of all men, its existence
must be pervasive; and the capacity to defend or assert rights must
be coëxtensive with the ultimate value of the rights enjoyed.   Otherwise, every franchise depends alone upon outside forbearance, or that
most fickle of all elements, falsely styled *policy*. It is therefore
accepted, that all citizens have a deep concern in every primary truth
that lies in the direction of national defense, or guides their judgment
to a right estimate of the national history, as compared with that of
other nations.   If peace, with its compensations and possibilities, its
sweet domesticities and its crowning glories, be indeed the sphere
wherein man can alone secure renewal of primeval perfection, there
must be large wealth of values in those deeds of self-sacrifice and
heroism which hasten its advent.

While the assurance of penalty acts as a preventive of crime, and
the capacity to vindicate rights wards off assault, so does true valor
rescue war from its most brutal aspects, and assimilate the guardian
of public peace to the administrator of law and justice.

The history of all legitimate warfare is instinct with the exhibition
of noble attributes and profound wisdom.   If the object of this volume were but the simple compilation of battle-narrative, there would
be no place for the present discussion; but the desire is, to place the
battles in the scales, and test their merits by the experience of other
nations and other great captains, in order that all non-military scholars who have set up false standards of judgment, or have presumed
upon the ignorance of past generations, may determine for themselves
as to the assumption advanced in behalf of the battles and battle-
direction of the American Revolution.

There are those who will reject the term, "science of war."
Some will deny to the soldier a higher purpose than self-support,
and ambition for place and power, and decry the profession as servile,
or denounce it as despotic.

There will not be wanting those who will treat the general education of Germany and the elastic resources of France, as at variance

with the assumption, that *nations habitually armed to the teeth are slowly bleeding to death.* Nevertheless, it is true that the normal condition of society is peace ; and in proportion as the resources of the state are diverted to warlike uses, except *in extremis*, or in the indispensable preparation for impending or contingent danger, society suffers, and suffers just in proportion as the obligations of God's law are imperative, and vital prosperity depends upon adherence to those obligations.

All similar and related questions of every kind are swallowed up in the fact, that as society suffers from internal violence, so nations as such, are put in peril. True wisdom lies in such a just and honorable discharge of every duty that war without just cause, is only possible, as an outrage, which humanity at large would condemn and resent.

Should any maintain that the time has passed for rendering homage to military attainment, it must be first made to appear that all nations are prompt to render justice, and to accept and practice the cardinal principles which Montesquieu declares to be the spirit of laws, or, that the higher refinement of duty which attaches to the precepts of the Saviour himself, has already blossomed into fruit. The great fact is, that true life is made up of struggle. Emulation in labor, resolution as against oppression, and ambition for preferment are parts of all inner life. When these partake of self-sacrifice and exposure for holy ends, at the risk of life, the subject is lifted above the plane of mere living, to that of monumental worth and bright example. Where these elements work evil, and assail the rights of man, the issue must be squarely met by every agent available for their suppression.

No nation rises by easy spring to well balanced independence. Injustice and wrong assert their claims, and unless a people will so far indicate their self-respect as willingly to understand their duty under any possible phase of the future, there will be brought home to their experience the bitter lessons which have involved so many listless, corrupted, and conceited nations in remediless ruin.

If a nation, like the man, be doubly armed, in a just cause, so the conscious dignity that follows an assured ability to maintain that cause, is strong assurance of independence, and a stern warning to aggressors. No student of history will fail to see that the profession of arms has ever been esteemed honorable.

The sacred record which lies at the foundation of society itself, and thus becomes the vitalizing and essential element of all true progress, bears honorable testimony to the prowess of those who bore arms against unrighteous violence.   The Bible, therefore, recognizing the necessity for those who bear the shield in the front of battle, both records and honors their triumphs.   Where, in classic epic, will be found more jubilant refrains over victories won, than the song of Deborah ! and what can surpass the majesty and all-embracing fullness of the chorus of Miriam and Moses !

The very laws and usages of chivalry were predicated upon the idea that the true soldier represented the best type of refinement and honor.   Piety itself, now so exalted, self-denying, and precious, was once but a synonym for generous courage and true manhood.   In its manifestations of filial love, combined with brave deeds, was found the hero of Virgil.   There have indeed been periods of history, when the soldier knight was almost exclusively the scholar, and the cloister alone furnished those who, besides himself, could transcribe thought upon parchment or paper.

Bunyan and Milton assume the metaphors and terms of military life, while they delineate their highest characters, and expend the best efforts of their genius in forms which borrow strength and significance from the military profession.   Both sacred and profane history combine to honor him who honors himself in arms.   The " good fight " has not been fought out.   This is not the day for the gracious glories of millennial peace; neither should the military profession be crowned for other merit than that which attaches to its faithfulness to duty, as the conservator of just and sacred rights.

The ever increasing responsibilities that attend the rapid increase of the world's population, and the commercial enterprise which brings half-civilized and barbarous people into intimacy and interfusion with less populous, but better educated nations, are pregnant with issues which provoke human passion and human conflict.   Tidal waves of armed ignorance, superstition, and brutalism are not impossible because a select minority of the earth's inhabitants are enlightened and civilized.

History has recorded such events under circumstances no more difficult than the future may evolve.   So also, the irresponsibility of despotic power, and the fiery scourge of religious fanaticism, are not barred out because just now restrained.

There is already a relaxation of fealty to authority, an independence of individual obligation to the rights of the many, a jealousy of superiority, whether of mental or industrial attainment, which tend to anarchy; and these work in the same direction with the arrogant spirit of centralization and oppression, which gradually and inquiringly lifts its arm as in the middle ages.

The final issue must be resolved, either by intelligent recognition of a common moral obligation, and respect for the rights of all; or the conflicts of physical force will go beyond their true mission and introduce unparalleled conflict.

There is no aspect in which the knowledge of military science does not commend itself to the favor of the present generation. The lessons to be derived from history were never so pre-eminently useful as now, and they will hereafter hold a more solemn place in the mind of the thoughtful scholar. In introducing those principles which place military attainment in fellowship with true science, thereby stating the laws by which to test the deeds of the American Revolution, it can not be entirely foreign or discursive thus to blend their statement with honorable mention of its history.

CHAPTER V.

WARS BETWEEN NATIONS.

THE use of force to assert rights, or redress wrongs,—the interruption of friendly relations between states,—organized resistance to the supreme authority of a single state; and the sweep of some over-mastering passion or opinion, carrying with its ebullition violence and the upheaval of existing order, *alike bring war*.

Whether the rights asserted be just, and the wrongs alleged be real, is a matter that mainly affects that moral force which imparts to physical force its best assurance of success. Without this electric impulse, the superior in numbers and general resources may become the vanquished party.

Barbarism and *fanaticism*, alone, are unrestrained in war. One is the expression of the brute, the other of madness; and yet, by a strange anomaly in human nature, certain classes of wars among civilized nations partake of both elements.

Ex-President WOOLSEY defines a just war, as " one that is waged in the last resort, when peaceable means have failed to procure redress, or when self-defense calls for it."

The common-law rule for the magistrate in the execution of his duty, and for the citizen in self-defense, admits, however, of only the necessary force required for the immediate issue. This principle is agreeable to international law as best interpreted, and should be regarded as the standard of waste which a state can afford in exercise of the right of war. Excessive or vindicative force is retro-active upon the party exercising it, and is fatal to all concert of nations in relief of the hardships of war.

Vattel declares that, " whenever justice is done, all right of employing force is superseded." He divides wars into two sorts; lawful and unlawful, the latter being those undertaken without apparent cause and for havoc or pillage; all others being lawful.

Grotius makes the distinction between those solemnly undertaken by the state, and those *non-solemn*, that grow out of the acts of subordinate authority, not ratified by the head of the state.

Wheaton asserts that, if war be declared in form by one state, it entitles both belligerent parties to all the rights of war against each other, whether the war be just or not.

Halleck notices the distinction between perfect and imperfect wars, when, in one case, all the citizens of two states are placed in antagonism, and in the other, there is a limitation of persons, places, and things, as illustrated in the character of hostilities authorized by the United States against France in 1798.

The terms offensive and defensive have also been applied to distinguish wars, although more applicable to military *operations*, since every war of considerable magnitude or duration, has its alternations of attack and defense. Even in the shaping of cabinet policy, these terms are rather those of action than of type of contest, the verbal or diplomatic initiative being so aggressive as to compel protest and armed resentment.

An equivalent principle obtains at common law, where " verbal acts," so called, may warrant physical redress. It is not proposed to carry this discussion into the domain of international law, which is largely that of ethics, but to recognize the distinctions and energizing principles of battle-issues.

Writers have needlessly enlarged upon the classification of wars, and only a brief allusion is deemed necessary to cover all the ground which has real value to the citizen or student.

While wars vary in the manifestation and use of force, their success involves the same principles of the military art. The elements that inspire hostility, and tender the battle-issue, largely determine the character of the war, and decide whether a whole nation is to put its resources and existence at risk, or only to display a partial force for some temporary advantage to itself, or in behalf of another nation seeking its support. But when two nations, as two pugilists, employ their resources exhaustively against each other, the term *national war* has proper application. Such wars are peculiarly free from those heathenish exhibitions which attach to internecine types of conflict. The national honor, sensitive and forced to the issue, aims to pay respect to international law, and thereby to challenge the moral recognition of civilized neutrals.

It is not an error, in a qualified sense, to treat as national wars,

the struggles of a once vanquished people to regain their independence.   The suppressed nationality has its patriotic longings, and
although lacking public recognition until successful, the struggle partakes of a national character.   Poland and Hungary for example,
tried to resume their place among nations, so that revolt was not
merely insurrection, but assertion of national *entity*, kept in subjection
by the force of conquest.   Such cases differ, however, from a pretended re-assertion of national character in attempted disruption of a
union which had the consent of both parties, and where the merger
of individuality has been voluntary and complete.   Thus Scotland
became an integral part of Great Britain, and Texas became an
integral part of the United States by common consent.   Turkey has
repeatedly made war with Russia to ward off the accumulating force
which threatened her independence, her national life.

The struggle of the Netherlands against Spain, of the Spanish
peninsula against France, of France against the allies, are treated by
General Halleck as wars for independence, and yet those were
national wars, to perfect and vindicate national existence.   The war
of 1812, between Great Britain and the United States, has been treated
as a war for independence.   It was, however, largely the culmination
of misunderstandings, put at issue indeed by the dawning development of those rights of citizenship which in later years have gained
general acceptance.   The claim of America was no more an assertion
of independence from British control, than was that of Great Britain
a claim for independence in the control of her home-born subjects.
The former was the outgrowth of questions unsettled by the American Revolution, and the latter but the instinctive adherence to long
existing prerogative.   The former guaranteed to the adopted citizen
the full measure of national protection ; the latter claimed the perpetual allegiance of all once citizens, and the right to reclaim their
persons even on the high seas, whenever found.   The war, however,
was truly a national war.   A war for independence suggests its own
mission.   It is the struggle of a colony, a dependent section of the
state or of a distinct race, to obtain and maintain public recognition
as a distinct nation.   It finds its key in the first grade of Revolution
hereafter considered.

Baron Jomini declares that. " the spontaneous uprising of an
united nation, must not be confounded with a national defense, in
accordance with the institutions of the state and directed by the government."   His statement originates in the idea, that the govern-

ment may act independently of the people, and foreign to their interests or wishes.   He would thus limit national wars to popular outbursts in search of independence, or such as are necessary to save the national life which has been put in peril.   The statement ignores those states whose government is *representative*, and therefore the executive of the will of the people.   He adds: "The term *national*, can only be applied to such wars as are waged against an united people, or a majority of them, filled with a noble ardor, and determined to sustain their independence."   Wars, however, may be precipitated upon an entire nation by blunders of administration, misconception of conflicting issues, or want of that catholicity and generous negotiation which will generally command peace when nations really desire peace There may be realized in such cases only a lukewarm support of the government by the people ; but the *nation* is responsible for the war, and its government is responsible to the people.   Sometimes a war is begun which dishonors national character and strikes at the rights of other nations, without any reasonable equivalent to the party taking the aggressive.   *Wars for conquest* are of this type, and so are wars for the propagandism of ideas, whether political or religious. Upon the assumption, not to be thoughtlessly discredited, that every nation, as an abstract matter, has a rightful independence in legitimate pursuits of peace, but no right to enforce its domestic policy upon equally independent nations, all forms of propagandism by force of arms are destructive of society, and violate that international comity which, as between nations, is but the application of the wise restraint which governs citizens in the exercise of individual personal rights.

The Crusades and the Moslem wars were of the character adverted to, full of evil passions and evil fruit, and in defiance of all social and national rights.   Fortunately, wars for mere conquest have rarely perpetuated the state which committed the robbery.   The compensations of time under Providence brand conquest.   The mark of Cain shows itself.   To rob a nation of life, is not to be a glorious mission in the future.

Wars of Intervention, once so common in behalf of a so-called *balance of power*, are almost invariably of doubtful expediency, and can only be justified when there has been that willful violation of the law of nations, which calls upon the strong to protect or vindicate the weak from an attempt at conquest, or the destruction of rights which are fundamental and essential to national life.

The *true balance of power*, is that of moral and industrial excel lence. All else savors of the dark ages, and is as absurd in essence, as the impossible equality of individuals in wealth or accomplishments. Equality to-day, will end to-morrow, just in proportion as the deserving improve their acquisitions and the unthrifty and selfish waste them. When the French army shall equal the German, the German impulse will prompt a fresh expenditure to retain ascendency in the material of war, at the expense of domestic rest. Such are the considerations which, as a general rule, are to determine the character of national wars and indicate their limit.

A nation has in fact no right to go to war unless it can pledge its entire national resources to the hazard. Neither has a nation the right to go to war if there be any attainable settlement of controversy upon a just basis without war. As a general rule, one nation has no purpose to destroy or absorb its opponent, but only to wear it out a little, so that it will be too tired to keep up controversy. As an equally general rule, nations are left after war pretty much where they started in respect of the issue made, but fearfully poor in the elements of a truly national life

CHAPTER VI.

CIVIL WAR, DISTINCTION BETWEEN INSURRECTION, REBELLION, AND REVOLUTION.

CIVIL war is a war of one's own household, intestine, and full of bitter issues.

In proportion as a state conserves the rights of its citizens and dispenses even justice, a civil struggle has the same merit which the claim of any bodily member might assert against the supremacy of the head or the heart. Just as the mangled limb or deranged function imperils the whole system, and can only revive its normal use by wholesome acceptance of its dependence, and such treatment as subserves the welfare of the uninjured parts, so do civil feuds and strifes endanger the state at the expense of the disaffected members, crowning the struggle with the ruin of all alike.

Civil war proper, is a war of factions, not necessarily aiming at the integrity of the state, but involving separate aspirations to obtain control of the state, or at least supremacy over the rival faction. The South American States and Mexico furnish impressive examples of civil war. The English "War of the Roses," that of the League in France, and of the Guelphs and Ghibellines in Italy, are suggestive of the mischief to the body-politic which must attend an effort to push personal or party strifes to the usurpation of national authority. Success itself has no sound basis of perpetuity, because essentially maintained only in defiance of others' rights. Such wars were rife in feudal times; and more than once the powers of Burgundy and France were well-nigh paralyzed for national offense or defense, by the selfish strife of rival aspirants for local power or influence at court.

Civil war, however, has a general sweep which includes other and related classes; these having subjective relations while full of dissimilar elements, viz., INSURRECTION, REBELLION, REVOLUTION.

Each alike, belong to civil war, insomuch as the parties at issue belong to the state which is put in labor by their struggle.

(a) INSURRECTION is resistance to the authority of the state in contempt of existing law. It has no dignity no worthy aspiration, and is as lawless as it is illegal. It has none of the elements which make rebellion formidable, which vindicate revolution, and give to both rebellion and revolution a memorable place among wars.

The failure of a state to govern wisely, in accordance with divine obligation, may engender distrust, antagonisms, and ultimate overthrow ; but *insurrection* is limited to that style of popular outburst, which, with no possible hope of redress for alleged wrongs, or benefit to the complaining parties, puts the rights of all in peril.

It mocks at law and order and the remedies of the courts, and trifles with the rights of property and person. This statement is predicated upon the supposed existence of legitimate authority, and that the functions of the body-politic are working in the usual channels of a state of peace.

Jealousy of a superior social condition, conflict with wise social laws, sudden impulses to take crimes or political issues out of the sphere of their legitimate control and adjudication, and even political or religious *enthusia*, are among the causes of insurrection.

The violence is limited, and in a state which is upheld by a healthy moral sentiment on the part of the people, must be short-lived and fruitless except for evil. In this class of conflict occur those strikes of labor against capital, which both waste capital and degrade honorable industry ; and to this ephemeral and suicidal ebullition of passion the reckless partisan, with no ambition beyond office, is the incentive.

Insurrection has no apology, short of a condition where the resistance of an individual to lawless force is his only salvation ; and *then* insurrection is merged in the *duty* of Revolution. In a just, civilized state, there is redress, however slow, by legal methods, and deferred redress is better than law defied. The mob-law, which hangs a criminal in advance of legal process, breathes the spirit of insurrection, and its impulse may shift, and may in turn, strike the best friend of the state and people. History bears frightful testimony to the character of such demonstrations.

In 1358, the Jacquerie, on the assertion that the nobles were oppressive and guilty of all license, began an unqualified slaughter of all who had preëminence for education, station, or wealth, until the catalogue of outrages upon person and life became the synonym for all time, of the possibilities of insurrection in the degradation of man.

Under the cloak of religious zeal, an equal fury burned in the breasts of bigots during the middle ages, and the spirit has not yet taken its flight from earth *to its own place*. On the fifth of March, 1770, when the people of Boston were almost at open issue with the authorities, and the leaven of revolution was already working to the surface, a mob precipitated a needless quarrel with the soldiery, caused the death of Attucks and two other citizens, and threatened the entire city with fire and blood. The dignity of the courts, and the vindication of the soldiers by Quincy and Adams, alone restored order and averted extremes.

In December, 1786, Shays' rebellion broke out in Massachusetts. The claim that the Governor's salary was excessive, that the State Senate was aristocratic, and that taxes were odious, was pushed so violently and wildly, that courts were interrupted, and it seemed as if anarchy was to bury all memory of holy sacrifices made in the war which had so recently closed.

When a rightful duty was imposed upon spirits in 1795, the popular resistance set Pennsylvania on fire with similar demonstrations. The mails were robbed, and nameless crimes against virtue and innocence followed in the wake of pretended assertion of civil rights. It required the promptest exertion of President Washington and Governor Lee, and the employment of fifteen thousand troops to restore order, and society did not resume a placid surface for a long time thereafter.

No less conspicuous, in a military relation, were the uprisings of both British and American troops in New Jersey. In both cases, the exhibition of force had nothing to gain, but put in jeopardy the very interests which the men were sworn to uphold. In one case, the English proposition to compromise with the colonies, was the exclusive prerogative of the state; and in the other, the very ability of Congress to pay arrears due the troops, depended eventually and wholly upon the moral force which discipline could impart to the army. Moreover, the officers suffered equally with the men.

(*b*) REBELLION has a broader domain. While insurrection ignores or trifles with authority, and substitutes selfishness and passion for legitimate means of redress, the former disobeys and defies the authority of the state. Halleck defines rebellion as, " usually, a war between the legitimate government of a state, and portions or parts of the

same, who seek to overthrow the government or to dissolve the allegiance to it, and set up one of their own," citing the war of the Great
Rebellion in England, and that of the Southern States in America in
1861. Rebellion has organization and method, embraces more definite plans for prolonged resistance, and differs therein from insurrection, which expends its strength upon sudden and temporary expression, affecting good order, indeed, but lacking the coherence and comprehension of issues which characterize its development into open
rebellion against the state itself.

(c) REVOLUTION advances with purpose to overthrow the state
and substitute a new form of government, or a new dynasty. The
nominal *Right of Revolution* is asserted by many, as if it were a high
reserve franchise belonging to the people, and one which they may
exercise according to their choice. This is not true. There are
indeed, conditions under which a people may assert such a choice ;
but these conditions must have foundation in principles which underlie social organization itself. To vindicate the claim of the people to
be governed wisely and justly is one proposition ; but to admit that a
majority may exercise their choice as a matter of abstract right, and
by violence, is to strike a fatal blow at real liberty. The dogma savors
of the worst forms of civil war, gives dignity to insurrection, develops
formal rebellion, and refuses to the minority their equal rights with
the majority. The deliberate and matured modification of existing
forms. peaceably and constitutionally effected, is of course an entirely
different matter. The fluctuations of opinion which mark all truly
enlightened nations, are the true life of real development, and the
alternations of civil control which attend these conflicts of opinion,
are designed to work out ultimate peace and prosperity for the
entire body-politic. A false assumption as to this alleged right of
revolution has often disguised civil war, and has made Mexican Revolution an expression for license, insecurity, and general waste.
There are but two conditions which lift revolution to the dignity
of a right, and *then the law of duty compels the revolution.* It is not
sought, but comes as an inevitable assertion of the principle of
self-defense.

The first grade is that which devolves upon distant dependencies,
the assertion of INDEPENDENCE, when the controlling authority is
unable or unwilling to grant the people their rights and proper representation ; when laws are constraints without equivalents, and the
subjects are, in fact, slaves, without the filial relation which people are

to bear to the state, and which reciprocally binds the state to legis-
late for the common good of all who render homage.

The second condition is cumulative of the first; when the ab-
sorption of power in the governing authority is wholly set upon its
own aggrandizement in defiance of popular rights, and no redress
can be found through legislative or judicial sources.   Mere errors of
judgment in line of policy, or the administration of law through mistaken forms, is not a fair basis for overthrow of existing state sovereignty.   There must be such a condition that no redress is obtain-
able through established methods, and existing authority has lost its
legal hold upon its subjects, by subverting the principles which underlie and impart all authority.

There is a divine right of authority. That social crystallization
which enlarges the family relation and forms the state, carries with it
not only the obligation of wise control, but that of wise obedience.
The parent may outrage that relation, and the law will give to the
child a guardian, or emancipate it from the abused control.   It is
under just such a phase of civil suffering that the remedy lies in revolution and independence.   The obligation of the child to endure
until no other remedy is possible, is the type of the patience and
duty which must possess the citizen until the necessity of self-defense
demands the ultimate remedy

In its assertion there must be an unqualified search for a true
social peace, and not an ambition for independence such as a mind
would covet under the irksome restraint of wholesome or even
stringent control.

The whole history of continental revolutions is full of lessons of
warning to those who, for nominal changes, or nominal forms of government, make haste to overturn existing order without the moral
purpose or capacity to remedy the evils which are the burden of
complaint.

Authority is intrinsically arbitrary.   So long as men are fickle and
human, there will be a tendency to abuse that authority, and an
equally fatal tendency to despise all authority.   The power of the
many is no *less* despotic than that of the few ; and the law of man, is
to aim at the highest good of the greatest number, and not to fly in
the face of authority because of a fancied improvement through
coveted change.   Outside of this law of social life there is no stability,
no progress, no abiding peace.

Revolution is therefore a last resort, and the subordination of temporary issues or burdens to the general peace will bring ultimate benefit to any enlightened people who have legitimate avenues by which to control or shape the policy of rulers, without a spasmodic dash for its overthrow, and a plunge from bad to doubtful, or worse.

Revolution, like civil war in all its phases, involves cost, waste, and long stagnation of the offices of true peace. These must be risked in the last resort, but only when legitimate methods fail, and the issue hurries the solution to a crisis.

CHAPTER VII.

PROVIDENCE IN WAR ILLUSTRATED.

THE war for American Independence was marked by many critical events which were beyond human control or remedy. Some of these changed the relations of contending armies in a single night. More than once, a few hours of unexpected rain, wind or fog, were enough to assure lasting results. These determining events, because belonging to the sphere and operation of physical laws, are not beyond the recognition of nature's Master. They testify very clearly at least, the absolute uncertainty of the best human plans, whether for peace or war, and the value of the promptness which seizes every opportunity as it passes, and thus gives shape to material issues which are ripe for solution.

A few facts are grouped together in advance of their relations to specific battles, to illustrate the principle.

Early in the month of November, 1775, the expedition of Arnold to Canada was rashly pushed through a pathless wilderness to the shore of the river St. Lawrence. The possibilities of success were fair, if the invader could have struck the feeble and astonished garrison promptly upon arrival. Sleet and rain continuing for several days, kept the adventurer fast at Point Levi, and prepared the way for his signal failure.

On the morning of August twenty-eighth, 1776, just after the battle of Long Island, a drizzling mist, succeeded by heavy rain which continued for most of the day, retarded the approach of the British army to the American intrenchments at Brooklyn, and prevented the fleet itself from approaching New York. Toward evening the rain ceased, and work was resumed upon the British lines.

August twenty-ninth was a second day of rain; but every hour was improved by Washington to collect all kinds of boats, including sloops, scows, and row-boats, with view to rescue his army from impending capture. The masterly execution of the retreat was made possible by an unexampled fog, which lingered until the last detachment had taken passage. The wind itself, which threatened to drive the boats toward sea, shifted suddenly and quickened the transit. The fog lifted. The wind, so long unpropitious, had detained the British fleet at the Narrows, while by the change which had done so much for the Americans, that fleet was borne up the bay to assert control of the harbor and river passage, but too late to foil the movement of the American commander.

On the evening of the thirtieth of October, 1776, Earl Percy joined Lord Howe, then encamped in front of the American lines at White Plains, and it was resolved to storm the works at daybreak following. A north-easter came down upon the camps at midnight, raging wildly for nearly twenty-four hours; but before the advance was attempted, Washington had again rescued his army by withdrawal to the heights of North Castle, and occupied a position too strong to warrant assault.

On Christmas night, 1776, the parting ice at McConkey's Ferry, nine miles above Trenton, on the Delaware river, admitted of the safe passage and landing of one column of the American army, although other divisions were foiled in like attempts at ferries still nearer Trenton, and thus the battle of Trenton made its stamp upon the entire history of the struggle. It impressed all nations with respect for the prudence, courage, and faith of Washington, and relieved the American troops of the impression that the Hessians were a peculiarly fierce and invincible race.

The renewal of the offensive by Washington on the first of January, 1777, by again crossing the river, and in force, during comparatively mild weather, was followed by the abrupt closing of the Delaware, not sufficiently for safe retreat over the ice, but solid enough to threaten his entire force with destruction or capture. The same extreme cold froze the roads, made them passable for artillery and men, and the whole situation was so skillfully improved, that the action at Princeton followed, and his retreat to secure winter-quarters on the heights of New Jersey, not only saved his command, but threatened the British posts about New York and affected the entire New Jersey campaign.

The battle of Brandywine which occurred September eighth, 1777, was not accepted by Washington as decisive of the fate of Philadelphia. After a brief rest, the armies were again face to face September sixteenth, near White House Tavern, twenty miles from Philadelphia, Washington seeking the issue. General Howe skillfully turned the right flank of the American army, and skirmishing had begun, when a storm of unusual severity put arms and ammunition out of condition for use, filled the small streams, parted the combatants, and ultimately gave to the British the barren acquisition of the city.

The sudden renewal of the offensive at Germantown, on the fourth of October following, and with large promise of success, was neutralized and turned into a repulse by the interposition of dense fog which confused the troops and compelled a retreat, but thereby secured the column from the pressure of overwhelming forces which Cornwallis hastened from Philadelphia to the support of General Howe.

On the eleventh of October of the same year, when the army of Burgoyne had crossed the Fishkill, and was supposed to be in full retreat, General Gates pushed Morgan's rifle corps and the brigades of Nixon and Glover across the river under cover of a dense fog. A deserter gave warning and the movement was suspended. As the fog lifted, the entire army was seen to be in line of battle to meet the attack.

A succession of head winds delayed the fleet of Count D'Estaing during the voyage to America in 1778, so that Admiral Howe withdrew his squadron from the Delaware river. The prompt evacuation of Philadelphia by General Clinton, pursuant to orders, was thus the means of saving both army and fleet.

A propitious voyage of the French squadron would have been fatal to both. The squadron of Lord Byron, which was to have sailed from England, when information was received of the departure of Count D'Estaing from France, was detained until June the fifth, and was so disabled by a storm as to be compelled to refit before taking the offensive on the American coast.

On the tenth day of August, 1778, a storm disabled both British and French fleets off the harbor of Newport, Rhode Island, deprived General Sullivan of the support of the French troops in the siege of that city, and compelled both a retreat from the island itself, and abandonment of the siege. Almost immediately after, General Clinton arrived with a reinforcement of four thousand British troops.

The supposed insecurity of the southern coast during the fall months, forced Count De Grasse to a premature assault, followed by defeat, at Savannah in the month of October, 1779, when completed

trenches and adequate forces gave entire assurance of a successful
siege.   Two days after he left, his fleet was dispersed by a tempest.

On the ninth of January, 1780, General Lord Stirling took a force of
twenty-five hundred men from Elizabethtown, New Jersey, to Staten
Island in sleighs, crossing the river on the ice, for the purpose of
attacking the British in their quarters.   The harbor itself had been
closed so that heavy cannon had been hauled across on the ice.
Quite unexpectedly, the channel had opened between New York and
the island, so that the British posts had been reinforced during that
very day.   The snow was three feet deep, and nearly five hundred
men paid the penalty of frozen limbs for this mammoth midnight
sleigh-ride.

On the twenty-ninth day of January, 1781, Lord Cornwallis marching between Broad and Catawba rivers, pursued Morgan with the hope
of recapturing the prisoners which that officer acquired in the battle
of Cowpens.   The pursuit was successful.   Night came on, and it was
left for sunrise to assure the victory.   Morgan crossed the Catawba.
A heavy rain filled the river to its banks, and cut off further pursuit.

Morgan gained the banks of the river Yadkin on the second day
of February.   An equally sudden storm came on.   Morgan swam his
horses across the river, and transported his troops in batteaux, which
he secured on the other bank, so that his pursuer again failed of
success.

On the thirteenth day of the same month, Morgan having effected
a union with Greene, the whole command successfully crossed the
river Dan, and then renewed rain interposed the shield of an impassable barrier for a third time, and Lord Cornwallis, disheartened,
abandoned pursuit and retired to Hillsborough.

At the critical period when the Count De Grasse entered Chesapeake bay with a formidable fleet of men-of-war and transports, to aid
the American army in the reduction of Yorktown, a Franco-Spanish
fleet of more than sixty sail was on its way to the West Indies to
operate against the British colonies.   The former fulfilled its mission.
The latter, separated by storms, and thoroughly demoralized for any
concerted action, returned to Europe, leaving the record of a profitless
venture.

During the night of the sixteenth of October, 1781, when stillness
pervaded the air, and a calm surface invited the attempt, the vanguard
of the beleaguered army of Cornwallis crossed York river by boats
and landed safely at Gloucester Point.   It was the beginning of a

brave and earnest effort to extricate his army from impending surrender, and to make a bold push for New York by land. Suddenly,
without warning, a storm of rain and wind burst over the heads of
the hopeful garrison. The detachment already over, was safely recalled, and the drama of the war proceeded to its catastrophe.

Such facts as are thus grouped from the record of the war of
1775–1781, are not exceptional. Neither was the overthrow of the
Spanish Armada exceptional. The majority of large maritime expeditions have had similar vicissitudes, and the battle of Waterloo itself
vibrated under the strokes of the storm king.

Such facts step in along the life record of nations, to show on the
one hand, how utterly dependent are all human enterprises upon elements largely beyond human control, and on the other hand to demonstrate that wise and earnest men, resolute of will, and prompt to
execute, have converted storm itself and seeming misfortune into
permanent benefit, and have even rescued victory from the grasp of
the elements themselves. It is a part of the philosophy of war to
study such examples, and the American struggle is the history of
seven years of characteristic fluctuations which worked in the direction of American Independence, even when hardships and misfortunes seemed to alternate during the operations of the contending
armies.

It is not alone, however, in the realm of physical nature that life's
issues bear the impress of external force. *Opportunity* is given to men
and nations, and all probation is full of the neglect or improvement
of opportunity. Slight causes, no less than those more impressive
and prominent, give shape to issues and assure results. The statesmanship of war grapples with all classes of influences which work
for or against success, and a brief consideration of its principles and
obligations is regarded essential to the proper fulfillment of the
purpose in view.

CHAPTER VIII.

STATESMANSHIP IN WAR ILLUSTRATED.

WAR begins in the closet. The purpose to fight is definitely settled before the army moves to strike. The entire success of that army will largely depend upon the wisdom of the policy adopted by the state. While military men must bear the burden of field-work, and be held accountable for adequate preparation for all its contingencies, there is a kind of closet work which will make, or mar, the success of all field-work.

Inasmuch as the army is but the strong arm of the state, to be employed in last resort to support the state, so will there be a tendency on the part of the state to confound its own relations with those of the executive force, and usurp functions, or dictate action, which should be determined mainly by the exercise of military judgment, acting in harmony with a sound state policy. The primary principles which in the outset are to determine for or against war, belong peculiarly to the consideration of the statesman. Some of these principles are such as equally concern the soldier and bind him to the study of their relations as causes of war.

A fundamental condition of rightful war is, that it be essentially just, be absolutely necessary, and be prosecuted by just methods for its legitimate ends. There are circumstances which compel war. These have been sufficiently outlined in the consideration of wars between nations.

The present inquiry teaches the management of war which has been already determined upon by the state. The problem whether one state "shall be able with ten thousand to meet one that cometh against it with twenty thousand," involves the corresponding inquiry, "whether, while the other is yet a great way off, an embassage shall go forth to propose conditions of peace."

The parable of the Saviour is suggestive of that solemn deliberation which the contingency of war devolves upon the state.

The first consideration, therefore, which demands notice, is that of
the character, resources, and location of the force opposed. A state,
whether near or remote, having maritime relations, is not to be estimated as is a border state non-maritime and entirely restricted to
operations by land.

The whole question of supply for troops, and of the exclusion of
supplies from the opposing force, is largely affected by this single
question. It affects the selection of a proper base of operations for
the army itself, and no less determines the character of the force to be
retained at home for defense against a possible intrusion from hostile
fleets. The right and application of blockade is thereby brought under
serious notice, as well as many delicate questions concerning the rights
of neutrals, since the sea itself is the free highway of nations, and all
nations, even while at war, are under high obligations to protect all
other nations, so far as possible, from the waste and burdens which all
wars involve. If war ensue between border-states, the questions
which affect other nations are more restricted, and offenses against
neutrals are less likely to enlarge the field of war and involve those
nations whose interests lie in a continued peace. It is important
that the issues joined are not those of political or religious opinion.
There is *no natural end to such a contest*, and the passions aroused are
absolutely foreign to a fair settlement of legitimate international
differences. Hence it is the part of intrinsic wisdom, so to carry on
war, that neither the political nor religious opinions of the opponent
are stirred up and made the impelling force which resists the demand
for a fair settlement of the controversy begun.

There are times, however, but rare, when moral questions force
themselves into that " military policy " which is very properly classed
by Jomini as the statesmanship of war. The war which began in
1861, between different sections of the American Republic, involved
such a question, and its part in the war was the result of changing
condition, and not an original impulse of the national authority in its
assertions of national unity. The abolition of slavery was not a real
issue at the outset. A declaration of that issue as a purpose, would
not have rallied to its support an united citizenship, as did the vindication of the national flag and the national life. Its subsequent introduction into the contest was a matter of *military necessity*, on the
ground that the prolonged warfare compelled a blow at the vital ele-

ment upon which the resistance hinged. It took its place as an element of the war, because permanent peace under reinstated authority was impossible, so long as an abnormal social condition conflicted with the law and essence of pure individual and personal liberty.

The suppression of the Mamelukes in 1811, and of the Janizaries in 1826, became indispensably necessary to the maintenance of legitimate authority, because the creature usurped authority over the state, its creator, and would not accept the legitimate control which the state asserted. It will not be questioned now that the aspiration of slavery to hold perfect equality of footing with liberty, forced it into an attitude wholly at war with the charity which had so long tolerated its presence as a transmitted incubus upon the national life. Hence, it became an objective of attack.

The expulsion or suppression of the order of Jesuits by certain European states, is not predicated upon their holding certain religious faith, but upon their supposed organization to contravene the authority, or seek the overthrow, of the very state which affords them protection and a home. Neither of these exceptions are in conflict with the principles asserted.

In view of war once undertaken, it is equally important that regard be had to the social and moral circumstances of the state assailed. Its government may have forced the war, while its people oppose or reluctantly support it. The whole policy of operations is to be shaped by regard to such issues. A just advocacy of rightful claims, as between civilized and enlightened nations, will gradually constrain a people to put their own government in the right, and compel the admission of such claims, if there be no manifest aggression for selfish ends, and in disregard of a sound discussion of the issues made. Hence, an *unreasonable ultimatum*, propositions looking to *national humiliation*, or, a claim for vindictive, consequential damage for injuries alleged, is not only provocative of protracted, bitter resistance, but will leave heartburns, thirst for revenge, and seed for future conflict. Regard must be had even for national peculiarities. An issue with Turkey is not well presented if it offend Moslem prejudices, unless that state shall intrude such prejudices in the way of equal justice to non-Mohammedan nations. An issue with China is not well presented if it make war upon its social customs, irrespective of their relation to international intercourse. In a word, the instincts of christian gentlemen are not to be cast away by nations any more than by individuals when differences arise, and the rights of each are to be weighed in the balances of even-handed justice.

A policy that will allay passion, and impress the opponent with the justice of the claim at stake, will hasten peace and a final settlement of all interests involved. In harmony with this line of conduct, is such a course as strongly appeals to sound patriotism at home, and thus unites the people in a hearty support of the government which carries on the war on their behalf.

An attitude which vindicates a merely partisan ascendency, is repugnant to the sober judgment of an intelligent people, and such a war must soon languish and fail, or be fruitless of substantial benefit to the nation involved. It is therefore just that the cause of the war be fairly stated, and that the men who are to furnish lives and treasure to *feed war*, shall be in full sympathy with its prosecution. Mere national aggrandizement, or the reduction to a lower grade of a state which is confessedly superior, will not meet the requirements of sound statesmanship. "To live and let live," is the duty of nations as well as of individuals. Predicated upon such principles, and working in such channels, a war advances to execute its work. Shall the nation take the offensive or await the attack? This must be determined by the respective preparations of the parties, the location of objectives most susceptible of attack with view to hasten the final result, and the character of the issue itself. If a boundary be in dispute, a prompt occupation and armed possession of the territory involved may prove a virtual solution of the whole controversy.

Dispossession of a firmly established force may be more costly than a surrender of claim to the title. Barren points of this kind have cost many lives and large treasure. A state can not afford to go to war for barren issues, and when no national benefit can possibly ensue from the contest.

It is always bad statesmanship to make merely nominal issues, or to stake the settlement of differences upon questions of pride, as for instance, the occupation of an enemy's capital, or any other particular and merely formal success, which does not of necessity work to the quickest conclusion in peace.

It is equally wrong to over-ride the jurisdiction of military men to whom the armies are entrusted, by loading them down with instructions that are non-military, and too late for application when the issue of arms has been joined. Confidence must be given to the commanders when they have been wisely selected, or their success is put in hazard at the outset.

During the year 1861, the American Congress and a portion of the American press reiterated the cry of "on to Richmond" *ad nauseam*, until outside non-combatant energies largely precipitated the first battle of Bull Run, and even contributed spectators to see how thoroughly a brilliant triumph would vindicate the manifold criticisms upon the delay of the national army to move to the front.

The movement made at the close of the Mexican war to supersede Major-general Scott by appointment of a citizen to the grade of lieutenant-general, was an intrusion of folly into matters strictly military, and failed through its inherent simplicity.

It is already evident that strategical combinations, and considerations such as Baron Jomini calls "making war on the map in contradistinction to operations on the field," fall within the considerate regard of the statesman as well as of the soldier ; and much that belongs to the consideration of strategy proper, is eminently worthy of the study of that cabinet which rules the affairs of states, and acts by authority in initiating the war itself.

It only remains to add that wise statesmanship in war embraces a careful consideration of the military and financial resources of the opposing state, in comparison with those of the state making war, so that adequate means may be furnished for the purpose required, with the least possible drain upon the state, and the least possible suspension of the industrial pursuits of those not called upon to take active part in the war itself.

To break up a nest of pirates, to vindicate a wrong done to a citizen by a half civilized or barbarous state, would involve a very different expenditure of means and men from a contest with a state fully up to all standard improvements in the capacity to carry on war. Extravagant means, beyond the necessity of the end in view, always beget a suspicion that the state is only seeking an excuse to increase its warlike capacity at the expense of the people, and the demands of a healthy and permanent peace. Strong armaments beget occasions for their use, and true statesmanship in war is that which is best in peace.

Finally, let it be understood that "amenities in war," belong to the age. Christianity, which is the true life of all national life, only declares the demand which civilization now affirms, that war shall have its issue between real combatants only, and that in the effort to deplete the enemy of resources for continuing the struggle, there is to be recognized a high regard for life itself, and for those personal rights which belong to the family and society. Of this class are those which deal with prisoners of war and certain grades of private property. Plunder is no longer a just right of the individual soldier. Starvation or abuse of captives only rebounds to irritate the enemy, and make a good cause partake of all the dishonor and natural fatality of a bad cause.

High statesmanship in war, which includes statesmanship during its inception and looking to its prevention, affords the best promise that the time will hasten when reason and charity combined will disarm the nations, and leave the settlement of national issues to that kind of arbitrament which long since abolished the " wager of battle," and the duelist's senseless " code of honor."

CHAPTER IX.

PRINCIPLES DEFINED. STRATEGY ILLUSTRATED.

WAR may be formally declared,—may start in the collision of armies stationed on the border, or may be forced by invasion or some other aggressive act of another state. The United States and Mexico were put at war with each other in 1845 by the advance of General Zachary Taylor upon territory then in controversy. Napoleon III. hurled the announcement of war against Prussia in 1870 only as he advanced his army of invasion.

Lexington and Concord opened the war of 1776-1781. The principles involved by the beginning of war are, however, entirely within the sphere of international law, except so far as policy or the statesmanship of war has considered the issue, for the purpose of determining what methods shall be adopted for its prosecution.

At this period physical force enters the arena. Practical questions take the place of theory. Shall the state take offensive measures, thereby to make the struggle upon foreign soil, or limit its action to defense of its own soil?

The offensive not only bears to the territory of the adversary the local waste of war, but carries with it the incentive which attends a first success. It assumes a superiority by assertion of the aggressive, and often excites enthusiasm at home while discouraging the adversary. The offensive must work by careful plans, with close counsels, and thus keep the enemy busy to meet them as they unfold. But it must be followed up with vigor and with adequate resources. These resources, whether of men, munitions, provisions, or transportation, must be continually renewed and continually protected. Otherwise, the advancing force will be so wasted by casualties as to become inferior to the resisting force, and will then fall an easy prey to a revived adversary backed by an aroused people, restored to a fresh consciousness of their ability successfully to resist.   Failure to sustain the offensive is generally the prelude to ultimate defeat.   The defensive, on the other hand, inspires a nation to earnest resistance, if its people are united in thought and policy, and if there be no elements in the issue which prompt a sympathy with the cause of the invaders and induce a *lukewarm* resistance.

Supplies are more readily at hand.   The superior knowledge of the country is of great use in keeping up communications and disturbing those of the enemy.   The social instincts, obligations, and sympathies, are more closely bound to every incident of the struggle, and the national life itself may be so imperiled as to evoke the maximum of resistance which the state and people combined can possibly put forth.   Many classes of supplies which are essential to invasion, can be largely dispensed with under many phases of a simple defense.

When the defensive by adequate resistance is enabled to assume the offensive in return, and to follow this with vigor and resources adequate to the opportunity, the war may be considered as near its final crisis.   But the passive or persistent defensive will ultimately be fatal in any struggle, whenever the aggressive force patiently maintains its pressure.

The terms offensive and defensive have pointed application in single actions, which are often decisive of a campaign, or of the war itself, whatever may have been the original policy of the state which took the initiative at the outset of hostilities.

Washington at Princeton, and Clinton at Monmouth, alike returned the offensive, under circumstances which accomplished for each the object in view, and alike testified of their courage, conduct, and military skill.   In the war of 1775–1781, there were peculiar circumstances to give value to the *defensive*, having offensive return. The territory was quite generally thickly wooded ; bridges were infrequent, the population was scattered, roads were poor, water courses were not only numerous and large, but were peculiarly susceptible to overflow, because of the mountains and hills which everywhere abounded.

In regions not hilly, or near the sea-coast, the numerous swamps interposed equally serious obstacles to the movements of organized commands, and afforded special opportunity for that partisan species of warfare which is then so efficient in defense, and so annoying to an invader.

War having in fact begun, the elements which control its destiny are embodied in simple propositions.　These embody five universally recognized divisions of the art of war, and will be defined as follows:

I. Strategy.

To secure those combinations which will assure the highest possible advantages in the employment of military force.

II. Grand Tactics.

To handle that force on the battle-field.

III. Logistics.

The practical art of bringing armies fully equipped to the battle-issue.

IV. Engineering.

The application of mathematics and mechanics to the maintenance or reduction of fortified places, the interposition or removal of natural or artificial obstacles to the passage of an army, and the erection of suitable works for defense of territory or troops.

V. Minor Tactics.

The instruction of the soldier individually and *en masse*, in the details of military drill and the perfection of discipline.

With regard to the last two divisions, it is only necessary to notice that the early drill of Washington, as a practical civil engineer and frontier officer, was made conspicuously useful in the selection of military positions for his army in the progress of the war of 1775–1781. Although he had the coöperation of several foreign officers of real attainment, he gave his personal attention to the location of field-works on occasions of great necessity.　He had strong faith in a system, now so indispensable, of casting up light earthworks when his army halted, and an enemy was within a short march of his lines. Baron Steuben and Generals Lee, Greene, Wayne, Varnum, and Maxwell, were among his most skillful and urgent officers in imparting instruction in the details of minor tactics.　The success was only limited by the fluctuations of army organization, and the short terms of enlistment.　The continental troops which were enlisted for the war, very properly styled the "American Continental Army," vindicated their drill and discipline in the field.　The first three divisions of the art of war, in their order as named, will receive brief consideration.

Strategy deals first with the *theatre* of war.　This involves a clear consideration of several included topics, *viz.*,—the character of the country, its natural resources, its topographical features, its means of inter-communication, in short, all elements which form or impede the movement of an army under the changing circumstances which affect all armies in the field.

During the war of 1775–1781, the theatre of war extended from the St. Lawrence river to Florida, and from the Atlantic ocean nearly to the Mississippi river. It was not then, and never is, enough simply to take cognizance of the theatre of active operations.

In the contingency of a collision between England and the United States, Canada would be, as then, a possible base of British operations, requiring observation at least as a hostile border, if it did not become an actual field of operations by intrusion of American troops.

Equally important, in case of trouble between the United States and Spain, would be such a naval observation of Cuba as to anticipate a concentration of troops on the island and a descent upon the American coast. Either Canada or Cuba might become a field of active operations, and neglect to anticipate these contingencies, would violate the demands of sound strategy as well as wise statesmanship.

Arnold's fatal attempt upon Quebec will be hereafter considered in connection with the battle record proper. Sufficient to say in this connection, that it had but one possible element of merit, and that, the wild conjecture that Canada had a common interest, and was willing to make common cause in the issue with the mother country.

In a wise examination of the *theatre of war*, the outlook must include *natural strategic positions*, just as in the operations of a campaign there will be found *accidental and conditional strategic positions*, having their sole value in the temporary strength or opportunity which they afford to one army, and the temporary detention or reverse which they involve for the adversary force.

The wise location of an army at the end of a day's march, will often secure determining positions which directly involve ultimate success, while a corresponding error will bring a quick attack and a speedy reverse.

Compactness, so that the whole force can be handled, and such disposition, that no surprise can be effected, are alike indispensable to such a position. West Point was a natural strategic point in respect of operations along the Hudson river. Forts Lee and Independence had a similar element of value, inasmuch as these positions, if substantially supported, were links to assure speedy communication between New England and the other colonies, and impart to each section the confidence which a prompt mutual support would engender.

Their early reduction, and that of Forts Clinton, Montgomery, and Stony Point, crowded this link of inter-communication far up the Hudson river. Such positions as the "straits of the Dardanelles" have a similar permanent strategic value, to be regarded, whether actually occupied or not.

Strategic movements have as their philosophy the use of all measures, other than those of detail and the mere physical struggle of the field, which tend to enhance success, and reduce to their lowest grade of destructive force the resources of the enemy. Thus a victory may be won without a battle, whenever a prompt and felicitous strategic movement, or the timely seizure of a single position, shall compel an enemy to abandon his own position as untenable, in view of the movement made.

The simulated attack upon New York by Washington, in 1781 which was carried so far as to have brick bread-ovens erected in New Jersey, opposite Staten Island, was a strategic movement which held the garrison fast to that city, induced a call upon Lord Cornwallis for reinforcements, and ultimately resulted in the capture of Yorktown. Thus the American army had substantially a double presence, represented a double force, and presented a double front,—one false, and one real.

The establishment of Washington's Head-quarters at Morristown was of high strategical value, inasmuch as New England, New York, New Jersey, and the Southern States, were all on *radii* from that centre, and almost equally accessible by his command. On the other hand, the occupation of Philadelphia by General Howe, lost the value which was predicated upon the movement, for want of adequate force by which to reduce the army of Washington still in the field. It simply afforded a comparative rest in comfortable winter quarters, but was barren of military results.

Lord Rawdon exercised sound strategy at the battle of Camden, when he secured for his army the protection of both flanks by an impassable marsh, while maintaining communication with his base, as the means of turning the American left.

A base of operations is of prime importance to an invading army, and is equally important in the consideration of suitable and determining objective points.

The general purpose of the campaign will largely determine the choice of the base and the immediate objective. *Jomini* declares that "it is important to establish the base upon those points where it can be sustained by all the resources of the country, and at the same time insure a safe retreat."

During the American war of 1861–1865, when the federal troops of the middle zone of operations made Louisville, Kentucky, their military base, as well as the base of supplies, with Nashville as the objective point to be reached, it became necessary first to drive the confederate force from Bowling Green, a fortified position between Louisville and Nashville, and then to reduce Forts Donaldson and Henry on the Cumberland and Tennessee rivers. The former was directly on the railroad line to Nashville. The latter made possible the control of the Ohio river by hostile vessels, or a flank movement to the rear, by land, and the loss of the base itself. Their capture gave a second line of operations by water, in concert with the main movement upon Nashville, which lay on the left bank of the Cumberland, and thus realized the desired result.

New York was made the chief base of General Howe's operations not long after the evacuation of Boston. In one sense it was a *double* base. While Staten Island gave peculiar facilities for operations towards Philadelphia and the south, the control of New York Island and of the accompanying entrance to Long Island Sound, was equally valuable in view of operations up the Hudson river and toward New England. As a depot of supplies and the general rendezvous of the British naval forces, it also operated as the primary base for all enterprises in the direction of Georgia and the Carolinas.

One objective, as already stated, was the capture of Philadelphia. Although this result was finally consummated, only by a detour through Chesapeake bay by aid of the fleet; the movement was originally organized as an operation by land. This involved the military occupation of New Jersey.

Washington's *offensive return* at Trenton and Princeton, modified the original purpose, and his command was suffered to hold the position at Morristown in the very heart of New Jersey, and to become a source of constant uneasiness and even of danger to New York itself.

The selection and successful occupation of Charleston, South Carolina, as the immediate base of operations in the Southern States was eminently wise and timely, but was not supported by a force adequate to the necessities of the movement.

Canada was made a base for a third line of operations, threatening the separation of New England from the other colonies; but the failure to destroy the army of Washington, which remained on the alert, within striking distance of New York, still paralyzed the arm which was to strike with Burgoyne, and his operations closed at Saratoga. While a base resting on the sea must be adequately supplied, as was New York, through superior maritime resources, it is equally true that an army forced back *upon* the sea by a competent force, as was that of Cornwallis, is lost.

CHAPTER X.

STRATEGY IN WAR CONTINUED.

THE prime objective of the war of 1775–1781, was the reduction of the colonial armies and enforcement of the authority of the crown. The occupation of territory or cities by an inadequate force, while the opposing armies kept the field, was therefore of transient benefit.

Philadelphia was made the objective of the British army during the campaign of 1777, mainly because it was the capital of the enemy. Congress removed to Wilmington,—Washington struck a blow at Germantown, close to the city, and the issue was as far as ever from conclusion. A single remark is therefore proper as to the value of a national capital as a chief military objective.

Colonel Hamley, commandant of the British Staff College, in his excellent volume upon " The Operations of War," (edition of 1875) states the proposition very precisely. " The mere possession of the capital is not final, so long as the enemy can still make head in the field. It is when the seizure of the capital is coupled with such ascendency over the defensive armies that they can never hope to retake it, that further resistance is felt to be hopeless, as leading only to national extinction, and that any terms not absolutely unendurable, are accepted by the vanquished."

This, as a general rule, is true as between independent nations. During the American war of 1861–1865, another element entered into the question. If Washington, with its archives, public buildings, and foreign representation, had fallen under Confederate control, especially as its soil was within the original territory under influence of Southern sympathy, there would have been a claim on the part of the successful party, that the Confederacy was, *de facto*, the United States. Neither would there have been wanting a certain extent of foreign sympathy with the demand, and also a color of right. On the other hand, Richmond, while a legitimate base of operations, was not a national capital, in any permanent sense. The transfer of its executive and of its legislative body to Montgomery, was not analogous to that of the removal of the American Congress to Baltimore, during the war of 1775–1781. The popular pressure for the premature occupation of Richmond at great hazard, on the ground that it was a capital was *sentimental* and unsound. Its sole value was in its character as a military base, having solid relations to an advance upon Washington. Moreover, European capitals have been repeatedly occupied, with no permanent benefit to the invader, and with no appreciable effect upon the issues of the war itself.

Immaterial objectives only impair general operations. The various British expeditions to Connecticut and Virginia committed waste, but accomplished nothing else, except to embitter the struggle and arouse fresh passion to resist.

Lines of operations are the *pathways of armies*, and include such contiguous territory as render the march secure and practicable.

Deep lines are those which advance far beyond the base. Napoleon's march to Moscow is the type of an *extreme* line. The Burgoyne campaign was another instance in point. It assumed impossible data as certain. It threw away communication with its base, which also included its base of supplies, since the supply-train was too limited for the entire movement; it over-estimated the resources of the country invaded, and depended upon the support of another far distant army for success, while that army was to operate from an opposite base, with no such assured readiness of communication as to assure the concert of action indispensable to the result. That *other army* projected a line of operations one hundred and fifty miles beyond its base, with the positive knowledge that if the movement were made with adequate force, it must imperil that base, and put the whole purpose of the war in peril. Justice to the high military qualities of Burgoyne and Clinton, requires the statement that this measure was at the dictation of bad statesmanship which controlled the English commander at New York.

Lines of operation may be *parallel* with or perpendicular to the base, this depending upon the strength of the forces, and the topography of the country occupied. It may be along a river, or through a region which gives strategic value to the movement, and thereby gain additional advantages to that of a mere advance. Thus the river Raritan, in New Jersey, repeatedly exercised a marked influence in giving direction to the lines of operation respectively adopted by the British and American armies in their movements to and from the Delaware river.   Washington's retreat from Fort Lee, in 1776, was secured only by a prompt withdrawal behind the Hackensack, and a movement down its right bank, holding the river itself as a cover from the left flank of the army.

A *front of operations* includes not merely the territory occupied towards the enemy, but so much as must be observed, in order to anticipate a hostile advance, while also affording margin for counter manœuvers.   *Jomini*, as well as other writers, limits this front to the equivalent of a two days' march.   This is, however, an artificial distance, wholly dependent upon the nature of the country.   The strict front of the army itself, has been called the *strategic front*.   If an army be behind an impassable stream, its front is sharply defined. This becomes an indication of the tract within which the army may operate with decisive advantage, so that the actual front and the strategic front may thus coincide.

As a matter of fact, there is little value in maintaining the distinction, since it must be assumed of any wise commander, that he will pay special attention to an issue which presents such a pressing demand as the presence of an enemy within easy striking distance. It often devolves upon a commander to maintain a double strategic front.   This invariably attends the presence of a substantial force upon either flank.   It may also become necessary by the very configuration of the country, and this necessarily increases as the army advances into an enemy's territory.   This involves the separation from the command of large detachments.   The failure of General Sullivan to maintain such a front to the right flank of the American army at Brandywine, coupled with defective reconnoissance, precipitated that action before the army could be adjusted to meet the skillful flank movement of Generals Howe and Cornwallis.

A *line of defense*, independent of the base, is not always indispensable, when the protection of the base is adequate, and the forces in hand are equal to any required advance movement.

Washington's policy being the preservation of his army, he adopted a line of defense across the New Jersey hills, which not only served as a base, but gave a definite character to his operations, and repeatedly saved that army.   Natural or artificial obstacles should be made to serve as supports to the army when driven to the stationary defensive.   Rivers often form lines of defense, as in repeated instance!

during the campaign of 1781 in the Southern States. The winter quarters of the American army at Valley Forge, 1777–8, were a line of defense no less than a peculiarly well selected strategic position. A large back country was accessible for supplies, although greatly impoverished by the waste of war, and the distance from the British army at Philadelphia fulfilled all the conditions which were necessary to secure reasonable safety, keep the troops on the alert, and afford both opportunity and inducement for observation and operations to the front.

A line of defense should be as compact as possible, with a strategic front so limited as to give prompt concentration of the army upon critical points. One consideration is worthy of suggestion to the student who would rightly estimate the merits of an issue, when one army is assured of artificial means of defense. If forces be otherwise equal, that army which holds a firm position, has *plus* strength equal to the advantage of that position, while the assailant has *minus* strength equal to the estimated loss involved in forcing that position. In an open field where successful movements and hard fighting make up the issue, the force of discipline and both the moral and physical elements which command success are left to their free exercise.

No line of defense should be *passively* occupied. The advance of La Fayette to Barren Hill, and Washington's attack at Germantown, were expressions of force which gave value to the position at Valley Forge, exalted its defensive properties, and put the British army itself upon a *quasi-defensive*. The latter army during the New Jersey campaign, had *two* ultimate lines of defense. The banks of the Delaware, with the *cordon* of posts extending to New Brunswick and Perth Amboy, formed one, and the river Raritan on the right, was auxiliary to the former, so long as the fleet controlled the waters about Staten Island. The latter was practically an advanced base for operations working southward from New York, with a strategic front looking to the movements of Washington's army which occupied the heights of middle New Jersey.

Zones of operation are belts of territory controlled by moving columns, or those within which columns can act in real concert. Several lines of operation may fall within one zone.

During the war of 1775–1781, New Jersey and Pennsylvania were within the centre zone, while Georgia and the Carolinas belonged to the left.

During the American war of 1861–1865, the trans-Mississippi

states filled the right zone ; the country eastward to Virginia, indicated the centre ; while the Atlantic belt, with operations on Richmond, determined the zone of the left.

It is possible, with the modern telegraph and railroad system, for a competent commander to ordain a general policy, by which operations in different zones may determine together toward the general result.   Thus General Grant on the left, and General Sherman in the centre, acted in full concert during the spring and summer of 1864, so to occupy the Confederate forces as to neutralize the benefit which otherwise enured to the latter by virtue of a series of interior railroad lines, which inabled their armies to operate alternately against the Federal armies of either zone, by a shorter route than was available for the latter troops.

During July, 1862, the author was instructed by competent authority, to meet Generals Halleck and Pope on their arrival at Washington, to which place they had been called by telegram, and to inform them that an immediate interview was desired by the President, then at the Soldiers' Home, a short distance from the city.   The whole object of the proposed interview was, that the President might determine in his own mind whether the different operations in Missouri, Kentucky, and Tennessee, were the result of *one forecast*, or judgment, or merely accidental.   As the result of their arrival, General Halleck was placed in general command, under the style of chief of staff to the President, who thereby asserted his constitutional prerogative as commander-in-chief, upon the assumption that General Halleck had the mental scope and executive ability to handle all the armies over the entire theatre of war.   General Pope was also assigned to a highly responsible sphere of duty.

The details of separate zones are necessarily distinct, as are many operations of single armies moving on separate lines in the same zone. General Sherman's march to the sea was practically but one line of operations, because he kept up such constant communication with his entire command, that it was at all times in hand for concentration, and the efficient accomplishment of his plans.   If it be regarded as the equivalent of two lines of operations acting together within one zone, it had the perfect accord of purpose and action, which under skillful hands, makes every key in music to vibrate in harmony together. The grand divisions of his army moved as a unit, on their mission.

During the war of 1775–1781, the operations of General Clinton were marked by great wisdom, and a fixed purpose to secure a sufficient concentration of force to realize success on the three zones of proposed operation. The right zone, bounded on the left by the Hudson river and its defenses, was favored by Lord George Germaine, but at the sacrifice of results elsewhere, and without an appreciation of the resistance with which he had to cope, and the character of the country in which the war was carried on.

Although Massachusetts was left unassailed by British troops, after the evacuation of Boston, a base was secured at Newport, Rhode Island, which was far more eligible for operations in that zone than was Boston itself. Its distance from that city was but seventy miles. General La Fayette went from Newport to Boston, during the siege of Newport in 1778, in seven hours, and returned in six and a half hours. It was sufficiently near to threaten the former city, and to somewhat restrict Massachusetts in contribution of troops to the central army of Washington. The harbor was excellent. Long Island Sound afforded a safe interior passage to the head-quarters at New York, so that the success of the apparently useless diversions into Connecticut would have had substantial method, if troops had been furnished up to the demand of the British General-in-chief. Herein, as elsewhere, the military judgment was superseded in operations strictly military, by a purely civil control. If military policy was considered in the English cabinet at all, it omitted to make the movement independent by the supply of means adequate to assure results.

Lines of communication are defined by their title. Modern science has facilitated the connection of armies with their base and with each other. It was with difficulty that Colonel Hamilton, *aid-de-camp* of General Washington, could determine the position of his own flanking parties, which were watching the movements of General Clinton's army during the retreat of that officer from Philadelphia in the year 1778; and it was not until the afternoon before the battle of Monmouth, that he could report the exact facts.

Interior lines, exterior, concentric, and *divergent lines*, are also self-expressive. It is obvious that in covering a capital or any other commercial centre, which is approached by different army corps on different roads, the defense can concentrate a superior force more speedily than the advancing army, unless the advance be made a surprise, or with greatly superior numbers.

In the advance upon Germantown, during October, 1777, the extreme left wing of the American army was too widely spread, so that the right wing of the British army actually reinforced the centre, and settled the issue without receiving a single blow from the force which had been sent to occupy its attention during the main attack.

On the British left a similar concentration took place, the observing party sent by General Washington to engage the Hessian forces having utterly failed to follow up the enjoined movement.

The inferior forces employed during the war of 1775–1781, as compared with great continental armies, limited the *range* of *strategic* operations, although demanding the right use of all general principles; and while army formations have been modified, and greater mobility has been secured during the century and more which has passed since that struggle began, the review of the actions themselves will prove that the lessons of antecedent warfare were carefully studied, and judiciously applied, up to the extent of the then realized facilities for war.

CHAPTER XI.

GRAND TACTICS ILLUSTRATED.

"TO handle well a military force on the battle field," which the author offers as a concise exposition of the term "Grand Tactics," involves several principles which all military writers accept as fundamental.

Although these truths have been elaborated and illustrated by eminent scholars of modern times, they obtained recognition and application at very early periods, and thus imparted success to military enterprise as long ago as the days of Hannibal and Cæsar. *Their maxims*, and *their instructions to commanders* are sound and practical *now*, as they were *then*. Baron *Jomini* states them thus:

First. "To throw by strategic movements the mass of an army successively upon the decisive points of a theatre of war, and also upon the communications of the enemy as much as possible, without compromising one's own."

Second. "To manœuvre to engage fractions of the hostile army with the bulk of one's forces."

Third. On the battle field, to throw the mass of the forces upon the decisive point, or upon that portion of the hostile line which it is of the first importance to overthrow."

Fourth. "To so arrange that these masses shall not only be thrown upon the decisive point, but that they shall engage at the proper time and with energy."

To apply military force upon these conditions, involves the highest wisdom,—a keen perception of the relations and circumstances which attend the changing issues of war;—a lightning-like logic, by which to interpret both relations and circumstances, and both skill and nerve to strike home the blow, with precision and force.

The introductory chapters have demonstrated the philosophy which underlies the conduct of war.

As with all theories, however perfect, the issues themselves are often confronted with facts which no human foresight can anticipate. If all great battles could be traced through the minute details which marked their progress, the human mind would be humbled by the evidence, that very often, an unexpected and apparently trivial event has been the pivot upon which the entire event changed its drift and destiny.

Notwithstanding these contingencies, common to all pursuits in life, the operations of the battle field have general features which work in the direction of the conditions laid down, and these are entitled to a brief review.

The war of 1775–1781, afforded illustrations of the changes which have characterized modern warfare from the time that Frederic William, of Prussia, father of Frederic the Great, combined rigid drill and exact discipline, with swift and impetuous movement upon exposed or cramped bodies of the enemy.

The British Light Infantry and Light Dragoons were active troops, and both mobility and flexibility began to take the place of those heavy strokes which simply measured the relative momentum of colliding bodies.

Braddock's campaign was a type of the old method. Tarleton's operations were characteristic of that new system which gained fresh spirit during the French revolution and afterwards distinguished Napoleon I.

The first Italian campaign of that commander, which, in a mere handful of days, made memorable the names of Legnano, Castiglione, Mendola and Mantua, has the magic thrill of romance. Like Habib, of the Arabian Nights, he seemed to wield the sword of Solomon, and at every stroke, its talismanic emblem, "*power*," only shone forth with increasing lustre,—disenchanting all machinations to check his advance, and melting all barriers of men, or matter, as the summer sun dissolves, dissipates and bears away the lingering, contending snows of winter.

It was in the maturing ascendency of this new system of tactics, that the British and American armies came to an issue. The colonists had been thoroughly proven in the skirmishing warfare of the Indian, had acquired signal skill in the use of the rifle, and by contempt of exposure and repeated battles upon the frontier, had been taught many lessons which were wild, but impressive, in the direction of attack and defense.

Upon this training, if but slowly, the stern discipline and military vigor of Washington, Greene, Steuben and Lee were to be grafted.

Another element gave character to the American army, and made soldiers quickly. Independently of the spirit of the struggle itself, the colonists possessed unusual intelligence and mental culture for men of that period ; and those who controlled the public policy were men whose capacity and moral worth were preëminent above all others.

The great skill in manœuvre which characterized Frederic was well represented by Clinton, Knyphausen, Percy and Tarleton, and the German troops came promptly up to duty in accordance with the methods of severe schooling to which they had been trained.

Washington, Greene, Lee, Maxwell, and other competent commanders, both American and foreign, who took the American army in hand, were compelled to enter the contest before their soldiers, however well-drilled, individually, could possibly acquire that concert of action which makes of an educated army a perfect machine.

This affords the clew to many disasters which attended operations in the field. An illustration of recent date will define the point in view.

Before the battle of Bull Run, in the American war of 1861–1865, the single regiments of the Federal army had been thoroughly instructed in battalion drill. These movements were exact. Brigade commanders had been assigned, so far as possible, from the colonels of the regular army, and evolutions of the line, in skeleton and by divisions, had been commenced and well advanced. Practically, however, the regiment was the unit, and these units largely maintained their organic coherence, when the freshly organized brigades and divisions, *parted*, in the first trial at arms with an earnest adversary. The general commanding, McDowell, himself a model type of the complete soldier, was crowded to the front, and did all that any great captain could have done with an army not yet perfected in that discipline which must inter-penetrate all parts and hold them fast to system, even in the decimation of battle.

But, as with that army, so with the army of Washington, the opportunity was forced, while the exigencies were too pressing to give time to make a really *perfect army*, and *that result* had to be evolved out of the battle struggle itself.

The most difficult position which troops can hold, is that which requires them to stand under fire, in passive waiting but with entire confidence that this position is for eventual benefit, whenever the controlling mind shall unfold his purpose. A "*forlorn hope*" has a stimulus. The other demands supreme steadiness, the hardness of adamant. This text is not discursive, nor without interest and direct relations to the battle narrative hereafter furnished. All that has been said is but a meagre indication of that exhaustive drain which war makes upon all possible resources that can apply force to the resolution of battle issues.

As grand tactics deals with the conflict of armies, so their organization and composition is worthy of consideration. Moreover, it involves good combinations before, as well as during the progress of battle.

It is to be noticed, in passing on, that military nations promptly seize and apply all improvements that any single nation originate, so that the balance stands nearly the same as when war was waged under systems of an earlier period. Brain and muscle give force and value to all alike.

As a full discussion of the military art is reserved for a future volume, only those elements will be considered which afford a key to the battles of the period under review.

The chief branches or arms of military service, Artillery, Cavalry and Infantry, proportioned as in order named, from least to most numerous, have varying values, according to the service required, Infantry composing the fundamental strength of all armies.

Improvements in artillery have made impossible that mighty sweep of mounted troops, which now and then, in early days, bore down whole armies by their intrinsic weight. Swift desolation may still be carried over a wide range of country, communications may be cut off and distant points may be struck suddenly by such a force; but there can be no overwhelming assault, by cavalry, upon a strong army well supplied with well handled guns.

During the war of 1775–1781, a real restriction was imposed upon the movements of cavalry by the nature of the country, so that their service was largely confined to attack upon columns already broken, independent operations against similar forces, raids upon supply trains, or the dispersion of small detachments.

The British dragoons did substantial service at Germantown, Monmouth and Brandywine, although in the last named action they were not employed until after the division of General Sullivan was in full retreat. Some of the Royalist volunteer cavalry proved quite

efficient ; but Tarleton's Legion was especially known for its sleepless
activity, its keenness of scent in pursuit, and sometimes, for its relent-
less vigor of stroke.

During the early part of the war, the American army was deficient
in this arm of the service. Colonel Lee, known as " Light Horse
Harry," and Colonel Washington, handled mounted men with signal
ability, and the latter, at the battle of Cowpens, inflicted a blow upon
Colonel Tarleton which, according to his own " Narrative," almost
ruined " The Legion."   Sumter, Marion and Horry performed
brilliant feats and made their respective corps distinguished for a
semi-ubiquitous warfare in the swamp districts of the Carolinas.

It was rarely the case that artillery determined an action in the
field, simply by superior weight of metal and its destructive force.
The short range of the guns then in use, the difficulty of moving them,
and the general reliance upon infantry, in close action, limited the
supremacy of this great arm of war.

The infantry had its scouts and skirmishing parties, but such
detachments were more frequently mounted men ; and modern skirmishing was hardly known until the French initiated the system of a
thin line of sharp-shooters in advance of moving columns.

General Morgan's rifle command, or brigade, was the nearest
approach to a systematic skirmishing force, while equally efficient in
general action. The British army itself, especially in the southern
districts, followed the example of the Americans and organized independent rifle corps, which, more than once, did efficient service. The
brigades were generally small in numbers, often not exceeding eight
hundred men, and by this means the number of opposing forces was
often greatly over-estimated on both sides.

Although the artillery was then employed, as now, wherever
actually needed, it was habitually posted in the centre unless required
at the flank, and was used mainly to hold or assail positions occupied
by troops. It lacked the mobility which the light artillery of modern
times has attained. General Burgoyne was sharply criticised before
the " House of Commons " for taking too many heavy guns upon his
expedition from Canada, and yet, it appears from a careful review of
the evidence offered in his case, that he was simply cumbered with
the exact proportion which rigid precedent assigned to his command, irrespective of the field of service it was to be dragged
over.

The engineer corps of that period was well organized and well handled, and by virtue of the short range of guns, they had full as much active work in the trenches as in more modern times.

The Order of Battle varies with the features of the country, the position of the armies, and the object in view. Whether the movement be offensive or defensive, which circumstances alone can determine, there are certain prevailing methods of arranging a command to meet the issue.

The parallel order must have, on one or both sides, elective positions to be held or seized, or the issue will be simply one of physical strength and the contingency of superior numbers or skill. In this order, whether the centre or one wing be the object of attack, it is certain that the concentration must be prompt for the blow or it will fail, provided that the enemy is closed up, so as to be able, quickly, to reinforce the part assailed. It can rarely, if ever, be of indifferent value whether to strike the centre, or one wing, unless the force be so small as to meet either attack equally well.

At the battle of Germantown, Washington advanced with his main force upon the British centre, striking full at the outpost in the village, while large detachments were sent to confront each wing and hold them back from giving support to their centre.

The parallel order may be modified by reinforcement of the centre or either wing, and this will often happen during the manœuvers or feints, which are resorted to, that the enemy may not antici pate the genuine attack.

A *crochet* upon the flank like the letter L, is often of value, ⌐, ⌐, thus offering two faces for defense, or presenting a second front perpendicular to the first, for the purpose of turning the flank of the enemy or striking to his rear. The advance of the British right wing at Long Island secured the latter result, first capturing the American centre, and then cutting off the right wing and capturing its commander. In this action the flanking force swept the whole American line, routing it utterly.

The crochet proper is susceptible of being roughly dealt with, if the adversary can mass artillery at the angle ; and the movement generally is hazardous, unless to resist an attempt upon a flank, or the force be strong enough to take some risk in an advance.

The convex and concave orders of battle are self-expressive. One advances and the other refuses its centre. At the battle of Cowpens the display of the American centre, *as a feint*, followed by its prompt withdrawal, enticed Tarleton within a trap and it was sprung upon him.

The oblique order has advantages for an inferior force, as it may rapidly gather up the refused wing to support the advance, or concentrate rapidly if compelled to retire.

The order by echelon on the centre, or one wing, is flexible; and while holding the refused battalion as a reserve, affords prompt support by a direct advance, and so disposes the whole command that it may, with equal promptness, operate toward either flank, or to the rear.

Modifications of these forms are various, but unimportant in this connection. *The exact formation* of *parade* is never long-lived in real action. Whatever may be the form adopted, there must be care not to prolong the line beyond support and thus leave a gap which will admit a quick and intelligent adversary. This gap at Bunker Hill will be noticed hereafter. A wise determination of choice in this important matter, may enable an inferior force to retard a superior force, may persuade it to fight at disadvantage, or even force it to movements which will set the inferior force free from peril.

In this connection may be applied the suggestion, that both vanguard and rear-guard of armies which are on the verge of action, are to be especially warned of the importance of their trusts.

When Cornwallis approached Trenton in January, 1777, with full purpose to capture or destroy Washington's army, his rear-guard was dropped so far behind as to involve a severe contest to extricate it from the grasp of his adversary.

Before the battle of Camden, the van-guard of the two armies, each intent upon surprising the antagonist, met after midnight, and by their mutual surprise, hurried the American army prematurely into action, at bitter cost.

On the other hand the strong van-guard of the American army was so loosely handled at Monmouth, that Clinton put in jeopardy one half of the entire American army, and extricated his own army from a position of no little peril.

To these general remarks as to the battle-issue, there may well be added the opinion of Colonel Hamley. "Orders of battle establish the relations existing between the hostile lines before or during the encounter." "The great object in modern battles is to bring at a certain point of the battle field a superior number of troops to bear upon the enemy. The design is screened by false attacks, by features of the ground, by a general advance of skirmishers, and by deceptive formations and manœuvers. The attacking force must be strengthened at the expense of some other portion of the line. To engage that other part would be to offer to the enemy the opportunity of restoring the equilibrium of the battle which it has been the object of the manœuver to disturb. Therefore modern battles have been for the most part partial attacks, when the assailant puts his foot no farther than he can be sure of drawing it back again."

The following is a brief epitome of Baron Jomini's views upon the selection of tactical positions:

That it be easier to fall upon the enemy than for him to approach.

That artillery have all its possible effect in defense.

That the ground selected conceal subordinate movements from the enemy, while commanding a view of the movements of the enemy.

That the line of retreat be unobstructed, and the flanks well secured.

The matter of retreats will have brief notice in another connection. Those of the war under review were frequent and often masterly.

CHAPTER XII.

LOGISTICS.

LOGISTICS was defined as, " The practical art of bringing armies fully equipped into the field."

The primary necessity for a thorough preparation of all the ele ments which go to equip, transport, and sustain an army, is apparent without discussion.

It is equally obvious that while the strategist and tactician must have wisdom in all elements that make the successful soldier, it is impossible for all the details of army outfit and army movement to be under their immediate care, while laden with the burden of directing war and fighting battles.

The details of logistics are therefore more especially within the sphere of various staff duty, and that department of public trust which superintends army supply. But it is far from sufficient, that arsenals be filled, that provisions abound, that hospital supplies have accumulated, and that every possible item which can be needed in camp or field, in victory or defeat, by night or by day, has been provided, unless each item shall be accessible at the right time and at the right place. Certain materials must accompany the first advance of an army; some attend the main army, and others are supplied as contingency requires. All these must be at hand in fit proportion to the force, with no surplus to embarrass movements, and no deficit to retard them. The supply must never fail, but flow on as the army moves, smoothly, adequately, and inevitably.

It is in small details, numberless and perplexing, which worry men more than grave issues, that logistics finds its great burden. In one contingency, a box of horse-shoes may be of more value than a box of cartridges; and in another, a roll of lint may do more service than a bale of clothing.

The wants of the soldier as well as the requirements of the gen-

Parallel Order of Battle.

Re-inforced Wing.

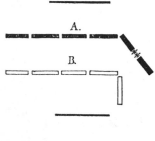

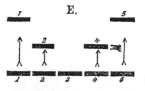

A.

B.

E.

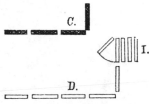

C.

I.

F.

D.

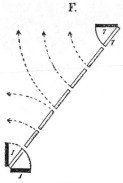

A. *Wheels left wing, with guns, to break
the Crotchet, made to the rear by B.*

D. *Makes re inforced Crotchet to the
front, to gain the flank. C makes a
Crotchet to the rear.*

E. *Echelon by both wings, refusing
the center, assimilated to concave
formation.*

F. *Oblique Order, giving ready formation to the Left, or Front.*

G. *In Echelon by the Right, indicating the readiness of Change of
Front to the left, perpendicular
to original formation.*

H. *Echelon by the right, and whole
line advanced, out of Echelon.*

I. *Advance in column to break Wing*

G.

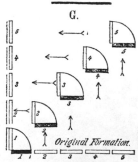

Original Formation.

H.

Front advanced

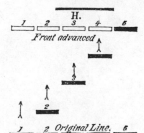

Original Line.

eral, are to be met promptly and sufficiently, or embarrassment must attend every movement, and the entire campaign will be imperiled or sacrificed.

It is not to be questioned that the failure of the movement of Napoleon III. upon Prussia, was considerably promoted by bad logistics, and that the success of the allies during the Crimean war was secured through excellent adjustments and prompt execution in this very branch of military art. The Prussian logistics in the Franco-Prussian war were admirable, and no operations of modern times, within a period so short and decisive, have evinced a more thorough preparation and adaptation of materials to meet the demands of battle-issues.

The Abyssinia and Coast of Guinea campaigns of Great Britain were marked by commensurate skill in adjusting the outfit of the command to its necessities, whether of service or climate. It would be difficult to estimate the expenditure of material which entered into the American war of 1861–1865. The several staff departments were severely tasked by the enormous drain upon their resources, and yet the exacting demand was fully met.

The division of labor alone made the result possible. The sphere of logistics however, is not bound up in merely mechanical work. In modern war the single direction of transportation requires the control of a master mind. Great talent is found at the head of railroad corporations; and similar capacity is necessary to move armies.

The Prussian railways moved more than six hundred thousand troops. The advance upon Paris involved the adjustments of rolling stock and material to different roads. Every department of bridge building and engineering was called into requisition, and such was the precision and omnipresent control, that accidents were rare, and the vast army was unfailingly supplied with all things essential to its comfort and its offensive work. The inspection of troops and of supplies belong to this department.

There can be no deficiency in the means of equipping an army that is not referable to bad logistics. To give effect to this responsible trust, there must be thorough concert of purpose and exact system in the execution. Overcrowded transports or trains, the indiscriminate shipment of supplies, the confusion of material belonging to different arms of the service, and the misdirection of these supplies are inevitable, unless the method be laid down clearly, and competent officers discharge the duty.   It is not, however, the whole of logistics to furnish the army in the manner indicated.

The duties of warehouse man, and forwarder of merchandise, however wisely planned and executed, are not up to the demands of the army.   Depots and hospitals are to be established and sustained ; a watchful eye must constantly guard against any deficiency at every point where the army will make its demands, and this demand is coëxtensive with every army movement whether of general or of minor concern.   The broken down bridge must find a guardian at hand to restore it promptly.

Siege-guns must be found, side by side with the means and talent necessary to put them in position ; the regulation of the movement of the troops themselves must be so discriminating and exact, that no conflict of route or orders shall cross the plan of the general commanding ; and the assignments for rest, for intrenching, or advancing, must be intelligently communicated to the officers who are respectively called upon to discharge these special duties.   The protection of all supplies, and their location and movement, so that they shall not be mere *impedimenta*, to cripple the general command, is equally important to the highest success.

No department of duty in military operations is more imperative in its necessities, or more painfully embarrassing under neglect, than the care of the sick and wounded ; and no other department, if neglected, is such a trying encumbrance during the active issues of a campaign.   Here logistics must come in with the fullest possible equivalent for distress that is inevitable, and here the stern machinery of war must have the appliances of a *great heart*, so that even in its rigid outline, the soldier shall feel that there is represented the abundant sympathy of the state for which he imperils life.

Independently of all these mechanical adjustments, however intelligently administered, there is a vast field of intellectual labor that is behind the physical facts.   Whatever may be the capacity of the master brain which directs the battle and shapes its antecedents, the *details* must be so conformed as to exactly accord with his purpose. Details themselves must be modified by circumstances, and the fluctuations of battle issues are often as critical as those of a game of chess, calling for new adaptation of material to meet the modified relations of the forces employed.

Clear instructions are indispensable to military success, and these must be as clearly understood by those who are to execute those

instructions.   Battle history is full of disasters which attach discredit
to great captains, when the responsibility properly belonged to those
who failed to appreciate, or accurately to execute, the will of the
commander.

It is authoritatively stated, that on the evening of July 4th, 1809,
before the battle of Wagram, the night being dark, and the rain falling in torrents, when one hundred and fifty thousand men were
pushed across the arm of the Danube, there one hundred and fifty
yards wide, by three bridges, that it was assigned to Davoust, who
commanded the right wing, to cross the centre bridge, and to Oudinot,
who commanded the centre, to cross the bridge to the right.   These
commanders obeyed the orders as received, and such was the marvellous discipline of the troops that the armies passed each other without disorder, and the movement was accomplished without knowledge
of the enemy.   While the error is attributed to Napoleon's haste in
dictating the order, Berthier is criticised for not observing the mistake, since he was called upon to make ten copies of the order for
information of the army.

Jomini broadly asserts, that " Napoleon made no provision for the
contingency of retreat, and lived, not only to demonstrate what *might*
be done, but *what* a good general should avoid."

It was in the sphere of logistics that the British army excelled, and
the American army was deficient.   The colonies had furnished army
contingents in the old French war, but these operated under the
control of experienced officers of the British army.

The sudden demand for the thorough equipment of twenty
thousand men designated for the siege of Boston, devolved vast military responsibilities upon inexperienced citizen militia.   The public
trusts which involved the purchase of supplies were too often confided to ignorant or dishonest parties.   The eager struggle for place
and preferment entered into the army at the outset, and almost as
soon as certain regiments received an outfit, the expiration of their
short enlistment involved a new issue of arms and equipments, or the
transfer of those already issued from the returning to the incoming
recruits.   Those considerations will find their illustration in the history of successive campaigns, and will be therefore passed by until the
effect of bad logistics shall mark the issues themselves.

The British army realized difficulties of a different kind in the
same general direction, until taught that the antagonist was one that
would enforce respect at their cost, if the full measure of military

preparation was not made to meet an enemy fully competent to test their mettle.

The first action itself, that of Breed's Hill (Bunker's Hill), was marked by carelessness, which amounted to gross neglect, the shot for the guns first landed being of larger caliber than the guns themselves.

The Army of Burgoyne, as already indicated, was inadequately furnished for the expedition, and many similar defects in preparation were predicated upon the supposition that the adversary was to be dealt with as an inferior in all military qualities, and therefore the risks taken were not unmilitary, but either economical or non-essential elements in the struggle.

A crowning element of logistics obtains in all truly military operations, and that is, that so far as possible, they shall be without the knowledge of the enemy. The battle of Bennington had its incentive in the purpose of General Burgoyne to complement his own scanty supplies from the depot, reported to have been accumulated near that place for the army of General Schuyler. Many of the minor operations of each army were predatory, and to secure rations for the needy troops. The British forces endeavored at times to live off the country, and the American troops during the scarcity of genuine money, were compelled to seize horses, cattle, flour, and other provisions which merchants and farmers refused to sell.

During the term that General Greene was quarter-master-general of the American army, the logistics were as good as possible under the changing circumstances of that fluctuating, uncertain force; and Colonel Alexander Hamilton, who had been introduced by General Greene to Washington as a young man of promise, gained deserved credit for his skill in the preparation of orders and accuracy in their distribution.

In this department, however, the remark which Baron Jomini applies to Napoleon, can with truth be said of Washington. "*He was his own best chief of staff.*"

CHAPTER XIII.

MISCELLANEOUS CONSIDERATIONS.

"A FINE RETREAT," says Baron Jomini, "should meet with a reward equal to that given for a great victory."

"A beaten army," says the Archduke Charles, "is no longer in the hands of its general."

"When an army makes a compulsory retreat," says Colonel Hamley, "it is not in a condition to renew the contest. The troops that have been driven from the field will be slow to form front for battle; confusion, too, will be added to despondency, for regiments will be broken and mixed, artillery will be separated from its ammunition, supply trains will be thrown into disorder by the sudden reflux, and the whole machine will be for the time disjointed."

In the American war, 1861–1865, the Federal retreat under General Banks from the Shenandoah Valley, and those of the Confederate army from Yorktown, Antietam, Corinth, and Murfreesboro, were signal for their good military dispositions and preëminent success.

But during the war of 1775–1781, the fluctuations of the tide of war induced retreats, under even more pressing exigencies and with equally skillful execution.

The march of General Clinton from Philadelphia to the shelter of the fleet near Sandy Hook, was in all respects a proof of his merit as a soldier and brave commander ; but while it was a retreat, it was not the *sequel* of *defeat*, and a desperate race for an asylum of safety. The transfer of his army to the original base with view to a new destination, was a prudential and strategic movement ; but failure to achieve anticipated results at Philadelphia, did not so demoralize his command as if it had been beaten out of its city quarters by a hostile force.

The retreats of Washington from Long Island to Pennsylvania,— from Princeton to the hills of New Jersey—and from the field of

Germantown—of Lafayette from Barren Hill, and of Morgan and Greene from the Carolinas, were made under circumstances of extreme peril. The rescue of the armies from impending ruin, was in each case quite material to the fate of the whole war. The most cursory reference to the maps will vindicate the claim of those officers to the tribute which introduces this chapter.

The movement of Cornwallis to Yorktown in 1781, while embracing ulterior plans, was substantially a retreat, and neither his generalship nor that of General Clinton is impeached by the circumstance which enforced his final surrender. The record will vindicate this position, and show that the misunderstanding between those officers which so long annoyed parliament and the British public, was unnecessary, provided that the burden of their failure had fallen where the responsibility belonged, upon the ministry.

The conditions of a wise retreat are many. The tendency is to panic. The whole matter of essential supplies is thrown into confusion. All facilities for food or rest are disturbed, and the only remedy lies in the self-possession, firmness, and daring of the commanding officers. Absurd panics have attended the best of troops. False alarms have converted a well organized retreat into a precipitate flight, and more than once the real victor has lost his laurels by failure to realize his success.

While the army of Washington was embarking at Brooklyn for passage to New York, on the night of September twenty-ninth, 1776, that general dispatched an *aid-de-camp* to General Mifflin, who was superintending the movement, with orders to hasten all the troops on their march. This order, given in the broadest sense, started the very troops which had been posted in the redoubts and trenches, to keep up the appearance of vigilant watch over the movements of the enemy. These men, impressed with the necessity of haste, pushed for the landing; but Washington's prompt measures suspended their march, and they coolly resumed their positions. This temporary desertion was not known to the beseigers, and thus the retreat was secured and the army saved. It is just such crises which dignify retreat, and exalt the wisdom and heroism of its execution.

The rear guard in a retreat, while adequate to check pursuit, must not be so strengthened as to recall the whole army for its support, unless some position be secured which will warrant a renewal of battle. The elements as stated by Colonel Hamley, are too significant to warrant hope of such coolness and concentration of material and men.

as will warrant success under the ordinary phases of a positive retreat from a beaten field.

The *pursuit* of a *retreating army* involves hardly less wisdom, unless the victor has sufficient cavalry to harass his adversary, successfully cut off all fugitive detachments, and occupy the rear guard until adequate force can be brought up to induce a new action. The pressure, however, upon the retiring force, should be so constant and earnest as to keep it too busy, in escape, to allow time for the destruction of bridges and the interposition of obstacles to the pursuit. Cavalry and artillery may thus be stopped for a sufficient length of time to save the army pursued.

It is of high importance that the pursuit shall be so directed by flank movements, as to crowd the retiring army upon rivers or portions of country which check their progress, and give strategical advantage to the adversary pursuing.

Diversions, such as those made by the British army from New York into Connecticut, are calculated to interfere with the general plans of the adversary. They have value in proportion as that result is effected, and the army which spares the detachment still retains an adequate force for its general operations. It is due to General Washington to state, that he was so bent upon his purpose to strike those armies which kept the field in force, that he could not be diverted from chief and paramount objects by those which were minor and transient, even while such movements inflicted local waste and real loss in property and life.

The diversions of Gréene and Morgan in 1781, which threatened Ninety-six and other posts to the rear of the British headquarters at Camden, really exposed the army to be beaten in detail. The feint was however successful. Fearing lest the base so far advanced from Charleston would be imperiled, and every benefit of the recent victory over Gates would be lost, the army was divided for the protection of the threatened posts, and the American detachments rejoined the army with safety.

Improvement of success. After the battle of Bennington in 1777, the American troops, elated with the result of the day's fight, occupied themselves so intently with the plunder of the battle field, that the artillery of Colonel Breyman, alone, aroused them to the conviction that another enemy was on their hands, and that victory itself was well nigh lost.

General Howe habitually failed to realize the best fruits of success

It was characteristic of Wellington and Napoleon, as of Marlborough and Frederic, that there was *no rest after victory*. What next? Strike on and finish war, that peace may replace conflict. If either of these great captains failed to achieve the highest possible results, it was Napoleon, when ambition and restless pursuit of military supremacy would not let him rest when peace was within reach, and when its blessings were most of all things essential to the well being of France.

Passage of rivers. The multiplication of machinery and the great respect paid to mechanical skill, have greatly facilitated the passage of streams. The British army transported a bridge of boats and pontoons to New Jersey in December, 1777, but returned it to the coast, as soon as Washington refused to be enticed from the fastness of Morristown. Upon his original retreat to Pennsylvania, he had cleared the left bank of every accessible craft, so that although he was landing his rear guard as the British troops reached the river, there were no facilities for further pursuit.

While at Valley Forge, the American army established a bridge across the Schuylkill, for the double purpose of communication with the country, and to secure a means of retreat in case the British army should threaten his camp.

During the war of 1861–1865, "The Board of Trade Battery," and regiment from Chicago, was so thoroughly composed of skilled mechanics, that their bridge building and their coöperation in the passage of streams by the armies of the middle zone was *simply wonderful.*

Such movements are generally to be anticipated, or covered by light earthworks or bridge heads—*têtes de pont.* A memorable instance of the value of such a position is that of the defense of the bridge-head and a light earthwork at Franklin, Tennessee, just after the principal action, November thirtieth, 1864, when a Federal corps commanded by General Schofield, crowded by the entire army of General Hood, successfully crossed the Harpeth river, and effected their retreat upon Nashville together with artillery and baggage. The river banks were precipitous, the stream was not fordable, a single railroad bridge had to be adapted to the pressing emergency; and the assailing force, more than double in numbers, was that army which immediately after attempted the capture of Nashville itself.

The neglect to establish a sufficient rear guard and light earthwork at Cowan's Ford, in 1781, especially ordered by General Greene, gave to the advance of Cornwallis a brilliant success.

The passage or attempted passage of rivers, is often a *feint* to mislead an enemy. Such movements involve strategical no less than tactical considerations, and this in proportion as the hostile force, the character of the river, and the immediate issue assume importance. The passage of the East river at New York, September twenty-eighth, 1776, and of the Delaware river on Christmas night of the same year, are characteristic operations in the passage of streams.

Obstructions. In the war of 1775–1781, the movements of armies were largely affected by that class of labor, which, without fighting, gave distinctive shape to more active operations by obstructing the advance or retreat of armies. The destruction of bridges, the felling of trees, and other obstructions were of signal service. The policy of the British army was to strike quickly and hard, before the colonies could concentrate men, improve discipline, procure arms, and inter-pose substantial defense. The American army was, constructively, on the defensive. *Its* policy was to delay and wear out its opponent, postpone premature collisions, and as far as possible, only to engage under such local advantages as would encourage troops and enhance the promise of success. Familiarity with the country, the scarcity of skillful engineers at the outset, and a large experience in frontier war-fare encouraged them to pursue this policy with success.

In every struggle when invasion threatens the homes of a people, there has been this spontaneous movement, even of non-combatants, thus to add to the efficiency of military defense and imperil the hostile advance. It becomes the *business* of *everybody*, and the troops in the field are both stimulated and strengthened by all such mani-festations of popular zeal.

Guards and outposts. A single word only is required to magnify the office of scouts and pickets. Vigilance, obedience and nerve mark the true picket-man. In darkness and storm he is the uncompro-mising guardian of the safety of the entire army. *Indifference is trea-son !* To sleep on post in an enemy's presence is worthy of death, its established penalty. He holds the key of the outer door. He has the pass-word ! The Sacred record thus testifies of the faithful and the faithless watchman.

"Son of man, I have made thee a watchman unto the House of Israel, therefore hear the word at my mouth, and give them warning from me."

" His watchmen are blind ; they are all ignorant; they are all dumb dogs, they can not bark ; sleeping, lying down, lying down to slumber !"

Thus signals of alarm, often by watch-fires and smoking beacons, had early introduction, and there will appear in this narrative more than one instance when the salvation of armies and detachments entirely hinged upon skillful reconnoissance and faithful picket duty.

The use of spies very naturally comes within this general class. Prisoners of war are also the source of valuable information. Each class is a doubtful dependence, unless corroborating circumstances confirm their statements. The memories of Andre and Hale are embalmed. Their loyalty to their cause, their intrinsic excellence as men, and their noble conduct in the extreme hour, have given them a like place of honor in British and American history. If Greene blotted his final signature to the order for Andre's execution with a tear, it was but the tribute which many an English soldier paid to the memory of Hale.

The sinews of war. The fluctuation in *the numbers* of the American army, was not more striking than their uncertainty of pay, and the scarcity of arms and proper equipments. Several battles were affected by their skill as marksmen. Others were changed at critical moments by possession and prompt use of the bayonet. If as a general rule, the American soldiers were individually better " *shots*," and could give an effect to the rifle which was beyond the reach of the " king's arms," the opposing force had the advantages which the bayonet and a complete equipment afforded. It had adequate supplies of powder, suitable camp equipage, an organized commissariat, and *money*. The history is not more instructive and interesting in respect of the particular deeds done, than in the really extensive operations compassed through disproportioned means and under discouraging circumstances.

Neither side was ready for war when it began. The British army fought with inadequate forces. The American army fought with inadequate means, only complemented by numbers and faith in their ultimate independence. This last consideration was the potent magic which transmuted continental paper into a semblance of money, and dignified semi-starvation into a heroic waiting for the rewards of the future.

The assumption of independence, so long merely nominal, was found to be a poor antidote for hunger and rags, and Congress finally instituted that system of bounties so largely adopted in the war of

1861–1865, and clothed Washington with dictatorial powers, which were absolute and supreme. As the war progressed, artillery and other material of war were furnished by France, and the timely contribution of six million dollars by Louis XVI., as well as a loan then effected, inspired some fresh sentiment that nationality was at last *real.* This practical support, in addition to its moral value, greatly enlarged the facilities for carrying on this conflict.

Alliances. The history of nations is full of treaties of alliance, offensive and defensive. They need no explanation. That of France with the United States had as its incentive the reduction of British power, and was not intrinsically an assurance of sympathy with the primary causes of the American war and of the principles which it asserted. That some phases of the asserted freedom reacted upon France, and made Louis XVI., and Lafayette indeed, to suffer under that license which affected the form of liberty, is a fact. That the French revolution reacted in like manner, and threatened America with the supremacy of a fanatical, godless, and irresponsible democracy is equally true. The names of Washington and Genet embody the whole history of that event.

The *proposition announced*, does not lie in the discussion of the political issues of that period. *It states that few alliances have a natural and binding force.* The interests of few families are exactly common. Those of nations are common only within the province of rightfully accepted international law, just as families have a common relation to social law.

The French alliance, valuable, and to be honored for real aid rendered, was repeatedly put in jeopardy by distinctness of interests; and the proposed diversion of a portion of the American army to reassert and enforce French sovereignty over Canada was but one illustration in point. The extraordinary tact, unselfishness, and solid judgment of Lafayette are monumental, as determining elements which gave to the alliance much of its harmony and enhanced its value.

If the coöperation of several powers in the Crimean war be cited as disproof of the proposition, let it be noticed that the Crimean war was based upon the supposed purpose of Russia to control the Dardanelles at the expense of Turkey, and of all interested maritime nations, and was predicated upon a principle similar to that which binds society to protect its members against lawless assault. It was another protest against a war for *conquest.*

Military commanders. The selection of men who shall vindicate the authority of the state, and apply military force in the battle-issue tasks the highest capacity. Probity, wisdom, unselfishness, and energy belong to such a trust. Appreciation of the issue, and intelligent comprehension of the resources of either contestant, and a cordial adoption of sound military policy, which is in harmony with the best interests of the state, are vital to the highest success.

Baron Jomini says:—" He must have a physical courage which takes no account of obstacles, and a high moral courage capable of great resolution. Unfortunately, this choice of a general is influenced by so many petty passions, that chance, rank, age, favor, party spirit, jealousy, will have as much to do with it as the public interest and justice."

If this eminent scholar, so long confidential with Alexander of Russia, as well as with Napoleon, can so broadly state his conviction, it might be a source of congratulation both for Great Britain and the United States, and indeed for civilization itself, that in the fore-front of the battles of 1775–1781, and during the introduction of the Great Republic to a place among nations, there stands in bold relief the name of WASHINGTON.

Leaving to the battle record, however, the test of battle direction, it is not impolitic or discursive to state the training of one single general of that period, thus to indicate the type of mind and preparation which the period developed.

A Quaker youth of fourteen spared time from the forge to master Euclid and geometry. Providence threw in his way Ezra Stiles, president of Yale College, and Lindley Murray, the grammarian. They became his friends and advisers. Before the war began, and while yet a young man, he carefully studied Cæsar's Commentaries, Marshal Turenne's Works, Sharp's Military Guide, Blackstone's Com mentaries, Jacob's Law Dictionary, Watts' Logic, Locke on the Human Understanding, Ferguson on Civil Society, Swift's Works, and some other models of a similar class of reading. In 1773 he visited a Connecticut militia parade to study its methods. In 1774 he visited Boston, to watch the movements of British troops, and took back to Rhode Island a British sergeant who deserted, as the instructor of the Kentish Guards, a militia company of which he was a member. Such was the proficiency attained by this company, that more than thirty of the private members became officers in the subsequent war. He commanded the brigade of sixteen hundred men which Rhode Island sent to the siege of Boston.

Modest, faithful, dignified, cool in danger, unprovoked, and undaunted by rebuffs or failures, equable, self-sacrificing, truthful, and honest, a man like General George H. Thomas in simple grandeur of character and the fullness of a complete manhood—such a man for the hour, the peril and the duty, was NATHANIEL GREENE.

6

CHAPTER XIV.

THE HOUR OF PREPARATION.

AT length, the thrill of action drove forth on errands of war the long smothered passions which so slowly deepened into a settled conviction that peace could never smile upon the colonies while the supremacy of Great Britain endured. Multiply all assumptions of superiority, all public tokens of contempt, all enforcements of unpalatable law, all restraints upon provincial commerce, and all espionage upon the brain-work which really wrought in behalf of peace, seeking a fair reconciliation with guarantees of representation and personal rights, and their product represents that incubus whose dead weight was upon the American colonies.

That is the statement of history. The longer that burden remained, the heavier it felt. It fretted, then aroused, then inspired, and at last set free the pent-up fires which cast it off forever. Rocked to and fro by the heaving of the heart it would smother, it was compelled to increase its force in proportion as the real vitality of a true soul life pervaded the masses. British will was firm and daring in the child as with the parent.

The legacies of English law, the inheritance of English liberty had *vested* in the colonies. Their eradication or withdrawal was impossible. The time had passed for compromise or limitation of their enjoyment. The issue long before fought out on English soil, and bearing fruit in English ascendency almost world-wide, had to be renewed ; and the authority which might have gladly welcomed the prodigious elasticity and growth of the American dependencies as the future glory of Great Britain, was armed to convert the filial relation into one of slavery.

Lord *Chatham* announced that, " it would be found impossible for freemen in England to wish to see three millions of Englishmen slaves in America "

Lord *Dartmouth* declared, " the effects of General Gage's attempt at Concord to be fatal."

Granville Sharpe of the Ordnance department resigned rather than forward stores to America.

Admiral *Keppel* requested not to be employed against America.

Lord *Effingham* resigned his commission when he learned his regiment was ordered to America.

It was such demonstrations as these that indicated how deeply the mother country was jealous, even of the efforts of her own government to assert a doubtful policy by force of arms.

John Wesley declared, that neither *twenty, forty*, nor *sixty* thousand men could end the dawning struggle. Thus revolution alone could roll off oppression.

The year 1774 witnessed the formation of new militia companies in all the colonies. New England had made especial progress in that direction. The noiseless arming of the people, and the formation of independent organizations was of still earlier date. The experience of the old French war had developed a necessity for fair military acquirements, and had educated many leaders fully competent for small commands ; while a growing uneasiness, in view of the increasing influx of British troops, inspired others to a studious preparation for the probable issue of force with the mother country.

The attempts of official authority to prevent the people from obtaining arms and munitions of war, and to seize those already in their possession, were not limited, as will hereafter appear, to Massachusetts and other New England colonies.

The fortification of Boston Neck by General Gage had elicited from the first Continental Congress, which met on the fifth day of September, 1774, an unequivocal declaration of sympathy with the people of Boston and Massachusetts, and thus the local struggle was swiftly changing its character, and becoming the basis for organized general resistance.

It has been noticed during comment upon the affairs of Lexington and Concord, how rapidly the provincial congress, which succeeded the Massachusetts assembly, developed its purpose to place its militia on a war footing.

During September, 1774, a report had become current that Boston had been attacked. The removal of powder from Cambridge and Charlestown, which belonged to the colony, was magnified, and taken as the open offensive, until the whole country was excited. One author states that, "within thirty-six hours, nearly thirty thousand men were under arms," and a profound impression was made even upon the American Congress then in session in Philadelphia. This only indicated the breadth of that feeling which already panted for armed expression.

On Sunday, the twenty-second day of April, 1775, Massachusetts declared a necessity for the employment of thirty thousand men in defense, and called upon adjoining colonies for their proportional quota, assuming as her own burden the enrollment of thirteen thousand six hundred men.

On the twenty-fifth day of April Rhode Island devoted fifteen hundred men to "An army of Observation."

On the day following, Connecticut voted a contingent of six thousand men.

On the twentieth day of May, New Hampshire tendered her proportion, which was two thousand men.

Each colonial contingent went up to Boston as a separate army, with independent organization and responsibility. The powder and food of each of these armies was distinct, and there was little that was homogeneous, except the purpose which impelled them to concentrate.

Massachusetts selected Artemas Ward, who had served under General Abercrombie, to be general-in-chief, John Thomas to be lieutenant-general, and Richard Gridley, an experienced soldier and engineer, to organize artillery and act as engineer in chief.

Connecticut sent General Putnam, whom active service in the old French war and in the West Indies, had inured to daring and exposure; General Wooster, an old veteran of the expedition to Louisburg thirty years before, who had served both as colonel and brigadier-general in the French and Indian war, and General Spencer.

Rhode Island entrusted her troops to General Greene; with Varnum, Hitchcock, and Church as subordinates.

New Hampshire furnished General Stark, also a veteran of former wars.

Pomeroy and Prescott were also experienced in the operations of the old French and Indian wars.

Thus these armies came together, and General Ward was by courtesy accepted as acting commander-in-chief. It was there before Boston, early in June, 1775, that General Greene declared that there were six indispensable conditions to the promptest success.

First. That there be one General-in-chief.

Second. That the army should be enlisted for the war.

Third. That a system of bounties should be ordained which would provide for the families of soldiers absent in the field.

Fourth. That the troops should serve wherever required through the colonies.

Fifth. That funds should be borrowed equal to the demands of the war, for the complete equipment and support of the army.

Sixth. That Independence should be declared at once, and every resource of every colony be pledged to its support.

The history of the war furnished its indorsement of the wisdom of these propositions. His patriotism was like that of Patrick Henry, who declared that "landmarks and boundaries were thrown down, that distinctions between Virginians, Pennsylvanians, New Yorkers, and New Englanders were no more," adding, "*I am not a Virginian, but an American.*"

By the middle of June, and before the battle of Breed's Hill, the colonies were substantially united in the war. During March, 1775, Richard Henry Lee offered resolutions before the second Virginia convention, "that the colony be immediately put in a state of defense," and advocated "the reorganizing, arming, and disciplining of the militia."

The winds seemed to carry the sound of the first conflict. In six days it aroused Maryland. Intermediate colonies in turn responded to the summons. Greene's company of Kentish Guards started the morning after the Lexington skirmish. The citizens of Rhode Island took possession of more than forty cannon, and asserted their claim to control all colonial stores.

NEW YORK organized a committee of one hundred, and then of one thousand leading citizens, to assure her support in the struggle, declaring, that "all the horrors of civil war could not force her submission to the acts of the crown." The City Hall and Custom House were seized by the patriots.

Arming and drilling were immediate. "An association for the defense of colonial rights" was formed, and on the twenty-second day of May, the colonial assembly was succeeded by a Provincial Congress, and the new order of government was in full force and effect.

In NEW JERSEY the people seized one hundred thousand dollars which were in the Provincial treasury, and devoted it to "raising troops to defend the liberties of America" The news reached Philadelphia on the twenty-fourth day of April. Prominent men at once accepted command, among them General Dickinson, afterwards prominent in duty ; and on the first day of May, the assembly made an appropriation of money to raise troops.   Dr. Franklin, just returned from England, was made chairman of the committee of safety, and the city was fully aroused to a hearty support of the common cause.

In MARYLAND, the inhabitants seized the Provincial magazine and fifteen hundred stand of arms, enrolled " volunteers for the army about Boston," appointed a committee of observation, " and recommended a system of economy, and abstinence from horse-racing, fairs, and other extravagant amusements as derogatory to the character of patriots at that solemn hour."

VIRGINIA was as tinder, ripe for the spark.   A positive issue had been made between Lord Dunmore and the people.   The former had sent powder of the colony on board of a vessel lying in the harbor. The militia gathered in force under Patrick Henry.   The powder was paid for by way of compromise, but Henry was denounced as a traitor. The storm gathered hourly, and Lord Dunmore took refuge on board of the *Fowey*, ship of war, then lying in York river.

The governor of NORTH CAROLINA had also quarreled with the people, in his effort to thwart the organization of a Provincial Congress in April.   It was organized, however, and while the people were consulting as to a permanent separation from Great Britain, the message from Boston intensified their purpose and ratified their judgment.

In SOUTH CAROLINA, on the twenty-first day of April, committees appointed for the purpose, took eight hundred stand of arms, and two hundred cutlasses from the magazine for the use of the patriots, upon receiving information that orders had been sent to all governors to seize the arms and ammunition of the colonists.   This order was based upon the act of parliament forbidding the exportation of arms to the colonies.   The news from Lexington, received twenty days after that skirmish, added fuel to the flame.

At Savannah, GEORGIA, six members of the " council of safety," broke open the public magazine, seized the powder, placed it in secret places for safety, and thus testified of their readiness to meet the grave future with decision and spirit, and this, before receiving news of the beginning of war.

Such is the briefest possible outline of the state of concurrent feeling and preparation, which harmonized with the resistance offered at Lexington and Concord.

The first Colonial Congress had authorized the formation of an

"American Association," under a "declaration of colonial rights," having for its purpose entire non-intercourse with Great Britain, Ireland, and the West Indies. This was a measure of policy designed to force a financial crisis before the British cabinet, and compel a modification of its laws ; but it also was aggressive in spirit, and gave warning of ulterior measures in reserve. The second Continental Congress met on the tenth day of May, 1775, immediately after Allen's capture of Ticonderoga.

Prompt measures were taken for the purchase of materials for the manufacture of powder and of cannon. Authority was given for the emission of two millions of Spanish milled dollars, and a resolution was adopted that the " *Twelve Confederate Colonies* " be pledged for the redemption of bills of credit, then directed to be issued.

A formal system of " Rules and Articles of war " was adopted, and due provision was made for raising an additional armed force, sufficient to meet the British reinforcements then expected from England, for the enforcement of acts of parliament which were denounced as " unconstitutional, oppressive and cruel."

Meanwhile, the colonial troops continued in position before Boston, and the state of war was so fully accepted, that a regular exchange of prisoners was made on the sixth day of June.

On the twelfth of June General Gage offered pardon to all, Samuel Adams and John Hancock excepted, who would lay down their arms, following this proclamation with a declaration of martial law.

This second Continental Congress promptly adopted the forces before Boston, and such as should be afterwards organized, as THE AMERICAN CONTINENTAL ARMY.

A light infantry organization was authorized on the fourteenth of June, to consist of " expert riflemen," of which six companies should be raised in Pennsylvania, two in Maryland, and two in Virginia, who should join the army at Boston as soon as possible. Additional companies were authorized before the adjournment of Congress.

On the fifteenth of June, the appointment of commander-in-chief of all continental troops then raised, or to be raised, was authorized, and George Washington was unanimously elected upon a vote by ballot.

A brief outline of the personal and military antecedents of that officer is highly proper, since his identification with the struggle for American Independence is a memorial lesson for his countrymen to study, and no less valuable to the intelligent appreciation of American history by the world at large.

The author does not propose to fill up his volume with biography, or to enlarge upon civil issues. All readers have access to complete histories. He exercises a choice, freely to use whatever his limits will warrant in carrying out his own purpose.

Washington was ready to enter the British navy as a midshipman at fifteen years of age, but withdrew from his chosen profession upon his mother's request.

At the age of nineteen, full of zeal in military studies, and those relating to civil engineering, he accepted an appointment as an Adjutant-general of Virginia, with the rank of major.

In the year 1753, while organizing militia for frontier service, he was detailed by General Dinwiddie upon a delicate mission to the French commandants of the frontier posts, and made the trying journey through a country infested by hostile Indians, with signal credit. During this journey he selected the forks of the Monongahela and Alleghany rivers as the proper site of a fort, subsequently established by the French as Fort du Quesne, (now Pittsburgh).

The journal of that winter's expedition is marked by critical notes of the military features of the country; and that journey without doubt, formed the basis of that peculiar skill and strategical exactness with which he adopted military positions during his subsequent career. At Great Meadows, Fort Necessity, and during Braddock's campaign he gained a high reputation for sagacity, practical wisdom, knowledge of human nature, and courage. These operations were followed by a careful inspection of all posts, and the careful organization of the Virginia militia, which was widely dispersed in small parties over an extensive range of wild country.

During these inspections he caused the posts to be made more secure by felling trees which would cover an advancing enemy, and otherwise instructed officers and men in the details of a peculiarly trying service. With a thousand men, he was charged with the care and defense of four hundred miles of frontier.

His formal suggestions as to army organization, movements, and supply, made from time to time, furnish maxims which are the equivalent of those which obtain with standard modern writers, and indicate the thoroughness of his study, and the practical use he made of real experience. After his occupation of Fort du Quesne, abandoned by the French, and the establishment of comparative quiet along the frontier, he became commander-in-chief of all the troops raised in Virginia.

As an engineer and disciplinarian he achieved credit, and when summoned to the command of the Continental army, he brought to the public service those qualities which enforced success.

The officers who were associated with Washington in high command were as follows :

MAJOR GENERALS.

1st. Artemas Ward ; already noticed.

2d. Charles Lee ; an officer once in the British army, and well skilled in military affairs.

After a life of rare adventure a soldier of fortune from his eleventh year, a professional adventurer, he still possessed remarkable faculties as a disciplinarian, and at least brought to the army such a reputation for brilliant deeds in various European service that strong endeavor was made to give him the first command in place of General Ward. His aspirations were even higher still.

3d. Philip Schuyler ; a man of rare excellence of character, who served in the French and Indian war, took part in Abercrombie's campaign against Ticonderoga, and was a member of the Continental Congress from New York at date of his appointment.

4th. Israel Putnam ; already noticed.

BRIGADIER GENERALS.

1st. Seth Pomeroy ; already noticed.

2d. Richard Montgomery ; who had served gallantly under Wolfe, and in the West Indies in 1762.

3d. David Wooster ; already noticed.

4th. William Heath ; who before the war was a vigorous writer upon the necessity of military discipline and a thoroughly organized militia.

5th. Joseph Spencer ; who had served as major and colonel in the French and Indian wars.

6th. John Thomas ; also a soldier of the old French and Indian war already in camp at Boston, at the head of a regiment recruited by himself.

7th. John Sullivan ; a lawyer of New Hampshire, of Irish blood, a member of the first Continental Congress, and a man quick in sympathy with the first movement for the organization of armed resistance.

8th. Nathaniel Greene; then at the head of the Rhode Island troops before Boston, and already noticed.

Congress elected Horatio Gates as adjutant-general. He had served in the British army, commanded a company during Braddock's campaign, accompanied General Monckton as *aid-de-camp* to the West Indies, and gained laurels at the capture of Martinico.

Both Gates and Lee had settled in Virginia after leaving the British army, and had there formed the acquaintance of the future commander-in-chief.

On the twenty-first of June, Washington left Philadelphia for Boston, and on the third of July assumed command of the Continental army with head-quarters at Cambridge. Thenceforth the war proceeded with slow but steady progress to its accomplishment.

At this point the mind instinctively turns from the general retrospect of these wide-spread pulsations, to again look upon the immediate theatre of active force. For two months the yeomanry of New England laid a close grasp upon all land approaches to the city of Boston. The pressure, now and then resisted by efforts of the garrison to secure supplies from the surrounding country, only brought a tighter hold, and incited a prime purpose to crowd that garrison to an escape by sea. The islands of the bay were miniature fields of conflict, and the repeated efforts to procure bullocks, flour, and other needed provisions, through the use of boats belonging to the British fleet, only developed a counter system of boat operations which neutralized the former, and gradually limited that garrison to the range of its guns.

And yet, the beleaguering force fluctuated every week, so that few of the hastily improvised regiments maintained either identity of person or permanent numbers. The sudden summons from industrial duty was like the unorganized rush of men upon the alarm of fire, quickened by the conviction that there was wide-sweeping and common danger to be withstood, or a devouring element to be mastered. That independence of opinion, however, which began to assert a claim to independent nationality was impatient of restraint, and military control was irksome, even when vital to success. Offices were conferred upon those who raised companies, regardless of character or other merit.

Jealousies and aspirations mingled with the claims of families left at home, and many local excitements threatened disorder wherever officers of the crown were stationed.

The flash of Lexington, and the hot heat of its fire had passed by, and it was dull work enough to stand guard by day, lie upon the ground at night, live a life of routine, receive unequal and indifferent food, and wonder when, and how, the affair would end.

These elements, however, were not sufficiently depressing to let loose the pent-in British forces. Strong wills carried men of strong convictions everywhere among the people. The raw troops were under wise guardianship!

The integrity and far reaching forecast of great citizens, united their influence with that of a few real soldiers, to keep an adequate force in the field. The idle were at length set to work. Occupation lightened the restraints of camp life. Earthworks and redoubts gradually unfolded their purpose, and out of seeming chaos there was lifted into perpetual remembrance the issue of Bunker Hill.

CHAPTER XV.

BUNKER HILL. THE OCCUPATION.

THE peninsula of Boston connects with Roxbury by the narrow neck of land which had been fortified by General Gage as early as October, 1774.

North of Boston, and separated by the Charles river, is a second peninsula, fully a mile long, and a little more than half a mile wide; also connected with the main land by a narrow isthmus, formerly subject to overflow at unusually high water.

By reference to the maps,—" *Boston and vicinity*," and "*Battle of Bunker Hill*,"—the reader will gain a fair impression of the topography of the immediate field of operations. The positions there assigned to American commanders are such as were established after the arrival of General Washington; but the entire circuit, with the exception of Dorchester, was in possession of the Provincial troops at the date of the battle of Bunker Hill, although with less completeness of earthworks and redoubts than after the investment was permanently developed.

Morton's Hill, at Moulton's Point, where the British army landed on the seventeenth day of June, 1775, was but thirty-five feet above sea level, while "Breed's pasture," as then styled, and Bunker Hill, were respectively seventy-five and one hundred and ten feet high. The adjoining waters were navigable, and under control of the British fleet.

Bunker Hill had an easy slope to the isthmus, but the other sides were quite steep, the position having control of the isthmus itself, as well as commanding a full view of Boston and the surrounding country. The strategic value of this summit was very decided for either army, yet it had been overlooked or neglected by the British commander, even although the arrival of Generals Howe, Clinton and Burgoyne, with reinforcements, had swelled the nominal strength of the garrison to about ten thousand men, and the importance of aggressive movements upon the colonial militia had been carefully considered and rightfully estimated.

This garrison had been gradually weakened by constant skirmishes, by sickness and other causes, leaving an effective force, even for garrison duty, of hardly eight thousand men. Scarcity of supplies, especially of fresh meat, bore some share in a depreciation of physical fitness for the field. The troops, however, that were fit for duty, were under excellent discipline and ably commanded.

The American army received information the thirteenth of June, that General Gage had definitely decided to take immediate possession of the Charlestown peninsula, and also of Dorchester Heights.

As early as the middle of May, however, the "committee of safety," and the "council of war," had resolved to occupy and fortify Bunker Hill as soon as artillery and powder could be adequately furnished for the purpose; while from want of definite knowledge of the military value of Dorchester Heights, a committee had been appointed for examination and report, respecting the merits of that position as a strategic restraint upon the garrison of Boston.

On the fifteenth day of June, the "Massachusetts committee of safety," and the same "council of war," voted to take immediate possession of Bunker Hill. This action was predicated upon positive information that the British council of war had resolved upon a similar movement, and had designated the eighteenth day of June for execution of that purpose.

There is no more significant fact of the want of thorough military oversight and system in the then existing Provincial army, than the looseness of discipline with which the enterprise under consideration was initiated, and the want of specific responsibility which attended its execution.

It is unquestionably true that the presence of Doctor Warren was one of the chief elements which inspired the prolonged resistance after the action began; and the chief credit at the redoubt belongs to Colonel Prescott. There was at first no unanimity in approval of the plan, no thorough support of the detachment sent upon so serious an expedition, and there was a complete failure to furnish that detachment with adequate means to maintain a serious contest with an enemy of considerable force.

More than a hundred writers have made this action the theme of diverse criticism, and many of them have run tilts for or against some candidate for special honor in connection with the first formal battle-issue of the war of 1775–1781.

The peculiarly loose *organization* of the army, also, had much to do with the inefficiency of the movement upon Bunker Hill; and yet, the specific work of the detachment, independent of the want of support to back the movement, was well done.

There were special considerations that undoubtedly exerted their influence at the time when the expedition was first considered. The supineness of the British army, the limitation of its outside demonstrations to simple excursions for supplies, and the impression that it was unable, or unwilling, to renew active hostilities against the force which controlled the main land and surrounding country, must have had effect upon the officers in command of the American army.

If the contingency of a battle, such as transpired; that is, of an attempt in force, to dislodge a successful occupation of the hill, had any consideration whatever, there was terrible neglect, in failure to supply ammunition and rations for that emergency. That the occupation of Breed's pasture, instead of Bunker Hill proper, was a departure from the *text* of the original instructions, is undoubtedly true; but a prompt and sufficient support would have assured the control of both, and have realized the complete repulse of the British assault. It will appear hereafter, that under all the circumstances, the judgment of Colonel Gridley, who laid out the intrenchments, was eminently wise and proper.

The narrative will be cleared of extrinsic issues, and no attempt will be made to supply facts which history omitted and the grave buried.

Few modern battles are described alike by different critics, and many a general would be puzzled to know whether he was in an action, where he actually commanded, if he sought information from contestants who scramble for honors beyond their experience or reach. The controversy as to General Putnam's relation to the battle of Bunker Hill alone, has burdened the minds of many authors, and tried the brains of thousands of readers who could not see the importance of the discussion. But, Bunker Hill was to be occupied. The decision was made. The emergency was pressing.

General Ward, advanced in years and feeble in body, was unequal to active service, and lacked that military acuteness and decision which the crisis demanded. He had no alternative but to obey the instructions of the committee of safety and the council of war.

Mr. Bancroft clearly states an important element of pressing im·
portance at the time. " The decision was so sudden that no fit preparation could be made. The nearly total want of ammunition
rendered the service desperately daring."

The decision to occupy the hill *pledged support*. As in fact transpired, the success was only limited by scarcity of powder. That
should have been furnished or the expedition withdrawn. Prescott
and Putnam had favored the movement, and urged it upon the council of war. Ward and Warren wished to avoid a general engagement,
and the expenditure of powder necessarily involved in occupying a
post so exposed to British attack. The latter, however, concurred in
the final decision, and on the day of action left his place as president
of the Provincial Congress, and traveled seven miles to bear part, as
he offered his life, in the battle of Bunker Hill.

Formation of the command. Colonel William Prescott, of Pepperill,
Massachusetts, was eager to lead the enterprise, and was intrusted
with its execution. The men detailed to form the detachment, were
for the most part from his own regiment and those of Colonels Frye
and Bridge. The three colonels were members of the council of war
which had been organized on the twentieth day of April, when General Ward assumed command of the army about Boston.

Captain Thomas Knowlton, of Putnam's regiment, who afterwards
fell in gallant fight on Harlem Plains, at the head of the Connecticut
Rangers, " Congress' Own," was to lead a detachment of two hundred
men drafted from the Connecticut troops.

Colonel Richard Gridley, chief engineer, with a company of artillery, was also assigned to the command. An order was, in fact, issued
for the first named regiment to parade at six o'clock on the evening
of the sixteenth, " with all the intrenching tools in the encampment."
The original purpose was also to have the detachment number one
thousand men. The field-order, however, covered about fourteen
hundred men. Frothingham, in his valuable " Siege of Boston,"
shows conclusively that the force as organized, including artificers and
drivers of the carts, was not less than twelve hundred men.

Cambridge Common was designated for the rendezvous. Beneath
the elms, solemn with that occasion, that band of earnest men, fresh
from peaceful homes, but hurrying into the face of battle for home and
country, was formed in perfect silence for the last duty which was to
precede the onward movement.

Rev. Samuel Langdon, president of Harvard College, invoked the

favor of high heaven upon their mission, and with a benediction peculiar to his stern and stately carriage, dismissed them to their silent
march.

"It was soon after sunset," says Bancroft;—"then—as the late
darkness of the mid-summer evening closed in, they marched for
Charlestown, in the face of the proclamation issued only four days
before, by which all persons taken in arms against their sovereign, were
threatened, under martial law, with death by the cord as rebels and
traitors."

The command moved silently but rapidly, crossed Charlestown
Neck, and then halted for consultation and definition of the enjoined
duty. Major Brooks, of Colonel Bridge's regiment, here joined with
a small detachment, as well as a company of artillery with their guns.

Orders. The confused account of instructions given on this
expedition is significant of the want of system then existing in the
American camp. There has also been a needless worry about the
matter, according as partisan authorities have selected favorites for
the honors of the day. No general officer was embraced in the detail,
and no general officer asserted authority over the operations of the
eventful twenty-four hours that followed the advance movement.

Such as were present at any time, advised as occasion required,
worked hard and well, but enforced no personal authority over the
command especially assigned to the duty.

Frothingham furnishes ample evidence, that written orders from
General Ward designated Bunker Hill as the summit to be occupied,
and that these orders were to be communicated to the command
after crossing the isthmus. The first order issued after the halt, was
the detail of Captain Nutting's company with a small detachment of
Connecticut men, to patrol Charlestown and the adjoining shore. A
second consultation took place after the command reached Bunker
Hill. Captain Maxwell's company, from Prescott's own regiment, was
detailed for patrol of the shore, and to keep watch of the British
works at Copp's Hill, directly opposite, and of the ships of war
then anchored within a short distance of the peninsula.

The Annual Register, 1775, thus indicates the fleet; *Somerset*, 68
guns, Captain Edward Le Cros; *Cerberus*, 36 guns, Captain Chads;
Glasgow, 34 guns, Captain William Maltby; *Lively*, 20 guns, Captain
Thomas Bishop; *Falcon*,—— guns, Captain Linzee, and the *Sym-
metry*, transport, with 18 nine-pounders.

The details thus made, not only to watch those vessels, but to occupy Charlestown, not only discharged their duty well, but by availing themselves of houses, proved active annoyances to the left wing of the British army in its ultimate advance upon the American works.

Occupation of the heights. The chief engineer, Colonel Gridley, laid out the intrenchments at "*Breed's pasture*" shortly after, first known as Breed's Hill. This was done after careful consultation with Colonel Prescott, Captain Knowlton, and other officers, and for the purpose of establishing a position giving the quickest control of the beach, in case of the landing of British troops. The eligibility of the situation will be noticed in the "military notes" belonging to the record of the action.

Packs were unslung, arms were stacked, the intrenching tools previously unloaded from the carts, were brought forward, and the troops were noiselessly distributed for duty. The bells of Boston struck *twelve;* and the new day, so fatal, so memorable, began its history, to the *dull thud* of the pick-ax and the grating of shovels. *Those men knew how to handle their tools !*

Martin states, as appears from a foot-note in Frothingham's history, that " about a thousand men were at work," and that "the men dug in the trenches one hour, and then mounted guard." All night that work went on, in solemn stillness, only relieved by the sentries' monotonous and encouraging "*all's well,*" which sounded from the battery across the river, and from the decks of the shipping. At dawn of day, the redoubt, about eight rods square, had been nearly closed, presenting a face nearly six feet high, with such hasty accommodations behind the parapet, as would bring the men to a convenient position for delivering fire.

More than once, Colonel Prescott and other officers quietly drew near the river, to be assured that no small boats were afloat, and that the apparent security was not the prelude to a surprise. He was everywhere present to inspire zeal and hope, and Bancroft's statement that General Putnam himself visited the works during the night and encouraged the men, is verified by respectable authority, and the contemporaneous statement of soldiers who had no possible inducement to befog the narrative of events. The character of his aid rendered during the entire day is perfectly consistent with this statement.

The situation. With daylight, the outline of the intrenchments, and the throng of busy workers, brought to the notice of British sentries the night's aggressive work. It had veiled the work of the

7

advancing patriots.   The colonists were in earnest!   The *Lively* put
a spring on her cable and opened fire.   The battery of Copp's Hill
responded.   The roar of cannon awoke the sleeping garrison of
Boston ; and while the streets resounded with the swift transit of
messengers, and the tramp of assembling battalions, and the house-
tops were crowded with anxious observers, the quickened and patient
laborers were perfecting their preparations, resolute of purpose to
meet face to face the veteran troops of George the Third.   The vigorous action of the land batteries and ships, only wasted their powder
and ball.   One man fell, and to convince his comrades that there was
no time for fear or rest, Colonel Prescott walked the parapet, openly
exposed, and re-inspired the men.

Continuous labor, under high pressure, began to wear upon the
stoutest.   At nine o'clock a council of war was called.   The activity
of the Boston garrison, the accumulating array of boats, and all the
activities of that city, were prophetic of a resolute purpose to resent
the offensive movement of the Americans, and still no reinforcements,
no relieving party, had appeared.

The rations hastily issued for twenty-four hours of duty, had, as
usual with raw and over-worked troops, become nearly exhausted, and
urgent requests were made that men should be relieved by others
who were fresh, and that reinforcements should be sent for, with an
ample supply of food.   In this emergency Major John Brooks was
dispatched to head-quarters to present these demands.

NOTE. As with the shield, one side *gold*, the reverse, *silver ;* so may critics ignore the
double aspect of the command at Bunker's and Breed's Hills.   The credit which is due to
Prescott, for occupying and defending the latter, is perfectly consistent with the universal
industry of Putnam, elsewhere.   Extreme partisans of either must violate the laws of evidence and impeach witnesses who are the chief authority for other, more important facts of
American history.

NOTE. *Moulton's* Point or *Morton's* Point, both are family names of that period ; each
adopted by reputable authority.   The author has preserved both, in connection with Hill
or Point.   No injustice is done.   Life is too short and history too remiss, for settlement
of this doubtful point.

CHAPTER XVI.

BUNKER HILL. THE PREPARATION.

REINFORCEMENTS. General Putnam was very early at head-quarters of the army at Cambridge, and urged that an additional force be sent to Charlestown Heights to reinforce Colonel Prescott's command. General Ward finally consented, so far as to order one-third of Colonel Stark's regiment to the front. The sequel will show that this was timely aid.

Major Brooks met General Putnam and pushed forward on his errand, while the general himself proceeded directly to the field of danger.

General Ward gave little heed to the urgent demand of Major Brooks, declining further to reduce his own force, lest the British garrison should make a movement upon Cambridge, and thus imperil the safety of accumulating stores, and even that of the entire army. The committee of safety was in session. Richard Devons, one of its most valuable members, is credited with the influence which persuaded them to furnish additional reinforcements. Colonel Sweet states, that orders were also issued to recall from Chelsea the companies there stationed, in order to increase the force at head-quarters.

The committee rested under a grave responsibility. "Their entire supply of powder, which could be obtained north of the Delaware," according to Bancroft and other eminent authority, "was twenty-seven half barrels, and a present from Connecticut of thirty-six half-barrels more." Bancroft adds: "The army itself was composed of companies incomplete in numbers, enlisted chiefly within six weeks, commanded, many of them, by officers unfit, ignorant, and untried, gathered from separate colonies, and with no reciprocal subordination but from courtesy and opinion."

Fearful to waste ammunition, solemnly bound to have regard to the whole army and ultimate ends, as well as constrained to support the movement which they had themselves enjoined, it is not strange that calm deliberation foreran the decision of the committee when the appeal of Major Brooks was made.

It was therefore as late as eleven o'clock when the whole of the New Hampshire regiments of Stark and Read were ordered to reinforce Prescott. This detachment reached its destination in time to participate in the action although not until after the landing of the British troops.

Sweet credits the regiments of Colonels Brewer, Nixon, Woodbridge, and Major Moore, with a contribution of three hundred men each.

Frothingham shows conclusively that, "several of the companies of Little's regiment were elsewhere on duty, one at Gloucester, one at Ipswich, one at Lechmere's Point, and some at West Cambridge "; but adds that, " Lunt's company arrived on the field near the close of the battle."

Bancroft carefully compiles from official reports and depositions, a statement, approximately as correct as can be derived from existing evidence, and thus states the force which " hastened to the aid of Prescott.

" Of Essex men, (Little's regiment) at least one hundred and twenty-five ; of Worcester and Middlesex men, (Brewer's) seventy or more, and with them, Lieutenant-colonel Buckminster ; of the same men, (Nixon's) fifty men, led by Nixon himself; forty men (Moore's) from Worcester ; of Lancaster men, (Whitcomb's) at fifty privates, with no officer higher than captain."

The hot day wore out its hours, as the tired troops resting from their assigned duty,—panted for water, hungered for food, and waited for the enemy ; and neither food nor reinforcements appeared in view, while the hostile forces were rapidly marshaling for attack.

The surrounding waters were salt sea water, or its brackish mixture with the flow from the Charles and Mystic rivers, and no fresh water was easy of access. A conviction that they were deserted began to spread through the ranks, that they had been pushed forward rashly, upon an ill-considered enterprise, and that there was wanting the disposition or nerve to undertake risks for their support or rescue.

It was at such a moment, terrible in its doubts and grand in its resolution, that Seth Pomeroy, then seventy years of age, having wisely declined his commission as Brigadier-general, found his way to the redoubt, musket in hand, to fight as a private volunteer.

And it was just then that Dr. Joseph Warren, President of the Provincial Congress, loved and honored of all, the undoubted patriot, and already monumental for worth and courage, added his presence and the beams of his animation to cheer the faltering and faint. He also declined command, served under Prescott, and plied his musket with the best when the crisis came on.

Ward himself, when the embarkation of the second British detachment furnished evidence that Cambridge was not in peril, hurried other troops toward the isthmus, but too late to avert the swift catastrophe.

Disposition of the American forces. Upon completion of the redoubt, it became painfully evident that the preliminary work was not yet complete. A new line of breastwork, a few rods in length, was hastily carried backward and a little to the left ; and very hasty efforts were made to strengthen a short hedge, and establish a line of defense for a hundred and twenty rods in the same direction, thereby to connect with the stone fence and other protection which ran perpendicularly toward the Mystic river. This retreating line was begun under the personal direction of Prescott himself, but was never fully closed up. A piece of springy ground on this line was left uncovered by any shelter for troops acting in its rear, or passing to and fro behind the main lines. The stone fence, which took its course nearly to the river, was like those so common in New England at the present day. Posts are set into a wall two or three feet high, and these are connected with two rails, making the entire height about five feet.

Freshly mown hay which lay around in winrows or in heaps, was braided or thatched upon these rails, affording a *show* of *shelter*, while the top rail gave resting place for the weapon. In front of this, an ordinary zig-zag, "*stake and rider*" fence was established, and the space between the two was also filled with hay.

This line was nearly six hundred feet in rear of the front face of the redoubt, and near the foot of Bunker Hill. To its defense Prescott assigned Connecticut men under command of Captain Knowlton, supported by two field pieces on the right, adjoining the open space already mentioned.

Still beyond the rail fence eastward, towards the river, and extending by an even slope to its very margin, was another gap which exposed the entire command to a flanking movement of the enemy, endangering the redoubt itself, as well as the more transient works of defense.   To anticipate such a movement, subsequently attempted, an imperfect stone wall was quickly thrown together by the assistance of Colonel Stark's detachment, whose timely arrival had cheered the spirits of the worn out pioneer command.

Meanwhile, Putnam was everywhere present to encourage the men, and superintended the establishment of light works on Bunker Hill summit, to cover the troops in case of forcible ejection from the advanced defenses. He caused the intrenching tools, no longer needed at the front, to be taken to that position. In spite of his entreaties and commands, some who thus carried the tools, threw them down upon reaching the summit, and took refuge behind the isthmus ; others returned to their places at the front.

His movement, which would have been appreciated by well disciplined troops, carried with it the suggestion of a contingency which defeated its purpose in the hands of men not soldiers. Putnam's efforts accomplished nothing of value in the preparation of ulterior defenses.   The time was too short, the control of men too feeble ; and the organization and discipline of the reinforcements which arrived, were too slack for their immediate subjection to authority, while the advancing enemy began to absorb the whole attention.   Prescott's force at the redoubt had dropped off to less than eight hundred men when Colonel John Stark arrived.   " Next to Prescott, he brought the largest number of men into the field," says Bancroft.   The British were already landing, as they crossed the isthmus under a heavy fire. The execution of that movement was characteristic of their brave commander, and well calculated to impart the courage which afterward sustained his men.   When Captain Dearborn, advised a quick step, he decided, that " one fresh man in an action was worth ten fatigued ones," and then deliberately advanced to his position.

As he descended the southern slope of Bunker Hill, his eye took in the whole plan of preparation for the battle.   He saw, as he afterward related the affair, " The whole way so plain upon the beach along the Mystic river, that the enemy could not miss it."   He went to work.   Reed's regiment, which had been detailed with Starks' early in the morning, upon the importunity of Putnam, was at the rail fence with the Connecticut men.   With every possible strain upon the New Hampshire men, this last obstruction was not sufficiently perfected to cover Starks' command, so that their ultimate defense was made while many were kneeling or lying down to deliver fire.

No other troops than those already named, arrived in time to take part in the action, and the total force which eventually participated in the battle did not exceed fourteen hundred men.

Six pieces of artillery were in partial use at different times, but with inconsiderable practical effect, and five of these were left on the field when the retreat was made.

The landing. The embarkation of the British troops was the signal for renewed activity of the fleet.

The base of Breed's Hill, and the low ground extending to the river, was swept by a fire so hot, that no troops, if any had been disposable for such a movement, could have resisted the landing.

Perfect silence pervaded the American lines. A few ineffectual cannon shots were fired, the guns were soon taken to the rear, and a still deeper calm enveloped the hill. The day was intensely bright and hot. Barge after barge discharged its fully equipped soldiery, then returned for more. This brilliant display of force, nowhere surpassed for splendor of outfit, precision of movement, gallant bearing, and perfect discipline, was spread out over Morton's Hill in well ordered lines of matchless array. With professional self-possession, these men took their noonday meal at leisure, while the barges returned for still another division.

Simultaneously with this reinforcement, the roar of artillery was heard from beyond Boston. As if to threaten General Ward, then at Cambridge, and General Thomas, who with several thousand Massachusetts men was then at Roxbury, and to warn both that they could spare no more troops for the support of Prescott; or, from the apprehension that an attempt might be made by the Americans to force an entrance to the city over Boston Neck, the batteries which covered the Neck opened forth a heavy fire of shot, shell and carcasses upon the village of Roxbury and its defenses. It was no less an indication to the silent yeomen on the hill, that mortal danger demanded a supreme resistance.

The crisis was at hand. The veterans were ready. The people were also ready.

The shaft of war, in the grasp of the trained legions of Great Britain was poised, and to be hurled at last upon the breasts of Englishmen, whose offense was the aspiration to perpetuate and develop the principles of English liberty.

It was a blow at Magna Charta itself, a *home thrust*, suicidal, and hopeless, except for evil! Its lesson rolls on to attend the march of the centuries.

CHAPTER XVII.

BUNKER HILL. THE BATTLE.

IT was nearly three o'clock of the afternoon of the seventeenth of June, in the year of our Lord one thousand seven hundred and seventy five, that the solid mass of silent veterans which had landed upon Moulton's Point, and had prepared themselves with due deliberation to execute the order of the day, moved forward to attack the American army, then intrenched on the summit of Breed's Hill.

To General Howe himself was intrusted the responsibility of breaking up the American left wing, to envelope it, take the redoubt in the rear, and cut off retreat to Bunker Hill and the main land. The light infantry, therefore, moved closely along the Mystic river, threatening the extreme left, while the grenadiers directed their advance upon the stone fence, with their left wing demonstrating toward the unprotected gap which was clearly exposed between the fence and the short breastwork next the redoubt. General Pigot, who commanded the left wing, advanced directly against the redoubt itself.

The movements were heralded by a profitless artillery fire from Morton's Hill, but this soon ceased, for the solid shot all ready for use, were designed for twelve-pounder guns, and those in position had the caliber of sixes. The prompt order to use only *grape*, was followed by an advance of the pieces to the edge of an old brick-kiln, the spongy ground and heavy grass not permitting their ready handling at the foot of the hill slope, or even just to its right. The guns, thus advanced, thereby secured a more effective range of fire upon the skeleton defenses of the American centre, and an eligible position from which subsequently to effect a more direct fire upon the exposed portion of the American front, and upon the breastwork and redoubt themselves.

The advance of the British army was like a solemn pageant in its steady headway, and like a parade for inspection in its completeness of furnishment. This army, bearing their knapsacks and the full equipment for campaign service, moved forward as if by the very force of its closely knit columns it must sweep away all obstructions, and overture every barrier in its way. But *right in the way* was a calm, intense, and energizing love of liberty.

It was represented by plain men of the same blood, and of equal daring. Contrast marked those opposing Englishmen very distinctly that summer afternoon. The plain men handled plain fire-locks. Ox-horns held their powder, and their pockets held the bullets. Coatless, under the broiling sun, unincumbered, unadorned by plumage or service medals,—looking like vagabonds after their night of labor, and their day of hunger, thirst and waiting, this *live* obstruction was truly in the way of that advancing splendor. Elated, conscious, assured of victory, with firm step, already quickened as the space of separation lessens, there is left but a few rods of interval—a few steps only, and the work is done.

A few hasty shots impulsively fired, but quickly restrained, drew an innocent fire from their front rank. The pale men behind the mock defense, obedient at last to one will, answered nothing to that reply, and nothing to the audible commands of those steady columns, waiting still.

It needs no painter to make the scene seem clearer than it appears from the recital of sober deposition and the record of surviving participators on either side. History has no contradictions to confuse or explain away the realities of that fearful tragedy.

The left wing is near the redoubt. It is *nothing* to surmount a bank of fresh earth but six feet high, and its sands and clods can almost be counted, *it is so near, so easy,—sure !*

Short, crisp, and earnest,—low toned, but felt as an electric pulse from redoubt to river, are the words of a single man—of *Prescott !* Warren by his side repeats it ! That word runs quickly along the impatient lines. The eager fingers give back from the waiting trigger. " Steady men ! " " Wait until you see the white of the eye ! " " Not a shot sooner ! " " Aim at the handsome coats ! " " Aim at the waist-bands." " Pick off the commanders ! " " Wait for the word, every man, steady ! "

Those plain men, so patient, can already count the buttons, can read the emblem on the belt-plate, can recognize the officers and men whom they have seen on parade at Boston Common. Features grow more and more distinct. The silence is awful. These men seem breathless—*dead !* It comes, *that word*, the word, waited for— "*Fire !* " On the right, the light infantry gain an equal advance, almost at the same instant that the left wing was treading so near the humble redoubt. Moving over more level ground, they quickly make the greater distance, and have passed the line of those who marched directly up the hill. The grenadiers also move upon the centre with the same serene confidence, and the interval has lessened to the gauge of space which the spirit of the impending word defines. That word, *waits behind the centre and the left wing*, as it lingers behind the breastwork and redoubt. Sharp, clear, and deadly in tone and essence it rings forth—" *Fire !* "

From redoubt to river, along the whole sweep of devouring flame, the forms of brave men wither as in a furnace heat. The whole front goes down ! For an instant the chirp of the cricket and the grasshopper in the freshly cut grass, might almost be heard, then the groans of the suffering, then the shouts of impatient yeomen who leap over obstacles to pursue, until recalled to silence and to duty.

Staggering, but reviving, grand in the glory of their manhood and the sublimity of their discipline, heroic in the fortitude which restores them to self-possession ; with a steady step in the face of fire, and over the bodies of the dead, the remnant dare to renew the battle. Again, the deadly volley, and the shattered columns, in spite of entreaty or command, move back to the place of starting, and the first shock of battle is over.

A lifetime when it is past, is but as a moment ! A moment sometimes, is as a lifetime ! Onset, and repulse ! Three hundred lifetimes ended in twenty minutes.

Putnam hastened to Bunker Hill to gather scattering parties in the rear, and to facilitate the passage of reinforcements across the isthmus, where the fire from the British shipping was maintained with destructive energy. But the battle at last had to depend mainly upon the men who had toiled all night, and who had gained confidence and firmness by the experience of those eventful hours. Nothing could bring the reinforcements in time.

The British troops rapidly re-formed their columns. Never, on other battle fields, did officers more gloriously evince the perfection of discipline, and the perfection of self-devotion. The artillery was pushed to the front, and much nearer to the angle made by the breastwork next the redoubt, and the retiring line through the open gap to its left. The American officers animated their men, and added fresh caution not to waste a single shot. The guns of Gridley and Callender were temporarily employed at the unprotected interval near the breastwork, and then withdrawn to the rear. The company of the latter officer became scattered and never returned to the fight. The remainder of the line kept up to duty, and resumed the silent waiting which had been so impressive before the attack began.

The British columns again advanced, and deployed as before across the entire extent of the American lines. The ships of war redoubled their effort to clear the isthmus of advancing reinforcements. Shot and shell cut up the turf, and dispersed the detachments which had reached the summit of Bunker Hill, and the companies which had been posted at Charlestown to annoy the British left, were driven to the shelter of the redoubt.

Charlestown had already been fired by the carcasses which fell through its roofs, and more than four hundred wooden houses kindling into one vast wave of smoke and flame, added impressiveness and terror to the scene, while a favoring breeze swept its quivering volume away from the battle field, leaving to the American forces a distinct and suggestive view of the returning tide of battle.

Nearer than before, the British troops press on! No scattering shots anticipate their approach this second time. It is only when a space of hardly five rods is left, and a swift plunge could almost forerun the rifle's flash, that the word of execution impels the bullet, and the front rank, entire, from redoubt to river, is swept away. Again, again, the attempt is made to inspire the paralyzed troops, and rally them from retreat; but the living tide flows back—flows back even to the river.

Another twenty minutes, hardly twenty-five, and the death angel has gathered his battle harvest, five hundred sheaves of human hopes, as when the Royal George went down beneath the waters with its priceless values of human life.

At the first repulse, the 38th regiment had halted under the shelter of a stone wall by the road which passes around the base of Breed's Hill, between the slope and Morton's Hill. At the second repulse, the same regiment supported on its left by the 5th, held a portion of its command in check, just under the advanced crest of the hill, and gradually gathered in the scattering remnants for a third assault.

The condition of the British army is one of grave responsibilities and grave issues. That which had the color of a simple dispersion, and

punishment of half organized and half armed rebels, begins to assume
the characteristics of a "*forlorn hope*," in a most desperate struggle.

"*A moment of the day was critical,*" said *Burgoyne*.

"A continuous blaze of musketry incessant and destructive," says
Stedman.

The British officers pronounced it, "downright butchery to lead
the men afresh against those lines," says *Gordon*.

"Of one company not more than five, and of another not more
than fourteen escaped," says *Ramsay*.

"Whole platoons were laid upon the earth like grass by the mow
er's scythe," says *Lossing*.

"The British line totally broken, fell back with precipitation to
the landing place," says *Marshall*.

"Most of our grenadiers and light infantry, the moment they
presented themselves, lost three-fourths, and many nine-tenths of
their men. Some had only eight and nine men a company left, some
only three, four, and five," is the statement of a British letter, dated
July 5th, 1775, and cited by *Frothingham*.

"A shower of bullets. The field of battle was covered with the
slain," says *Botta*.

"A continuous sheet of fire," says *Bancroft*.

"The dead lay as *thick as sheep* in a fold," said *Stark*.

It was just at this protracted interval, yet less than a single hour,
that each army evinced the great qualities of their common blood.

Clinton and Burgoyne had watched the progress of events from
Copp's Hill, and with true gallantry and courage, the latter threw himself into a boat with reinforcements, and volunteered to share the
issue of a third advance. Four hundred marines additional to the
1st battalion which had remained at the landing place, hurried across
the narrow river, and these united with the 47th regiment under
General Clinton, were ordered to flank the redoubt, and scale its face
to the extreme left, while General Howe with the principal part of the
grenadiers and light infantry, supported by the artillery, undertook
the storming of the breastworks bending back from the mouth of the
redoubt, and so commanding the entrance.

The remnants of the 5th, 38th, 43d, and 52d regiments under
General Pigot, were ordered to connect the two wings, and make an
attack upon the redoubt in front.

A demonstration was also made against the American left, more
to occupy its attention than to force the defenses. The artillery was

to advance a few rods, and then swing about to the left, to sweep the
breastwork for Howe's advance.

The preparations were nearly complete. It only remained to bring
the men to their duty. Knapsacks were unslung, every needless
incumbrance was laid aside, and the troops moved forward stripped
for fight.

The power of discipline, the energy of wise commanders, and the
force of every possible incentive which could animate British veterans
of proud antecedents, and established loyalty, combined to make the
movement as memorable as it was momentous.

Within the American lines the preparation involved equal responsibility, but under fearful discouragement. Few of the troops had
three rounds of ammunition left. During the second attack a part
of the men loaded while others fired, and the expenditure of powder
was commensurate with the results. The remaining cannon cartridges
were economically distributed, and there was no longer any hope that
substantial aid would come to their relief. There were less than fifty
bayonets to the entire command, and gloomy apprehensions began
to be entertained, but not at the expense of a firm purpose to fight
to the last.

During the afternoon General Ward sent forward his own regiment
and those of Patterson and Gardner. The last named officer led three
hundred of his men safely across the isthmus, reached Bunker Hill,
and commenced to throw up earthworks under the direction of General Putnam, but was soon ordered to the lines, and was mortally
wounded while executing the order. Few of his men actually participated in the fight, the majority, after his fall, returning to Bunker
Hill. Adjutant Febiger, a Danish officer, gathered a portion of
Colonel Gerrish's regiment, reached the redoubt as the last action
commenced, and did good service, but the other regiments were too
late.

Putnam, impressed with the critical nature of another attack, devoted himself wholly to an attempt to establish another position on
Bunker Hill for accumulation of reinforcements, and a *point of resistance*, in case the advanced positions should be abandoned, but he
could accomplish nothing in the face of the activity of the shipping,
now delivering its fire at short range.

Within the redoubt itself, and along the slender line, all was
resolution and attention to duty. Colonel Prescott appreciated
thoroughly the purpose of the enemy as soon as the sudden wheel of

the British artillery to the left, indicated their power to concentrate its fire upon his lines of retreat, and the reduction of the redoubt. The order was given to reserve every shot until the enemy should come within twenty yards. One single volley was delivered as the attack was made at the same moment upon three sides of the ill-fated work. For an instant the columns were checked, but in another they dashed forward with bayonets fixed. Those who first surmounted the parapet fell. Major Pitcairn was mortally wounded as he entered the works. Lieutenant-colonel Abercrombie, Majors Williams, and Speedlove shared his fate. A single artillery cartridge was distributed for a last effort, and then, intermingled with the assailants, fighting with clubbed guns and stones, the garrison yielded the contest, and each for himself, under Prescott's order, made a quick retreat. Prescott and Warren were the last to leave, and the latter, just without the redoubt, shot through the head, gave life to the cause he had so valiantly defended.

But with the capture of the redoubt, the struggle was not ended. Major Jackson rallied Gardner's men on Bunker Hill, and with three companies of Ward's regiment and Febiger's party, an effort was made to cover the retreat, and a vigorous fire was for a short time maintained upon the advancing enemy. It saved more than half of the garrison.

At the rail fence and clear to the river, Starks', Colt's, Reed's, and Chester's companies twice repulsed an attack, and by a resistance, prolonged as long as their powder held out, they afforded opportunity for the fugitives from the redoubt to make good their retreat. Then they also fell back, in no precipitate flight, but with a fair front, and a steadiness worthy of their brave resistance.

Putnam made one more effort to halt the men at Bunker Hill, but without bayonets or ammunition, worn out in physical strength, and hopeless of a successful resistance, the retreat became general, and the day closed with their occupation of the field works of Prospect Hill, and other defenses nearest of approach.

The British army occupied Bunker Hill, but did not pursue beyond the isthmus. General Clinton advised an immediate attack upon Cambridge, but General Howe declined the attempt. Both armies were too worn out to renew battle, and Colonel Prescott's gallant offer to retake the position if he could have three fresh regiments, found no response from the committe of safety and council of war. Both armies lay on their arms all night, equally apprehensive of attack.

The losses are given as officially stated, and as adopted by Sted
man, and Bancroft.

British casualties.   Nineteen officers killed, and seventy wounded :
of rank and file, two hundred and seven killed, and seven hundred and
fifty-eight wounded.   *Total casualties,* 1054.

American casualties.   One hundred and forty five killed and missing, and three hundred and four wounded.   *Total casualties,* 449.

Thus each army lost nearly one-third of the forces brought into
real action.

Thus brief is the record of a battle, which, in less than two hours
destroyed a town, laid fifteen hundred men upon the battle field,
equalized the relations of veterans and militia, aroused three millions
of people to a definite struggle for National Independence, and fairly
inaugurated the war for its accomplishment.

NOTE.   The prompt occupation of Prospect Hill, referred to in the text, was in keep
ing with General Putnam's purpose to resist at every point ; and the ultimate value of this
position which he occupied, as he stated to the " Committee of Safety," " without having
any orders from any person," was very determining in its relations to the siege.   Its
advanced flanking posts of Lechmere Point, Cobble Hill and Ploughed Hill, afterwards
developed by General Washington, combined their cross fire, and thus sealed Charlestown
Neck.   A protracted halt on Bunker Hill, as appears from notes on the battle, would have
been fatal to the whole detachment : but his occupation of Prospect Hill was eminently
judicious.

NOTE.   General Washington's report to Congress states the casualties at Bunker
Hill, by regiments.   It has already appeared that the organization of the command was
loosely and hastily effected : but the purpose was so far realized that about the required
number of men accompanied Colonel Prescott.

COLONEL OF REGIMENT.	KILLED.		WOUNDED.	MISSING.
Fryes	10		38	4
Little	7		23	..
Brewer	12		22	..
Gridley			4	..
Stark	15		45	..
Woodbridge	..		5	..
Scammon	..		2	..
Bridge	17		25	..
Whitcomb	5		8	2
Ward	1		6	..
Gerrishe	3		5	..
Reed	3		29	1
Prescott	43	K. & M.	46	..
Doolittle	6		9	..
Gardner	..		7	..
Patterson	..		1	..
Nixon	3	K. & M.		..

CHAPTER XVIII.

BATTLE OF BUNKER HILL. NOTES.

THE siege of Boston was protracted until the spring of 1776. It will be well, therefore, to devote a short space to the examination of the military relations which the battle of Bunker Hill sustained to the investment of that city. It will also afford material for a clearer appreciation of the battle itself.

The evacuation of Boston was made *necessary* by the ultimate American occupation of Dorchester Heights. The decision of the British council of war made during the month of April, in which Clinton, Burgoyne, and Percy concurred, and which decision affirmed the necessity of an immediate occupation of Dorchester Heights, was therefore correct; but Howe postponed action until a peaceable occupation was impossible.

The corresponding course of the " Committee of Safety " in that direction, showed a like appreciation of the strategic value of the position; but their means were too limited, and the time had not arrived for their action. The Americans burned their harbor lighthouse quite early during the investment, and the inner harbor itself was unsafe, unless absolutely under the control of the British forces. Charlestown Heights was therefore more important for protection of the shipping, and afforded a better base for active operations than did Boston itself. It was therefore sound military policy for the British army to seize the positions named as soon as the first attempt was made to invest the city.

The ostensible theory of the crown was to reconcile the colonies; but the actual policy and the physical demonstrations repelled, and did not conciliate. Military acts which were done easily by force, and which should have remained undone, were done ! Military acts which were sound upon the basis of anticipated resistance were not done. Threats and blows toward those supposed to be incapable of defense

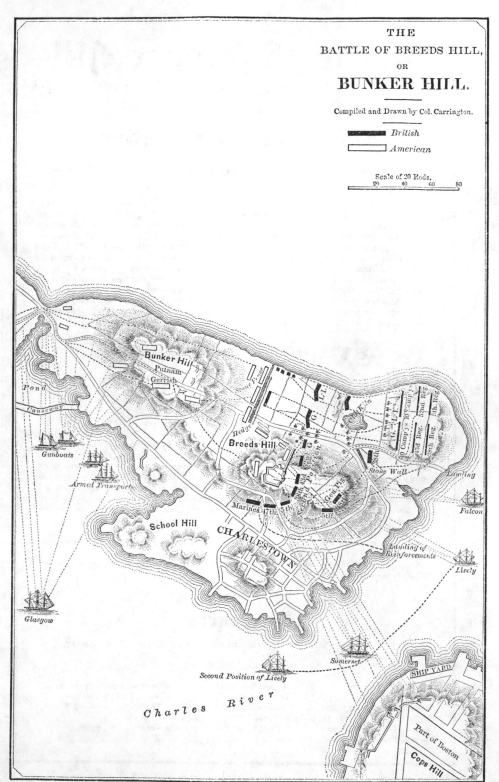

THE
BATTLE OF BREEDS HILL,
OR
BUNKER HILL.

Compiled and Drawn by Col. Carrington.

British
American

Scale of 20 Rods.
20   40   60   80

Bunker Hill
Putnam
Gerrish
Stone Fence
Pond
Causeway
Gunboats
Armed Transports
Hedge
Breeds Hill
Central Position
Gen Pige
Marines 47th 5th
Stone Wall
Lowling
Falcon
School Hill
CHARLESTOWN
Landing of Reinforcements
Lively
Glasgow
Second Position of Lively
Somerset
SHIP YARD
Charles River
Part of Boston
Cops Hill

Battle of Bunker Hill

JUNE 17th, 1775

American Commanders

PUTNAM   **PRESCOTT**   STARK

Strength, 1,400. Casualties, 449.

NOTES.—The spirited skirmishes at Lexington and Concord, April 19th, encouraged the "Massachusetts Committee of Safety" and the "Council of war" to seize the heights behind Charlestown, and thus anticipate a like movement proposed by the British for June 18th. The troops organized at Cambridge, just after sunset, June 16th, and moved under their commander, Col. PRESCOTT, for Bunker Hill; but, by advice of Engineer Gridley, Breeds Hill was substituted as more eligible for resisting a British landing. PUTNAM accompanied the expedition, returned to headquarters in the morning for reinforcements, regained the peninsula, with STARK, and was conspicuously active in encouraging the troops during the day. Stark held the left, supplementing what was defective near the Mystic, while Prescott fought at the redoubt. A small trench had been begun, eastward from the entrance, to be returned northward and join the main line. The presence of a small pond seemed partially to protect that flank, and there was no time for more elaborate entrenchments.

British Commanders

CLINTON   **HOWE**   PIGOTT

Strength, 3,800. Casualties, 1,054.

NOTES.—The British landed at Moulton's Point, and formed on Morton's Hill.

The first advance, at three o'clock P. M., was promptly repulsed. The artillery was of little service, having been carelessly supplied with balls of larger calibre than the guns. The 38th Regiment, upon their repulse, took lodgment behind a stone wall. Reinforced by the 5th Regiment, Gen-Pigott again approached the redoubt, but again the whole line is repulsed, and his division reforms under cover of a lower ridge of Breeds Hill. Charlestown is in flames. Clinton and Burgoyne cross over and take part in the action. The 47th Regiment and marines, freshly arrived, unite with the 43d and 52d to support the 5th and 38th in a combined attack upon the redoubt, while the grenadiers, light infantry and artillery, complete the general line of advance. Howe turns two available guns upon the entrance to the redoubt. The Americans, now being without ammunition, retreat. Putnam attempted to provide a rallying place on Bunker Hill, but found it impracticable.

Gen. Warren, present as a volunteer, was killed near the entrance of the redoubt, and each army engaged lost nearly a third of its force.

MEM.—*The British landing should have been made from the Mystic, in rear of Bunker Hill, or from the isthmus, under cover of the fleet.*

References

CARRINGTON'S "BATTLES OF THE AMERICAN REVOLUTION," pp. 92-117.

School Histories:

Anderson, ¶ 20; p. 70.
Barnes, ¶ 3; p. 108.
Berard (Bush), ¶ 41-42; p. 143-4.
Goodrich, C. A. (Seaveys), ¶ 9; p. 115.
Goodrich, S. G., ¶ 4-15; pp. 193-4.
Hassard, ¶ 10-19; p. 159-62.

Holmes, ¶ 8; p. 111.
Lossing, ¶ 10-14; p. 132-3.
Quackenbos, ¶ 294-7; p. 209-12.
Ridpath, ¶ 8-12; pp. 189-90.
Sadlier (Excel), ¶ 16-18; p. 17-980
Stephens, A. H., ¶ 3; p. 173-4.

Swinton, ¶ 79-84; p. 120-1.
Scott, ¶ 5-8; p. 161-3.
Thalheimer (Eclectic), ¶ 239-4;
     p. 134-5.
Venable, ¶ 123; p. 96.

were freely expended. Operations of war, as against a competent and skillful adversary, were ignored.

Inasmuch as the British authorities assumed that their force was adequate for any military purpose, when opposed to the Provincial militia, the battle of Bunker Hill in all its phases must be judged critically as a military demonstration.

The occupation of Charlestown Heights, which had been pronounced *necessary*, was also assumed to be *feasible*, and without risk to Boston itself. It was undertaken with the purpose announced by General Gage in advance, that he would burn Charlestown if its citizens committed overt acts of hostility. To say nothing of the value of the town to a British garrison for Bunker Hill, its destruction had no value as a military measure. It was one of those wanton acts which treated men, women, and children, as parts of an openly hostile force, and the town itself as part of a hostile country. It expressed vengeance, not the spirit of negotiation. Its destruction violated every element which bore in the direction of restored British supremacy, and had no apology consistent with a sincere desire for the honorable pacification of aroused passions.

A still greater mistake was made in the conduct of the occupation itself; and its mere statement shows how daring was that pre-occupation by the Americans, and how utterly the British commander failed to appreciate the character of the men with whom he was waging war. It may very well be suggested that General Howe had largely imbibed his impressions of the real state of affairs from General Gage, whose ill-judged conduct had precipitated, if it had not largely induced, the conflict.

The mistake is thus stated. Irrespective of inexcusable delay after the movement had been pronounced necessary, the method adopted was only an armed expression of contempt for the opposing militia, entirely unbecoming any wise commander. The law of military action requires the use of adequate force for a proposed end, but does not imply or warrant a needless waste of life or property.

General Clinton, when advised of the action of Colonel Prescott, promptly suggested the proper counter movement. Precisely as the fire of the shipping cut off reinforcements for the Americans on the seventeenth of April, so would a prompt occupation of the isthmus, under the guns of the fleet, have enabled the British commander to have seized Bunker Hill summit in the rear of the American works, and would have placed those works at his mercy. A similar landing along

8

the Mystic river behind the slender defenses, would have accomplished the same result. The advance as made, had the single element of supposed invincibility, as against a timid, unorganized, and ill-armed adversary. As against a mere mob, it would have carried moral weight,—would have been just the thing. Assertion of authority *then*, is not merely to vanquish force, but to restore public confidence in law. Its very momentum, when put in motion, generally does the work. As against a detachment out of nearly twenty thousand men who represented public sentiment itself, and would make no terms while arms were used to assert prerogative, it was unmilitary, mere waste—*madness*. It had physical courage, without the moral sanction which is so essential to highest military success.

The movement wrongly begun, was badly managed. It was Clinton's own suggestion, made at the moment of his gallant enlistment in the enterprise, and when the risk seemed extra hazardous, that secured the degree of success actually attained. He advised concentration of the assault upon the redoubt, because it commanded the other defenses. Even this movement would have been of doubtful success, if the Americans had been supplied with ammunition—if two half-barrels of the Connecticut powder then at Cambridge, could have been poured through the gun-barrels of the earnest defenders.

The *delay* of the movement was equally faulty. The force assigned to the attack was, after it had landed, deemed insufficient, and re-inforcements were obtained. One half of the force that first landed, could have passed along the shore of the Mystic river unobstructed, and could have turned the American left long before Colonel Starks' command came upon the field. When the British troops were leisurely dining, the question of sending re-inforcements had been only a little while decided in the American camp.

The British general, with a good military training, and as will more fully appear hereafter, with sound strategical conceptions as to army operations, and of undoubted physical courage, was seldom ready at the right time, invariably waited for reinforcements, and *never improved success*.

His army fortified Bunker Hill, but besides the loss or disabling of more than a thousand men, to demonstrate the invincibility of his troops, he had actually thrown away all the prestige of their past reputation, and enfeebled the power of his own will, as well as the capacity of the troops, for offensive measures against the American army.

It is of interest to the reader to notice the characters who figured in this action, that they may see how far its lesson made an impression upon their future military operations in America.

General Clinton proved his capacity to apprehend the situation, to devise and execute a purpose. General Burgoyne saw the whole battle, and knew that Provincials would fight. Lord Percy afterward commanded a division at Long Island, White Plains, Brandywine, and in other important actions. Lord Rawdon, then a lieutenant, who received in his arms the body of his own captain (Harris of the 5th infantry), as he was shot from the parapet of the redoubt, was afterwards to win his laurels at Camden and Hobkirk's Hill.

If the battle be examined with regard to the original occupation of the heights by the American forces, some additional elements are exposed. It is known that after due consultation, Colonel Gridley deemed best to fortify Breed's Hill ; and at the same time, it was the intention to establish a second position upon Bunker Hill, as soon as re-inforcements should come upon the ground. The spirit of the order was the occupation of the Charlestown Heights. At that time the local distinctions afterwards recognized did not obtain, and Breed's Hill was known as a pasture, a dependent slope, if not essentially a part of Bunker Hill, which represents the summit of the peninsula. It was impossible for Prescott not to anticipate the arrival of re-inforcements in time to hold the summit also; and in that view, he fortified the proper position to prevent a permanent lodgment of the British troops.

If he had occupied Bunker Hill proper, the British forces if wisely led, would have gained Breed's Hill without loss,—would have secured a safe position for accumulating their forces, and an equally good position for a battery to play against the summit.

It is profitless to go back and inquire whether the Americans were justified in their offensive movement, in view of the crude organization of their army, and the scanty supply of powder then in store. The danger that the British garrison would assail their incomplete intrenchments, was in fact averted by the expression of conscious power which the American advance and resistance indicated. Its moral effect was as great as if their large numbers represented similar courage, similar capacity, and the military resources to back them. The committee of safety and the council of war, seem to have apprehended the situation, and by the application of proper courage and that good sense (which largely underlies all military success) to have struck a blow which in fact intimidated the British commander, and dissuaded him from any further tilts with provincial militia.

It made a square issue between the country and the British army. It was no longer an issue between citizens and the state. Franklin stated truly, when advised of the facts,—" The king has lost his colonies." English statesmen made the same assertion.

It is true that the American army, then encamped about Boston, was at no point fully prepared to meet veteran troops. The hesitation of the British army to force their defenses, however, was one of the strongest elements of that defense ; while assumption of the offensive was not only the best employment of the half idle and impatient militia, but the best method of insuring success.

Only disciplined men can patiently stand fire under exposure. Habit renders the casualties but the necessary incidents to duty. Raw troops, however, must be pushed forward ; and in the enthusiasm of an advance, the casualties are lost sight of, and thus militia sometimes equal the most brilliant efforts of veterans in the line of daring adventure.

Men thus pushed forward, rarely know exactly when they are defeated, and take a victory by surprise. If they *halt*, they recognize danger, feel its power, and defeat is certain. It was thus that the Americans were enabled to realize from the offensive a result beyond the real scope of their military training ; and by the memory of Lexington they were led to rightly estimate both the offensive and defensive value of protecting earth-works, however inartificial and defective. The *individual* was thus enabled to do his best.

The company organizations were so crude, that the men of different companies were intermingled, and the pressure of imperative necessity became the substitute for organization and discipline. They had few officers, these for the most part inexperienced, and each man acted for himself, under the general direction of Prescott and his chief associates. The file-firing of regular troops could not have surpassed the intense vigor of that actually delivered.

The result was the best possible end of the conflict. The impatience of the two armies to have a fight was gratified ; the British army was practically shut up in Boston, and the American army, as they now realized the necessity for more thorough training, and the accumulation of military supplies, secured opportunities to perfect their defenses, and thereby compel the evacuation of Boston.

CHAPTER XIX.

THE NORTHERN CAMPAIGN. PRELIMINARY OPERATIONS.

NO expedition during the American Revolution had less elements of permanent value than those which were undertaken against Canada during the year 1775. Great results were anticipated, but none were realized. The obstacles were too substantial, and failure was inevitable. Wonderful endurance and great physical courage were manifested, and these were accompanied by a prodigious amount of faith, but there was neither ability nor opportunity for works commensurate with the faith. Certain Acts of Parliament, known as the Canadian Acts, were as offensive to Canadians as other legislation was to Americans; but the former were not pressed to the extremity of armed resistance. The people themselves having no harmony of religious or political views, were equally divided in language and race.

Neither did the Canadians invite the aid of the colonies. The hypothesis that Canada would blend her destiny with that of New England, and would unite in resistance to the crown, certainly involved some identity of interest as well as of action. But the characters of the two people were too unlike to be unified by simple opposition to English legislation, and Canadians had no antecedents such as would prompt a hearty sympathy with New England and its controlling moral sentiment. Neither was there such a neighborly relation as admitted of prompt and adequate aid from one to the other, in emergencies calling for a combined effort.

As a base of operations for a British army moving upon the colonies, Canada had the single advantage of being less distant from England than an Atlantic base, and many supplies could be procured without the expense and delay of their transportation across the Atlantic; but between Canada and the American colonies there was an actual wilderness.

Hence a British offensive movement from Canada involved con-

stant waste of men and materials, a deep line through an uninhabited
or hostile region, and such a constant backing, as was both inconsistent with the resources of the base, and with a corresponding support
of armies resting upon the sea coast.

The British government was not ready for operations so extensive
and so exhaustive of men and treasure; neither did it realize the
necessity for that expenditure. There were two alternatives, one
illustrated by General Carleton's plan, viz., to hold the forts of Lake
Champlain, as advanced, defensive positions; and the other, that of
Burgoyne, to strike through the country and depend upon support
from the opposite base.

The true defense of the colonies from such expeditions, depended
upon the prompt seizure and occupation of the frontier posts. An
American advance upon Canada, was not only through a country
strategically bad, but the diversion of forces for that purpose endangered the general issue, and entrusted its interests to the guardianship of an army already insufficient to meet the pressing demands
of the crisis.

The occupation of New York in 1775, by an adequate British
force, would have infinitely outweighed all possible benefit from the
complete conquest of Canada. At the very time when Washington
could hardly hold the British garrison of Boston in check,—when he
had an average of but nine rounds of ammunition per man, he was
required to spare companies, ammunition, and supplies for a venture,
profitless at best,—with the certainty that reinforcements could not
be supplied as fast as the enemy could draw veteran regiments from
Great Britain and Ireland, to defend or recover Canadian soil.

In giving a rapid outline of this first attempt of the colonies to
enlarge the theatre of active operations, it should be noticed that the
initiative had been taken before General Washington had been elected
commander-in-chief, and that Congress itself precipitated the final
movement.

A passing thought is noted, as historic characters now come into
view.

The crater of passion casts out every kind of element that has
been seething and boiling under pressure. So the impulse from Lexington and Concord brought to the surface some elements of great
variety of value and endurance. Arnold, then living at New Haven,
and commanding the company still known as the " Governor's Guards,"
was so heated; that he could not wait for orders or preparation; but

after taking ammunition by force, started with forty of his men for Cambridge on the third day after those skirmishes occurred. He rushed for Ticonderoga without men, as soon as he could handle a commission. He was one of the heroes of Quebec.

Lee was another man, who with hardly less ambition, eccentricity, and lack of moral force, had every volcanic symptom,—with more of military knowledge, and sufficient worldly wisdom to be careful that Congress made up the loss of income which his patriotism would involve. What Arnold was to the northern expedition, Lee fore-promised for a more rational, and a truly legitimate expedition to the southern colonies, when they were afterwards threatened by Clinton and Parker.

This digression purposely associates with two prominent early military movements, the two men who started forth at the outset as meteoric lights, challenging place as stars of the first magnitude, and going out in darkness.

The two expeditions to Canada only anticipated the fate of their leaders. Both expeditions are associated with other and related operations which give character to the campaign of 1776,—the first of the war.

The facts are as follows:

Arnold arrived at Cambridge, and immediately proposed to the Committee of Safety, that he should be sent to capture Ticonderoga. He was promptly commissioned as colonel, was supplied with money, powder, lead, and ten horses, and was authorized to enlist not to exceed four hundred men for the enterprise. Learning that a similar expedition had already started, he entrusted his recruiting to parties selected for the purpose, and joined the other enterprise at Castleton, its place of rendezvous. Here he found Ethan Allen in command, and after a vain effort to assert authority by virtue of his commission, he followed its destinies as a volunteer. Upon reaching the head of Lake Champlain, it was found that boats could not be procured for the whole force, and Allen, who took the lead with less than ninety men, crossed over to the fort, surprised the small garrison by night, and on the morning of the tenth day of May took command of Ticonderoga. Nearly two hundred cannon of all sorts were included among the trophies of the capture. The original inventory of trophies in the handwriting of Arnold, is now in the possession of Dr. Thomas Addis Emmett, of New York. Seth Warner, a volunteer at the battle of Bunker Hill, and afterwards dis-

tinguished in active service, was associated with Allen in this enterprise. On the morning of the twelfth of May, Warner embarked a
small force in boats, and captured the fort at Crown Point, which had
been left with only a nominal garrison to protect the public property.

At this juncture, Arnold reasserted his right to command, but the
colony of Massachusetts recognized the prior claims of Allen. Having been joined by fifty recruits whom his agents had enlisted, he
embarked this force upon a schooner belonging to Captain Skene,
placed cannon on board, and captured St. John's with its nominal
garrison, and a king's sloop then lying in the river near the fort.

Allen, who had started with one hundred and fifty men in bateaux
upon the same errand, was outstripped by the schooner, and met
Arnold, as he returned from the conquest. An attempt to occupy
St. John's permanently, was given up as soon as advised that adequate
forces had been ordered from Canada to maintain the post.

Arnold's force gradually increased to one hundred and fifty men.
With these he manned a small fleet, and assumed command of this
miniature navy as well as of Crown Point. Protests against his
assumption of so large authority, brought a committee from the Connecticut Provincial Assembly; and Massachusetts decided that the
conquest belonged to Connecticut, so that Arnold was not rightfully in
command. The latter colony at once forwarded four hundred men to
garrison the two posts. Arnold discharged his men, and returned to
Cambridge, highly offended. Before leaving Crown Point in June, he
wrote to the Continental Congress stating that General Carleton's
force in Canada was less than six hundred men, asking for the command of two thousand troops for the capture of the whole of Canada,
and assumed responsibility for success. He had formerly traded with
citizens of Quebec, was familiar with the city, and claimed to have
assurance of hearty support if he could have a small nucleus for further operations. On the second day of June, Allen made a proposition to the Provincial Congress of New York, embodying a similar
undertaking.

Allen and Warner also visited Congress, and requested authority
to raise new regiments. This authority was not given, but a recommendation was made to the Provincial Congress of New York, that
the "Green Mountain boys," so styled, should be recognized as regular forces, with the privilege of electing their own officers.

A formal expedition against Montreal was also authorized, and
Generals Schuyler and Montgomery were assigned to its command.

The force to be employed consisted of three thousand New York and New England troops, which were ordered to rendezvous at Ticonderoga during the month of August. Allen and Warner joined this command.

During the same month a committee from Congress visited Cambridge, and persuaded General Washington to send a second army to Canada, *via* the Kennebec river, having for its objective the capture of Quebec. Gardner, a town on the Kennebec, was made the base of departure; and skillful carpenters were sent forward to prepare two hundred bateaux for the use of the troops.

Arnold prominently urged the movement, earnestly solicited, and finally received the command, with the rank of colonel in the Continental army. Ten companies of New England troops under Lieutenant-colonels Enos and Christopher Green, and Majors Meigs and Bigelow, and three companies of riflemen, one from Virginia, and two from Pennsylvania, under the command of captain, afterwards General Daniel Morgan, composed this army of invasion. The aggregate force was eleven hundred men, furnished with rations for forty-five days. Aaron Burr, then but nineteen years of age, accompanied the expedition.

CHAPTER XX.

EXPEDITIONS TO QUEBEC AND MONTREAL. THEIR VALUE.

ON the seventeenth day of September, 1775, Arnold's command marched from Cambridge to Bedford; sailed from Newport on the nineteenth, and on the twentieth, entered the Kennebec river, and landed at Gardner, Maine.

A small scouting party was sent forward to *blaze* the trees, and thus mark out a route to Lake Megantic, at the source of the Chaudière river; and another party was dispatched to Dead river to select the best point for transferring the bateaux from the Kennebec. A glance at the map, " Outline of the Atlantic coast," will indicate the route pursued.

Morgan's corps of riflemen was assigned to the advance, and started on the twenty-third day of September. The rest of the command embraced three divisions, which marched at a day's interval between them, each having charge of its own support. Lieutenant-colonel Enos with three companies commanded the rear division.

The progress of the army was impeded by a swift current, and from the third day it became necessary for men to wade in deep water and force the boats along by main strength. Upon reaching Norridgewock Falls, the real difficulties of the march began. Seven days were consumed in carrying the boats and provisions around the falls, a distance of only a mile and a half. Precipitous rocks bounded the river on either side, and the transfer was not completed without injury to boats as well as provisions. The swift current of the river was confined within closer banks as they advanced: the eddies and exposed rocks rendered it necessary almost daily to drag or carry the boats along the shore, and on the tenth of October, when the army reached the *divide* between the Kennebec and Dead rivers, it was found that the force had been reduced by desertion and sickness to nine hundred and fifty effective men.

On the thirteenth of October, Arnold wrote to the commander of the expedition from Ticonderoga, giving his plans, and also sent an Indian messenger to his correspondents at Quebec, with report of his purpose and progress. This messenger betrayed his trust.

The march of fifteen miles across to Dead river was one of severe trial. Three shallow ponds which were choked with fallen trees, many ravines, quagmires, and swamps, lay in the way; the mud was often knee deep,—the water was up to the arm-pits; and even when oxen were used for hauling, the men were required to render aid and extricate the loaded boats from the mire.

October fifteenth, the boats were launched into Dead river, a comparatively still stream, but broken by shallows, falls, and ripples, so that in a distance of eighty-three miles, the boats had to be carried seventeen times, with constant loss of supplies and injury to the boats. Men deserted daily, some froze to death, others who were sick were left behind in charge of one or two convalescents, and still the army moved on.

October twenty-second, rain fell in torrents.

October twenty-third, continued rain raised the river nearly eight feet—seven boats were overturned and their contents lost. Rations for only twelve days remained on hand, and the army was still thirty miles from Lake Megantic.

A council of war was held. Orders were sent to Lieutenant-colonels Green and Enos to forward every able bodied man for whom rations for fifteen days could be made up, and to send all others back to Norridgewock Falls. Enos, short of provisions, as he afterwards claimed, marched his division of three companies back to Cambridge.

Suddenly rain changed to snow! The ponds froze over, and the ice had to be broken with the butts of muskets to effect a passage for the boats.

The barges had been hauled one hundred and eighty miles, and had been carried forty miles. The men began to go without shoes. Clothing was in rags; their limbs were torn by briars; provisions became scarce; their dogs were eaten for food as well as all their cattle; fish, plants, and roots made up their chief diet. Blankets not worn out, were continually wet or frozen, and hemlock boughs supplied the demand for shelter and bedding. Marvellous was the endurance of those men; and as if in his element, Arnold's courage never abated, his confidence in success never failed him. It was indeed a great ordeal, but a great triumph would compensate for the suffering, if it only secured the surprise of Quebec and the conquest of Canada.

For three days the army rested near Mount Bigelow. A quaint tradition is cited by Lossing, which asserts, " that this officer whose name is still identified with the mountain, visited its top to behold the towers of Quebec."

Lake Megantic was reached, and another inventory of supplies was taken. Less than three days' rations remained. Starvation seemed to be the inevitable destiny of the entire command.

October twenty-seventh, Arnold started with five boats, some *dug-out* canoes, and less than seventy men, to seek the nearest French settlements for the purchase of provisions. The government had furnished him with a thousand dollars before his departure, so that he felt confident of success among the French provincials. The Chaudière river flowed with impetuous velocity, three of the boats were dashed in pieces upon rocks, and the party were in the utmost peril.

October thirtieth, they reached Sertigan, seventy miles from Lake Megantic, were kindly received, purchased flour and cattle, and sent them back to the army in charge of some Canadians and Indians. In a few days, the troops, having lost all their boats, gathered by small detachments at Sertigan, and the army, reunited, was within twenty-five miles of Quebec. For thirty-two days of that march, no human being had been met with in the wilderness, and the trail made by the troops was obliterated as soon as made. Retreat had become worse than to advance.

November ninth, the remnants of the expedition reached Point Levi, opposite Quebec, and there established their base of operations for the conquest of Canada. But the garrison of Quebec, small as it was, had been forewarned; the outworks were undergoing repair, and all boats had been removed to the other side of the river. An immediate advance just at that time, might have secured the capture of the city. The garrison, or such officers as had been entrusted with the news of Arnold's expedition, had no faith in his ability to complete his march, and the people were so apprehensive that resistance would involve the ruin of the city, that the opportunity was ripe for an immediate and bold assault. But Arnold had to build, capture, or purchase boats before he could advance to conquest. His resolution was still equal to the emergency, and the men were put at work.

As if to test his endurance to the utmost, a furious tempest of wind, rain, and sleet set in, and the army was again in peril. He might overcome the terrors of the wilderness, but the tempest was his master!

The expedition to Montreal was being organized at Ticonderoga, when the attention of the reader was invited to Arnold's journey through the wilderness.

General Schuyler's ill health greatly retarded operations, and he soon found that the strength of the army which was hastily gathering at that post was only in mere numbers and the physical capacity of individual men. There was no discipline, no respect for officers, but a perfect independence of thought, judgment, and action, with no time for proper preparation and instruction. Unless the advance could be nearly simultaneous with that of Arnold, both expeditions would lose the objective in view.

It is just here that some attention may be given to the theory which led General Washington to authorize these demonstrations against Canada.

He believed that the occupation of Montreal and Quebec, while they were almost destitute of regular troops, and the season of the year precluded reinforcements from England, would afford the best opportunity for testing the people of Canada, and would also furnish them a basis for the assertion of independence, if they were ripe in sentiment for such a movement. His well-conceived circular addresses which were largely distributed, as well as the policy which he enjoined upon the officers and men of both expeditions, were eminently wise and inspiring. He judged the Canadian opponents of British policy by the expression of feeling which pervaded the colonies, and assumed that very many would gladly avail themselves of the opportunity which the presence of colonial troops would afford for throwing off the yoke of the mother country. It seemed clear that General Carleton, having no fears for Quebec, would concentrate at Montreal all effective forces for the recovery of Ticonderoga and Crown Point. Upon the supposition that Carleton's troops did not exceed seven or eight hundred regulars, and as many provincials, he decided that an army of three thousand men would be adequate for operations from Lake Champlain to Montreal. This estimate was a correct one. Popular demonstrations had indeed been made in the portion of Canada lying south from Montreal, which indicated sympathy with the American movement. This expression of feeling, however, was rather for the purpose of keeping on friendly terms with the American troops who threatened the border, than to indicate their readiness to take up arms for themselves as a people.

Arnold had freely declared his opinions, and claimed to have positive knowledge, that the provincials desired to act in full concert with the American forces. The occupation of Montreal was therefore regarded as both practicable and wise ; and it was near enough to the Sorel river and Lake Champlain to be well supported, so long as the British army was not augmented along the Atlantic coast.

There was still another consideration. The navigable waters of the St. Lawrence exposed Montreal, which was on the north side of the river, to naval attack ; and the strategical character of Quebec was so positive, as to make the occupation of any part of Canada very hazardous, so long as that fortress was left for a base and rendezvous of British armies and fleets. Thus the capture of Quebec, as well as of Montreal, was necessary to any substantial control of Canada itself. The concurrence of Washington in the proposed expedition of Arnold, was therefore predicated upon the possibility of striking quickly, and by surprise, before a substantial defense could be interposed, and did net provide for the contingency of a formal siege. No artillery was furnished, because not within the scope of the proposed duty, and its transportation would have been impossible.

Upon the assumption that Congress was rightly advised of the sentiments of the Canadian people, the expedition was rightly planned. As a matter of history, its signal failure repressed the public avowal of Canadian sympathy with the American Revolution, and demonstrated the bad policy of attempting such distant enterprises as were not essential to colonial defense proper.

Still another element entered into the calculations of the American Congress and affected its action. That body early in June, disclaimed all purpose to operate against Canada.

Bancroft states, that the invasion of Canada was not determined upon until " the proclamation of martial law by the British governor, his denunciation of the American borderers, and the incitement of savages to raids against New England and New York, had made that invasion a substantial act of self-defense."

The letters of Washington to Schuyler, Arnold, Wooster, Montgomery, and to Congress, show clearly that he estimated the difficulties that attended both expeditions, and the contingencies which awaited their execution.

Washington wrote earnestly on the fifth of October, "that if Carleton is not driven from St. John's, so as to be obliged to throw himself into Quebec, it must fall into our hands, as it is left without a regular soldier, as the captain of a brig from Quebec to Boston says. Many of the inhabitants are most favorably disposed to the American cause, and that there is *there* the largest stock of ammunition ever collected in America."

A second letter of the same date states that "Arnold expected to reach Quebec in twenty days from September twenty-sixth, and that Montgomery must keep up such appearances as to *fix Carleton*, and prevent the force of Canada from being turned on Arnold," but, "if penetration into Canada be given up, Arnold must also know it in time for retreat." And again, "This detachment," Arnold's, "was to take possession of Quebec if possible; but at any rate to make a diversion in favor of General Schuyler."

The narrative will now follow the second expedition in its course.

In spite of bad health, Schuyler worked vigorously to hasten the organization of his army.

The Green Mountain boys reorganized on the twenty-seventh of July, and elected the gallant Seth Warner as their lieutenant-colonel, in place of Ethan Allen. Boats were built with great rapidity, and yet, as late as the sixth day of August, the maximum force that was willing to cross the border did not exceed twelve hundred men, and the supply of powder was insufficient even for these. Washington then wrote to Schuyler: "In the article of powder we are in danger of suffering equally with you."

Meanwhile, Major John Brown, a discreet and brave officer, had been sent to Canada to learn the condition and disposition of the British troops. On his return about the middle of August, he reported the number of regulars in Canada to be about seven hundred men; that nearly half this number was at St. John's, and that the Canadian militia were disaffected towards their officers, who had been purposely selected from the old French nobility of the frontier.

On the seventeenth day of August, Montgomery arrived at Ticonderoga.

Upon receiving a letter from Washington that "not a moment of time was to be lost," Schuyler suspended his negotiations with certain Indian tribes whom he had met in council at Albany, and joined the army. The first objective point of importance was the reduction of St. John's, already well garrisoned, and greatly strengthened since the visit of Arnold in the spring.

Montgomery started with a little more than a thousand men, but was so retarded by storms as not to reach Isle La Motte until September third. On the fourth Schuyler joined him, and they advanced to Isle Aux Noix. On the sixth they embarked for St. John's. The enterprise, undertaken without artillery, failed, as did a second attempt of a similar force on the tenth.

Schuyler's ill health compelled his return to Ticonderoga, but with infinite resolution, system, and patience, he pushed forward supplies to Montgomery, who assumed the active command with a force augmented to about two thousand men. Week after week passed by, and little progress was made in the reduction of the fort. The difficulties of his position were mainly those of discipline. All wanted a voice, and few recognized the fact that in a regiment of five hundred men, there could not be five hundred *colonels*. The single question of the location of a battery was made to hinge upon what the men, not the commander, deemed best. An unauthorized and unfortunate enterprise occurred just at this moment, still more to embarrass the army.

Ethan Allen was endeavoring to recruit Canadian volunteers near Chambly. After partial success, and without consulting Montgomery, he resolved to surprise Montreal as he had captured Ticonderoga. He failed, was taken prisoner by General Prescott and sent to England. His hasty enterprise, undertaken with inadequate forces, compromised many Canadians, and repelled others who had been ready to join his command.

On the twenty-sixth of October, General Washington wrote to Schuyler the following consolatory words: " Colonel Allen's misfortune will, I hope, teach a lesson of prudence and subordination to others who may be too ambitious to outshine their general officers, and regardless of order and duty, rush into enterprises which have unfavorable effects on the public, and are destructive to themselves."

Justice to Allen requires the statement that Major Brown had pledged his aid in the enterprise, and to furnish two hundred men Brown had assured him that Montreal was practically defenseless Allen crossed the St. Lawrence from Longuenil, September twenty-fourth, upon the supposition that Brown had crossed the river higher up, and was waiting for his arrival.   Major Brown must have known that such an enterprise needed Montgomery's sanction, and was unwise ; but his failure to support Allen, compelled the latter to fight against overwhelming numbers.   General Carleton also collected nearly a thousand Provincial militia, but their desertion was so imme- diate that he was soon left with only a nominal command of less than three hundred men.   At this juncture he wrote to General Howe that " the Americans had poisoned the minds of the Canadians."

On the eighteenth day of October, Major Brown, aided by many citizens, then organized as a battalion under James Livingston of New York, who had resided at Chambly, and was very popular with the people, captured the fort at that place, sent the prisoners to Connecti- cut, and turned over to the American army the trophies, which included nineteen cannon, and most valuable of all, one hundred and twenty barrels (six tons) of powder.

General Wooster arrived just at this time, approved of Mont- gomery's general plans, aided him to advance his batteries to a com- manding position, and thereby made the investment of St. John's complete.   The garrison had no hope except from Canada.

General Carleton had by this time again collected a mixed and unreliable force of nearly eight hundred men, and made an attempt to cross the St. Lawrence at Montreal, but was thrust back by War- ner's Green Mountain boys, and a portion of the second New York regiment.   On the third day of November the garrison of St. John's, consisting of nearly five hundred regulars, more than half the British regular force then in Canada, and a hundred Canadians, became prisoners of war, among them *Andre*,—and this siege of fifty days ended.

As an evidence of the peculiar state of the regiments at that time, it is to be noticed that one of them mutinied because Montgomery allowed the prisoners to retain their extra suit of clothing, instead of treating it as plunder.

On the twelfth of November, Montgomery took possession of Montreal, and the expedition of the left zone of operations attained its objective.

The British flotilla was also captured, together with General Pres- cott, the captor of Allen, but General Carleton escaped under very favoring circumstances, and thus was enabled to participate in the defense of Quebec.

9

CHAPTER XXI.

THE ASSAULT UPON QUEBEC.

"THE drums beat to arms, and the city was thoroughly aroused." It was hardly daylight on the morning of November ninth, 1775, when Arnold's men appeared upon the river shore, just opposite the citadel of Quebec. His daring spirit was moved to an immediate advance. That instant of time was one of those which contain vast possibilities, and Arnold was a man peculiarly prompt to seize opportunities for daring adventure.

He resolved to cross at all hazards, with numbers however small, if canoes or any other floating fabric could be applied to the movement of men; but it was just then, as already stated, that the Storm King held mastery by day and by night for three successive days, and even Arnold must obey and wait.

During this interval there occurred substantial changes in the character and condition of the garrison of Quebec.

Colonel Allen McLean, who had been operating with General Carleton in the western zone, had abandoned it upon the successful advancement of Montgomery's army to Montreal, and retreated in safety to Quebec, reaching that fortress with one hundred and seventy "Royal Scotch," on the twelfth day of November.

On the fifth, one hundred carpenters arrived from Newfoundland. The deputy-governor, Cramahe, had in fact commenced to repair the defenses as early as September, and the arrival of Arnold was at the last moment of possible success. Two vessels of war, the Lizard and the Hunter, lay in the harbor, and the crews of merchant vessels were also impressed into the service.

Arnold, unapprised of the reinforcement of the garrison, took advantage of his enforced delay, and secured thirty birch-bark canoes for the use of his troops. On the night of the thirteenth of November, by making three trips for the purpose, he crossed the river with seven hundred and fifty men. Daylight revealed his movements, and prevented his return to Point Levi for the last detachment of one hundred and fifty men, and all the ladders which had been prepared for storming purposes.

The landing had been made at Wolfe's cave, a deep notch in the bank up the river just below Sillery, and indelibly associated with the name of that brave soldier who captured Quebec in 1759. Was the name suggestive? That was indeed a little army which Arnold was about to hurl against the parapets, where Wolfe "*died happy*" in victory.

They climbed the steep ascent undisturbed, took their position about half a mile in front of St. Ursula bastion, between the gates of St. John and St. Louis, aroused the garrison by loud huzzahs, and sent forward a formal flag with the demand for immediate surrender.

At that very moment, the army of Arnold was but poorly prepared for meeting an enemy. Over one hundred of their muskets were unserviceable, many cartridges were ruined, and much powder was spoiled. A careful inspection disclosed the fact that the sound ammunition only averaged five rounds per man.

The flag elicited no reply; and a second flag, accompanied by threats of terrible things unless the surrender should be immediate and complete, was fired upon.

It was entirely unnecessary for McLean's Royal Scotch to make a sortie upon the American army. Their steadfast hold upon the city, not only repressed any efforts of disaffected citizens to open the gates to that army; but was a warning to Arnold that his victory must be won by storming the fortress itself.

It is historically true, that Morgan, Febiger and other officers of equal merit, painfully realized the contrast with those expectations which had inspired their departure from Cambridge, and had sustained them in the perils of the wilderness.

Arnold now learned, for the first time, of the re-inforcements which had reached Quebec; and was also advised, by personal acquaintances, that a sortie from the city would soon be made, and that general Carleton had escaped from Montreal and was on his way to the city.

For two or three days the formalities of a blockading force were kept up, guards were posted upon the roads leading to Lorette, St. Foy and Three Rivers, thus cutting off all country supplies of wood or meat which were intended for the garrison; but on the nineteenth

Arnold retired to Point Aux Trembles, to await the arrival of Montgomery.

On that very day, Washington sent a communication to Congress, in which the following words occur:

"It is likely that General Carleton will, with what force he can collect, after the surrender of the rest of Canada, throw himself into Quebec, and there make his last effort."

Carleton was at Aux Trembles in the morning, barely missed Arnold, and entered Quebec during the afternoon of the nineteenth. His first official act was to require all persons who refused to aid in defense of the city, to leave it within four days. Upon removal of these dangerous elements, his available force consisted of at least three hundred regulars, three hundred and thirty Anglo-Canadian militia, five hundred and forty-three French Canadians, four hundred and eighty-five seamen and marines, and one hundred and twenty artificers, fit for duty.

The sole dependence of Arnold was now upon Montgomery, and he sent Captain Ogden with an urgent request, that he would come to his aid with artillery and at least two thousand men.

That officer had indeed occupied Montreal, which was an open city, but by reason of the expiration of terms of enlistments and the unwillingness of the troops to serve any longer, so far from home, he was left with only about eight hundred men as the month of November drew to its close. Even the Green Mountain boys had returned home, greatly to his disgust. The loss in numbers, however, did not represent the real state of his army. Officers and men were alike fractious, dictatorial and self-willed. They claimed the right to do just as they pleased, and to obey such orders only as their judgment approved.

General Schuyler's letter books, and orderly book, and the letters of Montgomery written during that campaign, are very extraordinary exhibitions of the characters of the two men, of their appreciation of the issues of the day, and of their wise and unremitting efforts to secure an exact and thorough army discipline. The aspiration for national liberty had evoked a sense of personal liberty, which was eminently destructive of all real liberty.

The American army at Montreal, at Ticonderoga and at Cambridge, was so intractable and so short-sighted, as very nearly to fulfill Milton's apothegm, "*License* they mean, when they cry Liberty!"

The effort of Montgomery to provide humanely for prisoners of war, was not only treated with contempt, but was made the excuse for insubordination and outrage. On one occasion he tendered his resignation; but canceled it when due apology was made. Schuyler had trouble in the same direction, and officers refused to take clothing and food to suffering prisoners until he made his authority stringent.

Another difficulty grew out of the refusal of troops to serve under generals from other colonies than their own. Colonies had their distinctive military codes, which limited the obligation of the men. To serve in the continental army involved some abnegation of self, and the surrender of the individual will to that of authority.

Montgomery could not, at that time, go to the support of Arnold, without leaving a competent officer in command. It seemed as if the armies at Ticonderoga and Montreal were about to melt away entirely; and both generals were ready to retire from the service, when Washington addressed them a letter, quite characteristic of himself and of the crisis.

"God knows," wrote Washington, "there is not a difficulty that you both (Schuyler and Montgomery) complain of, which I have not, in an eminent degree, experienced, that I am not every day experiencing; but we must bear up against them and make the best of mankind as they are, since we cannot have them as we wish. Let me therefore conjure you and Mr. Montgomery to lay aside such thoughts (of leaving the service); thoughts injurious to yourselves and extremely so to your country, which calls aloud for gentlemen of your abilities."

Late in November, General Wooster arrived at Montreal. With a patriotism characteristic of the man, and especially complimented by Washington, this officer waived his rank in the Connecticut army, and accepted continental assignment, which was below that of Montgomery by one day's date of commission. He took command of the Montreal district, and Montgomery with about three hundred men and a few pieces of artillery, started for the relief of Arnold and the capture of Quebec. A sufficient supply of clothing which had been captured upon the first occupation of the city, was taken on board the vessels for Arnold's command.

Montgomery landed at Point Aux Trembles, on or about the first day of December, and swelled the combined army to a force of nearly one thousand men. This included the detachment originally left at Point Levi, which had subsequently crossed the river with safety.

The strongest fortress in America defended by two hundred heavy cannon, and a garrison of nearly or quite two thousand effective men, was to be subjected to the assaults of this handful of men.

The advance was made during a driving snow storm, through drifts ten feet high; and yet the army was quartered in houses of the suburb of St. Roche, on the Charles river, before dark, December fifth.

December sixth, Montgomery demanded the surrender of the city. This communication eliciting no response, another was sent. This contained exaggerated statements of his force, and threatened dire results, if resistance should be prolonged. No reply was made.

December ninth, a battery of six small guns and two mortars was established about seven hundred yards from St. John's gate. The ground was too hard for earthworks, and snow with water poured over it and frozen, supplied the filling, which with gabions and fascines was made to answer for cover to the battery. The small caliber of the guns rendered them useless, and on the sixteenth of December it was determined to resort to assault, as the only means of gaining access to Quebec.

At this juncture, three of Arnold's captains refused to serve under him any longer. Their time of service would expire at the end of the month, and there was every indication that open mutiny would replace the harmony which had thus far prevailed. An earnest appeal from Montgomery restored them to duty.

The weather had become so cold that men could not handle their arms except for a few minutes at a time, and the month was drawing to its end. On Christmas, the officers held a council, and resolved to make an assault as soon as the weather would permit. The next night was one of intense cold even for that latitude, and great suffering ensued. Succeeding moderation of temperature induced immediate preparation for offensive action; but it was not until the night of the thirtieth, when but one day of legal service remained for a large portion of the troops, that the preparations were complete.

The army was divided into four divisions. The Canadians about two hundred in number, under Colonel Livingston, of Chambly, and Major Brown with his own companies, were to demonstrate in front of St. John and St. Louis gates, and at Cape Diamond bastion, while Montgomery and Arnold were to make *bona fide* attacks through the lower town. The signal for these attacks was to be a discharge of rockets at Cape Diamond.

Montgomery commanded the New York militia and a part of the Eastern. He was to advance from the south and west, directly under Cape Diamond, while Arnold from the north and west, with Lamb's artillery, Morgan's riflemen, and other troops, was expected to pass along the head of the stone jetty, and meet Montgomery at Mountain street, when an attempt would be made upon the city by the rear, at Prescott gate.

Montgomery moved his men to Wolfe's cave, and at least two miles up the river, and then followed the narrow passage which is left between Cape Diamond and the river. His course was almost directly north-east, and in the face of drifting snow, which soon changed to fine hail, rendering it impossible to recognize his men at the distance of a few feet, and equally impossible to communicate orders except by messengers. Men's breathing soon covered the face with ice, the single trail became hard and slippery after a few had led the way, and the march was along a ledge where a single careless step would precipitate a man to an abyss on the right.

Unexpectedly, and half an hour too soon, the rocket signal put the garrison on the alert. Lanterns flashed on the parapet, and Montgomery with a mere handful of men had just passed under Cape Diamond, while his principal force, with the ladders, still struggled through the snow half a mile in the rear. It was a moment of intense interest!

The first barrier of timber and pickets extending from the slate rock upon which Cape Diamond rested, to the river precipice, had been left to its intrinsic excellence as an obstruction, and was without a guard.

Hatchets and saws made quick work! Sending a messenger to the rear to hurry men forward, Montgomery with his aid, McPherson, and parts of Cheeseman's and Mott's companies, pushed through this barrier, and advanced upon the second, which consisted of a log-house, loop-holed for muskets, and defended by two pieces of cannon.

The pathway now descended and approached the foot of King's Yard. Only three or four men could march abreast, yet Montgomery, as soon as sixty men were collected, advanced to force the defenses. A master of a transport with a few seamen, and not more than thirty-eight militia, manned the block-house. The forlorn hope was already within a hundred feet of the barrier. Montgomery shouted, "Men of New York, you will not fear to follow where your general leads: push on, Quebec is ours!" Suddenly the lighted matches sparkled like fire-flies in the gloom; a whirl of grape-shot swept the narrow pathway, and Montgomery, McPherson, Cheeseman, and ten others were instantly killed!

In vain, Captain Mott urged the survivors to renew the advance. A continuous fire from the loop-holes of the block-house and repeated discharges of grape, were followed by the descent of fire-balls from the heights to light up the scene of conflict, and as daylight began to appear, the whole detachment could be seen in full retreat.

Montgomery lay stiff and cold in death ; but his memory, honored by the garrison which rescued his body, and buried it with the honors of war, is ever a theme of praise ; and that perpetual tribute is the spontaneous offering of foes and friends alike.

Arnold moved on his errand with equal promptness, and under equally trying risks. The ice had gorged, and had been forced upon the shore by the heavy tides, so that his men also were confined to a narrow passage along the rock. The north-east storm beat with un-broken force upon their left flank, and the eddies of wind which curled about the cliff, lifted great drifts in their path.

Arnold led the advance with merely five picked men. Morgan's riflemen and Lamb's artillery followed, the latter dragging a field-piece on a sled. It was soon abandoned.

Already they had passed the stone jetty ; had passed the Palace gate, and were pushing forward into the narrow street of Sault au Matelot, where, under a projecting rock in a narrow passage, a barrier had been established and was strongly supported.

The advance had been so far made, and as yet no report of fire-arms gave notice that Colonel Livingston had made his demonstration before St. John's gate, to occupy the garrison, and divert their atten-tion from the assault upon the Lower town. But in its place, the beat of drums, and the roar of cannon, gave warning of the hot wel-come which awaited the assailants.

A storm of grape and musketry received Arnold's advance ! At the first discharge his right knee was shattered by a musket ball, and he was carried back to St. Roche. Morgan and Lamb passed on, planted ladders, and the first barrier was gained.

At the end of the same street, and not far from the anticipated union with Montgomery's column, a second barrier, supported by a well defended stone house, was in the way. Once it was surmounted by Morgan, but only to learn that a strong force was posted in its rear. Seizing houses for cover, and answering back the fire from other houses across the street, the fight continued for nearly four hours. Ignorant of the localities, but determined not to recede, Morgan fought on. Lamb was wounded, nearly sixty of his men had fallen, and still the expected command of Dearborn did not come to his support. A well conceived sortie from the Palace gate had been made under General Carleton's orders, and Dearborn's company, divided into two detachments, were already prisoners of war.

Hopeless of success, unsupported, destitute of ammunition, and without bayonets, apprised of the fate of Montgomery and his companions, Morgan also surrendered his command, and entered Quebec, but as a prisoner of war. Thus failed the second movement as the first failed; and four hundred and twenty-six officers and men, one half of the entire American force, were with him prisoners of war.

They were captives, but let it be recorded to the perpetual memory of General Carleton, that these captives were treated with soldierly respect. When his officers complained of his kindness toward rebels, his answer was characteristic, and more and more to be valued as England and America enjoy the fruits of comity and peace.

"Since we have tried in vain to make them acknowledge us as brothers, let us at least send them away disposed to regard us as first cousins."

Arnold withdrew to a distance of three miles from the town, intrenched himself as well as he could, confined his operations to shutting the city off from supplies, and his share in the campaign of 1775 closed.

The invasion of Canada came to a full stop. The invasion of the colonies was to follow its abandonment. Of the brave men who took part in those exciting events, many had a future history; and their after conduct will bear testimony of the value of the experience which so thoroughly tested their patriotism and valor.

Morgan was General Morgan, of Morgan's riflemen.

Meigs and Febiger are associated with the forlorn hope of Stony Point.

Greene defended Red Bank on the Delaware.

Thayer was heroic at Fort Mifflin.

Lamb fought at Montgomery and Yorktown.

Oswald is identified with Monmouth.

Porterfield was killed in the battle of Camden.

Many of these began their training at Bunker Hill, and, through the wilderness and before Quebec, continued their education in the art of war.

CHAPTER XXII.

CAMPAIGN OF 1775.—BRIEF MENTION.

THE campaign of 1775 was characterized by greater offensive activity on the part of the colonists than of the British troops. The defensive returned the offensive. The occupation of Charlestown Heights was supplemented by the invasion of Canada. The impulse which surrounded Boston with the militia of New England necessarily made that camp the head-quarters of the American army, and the capture of Boston its primary objective.

At all other sea-port cities there was disaffection of the people, and partial assertion of force ; but there were no British garrisons to support the British governors, and few occasions for open rupture. The policy of Congress still comprehended the possibility of an amicable settlement of the difficulties with the mother country.

The fact is also to be noticed, that the militia from Northern New England were peculiarly concerned in the defense of their own border, because the forts upon Lake Champlain, its navigable waters, and the presence of British troops in Canada, afforded the only then existing opportunity for British offensive movements. There was no external force which could be employed to disturb the investment of Boston, and none which was disposable for occupation of Atlantic ports. It was therefore a wise strategic movement, to take the control of Lake Champlain, to hold its forts for defensive purposes, and so demonstrate, in force, as to ward off British attack. An adequate army of invasion from Canada, if in secure possession of Ticonderoga and Crown Point, supported by armed vessels, would be a constraint upon New York, the Green Mountain country, and New Hampshire.

These elements dictated the military movements of 1775. The few minor operations of the year, including that at Great Bridge, Virginia, in December, were only significant of an increasing sentiment of hostility to any compromise. On the other hand, wherever there

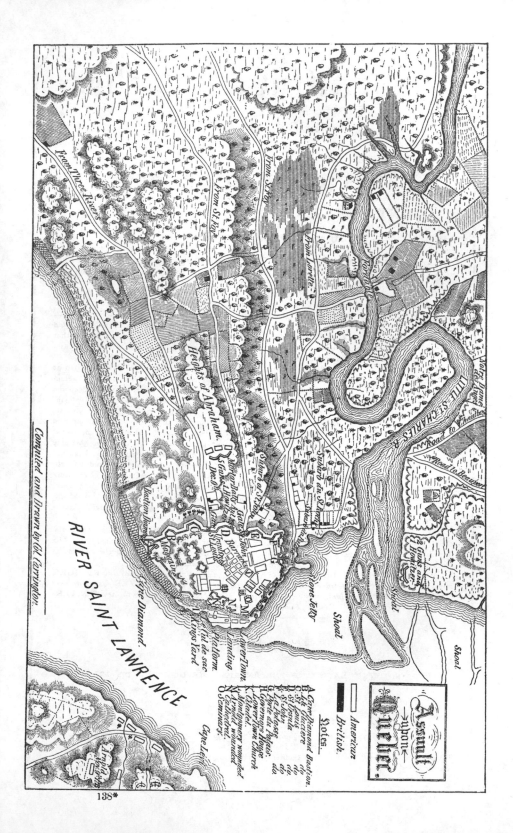

Assault upon Quebec.

Notes

American
British

A Cape Diamond Bastion.
B St Louis do.
C St Ursula do.
D St John do.
E La Potasse do.
F La Joliste do.
G Porte du Palais do.
H Governors House
I Governors House
K Citadel
L Montgomery wounded
M Arnold wounded
N Cathedral
O Seminary

RIVER SAINT LAWRENCE

Compiled and Drawn by Col. Carrington.

138*

Assault upon Quebec

DECEMBER 30, 1775

American Commanders

MONTGOMERY   ARNOLD

Strength, 1,300.   Casualties, 750.

NOTES.—ARNOLD left Cambridge Sept. 17th, sailed from Newport Sept. 19th, entered the Kennebec River Sept. 20th, sent scouts to Dead River and Lake Megantic (see map 1), and advanced Morgan's riflemen on the 23d. This command of 1,100 men, with rations for 45 days, was expected to make the march to St. Lawrence River in 20 days. Storms, swamps, thickets, freezes, hunger and desertions reduced the number one fourth, and Point Levi was not reached by the survivors until Dec. 9th. On the 13th, at night, 750 men crossed in birch bark canoes, but daylight having revealed the movement, the residue, with ladders already prepared for storming purposes, was left behind. Arnold picketed the roads from Lorette, St. Foy and Three Rivers, to cut off supplies for Quebec; but finding that the garrison had been strengthened during his protracted march, he retired to Point Aux Trembles on the 19th, to await the arrival of Montgomery.

MONTGOMERY succeeded Schuyler (sick) in command of a second expedition, organized at Ticonderoga to invade Canada *via* Montreal, captured that city November 12th, left Wooster in command, and joined Arnold about Dec. 1st. Advancing through snow drifts ten feet deep, he quartered his men in houses of the suburb of St. Roche, on the Charles River, before dark, Dec. 5th. On the 6th he demanded the surrender of Quebec, but received no reply. On the 9th a battery of six guns and two mortars was planted before St. John's gate. The hard frozen ground and extreme cold rendered regular approaches impracticable, and the small calibre of the guns rendered them useless for breaching purposes. On the 16th an assault was planned. On the night of the 30th one column demonstrated against St. John's and St. Louis' gates; one column against Cape Diamond bastion, while one, under Montgomery, toward Kings Yard, beneath Cape Diamond, and a fourth under Arnold, through the lower town, by Porte de Palais, made the chief attacks. Premature signals alarmed the garrison, and in spite of desperate valor, both assaults failed. Montgomery, McPherson, Cheeseman and ten others were killed by one discharge of grapeshot. Arnold was wounded, and Morgan, who accompanied him, was taken prisoner with 426 officers and men. Arnold retreated, and the siege was practically abandoned until spring.

SIR GUY CARLETON, Governor of Canada, distinguished himself by kindness to the prisoners. He had withdrawn from Montreal in safety, at the attack of Montgomery, reached Point Aux Trembles the same day as Arnold, just missing him, and by his arrival increased the garrison of Quebec to about 2,000 men. Two hundred guns defended the works.

MEM.—*Of the brave men in the assault, the following deserve notice;* MEIGS and FEBIGER *stormed Stony Point with Wayne ;* Col. GREEN *defended Red Bank ;* THAYER *fought at Fort Mifflin ;* LAMB *at Fort Montgomery and Yorktown :* OSWALD *at Monmouth, and* PORTERFIELD *at Camden,* STEVENS at Ticonderoga, Saratoga and Yorktown.

References:

CARRINGTON'S "BATTLES OF THE AMERICAN REVOLUTION," pp. 121-137.

School Histories:

Anderson, ¶ 25 ; p. 72.
Barnes, ¶ 2 ; p. 112.
Berard (Bush), ¶ 48-9; pp. 146-7.
Goodrich, C.A. (Seaveys), ¶ 14, p. 117.
Goodrich, S. G., ¶ 8 ; p. 200.
Hassard, ¶ 5 ; p. 164.

Holmes, ¶ 11 ; p. 113.
Lossing, ¶ 21-2 ; p. 137.
Quackenbos, ¶ 302 ; p. 216.
Ridpath, ¶ 19 ; p. 191.
Sadlier (Excel), ¶ 21 ; p. 180.
Stephens, A. H., ¶ 10 ; p. 177.

Swinton, ¶ 94 ; p. 124.
Scott, ¶ 14 ; p. 165.
Thalheimer (Eclectic), ¶ 246-7 ;
      p. 137-8,
Venable, ¶ 126 ; p. 98.

were no expressions of force, and no committal of overt-acts, there was evidence afforded through many citizens, that they wished to avoid such acts and constrain some settlement with Great Britain.

It needed just such a protracted suspension, or withholding of open hostilities, over the country at large; and just such a display of force about Boston, to prepare the colonies for real war, and at the same time develop an army and test both officers and men. The army was *organized* at Cambridge. Washington was so doubtful of some of the appointments of general officers that he withheld for a time the delivery of commissions which had been entrusted to his charge when he left Philadelphia to assume command.

The character and composition of the army, or, the *armies*,—the various and distinctive systems adopted, and the jealousies and antagonisms which prevailed, have been illustrated by incidents of the northern campaign.

They were infinitely provoking and provokingly constant! General Schuyler affirmed that " if Job had been a general, in his situation, his memory had not been so famous for patience." Washington assured him that " he," Schuyler, " only had, upon a very limited scale, a sample of his own perpetual trials."

No sooner had the troops assembled than a set repugnance was manifested to all proper instruction in the details of Minor Tactics. " They had been trained to have their own way too long," said Washington. Guard duty was odious! Superiority by virtue of rank, was denied! The abuse of places of trust, and their prostitution for selfish ends, was constant. Profanity, vulgarity, and all the vices of an undisciplined mass became frightful, as soon as any immediate danger *passed by*.

The good, the faithful and the pure were hardly less restless under the new restraint; and few appreciated the vital value of some absolutely supreme control. The public moneys and public property were held to belong to everybody, because Congress represented everybody. Commands were considered despotic orders, and exact details were only another form for slavery.

Such was the state of things when Washington assumed command at Cambridge.

Even officers of high position, whether graded above or below their own expectations, found time to indulge in petty neglect of plain instructions, and in turn to usurp authority, in defiance of discipline and the paramount interests of the colonies at large.

Washington gave the army work in perfecting earth-works, build-ing redoubts, and policing the camp,—enforced the observance of the Sabbath, court-martialed officers, and tried soldiers for swearing, gambling, fraud, and lewdness; introduced a thorough system of guard and picket duty, and made the nights subservient to proper rest, in the place of dissipation and revelry. Good order, *discipline*, was the first purpose of the commander-in-chief.

These statements fall far below a fair review of the situation as given by Washington himself.

The *logistics* of war became his next care. The army was deficient in every element of supply. The men who held their colonial obliga-tions to be supreme, came and went, just as their engagements would permit, and the comfort of their families required. Desertion was considered as nothing, or at the worst but venial, and there were times when the American army before Boston, through nine miles of investment, was less in numbers than the British garrison within the city.

The deficiency in the number of men was not so conspicuous as in the matter of powder, lead, arms, tents, horses, carts, tools, and medical stores. Ordinary provisions were abundant. The country about Boston fed the men generously; but it was difficult to convince the same men that all provisions must go into a general commis-sariat, and be issued to all alike, and that stores must be accumulated, and neither expended lavishly, nor sold at a bargain as soon as a sur-plus was on hand.

Such items as cordage, iron, horse-shoes, lumber, fire-wood, and every possible article that could be used by an army for field or frontier service, were included in his inventory of essential stores; and in his own expenditure of the most trivial item of public property, he kept a detailed and exact account.

Of the single article of powder, he once stated that, "his chief supply was furnished by the enemy," as during one period, the armed vessels which patrolled the coast captured more powder than Con-gress had been able to furnish in several months.

On the twenty-ninth of November, Captain John Manly, who was the most prominent officer of this hastily improvised navy, captured a British store-ship containing a large mortar, several brass cannon, two thousand muskets, one hundred thousand flints, thirty thousand shot, thirty tons of musket shot, eleven mortar beds, and all necessary implements for artillery and intrenching service.

The strategical value of the operations during 1775, was limited by defective discipline, bad logistics, and the changeable character of the army. Schuyler and Montgomery, who deservedly shared his confidence and commanded his respect, performed their work fully up to the limit of the means furnished.

The feeble results realized from the invasion of Canada, do not impair the proposition, that its direction from head-quarters showed a clear conception of the strategical relations of the points involved, and the proper methods by which to attain success.

The deep line of operations which left no track through the wilderness would have been a memorable folly as an independent movement. When it attempted to strike the capital of Canada, which was at the same time the base of operations and of supplies for the entire British provinces, at a time when its last garrison was far advanced towards Lake Champlain, it had *method*.

When taken in connection with the American movement on the left, which had for its purpose the destruction or capture of those advanced troops, it became a bold enterprise of a thoroughly scientific and well related value.

When it had the supposed assurance that the people of Canada were ready, and only needed the nucleus for organization and practical revolution against a common adversary, it combined sound strategy with the wisest *military policy*.

When it contemplated the fact that the principal military stores of North America were at Quebec, and that its possession substantially controlled the St. Lawrence, overawed all Canada, and compelled England to employ a great army to recover its possession, if recoverable at all, it becomes memorable for its conception and its illustration of the science of war.

The following is an extract from Washington's Orderly book: " November fifth. As the commander-in-chief has been apprised of a design formed for the observance of that ridiculous and childish custom of burning the effigy of the Pope, he cannot help expressing his surprise that there should be officers and soldiers in this army, so void of common sense as not to see the impropriety of such a step at this juncture, at a time when we are soliciting, and have really obtained, the friendship and alliance of the people of Canada, whom we ought to consider as brethren embarked in the same cause, the defense of the general liberty of America. At such a juncture and in such circumstances to be insulting their religion, is so monstrous as not to be suffered or excused ; indeed, instead of offering the most remote insult it is our duty to address public thanks to those our brethren, as to them we are so much indebted for every late happy success over the common enemy in Canada."

The closing events of the year were full of discouraging features.

As early as September there was no money, and but little clothing. Economy in the use of powder was more than balanced by its poor quality and its waste through bad management and inadequate store-houses for its protection.   Fire-wood was scarce, and the troops whose time was soon to expire were unwilling to work in advance for the comfort of those who were to succeed them.   A large number of the Connecticut troops had been enlisted for six months, and their time would expire November thirteenth.

Washington was determined to make a decisive movement while the army was at its best estate.   The British had advanced their works beyond Charlestown Neck, upon the main land.   As a counter-movement, with the hope that it would be resisted, Washington put his army in readiness to resist an attack, and commenced the thorough fortification of Ploughed Hill and Cobble Hill, and also increased the strength of works at Lechmere Point, hoping to elicit an attack from the enemy.

The British troops, however, made no counter demonstration, and after twenty-four hours of preparation, these redoubts were capable of defense against the whole British army.   He also entertained a purpose to assault Boston itself and to burn the city if it seemed to be a military necessity.   Lee opposed the movement as impossible, and the council of war concurred in the postponement of such an enterprise.

Meanwhile the citizens of sea-coast towns began to be anxious for their own safety.   A British armed transport cannonaded Stonington, and other vessels threatened New London and Norwich.   All these towns begged Washington to send them troops.   Governor Trumbull, of Connecticut, whose extraordinary comprehension of the military as well as the civil issues of the day, made him a firm supporter of Washington's policy, ever reliable and ever just, inquired his opinion upon this very matter.

Washington wrote : " The most important operations of the campaign cannot be made to depend upon the piratical expeditions of two or three men-of-war privateers."

Gage had been ordered home, and left October tenth.   General

Howe assumed command over all the Atlantic Colonies from Nova Scotia to West Florida inclusive.

Offensive proclamations, bad in policy, fruitless for good, and involving the immediate crushing out of all sympathy from those who were still loyal to the crown, marked his advent to command. He threatened with military execution any who should leave the city without his written consent, enjoined all the citizens to arm, and placed Washington under the necessity of taking active measures against all " who were suffered to stalk at large, doing all the mischief in their power." Up to this time the officers of the crown and neutral citizens had not been interfered with by the American authorities. Acting under his orders, Admiral Graves determined to give greater efficiency to his small fleet, and Lieutenant Mowatt, under general instructions to burn all towns that fitted out or sheltered privateers, began his work by the destruction of Falmouth, now Portland, Maine.

An American privateer, soon after sent by Washington to the St. Lawrence river, to cut off two brigantines which had left England with supplies for Quebec, plundered St. John Island. Washington sent back the citizen-prisoners, and restored all their private effects, denouncing the movement as a violation of the principles of all civilized warfare.

Crowded by these multiplying demands upon his resources, and equally conscious that there would soon be neither army nor supplies, equal to the emergency, he made an independent appeal to Congress, covering the whole ground of his complaints and his requisitions.

He wanted money,—a thoroughly organized commissariat,—a permanent artillery establishment,—more adequate control over all troops,—a longer term of enlistment,—an enlargement of the rules and articles of war, and power to enforce his will. He also asked for a separate organization of the Navy, and that it be placed upon a sound footing, as to men and vessels.

Congress acted upon these recommendations. On the fourth of October, a committee, consisting of Benjamin Franklin, Thomas Lynch, of South Carolina, and Benjamin Harrison, of Virginia, started for Washington's camp, with three hundred thousand dollars in Continental money, and after a patient consideration of his views, advised the adoption of his recommendations by Congress. A council of the New England Governors was called to meet this committee.

At this interview, a new organization of the army was determined upon, fixing the force to be employed before Boston at twenty-three thousand, three hundred and seventy-two, officers and men.

Washington submitted to this committee his plan for attacking Boston. It was approved, and Congress soon after authorized him to burn the city if necessary to the prosecution of military operations against the British army.

October thirteenth; Congress authorized the building and equipment of one cruiser of ten and one of fourteen guns.

October thirtieth; one vessel of twenty and one of twenty-six guns was authorized. A naval committee was appointed, composed of such men as Silas Deane, John Langdon, Christopher Gadsden, Stephen Hopkins, Joseph Hewes, Richard Henry Lee, and John Adams.

November twenty-eighth; a code of regulations was adopted for the navy, and on the thirteenth of December the construction of thirteen vessels of war was authorized. As some of these vessels are necessarily noticed in the course of the narrative, their names, themselves memorial of the crisis, are given.

"Ordered to be built at Philadelphia, the Washington, 32 guns; Randolph, 32; Effingham, 28, and Delaware, 24; at Portsmouth, the Raleigh, 32; at Boston, the Hancock, 32, and the Boston, 28; at Providence, the Warren, 32, and the Providence, 28; at Annapolis, the Virginia, 28; at New London, the Trumbull, 28; at Poughkeepsie, the Congress, 28, and the Montgomery, 24 guns.

Among the officers commissioned December twenty-second, Nicholas Biddle appears in the list of captains, and John Paul Jones among the lieutenants.

As the year approached its close, the British leveled their advanced works on Charlestown Neck, and concentrated their right wing in a strong redoubt upon Bunker Hill, while their left wing at Boston Neck was more thoroughly fortified against attack.

Congress now intimated to Washington that it might be well to "attack on the first favorable occasion and before the arrival of reinforcements."

Washington replied that he "must keep his powder for closer work than cannon distance."

November nineteenth, Henry Knox was commissioned as Colonel *vice* Gridley,—too old for active service; two lieutenant-colonels and two majors, as well as twelve companies of artillery, were authorized, and thus the American artillery, as well as the navy, was put upon a substantial basis, with Knox as its chief.

The year closed, with the prospect that the army would be immediately replaced by raw troops ; and in spite of the advances made toward a substantial paper organization, the period was one of the most perilous of the war.

NOTE. The fate of the American navy is worthy of record.

*Washington, 32, destroyed by the British in the Delaware........................ 1778
Randolph, 32, blown up in action with the Yarmouth, 64.......................... 1778
*Effingham, 28, destroyed by the British in the Delaware........................ 1778
Delaware, 24, captured by the British in the Delaware............................ 1777
Raleigh, 32, captured by the Experiment 50, and Unicorn, 22......... 1778
Hancock, 32, taken by Rainbow, 44, and Victor, 16.............................. 1777
Boston, 28, captured at Charleston...........   1780
Warren, 32, burned in the Penobscot by the Americans........................... 1779
Providence, 28, captured at Charleston... 1780
*Virginia, 28, taken by British fleet near Cape Henry........................... 1778
Trumbull, 28, taken by Isis, 32, and General Monk, 18... 1781
* Congress, 28, burned in the Hudson to avoid capture........................... 1777
*Montgomery, 24, "   "   "   "   "   "   "   1777
Andrea Doria, 14, burned in the Delaware to avoid capture....................... 1777
The Alliance, 32, (afterwards built and identified with La Fayette, was sold after the
    war, and converted into an Indiaman.
The Confederacy, 32, was taken, off Virginia, by a ship of the line................. 1781
Queen of France, 18, captured at Charleston....................................... 1780

* *Never went to sea.* (Reference is made to Cooper's naval history, for the fate of the other vessels, not incidentally mentioned in connection with the British occupation of the Atlantic ports.)

10

CHAPTER XXIII.

THE year 1776 enlarged the theatre of operations. The demonstration before Boston attained its objective; and the city was evacuated by the British troops. At all other points of active service the Americans were driven to the defensive; and it was not until the month of December, of that year, that the *offensive return*, at Trenton, imparted a new character to the struggle and interrupted the general success of the royal forces.

On the thirtieth day of December, Admiral Shuldham brought reinforcements to General Howe and at the same time took command of all naval forces, *vice* Graves, relieved.

The troops in garrison were kept under the most rigid discipline. General Howe exacted the most formal observance of all military ceremony, and issued orders, sharply reprimanding some soldiers, who had been careless in minute details of personal neatness and outfit. An order of January thirteenth particularly calls those to account, "whose hair was not smooth, but badly powdered; who had no frills to their shirts, whose linen was dirty, whose leggins hung in a slovenly manner about their knees, and other unsoldier-like neglects,"— "which must be immediately remedied."

Amusements were also provided for the entertainment of the troops, a theatre was opened, and a sense of perfect security pervaded all ranks.

The condition and style of doing things, in the adversary army, was quite in contrast with all this nursing process, so good in itself— so inefficient for real work at the time.

For many weeks it had been a matter of the greatest concern with Washington, how to keep up appearances of military preparation, while all things were in extreme confusion. He had to demonstrate, as if urgent to attack the city at the first moment, while the extraordinary operation was going on, of disbanding one army and creating another in its place, directly in front of an enemy.

Enough has been said to indicate the difficulties of that operation.

Washington, as well as Howe, had ideas respecting military discipline, and he, also, issued orders upon the habits, personal bearing and want of neatness among the men, closing on one occasion thus emphatically, " Cards and games of chance are prohibited. At this time of public distress, men may find enough to do, in the service of their God and country, without abandoning themselves to vice and immorality." " It may not be amiss for the troops to know, that if any man in action shall presume to skulk, hide himself, or retreat from the enemy without the orders of his commanding officer, he will be instantly shot down as an example of cowardice ; *cowards having too frequently disconcerted the best formed troops by their dastardly behavior.*"

Meanwhile, General Greene kept his little army well in hand. On the fourth of January, he wrote, from Prospect Hill,—" The night after the old troops went off I could not have mustered seven hundred men, notwithstanding the returns of the new enlisted troops amounted to nineteen hundred and upward. I am strong enough to defend myself against all the force in Boston. Our situation has been critical. Had the enemy been fully acquainted with our situation, I cannot pretend to say what might have been the consequences."

Washington wrote to Congress January first, leaving the last word *blank*, lest the letter should miscarry. " It is not perhaps in the power of history to furnish a case like ours ; to maintain a post within musket shot of the enemy, within that distance of twenty old British regiments, without ———."

The winter was memorable for its mildness.

" Give me powder or *ice*," was Washington's ejaculation, when writing to a friend. It was his intention as soon as the river froze over to march directly to Boston, across the ice. The presence of ships of war prevented any attempt by the use of small boats while the river remained open. There had been " one single freeze, and some pretty strong ice," and he suddenly proposed to the council that the opportunity be seized at once to cross over and take or burn Boston. On the twenty-sixth of February, he wrote to Joseph Reed, saying,—" Behold, though we have been waiting all the year for this favorable event, the enterprise was thought too hazardous. I did not think so, and I am sure yet that the enterprise, if it had been undertaken with resolution, must have succeeded ; *without it any would fail*, and I am preparing to take post on Dorchester Heights, to try if the enemy will be so kind as to come out to us."

" What I have said respecting the determination in council, and the possessing of Dorchester Heights, is spoken *under the rose*."

A great improvement had been made in the ordnance department, through the great business capacity of Colonel Knox. He made a journey to Fort George during the preceding December, and by the latter part of February, had hauled, upon sleds over the snow, more than fifty pieces of artillery from that fort to Cambridge. This had enabled him to make the armament at Lechmere Point very formidable, and by the addition of several half-moon batteries between that point and Roxbury, it was possible to concentrate nearly every mortar which the army had upon the city itself.

During the first week in January, Washington was advised that General Clinton, relying upon the new troops which arrived with Admiral Shuldham, was to be detailed with an independent command for some remote expedition, or at least beyond the waters of New England.

Believing that New York must be the immediate objective of such a movement, he ordered General Lee, then upon detached service in Connecticut, "to take such volunteers as he could quickly assemble on his march, and put the city of New York in the best posture of defense, which the season and circumstances would admit of." Lee had already written to the commander-in-chief, urging " the immediate occupation of that city, the suppression or expulsion of certain tories from Long Island," and that " not to crush the serpents before their rattles are grown would be ruinous."

The control over disaffected citizens on Long Island had already been desired by the New York convention, and Lord Sterling, then at Elizabethtown with his regiment, was ready to coöperate with any other forces that might be available for the purpose, as " none could be spared from Cambridge."

Lee entered New York with two regiments from Connecticut, amounting to nearly fifteen hundred men, on the same day that Clinton cast anchor near Sandy Hook. Notwithstanding the assurances of that officer that he called to consult with Governor Tryon, and that he was imperatively ordered to the south, fortifications were immediately begun at New York and Brooklyn Heights. This was timely, and a matter of military obligation.

It must be noted in this connection, that General Lee had secured troops from Connecticut, and placed them upon a continental basis of service, when he was instructed only to assemble volunteers for a special duty, and thereby deliberately exceeded his authority. One of these regiments had been disbanded by order of Congress ; and its reassembling as a regiment of the continental army, although countenanced by the authorities of the colony, was a breach of military subordination on the part of Lee. Neither did he hesitate as to the style of language in which he spoke of Congress itself. He was equally unjust to the leading men of the New York convention. The exact condition of Manhattan Island must be stated in this connection, as some writers persistently claim that New York failed in duty at this juncture. The British fleet controlled the adjoining waters. It could destroy the city; but the city had neither the numbers nor the guns to make any substantial resistance. There was a general understanding that each party should attend to its own business ; that the officers of the crown would keep within the technical line of their duty, and that the citizens would not interfere. Congress had no troops to spare, and there was a general suspension of public arming, except to keep up the armies already in the field. This was of itself a great undertaking. The precipitation upon Congress, or upon special localities, of exacting issues, was therefore unwise. The disaffected citizens of New York were *not* forgotten ; neither were the patriotic leaders who responded promptly in 1775.

The movement of Clinton was a fortunate opportunity for bringing this condition of armed neutrality to an end, and it was accomplished peaceably and at the right time.

It is to be admitted, however, that Lee asserted a very high prerogative in this his first independent command, and that it called forth criticism from Washington as well as Congress. A committee of that body met him at New York and accommodated the occupation to the judgment of all well disposed citizens. His denunciation of the "accursed Provincial Congress of New York" was characteristic of Lee's temperament, his erratic career, and his subordination of all things to the wishes of Charles Lee, but it was neither politic nor becoming a great commander.

On New Years day, Norfolk, Virginia, was bombarded and burned under the direction of Lord Dunmore. This was one of a series of acts perpetrated by the colonial governors, which induced a second series of southern demonstrations in behalf of independence, very similar to those which attended their attempt to disarm the people during the spring months of 1775.

Sparks embodies the matter thus clearly. "These expeditions were undertaken at the suggestion of the colonial governors and zealous partisans, whose hopes and wishes betrayed them into a deplorable ignorance of the state of the country and character of the people." Lord Dartmouth himself planned this expedition, and sent instructions to Lord Howe under date of October twenty-second, 1775, directing him, " to gain possession of some respectable post to the southward, from which to make sudden and unexpected attacks upon sea-coast towns during open winter." Clinton had orders " to destroy any towns " that refused submission. Lord Dunmore protested against sending seven regiments from Ireland to North Carolina upon the solicitation of Governor Martin of that colony, while he was living in the very hot bed of rebellion itself, and almost defenseless.

Lord Howe himself advised that New York should be the first objective of attack, and the permanent base of future army movements.

After these essential diversions to contemporaneous matters, which had their quickening element to inspire Washington to offensive measures, the narrative takes up the closing scenes of the siege of Boston.

The month of February was drawing near its close. Washington determined to delay no longer to test his strength against the garrison of Boston. He collected forty-five bateaux, each capable of transporting eighty men, and built two floating batteries of great strength and light draught of water. Fascines, gabions, carts, bales of hay, intrenching tools, two thousand bandages for wounds, and all other contingent supplies that might be needed were gathered, and placed under the guard of picked men.

General Thomas Mifflin, quartermaster-general, who had originally accompanied him from Philadelphia as an *aid-de-camp*, was thoroughly aroused to the importance of the impending movement. He shared the confidence of Washington.

The movement was carried through with that inflexibility of purpose which marked Washington's career during crises of imminent peril. It seemed as if the very fact of his submission of a military movement to a council, awakened questions as to its feasibility. *Jomini*, in connection with his statement, that Napoleon never seemed to provide for a retreat, adds, that " when Napoleon was present no one thought of such a provision."

The great acts of Washington's career were performed when he was clothed with ample authority by Congress, or the emergency forced him to make his own will supreme. This was the reason which led Congress at last to emancipate him from the constraint of councils. If he doubted, others doubted; if he was persistent, he inspired the courage and nerve which secured results. He was in such a mood on the first day of March, 1775. He had a plan, a secret, and he kept it secret until the hour for execution.

Just after sunset of that New England spring evening, from Lechmere Point, past Cobble Hill, and through the long range of encircling batteries, clear to Roxbury lines on the right, every mortar and cannon which could take the range opened their fire upon the quiet city. It was a test of the location, range, and power of the adversary's fire. That fire was returned with spirit, and when morning dawned the American camp resumed its quiet, the men were kept within their lines, and only behind the head-quarters at Cambridge was there ceaseless activity, where Putnam, Thomas, Knox, and Mifflin were "putting the house in order for moving day."

On the night of the third of March, the bombardment was renewed, with equal vigor, and as promptly answered; and again the camp was still and patient. One shot had reached Prospect Hill but no appreciable damage accrued to the American works. Some houses had been penetrated in Boston, and six soldiers were wounded in one guard-barrack. Places of safety began to be hunted out; and artificial obstructions were arranged for a cover from the random shot and shell; but no special parade was ordered, no detail was moved forth, to silence the offensive batteries, no scheme was put on foot, to break up the investment. No excited commander tendered his services, to lead a forlorn hope against Cambridge, to seize and try for treason the arch-commander of the defiant Colonists. Bunker Hill was in sight! Red uniforms were conspicuous in the sun-light; but these had no promptings to an assault upon earth-works, which screened twenty thousand men and were the work of months.

The fourth of March closed, and the night was bright, mild and hazy. The moon was at its full. It was a good night for rest. Surely the Americans cannot afford such waste of powder! They impoverish themselves: but Boston is safe!

But on the night of the fourth of March, and through all its hours, from "candle-lighting time," to the clear light of another day, the same incessant thunder rolled along, over camps and city; the same quick flashes showed that fire was all along the line, and still, both camps and city dragged through the night, waiting for the day-light to test the work of the night, as day-light had done before.

Two strong redoubts capped Dorchester Heights !

" If the Americans retain possession of the heights," said Admiral Shuldham, " I cannot keep a ship in the harbor." Howe wrote to Lord Dartmouth, " It must have been the employment of at least twelve thousand men." " They were raised," wrote an officer, " with an expedition equal to that of the Genii, belonging to Aladdin's lamp."

" The rebels have done more in one night than my whole army would have done in a month," said Lord Howe.

" Perhaps," said Heath, " there never was as much work done in so short a space."

The works were *very simple* of construction. The earth was frozen to the depth of eighteen inches. But hurdles, fascines, and bundles of branches, and abatis, cut from apple orchards, had been supplied in great quantities, and large bales of compressed hay, which were proof against any ordinary cannon ball, had also been furnished, so that the heaping up and arranging of these, under the direction of Rufus Putnam, according to a plan thoroughly digested, was but easy work for a class of soldiers peculiarly handy with the material employed. On the tops, there were barrels, filled with stones, having for their ultimate purpose—to be rolled down hill, and thus disconcert the advance of any regulars from Boston. The manner of doing this work was also very simple.

Eight hundred soldiers marched very quietly out of Roxbury, after dark, on the previous evening, and placed themselves, a part between Boston and Dorchester Heights, and a part at the east end of the peninsula, opposite Castle Island. Men with tools, and a working party of twelve hundred soldiers under General Thomas, followed the advance. Then three hundred carts, loaded with the proper material, followed.

To thwart curiosity, and prevent impertinent interference with the work which Washington had ordered to be done, some of these large bundles of hay had been placed in a long row along the most exposed part of the way, so that carts passed to and fro all night behind this cover, and the moon itself was unable to betray the secret, even if some sentry at Boston Neck had accidentally allowed his eyes to turn away from the rival exhibition of shot and shell practice.

There was a north wind that night which took all the sound of the rolling carts into the country below Boston. This was also very matter of fact, but of real service.

During this time, Generals Greene and Sullivan were standing in front of four thousand men near Fort Number Two, as indicated on the map, with bateaux and floating batteries manned for crossing to Boston, if the garrison should move out and interfere with the order of the day. The incessant firing all night seems to have been but playing a trick upon the garrison. It was of course a *feint*.

The silent movement of the two thousand men, and of the three hundred carts was not as at Bunker Hill, a forlorn hope affair. It was not hurried nor expensive of strength and patience. Reliefs came and went, and the system, order, and success that marked each hour, could not have been better realized by daylight. An eminent historian explains this movement in a few words, and tells it all.

" One unexpected combination concerted with faultless ability, and suddenly executed, had in a few hours made General Howe's position at Boston untenable." This was " Grand Strategy."

General Howe immediately detailed Lord Percy with twenty-four hundred men to dislodge the Americans from Dorchester Heights. The command moved by boats to Castle Island first, for the purpose of making a night attack. During the afternoon a storm came up from the south, increasing to a gale ; rain poured in torrents all night : some of the boats were driven on shore and the project was abandoned.

By the tenth of March the Americans had fortified Nook's Hill, and this drove the British troops from Boston Neck. Eight hundred shot and shell were thrown into the city during that night.

On the morning of the seventeenth of March, the British troops embarked in one hundred and twenty crowded transports for Halifax, the total force including seamen of the fleet being not quite eleven thousand men. It is proper to say that historians differ as to the damage done to private property by the retiring garrison. Distinctions of property are always lost sight of in war. This evil attaches to its skirts and follows its track. General Howe issued an order forbidding plunder, and he is entitled to this credit. Washington did not give him time to watch its execution, but took charge of the city himself as soon as possible.

Five thousand troops under Ward entered as the last boats left.

General Putnam was placed in command, and on the twentieth Washington entered at the head of the whole army.

For ten days the British fleet was weather bound in Nantasket Roads, then bore away for Halifax. Valuable stores were left behind, including two hundred and fifty cannon, half of them serviceable, and these were still farther increased by the capture of store-vessels which entered the harbor without knowledge of the evacuation of the city.

The siege of Boston was at an end. Less than thirty lives had been lost during the investment, and New England was freed from the presence of British troops.

NOTE. A manuscript narrative of the experience of Mr. Edward Stow during the siege of Boston, besides portrait sketches of the British commanders, relates his attending upon a performance of the play, " Boston Besieged," at Faneuil Hall, in company with his mother, upon the invitation of Lieutenant Haley of the British Fourth regiment. During the play, composed by General Burgoyne, and on the night of March 3d, " one cannon ball from the American batteries whizzed directly over the roof," " another struck Dr. Cooper's Meeting House." It was the first demonstration that the city was in real danger. Mr. Stow was then but a boy, but states, that he remembers perfectly well that " General Burgoyne suddenly came upon the stage, and ordered the officers to their posts," and that himself and mother were indebted to the kindness of a sentry, who met them near the Liberty tree, for a safe escort home. Several of the officers were his mother's guests, Colonel Cleveland among the number. On one occasion he accompanied one of the officers to the Neck where the British artillery made a test of the Roxbury lines. The author acknowledges the courtesy of Mr. A. S. Barnes for the perusal of the manuscript, which abounds with incidents of interest.

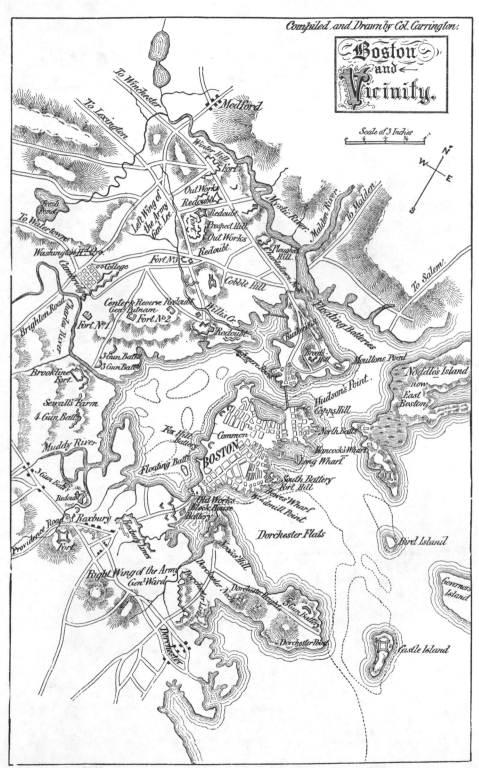

Compiled and Drawn by Col. Carrington.

Boston
and
Vicinity.

Scale of 3 Inches

To Winchester

To Lexington

Medford

Winter Hill

Fort

Out Works
Redoubt

Left Wing of the Army Gen'l Lee

Fresh Pond

Redoubt

Prospect Hill
Out Works
Redoubt

Mystic River

To Watertown

Ploughd Hill

To Malden

Washington H'd Qrs

College

Fort No 3

Cobble Hill

Charlestown Neck

Floating Batteries

To Salem

Brighton Road

Cambridge

Charles River

Center & Reserve Redoubt
Gen'l Putnam
Fort No 2

Willis's Cr

Redoubt

Bunker Hill

Breeds Hill

Moulton's Point

Noddle's Island
now
East Boston

Fort No 1

3 Gun Batt'y
3 Gun Batt'y

Charlestown River

Hudson's Point

Copps Hill

Brookline Fort

Sewall's Farm
4 Gun Batt'y

Fox Hill Battery
Common

North Batt'y

Muddy River

Floating Batt'y

BOSTON

Hancock's Wharf
Long Wharf

3 Gun Batt'y

Redoubt

Old Works
Block House
Battery

South Battery
Fort Hill
Hewes's Wharf
Windmill Point

Bird Island

Governors Island

Providence Road

Roxbury

Fort

Washington Tree

Right Wing of the Army
Gen'l Ward

Dorchester Flats

Roxbury Hill

Dorchester Neck

Dorchester Hill

Dorchester Heights
3 Gun Battery

Castle Island

Dorchester

Dorchester Point

154*

Siege of Boston

From JUNE 20th, 1775 to MARCH 17th, 1776

American Commanders

WASHINGTON

WARD, LEE, PUTNAM, GREENE, SULLIVAN, THOMAS, R. PUTNAM, MIFFLIN.

Strength, 23.372   Casualties 30

British Commanders

HOWE

PIGOTT   **BURGOYNE**   **CLINTON**

Strength, 9.147   Casualties, Nominal

NOTES.—Immediately after the action at Breeds Hill, Putnam fortified Ploughed Hill and Prospect Hill, so effectually, that no successful sortie was made across the isthmus, by the British force on Charlestown Heights.

The position of the American divisions appears from the map. The environment was complete. During the winter, Washington waited, in vain, for such thickness of ice as would enable him to cross and attempt the city by assault. The strategy, which was finally successful, commanded universal praise from contemporary soldiers.

After sunset, March 1st, and again during the entire night of March 4th, all batteries within practical range, opened fire upon the city, and with such effect as to compel the garrison to keep under cover. By daylight of March 5th, two redoubts crowned Dorchester Heights. Generals Greene and Sullivan were in position at Fort No. 2, near Putnam's headquarters, to resist any attack, in case the British discovered the proposed movement before its execution. Eight hundred picked men, well armed, and a working party of twelve hundred, marched silently, under command of General Thomas. Three hundred carts, with picks, tools and fascines, had been provided by Quartermaster Mifflin, who had been in Washington's confidence, during preparation for the movement. Rufus Putnam acted as Chief Engineer.

The British made one effort to dislodge the Americans from the Heights, but their boats were dispersed by a storm, and the attempt was not repeated.

By March 10th, the Americans had fortified Nook's Hill, and during that night, eight hundred shot and shell were thrown into the city.

On the 17th General Howe evacuated, and on the 20th General Washington entered Boston.

References :

CARRINGTON'S "BATTLES OF THE AMERICAN REVOLUTION," pp. 146-154.

School Histories :

Anderson, ¶ 28 ; p. 73.
Barnes, ¶ 3 ; p. 112.
Berard (Bush), ¶ 53 ; p. 148.
Goodrich, C. A.(Seaveys) ¶ 16; p. 117.
Goodrich, S. G., ¶ 7-8 ; p. 204-5.
Hassard, ¶ 12-13 ; p. 167.

Holmes, ¶ 14 ; p. 114.
Lossing, ¶ 13 ; p. 140.
Quackenbos, ¶ 307 ; p. 219.
Ridpath, ¶ 3-5 ; p. 193.
Sadlier (Excel.), ¶ 25 ; p. 182.
Stephens, A. H., ¶ 13 ; p. 172.

Swinton, ¶ 97-8 ; p. 124-6.
Scott, ¶ 2-5 ; p. 167.
Thalheimer (Eclectic), ¶ 248 ; p. 13³.
Venable, ¶ 127 ; p. 98.

CHAPTER XXIV.

WASHINGTON AT NEW YORK.—APRIL TO JULY, 1776.

THE British troops evacuated Boston on the seventeenth of March, 1776, but did not leave Nantasket Roads until ten days afterward.

Washington had reason to believe that General Howe would make New York his immediate objective. His movement to Halifax was such a grave military error, that its apology must be derived from the fact that his fleet transported more than a thousand loyalists, and a large quantity of their personal effects.

The British government, however, had not held on to Boston so long, without some suspicion that it was attaching a false value to that occupation. It was treating a post as vitally important, which had no strategic value whatever in determining the result of the war. As soon as it became impossible to break up the investment, the base should have been changed to one which had real offensive value. Failure in an immaterial issue only gave to that failure a gravity far beyond the importance of the issue itself, impaired their own strength, and developed an adversary army of permanent resistance.

During the fall of 1775, Lord Dartmouth, as appears from the British archives, expressly advised that Boston should be evacuated, and that Newport or New York, or both, should be occupied by strong armies well supported by a competent naval force. This was not a random suggestion, but it appears from one of his letters, that he considered Newport as the key to an absolute control of all the New England colonies. This matter has been adverted to under the topic, " Base of operations," and is again mentioned in connection with the events which immediately followed the enforced evacuation of Boston.

Within twenty-four hours after General Howe embarked his command, Washington began to plan for the future.

On the eighteenth day of March, and before the main army had entered Boston, General Heath was ordered to march to New York with five regiments of infantry, and a portion of the field artillery.

On the twenty-seventh, when the British fleet actually put to sea and left the coast, he ordered the whole army to the south, with the exception of five regiments, which were left as a garrison command, under Major General Ward. On the same day General Sullivan marched. Another division marched on the first of April; and on the fourth of April, General Spencer left, with the last brigade. General Washington started for New York that evening.

Owing to the badness of the roads, which threatened to delay the troops, and the great number of small inlets from Long Island Sound which had to be crossed, or avoided by a march through Connecticut, Washington requested Governor Trumbull to reinforce the New York garrison with two thousand men from western Connecticut, and also requested the commanding officer at New York to apply to the Provincial convention, or Committee of Safety of New Jersey, to furnish a thousand men for the same purpose. As an apology for this additional expense, he wrote to Congress—"Past experience, and the lines in Boston and on Boston Neck, point out the propriety and suggest the necessity of keeping our enemies from gaining possession and making a lodgment.

Before leaving Cambridge, he had perfected his arrangements for the movement of the army, so that vessels should meet the regiments at Norwich, Connecticut, and thereby save one hundred and thirty-seven miles of land travel; had written to General Lee, who had been assigned to the command of Canada and then to the Southern Department, that he must not take south with him the guard which had been detailed from regiments, to escort him to New York: had prepared detailed instructions for Colonel Mifflin, Quarter-master General, under which he was to procure barracks, forage, quarters and supplies for the army, by the time of its arrival at New York: had ordered two companies of artillery, with shot and shell, to report to General Thomas, then ordered to Canada, *vice* Lee, ordered south: had so digested an *itinerary* for the marching divisions and brigades that they would not crowd one upon another during their march: had instructed Arnold, recently promoted, that shot and shell might be made at a furnace not far from Montreal: had proposed a new and more complete system for keeping the pay accounts of officers and men   had corresponded with the governors of all the New England States, upon the necessities and possible contingencies of the crisis, and had-provided for the anticipated incursions of small bodies of the enemy upon the exposed towns of the New England coast.

Such were some of the branches of Logistics which underwent review, and left him free to go to his new head-quarters, with all ante-cedent details in process of execution. One of his last acts was to inquire into an alleged instance of an officer carrying on trade in sup-plies while holding a commission in the army.

All the acts referred to are particularly noteworthy at this early stage of the army organization, before field operations had been prop-erly commenced.

Washington's journey to New York was made *via* Providence, Norwich and New London, for the purpose of inspecting and expe-diting the embarkation of the troops. His first act, after arrival at his destination, was to detail four battalions as a reinforcement to the army in Canada, sending them by water to Albany, "to ease the men of fatigue." He also sent five hundred barrels of provisions to Schuyler's command. Brigadier General Thompson, with Colonels Greaton, Patterson, Bond and Poor, accompanied the division, which sailed from New York April twenty-second.

An immediate communication to the New York Committee of Safety laid down the law that further correspondence with the enemy must cease: that "we must consider ourselves in a state of peace, or war, with Great Britain," and enforced his views, with emphasis.

Late at night on the twenty-fifth, Washington received an order from Congress to send six battalions to Canada, in addition to four already sent, and requested him to report, at once, whether addi-tional regiments could be spared for that purpose. General Sullivan accompanied this division, and with him were such men as Stark, Reed, Wayne and Irvine. Washington declared that "there was danger by this division of forces, that neither army,—that sent to Canada, and that kept at New York,—would be sufficient, because Great Britain would both attempt to relieve Canada and capture New York, both being of the greatest importance to them "*if they have men.*"

On the twenty-eighth of April, the whole army at New York amounted to ten thousand two hundred and thirty-five men, of whom eight thousand three hundred and one were present, and fit for duty.

The Orderly Book at this time rebukes certain disorderly conduct of the soldiers, in these memorable words. "Men are not to carve out remedies for themselves. If they are injured in any respect, there are legal modes to obtain relief, and just complaints will always be attended to and redressed."

Rhode Island called for troops to protect her ports, and two regiments of her militia were taken into continental pay.

During the month of May, advices were received that Great Britain had made a contract with various European States, for certain military contingents :—that the sentiment in Canada had been changed to that of antipathy, and that continual disaster was attending all military operations in that Department. On the twenty-fourth of May Washington wrote to Schuyler: "We expect a very bloody summer at New York and Canada, as it is there, I presume, that the great efforts of the enemy will be aimed, and I am sorry to say that we are not either in men or arms prepared for it."

General Putnam was placed in command at New York, and General Greene took charge of the defenses on Brooklyn Heights and of their completion.

June first, Congress resolved that six thousand additional militia should be employed from Massachusetts, New Hampshire, Connecticut, and New York, to reinforce the army in Canada, and that two thousand Indians should be hired for the same field of service.

Three commissioners, Messrs. Franklin, Chase, and Carroll, had been appointed by Congress February fifteenth, with instructions to visit Canada, and learn the actual condition of the army and the temper of the people. These gentlemen accompanied by Rev. John Carroll, afterward archbishop of Baltimore, arrived at Montreal on the twenty-ninth day of April, and reported that "negligence, mismanagement, and a combination of unlucky incidents had produced a confusion and disorder that it was now too late to remedy." The ill health of Dr. Franklin compelled his immediate return ; the others remained until the army began to evacuate Canada.

To the proposition to hire Indians, General Schuyler replied that, "if this number, two thousand, can be prevented from joining the enemy it is more than can be expected. They have but one maxim in their alliances with the whites, which is to adhere to the strongest side, where they are paid most liberally and run the least risk."

The commissioners wrote from Montreal, giving a most terrific picture of the condition of the troops, "who were thoroughly disorganized, half-starved, and visited by the scourge of the small pox."

General Wooster was recalled as too old, inefficient, and ill-suited to the command.

General Thomas died of the small pox on the second day of June, and was succeeded in command by General Sullivan. This officer had already written letters to General Washington, " clearly indicating that he was aiming at the command of Canada," but he failed to advise the commander-in-chief of the actual extremity to which the army had been reduced. These letters, although marked personal, were forwarded to Congress with the following comment.

" He (Sullivan) is active, spirited and zealously attached to the cause. He has his wants and his foibles. The latter are manifested in his little tincture of vanity which now and then leads him into embarrassments. His wants are common to us all. He wants experience to move on a large scale ; for the limited and contracted knowledge which any of us have in military matters stands in very little stead, and is quickly overbalanced by sound judgment and some acquaintance with men and books, especially when accompanied by an enterprising genius, which I must do General Sullivan the justice to say, I think he possesses. Congress will therefore determine upon the propriety of continuing him in Canada, or sending another as they shall see fit."

Gates was immediately sent to take command of the troops of the United Colonies in Canada, with power to appoint his own staff and a department staff, and a large discretion over officers as well as troops, and over their appointment, discipline, and removal for cause. To General Schuyler, still in command of the northern department below Canada, was entrusted the responsibility of making a treaty with the Six Nations, and the earliest possible completion of Fort Stanwix.

On the third of June, Congress resolved to reinforce the army at New York by thirteen thousand eight hundred militia from Pennsylvania, Delaware, and Maryland.

By the twenty-ninth of June, forty British ships were reported as having been sighted off Sandy Hook. The crisis which had already visited Canada was on the wing for New York.

Washington in connection with Putnam had previously laid out the fortifications which bore his name, had critically inspected the progress of all defenses about New York, and entered so closely into calculations of their value as to lay down the following instructions for officers and men.

" Not to throw away fire ; fire first with ball and shot," —" that the brigadiers should order a circle to be marked round the several re-doubts, by which their officers are to be directed in giving orders for the first discharge." " Small brush to be set up to mark the line more distinctly, and make it more familiar to the men, who are by no means to be ordered to fire before the enemy arrive at the circle."

Such are some of the leading military features of Washington's career while at New York during the early summer of 1776.

The colony felt confidence in his capacity and judgment, and with the exception of certain special localities, the people were meeting his demand for means and supplies with as much promptness and cheer-fulness as could have been expected.

Throughout the colonies there was a rapid gravitation toward a permanent union and the assertion of national independence.

That Declaration was made on the *Fourth of July*, 1776. It was a birthday of momentous peril. From Canada to the Carolinas, the armies and fleets of Great Britain were about to strike together, and still the people faced the responsibility squarely.

Within a few weeks at furthest, the blow would reach New York, and yet, before it fell, the other fields of operation were to be heard from, and their impressions were to give character to the struggle.

The narrative will now take up the history of operations within the two extreme zones of active war, and then resume the history of the expedition against New York.

NOTE. It has not been deemed necessary to enter into the details of General Lee's brief administration while at New York, *en route*, to the South. The visit of Sir Henry Clinton, ostensibly to visit Governor Tryon, inspired fears that he would bombard the city. Lee threatened summary destruction to the prisoners and property of loyalists, if a gun were fired. He was energetic, self-willed and efficient ; but forever bore with impatience the yoke of responsibility to Congress for his official acts.

CHAPTER XXV.

AMERICAN ARMY DRIVEN FROM CANADA.

FIVE thousand men perished by disease or the casualties of battle during the last two months of the campaign for the conquest of Canada, which commenced in 1775 and ended early in the summer of 1776.

Arnold's expedition reached Quebec. Montgomery also reached Quebec. At the end of their assault, the remnant of both commands was less than five hundred effective men. Up to March first, 1776, including all reinforcements, the number never exceeded seven hundred able-bodied men, present at one time for duty.

During the month of March the army increased to about seventeen hundred effective men. The detached guards, upon Orleans Island, at Point Levi and on both sides of the river, left but a small force to protect earth-works, to say nothing of the absurdity of any assault upon Quebec.

Small-pox broke out in the camp. Many enlistments were to expire April fifteenth, and no rational reason could be urged upon the dispirited men to induce their reënlistment.

Supplies became scarce, and continental money had no value. Arnold made proclamation on the fourth of March, that paper money then put in circulation, would be redeemed in four months, and that those who refused to take it should be treated as enemies. Already every promise of sympathy from the people had vanished, and when General Wooster arrived to take command on the first of April, he found that the army itself was fast melting away. That there had been much kind feeling toward the colonies on the part of very many Canadians is manifest from the success which attended the efforts of Colonels Livingston and Allen and Major Brown to organize Canadian battalions as soon as Montgomery appeared in force before St. John. Ramsey writing in 1793, particularly notices the fact that the American express messengers freely passed between Montreal and Quebec without molestation, every where receiving kind treatment; and that a Mr. Price actually advanced five thousand dollars in specie to relieve the embarrassments of the officers who could not purchase supplies with continental money. This was a large amount when it is considered that Congress was able to send but a little over sixteen thousand dollars, at a time when a hundred thousand was actually needed.

On the second day of April General Wooster examined the British works and declared his purpose to begin active work. A few small cannon and two small mortars, then in position, were vigorously exercised to see what they could do : but their light metal was simply insignificant and made no impression upon the parapets of Quebec.

During this time, scattered all the way from Albany on the Hudson river to Montreal, there could have been found companies of the regiments which Congress had sent to *Canada*, and which Washington and the colonies could so poorly spare at such a crisis.

On the day of Wooster's sham cannonading, Arnold's horse fell with him and bruised his wounded limb, so that he was confined to the bed, and to his reflections upon the progress of the campaign thus far realized. As soon as able to move he retired to Montreal on leave of absence.

As spring approached and the ice broke up, the ground thawed, and it became simply impossible to move troops over the intermediate country to their support, and the river was not sufficiently open for transportation purposes. On the first of May, General Thomas, a man of culture, wisdom and courage, assumed command of the troops, then amounting to hardly nineteen hundred men, of whom less than a thousand, including officers, were fit for duty. Among those really effective, not less than three hundred claimed a discharge, their term of legal service having expired. The previous separation of the army into detachments, for the sake of blockading Quebec and cutting off supplies from the country, involved the constant use of three ferries, so that it was impossible upon any short notice to rally more than three hundred men to resist an attack, and even the medical appointments could not be kept up to their best efficiency.

At the time of his arrival the army was increased to the nominal strength, all told, of about three thousand men; but this accession was simply a contribution to the grave, a stimulus to the growing dislike of the provincials, and the assurance of a more speedy expenditure of supplies and an ultimate retreat.

The ice was moving rapidly. Reinforcements were known to have left England and Ireland, and there was no possibility of substantial, *offensive* activity.

A fire-ship was prepared and floated toward the shipping then in the channel, but it did no harm, and the men in charge had a narrow escape from capture. The supply of powder had been reduced to one hundred and fifty barrels, and the store of provisions on hand was barely sufficient for six days of economical use.

A council of war was held, and an immediate retreat to the Three Rivers was decided upon as the only means of saving the army from starvation or capture.

Orders were issued for the embarkation of the sick and the artillery except one gun ; and orders were also sent to Orleans Island, Point Levi, and other points where detachments were stationed, in order to make the utmost expedition before the garrison should learn of the design.

On the very next day, during the confusion incident to the emergency, the frigate Surprise, the Isis, 54, and the sloop of war Martin, arrived with two companies of the Twenty-ninth regiment, which were promptly landed as well as a considerable force of marines.

General Carleton did not wait for these new forces to rest, but sallying forth at one o'clock in the afternoon with nearly a thousand men and six pieces of artillery, he made a vigorous attack upon the American position. One piece of artillery, and about three hundred men constituted the resisting force then available, and General Thomas wisely retreated, and in order, but with necessary precipitation.

Nearly a hundred prisoners, beside the sick in hospital, his stores, baggage, and artillery were captured, and with these, nearly two tons of powder, and five hundred muskets, which had arrived that very morning from General Schuyler. Some of the sick, many of them still suffering with the small-pox, dragged themselves along, thoroughly desperate in their purpose to work their way homeward rather than remain as captives, and the retrograde movement was not interrupted until the army reached Deschambault, about fifty-eight miles toward Montreal. The command made no halt during the march, and the night was one of fearful terrors to the hungry and weary command, staggering through woods, streams, and swamps, with everything to discourage, and nothing to hope for except to escape from the conquest of Canada.

Dr. Gordon writing from Roxbury, July nineteenth of that year, says, " Their condition could not be expressed in words."

The army rested a few days at Deschambault. A council of war decided that there could be no safety short of Sorel. The British fleet had followed fast after them, and were even then at anchor at Jacques Cartier, only nine miles below their camp. This fleet had been largely increased. On the eighth of May, the Niger ship of war arrived from Halifax, convoying three transports and bringing the Forty-seventh regiment, and on the tenth the Triton arrived with other transports loaded with veterans and the European contingent.

General Thomas proceeded directly to Sorel, where he found four regiments awaiting orders. Additional battalions arrived in a few days. Here he was taken down with the small-pox, and died on the second June.

On the first of June, General Reidesel arrived with Brunswick troops, and Burgoyne with troops from Ireland. These reinforcements swelled the command of General Carleton to nine thousand nine hundred and eighty-four effective men, and preparations were made to take the offensive in force, and expel the American troops from Canada.

General Sullivan arrived at Sorel on the sixth of June, and assumed command. His words were to the point. " I can reduce the army to order, and put a new face upon our affairs here."

To Washington he wrote,—" I am determined to hold the most important posts, so long as one stone is left upon another." He did not appreciate the position, neither did Congress.

A single minor operation of this disastrous campaign is worthy of mention at this stage of the narrative.

There is a narrow pass in the St. Lawrence river above Perrot Island, nearly forty-three miles above Montreal, and a projecting point called the Cedars.

Sir John Johnson, who had previously stirred up Indian aggression upon New York settlements, had received a British commission as Colonel, and was engaged in exciting the Indians of the north-west, and from Detroit eastward, to offensive movements against the American forces then in Canada.

Colonel Bedell of New Hampshire, who had been associated with Colonel Livingston and Major Brown in the capture of Chambly, during 1775, had been assigned to post command at the Cedars with a garrison force of three hundred and ninety troops and two field pieces.

On the fifteenth of May a hostile force consisting of forty regulars of the Eighth regiment from Detroit, one hundred Canadians, and five hundred savages under Colonel Beadle and Captain Foster, but without artillery, descended from the lakes and approached the fort.

Colonel Bedell hastened to Montreal for reinforcements, leaving Major Butterfield in command.

Major Sherburne started for the fort the next day with one hundred and forty men, and was soon followed by General Arnold with a still larger detachment. The facts as stated by Gordon, Stedman, Marshall, Bancroft, and other writers, British and American, do not substantially differ from the finding of the standing committee upon Indian affairs which was reported to Congress, and adopted by that body on the tenth of July, 1776, except as to the extent of injury done by the Indians. Congress received an exaggerated report of the matter. A brother of General Sullivan, who was one of the prisoners, wrote shortly after the so-called massacre that " Captain Foster treated them well after the surrender, or *to the utmost of his ability.*"

The transaction is memorable as one of the incidents attending the evacuation of Canada, and more particularly as the occasion of a formal notice to Generals Howe and Burgoyne on the part of Congress, that the Americans would measure out exact and literal retaliation for any departure from the rules and usages of honorable warfare. Major Butterfield having plenty of ammunition and provisions for nearly thirty days, without permitting his officers to sally out and attack the enemy as they desired to do, surrendered his whole command upon the simple condition that they should be prisoners to the British forces and not to the Indians, and that their baggage should not be plundered.

On the day following, Major Sherburne, who brought reinforcements, was attacked as he approached the fort, and fought with great courage for nearly an hour, but finally surrendered, when hotly pressed by superior numbers, and upon advices of the fate of the garrison. A cartel of exchange was enforced, coupled with the condition that " they would not in words, writing or signs, give the least information to government enemies, or to their adherents now in arms, in the least prejudice to his majesty's service," thus practically doubling the exchange, and this was made the condition of their exemption from Indian outrage.

Captain Foster stated in the preamble to the cartel, that he " found from their threats and menaces that the inevitable consequences of savage custom, to put prisoners to death, would ensue ;" hence the stipulations made.

The British took a strong position at Vaudreuil and Perrot Island. Arnold, with seven hundred men, made an attempt to dislodge them and rescue the prisoners, but the British commander so positively threatened to turn the prisoners over to the Indians in case of attack, that Arnold himself signed the proposed cartel, withdrew from St. Anne to La Chine and then returned to Montreal. It was an illustration of the far reaching effects of the cowardice or incompetency of a single post commander.

The narrative left General Sullivan at Sorel, and General Carleton on the eve of aggressive action.

The rendezvous appointed for the advancing British troops was at Three Rivers, about equally distant from Montreal and Quebec, and General Fraser had taken command of that station.

Burgoyne, Riedesel and Phillips had started by land and water, to concentrate the army at that point.

General Nesbit was near Three Rivers, on transports, under convoy. Gordon puts the British effective force at thirteen thousand men but he makes no allowance for the percentage of non-effectives, clerks and detachments, which reduce an army within twenty-four hours after a regular muster. Few of the battalions sent to America were full, and any estimate of forces based merely upon the number of battalions, is invariably an error.

At this stage of affairs, General Sullivan having a force of about five thousand men at Sorel, called a council of war and resolved to occupy and hold Three Rivers. He was under the impression that the British force at that post was less than seven hundred men, probably not more than five hundred for duty.

Colonel St. Clair was already at Nicholet with nearly eight hundred men. Colonels Wayne, Maxwell and Irvine, with sufficient force to make an aggregate of two thousand men, were sent down the river and through Lake St. Peter to join him. The command of the expedition was assigned to General Thompson.

Chief Justice Marshall, in his life of Washington, supplies a fact in this connection which reconciles other historical accounts, and shows that during the four days which intervened between the death of General Thomas and the arrival of General Sullivan, General Thompson was in command, and that he sent St. Clair to Nicholet for the purpose of surprising the British post at Three Rivers. General Thompson, under the order of General Sullivan, whom he must have advised of the state of affairs, on his arrival, reached Nicholet, a little after midnight, or early in the morning, of the seventh of June.   He kept his command under cover during the day, and crossed the St. Lawrence early in the evening of the seventh, landing at Point Du Lac. Their movement was not a secret.   If it had been, the result would have been fully as disastrous.   With morning light they found themselves flanked by a swamp and compelled to march along the river. This exposed them to the fire of the shipping which they had safely passed under cover of the night, to the fire of artillery which had been landed on the beach by General Fraser, to conflict with a force three times their number, and to a class of risks never contemplated in their detail " to take and occupy Three Rivers."

Where Wayne went there was a fight, always.   That was his business.

Bancroft thus sums up the scene : " The short darkness of that latitude was soon over ; as day began to appear, the Americans, who were marching under the bank of the river, were cannonaded from the ships ; undismayed they took their way through a thickly wooded swamp, above their knees in mud and water ; and after a most wearisome struggle of four hours reached an open piece of ground, where they endeavored to form.   Wayne began the attack and forced the party to run ; his companions then pressed forward in column against the breast-works, which covered the main body of the enemy.   They displayed undisputed gallantry ; but being outnumbered three to one, were compelled to retire."

The battle was soon over.   One hundred and fifty prisoners were left in the hands of the British troops, including General Thompson and Colonel Irvine.

The men, scattered and disheartened, found their boats, and Three Rivers was not taken.

Sullivan wrote—" I now think only of a glorious death, or a victory obtained against superior numbers."

The Congressional commission had already advised that Canada be abandoned.   Congress, however, voted to sustain the offensive and was still legislating to maintain that army as late as July eighth.   Sullivan's officers finally advised retreat.

The British fleet came up the river under a favorable wind on the fourteenth of June, and when they were within one hour's sail of Sorel, Sullivan broke up his camp and started for St. John's.

Arnold held on to Montreal with three hundred men until the fleet was within twelve miles of the city, and then crossed to La Prairie, without interruption.

Sergeant Lamb, of the Royal Welsh Fusileers, then a private soldier, published his diary of the events of that campaign. He says— "The sufferings of the Americans were indeed great, obliged to drag their batteries up the rapids of the Sorel, by mere strength, often to their middle in water, and encumbered with great numbers laboring under that dreadful disease, the small-pox, which is so fatal in America. It was said that two regiments, at one time, had not a single man in health, another had only six, and a fourth only forty, and two more were nearly in the same condition. While the Americans were retreating, they were daily annoyed by the remonstrances of the inhabitants of Canada, who had either joined or befriended them. Many of the Canadians had taken a decided part in their favor, rendered them essential services, and thereby incurred the heavy penalties annexed to the crime of supporting rebellion. These, though Congress had assured them but a few months before, that, they would never abandon them to the fury of their common enemies' were from the necessity of the case, left exposed to the resentment of their rulers."

On the seventeenth, says Bancroft, "all that was left of the invading army met at St. John's."

"On the eighteenth, the emaciated, half-naked men, broken in strength and in discipline, too weak to have beaten off an assault from the enemy, as pitiable a spectacle as could be seen, removed to Isle Aux Noix, where Sullivan proposed to await express orders from Schuyler." This island was low, badly supplied with water, and so unhealthy, that Sullivan retired to Isle La Motte, where he received orders from General Schuyler to retire to Crown Point, which post he reached during July.

Colonel Trumbull visited the post, and thus states the condition of the troops. "I did not look into a tent or hut in which I did not find either a dead or dying man." "I wept till I had no more power to weep," said a physician who attended the troops.

"Everything about them, their clothes, their blankets, the air, the very ground they trod on, was infected with the pestilence." "More than thirty new graves were made every day."

Sergeant Lamb's statement was not exaggerated. The official muster rolls showed that on account of sickness or inoculation, there were single regiments without a man fit for duty.

Canada was free from the pressure of American troops. Burgoyne re-occupied St. John's. Gates had superseded Sullivan, and he was promised additional troops to the number of six thousand men, viz., three from Massachusetts, fifteen hundred from Connecticut, seven hundred and fifty from New Hampshire, and seven hundred and fifty from New York ; but none entered Canada. The death of Montgomery was the pivot event of the entire campaign.

His plan contemplated the establishment of strong posts at Jacques Cartier, the Narrows, and at Montreal, and the occupation of the plains of Abraham by ten thousand men. More than this number was actually assigned to operations in Canada, but if all had reached Quebec, they could not have been maintained at that number, unless all other operations were sacrificed.

A committee of Congress gave good reasons for the failure of the invasion, viz., *undertaken too late in the fall,— enlistments too short* and the consequent haste which *forced immature expeditions* for fear there would be no men to undertake them—*want of specie, and the small-pox.*

CHAPTER XXVI.

BRITISH PREPARATIONS. CLINTON'S EXPEDITION UNFOLDED.

IT will give interest to the narrative to introduce to the reader those British regiments which were assigned to duty in America, early in the year 1776, so that they, as well as the American officers who figured early in the war, may be recognized as acquaintances when the battle issues shall bring them face to face.

STATIONED IN BOSTON.

17th Dragoons .	Preston's.	43d Foot . . .	Cary's.
4th Foot . .	Hodgsin's.	44th " . . .	Abercrombie's.
5th " . .	Percy's.	45th " . . .	Haviland's.
10th " . .	Sandford's.	47th " . . .	Carleton's.
22d " . .	Gage's.	49th " . . .	Maitland's.
23d " . .	Howe's.	52d " . . .	Clavering's.
35th " . .	F. H. Campbell's.	63d " . . .	T. Grant's.
38th " . .	Pigot's.	64th " . . .	Pomeroy's.
40th " . .	Hamilton's.	65th " . . .	Armstrong's.

A detachment of the 65th regiment was then at Halifax.
Five companies of the Royal Artillery were also stationed at Boston.

THEN IN CANADA.

7th Foot . . .	Berlier's.	26th Foot, .	Lord W. Gordon's.
8th " . . .	Armstrong's.		

This regiment was in charge of the upper, or western parts of Canada, including Niagara and Detroit. One company of Royal Artillery was at Quebec, one at Montreal, and one "*invalid*" company at Newfoundland. McLean's regiment was partially organized in Canada, and its service has already been noticed.

AT ST. AUGUSTINE.

One company of Royal Artillery, and part of the 14th Foot, Cunningham's. The other companies were with Lord Dunmore in Virginia, or at Halifax.

ON THEIR PASSAGE FROM IRELAND TO BOSTON.

17th Foot . .	Monkton's.	46th Foot . . .	Vaughan's.
27th " . . .	Massey's.	53d " . . .	James Grant's

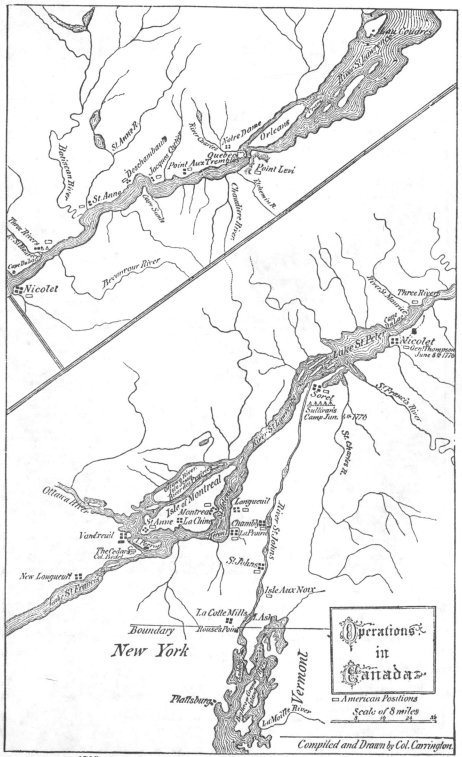

Operations in Canada

□ American Positions

Scale of 8 miles

Compiled and Drawn by Col. Carrington.

170*

Operations in Canada

From SEPT. 1755, to JULY 1776

American Commanders

Schuyler, Montgomery, Wooster, Thomas, Sullivan

ARNOLD, J. & H. B. LIVINGSTON, WAYNE, Col. GREEN, OSWALD, MORGAN, WARNER, IRVINE, PORTERFIELD, ALLEN, THAYER, THOMPSON

British Commanders

CARLETON   BURGOYNE

PHILLIPS, RIEDESEL, PRESCOTT, FRASER, NESBIT, McLEAN

NOTES. The Canada campaign was based upon the theory that the people of that country were fully in earnest to resist the enforcement of certain Acts of Parliament, which were reported to be as offensive, in practical application, as those which irritated the other colonies. The garrisons at Montreal and Quebec were known to be small, and the acquisition of Canada would leave no independent land base for British operations on the continent. The people of Canada did not respond, in force. The expeditions were too feeble to command their respect, or act independently, and the season of the year was exceedingly unpropitious for field service.

Governor Carleton had moved southward to St. Johns, intending to secure Ticonderoga and Crown Point, which had been seized by Allen and Warner on the 10th and 12th of May. Schuyler was entrusted with command of the column against Montreal. It reached Isle La Motte Sept. 3d, Isle Aux Noix Sept. 4th, and embarked for St Johns Sept. 6th. Montgomery at once succeeded to the command, as Schuyler was compelled to return to Ticonderoga on account of sickness. October 18th, Livingston (James) and Major Brown, with a local force, seized Chambly, and large supplies. General Wooster then joined Montgomery, and, after a siege of fifty days, captured St. Johns, Nov. 3d, and 600 prisoners, André among the number. Nov. 12th, Montgomery occupied Montreal, and Carleton retired to Quebec. On the 1st of April, 1776, Wooster assumed command in Canada, and attempted to reduce Quebec. Arnold injured his wounded limb by a fall from his horse, and returned to Montreal with Wooster, who took a sick leave, while Thomas took command. On May 1st, Carleton made a prompt sortie, in force, and the American army, after much loss, retreated to Dechambault, 58 miles below Montreal, and on the 2d of June reached Sorel. Here General Thomas died, and Sullivan took command on the 6th. The battle of the Cedars, near Montreal, had already been disastrous to American prestige in that vicinity. On the 1st of June, the British army in Canada had been increased to 9,984 effective men, and General Fraser advanced nearly to Three Rivers, to take the offensive. Sullivan, underestimating Fraser's force, reinforced St. Clair, who was at Nicholet, with 800 men, by sending Wayne, Maxwell and Irvine, under General Thompson, down the river and through Lake St. Peters, to attack the British column. They effected a landing at Cape Aux Lac, but not undiscovered, and left Thompson, Irvine and 150 other prisoners with the enemy.

The British ships ascended the river, and on the 14th of June, Sullivan withdrew his army, already demoralized and enfeebled by the scourge of smallpox, reaching St. Johns on the 18th of June, and Crown Point early in July. Arnold remained at Montreal with 300 men, until the British fleet hove in sight. The British army, under Burgoyne, re-occupied St. Johns, and the Canadian campaign, which had cost over 5,000 men, and so persistently depleted the army which Washington needed at New York, came to an end.

References :

CARRINGTON'S "BATTLES OF THE AMERICAN REVOLUTION," pp. 92-117.

School Histories:

Anderson, ¶ 26; p. 72.
Barnes, ¶ 4; p. 111.
Berard (Bush), ¶ 47-52; p. 146-7.
Goodrich, C. A. (Seaveys), ¶ 13; p. 117.
Goodrich, S. G., ¶ 1-10; p. 201-2.
Hassard, ¶ 2-6; p. 163-4.

Holmes, ¶ 9; p. 112.
Lossing, ¶ 19-22; p. 136-7.
Quackenbos, ¶ 299-303; p. 214-17.
Ridpath, ¶ 17-20; p. 191-2.
Sadlier, (Excel), ¶ 20; p. 180.
Stephens, A. H. ¶ 7-13; p. 174-6.

Swinton, ¶ 93-5; p. 123-4.
Scott, ¶ 12-16; p. 164-5.
Thalheimer (Eclectic), ¶ 246-7; p. 137-8.
Venable, ¶ 126; p. 98.

READY TO SAIL FROM CORK TO AMERICA.

15th Foot . . .	Cavans'.		42d Foot	Lord Murray's.
33d " . .	Cornwallis'.		54th " . . .	Frederick's.
37th " . .	Coote's.		57th " . . .	Irwin's.

ORDERED FOR BOSTON.

16th Dragoons, Burgoyne's, and one thousand of the King's Guards, to be drafted from three regiments, to be commanded by Colonel Matthews.

The 29th Foot, destined for Quebec, were ordered to sail so as to arrive as early as the navigation of the St. Lawrence would permit. It has been already noticed how that regiment obeyed the order to the very letter.

ORDERED TO BE IN READINESS FOR EMBARKATION TO SAIL FROM IRELAND TO QUEBEC IN APRIL, 1776.

9th Foot . . .	Ligonier's.		34th Foot . .	Lord Cavendish's.
20th " . . .	Parker's.		33d " . .	Elphinstone's.
24th " . . .	Taylor's.		62d " . .	Jones.

The two Highland battalions, viz., Lord John Murray's and Fraser's, were to consist each of one thousand men. The marching regiments for the American service were to consist of twelve companies of fifty-six rank and file, each company, while two companies of each battalion were to remain in Great Britain and Ireland for recruiting purposes.

It will be seen that each battalion sent to America only six companies, instead of eight, two battalions forming the regiment. The use of the term battalion in connection with the British army, will therefore be construed nominally as half a regiment; while the American regiments had but one battalion, and the terms are, ordinarily, convertible expressions when referring to the latter army.

The nominal colonel of a British regiment then, as since, may also be a general officer, and the American reader will do well to bear this in mind, since Percy, Grant, Cornwallis, Pigot, and many colonels already named, are scarcely known to popular history, except by their high rank, which was in the nature of a brevet.

The recruits for the regiments ordered to America were especially enlisted to be discharged at the end of three years, or at the end of the war, at the option of the king.

During the winter of 1775–6, the British government entered into treaties with the landgrave of Hesse Cassel, the Duke of Brunswick, and the hereditary prince of Hesse Cassel, ruling the principality of Hanau, by which men were hired to do military service in America. This was done by arbitrary impressment. The force thus furnished amounted to seventeen thousand and three hundred men.

The prince of Waldeck also tendered a regiment which was accepted, and with other troops from that state was sent forth under the command of the veteran Baron Riedesel.

There never was a doubt among military men as to the bad military policy of this arrangement. The men were paid by their own state, but the state was paid a much larger rate by Great Britain, so that it was a speculation entirely; but it robbed the English crown of prestige, maddened the colonists, and was unworthy of a great nation which was still claiming from the colonies the allegiance due to paternal authority.

These treaties were stubbornly opposed in both houses of parliament. A few extracts from the debate will illustrate the principles laid down under the title "statesmanship in war."

" An army of foreigners is now to be introduced into the British dominion, not to protect them from invasion, not to deliver them from the ravages of an hostile army, but to assist one half of the inhabitants in massacring the other," said the duke of Richmond, adding: "Unprovided with a sufficient number of troops for the cruel purpose designed, or unable to prevail upon the natives of this country (England) to lend their hands to such a sanguinary business, ministers have applied to those foreign princes who trade in human blood, and have hired armies of mercenaries for the work of destruction." "The colonies themselves, after our example, will apply to strangers for assistance."

The bill passed the Commons by a vote of 242 to 88, and the House of Lords by a vote of 100 to 32. A protest was made in strong words, one single sentence of which will illustrate the folly of the policy, and its bearings upon the future. " We have reason to apprehend that when the colonies come to understand that Great Britain is forming alliances and hiring foreign troops for their destruction, they may think that they are well justified by the example in endeavoring to avail themselves of the like assistance, and that France, Spain, and Prussia, or other powers of Europe may think they have as good right as Hesse, Brunswick, and Hanau to interfere in our domestic quarrels.

Lord Inham declared, that, " the landgrave of Hesse had his prototype in Sancho Panza, who said that if he were a prince he should wish all his subjects to be blackamoors, so that he could turn them into money by selling them ; that Hesse and Brunswick rendered Germany vile and dishonored in the eyes of Europe,—a nursery of men for those who have most money."

The King wrote personal letters to Catharine of Russia, asking for twenty thousand men. She replied " that there were other means of settling the dispute in America, than by force of arms," and declined to furnish any, although the application was made for a much less force, subsequently to the first refusal.

The States-General of Holland were also requested by the king to dispose of their Scotch brigade, for service in America; but the proposition was declined and strict neutrality was maintained.

During the war that followed, Brunswick furnished a total of seven thousand and twenty-three men, " amounting," says Bancroft, " to more than one-sixth of the able-bodied men of the principality."

The Hessian force originally designated at four thousand men, was ultimately increased to twelve thousand, besides three corps of artillery, three hundred chasseurs and three hundred dragoons.

Lieutenant Generals De Heister and Knyphausen commanded these troops, the former having senior command. Among the Colonels, Donop, Rahl, Wurmb-Minigerode and Loos were better known than others, in their connection with the wars.

If Great Britain had drafted from England and Wales, a quota of troops, proportionally equal to the drain made upon the industry of Hanau and Hesse Cassel, through those treaties, she would have raised an army of more than four hundred thousand men.

It is the affirmation of history that Hesse Cassel, Brunswick and Hanau matured bitter fruit by their sale of men, and that it did not pay.

According to the estimate laid before parliament, there would be, including the foreign mercenaries, about fifty-five thousand men for American service without counting Canadians, Indians and other Loyalists, who were estimated at four thousand more; and that the greatest possible allowance for possible deficiencies could not reduce the number below forty thousand.

These troops were put in motion with commendable activity. Sir Peter Parker and Earl Cornwallis were ready to sail from Cork by the twentieth of January, but were detained until the thirteenth of February, through technicalities as to the authority of the king; and legislation was deemed necessary by the Lord Lieutenant of Ireland before he would permit the departure of the expedition.

The squadron consisted of forty-three vessels and more than twenty-five hundred troops; but it had not left the Irish Channel before a severe storm drove many of the ships to Cork, Plymouth,

Portsmouth and other harbors for refuge. The larger portion was speedily collected and sailed for Cape Fear river, North Carolina.

Meanwhile, the loyal governors of Virginia and North Carolina were doing their part in the preparation for active operations under instructions from the king. In the former colony, Lord Dunmore had already armed slaves and thus held out the threat of a servile war; but the influence of Lee and Henry and other men of strong will, and their self-sacrifice and wide-spread popularity, kept him under some restraint, since he had not the force for a boldly offensive action.

Governor Martin, of North Carolina, had promised the king to raise ten thousand men and that number of arms had been ordered to the colony. Upon receiving positive assurance that the regular troops, applied for during the fall of 1775, had been detailed, and ordered to sail for Wilmington, he began to assert vice-regal powers. Not daring to trust himself away from Wilmington and the ship which was both his head-quarters and home, he appointed one Donald McDonald to the office of Brigadier General, gave Donald McLeod the next position, and sent them out with thirteen other Scotchmen, to raise an army for the king. They induced him to believe that at least four thousand men could be put under arms before the arrival of regular troops. A force of nearly eighteen hundred men was gathered, and on the twenty-seventh of February they attacked the Wilmington and Newbern minute-men and the militia of Craven, Johnson, Dobbs and Wake counties, who were under the command of Colonel Caswell, afterward Brigadier General, and Colonel Lillington, at Moore's Creek Bridge.

The result of this hot skirmish was quickly determined. McDonald was taken prisoner; McLeod, Campbell and several other leaders were killed, and the whole command was dispersed. Thirteen wagons, three hundred and fifty muskets, nearly fifteen hundred country rifles and two medicine chests, just from England, were among the trophies which the colonists bore away in triumph. A box of gold of the value of fifteen thousand pounds sterling, which was the chief reliance of McDonald in his work of recruiting, was another acquisition of the day.

This event happened quite opportunely for the Americans. General Lee had been ordered to the Southern department, and it was known that General Clinton intended to attack the coast at some eligible point. During the few weeks following the affair at Moore's Creek Bridge, nearly nine thousand citizens of the colony organized in behalf of the common cause of colonial independence.

It is worthy of note that North Carolina ever after was conspicuously faithful to her obligations, and no local organization gained any considerable headway against the national sentiment of the people.

Colonel Moore was in command of the Continental regulars, and the advent of Clinton was anticipated without apprehension. The colonists were ready.

On the third of May, Sir Peter Parker and Earl Cornwallis entered Cape Fear river with twenty transports.

General Clinton had already reached Wilmington. After leaving New York, he first entered Chesapeake Bay to have a conference with Governor Dunmore.

During the month of April, beginning with the eighteenth, when the Ann and Isabella arrived with a part of the Seventeenth regiment, thirteen transports had reached Cape Fear river in advance of the flag-ship.

The united forces of Clinton, General Vaughan, and Earl Cornwallis were too large to be of special service upon the North Carolina coast, and Charleston was finally adopted as objective of attack. Before his departure, Clinton, acting under instructions from the king, issued from on board the Pallas transport, a formal proclamation of an unpopular nature, denouncing persistent rebels, conventions and congresses; offering pardon to all penitents except Colonel Howe, of the continental army, and Mr. Cornelius Harnet, and closed his duties at Wilmington by sending Cornwallis on shore with nine hundred men, to lay waste Brunswick. Colonel Howe's house and mills were burned, and some injury was done to the town of a profitless nature, only aggravating the people, and the army took sail for Charleston harbor

CHAPTER XXVII.

THE REPUBLIC OF SOUTH CAROLINA. PREPARATIONS FOR DEFENSE.

A QUAINT old map bearing date August 31st, 1776, was found in London during the year 1875. Eleven companion maps were found with it in a rude atlas called "The North American Pilot," which the tremulous old man who guarded the street book-stand said, "ought to be worth a shilling." His judgment was respected, and a shilling bought the relic!

Those maps proved to be the record of official work done by Gascoine, Fisher, Blamer, and other officers and pilots in his majesty George the Third's service, for the special information of officers, soldiers, and seamen who should have occasion to perform military duty anywhere upon the coast of North America.

The special map which bore the date already given, was "An exact plan of Charleston and harbor; From an Actual Survey, with the Attack of Fort Sullivan on the 28th of June, 1776, by his Majesty's Squadron commanded by Sir Peter Parker."

The soundings and bearings are profusely indicated, as they were tested during June, 1776, for the use of the fleet which subsequently made the attack, and with due allowance for an extraordinary perspective view of the city, which seems to have puzzled the ingenuity of the draughtsman himself, the chart is excellent and very complete.

In the attempt to throw ourselves more than a century into the past, to study its facts and their lessons, it is certainly but just that we include the topography of places as it was then viewed by contemporaries, so that we may seem to stand by their side as the scenes and actors pass by.

On the right of the harbor entrance to Charleston, there was then, as now, a low sandy island called Sullivan Island. Marshes, thickets, and trees abounded.

Northward, near by, but up the coast a short distance, there was then, as now, a larger island called Long Island. To the left of the harbor entrance, there was then, as now, a large island of several thousand acres, with Cummins Point and Fort Johnson defined, and this was James Island.

Upon Sullivan Island a fort had been begun, and was " unfinished," according to the quaint old map ; but on either side of it was a small redoubt, and near the entrance of the fort was a " mark-tree," to guide pilots as they made the port. Just across the intervening water and marsh, a little more than a mile, was another redoubt at Mt. Pleasant, (Haddrell's point), and close by two houses, marked Jonathan Scott's, and Mr. Poang's, was " The American Army."

The channel mark shows seven feet of water at low tide, between Sullivan Island and the " American Army." At the north end of this island there appear to be some earth-works, and these are occupied according to the map, by fifteen hundred Provincials, " *intrenched*," to oppose the landing of Clinton's army.

On Long Island appears " British forces, fifteen hundred men under General Clinton, landed June the ninth," which were to attack Fort Sullivan by land. Between Long Island and the main land there is indicated deep water, and between Long Island and Sullivan Island the water varies from eighteen inches to seven feet at low tide.

The deepest water of the harbor entrance is in the north channel close by Sullivan Island, and very near to the " unfinished " fort, and thirteen feet of water is indicated.

" On the bar, the low water at neap tides is twelve and a half, and high water is seventeen and a half feet. At spring tides, low water is eleven and a half, and high water is nineteen feet." All other channels range from five to nine feet of water, so that ships had to go near where the fort was built if they were bound to Charleston, and for this reason Colonel Moultrie built the fort at that point. Such is a brief suggestion of the attack upon Fort Sullivan, and of the cause of its failure.

It is obvious that there is no depth of water which will give to a naval force a choice of position or room to wear on or off at will ; that a landing which can not be made through the marshes of the main land, must be made upon Sullivan Island, so as to control the bridge of the Americans if possible ; that the small channels with seven feet of water must require boats for a passage, and that there must be some solid landing place, or there can be no efficient landing at all under fire.

12

The historical antecedents of Fort Sullivan and its defenders require some attention, and then a narrative of the attack and defense will test the accuracy of the quaint old map.

The attack upon Fort Sullivan was but four days after Congress had solemnly asserted that " all persons abiding within any of the United Colonies, and deriving protection from its laws, owed allegiance to the said law," and charged the guilt of *treason* upon " all members of any of the United Colonies who should be adherent to the king of Great Britain, giving to him aid and comfort."

Its issue was as expressive as that of Bunker Hill, of the stubbornness of the defensive, and it afforded an example well calculated to inspire the troops which were then at New York awaiting an attack in force. The people of South Carolian were ripe for just such a deed of valor, and deserved success.

It will be remembered that during April, 1775, a secret committee of citizens took the colonial muskets and cutlasses from the public magazine for the use of the patriots. This act was followed by seizure of powder, and a wide-spread effective organization of the militia.

Thomas Corbett, one of the committee, and acting by its authority, took possession of a mail package just from England, and obtained from it the private dispatches which announced the purpose of the British ministry to subdue the colonies by force of arms.

These dispatches were addressed to Governor Dunmore, of Virginia, Governor Martin, of North Carolina, Governor Campbell, of South Carolina, Governor Wright, of Georgia, and Governor Tonyne, of Augustine. These dispatches were sent to Congress, and had a positive effect upon their action, but they were especially influential in stirring up the people of Charleston to prepare for the worst.

A dispatch had previously been found upon a vessel captured in northern waters, dated at Whitehall, December twenty-third, 1775, stating that seven regiments were in readiness to proceed to the Southern colonies, and that they would in the first place proceed to North Carolina, thence to Virginia or South Carolina as circumstances should point out.

A letter from Governor Wright himself, addressed to General Gage, and requesting " that a detachment of troops be sent to awe the people," was also intercepted, and another was substituted with a counterfeit of his signature, saying that " the people were again come to some order, and there would be no occasion for him to send troops."

The excitement attending the news from Lexington did not subside, but seemed to decide the people of South Carolina to make it the occasion for permanent resistance to British supremacy. Two regiments of foot and one of rangers were organized. The field officers of the First regiment were, Colonel Christopher Gadsden, Lieutenant-colonel Isaac Huger, and Major Owen Roberts; and of the Second regiment, Colonel William Moultrie, Lieutenant-colonel Isaac Motte, and Major Alexander McIntosh. Among the captains were Charles C. and Thomas Pinckney, Francis Marion, Peter and Daniel Horry, William and Benjamin Collett, Francis Huger, and Charles Motte. William Thompson was elected colonel, and James Mayson was elected lieutenant-colonel of the Rangers.

A council of safety was appointed by the Provincial Congress, June sixteenth, 1775, consisting of Henry Laurens, Charles Pinckney, Rawlins Lowndes, Thomas Ferguson, Arthur Middleton, Thomas Heywood Jr., Thomas Bee, John Huger, James Parsons, William H. Drayton, Benjamin Elliott, and William Williams.

During the month of July, seventeen thousand pounds of powder was taken from a brig near Augustine, and by the twentieth of August more than thirty thousand pounds had been accumulated in the storehouses of Charleston and Dorchester. The militia of Georgia had secured nearly an equal amount.

After midnight of the fourth of September, James Island was occupied, including Fort Johnson, under the direction of Henry Laurens, President of the Provincial Congress, and Colonel Gadsden's regiment became its garrison.

Colonel Moultrie occupied Sullivan's Island, and during the month of November, a regiment of artillery was organized, and the work of fortifying all prominent points of the city and adjacent islands was systematically commenced. Haddrell's Point, was occupied for this purpose on the seventeenth of December. During January, 1776, Colonel Moultrie began to build a fascine battery on Sullivan's Island, and on the fifteenth, the discipline of the troops had become so well advanced that every company had its designated rendezvous in case of alarm, and nearly seventy guns were in position. Moultrie states in his memoirs, that "everybody supposed that two small armed ships could take Charleston," but he never believed that *they* could not sink ships, as well as Frenchmen or Spaniards could do it. This impression however, had its good effect. The men were drilled in the exercise of extinguishing fires, planting ladders and whatever might be required in case the city was shelled and set on fire. Governor

Campbell, successor to Governor Wright, had by this time become a resident upon the sloop of war Lamar, as the Governors of Virginia and North Carolina had already made ships of war their place of refuge, and thus declared their distrust of the people and inability to conciliate or govern them.

The council of safety ordered the detachment on Sullivan's Island "to fire upon ships, boats or other vessels which should attempt to pass, approach, or land troops on the island." Moultrie describes the island, as " quite a wilderness and a thick, deep swamp where the fort stands, with live oak, myrtle and palmetto trees.

On the second of March he began to build a large fort capable of containing one thousand men. Two regiments of riflemen were also authorized, and these were officered, respectively, by Colonels Isaac Huger and Thomas Sumter.

South Carolina thus boldly led the way to general independence by asserting her own, under John Rutledge as President, with Henry Laurens as Vice President, and William H. Drayton as Chief Justice. An army and navy were created ; Privy Council and Assembly were elected, and the issue of six hundred thousand dollars of paper money was authorized, as well as the issue of coin: and the first Republic of the New World began its life.

Laurens, as well as Moultrie, Huger, Pickens and Warren, already commissioned in the colonial militia regiments, had served with credit in the old Cherokee war of 1760-1.

Massachusetts had begun the year with substantial freedom. South Carolina put all the machinery of a nation into operation with the opening spring.

By the twenty-sixth of April one hundred heavy guns were in position.

On the thirty-first day of May a large British fleet had been reported as within twenty miles of the harbor's mouth, and on the first day of June the squadron of Admiral Parker began to appear within view from Haddrell's Point.

The month of June, 1776, was an important period in the life of the young Republic of South Carolina.

The men who toiled, endured, and fought out an issue which secured the inviolability of her soil for nearly three years of the national struggle, were men who had entered upon military service with a real purpose to make themselves acquainted with the art of war. Their long period of preparation and drill was destined to bear its natural fruit and to confer perpetual honor upon those who had so early anticipated, appreciated and prepared for the struggle.

The militia about Boston had been suddenly summoned to become soldiers and to meet all the demands which military service exacts of disciplined troops, without the antecedent preparation for so formidable a responsibility, and this at the very outset of the war, before experience had demonstrated the importance of system, obedience and self-sacrifice, if physical force were to be employed to advantage, against the thorough veterans of Great Britain.

The orders and familiar instructions which had been given as guides to Moultrie's, Gadsden's and Thompson's regiments, bore the impress of careful thought ; and there was a deliberate steadiness, in the preparation for invasion, which was nowhere surpassed in colonial experience.   The material was quite homogeneous and the men who were selected as officers, were so selected, as it was claimed, for the very purpose of getting the best men for their respective trusts.   The contest was so largely dependent upon her own citizens in the first place, that there was very little of jealousy, or the clashing of personal ambition at the time, and the lessons of more than a year of national struggle were not lost sight of in the hour of peril.

President Rutledge, afterwards Chief Justice of the United States, was endowed with a rare faculty of judging men and issues by practical tests, and his sagacity, nerve and inflexible will, more than the valor of Moultrie and his companions, secured the victory achieved. It was through his deliberate and unchanging purpose, that Moultrie was enabled to achieve.

The month of June was full of that type of painstaking and cheerful waiting which gave to Bunker Hill its possibility and its history.

General Armstrong arrived from the north late in April, assisted with his counsel, and was practically, if not formally, in command of the South Carolina troops upon the arrival of the British fleet.

On the first day of June, 1776, the city of Charleston was full of life and labor.   Colonel Pinckney's regiment was prompt to take the places assigned to the companies upon an alarm.   Negroes were on duty with the fire-engines, bringing fire-hooks, axes, and all things before provided for an emergency ; the batteries were manned, and additional defenses were begun.   Traverses were made in the principal streets, and light works were thrown up at every point which afforded a ready landing from boats.

The lead sash, then so common, were taken from churches and

houses to be run into bullets, while in response to swift messengers sent into the country, the minute-men began to assemble and go to the places which were to be partially under their charge. Warehouses and other buildings along the river front were demolished, and their sites and materials were used to establish additional defenses. Wherever any necessary work was to be done, however humble, sergeants were sent with a guard detail, and the duty was performed with expedition and system.

On James Island, Colonel Gadsden, then the commanding officer at Charleston, had established a well arranged camp, with tents and all necessary protection for the ordinary garrison of five hundred men.

That force was now increased, and a battery was established directly opposite the city for the use of the artillery companies which reported to him in case the shipping should pass Fort Johnson in safety.

Colonel Moultrie was rapidly completing the exposed faces of Fort Sullivan, and new works were begun along the coast east of Mount Pleasant, to command the shore opposite to Sullivan and Long Islands. Sumter's and Thompson's regiments had reported to Moultrie for duty. June third, he notified President Rutledge that a tender, which had been in company with two large ships and a schooner, was taking soundings from near the post of his advanced guard all along Long Island.

June fourth, General Charles Lee arrived, and on the ninth was placed in general command. He had kept pace with Clinton from Boston to New York, thence to Virginia and North Carolina, and arrived at Charleston just as that officer was approaching its coast to join in the effort to capture and occupy its harbor defenses.

Lee was in his element, that of independent command, only restrained by the authority of President Rutledge, who was as resolute as Washington himself when convinced of duty. Lee made immediate inspection of all preparations, and was tireless in his work. He insisted from the first that Fort Sullivan would be a mere " slaughter pen," and must be abandoned. This opinion he maintained until the fort had actually repelled the enemy ; and only Moultrie's persistency and faith, backed by the president, prevented the abandonment of that position and the inevitable loss of the city.

Moultrie says in his memoirs, " I never was uneasy on not having a retreat, because I never imagined that the enemy could force me to that necessity." Notwithstanding Moultrie's faith in the sufficiency of his defense, Lee never rested easy until a large force had been employed to begin a second bridge to Sullivan Island; the first, which had been made of floating hogsheads with plank stretches, having proved capable of sustaining less than two hundred men at a time.

Lee brought great reputation; equal, said Moultrie, in its encouragement of the troops, to a reinforcement of a thousand men. He adds, "The officers could not at first reconcile themselves to his hasty and rough manners, but he taught us to think lightly of the enemy, and gave a spur to all our actions."

Lee had fears that Colonel Moultrie's "good temper and easy nature" interfered with proper discipline, and repeatedly calls attention to this matter in letters written to him before the battle. His own orders to the troops indicate a sound appreciation of all that constituted a good soldier, and his experience before Boston had prepared him to find a body of militia of the same character as those which first invested that city. A few extracts from his official papers illustrate his views. "Soldiers running at random wherever their folly directs, is an absolute abomination not to be tolerated." "When you issue any orders, do not suffer them to be trifled with." "Let your orders be as few as possible; but let them be punctually obeyed." "Do not tease men with superfluous duties or labor, but enforce whatever is necessary for the honor and safety of your garrison." "Post a commissioned officer at the beach to prevent the monstrous disorders I complain of." "If you expend your ammunition without beating off the enemy, spike your guns, and retreat with all the order possible." "Never fire without a moral certainty of hitting. One hundred and fifty yards is the maximum for muskets, and four hundred for cannon." "Distant firing encourages the enemy, and adds to the pernicious persuasion of the American soldiers that they are no match for their antagonist at close fighting. It makes them cowards, is childish, vicious, and scandalous."

Lee was vigilant, by night and day, and as soon as he understood exactly what was expected to be done through his authority, he discharged his duty promptly and efficiently, and was one of the first to congratulate Colonel Moultrie upon his final success.

June seventh, a flag from Admiral Parker was fired upon by an ignorant sentry, but Moultrie apologized for the oversight on the following day. General Clinton, in return, sent a proclamation to the colonists similar in character to that issued at Wilmington.

June eighth, Colonels Thompson's and Sumter's regiments were ordered to Long Island to dislodge the British troops who were effecting a landing; but this impracticable order of General Lee was modified, and they took position upon the northeast end of Sullivan Island.

June tenth, the British fleet came over the bar, except two vessels. On the eleventh, the North Carolina and Virginia Continental troops arrived, increasing the American forces to six thousand men, of whom twenty-five hundred were regulars. On the twelfth the British fleet made a demonstration as if to attack, but were driven off by a heavy squall of wind. On the fifteenth General Lee placed General Armstrong's command at Haddrell's Point and ordered Moultrie to report to him as his immediate commanding officer. On the twenty-third the fleet made movement preparatory to an attack, but a contrary wind defeated their purpose. On the twenty-fourth the Muhlenburg regiment arrived from Virginia well equipped and in a high state of discipline.

On the twenty-fifth Clinton made a vain effort to reach the main land. On the twenty-sixth the Experiment, 50, also crossed the bar. On the twenty-seventh, Lee sent scouting parties in boats, along the coast, and an effort was made under his orders, to remove the buoys which had been established by the surveying parties sent from the fleet. The enemy made no movement that was not watched, and four miles of earth-works had been completed along the shore.

Thus four weeks of preparation passed by.

The American forces gained confidence, numbers and discipline: while the British fleet and army had just reached the positions which were necessary for offensive action.

Horry's and Clark's regiments were on the island or at Haddrell's Point, while Isaac Motte and Francis Marion, were comrades of Moultrie in the hour of final danger.

It was the eve of battle. Admiral Parker had drilled his marines and seamen in the motions of climbing the parapet of the fort and entering the embrasures, and he was confident that two rounds of fire would prepare the way for an assault; while Clinton, too heedless of warnings as to the depth of intervening water, had his army in hand as he confidently hoped, for occupation and victory.

CHAPTER XXVIII.

CLINTON'S EXPEDITION. ATTACK ON FORT MOULTRIE.

FORT Moultrie was laid out for four bastions, but on the twenty-eighth day of June, 1775, the west and north faces of the main work were nearly open, and only the two bastions on the channel front had been sufficiently advanced to receive guns. The soft and spongy but tough palmetto trees which abounded on Sullivan Island, had been dove-tailed together in a series of connecting pens, and these were filled with sand, so that the parapet was sixteen feet in thickness, and sufficiently high to protect the gunners and garrison. Thirty-one guns were in position. Only twenty-one could have a combined fire at the same time, and the ammunition on hand at the commencement of the action of that date did not average thirty rounds to the piece.

It was evident very early in the morning, that an immediate assault was impending. Colonel Moultrie visited the advance guard, which was on the northern extremity of the island three miles from Sullivan, very soon after the break of day.   He found that Colonel Thompson had completed the light breastworks which were to face the channel between Sullivan Island and General Clinton's camp, and that one eighteen and one six pounder gun had been well located for resisting a landing by the British troops. In the myrtle bushes near the beach, and well covered by some drifted sand hills, there had been secreted a company of expert riflemen.   Three hundred "good shots" from Thompson's own regiment, supported by nearly as many from Colonel Clark's North Carolina regiment, two hundred of Horry's men, and the "Raccoon Rifles," made up the entire command, and their officers manifested full confidence in their ability to resist any attack.

Moultrie had just finished his inspection of these preparations when the movement of the troops from the opposite beach to their boats and floating batteries, warned him that the time had come for him to be at his own post of danger.   Motte, his second in command, and Marion who had been his lieutenant in the old Cherokee war, were anxiously awaiting his arrival.   Already the flag-ship of Commodore Parker was flying signals for Clinton's army to cross Breach inlet to Sullivan Island, and attack the main fort in the rear, and the ships had shaken out top-sails in readiness to advance to their own proper position in the channel nearest the fort.

Moultrie was on horseback.   He says, " I hurried back to the fort as soon as possible.   When I got there I found that the ships were already under sail.   I immediately ordered the long roll to beat, and officers and men to their posts, when the ships came sailing up, as if in confidence of victory.   We had scarcely manned our guns.   They were soon abreast of the fort, let go their anchors, and began their attack most furiously."

The fort was designed for a thousand men, but was occupied by Moultrie's own regiment only, and part of one artillery company, making a total of four hundred and thirty-five, including officers and men.

General Armstrong was in command of a force of fifteen hundred men, and a portion of the artillery regiment at Haddrell's Point, and General Lee took up his head-quarters for the day at that post.   The First regular South Carolina regiment, under Colonel Gadsden, still occupied Fort Johnson, on James Island, and a force of nearly, or quite twenty-five hundred men was properly disposed for the protection of the city itself, and its earthworks and batteries.   A large force of negroes was briskly at work endeavoring to complete some additional works; and another body had charge of the fire-engines and other fire-apparatus, as when the first alarm four weeks before had called the city to arms.

The quaint old map referred to, so accurate in its description of the harbor, and in all chief respects in full harmony with official reports, is erroneous as to Clinton's force, which consisted of over twenty-one hundred foot, light infantry, and grenadiers, and nearly seven hundred seamen, making a total of nearly three thousand men. But the old map thus correctly represents the location of the advancing vessels.

The Solebay, 28, Captain Thomas Symonds, led the van of the first division; the Experiment, 50, Captain Alexander Scott; the Bristol, 50, flag-ship of Sir Peter Parker, Captain John Morris; and the Active, 28, Captain William Williams followed.   A second division of three light frigates; the Sphynx, 20, Captain Anthony Hunt; the Actæon, 28, Captain Christopher Atkins; and the Syren, 28, Captain Tobias Furneaux, moved on a course further to the south, with orders to pass the line of battle ships, and gain a position westward of the fort, so as to sweep its open side with an enfilading fire, and give their larboard broadsides to the redoubts and earthworks on Haddrell's Point. The Thunder Bomb, mortar ship, 8, Captain James Reid commander, took its position south-east by south from the salient angle of the east bastion, with Colonel James, throwing shells, and covered by the Friendship, 22, Captain Charles Hope. The Ranger, sloop, Captain Roger Willis, and the St. Lawrence schooner, 8, Lieutenant J. N. Graves, lay off Breach inlet, which separated Sullivan and Long Island, to act in concert with the small boats which were to land the troops of Clinton.

The plan of attack was well conceived, and was sustained with a persistent gallantry nowhere surpassed in naval annals.

It was nearly eleven o'clock when the first division advanced under easy sail, and disregarding the first few shots delivered from the fort, let go their anchors and opened fire. The Thunder Bomb was already at work, and the roar of guns from the northward, brought notice to the quickened garrison that this double effort to win their post was at its issue. That garrison, under the order of Moultrie, " mind the commodore," " mind the fifty gun-ships," wasted few shots upon the frigates, but steadily, and as rapidly as the supply of powder would give them chance, swept the quarter decks of the heavy vessels, from about noon until sunset.

The first broadside firing from the fleet embedded balls in the palmetto logs; but scattered no splinters, displaced no material and afforded no hopeful sign of the anticipated victory. Moultrie writes, " The Thunder Bomb had the bed of her mortar soon disabled, she threw her shells in good direction, and most of them fell within the fort; but we had a morass in the middle that swallowed them up instantly, and those that fell in the sand, in and about the fort, were immediately buried, so that very few bursted among us."

In the midst of the action the flag ship swung round, with her stern to the fort. Every available gun was trained upon the ship and with terrible effect. Captain Moore lost an arm and was carried below. " At one time," says Edmund Burke, then editor of the Annual Register, " the quarter deck of the Bristol was cleared of every person but the Commodore, who stood alone,—a spectacle of intrepidity and firmness which have seldom been equaled, never exceeded."

Until the position of the ship was shifted, there was every probability that she would be sunk at anchor.

It was just then that the fire from the fort began to slacken, for want of powder; but within an hour it was resumed with increased vigor. Rutledge had not forgotten Moultrie, neither had he lost faith in his capacity and skill. The following note, written in pencil, conveyed his sympathy with the successful resistance thus far sustained.

"DEAR SIR,

I send you 500 pounds of powder. You know our collection is not very great. I should think you may be supplied from Haddrell's Point. HONOR and VICTORY, my good sir, to you, and our worthy countrymen with you. Yours,

J. RUTLEDGE."

"P. S. Do not make too free with your cannon."
"Cool and do mischief."

This wise postscript was a caution against that rapid firing so common with unskilled gunners who over-heat their pieces, endanger the lives of their comrades, and impair the accuracy of the aim and ranges. It was now three o'clock in the afternoon. The firing, to the northward, which began at the time of the naval attack, had ceased. Clinton had loaded his boats and attempted to cross to Sullivan island. The men could not wade through the deep water: and the loaded boats could do nothing upon intermediate shoals, with a depth of less than eighteen inches. The withering fire of the American riflemen who were under close cover, rendered every vigorous effort to force the army to the shore, a sure delivery of the command to entire destruction.

William Falconer, writing on the thirteenth of July from Long Island, where Clinton remained until his departure for New York, says, "If the ships could have silenced the battery, the army was to have made an attack on the back of the island, where they had about one thousand men entrenched *up to their eyes*. They would have killed half of us before we could have made our landing good."

General Clinton made two attempts, and finding that it was equally impossible to reach Sullivan island or the main land, on account of the marshes, he very wisely saved his troops from further effort.

The second division of the squadron, under top-sails only, sailed smoothly by the flag-ship, and by the Solebay, while the broadsides of those ships were first testing the palmetto fort. The quaint old map, locates them a little time after that, *thus*—"*A—ground.*" They had run upon the "middle ground shoal," near where Fort Sumter was afterward built. "*These three frigates were to have gone to the westward of the fort.*" "*Actæon scuttled and set on fire on the 29th.*"

Lee crossed to Sullivan Island during the fight, to inquire into the condition of the fort, and returned with the conviction that the defense would be successful. Moultrie says, "we opened our temporary gate, to admit General Lee. Several of the officers as well as myself were smoking our pipes and giving orders ; but we laid them down when he came in."

The day was memorable for its incidents. Captain Scott of the Experiment, as well as Captain Morris, lost an arm. Forty were killed and seventy-one were wounded on the Bristol ; her hull was struck seventy times, the masts and rigging suffered severely, and a half hour of additional exposure would have been fatal. The Experiment had twenty-three killed and fifty-six wounded. The vessels slipped their cables at dark, and retired nearly three miles from the scene of conflict.

Within the fort, behind the palmetto logs and sand, where the people in shirt sleeves were handling cannon, there were heroic deeds performed well worthy of record with those of the battle deck. "At one time," says Moultrie, "three or four of the men-of-war broadsides struck the fort at the same instant, which gave the merlons such a tremble that I was apprehensive that a few more such would tumble them down." "Our flag was shot away! Our friends gave up all for lost! Sergeant Jasper perceiving that the flag (blue, with a silver crescent in the dexter corner, corresponding with the cap ornament of the South Carolina troops) had fallen without the fort, jumped through one of the embrasures and brought it up through heavy fire, fixed it upon a sponge staff, and planted it upon the ramparts again." Twelve men were killed, and twenty-four were wounded, nearly every casualty having occurred from shot which entered the large embrasures of the fort. When Sergeant McDonald received his mortal wound, addressing the soldiers who were carrying him to the doctor, he begged them "never to give up, they were fighting for liberty." His words are to be remembered with those of another of the same blood, "England expects every man will do his duty."

With the next morning, there came a clearer view of the result of the battle. The Actæon was burned by her crew as they abandoned her. The Sphynx had fouled with the Syren and lost her bowsprit.

Both vessels went off with the tide and joined the first division, and the flag-ship which was also disabled for further offensive operations.

The British troops lingered on Long Island for nearly three weeks. Falconer thus describes his own condition under date of July thirteenth. " We have been encamped on this island for nearly a month past, and have lived upon nothing but salt pork and pease. We sleep upon the sea-shore, nothing to shelter us from the violent rains but our coats and miserable paltry blankets. There is nothing that grows upon this island, it being but a mere sand bank, but a few bushes which harbor millions of mosquitoes. Our killed and wounded number between two and three hundred, and numbers die daily of their wounds."

General Clinton, with his command, left under the convoy of the Solebay frigate, and reached Staten Island on the first of August. Useless differences arose between that officer and Commodore Parker. Each did his duty gallantly and well. Neither had the right to blame the other for the alternations of deep and shoal water, which rendered impossible the success of either.

South Carolina and the American Congress united their testimonials of gratitude and honor to the men who achieved the victory, and after more than a century of national life, the American Republic reaffirms the tribute which was given by the Palmetto State ; and the fort on Sullivan Island is only to be remembered as FORT MOULTRIE !

CHAPTER XXIX.

THE TWO ARMIES IN JULY AND AUGUST, 1776.

THE month of July, 1776, began with the saddest show for a vast expenditure of men and money that could oppress a people just entering upon a great war. The story of the expedition to Canada was a tragedy of woe which carried mourning to many households, and demanded great wisdom, endurance, and faith, if the costly sacrifice was to be converted into hopeful promise for the future.

The lesson was one which had for its text the primary importance of thorough discipline as the chief requisite of well applied physical force, and most impressively declared a fact, that the casualties of the battle-field are but few, when compared with the waste which belongs to bad *logistics*.

Individual courage was not wanting. Capacity, self-sacrifice, and great daring were well supplied; but these elements had not been sufficiently combined, systematized and concentrated, at the expense of all individual choice and preferment. It was hard to make it understood that even veteran soldiers are like obedient *children*, at the same time strong and weak. They obey, but expect a complete outfit of food, clothing, and all the essential elements of success. Improvidence in expenditure will necessarily result where there is a lavish supply, which costs the individual nothing; but with fresh troops who have not learned to husband everything, *even short intervals for rest*, the dependence upon authority is constant and absolute, even in minute matters which would be absurd in civil life.

These remarks furnish a brief epitome of the experiences of the American army up to July, 1776. The fireside mourning over the Canadian sacrifice had not so depressed the people, however, that hope was laid aside. The impending contest at New York began to absorb attention, and awakened fresh energy and will. It was at such an hour, when the consciousness of great disaster was lost sight of in the demand for a still greater effort, that the reverberations from Fort Moultrie reaffirmed the lesson, that the individual soldier was fully equal to duty, if his personal independence could be once merged in the national independence just asserted.

To accomplish this essential condition of success, was the task which had to devolve upon some adequate responsible authority, and the American Congress laid this burden upon the commander-in-chief of its armies.

The British government had placed its share of the issue in the hands of Admiral and General Howe, tacking on to their instructions, however, the contingency of concurrent operations from Canada also.

A brief statement of the relations of both armies will be the introduction to the skirmishes which made up the battle of Long Island.

General Howe's fleet of transports sailed from Halifax June tenth, under strong convoy, made offing at Sandy Hook on the twenty-ninth, and on the second day of July dropped anchor. On the fifth, this fleet of one hundred and twenty-seven square-rigged vessels, besides smaller crafts, effected the landing of General Howe's army on Staten Island. A portion of the Scotch brigade, three companies each of the forty-second and seventy-first regiments joined the squadron off Nantucket, having made for Boston, direct from England, and the total force amounted to about nine thousand two hundred men, under Generals Howe, Pigot. Grant, and Jones. During the voyage, two of the transports carrying the Scotch brigade were captured by American armed vessels after a short engagement, and taken into Boston. Lieutenant colonel Campbell of the seventy-first, with sixteen other officers, and four hundred and fifty men were reported by General Howe as among the missing then taken captive, including General William Erskine. General Howe himself reached Sandy Hook on the twenty-fifth of June, in the fast sailing frigate Greyhound, and held a secret conference with Governor Tryon on board the ship. As the result of this interview, he determined to land his entire force at Gravesend, and the fleet actually took position in the Gravesend cove on the first of July for that purpose. The key to his change of purpose is found in some letters sent to Lord Germaine by a dispatch vessel, July seventh. He wrote as follows: " I had been informed during the night of a strong pass upon a ridge of craggy heights, covered with wood, that lay in the route the army must have taken, only two miles from the point of the enemy's encampment, and seven from Gravesend, which the rebels would undoubtedly have occupied before the king's troops could get up to it; and from the minutest description, judging an attack upon this post so strong by nature, and so near the front of the enemy's works, to be too hazardous an attempt before the arrival of the troops with Commodore Hotham, daily expected, I declined the undertaking." "I propose waiting for the English fleet or the arrival of Lieutenant-general Clinton, in readiness to proceed, unless by some unexpected change of circumstances in the meanwhile, it should be found expedient to act with the present force." "In case Lieutenant-general Clinton's southern operations should prevent his joining the army here, I am apprehensive the possession of Rhode Island, though of the most important nature, must be deferred until the arrival of the second embarkation from Europe, unless General Carleton should penetrate early into this province, which may enable me to spare a corps adequate to that service"; "But, as I must esteem an impression upon the enemy's principal force collected in this quarter, to be the first object of my attentions, I shall hold it steadily in view, without losing sight of these which comparatively may be esteemed collateral." These quotations show that the very best possible strategical movements had been selected by the British Cabinet and its advisers, for the prosecution of the war. The adequate force was not supplied. The fate of Clinton's expedition southward was unknown at date of the dispatch of General Howe.

It will be seen that four armies were to act with substantial unity of time, and so widely apart that the American army could not give alternate attention to any two of the four. Three of these operations, those at Newport, New York, and southward, were supported by fleets; the third was to descend from Canada with the moral support which the failure of the American invasion conferred upon the veteran legions of the British army.

One signal restraint upon a general plan of operations, otherwise excellent, was the monstrous under-estimate of the courage, numbers and purposes of the American people, which stuck so fast to the ministry that it was with the greatest difficulty that Yorktown itself could make the error intelligible. Admiral Howe arrived July twelfth with an admirably equipped squadron and nearly one hundred and fifty transports loaded with troops. On the same day, two men-of-war, the Phœnix, 40 guns, and the Rose, 20 guns, safely passed the batteries at Paulus Hook and Greenwich, and thus early interrupted Washington's communication with Albany, and the northern army.

13

On the next day a flag was sent to the American head-quarters for the purpose of opening negotiations for a settlement of the issues between the mother country and the colonies. Admiral Howe had been deputized to act jointly with his brother, as commissioners, in this behalf. The proposition was so weak that it had no favor whatever. General Washington described their errand, in a letter to General Schuyler, in these terms, " Commissioners to dispense pardon to repenting sinners."

Much unreasonable censure has been cast upon General Howe and his brother, for their reluctance to address Washington in his official character, as if it implied discourtesy on their part, or the fear that they would waive some legal rights of the crown, by the most ready access to the American authorities. It is only necessary to cite the American war of 1861–5, when the same reluctance of the United States to address the Confederate officers by their title, embarrassed the exchange of prisoners, as in 1776, while it had not the weight of a feather in determining the real status of the parties, or the battle issues themselves. Adjutant-general Patterson, of the British army had an interview with Washington, on the twentieth day of July ; mutual courtesies were exchanged, but no business was done, as there was no real basis of compromise in the instructions of Lord Howe.

Admiral Howe says of Colonel Patterson's interview : " It was more polite than interesting ; however, it induced me to change my superscription of the address upon the letter, which had been George Washington, Esqr., for the attainment of an end so desirable ;—referring to the effort to secure the exchange of General Prescott, who had been taken prisoner at Montreal, and of the officers and men of the seventy-first regiment, just captured at sea.

Congress had its own Declaration of Independence engrossed upon parchment on the nineteenth of July, for the signature of members, and freely disseminated Lord Howe's proposition throughout the colonies, so little did they regard it as having a single element of value in the interests of peace. There was another good reason for the free publication of the document. Rumors of a sensational character were as thick and absurd as in more modern times. General Roberdeau notified Washington, on the nineteenth of August, in all seriousness, that a " post-rider had told with great confidence that General Howe had proposed to retire with the fleet and army, and was willing to settle the present dispute on any terms asked by Washington : that this came from an officer who was ready to swear to it, but as it might have a tendency to lull the inhabitants, he made it the subject of an express."

This was based upon another rumor that England and France were at war. General Washington was compelled to publish an order rebuking the recklessness of gossip-mongers. This was more important, since many of those who opposed the war on account of business relations with the British civil authorities, were most active in words, while lacking courage to take up arms on either side.

On the first day of August, Generals Clinton and Cornwallis reached Staten Island with their united command. On the twelfth Commodore Hotham arrived, having convoyed a fleet of transports which landed twenty-six hundred British troops and eight thousand four hundred Hessians, and a supply of camp equipage for the entire army. On the fifteenth Sir Peter Parker arrived with twenty-four sail from the south.

Admiral Howe made one more effort to press the proposition of the British Cabinet to a favorable consideration by the American Congress, but without effect. His high character and sincere desire for peace are ever to be honored, no less than his real merit as a naval commander.

The American preparations were far less perfect, but equally earnest with those of the British army.

The Declaration of Independence, made on the fourth day of July, was favorably adopted by Maryland on the sixth, on the ground that " the king had violated his compact," and the people were without a government; thus starting out upon the original basis of all government, as heretofore discussed. Pennsylvania and New Jersey followed on the eighth and New York on the ninth. Other colonies rapidly accepted the action of Congress and entered upon a more systematic organization of the militia.

On the ninth of July, Massachusetts was engaged in hurrying three additional regiments to the Northern army, then having its headquarters at Crown Point, and Congress ordered fifteen hundred additional troops to be raised for the same destination. On the nineteenth, Washington ordered three of the eastern regiments to join the northern army.

Crown Point was soon abandoned, in accordance with the recommendations of a board of officers convened July seventh, acting upon the advice of General Gates, but contrary to the judgment of Washington ; and Ticonderoga alone of the northern posts, remained in the occupation of the American army.   The evacuation of Crown Point is mentioned in this connection as only one of the annoying elements of the crisis, when each detached officer seemed ready to exercise the prerogative of a commander-in-chief.   There were sanitary considerations to be regarded, on account of the remains of the scourge of the small-pox, but General Carleton deemed its possession of such military importance that he soon occupied it for his head-quarters.

The defense of Brooklyn Heights was decided to be essential to the most efficient prosecution of the war.   To give value to this decision, it was necessary to provide for all possible demonstrations which lay within the reach of the British naval forces.   From Brooklyn to Kings Bridge the distance was nearly fifteen miles, with the navigable waters of the Hudson, East river and Harlem creek, to be watched, and their shores to be amply guarded.   The battery on Paulus Hook, then an island, was on the New Jersey shore, making two ferries for communication with Brooklyn, and the entire force of the regular artillery regiment of Colonel Knox was reported at only five hundred and eighty-five men.

The official army return for the third of August, 1776, gives the strength of the American army as follows.   Commissioned officers and staff, twelve hundred and twenty-five ; non-commissioned officers, fifteen hundred and two ; present for duty, ten thousand five hundred and fourteen ; sick, present and absent, three thousand six hundred and seventy-eight ; on furlough, ninety-seven ; on command, two thousand nine hundred and forty-six, making a total of seventeen thousand two hundred and twenty-five men.   Less than one-third of this force had served from the beginning of the war, and the arms were not only insufficient in numbers, but many of those treated as serviceable would have been condemned, upon inspection for issue to regular troops.   The crudeness of the army organization, and the short terms of service engendered neglect of such as they had, and the army had not learned that a gun must be kept in order, even if the soldier goes barefoot.   The artillery was of various patterns and caliber, second hand and neglected, or hastily fabricated, and the men, who were excellent riflemen, knew very little about the range or management of field or siege pieces.   It was just then that the American army was to renew the contest, no longer trusting in numbers, but against superior forces fully equipped.

Two days after the muster of the army above referred to, Governor Trumbull of Connecticut assured Washington that "he did not greatly dread what the enemy could do, trusting Heaven to support us, knowing our cause to be righteous." On the seventh, Washington sent him a copy of his "Return," with the laconic suggestion, that "to trust in the justice of our cause without our own utmost exertions, would be *tempting* Providence." Trumbull responded in his usual practical way, and although five regiments had already been sent forward, he very soon called out nine regiments more, and sent them, averaging three hundred and fifty men each, in time to be present when the British troops subsequently landed in Westchester county.

Two regiments, including Colonel Prescott's, were detailed as the garrison of Governor's Island. The works upon Brooklyn Heights had been begun by General Lee, but prosecuted under the personal direction of General Greene, who had explored the country thoroughly, and knew the range of each piece as well as the character of the approaches to the works. He was a soldier by choice, subordinate at all times, and ambitious to attain excellence for himself and proficiency in his men. A redoubt of seven guns crowned the heights. The exposed point of Red Hook, which was a combination of marsh and thicket and solid land, was supplied with five guns, and the intrenchments, more than half a mile in length, were protected by abattis and four redoubts, which mounted twenty guns. Greene occupied these redoubts and lines with two regiments of Long Island militia, and six Continental regiments, none of which exceeded four hundred men for duty. The lines extended from Wallabout Bay, the present navy yard, to the creek then setting in from Gowanus Bay, and some adjoining marshes, which were impassable at high tide, and at all times miry, and difficult of approach.

The Pennsylvania rifle battalion, Colonel Atlee, Smallwood's Maryland, and Haslet's Delaware, which had just joined the army from the south, were added to the garrison, and were placed in Stirling's brigade on the morning of the twenty-seventh, before the attack was made.

The total nominal strength of the American army about New York on the twenty-sixth of August, including the sick, non-effectives of all kinds, and those without arms, was a little over twenty-seven thousand men. The Connecticut regiments which last joined, brought such arms as they could provide for themselves, and were but so many citizens, with nominal organization, but neither discipline nor experience in military drill.

On the fifteenth of August, Greene, " then confined to his bed with a raging fever," wrote to Washington that " he hoped through the assistance of Providence to be able to ride before an attack should be made, but felt great anxiety as to the result."

Such was the relative state of readiness with which the British and American armies awaited conflict. Repeated storms and high winds postponed the landing of the former troops, and the latter army was accumulating in numbers, but anticipating the coming issue with the conviction that the ordeal would be one of surpassing trial and danger.

CHAPTER XXX.

BATTLE OF LONG ISLAND.—PREPARATIONS.

THE British commander-in-chief determined to attack the American works on Brooklyn Heights and thereby secure a land-footing for operations against the city of New York, which was directly across East River and less than three-fourths of a mile distant.

The defense of Fort Moultrie had indicated the kind of resistance which provincial troops could oppose to an attack by naval forces, and the advance had to be made across Long Island, unless a combined movement should be attempted through Long Island Sound and up the Hudson river, to occupy the country north of Manhattan, or New York, island. The latter plan would enclose the American army, as the British army was caught at Boston; while the occupation of the heights of Brooklyn would be a counterpart to the American possession of Dorchester Heights during the previous June.

The movement was well devised, well supported and faithfully executed. In determining the force actually employed in the attack, reference is made to the report of Admiral Howe, who states, that "on the twenty-second of August the whole force then destined for this service, consisting of about fifteen thousand men, was landed before noon: and that on the twenty-fifth, an additional corps of Hessian troops under General De Heister, with their artillery and baggage, were conveyed to Gravesend Bay." This made the effective force twenty thousand men, leaving at least four thousand upon Staten Island, besides the sick. The latter force included one brigade of Hessian troops. On the twenty-seventh day of August, General Howe made official report of the rank and file of his army, as twenty-six thousand two hundred and forty-seven men, exclusive of the battalion of royalists under Brigadier-general De Lancey. In quoting the Returns of General Howe which were laid before the House of Commons, General Clinton says, that "he (Howe) had 24,464 *effectives* fit for duty;—a total of 26,980, officers not included, who, when added, amount to 31,625 men." Sir George Collier, who was present at the landing of the army, says, that "the army with Howe on Long Island amounted to upwards of twenty thousand besides those who remained on Staten Island."

The admirable logistics exhibited in the whole movement requires fuller detail of narrative than would be desirable in a more general history.

The British army proper consisted of an advance corps, a reserve, and seven brigades, constituted as follows:

The advance corps :—Four battalions of light infantry and the light dragoons. *The reserve :*—four battalions of grenadiers, with the 33d and 42d regiments of foot.

First Brigade : the 44th, 15th, 27th and 45th regiments.

Second Brigade : the 5th, 28th, 55th and 49th regiments.

Third Brigade : the 10th, 37th, 38th and 52d regiments.

Fourth Brigade : the 17th, 40th, 46th and 55th regiments.

Fifth Brigade : the 22d, 43d, 54th and 63d regiments.

Sixth Brigade : the 23d, 44th, 57th and 64th regiments.

Seventh Brigade : the 71st Highland regiment, New York companies and the Royal Artillery.

Colonel Donop's corps embraced the Hessian grenadiers and chasseurs ; and General De Heister's command consisted of two brigades.

Some of these regiments are at once to be recognized as among those which were largely depleted in the action on Breed's Hill ; but the number of battalions which landed, confirms the estimate given by Admiral Howe and Sir George Collier.

The debarkation was signally perfect. More than four hundred transports were within the arms of Sandy Hook. Ten line-of-battle ships and twenty frigates were their escort and protection. Seventy-five flat boats, eleven bateaux and two galleys, all built for the purpose, in ten distinct, well-ordered divisions, simultaneously touched the beach and landed the reserves and advance corps, four thousand strong, near the present site of Fort Hamilton, and within two hours after the signal had been set. Five thousand additional troops were landed with equal celerity and order, a little further down the bay. The transports came up in their designated succession to deliver the regiments to the long line of waiting boats, and before twelve o'clock of the twenty-second of June, fifteen thousand men, with artillery, baggage and stores, had been placed on shore, without mishap or delay. On the twenty-fifth, the division of General De Heister was transported to Gravesend cove, and made their landing with equal skill.

On the twenty-sixth, a naval diversion was attempted up New York Bay, to alarm the posts on Governor's Island and Red Hook, and induce the belief that an attack was to be made upon the city itself. It so far succeeded as to delay the movement of reinforcements then under orders for Brooklyn ; but a strong north-east wind compelled the fleet to drop down the bay and come to anchor. The Roebuck alone reached Red Hook, but accomplished no mischief, and soon dropped out of fire.

General Cornwallis, with the reserves, ten battalions of light infantry, and Donop's corps of Hessians, had been advanced to the vicinity of Flatbush immediately after landing on the twenty-second, to learn whether the pass through the hills at that point had been occupied by the Americans. Upon finding that it had been so occupied, and that a redoubt and intrenchments had been interposed in his way, his command was not pushed to an attack, but encamped in front of Flatbush. The main army occupied a line extending from the coast through Gravesend to Flatlands, and active preparations were at once made for an immediate advance.

The long range of hills extending from the Narrows to Jamaica was known to have four passes available for the movement of troops with artillery. The most direct road was that along the bay, cutting through the hills just back of Red Lion, where Martense's Lane joins the usual thoroughfare, at the edge of the present Greenwood cemetery. A second was directly in front of Flatbush, and this road led directly to the American intrenchments. The third was by the road from Flatbush to Bedford. The fourth, which extended as far as Flushing, crossed the Bedford and Jamaica road nearly three miles east from the first named town. Reference to the map, " Battle of Long Island," which is built upon the United States Coast Survey Chart, will indicate the respective relations of these roads to an advance upon the American position. The disposition of the British army is to be particularly noticed for its exact comprehension of the situation, and the assurance of success which that disposition secured.

During the morning of the twenty-second, at the time of the first landing, Colonel Hand's American regiment had deployed along the coast for the purpose of checking the movement, if attempted only by a moderate force ; but the regiment fell back to Prospect Hill as soon as advised of its real character. It does not appear from the official archives, or other responsible authority, that he advised the commanding general of the landing of the additional corps on the same day, nor that any adequate vidette system was employed to secure an intelligent impression as to the ultimate design of the British army.

On the twenty-sixth, General De Heister occupied Flatbush, and thereby greatly strengthened the conviction that an advance would be made in force from that point, but during the evening, Earl Cornwallis withdrew his own command, and joined General Clinton at Flatlands.

Shortly after nine o'clock, General Clinton with the light dragoons, two battalions of light infantry, the reserve under Cornwallis, (except the forty-second regiment which had been detached to the left of General Heister,) and the portion of the seventy-first regiment which escaped capture at sea, with fourteen pieces of artillery, moved through New Lots, near the present East New York, and before three o'clock in the morning, arrived within half a mile of the pass which he intended to force. A narrow causeway built through a marsh, and known as Shoemaker's bridge, which only admitted of the passage of a single column at a time, was passed without interruption, and a halt was then ordered for re-formation of the command.

Lord Percy followed with the main army, which consisted of the Guards, the Second, Third, and Fifth brigades, and ten field pieces. The Forty-ninth regiment, with four medium twelve-pounders, and the baggage brought up the rear. Percy joined Clinton at least a half hour before daybreak. A small American patrol was captured, the pass was occupied, the heights were reached, and the troops were allowed an interval for rest and refreshments, preparatory to a further advance.

There was now open before this powerful column, a clear and direct route to Brooklyn Heights by the rear of all advanced posts. Thus far, the British right wing had profitably employed the hours and realized its immediate objective, without loss or alarm to the enemy. An immediate advance upon the American intrenchments would have been successful, but costly in life. This was not the original purpose, and the success already realized was more than should have been anticipated.

During this time, General De Heister, under instructions, only *demonstrated* toward the American force which held the Flatbush pass, and Colonel Miles of the American army, who was posted toward the Bedford road, and Colonel Wyllis, who was posted across that road, seem to have had no intimation that a British force had already turned their flank, and was advancing between their own position and the American lines.

Occasional firing took place about Flatbush, but no more than was incident to antagonistic forces occupying positions within short range. They seem to have regarded the Flatbush pass as seriously threatened, and the heavy force in front gave color to this opinion. General Grant's command could be seen from Prospect Hill, and the comparative passivity of Heister's division would have suggested that he was withholding attack, in order to give General Grant an opportunity to advance by the harbor road.

General Grant also moved late in the evening with the Fourth and Sixth brigades, and reached Red Lion just before midnight. His advance was promptly checked by a lively fire from a detachment of militia properly posted before the pass. This skirmishing was maintained until early dawn. He advanced slowly, without crowding the American pickets, yet pressed firmly on, as if assured of abundant support.

Washington had been advised of the landing effected on the twenty-second, and that " Colonel Hand had fallen back to Prospect Hill, burning wheat and such other property as might be of immediate use to the British troops." Six regiments were sent to reinforce the garrison on the heights. These regiments ranged in number from three hundred to four hundred men. Orders were sent to General Heath, then at the north end of Manhattan island, to be prepared to forward additional troops, and five regiments from the city force were placed in readiness to cross East river, as soon as it should be clearly determined whether General Howe was making a final movement to cover a positive attack upon New York, or really designed to make the occupation of Brooklyn Heights his single immediate objective. The absence of General Greene became a matter of serious concern. In a letter to Congress, dated the twenty-third, Washington says, " I have been obliged to appoint General Sullivan to the command on the island, owing to General Greene's indisposition."

When Colonel Hand fell back to Flatbush on the twenty-second, and gave notice of the first landing, the small picket force at that pass was increased, by order of General Sullivan. In a letter to Washington, written on the twenty-third, he says, " This afternoon the enemy formed, and attempted to pass the road by Bedford. A smart fire ensued between them and the riflemen. The officer sent off for a reinforcement which I ordered immediately. A number of musketry came up to the assistance of the riflemen, whose fire, with that of the field pieces, caused a retreat of the enemy. I have ordered a party out for prisoners to-night. We have driven them a mile from their former station. These things argue well for us, and I hope are so many preludes to a general victory." This confidence of General Sullivan was hardly less unfounded than his faith in the success of operations in Canada, and, as in that case, he was immediately superseded.

On the next day General Putnam was assigned to the command. On the twenty-sixth, Washington wrote to that officer, to " stop the scattering, unmeaning and wasteful firing, which prevents the possibility of distinguishing between a real and false alarm, which prevents deserters from approaching our lines, and must continue so long as every soldier conceives himself at liberty to fire when, and at what he pleases." " Guards are to be particularly instructed in their duty." " A brigadier of the day is to remain constantly upon the lines, that he may be upon the spot, to command and see that orders are executed." " Skulkers must be shot down on the spot." " The distinction between a well regulated army and a mob, is the good order and discipline of the former, and the licentiousness and disorderly behavior of the latter." " The men not on duty, are to be compelled to remain at, or near their respective camps, or quarters, that they may turn out at a moment's warning: nothing being more probable than that the enemy will allow little time enough to prepare for the attack." " Your best men should at all hazards prevent the enemy passing the woods and approaching your works."

On the twenty-sixth Washington reported to Congress, that, " the fleet had fallen down to the Narrows, that the tents had been struck on Staten Island, and he was led to believe that the main army had landed upon Long Island and would make their grand push there."

The force on Long Island at the time of the battle, was not quite eight thousand men, inclusive of Stirling's brigade, which crossed the river in the morning. During the subsequent debates upon this battle in the British House of Commons, and the examination of witnesses who had participated in the action, Cornwallis testified, " It was reported that they (the Americans) had six or eight thousand men on Long Island." General Howe, on the other hand, reported the American force which occupied the woods alone at ten thousand men   This was nearly one-half of the effective force of the whole American army about New York. While the exact number may not be ascertained, it is best to settle upon some final standard, so that an approximate estimate can have its place in history. That standard must be the official returns, with only those qualifications which equally valuable contemporaneous judgment will warrant. The "ration returns" then made, vindicate the above judgment of the force at the post. The disposition of the American advance posts before Brooklyn was of the feeblest kind, in view of the impending advance of the British army.

Johnson's New Jersey, and Handshaw's Massachusetts regiments were established at Prospect Hill. Colonel Hand's was also there ; Miles' Pennsylvania rifles, and Wyllis' Connecticut were at or near the Bedford pass. Three field pieces, and one howitzer were in the redoubt and intrenchments before Flatbush. General Sullivan's report contains the following : "Lord Stirling commanded the main body without the lines. I was to have commanded under General Putnam within the lines. I was uneasy about a road, through which I had often foretold that the enemy would come, but could not persuade others to be of my opinion. I went to the hill near Flatbush to reconnoiter, and with a picket of four hundred men was surrounded by the enemy, who had advanced by the very road I had foretold, and which I had paid horsemen fifty dollars for patrolling by night, while I had the command, as I had no foot for the purpose." "I often urged, both by word and writing, that the enemy would first try Long Island ; and then New York, which was completely commanded by it, would fall of course. In this I was unhappy enough to differ from almost every officer in the army, till the event proved my conjectures were just." General Sullivan was second in command. Lord Stirling was at the fort, until awakened at three o'clock on the morning of the twenty-seventh, and assigned to duty on the extreme right. The standing order of Washington required a general officer to be always on the lines. General Sullivan, in the absence of all other officers, and as so recently responsible for the whole command, does not successfully limit his responsibility to that of fighting well the little escort to his reconnoitering trip.

General Putnam already advanced in years, and wholly unacquainted with the outposts, seems to have left undisturbed the existing picket arrangements when he took command. It has been seen that Washington had ordered the careful observation and guard of all approaches. As General Sullivan claimed that he always expected the British advance to be made upon Brooklyn, he must as a soldier be held to certain implied presumptions which he alone could, and never did, adequately explain.

The simple facts are that the Jamaica road was overlooked. The force at all outside posts up to the attack upon the pickets at Red Lion, on the harbor road, was but a little over three thousand men; and when that attack was made it was assumed to be conclusive of the purpose of General Howe to make that route his line of operations against the American works. There is no other hypothesis which would warrant the exposure of troops on that road, subject as they would be to lose their line of retreat, if General De Heister should advance upon the centre. He was in fact nearer the fort than Red Lion was.

The British army was prepared to fulfill its duty. The American army, without Greene, failed to understand the position, and was not ready for duty.

CHAPTER XXXI.

BATTLE OF LONG ISLAND.

THE twenty-seventh day of August, 1776, was a day of struggle from its first hour.

The narrative brought General Grant into conflict with the pickets of the American outposts on New York Bay, just about midnight of the twenty-sixth. The picket was commanded by Major Burd, of the Pennsylvania flying camp. This camp, it will be remembered, was established by authority of Congress for the concentration of ten thousand men who were to be placed under instruction, as an ultimate reserve. The exigency hurried many of these regiments to New York before they had in fact been fully organized.

The picket at Red Lion held firmly to their post, supported by a portion of Huntington's Connecticut regiment, and aided by the early presence of General Parsons, who had just before received the appointment as brigadier-general. He was a lawyer, without military antecedents, and had been with the army but a few weeks.

Major Burd was captured during the pressure of General Grant's advance guard upon the picket line. Messengers were dispatched to head-quarters, and at three o'clock General Putnam sent General Lord Stirling to the relief of the picket, with orders "to stop the advance of the enemy." Colonel Atlee, of the Pennsylvania musketeer battalion, was pushed forward to the crest of the hill by which the British must approach, and a portion of three companies uniting with the original advance guard, maintained such vigorous skirmishing just back of Red Lion, as to check the advance of the enemy until quite late in the morning. Nearly midway between the American lines and Red Lion, a well developed ridge extended from the general line of hills across the traveled road, nearly to the shore of the New York Bay. The ground in front, to the south-west, was low and marshy at places, while an orchard occupied the slight upland immediately in front of this ridge, which General Stirling selected as his *point of resistance*. In order to check the British advance, and give time for the formation of the troops then rapidly approaching from Brooklyn, Colonel Atlee promptly concentrated his regiment and the retiring picket guard upon the side of the main hills, so as to have a superior position from which to open fire upon the British columns, then preparing to descend from the summit near the pass to the low ground and orchard which they must cross in order to attack Stirling. This movement of Colonel Atlee to high ground which was well wooded and adapted to his design, was made under a fire of grape shot, with the loss, according to his report, of but one man.

It is necessary to state in this connection that the reports of Stirling, Atlee, and other officers, written on the night of the twenty-seventh, and on the twenty-eighth, while they were prisoners, are necessarily meager in detail, and have value simply for the facts within their immediate personal knowledge. Those facts only are here embodied which are consistent with the record as gathered from additional sources. Statements and omissions are therefore alike to be regarded, in order to make the narrative as full as the facts will warrant, and military orders themselves are to be largely inferred from acts done. Each claims for himself sufficient credit for good conduct, while none assume responsibility for neglect.

Colonel Atlee had barely reached the wooded slope referred to, when General Grant moved the twenty-third, forty-fourth, and a part of the seventeenth British foot to the right, up the hill, overlapping Atlee's command, and having as their evident purpose to flank him first, then to crowd him back upon Stirling, and so flank the entire command. Stirling had already formed his line. It consisted of Smallwood's Maryland battalion, Haslet's Delaware battalion, their colonels being absent as members of court-martial in New York, and a part of Kiechline's rifle battalion, just then coming upon the ground. Captain Carpenter with two pieces of artillery was already in sight, and soon after joined the brigade. Stirling sent Captain Stedman with two Delaware companies to support Colonel Atlee, with orders to take distance still more to the left, and prevent the enemy from gaining higher ground for their flank movement. General Parsons was also placed on the left with so much of Huntington's regiment as was on the ground. Two vigorous attacks were made upon Atlee without success. Both were repulsed with considerable loss, as the character of the ground and the intervening woods gave confidence and efficiency to the American troops.   After the second repulse, Colonel Atlee made a quick advance to force a good position which the British held, but was forced back by a heavy fire from a superior force.   His Lieutenant-colonel, Caleb Parry, was killed, as well as Lieutenant-colonel Grant, of the fortieth British foot.   The British loss in killed and wounded during these attacks was a little over sixty officers and men, including Lieutenant Colonel Monckton of the forty-first, dangerously wounded.

The British centre and left had now formed in two lines for an advance upon Stirling ; their left having been relieved from pressure, moved on in a single line as originally deployed.   Captain Carpenter's guns were promptly moved nearer the hill-side to command the road, and a spirited action was maintained, at arms' length, for nearly two hours, with considerable loss on both sides, and little advantage to either.   The distance to the American lines was much less than three miles, the disparity in force was not sufficient to warrant the sacrifice and risk of assault, and the general plan of the combined British movement, rendered such an attempt unnecessary.   It was enough for the British left wing to be able to hold Stirling fast where he was.

The sound of firing had already been heard in the direction of Flatbush.   Shortly before eleven o'clock it was heard to the rear of Stirling, and the real issue of the day approached its solution.   Stirling retreated hastily, but in order ; and was soon confronted with fresh columns which were rapidly advancing toward the road which ran from the Upper Mill, to Flatbush.   Orders were given for the men to seek their own safety, by crossing the marsh to the Yellow Mill, or otherwise, each for himself.   The tide was already coming in, and promptness alone could save any of the command.   Atlee and Parsons fell back, along the hill, skirmishing as they retired.   The ammunition wagon of Huntington's regiment had joined the detachment, but the increasing volume of fire gave imperative warning no longer to delay retreat.   Parsons, with a few men, attempted to cross the Flatbush road and retreat toward Hell Gate.   His men scattered and he entered the works in the morning, having escaped through the thick woods.   Atlee found himself in danger of capture by a Hessian detachment, and turning to the right surrendered to the forty-second Highland regiment, which was on De Heister's left, and had advanced over Prospect Hill.

General Stirling, with four hundred men of Smallwood's Maryland
14

battalion, faced his new opponent, and made a grasp to control the road which led into South Brooklyn and thereby cover the causeway at the Upper Mill. This would at least have secured a retreat for the other troops. It was too late. Cornwallis had already occupied the Cortelyou house, and held fast to his position with constantly increasing forces. An attempt was then made to force a passage to fort Box, the redoubt at the nearest point on the American lines, but this was foiled by the skillful interposition of a force of grenadiers and two guns.

Finding this avenue of escape closed, and that the army of Grant was fast approaching, Stirling moved rapidly into the woods to the right, up the slope of the hill, only to be confronted by a Hessian column which had crossed over from Prospect Hill. He surrendered to General De Heister in person.

Thus closed the operations of the right wing. It was marked by great courage, pertinacity and presence of mind, and the disposition of Stirling's brigade was such as to meet every requirement that could be expected of a force hardly exceeding seventeen hundred men.

A single detachment of prisoners had been taken. Lieutenant Ragg and twenty men, of the second regiment of Marines, as designated in General Howe's official report, although not named on the Roster of the army as landed, mistook the well equipped southern troops for Hessians, and fell into their hands as subjects of exchange.

The retreat was a trying one, but without considerable loss, except that of the battle-field and of prisoners. Exaggerated reports were current at that period, as to the number of men drowned, or suffocated, while crossing the head of Gowanus Bay. Many of the men abandoned their arms and equipments and swam the narrow belt of deep water, but no reasonable construction of official or personal information will place the number of drowned men at more than seven, and Colonel Haslet mentions only one. The Maryland and Delaware regiments fought like veteran troops, and maintained their reputation on subsequent battle-fields. A loss, in killed, wounded and missing, of two hundred and fifty-nine, tells the whole story; and in the last struggle to force the lines of Earl Cornwallis, the Maryland troops made repeated assaults under a heavy fire, with commendable spirit and coolness.

While General Grant's division was thus actively engaged, the division of General Heister was contented with an active cannonading of the American redoubt and intrenchments, where General Sullivan was really and necessarily in command, before Flatbush.

Generals Howe, Clinton, Percy and Cornwallis, after resting their troops on the Jamaica road near Bedford, still undiscovered by the Americans, began their advance again at half-past eight o'clock in the morning. The light infantry and light dragoons passed beyond Bedford and bore to the left, and south, directly across the Flatbush road. The alarm had been already given. A detachment of the Guards and one grenadier company with three pieces of artillery soon joined them and commenced a spirited attack upon the alarmed troops who were rapidly retiring from Prospect Hill. The Thirty-third foot and another detachment of grenadiers pushed across the Heights under the very fire of the American lines to cut off Stirling's retreat and unite with General Grant. The Second grenadiers, and the detachment of the Seventy-first, followed, in time to defeat Stirling's last effort to escape. As soon as General Clinton's guns opened fire, De Heister, thus notified that the time had come for his action, ordered Colonel Donop with the Yagers to advance in open order, using only the bayonet, and put his whole command in quick motion to support this impetuous onset. Several light field pieces, charged with grape, were sent in advance to clear the way. The American army was between two fires. Single positions were held for a few moments with obstinacy and gallantry, but in a few moments more, the crushing force of two fronts, enveloped each party in turn, and the whole command broke up into small detachments, seeking personal safety in flight or hiding places.

The British loss, as officially stated, including Hessians and Marines, was five officers killed and twenty-one wounded and missing; fifty-eight non-commissioned officers and men killed, and three hundred and sixteen wounded and missing.

The British return of American prisoners made a total of one thousand and ninety-seven, including sixty-seven wounded officers and men.

Upon this list there are reported Generals Sullivan, Woodhull and Stirling. General Woodhull, with more than two hundred militia, was captured on the twenty-eighth, near Jamaica, as elsewhere stated, but appear on the return referred to.

Upon a muster of the two Pennsylvania rifle battalions, and Colonel Atlee's musketeer battalion, the day after the battle, "afterwards carefully compared with the accounts which came by a flag of truce," their total of killed, wounded and missing, added up two hundred and seventy-seven.

Upon a revision of the whole returns it appeared that the casualties of Stirling's brigade were one-half, and those of the Maryland battalion were one-fourth of the aggregate losses of the entire day.

The American casualties, exclusive of the Long Island militia, were, as nearly as can be ascertained, nine hundred and seventy officers and men, and the British casualties foot up just four hundred.

The battle of Long Island had to be fought. If the protracted resistance of Breed's Hill, and the successful defense of Fort Moultrie, created an undue estimate of the capacity of militia and raw troops when covered by breast-works, and thereby engendered a false confidence that the works on Brooklyn Heights could be also held against a well equipped veteran army, it certainly demonstrated that no resistance *at all* could be kept up, without complete discipline. The defense was doomed to be a failure from the first, independent of the coöperation of a naval force. The sole value of the advance posts and of careful pickets, lay in the assurance of prolonged resistance, and not in a finally successful resistance. The ultimate course of General Howe, that of regular approaches, was inevitable, and the result was almost certain. Washington was wise in his purpose " to make the acquisition as costly as possible to his adversary." He needed time to increase and discipline his army. Occupation and the stimulus of action alone could do this.

The people of the country demanded that New York should be held to the last possible moment.

Jay's proposition to burn and abandon it without a show of resistance was not the way to make the army strong for future endeavor. Its immediate abandonment would have involved the demoralization of the entire army, and would have been in marked contrast with his efforts to restore Boston to herself. The resistance so widened the breach between the parties at issue and made the necessity more pressing for the development of resources equal to the increased gravity of the struggle. General Howe checked his troops, as they acted under the impulse of success, and were ready to assault the American works. In this much criticised delay he was right. A repulse would have been ruin. Washington crossed the river with three regiments after the battle began, so that he could have met an assault with nearly as many men as could have been brought to the attack and thoroughly handled : but with characteristic resting after

an exertion, and habitual under-estimate of the sagacity and wakeful-
ness of his adversary, Howe failed to improve his suceess. His
enemy escaped ; other battle-fields were to illustrate the capacity
and military genius of the opposing General in chief, and other
neglects to improve success were to wrest from his, General Howe's,
hands, every substantial benefit which so often fell within their
grasp.

CHAPTER XXXII.

RETREAT FROM LONG ISLAND.

THE British army sat down before Brooklyn, opened lines of approach, erected adequate works to resist any sortie from the garrison, and awaited the operations of the pick and shovel.

Within the American lines, a critical examination of every defensive appliance or position was made by Washington in person. He had organized a strong detachment for the relief of Stirling at the time that officer made his earnest effort to gain the position occupied by Cornwallis at the Cortelyou house; but the swift movement of the British grenadiers across the face of the intrenchments, within full view of the garrison, rendered any reinforcement to Stirling simply impossible.

The night was spent by the men in strengthening the defenses, and in readiness to resist any attack. The officers and men who had disappeared during the day were among the best of the army. Of the general officers that remained, the Commander-in-chief alone inspired confidence. He spent the night in visiting the guard, and at early dawn of the twenty-eighth, he was again in the trenches, personally attentive to all details, and cheering the men by strong and hopeful words. General Mifflin arrived before noon with the well drilled regiments of Glover, Massachusetts, and of Shee and Magaw, Pennsylvania. The enthusiasm which greeted their arrival was an involuntary tribute of respect for those well equipped troops, who had been sneered at as fair weather soldiers, so " proud of fine arms and fine feathers." The garrison was now fully nine thousand strong. Rain began to fall heavily. " A northeaster " set in, and the afternoon was one of extreme discomfort and trial. The trenches through the low ground, filled with water, cooking was impossible, the troops were without tents or other shelter, the supply of blankets was inadequate for half the command, and the ammunition itself was greatly

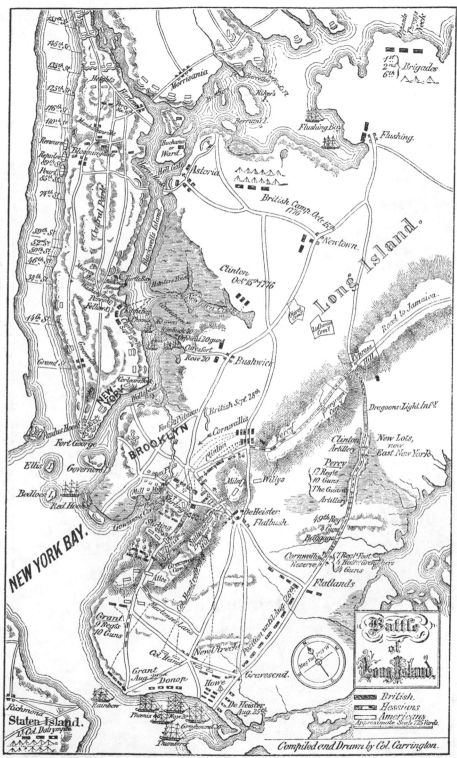

Battle of Long Island

AUGUST 27, 1776

American Commanders

SULLIVAN   **PUTNAM**   STIRLING

Strength, 9,380   Casualties, 997

NOTES.—Americans entrench on Brooklyn Heights, from Wallabout Bay to Gowanus Bay. *Righ wing*, under Stirling, is advanced along the harbor road, on shortest line of British approach. The *centre*, under Sullivan, is at Prospect Hill (now Prospect Park), to oppose British advance *via* Flatbush. The *left*, toward Jamaica, is unprotected and only negligently patrolled.

British Commanders

CORNWALLIS   **HOWE,**   CLINTON

DONOP   DeHEISTER   PERCY

Strength, 20,500   Casualties, 400

NOTES.—British, in force under Grant, press Stirling back, after a sharp action, near present Greenwood Cemetery. De Heister threatens Sullivan from Flatbush. The main army, under Howe, Clinton, Cornwallis and Percy, turns the unprotected American left flank, takes Sullivan and Stirling in the rear, and captures both. British entrench ; neglect to assault the works, and the American army retreats to New York, Aug. 29, without loss, under cover of night and a dense fog.

MEM.—*The examination of British and American Archives clearly shows the fact that the American loss in prisoners has been greatly over-estimated. The American force at Brooklyn has been under-estimated ; but these disparities are accounted for by careful study of the "Official Returns." The statement that many of Stirling's division were drowned in Gowanus Bay, is confronted by these Returns.*

References:

CARRINGTON'S "BATTLES OF THE AMERICAN REVOLUTION," pp. 198-213

School Histories :

Anderson, ¶ 33-4 ; p. 75.
Barnes, ¶ 3 ; p. 114.
Berard (Bush), ¶ 60-62 ; p. 151-2.
Goodrich, C. A. (Seaveys), ¶ 4; .p.120.
Goodrich, S. G., ¶ 3-6 ; pp. 211-212.
Hassard, ¶ 5-8; p. 176-7.

Holmes, ¶ 20 ; p. 119.
Lossing, ¶ 14 ; p. 135.·
Quackenbos,¶ 311-16; p. 224-27.
Ridpath, ¶ 7-12 ; pp. 188-90.
Sadlier (Excel),¶ 2; p.184
Stephens, A. H., ¶ 4-7 ; p. 192.

Swinton, ¶ 112-14 ; p. 128.
Scott, ¶ 8-9 ; p. 170-1.
Thalheimer (Eclectic), ¶ 239-4 p. 134-5.
Venable, ¶ 134 ; p. 101.

injured for want of proper protection. General Washington took neither rest nor sleep, but spent his entire time, by night and day, as actively on duty as if he were the sole picket upon whom the safety of all depended. Such little skirmishing fire as was practicable was encouraged, so that the British troops were kept under the impression that it was useless to risk small detachments outside of their own guard lines. This was compensated by their overrunning adjacent parts of the island. General Woodhull with more than two hundred militia were captured during the day, near Jamaica, by Delancy's provincial loyalists, who had crossed over from Staten Island, and took lively interest in all operations in small villages which were occupied by " revolutionists."

The rain was so incessant, and accompanied by a wind so violent, that the British troops kept within their tents, and their works made slow progress toward completion. During the entire night of the twenty-eighth, as during the previous night, Washington and his aids, made the entire sentry rounds with periodic exactness, attending to matters requiring notice, and imparting to the guard the confidence which such attentions alone could secure. The twenty-ninth was another day of clouds and storms. The British, however, improved every cessation of heavy rain, to prosecute work upon their trenches, which had been started at a distance of six hundred yards from Fort Putnam, the present Washington Park. If they had worked during the hours when the American troops stood in water unprotected, silently waiting upon the movements of the investing army, they could have opened fire by the evening of that day. More than once in subsequent campaigns, General Howe suspended movements at critical times because of rain, when his adversary, less comfortably provided for and protected, treated the rain as no obstacle in the way of impending possible duty.

It is just here, as one instance, that the voluminous discussions as to lines of policy and action have beclouded the narrative of the war for American independence ; and the opinions of councils of war, of general officers, of committees of public safety and of Congress, have been confused and made to declare irreconcilable inconsistencies, as if the retreat from Long Island and New York had no intrinsic necessity, but was the accident of majority opinions. The American and British archives and biography are full of contemporaneous letters and humble data, which it would require volumes to quote, but which have but one possible conclusion,—that Washington of his own judgment, and acting upon the same philosophy which made the defense of Brooklyn necessary in the first instance, resolved to evacuate the Heights in due time without a decisive battle.

Washington's policy was to postpone all issues which had a determining character, and were beyond mastery by his army, to wear out the offensive by avoiding its strokes, and thereby to gain the vantage ground for turning upon it, when thus worn out or over-confident, and off its guard. The necessities of the American cause called for *Grand Strategy*, and improved *Logistics* rather than *Grand Tactics*, because his army was unequal to the latter, and largely dependent for its success upon the wisdom with which its undoubted courage could be made available in the interest of the new nation. The retreat from Brooklyn was characteristic of this policy. The men were kept up to duty as if any hour would command their utmost energies in self-defense; but he had his own plan to develop, and this he did not submit to his aids or his officers, until it was matured and nearly ripe for execution. How well he kept his own counsel will be seen by his action.

The following order was sent to General Heath, then commanding officer at Kings' Bridge, through General Mifflin, very early on the morning of the twenty-ninth of August.

LONG ISLAND, AUGUST 29TH, 1770.

"DEAR GENERAL—We have many battalions from New Jersey which are coming over this evening to relieve others here. You will please therefore to order every flat bottomed boat and other craft at your post, fit for transporting troops, down to New York as soon as possible. They must be manned by some of Colonel Hutchinson's men and sent without the least delay. I write by the order of the General.

I am affectionately Yours,

"TO MAJ. GEN'L HEATH."   MIFFLIN."

Commissary-general Trumbull also bore an order to Assistant Quarter-master Hughes, by which he was instructed "to impress every kind of craft, on either side of New York, that could be kept afloat, and had either oars or sails, or could be furnished with them, and to have them all in the East river by dark."

After these officers had started upon their missions, Washington continued his watchfulness and visitations to all parts of the camp, summoning a council of officers, however, to an early evening interview. He submitted his plan to that council, and with this result: "At a council of war held at Long Island, August 29th, 1776, Present: His Excellency General *Washington ;* Major Generals *Putnam,*

Spencer, Brigadier Generals *Mifflin*, *McDougall*, *Parsons*, *Scott*, *Wadsworth*, *Fellows*.

It was submitted to the consideration of the council, whether, under all circumstances, it is not eligible to leave *Long Island*, and its dependencies and remove to *New York*. Unanimously agreed in the affirmative. General Putnam, Saml. H. Parsons, Thos. Spencer, Jno. Morin Scott, Thos. Mifflin, James Wadsworth, Alex. McDougall."

Eight reasons were also assigned for this action.

The date of the council shows that its action was not the origin of the retreat. General Heath acted with such promptness, that although more than fourteen miles from Brooklyn when he received the order for transportation, he properly conceived its import, and so faithfully executed it, as did Quarter-master Hughes also, that the boats reached the foot of Brooklyn Heights just at dark that afternoon.

At about eight o'clock the regiments were put under arms, as if to make a sally upon the British lines. General McDougall was stationed at the shore to regulate the embarkation. Colonel Glover's regiment, which had been recruited at Marblehead and other sea-coast towns of Massachusetts, was very appropriately distributed in the boats to act as seamen, and General Mifflin with the three regiments which he had brought over on the previous day, and those of Hand and Smallwood, were designated as the new guard and garrison of the intrenchments and redoubts. As the latter occupied the works the old guard passed directly to the heights, and the regiments last recruited, and least drilled, took the lead in crossing the river.

From about nine o'clock until nearly midnight, through wind and rain,—company by company,—sometimes grasping hands to keep companionship in the dense gloom,—speechless and silent, so that no sound should alarm the enemy,—feeling their way down the steep steps then leading to Fulton ferry, and feeling their way as they were passed into the waiting water-craft, these drenched and weary men took passage for New York. The wind and tide were so violent that even the seamen soldiers of Massachusetts could not spread a close reefed sail upon a single vessel; and the larger vessels, upon which so much depended, would have been swept to the ocean if once entrusted to the current. For three hours, all the boats that could be thus propelled, had to depend upon muffled oars. The difficulties of such a trip, on such a night, can be realized better by a moment's reflection. There is no record of the size of the waves, or of narrow

escapes from upset, no intimation that there was competition in entering
the boats and rivalry in choice of place—that each boat-load was
landed hastily and that the boats themselves were leaky and unsafe ;
but any person who proposes to himself an imaginary transit over
the East river under their circumstances, can supply the data he may
need to appreciate the process.

General McDougall himself doubted whether nine thousand men
could be thus transferred before morning and advised its postponement until another night, but there was to be no cessation of the task
until its proper work was done.

It was about midnight, just as the tide turned, that the north-east
wind which had steadily prevailed for more than three days, and had
kept the British fleet in the lower bay, spent its strength,—the water
became smooth, the sky was clear, and the boats " loaded to the
water's edge," and guided safely, began to make productive trips. A
south-west wind sprang up by one o'clock. Everything that could
carry sail now took its part in the movement, and with more than
four-fold celerity, the transfer of troops continued. It was in the
midst of this prosperous undertaking that there occurred one of those
unexpected incidents which for a time threatened the rear of the
army with destruction. Washington sent Colonel Scammel to General
Mifflin to hasten all the troops forward. The covering party was put
in motion, but returned promptly to their places; and the error was
not discovered by the British sentries. Reference was made to this
affair under the subject of " Retreats." Irving states that Washington calmly replied to Mifflin, who cited orders, " It is a dreadful mistake. Unless the troops can regain the lines before their absence is
discovered by the enemy, the most disastrous consequences are to be
apprehended." One soldier wrote, " when the order came, it was so
much sooner than we expected, that a rumor went through the battalion that the British Dragoons were at our heels, and some of the
men halted, kneeled down, and prepared to resist a charge." A heavy
sea-fog, driven in from the Atlantic, hung above Long Island and the
lower bay, while the peninsula of New York was uncovered. This
increased the danger of panic, but also prevented discovery of the
misadventure.

The military stores and all guns which were not too heavy to be
hauled through the mud, were safely placed on the transports, and
with the last boat-load, Mifflin, and last of all, Washington, took
passage.

On the day following the troops and stores were also removed from Governor's Island in safety, and the evacuation was complete.

"Whoever will attend to all the details of this retreat," says Botta, "will easily believe that no military operation was ever conducted by great captains with more ability and prudence, or under more favorable auspices."

General Howe states in his official report, that on the twenty-ninth, at night, the rebels evacuated their intrenchments and Red Hook, with the utmost silence. At daybreak of the thirtieth their flight was discovered, the pickets of the line took possession, and those most advanced reached the shore opposite to New York as their rear guard was going over, and fired some shot among them."

Prompt action as soon as General Howe had notice of the retreat, would have secured the capture of Washington himself. Stedman, after stating that General Howe was advised very early that the retreat was in progress, and delayed for some time before giving the order to Lord Percy to advance upon the works, thus wonderfully philosophizes upon the event: "In reviewing the actions of men, the historian is often at a loss to conjecture the secret causes which gave them birth. It cannot be denied that the American army lay almost entirely at the will of the English. That they were therefore suffered to retire in safety has by some been attributed to the reluctance of the commander-in-chief to shed the blood of a people so nearly allied to that source from whence he derived all his authority and power. We are rather inclined to adopt this idea and to suppose motives of mistaken policy, than to leave ground for an imagination that the escape of the Americans resulted from any want of exertion on the part of Sir William Howe, or deficiency in the military science.

In the range of "historical and military criticism" which the author has adopted, it is his purpose to furnish a correct record, and leave the facts to the interpretation which the principles stated will evolve. It is however but justice to General Howe's military knowledge to state, that the element of character heretofore unfolded, was the cause of his failure at Brooklyn. He was wanting *in details*, sluggish when *instant* action was vital, and could not *improve success*. The strategical features of his operations on Long Island were admirable; and the American army was saved, through equally admirable Logistics.

CHAPTER XXXIII.

THE AMERICAN ARMY RETIRES FROM NEW YORK.

THE retreat of Washington from Long Island saved his army. When the " forty-eight sleepless hours," during which he had been constantly in the saddle, or equally active on foot, had passed away, that army was indeed in New York, but under circumstances of hardly less peril than before.

"The militia," said Washington, " are dismayed, intractable, and impatient to return home. Great numbers have gone off, in some instances, almost by whole regiments, by half ones, and by companies at a time," and adds, " when their example has infected another part of the army, when their want of discipline and refusal of almost every kind of restraint and government, have produced a like conduct, but too common to the whole, and an entire disregard of that order and subordination so necessary to the well doing of an army, and which had been inculcated before as well as the nature of our military establishment would admit of, our condition is still more alarming, and with the deepest concern I am obliged to confess my want of confidence with the generality of the troops."

He made an urgent appeal to Congress to establish a regular army, or to enlist men for the war, and laid before them the difficulties of the situation, and the impending necessity of retiring from New York itself. He put the plain question, whether, in that event, the town should be left standing for British winter-quarters.

" The number of men present fit for duty, on the second day of September, was under twenty thousand." An order was issued on the same day, " for a new arrangement of the troops, in order that they might act with union and firmness." Three grand divisions were organized.

General Putnam's division, consisting of the brigades of Generals Parsons, Scott, Clinton, Fellows and Silliman, was assigned to duty in the city and its vicinity.

The center division, under General Spencer during Generâl Greene's illness, was ordered to be in readiness to march immediately to Harlem, to prevent the enemy's landing on the island. It consisted of the brigades of Nixon, Heard, McDougall, Wadsworth, Douglas, and Chester.

General Heath, with the brigades of General Mifflin and General George Clinton, were ordered to Kings Bridge and its vicinity. Colonel Haslet's regiment was assigned to Mifflin's brigade.

September third, Congress resolved that "two of the North Carolina battalions be ordered to march with all expedition under General Moore, to reinforce the army at New York, that one continental battalion be ordered from Rhode Island to New York, and that the States north of Virginia be recommended to send all the aid in their power."

On the same day, Putnam, writing from Bloomingdale, declares, "there are so many places where the enemy can land in superior force, that he advises the fortification of Mount Washington, Harlem Heights, and the Jersey shore, and to take all measures requisite to defend the passage of the North river." He adds, "I know that this doctrine gives up York to destruction, but what are ten or twenty towns to the grand object. If Howe gets to Albany, our northwestern army must quit Ticonderoga or fall a sacrifice. Burgoyne need never come from Canada."

September fourth, General Washington reprimanded such "diabolical practices as robbing orchards, gardens, and straggling without arms or purpose, and advises that the roll be called three times a day, to keep the men to duty."

September fifth, General Greene urged a general and speedy retreat from New York, and that a council be convened to take action upon that question.

September eighth, Washington reported the militia of Connecticut then with him, "as reduced from six to two thousand men, and in a few days their number was but nominal, twenty or thirty to some regiments," so that "they were discharged with a recommendation to Governor Trumbull that it was about time to begin dealing with deserters." On the same day he reported to Congress that a council which he had convened on the sixth was opposed to retiring from New York, although they acknowledged that it "would not be tenable if attacked with artillery," and adds significantly, that "some to whom the opinion of Congress was known, were not a little influenced in their opinions, as they were led to suspect that Congress wished it to be retained at all hazards."

Washington realized daily that it was useless labor and expense to line the rivers of New York with field-works, which would require a garrison of thousands, so long as the rivers themselves were under the control of a large naval force and a veteran army.

That army had already extended its right wing as far as Flushing and Hell Gate, with posts at Bushwick, Newtown, and Astoria. Montressor and Buchanan islands, now Ward's and Randall's, had been abandoned by the Americans and occupied by the British. Several frigates had passed between Governor's Island and the peninsula known as Red Hook, and smaller vessels took position at the head of Wallabout Bay, and Newtown inlet, where they found depth of water, and immunity from the fire of the American guns.

The entire East river front of New York island was thus exposed to incursions which could be made more quickly than troops could be concentrated for resistance. Appeals to the northern States were indeed favorably entertained, and Massachusetts made a draft of one-fifth of her able-bodied male population, certain exposed localities and certain classes of persons alone excepted ; and on the fourteenth, Congress authorized a total of eighty-five regiments to be enlisted for a term of five years. These were apportioned to the respective States. All this was of little immediate value to the army. Application had been made to Washington for troops to garrison Fort Montgomery, on the Hudson river, but none could be spared ; and the elaborate works erected at King's Bridge, and thence southward to Harlem Plains, were of no practical value to the army which occupied the lower part of the island.

In Washington's letter of the eighth of September the following words occurred : " Men of discernment will see that by such works and preparations we have delayed the operations of the campaign till it is too late to effect any capital incursions into the country. It is now obvious that they, (the British army) mean to enclose us on the island of New York, by taking post in my rear, while the shipping secures the front, and thus oblige us to fight them on their own terms, or surrender at discretion." " Every measure is to be formed with some apprehension that all our troops will not do their duty. On our side, the war should be defensive : it has even been called a war of posts ; we should on all occasions avoid a general action, and never be drawn into a necessity to put anything to risk. Persuaded that it would be presumptuous to draw out our young troops into open ground against their superiors in numbers and discipline, I have never spared the spade and pickaxe, but I have not found that readiness to defend, even strong posts, at all hazards, which is necessary to derive the greatest benefit from them. I am sensible that a retreating army is encircled with difficulties ; that declining an engagement subjects a general to reproach : but when the fate of America may be at stake on the issue, we should protract the war, if possible. That the enemy mean to winter in New York, there can be no doubt ; that they can drive us out, is equally clear : nothing seems to remain, but to determine the time of their taking possession."

The following is the journal entry upon receipt of the letter referred to :

"TUESDAY, *September* 10, 1776.

A letter of the eighth from General Washington, with sundry papers inclosed, was read : whereupon,

Resolved, That the president inform General Washington, it was by no means the sense of Congress, in their resolve of the 3d instant, respecting New York, that the army or any part of it should remain in that city a moment longer than he shall think it proper for the public service that troops be continued there."

The resolution referred to embraced this clause : "That General Washington be acquainted that Congress would have special care taken, in case he should find it necessary to quit New York, that no damage be done to the said city by his troops, on their leaving it : the Congress having no doubt of being able to recover the same, though the enemy should for a time have possession of it."

During the two weeks which succeeded the retreat from Brooklyn, the army was rapidly fading away, while raw recruits were gathering to supply the vacant files, as during the first week of the year, before Boston. The comparative inactivity of the British troops was made the occasion of new propositions for settlement of the difficulty between the two countries. General Sullivan was sent to Congress as bearer of Lord Howe's message. John Adams, Edward Eldridge and Dr. Franklin were elected as a committee to meet Lord Howe and state the position which the United States assumed. Franklin urged, that a recognition of American Independence, to be followed by a treaty of alliance and friendship, would be for the best interests of both nations. Lord Howe, thoroughly anxious to secure an honorable end to the conflict, was so limited by his instructions that submission was the indispensable element to success in his mission. The interview only re-asserted the impossibility of compromise.

By the tenth of September, Washington began the removal of valuable stores, preparatory to ultimate retreat from the city. On the eleventh Generals Greene, Nixon, Mifflin, Beall, Parsons, Wadsworth and Scott united in a request for a new council, for the purpose of re-considering their former action. On the twelfth, the council met. The vote is thus recorded. To reconsider: *Generals Beall, Scott, Fellows, Wadsworth, Nixon, McDougall, Parsons, Mifflin, Greene* and *Putnam.*

To adhere: Generals *Spencer, Clinton, Heath.* The council also decided that eight thousand men should be left for the defense of Mount Washington and its dependencies. A brief examination of the " Returns of the army " " in the service of the United States of America, in and near the city of New York," at that time, will have value in this connection. The weakest and strongest regiments of several brigades are selected as types of the general condition of the army, and the figures indicate the rank and file only.

In Parsons' brigade, the regiments of Huntington and Tyler are placed side by side, *Huntington's* regiment, Total 348. Sick 169. *Tyler's* regiment. Total, 567. Sick, 147. The former regiment had seen service: the latter was new. In Silliman's brigade. *Hinman's* regiment. Total 237. Sick, 179. *Thompson's* regiment. Total 416. Sick 243.

In Mifflin's brigade, composed of the regiments of *Hand, Shee, Magaw, Atlee, Miles, Ward, Hutchinson,* and *Haslet :* already familiarly known. Atlee's regiment. Total 243. Sick 60. Shee's regiment. Total 499. Sick 142.

In McDougall's brigade. McDougall's regiment. Total, 428. Sick, 108. Smallwood's, Total 584. Sick 161.

The columns, headed " wanted to complete," and " alterations since last return " have been used elsewhere, as the basis for estimate of the loss incurred in the skirmishes on Long Island.

The foregoing statement is impartial and indicates the condition of the army which was preparing to leave New York.

The Council had decided to retreat, just when the strong arm of force was ready to drive them out.

There was hardly time to do the work with decorum, to say little of military order.

On the thirteenth of September several frigates entered East river and commanded the works near the foot of Thirteenth street, and the whole army was engaged in removing stores and heavy artillery. General Putnam was detailed with a command of four thousand men to cover the retreat, while the remaining divisions moved to King's Bridge and Mount Washington.

On Saturday the fourteenth of September, while at his head-quarters at the house of Robert Murray, Washington noticed that " about sunset six more vessels, one or two of them men-of-war, passed up the East river to the station occupied by others on the previous day." " In a half an hour " he " received two expresses, one from Colonel Sargent at Horn's Hook (Hell Gate), giving an account, that the enemy, to the amount of three or four thousand, had marched to the river and were embarking for Montressor's Island, where numbers of them were then encamped "—the other, from General Mifflin " that uncommon and formidable movements were discovered among the enemy." " These having been confirmed by the scouts sent out by himself," Washington " proceeded to Harlem, where it was supposed, or at Morrisania opposite to it, the principal attempt to land would be made." His head-quarters were then transferred to the house of Roger Morris very nearly at the centre of the theatre of operations.

The night passed without an attempt at landing. Early the next morning three ships of war passed up the Hudson and took a position near Bloomingdale, thus " putting a total stop to the removal, by water, of any more provisions " and other stores. About eleven o'clock the ships in the East river began a heavy cannonading.

The British divisions which had been designated as the force which was to land, under cover of this squadron, had already embarked upon flat-boats, barges, and galleys, at the head of Newtown inlet, and were carried with a favoring tide directly to Kipp's Bay, where they disembarked.

The light infantry, British reserve, Hessian chasseurs, and grenadiers, constituted the first division under the command of General Clinton, having with him Generals Cornwallis, Vaughan, and Leslie, and Colonel Donop.

" At the first sound of the firing," writes Washington, " I rode with all possible dispatch towards the place of landing, when to my surprise and mortification, I found the troops that had been posted in the lines, retreating with the utmost precipitation; and those ordered to support them, Parsons and Fellows' brigades, flying in every

15

direction and in the utmost confusion, notwithstanding the efforts of their generals to form them. I used every means in my power to rally and get them in order, but my attempts were fruitless and ineffectual, and on the appearance of a small party of the enemy, not more than sixty or seventy in number, their disorder increased, and they ran away without firing a shot."

The indignation of Washington at this "disgraceful and dastardly conduct," carried him directly among the fugitives nearest the enemy, and exposed him to death or capture. More than once afterwards, a similar daring rallied fugitives, but the panic on this occasion was wild, unreasoning, and impossible of control. Its story has been draped with high colored fiction, until a credulous man's faith in one half of the camp rumors which stole into history, would convict the American commander of lunacy. That with drawn sword, impetuous command, and fearless exposure of his person, Washington did his best to retrieve the disaster, is undoubtedly true, so that he seemed, in the strong figure of General Greene, to seek death rather than life. All beyond this, so thoroughly examined by Mr. Bancroft, is foolish tradition or contemporaneous camp gossip. A court of inquiry which reported October twenty-sixth, failed to fix responsibility for the panic. It appeared from the testimony, however, that General Parsons rallied a portion of the troops under Washington's own eye ; but that almost immediately they got hold of some field rumor and ran in every direction.

Finding all efforts to check the retreat to be fruitless, Washington hastened back to Harlem Heights, put the army in condition to meet the enemy, sent out reconnoitering parties in all directions, and devoted himself to restoration of order and the exigencies of the hour. While confident that his new position was almost impregnable, a single paragraph in his report to Congress, which in his haste was unsigned and forwarded by his secretary, will indicate his greatest apprehension for the future. " We are now encamped with the main body of the army upon the heights of Harlem, where I should hope the enemy would meet with a retreat in case of an attack, if the generality of our troops would behave with tolerable bravery ; but experience, to my great affliction, has convinced me that this is a matter to be wished, rather than expected."

The disaster was the more humiliating, since the roster of the army shows that Parsons' brigade was composed of the regiments of Huntington, Prescott, Ward, Wyllis, Durkee, and Tyler, some of

which had behaved well under previous fire, and their returns showed
"present" at the previous muster, "fit for duty, or on command, an
aggregate of one thousand nine hundred and thirty-six, exclusive of
officers commissioned and non-commissioned and musicians." It is
another illustration of the strange pivot events that occur in all military enterprises.

General Putnam's command was greatly endangered by this misconduct. Colonel Donop's Hessians moved directly for the city, but
by the timely occupation of the road nearest the Hudson river, Putnam extricated his division without substantial loss.

The heavy cannon and a large quantity of provisions, camp kettles,
tents, and other essentials to the comfort of the army, were sacrificed
by the energetic action of Clinton, who almost invariably realized the
best fruits of success.

The British army at once marched to the heights of Inclenburg, or
Murray's Hill, and a subsequent debarkation of troops was advanced
so far northward as to make a chain of posts across the island from
Bloomingdale to Horn's Hook, near Hell Gate. General Howe established his own head-quarters at the Beekman mansion, not far from
those just vacated by General Washington on Murray Hill.*

Before four o'clock in the afternoon, the American flag disappeared
from Fort George, and New York was in the hands of the British
army.

* At the Murray house, Captain Nathan Hale, of Knowlton's Connecticut Rangers,
received his instructions from Washington to visit Long Island and obtain accurate knowledge of the movements of the British army. At the Beekman house on the twenty-second
day of September he was executed as a spy.

Lossing adds, " Hale was hanged upon an apple tree in Rutger's orchard near the present intersection of East Broadway and Market Streets."

CHAPTER XXXIV.

HARLEM HEIGHTS AND VICINITY, 1776.

THE American army spent its first night on Harlem Heights. A period of fifteen hours of labor was followed by many hours' exposure under rain, without tents, with limited rations, no utensils for cooking, and the consciousness that many comforts had been sacrificed by a needless panic.

On the following day a spirited skirmish revived their spirits, and evinced the value of courage and promptness in action.

The official accounts of this affair which were made up by the two generals-in-chief, while the facts were fresh in mind, are combined so as to indicate their respective appreciation of the real issue. They confirm the opinion that reports of officers, as to facts not within their personal knowledge, are second rate testimony ; that very humble data are often very material to the appreciation of an issue ; that the principal features of an engagement are necessarily the objectives of an official report, and that these may lack accuracy through the misdirection which a single error of fact may impart.

General Howe says, " On the 16th in the morning, a large party of the enemy having passed **under cover of the** woods, near to the advanced posts of the army, the Second and Third battalions of light infantry, supported by the **Forty-second infantry**, pushed forward and drove them back to their intrenchments, from whence the enemy, observing they were not in force, attacked them with near three thousand men, which occasioned the march of the reserve with two field pieces, a battalion of Hessian grenadiers, and the company of chasseurs and field pieces, repulsed the enemy with considerable loss, and obliged them to retire within their works. From the accounts of deserters it is agreed that they had not less than three hundred killed and wounded, and among them a colonel and major killed. We had

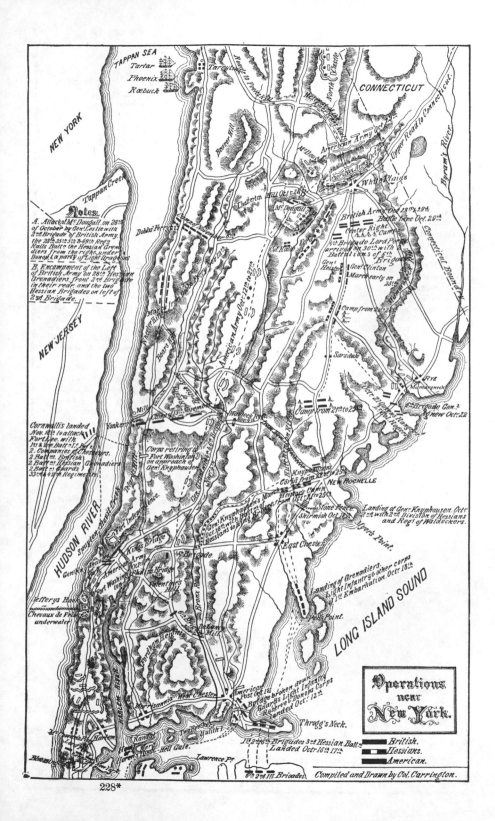

TAPPAN SEA
Tartar
Phoenix
Roebuck

Road to Peekskill

CONNECTICUT

NEW YORK

Tappan Creek

Tarrytown

Bemer Hill

North Castle

American Army Oct 29

American Army Oct 18

Upper Road to Connecticut

American Army Oct 21

White Plains

Chatterton Hill Oct 28

Mc Dougall

British Army Oct 18th & 24th

Battle Line Oct 29th

Center Right Camp

4th Brigade Lord Percy arrived on 30th with Battalions of 6th Brigade

Dobbs Ferry

Col. Rolle

Genl Heister
Genl Clinton
March early on 28th

Camp from Oct 24th

NEW JERSEY

Bear Hill

American Army Oct 21 to 27

Sarsdale

Notes

A. Attack of McDougall on 28th
of October by Genl Leslie with
2nd Brigade of British Army,
the 28th 35th 5th & 49th Regts
Ralls Batts the Hessian Grenadiers from the right, under
Donop & a party of Light Dragoons

B. Encampment of the Left
of British Army on 28th Hessian
Grenadiers front 2nd Brigade
in their rear, and the two
Hessian Brigades on left of
2nd Brigade.

RYE
Mamaroneck

Camp from 21st to 25th

6th Brigade Genl Rogers
knew Oct 22

Dear Brigade Lord Rogers

Camp Nov 13th November

Wadleck Corner Nov 5th

Corps retiring to
Fort Washington
on approach of
Genl Knyphausen

Knyphausens
Corps from Oct 21 to 25th

NEW ROCHELLE

Genl Knyphausens March Oct 21st to 25th

Cornwalls landed
Nov. 18th to attack
Fort Lee with
1st & 2nd Batts
2. Companies of Chesters.
2. Batts British
2. Batt. Hessian Grenadiers
2. Batt of Guards
33d & 42d Regiments

Yonkers

Fort Independence

HUDSON RIVER

Spuyten Duyvil

Kings Bridge

Genl Knyphausens
Oct 28th with Batts of the
Hessians to King

Stone House
Skirmish Oct 18

Landing of Genr Knyphausen Oct
22 with 2nd Division of Hessians
and Regt of Waldeckers.

Myers Point.

Genl Knox

American
Fort Washington
Phillips Bridge

4th Brigade

East Chester

Landing of Grenadiers,
Light Infantry & other corps
1st Infantry on Oct 18th
& 1st Embarkation Oct 18th

Valentines Hill

Jefferys Hook

Chevaux de Frise
underwater

Brom River

Jones Mill

Potts Point.

LONG ISLAND SOUND

Westchester

American
Post Oct 12
Bridge broken down
Guards Light Infantry
Reserve & Donops Corps
landed Oct. 12th

Hell Gate

Lawrence Pt.

Throgg's Neck.

1st 2nd & 4th Brigades 3rd Hessian Batts
Landed Oct 16th 17th

8th & 2nd Brigades

**Operations
near
New York.**

▬▬▬ **British.**
▬▬▬ **Hessians.**
▬▬▬ **American.**

Compiled and Drawn by Col. Carrington.

228*

Operations near New York

Harlem Heights. White Plains.

NOTES.

NOTE I.—Clinton lands at Kipp's Bay, September 15th, under cover of ships of war, indicated on map, and disperses the brigades of Parsons and Fellows, which Washington attempts, in vain, to rally. Three ships of war ascend the Hudson to Bloomingdale, to cut off retreat from New York. (Map 1.)

NOTE II.—Howe sends troops to Buchanan Island (now Ward's), and Montressor Island (now Randall's); also, beyond Flushing, to control outlet to Long Island Sound.

NOTE III.—Howe encounters Washington, near HARLEM HEIGHTS, Sept. 16th, greatly to the credit of the Americans.

NOTE IV.—The British army, at Staten Island, Aug. 27th, numbered 31,625 men. The American Army Return of Oct. 6th, gives a total, rank and file, of 25,735; absent, sick or on furlough, 8,075. Needed to complete regiments, 11,271. Knox's artillery numbered 580, and Backus' light horse 158. Some regiments made no returns.

NOTE V.—Washington retired from Harlem to the main land; left a garrison at Fort Washington; moved along the west side of the Bronx toward White Plains, to protect his supply depot, keep his communication with New England, and foil the plan of Howe to shut him up between the East River and the Hudson.

NOTE VI.—Howe leaves Percy at McGowan's Pass, lands at Throgg's Neck; finds the passage to the main land well guarded; reembarks; lands at Pell's Point; on the 16th and 17th, has a skirmish beyond East Chester, at a stone fence; passes New Rochelle on the 21st, and goes into camp.

NOTE VII.—On the 22d, Knyphausen, having arrived from Europe, lands at Meyer's Point; protects Howe's base, and moves toward Fort Washington on the 28th, on which date Howe gains a position at White Plains.

NOTE VIII.—Chatterton Hill, which commanded Howe's camp, as well as White Plains, and was occupied by McDougall and two guns of Capt. Alexander Hamilton, is stormed by Leslie and Rahl on the 29th. British casualties, 231. American casualties, 130.

NOTE IX.—Howe waits for reinforcements; loses one day, through a storm, and Washington retiring, attains a strong position on North Castle Heights. Howe, thus foiled, crosses to the Hudson River, at Dobbs Ferry, to operate against Fort Washington.

NOTE X.—The fight at Chatterton Hill is generally known as the "Battle of White Plains," at which place there was no actual collision between the armies.

References:

CARRINGTON'S "BATTLES OF THE AMERICAN REVOLUTION," pp. 228-234

CARRINGTON'S BATTLES; for other Details, pp. 214-242

School Histories:

Anderson, ¶ 35; p. 75.
Barnes, ¶ 1; p. 116.
Berard (Bush), ¶ 63; p. 153.
Goodrich, C. A. (Seaveys), ¶ 5; p.121.
Goodrich, S. G., ¶ 1; p 213.
Hassard, ¶ 9; p. 178.

Holmes, ¶ 21; p. 119.
Lossing, ¶ 18; p. 146.
Quackenbos, ¶ 319; p. 229.
Ridpath, ¶ 21; p. 197.
Sadlier (Excel), ¶ 4; p.187.
Stephens, A. H., ¶ 9; p. 193.

Swinton, ¶ 115; p. 128.
Scott, ¶ 12; p. 171.
Thalheimer (Eclectic), ¶ 254-6; p. 145-6.
Venable. ¶ 135; p. 102.

CARRINGTON'S "BATTLES OF THE AMERICAN REVOLUTION," (White Plains,) pp. 234-242.

eight officers wounded, fourteen men killed, and about seventy wounded."

Washington thus reports to Congress : " About the time of the post's departure with my letter of the 16th, the enemy appeared in several large bodies upon the plains about two and a half miles from hence. I rode down to our advanced post to put matters in a proper situation if they should attempt to come on. When I arrived I heard a firing, which I was informed was between a party of our rangers under the command of Lieutenant-colonel Knowlton, and an advance party of the enemy. Our men came in' and told me that the body of the enemy who kept themselves concealed, consisted of about three hundred men, as near as they could guess. I immediately ordered three companies of Colonel Weedon's Virginia regiment, under Major Leitch, and Colonel Knowlton with his rangers, to try and get in the rear, while a disposition was making as if to attack them in front, and thereby draw their attention that way. This took effect as I wished on the part of the enemy. On the appearance of our party in front, they immediately ran down hill, took possession of some fences and bushes, and a smart firing began, but at too great a distance to do much execution on either side."

" The parties under Colonel Knowlton and Major Leitch unluckily began their attack too soon, as it was rather in flank than in rear. In a short time Major Leitch was brought off wounded, having received three balls in his side, and in a short time Colonel Knowlton got a wound which proved mortal. The men continued the engagement with the greatest resolution. Finding that they wanted a support, I advanced part of Colonel Griffiths, and Colonel Richardson's Maryland regiments, who were nearest the scene of action. These troops charged. the enemy with great intrepidity, and drove them from the wood into the plain, and were pushing them from thence, having silenced their fire in a great measure, when I judged it prudent to order a retreat, fearing the enemy, as I have since found was really the case, were sending a large body to support their party. We had about forty wounded, the number of slain is very inconsiderable. By a sergeant, who deserted from the enemy and came in, I find that their party was greater than I imagined. It consisted of the Second battalion of light infantry, a battalion of the Royal Highlanders, the Forty-second regiment, and three companies of the Hessian riflemen under the command of Brigadier-general Leslie. The deserter reports that their loss in wounded and missing was eighty-nine, and eight

killed.   In the latter, his account is too small, as our people discovered
and buried double that number.   This affair, I am in hopes, will be
attended with many salutary consequences, as it seems to have greatly
inspirited the whole of our troops."

It appears that both generals were nearly correct as to the forces
ultimately brought into the field by the adversary.   General Howe's
attention was not called to the matter until the skirmish between
small picket detachments of the two armies had induced Washington
to advance with reinforcements, and this was taken to be an original
advance in force.   The English deserter, a sergeant, with professional
exactness, gave an accurate account of the condition of things as he
obtained it on the field; and the American deserters, terrified under
fire, as naturally over-estimated their danger, and the consequence of
the skirmish.   The fall of Knowlton and Leitch was known to them,
and after the loss of the two commanding officers they abandoned
their companies.   The sergeant's statement of the British casualties
was also substantially correct, and Washington's presence at the scene
of action enabled him to test it.   General Howe's ignorance of the
origin of the skirmish also lent color to the deserter's exaggeration
of American losses, and gave to the whole the character of a deliberate
assault upon his front, instead of the collision of advance guards supported by reinforcements as occasion required.   Another version
illustrates the difficulty of getting facts amid the excitements of a
campaign.

General Greene, in a letter to Governor Cooke bearing date the
seventeenth, states, that " on the previous day about a thousand of the
enemy attacked the advance post, and that by the spirited conduct
of General Putnam and Colonel Reed, Adjutant-general, our people
advanced upon the plain ground without cover, attacked them and
drove them back; that his excellency ordered a timely retreat, having
discovered or concluded, that the enemy would send a large reinforcement, as their main army lay so near by."

In connection with this letter there is a third history of the transaction, which indicates very strikingly that the American officers were
beginning to see the importance of having no more panics.   Adjutant-
general Reed wrote to his wife that " General Putnam, General Greene,
Mr. Tilghman and others were in it."   The excitement incident to actually chasing a party of British troops, had a very happy effect in restoring the confidence of the men.   Reed had his horse shot, and while
attempting to stop a runaway soldier, " the rascal presented his piece

and snapped it at him, at about a rod's distance." Seizing a musket from a soldier, the Adjutant-general snapped it, also, but it missed fire. He then "cut the coward over the head and hand with his sword, and the man was promptly tried and sentenced to death." He says, "I suppose many persons will think it was rash and imprudent for so many officers of our rank to go into such an action, but it was really to animate the troops who were quite dispirited and would not go into danger unless their officers led the way."

Colonel Knowlton was greatly mourned. His gallantry at Breed's Hill identified him with the first battle of the war, and he seems to have been as nearly fire proof and panic-proof as any man in the service.

For four weeks the American army maintained its position. While occasional skirmishing took place, the periodical home-sickness broke out again, with contagious virulence. Desertions, and the expirations of short enlistments, seemed to defy all attempts at thorough discipline. Orders were so frequently overruled or modified, that Washington was compelled to publish the following on the seventeenth of September: "The loss of the enemy yesterday would undoubtedly have been much greater if the orders of the Commander-in-chief had not in some instances been contradicted by inferior officers, who however well they may mean, ought not to presume to direct. It is therefore ordered that no officer commanding a party, and having received orders from the Commander-in chief, depart from them without counter orders from the same authority; and as many may otherwise err, through ignorance, the army is now acquainted that the general's orders are delivered by the Adjutant-general, or one of his aid-de-camps, Mr. Tilghman or Colonel Moylan, the Quarter-master General.

Brigade majors were required to report twice, daily, of the location and condition of their command; plundering and desertions were punished, the organizations of the medical staff, upon the basis of examination of candidates, was pushed forward, and the minutest details which conduced to the discipline, comfort or safety of the troops, entered into the routine of work which laid its own burden upon the Commander-in-chief.

The State of Massachusetts sent General Lincoln in command of her drafted men; General Greene, was placed in command across the Hudson river, in New Jersey, Generals Sullivan and Stirling were at once exchanged, and the armies were at comparative rest.

On the fifth of October the Army Return was made up by Adjutant-general Joseph Reed with the following exhibit ; Total of rank and file, twenty-five thousand seven hundred and thirty-five men, of whom eight thousand and seventy-five were sick or on furlough : wanting to complete the regiments eleven thousand two hundred and seventy-one. A foot-note states that "General Lincoln's Massachusetts Militia, computed at four thousand men, are so scattered and ignorant of the forms of returns, that none can be got." The fourteen brigades nominally comprised forty-four regiments. Major Backus' light horse numbered one hundred and fifty-eight, and Colonel Knox's artillery numbered five hundred and eighty rank and file, including sick and those on furlough.

On the eighth of October the army in New Jersey under General Moore, exhibited a total of six thousand five hundred and forty-eight officers and men, stationed at the Amboys, Woodbridge, Elizabethtown, Newark and Fort Constitution, afterward Fort Lee. On the ninth, the Phœnix and Roebuck safely passed the forts and went up to Dobbs Ferry and took possession of two vessels belonging to the Americans. On the tenth General Greene reported his " surgeons, as without the least particle of medicine," that " the regimental surgeons embezzle the public stores committed to their care so that the regimental sick suffer," and that " they should have the benefit of the general hospital."

On the eleventh, Adjutant-general Reed, in a letter to his wife, expressed his purpose to resign. He was disgusted with the predominating leveling spirit,—the equality between officers and men, and says, " Either no discipline can be established, or he who attempts it must become odious and detestable, a position which no one will choose. Yesterday morning a captain of horse who attends the General, from Connecticut, was seen shaving one of his men on the parade near the house. I have expressed myself of and to some people here, with such freedom, after the affair of the fifteenth, that I believe many of these wish me away. My idea is shortly this, that if France or some other power does not interfere, or some feuds arise among the enemy's troops, we shall not be able to stand them till spring."

Notwithstanding all that has been said and reiterated as to the looseness of discipline, the prime difficulty was not with the rank and file. In a report made to the Maryland Council of Safety, by Colonel Smallwood, he properly states what was still the chief bane of the army—" could our *officers* be brought to a proper sense of their duty and dignity, and the weight of the army, the enemy might be checked in their course; for this you may rely upon, however their parade may indicate the contrary, yet it is a fact, they are as much afraid and cautious of us, as we can be any of us of them. *Their officers alone give the superiority.* Our Commander-in-chief is an excellent man, and it would be happy for the United States if there was as much propriety in every department below him. It is not owing to any want of precaution in him that discipline is not exacted with more rigor. Much must depend, respecting this, on the superior officers next under him in command, and here there seems to be a total ignorance of and inattention to that system, so necessary to render an army formidable."

At this time General Howe himself notified Lord Germaine " that he no longer expected to finish the compaign until spring, that the provincials would not join the English army in any considerable numbers, that additional foreign troops should be hired, and that at least eight men of war should be sent from England by the February ensuing."

Such are a few of the incidents which attach to the four weeks of interrupted military action while the American army remained at Harlem Heights.

The location was admirable to resist an advance from New York itself. Three lines of intrenchments extended across the narrow neck of land, hardly half a mile wide, between the Hudson and Harlem rivers. These intrenchments were embraced within less than a mile, from near one hundred and forty-fifth street northward; and just within the upper line, was the house of Colonel Morris, occupied by Washington. Fort Washington was still a mile beyond. On the east side of the Harlem river, and as far as Frog's Neck, detached redoubts and earthworks, called alarm posts, were established, so that the whole front, from the Hudson to Long Island Sound was under guard.

October eleventh was designated by Washington for his personal inspection of the troops at their alarm posts. It was timely, and within twenty-four hours of the advance of the British army.

CHAPTER XXXV.

OPERATIONS NEAR NEW YORK, WHITE PLAINS, CHATTERTON HIIL.

ON the twelfth day of October, 1776, General Howe began the execution of his plan to cut off Washington's army from New England and upper New York, and fasten it to its own lines, for future capture. Unwilling to attempt the costly enterprise of storming the craggy and broken heights, where the whole country was defensive by small parties against superior force, and to force so many successive lines of earthworks and redoubts, he resolved to move from the coast of Long Island Sound, across to the Hudson river where his ships were lying, and also to occupy the entire rear of the American army by this movement. It was a repetition of the movements which gained Brooklyn Heights and New York City. It would also put him in water communication with New York and Staten Island.

The Guards, Light Infantry, Reserve, and Donop's Hessian corps, were embarked upon large vessels, and were transferred from the city to Frog's Neck, (once known as Throckmorton's, or Throck's Neck) on the same day, in safety. As soon as the landing had been effected, it was found that the tide swept behind the Neck and detached it from the main land, so that even at low tide it would be impossible to transfer the artillery without a bridge. Colonel Hand's American Rifles had already taken up the planks of the bridge which had been built to the Neck; and the causeway which led to the channel was covered by earthworks and the additional regiments of Colonel Graham and Colonel Prescott. Colonel Pepperill was also within supporting distance. One three pounder, under direction of Lieutenant Bryant, and a six pounder, in charge of Lieutenant Jackson, of the artillery, were trained upon the beach. General Howe placed the troops in camp, and awaited reinforcements.

Lord Percy had been left at McGowan's Pass, with three brigades to cover New York, and the troops at Flushing were ordered to cross at once. By reference to the map, " Operations near New York," the position of the army will be understood.

On the sixteenth and seventeenth, the Frst, Second, and Sixth brigades, and the Third Hessian battalion joined from Flushing, and on the eighteenth, the combined commands, including also the grenadiers, were transferred to Pell's Point, thereby turning the position at Westchester, and landing near the mouth of Hutchinson river. This entire country, rough and broken as it was, was also divided, wherever cultivated, by stone walls or fences, as in later times, so that when the army advanced toward New Rochelle, skirmishing became frequent. Colonel Glover with his regiment made so persistent a resistance with a force of seven hundred and fifty men behind one of these walls, as to check the advance guard until it was strongly reinforced, and earned for himself honorable mention in orders.

On the twenty-first, General Howe advanced his right and centre two miles beyond New Rochelle, where he remained in camp until the twenty-fifth, waiting for still additional reinforcements. General De Heister was left for the same length of time at the camping-ground which Howe had first occupied. During the same week, General Knyphausen arrived from Europe with the Second division of Hessians, the regiment of Waldeckers, one thousand strong, the Sixth foot, and the Third light dragoons.

These troops were promptly transferred from Staten Island, and landed at Myer's Point on the twenty-second, taking post near New Rochelle. This position secured the base of General Howe's further advance ; and, as will be seen by reference to the map, afforded the proper starting point for General Knyphausen's subsequent movement against Fort Washington.

As soon as General Knyphausen was established, General De Heister moved forward to overtake General Howe, and the army encamped within four miles of White Plains, their fixed objective. On the morning of the twenty-eighth, the army advanced within about a mile of the court-house and village. It had thus moved parallel with the river Bronx, over a distance of at least thirty miles of rough country, and was now ready to wheel to the left, cross to the Hudson, and cut off Washington's retreat, while at the same time excluding supplies for his army from Connecticut on the east. By this date the ships of war had pushed up the Hudson as far as Tarrytown, and from White Plains there was a good road across to that village.

It had been a difficult and embarrassing march from the first. The Bronx was narrow, but ran along a steep range of hills, thickly wooded, and as thickly set with undergrowth, thorn bushes, and briars. A brief rain storm easily made the stream impassable. There were no roads of even surface, and the American riflemen, now in their element, hung upon the left flank, and watched for opportunity to do mischief. A steady movement in column was impossible, and the officers had to depend entirely upon countrymen for information as to the character of the country and the location of the roads. Very much had been expected of the regiment of cavalry which had just arrived. They were at first a source of terror to new troops. Washington had instructed the men that in a country where stone fences, crags, and ravines were so numerous, the American riflemen needed no better opportunity to pick off the riders and supply the army with horses. A reward of one hundred dollars was offered any soldier who would bring in an armed trooper and his horse. The facts confirmed his judgment, and the cavalry were of very little service during that campaign. On the twenty-second, General Stirling sent Colonel Haslet out with a scouting party, which crossed the Bronx, attacked the Queen's Rangers, a royalist corps under Major Rogers, captured thirty-six, left as many on the field, and carried away sixty muskets. Colonel Hand's regiment also had a skirmish with the Hessian Yagers, near Mamaroneck, with considerable success and credit. Their entire march had been subject to such annoyances and interruptions.

While the British army thus advanced upon its mission, the American army had abandoned New York Island, leaving a small garrison at Fort Washington, still holding fast to King's Bridge. As soon as the British movement became general and well defined, and the main army reached the northern shore of Long Island Sound, Washington transferred his headquarters to Valentine's Hill, ordered all needed supplies to be forwarded to White Plains, and pushed his own army along the west bank of the Bronx, division by division, establishing earthworks at every prominent point, and making a chain of small posts throughout the whole distance. His object was to crowd the British army toward the coast, and use the shorter *interior* line, which was at his service, to thwart the plans of General Howe, and place himself in a position to fight his army on favorable ground of his own selection, and at advantage. Time was now an element of real value. Howe gained a fair start on the twelfth of the month, but lost five days at Frog's Neck, and four days more near

New Rochelle. Washington already had a depot of Connecticut supplies at White Plains, and prolonged his left toward that point with great vigor, as soon as he found that Howe would not attack from the east, as he had already declined to attack from the south.

On the twelfth, when first advised of the landing upon Frog's Neck, General Greene, then at Fort Lee, asked authority to cross with the brigades of Nixon, Clinton and Roberdeau, and take part in the coming issue. On the sixteenth Washington called a council of war. The record is given literally, to correct erroneous impressions as to the participants in proceedings which had important bearings upon future operations and responsibility therefor.

" PROCEEDINGS OF A COUNCIL OF GENERAL OFFICERS."

" At a council of war held at the head-quarters of General Lee, October 16th, 1776: Present, His Excellency, General Washington. Major Generals *Lee, Putnam, Heath, Spencer, Sullivan*, Brigadier Generals *Lord Stirling, Mifflin, McDougall, Parsons, Nixon, Wadsworth, Scott, Fellows, Clinton*, and *Lincoln*. Colonel *Knox*, commanding artillery."

" The General read sundry letters from the convention and particular members, of the turbulence of the disaffected in the upper part of the State : and also sundry accounts of deserters showing the enemy's intention to surround us."

"After much consideration and debate the following question was stated ; whether, (it having appeared that the obstructions in the North river have proved insufficient and that the enemy's whole force were in our rear, on Frog's Point) it is now deemed possible in our situation to prevent the enemy cutting off the communications with the country and compelling us to fight them at discretion."

" *Agreed ;* with but one dissenting voice (viz., General *Clinton*) that it is not possible to prevent the communication "being cut off ? " and that one of the consequences mentioned in the question must certainly follow."

" *Agreed ;* that Fort Washington be retained as long as possible."

Lee joined on the fourteenth, only two days before the council, and was assigned to the command of the grand division at Kingsbridge, with instructions to assume no direction in affairs, or active duty, until he should become acquainted with the existing arrangements and relations of that post.

Just before crossing the river to report for duty he wrote the following letter to General Gates:

FORT CONSTITUTION, *October* 14, 1776.

"MY DEAR GATES—I write this scroll in a hurry. Colonel Wood will describe the position of our army, which in my breast I do not approve. *Inter nos,* the Congress seem to stumble every step. I do not mean one or two cattle, but the whole stable. I have been very free in delivering my opinion to 'em. In my opinion General Washington is much to blame in not menacing 'em with resignation, unless they refrain from unhinging the army by their absurd interference.   *   *   *

The familiarity between these officers, it will be remembered, was entirely consistent with their intimacy before the war, and that both had been officers in the British army. This letter, however, in connection with subsequent correspondence, will have special value in determining the military subordination and *personal* discipline of the two men.

Several embarrassments attended the American movement at first. The conspiracy referred to, before the council, Tryon county and vicinity, was deemed of sufficient importance for a detail to watch the disaffected districts, but a more serious matter was the want of flour. Washington at once importuned Governor Trumbull of Connecticut, whose resources seemed as exhaustless as his patriotism and wisdom, to send a supply to White Plains, and it was sent.

On the twenty-second of October, while General Howe, for the second time, was "awaiting reinforcements," two miles above New Rochelle, General Heath's advance division made a night march, reached Chatterton Hill at daylight, and in the afternoon were engaged in strengthening the defenses at White Plains. General Sullivan's division arrived the next night, and General Lord Stirling immediately after. On the twenty-third Washington established his head-quarters at the same place. On the twenty-sixth Lee's Grand Division joined Washington, and the entire American army was awaiting General Howe's advance, behind rapidly augmenting breastworks, on eligible ground for defense.

Washington's position was not intrinsically the best for final defense; but he had selected an *ultimate* position, which fulfilled all the conditions of a possible retreat from the first. His left was protected by low ground, only accessible with difficulty. His right was met by a bend of the river Bronx, and while one line of earthworks was in front of and controlled the upper Connecticut road, the two successive lines to the rear were upon a gradual ascent very capable of vigorous defense. He also controlled the roads that led westward to the Hudson river. Somewhat advanced, and hardly a mile to the south-west, Chatterton's Hill was occupied by Haslet's regiment, supported by General McDougall's brigade, which contained two of the most reliable regiments in the army. Behind the interior line of the American encampment was still higher ground, entirely commanding the passes through tne hill by the Peekskill and upper Tarrytown roads.

General Lee criticised the position taken by the army on his arrival, but the strategic considerations which seem to have induced Washington to have taken his ground, in confidence that he had a secure ultimate defense in case of failure to maintain the first, were sound, and realized his purpose. It is to be especially noted that Washington, superior in numbers to his adversary, was in a situation and in one of his moods when he *courted* battle, and adopted the best course to invite attack.

On the twenty-eighth of October the armies thus confronted each other.

It will be noticed that a direct advance upon Washington's lines would subject General Howe's army to an attack upon their left flank or rear, unless the force on Chatterton's Hill should be first dislodged. And yet the difficulties of a descent from the hill would have weakened such a movement, and made it fruitless, if he had concentrated his army and broken Washington's centre. General Clinton would undoubtedly have made the attack. General Howe placed General Leslie in command of a division, with orders to dislodge the Americans and occupy Chatterton's Hill. This divided his force, and left the main body passive spectators of the movement. The division consisted of the second British brigade, Donop's Hessian grenadiers, the Hessian regiment Lossberg, and Colonel Rahl's Hessians, making a total force, according to General Howe's official report, of four thousand men, or very nearly one-third of the army. At the time of this detail, General Howe's army was superior in numbers to that in his immediate front, because of the occupation of the hill by the American extreme right.

The troops crossed the river Bronx with some difficulty, and then had to climb a difficult ascent. The British superiority in artillery was more than compensated by the American position, and artillery was of little practical value. Captain Alexander Hamilton served two light guns at the centre, and as the British brigade crossed the Bronx and ascended the hill he delivered effective fire ; and Smallwood's regiment supported by Ritzema's, made two successful charges down the hill and checked the advance. To spectators at White Plains, it appeared as if a final and complete repulse had been achieved. At this crisis, Colonel Rahl, by a sudden and well pressed movement to the left, reached and turned the American right flank and stood upon the summit, while Donop boldly charged up the face of the hill to the left of the British brigade. The American troops overwhelmed by this attack, fell back to a second position on the right of the army, and General Leslie could not pursue without throwing himself in the rear of Washington, or at least exposing himself to be entirely cut off from General Howe.

Haslet's Delaware, and Smallwood's Maryland had again confirmed their reputation, and with Brooks' Massachusetts, Webb's Connecticut, and Ritzema's New York had fought with commendable spirit, and as long as consistent with safety for themselves and the American right wing. General Putnam had been sent to their support as soon as the affair appeared doubtful, but was too late to redeem the contest.

Colonel Haslet afterwards wrote, that *he* was first assigned to the command of Chatterton's Hill with his own regiment and a force of militia; that the latter fled, and that three companies of Smallwood's Maryland also retreated precipitately; that General McDougall's command supported *him*, and was so dangerously placed in his rear, that he was in danger from their fire; that upon his advice General McDougall changed his position. Much is assumed by this officer, which is not supported by other authority. Colonel Graham, who commanded the regiment of New York militia, was tried before a court martial for unnecessarily abandoning two stone fences where he had been placed by Colonel Reed. The position would have had value if properly supported. The evidence was conclusive as to his personal bravery, although some of his officers failed him, and that his retreat was in pretty good order, and was directed by superior authority. Captain Hamilton also brought off his guns in safety.

Colonel Smallwood was wounded, and forty-six of his regiment were also among the killed and wounded. The total loss was reported at ninety, but Dr. Bird, who visited the hospitals, stated that it was not less than one hundred and twenty. Marshall says, " between three and four hundred." General Howe " estimated the American loss at two hundred and fifty." The returns and contemporaneous letters fix the loss at one hundred and thirty. General Howe's report at the close of the year mentions no prisoners as taken between the twelfth and the sixteenth of November; but under the caption "White Plains," enumerates four officers and thirty-five privates. As this number were taken early on the march, it does not enter into the casualties at Chatterton's Hill.

The loss of the British brigade was officially reported by General Leslie as one hundred and fifty-four. Lieutenant-colonel Carr, of the Thirty-fifth, Captain Goar of the Forty-ninth, and Deming of the Twenty-eighth regiments were among the killed. The Hessian loss increased the total casualties of the command to two hundred and thirty-one.

The heaviest portion of this loss was incurred in the attempt to scale the cliff, just after crossing the river.

On the twenty-ninth the armies rested. General Howe, "waited for reinforcements." Washington removed his sick to better quarters and prepared to move to his selected ultimate place of resistance. On the thirtieth, Lord Percy arrived with the third brigade and two battalions of the fourth brigade, and the next day was designated for an assault in force. The day was stormy, and for twenty hours the rain and wind suspended the movement. Batteries were planted, however, for a subsequent advance, "*weather permitting.*"

During that night Washington retired nearly five miles, to North Castle Heights, from which he could not be dislodged by the entire British force, and the "Battle of White Plains," had been fought at Chatterton Hill.

The Court-house at White Plains was subsequently burned by lawless Americans, for which the British troops were in no way responsible. Washington burned his excess of forage, and stores that could not be removed, and in a prompt order thus denounced the burning of the public buildings:

"It is with the utmost astonishment and abhorrence, the general is informed, that some base and cowardly wretches have, last night (November 5th) set fire to the Court house and other buildings which the enemy left. The army may rely on it, that they shall be brought to justice, and meet with the punishment they deserve."

The horrors of civil war began to develop fruit. The soldiers plundered towns, and the British took without discrimination of persons, what they wanted. Citizens became alarmed, and infinite issues were involved in the integrity and faithfulness of Congress and its defenders.

16

CHAPTER XXXVI.

OPERATIONS NEAR NEW YORK. WHITE PLAINS TO FORT WASH-
INGTON.

ON the second day of November General Knyphausen broke up
his camp near New Rochelle, and at evening encamped at the
north end of New York Island. On the fifth General Howe left
White Plains, and during the afternoon of the sixth encamped at
Dobbs Ferry, on the east bank of the Hudson river. Thus the army
abandoned the temporary base at New Rochelle.

General Howe drew his supplies from vessels which were already
at Dobbs Ferry, while the Hessian commander had direct water-
communication with New York city, by Harlem creek. By the
fourteenth General Knyphausen had accumulated a large number of
flat-boats and barges for the more rapid transportation of his troops
toward Fort Washington. Reference is had to maps entitled " Operations near New York," and " Capture of Fort Washington."

The barracks at Fort Independence had been burned by Colonel
Lasher, at three o'clock on the morning of the twenty-eighth of October, and three hundred stands of arms, out of repair, five tons of bar
iron, spears, shot, shell, and numerous additional valuable stores, had
been abandoned, in the hurried retreat to Kingsbridge. General
Greene crossed over and gathered as many as he could procure
wagons for, and intended to have used the lumber of the barracks, but
for their premature and improvident destruction. On the sixth,
Washington informed Congress of these different movements, and that
" he expected the enemy to lead their forces against Fort Washington,
and invest it,"—and that " Howe would probably make a descent
into New Jersey." A council of war, that day convened, unanimously
agreed, " that, if the enemy retreated toward New York it would be
proper to throw a body of troops into New Jersey, immediately : "—
that the troops raised on either side of the Hudson river should

occupy the side where they had been enlisted, and that a force of three thousand men would be necessary for the erection and defense of posts and passes in the Highlands, which included Peekskill, and all mountain spurs which commanded the river.

General Washington wrote to Governor Livingston that General Howe "must undertake something on account of his reputation, that he would probably go to New Jersey, and then urged that the militia be in readiness to supply the places of those whose term would soon expire." To Greene he wrote in the same terms on the seventh ; adding, "they can have no capital object in view unless it is Philadelphia." It was then known that General Carleton retired from Crown Point on Saturday the second of November, so that there was no danger of a British movement up the Hudson. On the eighth he wrote to General Greene, " The late passage of the three vessels up the North river is so plain a proof of the inefficiency of all the obstructions we have thrown into it," referring to sunken vessels with submarine abati, designed by General Putnam, " that I can not but think it will fully justify a change in the disposition which has been made. If we can not prevent vessels passing up, and the enemy are possessed of the surrounding country, what valuable purpose can it answer to hold a post from which the expected benefit can not be had ? I am therefore inclined to think it will not be prudent to hazard the men and stores at Mount Washington ; but as you are on the spot, leave it to you to give such orders as to evacuating Mount Washington as you judge best ; and, so far, revoking the order given Colonel Magaw to defend it to the last."

General Greene was also ordered to remove all stores not necessary for defense, adding, " if the inhabitants will not drive off their stock, destroy it, with hay, grain, etc., since the enemy would take it without distinction or satisfaction."

General Greene had anticipated a movement into New Jersey late in October. It was evident that there must be an end to the pursuit of Washington's army by General Howe, and he was well assured that that pursuit would end at White Plains.

On the twenty-ninth of October, he sketched an *itinerary* which is of value as giving a measure of distance by which to appreciate the subsequent movements, as reported at their occurrence. It is as follows :

"From Fort Lee to Hackensack bridge, nine miles ; water carriage from this place.

"From Hackensack to Equacanaugh, five miles; water carriage from this place.

"From Equacanaugh to Springfield, sixteen miles; to a landing at Newark.

"From Springfield to Boundbrook, nineteen miles; seven miles to a landing at Brunswick.

"From Boundbrook to Princeton, twenty miles; twelve miles land carriage to Delaware river.

"From Princeton to Trenton, twelve miles; water carriage to Philadelphia."

His estimates for stores of flour, pork, hay, and grain, including allowance for supplying troops passing and repassing from the different States, is given as an index of his forethought in the line of logistics.

"Two thousand men at Fort Lee for five months; at Hackensack a supply for the general hospital—the troops to have fresh provisions; at Equacanaugh, for the troops at Newark and Elizabethtown, and to subsist the main army in passing to Philadelphia; at Springfield a week's provisions for twenty thousand men on their way to Philadelphia; at Boundbrook the same; at Princeton the same; at Trenton to subsist twenty thousand men for three months." The period at which this forecast of the future was made is worthy of notice.

November ninth, President Hancock notified Washington of the restoration of a money allowance upon reënlistment, and of the passage of a resolution that the American army might be enlisted for three years or during the war.

At this time *more than one-half* the enlistments of the army were on the extreme limit of their service, and reports of its condition were freely circulated in New York. The militia of that State, then at Fort Washington, upon the pledge of General Howe that " he would guarantee to them the blessing of peace and a secure enjoyment of their liberties and properties, as well as a free and general pardon," were determined not to reënlist, and became fractious and insubordinate. Governor Livingston notified Washington, under date of November ninth, that he had received his letter above referred to, and that in case of an apprehended invasion he would call out the men to repel it.

On the same date with Livingston's letter, Greene admitted the failure of the river obstructions to do their work, adding, " but upon the whole I cannot help thinking the garrison is of advantage, and I cannot conceive the garrison to be in any great danger ; the men can be brought off at any time, but the stores may not be so easily removed ; yet I think they can be got off in spite of them, if matters grow desperate.   I was over there last evening ; the enemy seems to be disposing matters to besiege the place, but Colonel Magaw thinks it will take them till December expires before they can carry it."

On the same date Washington ordered the first division to cross the Hudson at Peekskill; the second to cross the day following.

A brief epitome of the details in logistics which occupied the attention of the American commander-in-chief during the last four hours before he followed these divisions into New Jersey, is pregnant with military and historical suggestions.

To General Lee he commits certain trusts ; " that all tools not in use be got together and delivered to the quartermaster-general ; that the commanding officer of artillery fix convenient places for the uninterrupted manufacture of musket cartridges ; that no troops be suffered to leave camp until army accoutrements and tents are accounted for, or delivered upon proper receipt ; that the contingency of an attack, in case the threatened movement to New Jersey be but a feint, be provided for ; and that all stores and baggage not for immediate use, be sent northward of the Croton river ; that in case of change of post, all hay be destroyed, so that the enemy can not get it ; that supernumerary officers of regiments greatly reduced be discharged, or annexed to some brigade ; that provisions and forage be laid in for winter quarters ; that it is important to remember in deliberation, that the militia of Massachusetts stand released from their contract on the seventeenth instant, and the Connecticut militia are not engaged for any fixed period."

The closing paragraph of this remarkable order, thus briefly outlined, is material to an appreciation of the future course of the officer intrusted with these duties.   It is given with official exactness, is placed in Italics, and reads as follows :

" *If the enemy should remove the whole or the greatest part of their force to the west side of the Hudson river, I have no doubt of your following with all possible dispatch, leaving the militia and invalids to cover the frontiers of Connecticut, etc., in case of need.*

" *Given at headquarters, near the White Plains, the* 10*th day of November,* 1776.

" GEORGE WASHINGTON."

" *To Major-general Lee.*"

Washington wrote to Governor Livingston in substance, that the bounties offered by New York would deter enlistments in States not giving bounties, because, " troops embarked in the same cause and doing the same duties, will not long act together with harmony for different pays."

To Colonel Knox he made a suggestion as to a partition of the artillery among different commands, unless Howe should throw his whole force into the Jerseys, and bend his course to Philadelphia, adding this paragraph :—

" It is unnecessary to add that if the army of the enemy should wholly or pretty generally throw themselves across the North river, General Lee is to follow." To General Mifflin : " that as enlistments are to expire, many will not reënlist, hence tents and stores delivered, are to be collected and safely deposited ; tents to be repaired against another season, intrenching tools to be collected or placed where General Lee should direct, and magazines of forage be provided."

To Governor Trumbull he sent a particular letter of detail, closing, " In case the enemy should make a pretty general remove to the Jerseys, that part of the army under General Lee will more than probably follow ; *notice of which I now give*."

To Ezekiel Cheevers, commissary of military stores :

" As the army, (at least part of it) is near the period of dissolution,"—army and other stores issued to continental troops or militia are to be recovered ; unserviceable arms that can not be repaired by the armorers of the army, are to be packed and sent to the Board of War, other stores to be put in a safe place near the winter quarters of the troops ; and, " it is unnecessary to add, that the troops of General Lee will also cross the Hudson river if it should be necessary, in consequence of their throwing their force over."

One general order reads like so many orders of later date, that it is referred to in connection with the historical statement, that the organization and support of the American armies in the war of 1861–65, was substantially based upon legislation which reproduced the system adopted during the war of 1775–1781. The order is as follows: " Colonels to examine the baggage of troops under marching orders ; tents and spare arms to go first in the wagons, then the proper baggage of the regiment ; no chairs, tables, heavy chests or other personal baggage, to be put in, as it will certainly be thrown off and left ; no officer of any rank to meddle with a wagon or cart appropriated for any other regiment or public use ; that no discharged men be allowed to carry away arms, camp kettles, utensils, or any other public stores ; recruiting officers so detailed, to proceed with their duty ; no boys or old men to be enlisted, and if so, to be returned on the hands of the officer, with no allowance for any expense he may be at."

On November twelfth, at Peekskill, just before crossing the river, Washington having spent the previous day in a visit to the Highlands in the vicinity of West Point, specifically instructed General Heath that " his division and the troops at Forts Constitution, Montgomery, and Independence, as well as Colonel Lasher's regiment, were under his command for the security of the above posts, the passes through the Highlands from this place, and on the west side of the river." General Heath at once convened a council of war and divided his troops in accordance with the tenor of Washington's orders. By the fourteenth all the troops of the army belonging to States which lay south of the Hudson river, excepting Smallwood's, already on its march, had been safely moved across the river, and Washington himself reached General Greene's headquarters that morning. At this time a fleet of nearly three hundred sail lay at Sandy Hook with a large number of British troops on board, and their destination was suspected to be Rhode Island, Philadelphia, or South Carolina.

On the twelfth, General Greene had written, " I expect General Howe will endeavor to possess himself of Mount Washington, but very much doubt whether he will succeed in the attempt."

When Washington arrived at Fort Lee, the British army had already removed from Dobbs Ferry to Kingsbridge. In his report of this fact to Congress, the following sentence directly follows the announcement : " It seems to be generally believed, on all hands, that the investing of Fort Washington is one object they have in view." " I propose to stay in the neighborhood a few days ; in which time I expect the design of the enemy will be more disclosed, and their incursions made in this quarter, or their investiture of Fort Washington if they are intended." This letter regards the anticipated investment very calmly. Washington established his headquarters at Hackensack bridge, nearly nine miles from Fort Lee. The garrison of Fort Washington had been previously reinforced from the flying camp and on the fifteenth it numbered nearly three thousand men. Washington's personal report placed the garrison at about two thousand. His estimate was too low, for at the close of the year, a revised list of the prisoners taken on the sixteenth, was made up and settled upon, as the basis of exchange, at two thousand six hundred and thirty-four.

The fort was commanded by Colonel Magaw, of Pennsylvania. He was a man of courage and capacity. Colonels Rawlings, Cadwallader and Baxter were his chief associates, and to each was entrusted a command bearing upon the defense of the fort. Major Otho H. Williams with a Maryland rifle battalion, was also attached to Rawlings' command.

*Fort Washington was a hastily built, open earthwork, and according to Graydon, "without a ditch of any consequence, and with no exterior defenses that could entitle it to the name of a fortress in any degree capable of sustaining a siege." There was no well within the fort proper, so that water was procurable only from the Hudson river, nearly three hundred feet below.

Southward, within less than two miles, were the interior lines of the old defenses which were built when Washington's army was on Harlem Heights. Colonel Cadwallader was stationed there. Eastward was a ridge called Laurel Hill, a part of Fordham Heights, and at its north end was a slight defense afterwards known as Fort George. Opposite, on the prolongation of the Mount Washington ridge, was a fort subsequently known as Fort Tryon. Between these somewhat commanding positions there was a deep and rocky ravine through which ran the old Albany road. The river ridge, with a slight interruption near Tubby Hook, continued as far as Spuyten Devil Creek, where light earthworks had been built, known as " Cock Hill Fort." Still northward, across the creek on Tetard's Hill, was Fort Independence. From the point where the Albany road left the pass and turned towards the Harlem river was a valley, and much marshy land; but across the Harlem river, opposite Fort George, and as far as Williams, or Dykeman's bridge, the ground was high again, and the British had erected two redoubts to cover the landing of Generals Matthews and Cornwallis. General Howe thus gave his opinion of Fort Washington : " The importance of this post, which with Fort Lee on the opposite shore of Jersey kept the enemy in command of the North river, while it barred the communication with New York, by land, made the possession of it absolutely necessary." This is the identical argument used by General Greene for its " retention to the last possible moment."

In Washington's report of November sixteenth occurs this paragraph : " Early this morning, Colonel Magaw posted his troops, partly in the lines thrown up by our army on our first coming thither from New York, and partly on a commanding hill lying north of Mount

Washington, *the lines being all to the southward.*" The paragraph now placed in italics, has significance, as the facts indicated enabled the British, who operated from the north and east, to enter the open sides; and in fact, practically, to disregard the greater portion of the nominal lines of defense.

Directly eastward of the redoubt itself, there was no defense, other than that assured by the steepness and roughness of the ascent. The fort was first built, in order to command the Hudson river; and the principal portion of the lines, immediately northward, had a river front, but was nearly open toward the rear.

During the afternoon of the fifteenth, the British arrangements having been perfected for an assault on the following day, Adjutant-general Patterson was sent to the fort with a peremptory demand for its surrender, with the alternative "*to be put to the sword.*" In reply, Colonel Magaw declared that "he would defend the post to the last extremity," very generously qualifying a portion of General Howe's ultimatum, as follows,—"I think it rather a mistake, than a settled purpose of General Howe to act a part so unworthy of himself and the British nation."

Greene ordered Magaw to "defend the place until hearing from him again"—ordered General Heard's brigade to hasten up—sent the despatch from Colonel Magaw to Washington, then at Hackensack, and crossed over to the fort.

Washington immediately returned to Fort Lee, and started across the river to determine the condition of the garrison himself. He says:—"I had partly crossed the North river when I met General Putnam and General Greene, who were just returning from thence, and they informed me that the troops were in high spirits and would make a good defense, and it being late at night, I returned."

The attack upon Fort Washington was admirably planned and admirably executed. "The Pearl was stationed in the North river," says General Howe, "to cover the march of the Hessian troops and flank the American lines." On the night of the fourteenth, thirty flat-boats under the command of Captains Wilkinson and Molly, passed up the Hudson, eluded the vigilance of General Greene and Colonel Magaw, entered Spuyten Devil Creek and thus reached King's-Bridge.

Three distinct assaults were ordered, and a fourth movement, which was at first intended as a feint, was converted into a **spirited** attack, at a critical moment. The marginal notes on the map, indicating the troops assigned to each column, are from General Howe's "Orderly Book."

From the north, along the ridge, scattering the little guard at Cock Hill Fort, Colonel Rahl, on the right, moved steadily upon Fort Tryon, crowding Colonel Rawlings back by weight of numbers, nearly to the fort itself. General Knyphausen with the left of the Hessian column took the side of the ridge even down to the ravine, and after considerable loss while fighting his way through woods and over rocks against a spirited resistance, joined Colonel Rahl near the fort.

Lord Percy advanced from the south, and was checked for a little while by Cadwallader, who having too small a force to defend the entire lines, was then compelled to fall back to the interior or northern line of works, which had no guns in position as support to his resistance.

At this advance the division of Matthews and Cornwallis, which had been in readiness, landed, although under heavy fire, pushed back the resisting force, and moved over Laurel Hill to take the works in the centre. As soon as advised that Lord Percy had carried the advance-work to the south, General Howe ordered Colonel Sterling to land and coöperate with Matthew's division. At this point of debarkation there were light earthworks also, which were stubbornly held by the Americans. Cadwallader, seeing that the success of this movement would interpose a force in his rear, sent a detachment to assist in opposing the landing; but upon failure to check it, the detachment too rapidly retreated, losing one hundred and seventy men as prisoners. Colonel Magaw also sent a detachment from the fort for the same purpose, when he saw the boats approaching the landing.

The whole weight of the British left and centre was now converged upon a direct assault up the steep ascent in front of the fort itself. It was made under heavy fire, but with unwavering steadiness and speedy success. All the British divisions were thus within the exterior lines, and the garrison was crowded into a space designed for only a thousand men. Surrender or rescue was inevitable. Magaw asked for five hours' parley. A half hour only was given, and the surrender ensued soon after; but Washington had been notified of the demand. Washington says, "I sent a billet to Colonel Magaw directing him to hold out, and I would endeavor this evening to bring off the garrison if the fortress could not be maintained, as I did not expect it could, the enemy being possessed of the adjacent ground."

Rawlings and Williams were wounded on the left, and Colonel

Baxter fell on Laurel Hill. Colonel Miller, of the Fifth Pennsylvania battalion, was also killed.

The American loss in killed and wounded did not exceed one hundred and thirty.

The British regiments lost in killed, wounded, and missing, one hundred and twenty-eight, and the Hessian troops, three hundred and twenty-six. Among the regiments engaged, the following were conspicuous in subsequent stages of the war: viz., those of Rahl, Donop, Losberg, Stein, Nessembach, and Dittforth.

On the seventeenth, an additional number of flat boats was sent up the North river by Admiral Howe, and on the eighteenth Cornwallis crossed over nearly opposite Yonkers, at a point not sufficiently watched and defended, with six thousand men. Fort Lee was abandoned, the American army falling behind the Hackensack, and then to Aquackanonck.

Two officers, one quartermaster, three surgeons, and ninety-nine privates were taken prisoners at Fort Lee.

The loss in public stores by the capture of these forts, including those taken at Valentine's Hill and left on the march, was a serious one to the American army, and embraced besides shot, shell, twenty-eight hundred muskets, and four hundred thousand cartridges, at least one hundred and sixty-one cannon, ranging from three to thirty-two pounders, and several hundred tents.

On the capture of Fort Lee, General Greene wrote to Governor Cooke of Rhode Island under date of December first, that " the enemy's publication of the cannon and stores then taken is a grave falsehood ; not an article of military stores was left there, or nothing worth mentioning. The evacuation of Fort Lee was determined upon several days before the enemy landed above, and happily all the most valuable stores were over."

General Washington's report of the twenty-first of November, the day after its capture, says, " we lost the whole of the cannon that were in the fort, except two twelve pounders and a great deal of baggage, between two and three hundred tents, and other stores in the quartermaster's department. The loss was inevitable. As many of the stores had been removed as circumstances and time would admit of. The ammunition (of Fort Lee) had been happily got away."

This apparent discrepancy of statement is given for the following reasons.

It indicates the purpose of the author to rely in the first instance

upon official Reports, Muster Rolls, and Returns, and to reconcile
conflicts by the use of contemporary papers and letters, and the application of governing principles ; and because, as seen by references to
operations at Brooklyn, Harlem, and Chatterton Hill, the tendency
of individuals to throw responsibility upon others when there was any
misadventure, was as common then, as at all other periods of human history from the day that the forbidden fruit was eaten in the region of
Paradise. It must be remembered, however, that the reports of commanding officers are very often but summaries of general results ; and
that only exceptional cases of merit or demerit attach to such reports.
It would be impossible to name *everybody*, and the nearer that attempt
is made, the more there will remain to be dissatisfied. Greene had,
in fact, removed the *general stores* and a portion of those of the Fort
proper; but the report of General Washington corroborates that of
General Howe. General Greene was smarting under malicious criticisms, and his strong language was erroneous in the letter, but just in
its general substance.

General Washington himself is not without some inconsistencies
of statement as to the capture of Fort Washington, and these are
important elements of justice in stating the matter exactly as it transpired. It was then that the first distinct insubordination of General
Lee had its expression, and calumny seems to have been the current
news of the crisis. No event during the war had called forth more
partisan discussion. It shows the importance of giving full credit to
real courage and general wisdom, and the folly of aggravating a
disaster or mistake of judgment into a charge of weakness or
incompetency.

In a letter to his brother, Washington says, " what adds to my
mortification is, that this post after the last ships went past it, was
held contrary to my wishes and opinions, as I conceived it to be a
hazardous one. . . . I did not care to give an absolute order for
withdrawing the garrison till I could get round and see the situation
of things, and then it became too late, as the fort was invested. . . .
I had given it as my opinion to General Greene, under whose care it
was, that it would be best to evacuate the place ; but as the order
was discretionary, and his opinion differed from mine, it unhappily
was delayed too long to my great grief."

Washington was not an entirely exceptional man, but a great man.
He must be dealt with by his merits. The facts are simply these.
Putnam, who built the post, and had great faith that he was to close

the river; Greene commanding on the Jersey side, who was anxious to have no more retreats; and Colonel Magaw, the brave post commander, must have *satisfied Washington* that he could, as he wrote on the seventh, " take some risk to hold it."

His letter written after his arrival, showed his intention to watch the British movements; and the investment had not *then* been made. It is to be inferred from his own letter that he could have withdrawn the garrison. His army, only three thousand men, was inadequate to reinforce it, without sacrificing all field movements and shutting himself up for capture. He was not prepared to take responsibility after the decided action of his general officers and Congress, and the drift of public sentiment was in a direction that would have made its early evacuation a greater disaster than its defense. Its loss quickened the action of Congress, and ultimately secured to Washington independence of action; but there is no occasion for converting this episode of the war into a harsh judgment of either Greene or Washington. The ordeal was one which would have tried any commander. Governor Jonathan Trumbull of Connecticut had *his* opinion, and his conscience and wisdom inspired many key-notes to the conduct of the war. He wrote to the American commander-in-chief as follows: " The loss of Fort Washington with so many of our brave men, is indeed a most unfortunate event. But though we are to consider and improve like disappointments, yet we are by no means to despair,—we are in this way to be prepared for help and deliverance."

CHAPTER XXXVII.

PLANS AND COUNTER PLANS. FORT WASHINGTON TO TRENTON.
1776.

GENERAL HOWE matured a plan of operations which clearly indicated that he comprehended the gravity of the undertaking which the British government had assumed. It had so much of true value that it would be difficult to improve it after more than a century of modern military experience. That plan proposed : that an army of ten thousand men should be established at Newport, Rhode Island, of which force at least three-fourths should act offensively against the New England States, particularly Boston and vicinity;—that twenty thousand men should be placed at New York, of which seventeen thousand men should be available for field service ; —that ten thousand men should coöperate with this army, southward ; and that ten thousand men should be sent to the Southern States. The New Jersey contingent was added, in order that an adequate force from the New York command might be directed up the Hudson river, to coöperate with troops having their own base on the St. Lawrence. This requisition for troops was sent to the British government. It bears upon its face, its significance ; and much of General Howe's indecision and carefulness of movement must be attributed to some maturing conviction of the character of the contest which had been driven into his mind during his career from Boston to Fort Lee. The modern reader must be impressed with the belief that such a force, so disposed, would have fulfilled all the strategic elements required for a vigorous prosecution of the war. It is certainly true that the necessity for such a requisition for troops must have restrained the British General in chief in his operations in New Jersey.

The elaborate controversy between Howe and Clinton does not impair his judgment in this respect ; and while constitutional temperament and certain vagaries of personal habit slipped in at nearly every

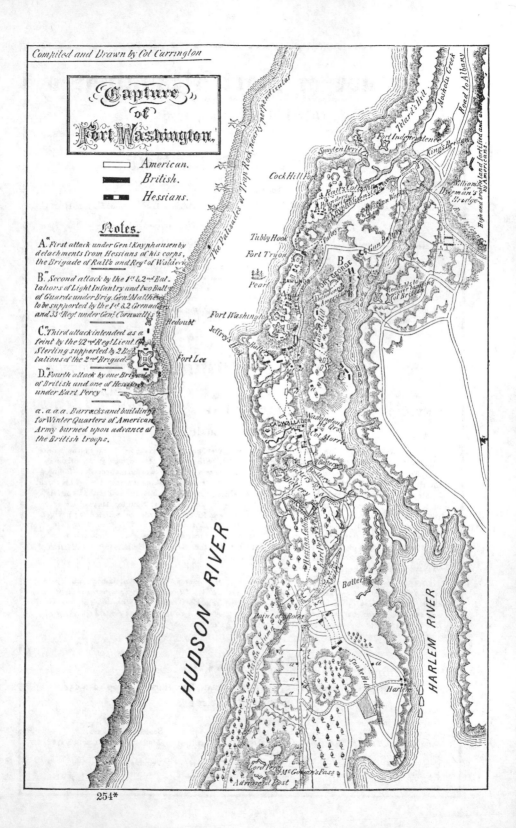

Capture of Fort Washington

NOVEMBER 16th, 1776

American Commanders
MAGAW
RAWLINGS   CADWALLADER   BAXTEP   MILLER

Strength, 2,764   Casualties 130   Surrendered, 2 634

NOTE.—Cadwallader was advanced southward to the old field-works near the Morris House, to resist British approach from New York. Baxter and Miller occupied Laurel Hill and the site of Fort George, overlooking Harlem River, to prevent the crossing of troops which approached from the direction of William's Bridge, on the east bank of that river.

Rawlings was on the Hudson River ridge, or bluff, northward, toward Kingsbridge. Fort Tryon and Cock Hill Fort were small, advanced works, in the same direction, but designed chiefly to command the Hudson River. Fort Washington itself, except the small redoubt, was open eastward, and unprotected from artillery, which might be used from Laurel Hill.

British Commanders
CORNWALLIS   **HOWE**   CLINTON

KNYPHAUSEN   MATTHEWS   RAHL   PERCY   STERLING

Strength, 9,000   Casualties, 454

NOTE.—One British column ascended the Harlem River, practically gained the rear of the works held by Cadwallader, and compelled him to retreat, with the loss of 170 men taken prisoners. Knyphausen and Rahl crossed at King's Bridge, took the two small out-works in succession, followed the Hudson River Heights, and thus were in the rear of Laurel Hill, making it untenable. This force had been augmented by troops which ascended the Hudson in thirty flat boats, and eluded the vigilance of Gen. Greene, then at Fort Lee, and Col. Magaw, and landed at Spuyten Duyvel Creek on the night of Nov. 14th. The landing from the Harlem River, eastward, was resisted with vigor. Baxter and Miller fell. Rawlings was wounded in the attack from the North.

A general assault compelled surrender. In storming the rear ascent, eastward, which was already commanded by guns placed in position on Laurel Hill, the Hessian regiments of Rahl, Donop, Losberg, Stein, Nesseaback and Dittforth lost 326 men. The great loss in tents and heavy guns was severely felt by the American army.

MEM.—*This Fort did not prevent the passage of ships of war up the Hudson, as had been expected, and its loss, except in men and materials of war, did not permanently injure the American cause. Its possession by the British, as an outpost of New York, continually required a garrison, and the Americans maintained communication with New England, through forts higher up the Hudson. The few incursions to Westchester had little effect on the war.*

References :

CARRINGTON'S "BATTLES OF THE AMERICAN REVOLUTION," pp. 242-254.

School Histories :

Anderson, ¶ 36 ; p. 76.
Barnes, ¶ 1 ; p. 116.
Berard (Bush), ¶ 66 ; p. 154.
Goodrich, C.A.(Seaveys),¶ 6; p. 121.
Goodrich, S. G., ¶ 4-5 ; p. 213.
Hassard, ¶ 4 ; p. 181.

Holmes, ¶ 22 ; p. 120.
Lossing, ¶ 20 : p. 147.
Quackenbos, ¶ 323; p. 231.
Ridpath, ¶ 23 ; p. 198.
Sadlier, (Excel), ¶ 4 ; p. 187.
Stephens, A.H. ¶ 10; p. 194.

Swinton, ¶ 116 ; p. 129.
Scott, ¶ 14 ; p. 172.
Thalheimer (Eclectic), ¶ 256 ;
   p. 146-7.
Venable, ¶ 136 ; p. 102.

crisis to rob him of the best fruits of skillful preparation, this single scheme for quickening the war to a conclusion, must go upon record to his credit as a soldier. It was in substance the cabinet policy; but indicated an appreciation of the means required to carry out that policy. A rapid summary of events up to the battle of Trenton is important in this connection so that the closing operations of 1776 may have their appreciative value in an estimate of the character and operations which entered into the permanent history of the struggle.

General Clinton sailed from New York December first and landed at Newport, Rhode Island, on the ninth, with a little over three thousand men. This was the squadron which had so long demonstrated near Sandy Hook, creating doubts in the mind of Washington as to its ultimate destination.

Major General Prescott and Lieutenant General Percy accompanied Clinton. Sir Peter Parker commanded the naval forces. The effect of this movement was to suspend for a time the movement of Massachusetts troops. Six thousand men were nearly ready to march to General Washington's support, under General Lincoln, in place of troops whose terms of service had expired.

The *Northern* American army had at that time two Major-generals on duty, each claiming command, but amicably settling the difference so far as surface manifestations were apparent. General Gates had joined Schuyler, and by the retreat from Canada, lost his distinctive department. He preferred to retain command of the troops which he brought back; but this was incompatible with the situation, which was handled by Schuyler with great integrity, patriotism and energy. Congress settled the matter by declaring that " they had no design to invest General Gates with a superior command to General Schuyler, while the troops should be on this side of Canada." Schuyler actively engaged in fitting out a fleet for the control of Lake Champlain, which was placed under the command of Arnold. This fleet was equipped, made a good fight with that of General Carleton, but was either captured or withdrawn to the south under the guns of Fort Ticonderoga. All operations in that department were suspended when General Carleton withdrew from Crown Point and returned to Canada. On the ninth day of November General Gates made an official report of the troops serving in the northern Department, showing a force of seven thousand three hundred and forty-five " effective rank and file," present for duty and on command, and three thousand nine hundred and sixty-one sick, present and absent. The terms of enlistment of many regiments were to expire between that date and the ninth of January ensuing, so that after General Gates joined Washington with a portion of the Northern army, there remained for duty at Ticonderoga, Mount Independence and Fort George, on the first of December, only two thousand three hundred and eighty-four men.   General Lee still commanded a grand division at North Castle Heights.   This force numbered on the sixteenth of November, when the assault was made upon Fort Washington, seven thousand five hundred and fifty-four " effective rank and file present for duty and on command."   His report of November twenty-fourth, shows the somewhat larger force, of seven thousand eight hundred and twenty-four men.   The enlistments of a great majority of these troops were however close to their limit, and he ultimately crossed the river with less than thirty-four hundred effective men.

The division of General Heath with headquarters at Peekskill, and commanding the North river defenses, was also reported on November twenty-fourth, as numbering, effective rank and file, present, and on command, four thousand and sixteen men.   The army of Washington was mustered at Newark on the twenty-third day of November, and amounted to five thousand four hundred and ten men for duty.

Colonel Bradley's brigade which was to go out of service December first, had but sixty men present.   The largest brigade, that of General Beall, twelve hundred strong, *also had but a week to serve.*   The enlistments of only twenty-four hundred and one men extended beyond January first, next ensuing.   On the first of December a general return of the army was made at Trenton, with the following result. The command consisted of four brigades, including sixteen regiments, and numbered with officers and staff, four thousand three hundred and thirty-four, of whom one thousand and twenty-nine were sick, and two-thirds of the sick were absent.

The foregoing official data are substituted for general statements as to the condition of the American army.   The army movements were as follows.   The American army, compelled to abandon the space between the Hackensack and Passaic, crossed the latter river at Aquackanonck on the twenty-first day of November, burned the bridge after a brief skirmish, and followed the right bank of the Passaic river to Newark, reaching that city on the twenty-third, and New Brunswick on the twenty-ninth.   Here also a vigorous skirmish took place with the columns of Cornwallis, which had orders " *to go no farther.*"   Washington moved on to Princeton, and then to Trenton, where he arrived on the third of December. He immediately obtained boats from Philadelphia, and for a stretch of seventy miles above that city, secured everything that could float, and on the fifth, having re- moved all heavy military stores, thus reported to Congress his action.

" As nothing but necessity obliged me to retire before the enemy, and leave so much of Jersey unprotected, I conceive it my duty, and it corresponds with my inclination *to make head against them so soon as there shall be the least probability of doing it with propriety*. That the country might in some measure be covered, I left two brigades, consisting of five Virginia regiments, and that of Delaware which had just arrived, containing in the whole about twelve hundred men fit for duty, under the command of Lord Stirling and General Stephen at Princeton, until the baggage and stores could cross the Delaware, or the troops under their respective commanders should be forced from thence. I shall now march back to Princeton, and then govern my- self by circumstances and the movements of General Lee." Wash- ington also stated that if the troops confidently expected (Lee's) had joined him, he should have made a stand both at Hackensack and Brunswick, and that " at any event the enemy's progress would have been retarded." Upon advancing toward Princeton, he met Stirling retreating before superior forces, and fell back to Trenton, and on the eighth he was over the Delaware.

On the twelfth, he heard that Lee was in Jersey with over four thousand effective troops ; but neither his own staff, nor a messenger sent by Congress, succeeded for some time in finding out the location and movements of that officer, although his letters invariably assumed great importance for his successive plans and positions.

An order had been sent to General Schuyler on November twenty- sixth, to forward all the Jersey and Pennsylvania troops then in his department to Washington. By the thirteenth of December, the British columns which had crossed the Hudson with Cornwallis, or joined from New York, were concentrated at Brunswick.

General Howe's " first design extended no further than to get and keep possession of East Jersey. Lord Cornwallis had orders " not to advance beyond Brunswick " ; " but on the sixth," continues General Howe, " I joined his lordship with the Fourth brigade of British, under command of Major-general Grant." On the seventh, Cornwallis marched with his corps, except the Guards, who were left at Brunswick, to Princeton, which the Americans had *quitted on the same day*. Corn- wallis delayed seventeen hours at Princeton, and was a whole day in

17

marching twelve miles more to Trenton.   This corps marched in two divisions, one of which reached Trenton just as the American rear-guard had crossed ; the other led by Cornwallis in person, broke off at Maidenhead and marched to Coryell's ferry, in some expectation of finding boats there and in the neighborhood, sufficient to pass the river ; but the enemy had taken the precaution to destroy, or to secure on the south side, all the boats that could possibly be employed for that purpose.   Cornwallis remained at Pennington until the fourteenth, when the cantonments having been arranged, the British army was placed in winter quarters," " the weather," as stated by General Howe, " having become too severe to keep the field."

Such were the relative positions of the retreating American army and the British army which followed its march.   It was hardly a pursuit, in the proper military sense.   General Howe, however, complimented Cornwallis in general orders as follows :   " I cannot too much commend Lord Cornwallis' good service during this campaign : and particularly the ability and conduct he displayed in the pursuit of the enemy from Fort Lee to Trenton, a distance exceeding eighty miles, in which he was well supported by the ardor of his troops, who cheerfully quitted their tents and heavy baggage, as impediments to their march."

In a careful estimate of probabilities, it is difficult to determine how Washington's army could have been saved, if General Howe had not limited Cornwallis by exact orders.   If the latter had left Brunswick and followed closely upon Washington's retreat, the capture of the American army, or its utter dispersion, would have been simply a matter of course.

A memorable episode of the war, which largely affected the campaign under notice, and had its sequel in subsequent events, must be considered in this connection.   On the fourteenth of December the armies were on opposite sides of the Delaware river, as already stated. On the previous day at a country house, three miles from his command, General Lee, who was second in command of the American armies, was leisurely resting after finishing a letter hereafter cited, when he was surprised and made prisoner of war by Lieutenant Colonel Harcourt, who was on a scout to find out that which puzzled Congress and its general in chief,—the location of General Lee.   He found General Lee at Baskingridge, the best possible location from which easily to have joined Washington.   Lee's division accompanied by General Sullivan, had marched to Vealtown, only about eight miles, on the previous day.   He left Chatham and rode at least three miles outside of the left flank and to the rear of his army, and spent the night at White's Tavern.   He was not at breakfast until ten, when he was summarily ordered out of his house and taken away in morning *dishabille*, without hat, boots or cloak, upon the horse of Major Wilkinson, then picketed before the house.   Major Wilkinson escaped.

From orders already cited it appears that General Washington, before undertaking his original movement southward, gave the necessary instructions that the main army then at North Castle Heights would soon follow.   The necessities of the crisis compelled him to advance in person, toward Philadelphia, and occupy the field of greatest danger.   The relations of General Lee as a subordinate officer, and the gravity of the issue, give significance to papers of which a few only are cited.   The letter referred to was written in the presence of Major Wilkinson, a messenger from General Gates, and was not folded when the capture was effected.   A former letter of Lee to General Gates, their relations before the war, and the flattering advance by Congress of thirty thousand dollars to General Lee to enable him to transfer his English property to America, force themselves to notice in connection with this paper.   The expletives are omitted.

BASKENRIDGE, *December* 13, 1776.

"MY DEAR GATES.—The ingenious manœuver of Fort Washington has com·pletely unhinged the goodly fabric we had been building.   There never was so——— a stroke :—*entre nous*, a certain great man is——deficient.   He has thrown me into a situation where I have my choice of difficulties.   If I stay in this province, I risk myself and army: and if I do not stay, the province is lost forever: .   .   . our councils have been weak to the last degree.   As to what relates to yourself, if you think you can be in time to aid the General, I would have you by all means go. You will at least save your army."

The above letter was not written by the American General-in-chief as might be supposed, neither was Lee's situation, however important in his own judgment, the pivot of the struggle.   As he was under positive orders, his safety was in obedience: and there was a commander-in-chief who based all his actions, at that very moment, upon such obedience, and Lee knew it.

On the twentieth of November the following official order, signed by Grayson, of Washington's staff, was sent to General Lee; "His excellency thinks it would be advisable in you to remove the troops under your command to this side of the North river and there await further orders."

On the twenty-first Washington wrote, " Unless some new event should occur or some more cogent reason present itself, I would have you move over by the easiest and best passage. I am sensible that your numbers will not be large and that perhaps it will not be agreeable to the troops. You will doubtless represent to them that in duty and gratitude, their service is due where the enemy make the greatest impression, or seem to do so."

Washington wrote on the twenty-fourth of November, to urge " the propriety of sending frequent expresses to advise of your approaches,"—on the twenty-seventh—" my letters were so full and explicit as to the necessity of your marching as early as possible, that it is unnecessary to add more on that head. I confess I expected you would have been sooner in motion ; "—" the force here, when joined by yours, will not be adequate to any great opposition ; "—on the first of December, " the enemy are advancing and have got as far as Woodbridge and Amboy, and from information not to be doubted, mean to push to Philadelphia. I must entreat you to hasten your march as soon as possible, or your arrival may be too late to answer any valuable purpose ; " on the third, " just now favored with your letter of the thirtieth ultimo. Having wrote you fully both yesterday and to-day of my situation, it is unnecessary to add much at this time. You will readily agree that I have sufficient cause for my anxiety, and to wish for your arrival as early as possible. . . . The sooner you can join me with your division the sooner the service will be benefited. As to bringing any of the troops under General Heath I can not consent to it ; —" I would have you give me frequent advices of your approach. Upon proper information in this instance, much may depend ;"—on the tenth of December,—" when my situation is directly opposite to what you suppose it to be, and when General Howe is pressing forward with the whole of his army, except the troops that were lately embarked . . I can not but entreat you, and this too by the advice of all the general officers with me, to march and join me with all your force, with all possible expedition. The utmost exertions that can be made will not more than save Philadelphia. Without the aid of your force I think there is but little if any prospect of doing it." On the eleventh of December,—" Nothing less than our utmost exertions will be sufficient to prevent General Howe from possessing it," meaning Philadelphia. " I must therefore entreat you to push on with every possible succor you can bring. Your aid may give a more favorable complexion to our affairs. You know the importance of the city of Philadelphia and the fatal consequences that must attend the loss of it."

On the twenty-first, with Washington's orders before him, Lee wrote to James Bowdoin, President of the Massachusetts Council. "Before the unfortunate affair at Fort Washington it was my opinion that the two armies, that on the east and that on the west side of the North river, must rest, each on its own bottom: that the idea of detaching and reinforcing from one side to the other on every motion of the enemy was chimerical; but to harbor such a thought in our present circumstances is absolute insanity. Should the enemy alter the present direction of their operations, I should never entertain the thought of being succored from the western army. We must therefore depend upon ourselves;" and again: "Affairs appear in so important a crisis that I think even the resolves of the Congress must no longer nicely weigh with us. There are times when we must commit treason against the laws of the State, for the salvation of the State. The present crisis demands this brave, *virtuous* kind of treason. For my own part (and I flatter myself my way of thinking is congenial with that of Mr. Bowdoin) I will stake my head and reputation on the measure."

Lee had written November twenty-fourth: "I have received your orders, and shall endeavor to put them in execution; but question much whether I shall be able to carry with me any considerable numbers. I sent Heath orders to transport two thousand men across the river; but that great man intrenched himself within the letter of his instructions and refused to part with a single file, though I undertook to replace them with a part of my own." Lee in fact wrote insultingly to Heath, who was as independent in command as himself, and even went to his post by virtue of rank, although only a guest, ordered two of Heath's regiments to join him, usurping authority, and only receded from his position when he realized the nature of his offense, and after being constrained to receipt for the troops, as "ordered away by myself, at this writing, commanding officer *in* the post."

He wrote to Heath on the twenty-sixth: "The commander in chief is now separated from us; I of course command on this side the water; for the future I will and must be obeyed." In the letter of the thirteenth, acknowledged by Washington, he wrote: "You complain of my not being in motion sooner. I do assure you that I have done all in my power, and shall explain my difficulties when we both have leisure. . . The day after to-morrow we shall pass the river. I do wish you would bind me as little as possible, . . . detached generals can not have too great latitude, unless they are very incompetent indeed "; on the fourth, "the northern army has already advanced nearer Morristown than I am. Shall put myself at their head to-morrow. We shall upon the whole compose an army of five thousand good troops in spirits." On the eighth of December he wrote from Chatham to Washington : " I am certainly shocked to hear that your force is so inadequate to the necessity of your situation. . . . It will be difficult, I am afraid, to join you, but can not I do more service by attacking their rear ? "

On the *same day* he wrote this reply to Richard Henry Lee and Benjamin Rush, a *committee from Congress* sent to hunt him up : "My corps that passed the North river will amount (for we are considerably diminished) to twenty-seven hundred ; in fact our army may be estimated at four thousand. If I was not taught to think that the army with General Washington had been considerably reinforced, I should immediately join him ; but as I am assured he is very strong, I should imagine that we can make a better impression by beating up and harassing their detached parties in the rear, for which purpose a good post at Chatham seems the best calculated."

On the ninth he wrote to Heath : " I think we shall be strong enough without you. I am in hopes here to reconquer, if I may so express myself, the Jerseys. It was really in the hands of the enemy before my arrival."

The following letter, dated at Morristown, December eleventh, indorsed "*From General Lee*," is added, "*We have three thousand men here at present, but they are so ill-shod that we have been obliged to halt these two days for want of shoes. Seven regiments of Gates' corps are on their march, but where they actually are is not certain.* General Lee has sent two officers this day, one to inform him where the Delaware can be crossed above Trenton, the other to examine the road toward Burlington, as General Lee thinks he can without great risk cross the great Brunswick road at night, and by a forced night march make the ferry below Burlington. Boats should be sent from Philadelphia to meet him. *But this scheme he only proposes if the head of the enemy's column actually pass the river. The militia in this part of the province seem sanguine. If they could be sure of the army remaining amongst them, I believe they would raise a considerable number.*

The italicized portions indicate the discrepancy with letters imme-

diately preceding, as declaratory of his settled purpose to act independently, and leave to Washington the responsibility for the loss of
Philadelphia, or other disasters. Letters to Reed, Greene, Heath,
Trumbull, and others are similar, or even worse in spirit, and while
tedious, portions of them are essential elements to a correct judgment
of this officer's conduct. Washington had provided boats, and acqui-
esced in Lee's suggestion not to cramp him by defining his exact route,
so that Washington, by Lee's secrecy, was wholly in the dark as to
every detail of his progress, and incurred repeated risks through the
expectation of seeing his troops arrive with promptness.

The capture of Lee was characterized by Washington thus mildly,
" It was by his own folly and imprudence, and without a view to effect
any good that he was taken." General Sullivan succeeded Lee in
command, and with Gates of the Northern army, who brought about
six hundred men, moved promptly to the Delaware, crossed the river
at Phillipsburg, and joined Washington. The army was reorganized
on the twentieth for further service. General Howe had returned to
New York on the thirteenth. The British cantonments embraced
Burlington, Bordentown, Trenton, Brunswick, and other small places.
Colonel Donop, acting brigadier, was stationed at Bordentown.

It will be seen that in one of the most critical periods of the war,
when the commander-in-chief himself was on trial, the man who next
commanded public confidence because of his military training, failed
him ; simply because Washington with the modesty of a true desire to
attain excellence in his profession, would not pass final judgment and
enforce his own will in disobedience to the will of Congress. Congress
itself began to realize however, that a deliberative civil body was not
the best commander-in-chief for field service, and that it would have
to trust the men who did the fighting. It adjourned on the twelfth of
December quite precipitately, and at the same time, " *Resolved*: that
until Congress shall otherwise order, General Washington be possessed
of full power to order and direct all things relative to the department
and to the operations of war."

CHAPTER XXXVIII.

WASHINGTON RETURNS THE OFFENSIVE. TRENTON HIS FIRST
OBJECTIVE. 1776.

ON the eleventh of December Washington learned that the British troops were repairing bridges below Trenton and had also rebuilt one which had been destroyed by the Americans at Crosswicks. While it seemed that this work was preparatory to an attempt to move down the river and cross it at a point nearer to Philadelphia, he regarded even such a movement as likely to expose the British post-detachments to attack, and began to make his plans accordingly. His army had increased to nearly six thousand effectives, rank and file. General Maxwell had been very faithful in collecting boats to secure the anticipated crossing of General Lee's command, and was familiar with the country, so that he was selected to command at Morristown, which was regarded as a valuable position for a permanent post. Meanwhile it was a rendezvous for troops coming from the north, and a considerable militia force was already assembling at that place.

To guard against surprise he divided the river-front into sections, under competent commanders. These orders were issued on the twelfth and thirteenth of December. The system adopted is worthy of notice. Besides light earthworks opposite ferries and exposed places easy for landing, and intermediate sentries, small guard posts were established at short intervals, and " constant patrols were ordered to pass." Points were assigned for a rendezvous in case of a sudden crossing where the force detailed was not capable of resistance. The troops were to have rations for three days always on hand, and all boats were to be protected and kept in good order.

General Ewing was to guard the river from Bordentown Ferry to Yardley's Mills where he lapped on to General Dickinson's section. Four brigades, each with artillery, under Stirling, Mercer, Stephens and De Fermoy, were posted from Yardley's to Coryell Ferry, in such manner as to guard every suspicious part of the river and to afford assistance to each other in case of attack. Colonel Cadwallader was posted above and below the Neshaminy river, as far as Dunks Ferry, at which place Colonel Nixon was posted with the third battalion of Philadelphia. An order was issued the same day, "requiring all able bodied men in that city, not conscientiously scrupulous about bearing arms, to report in the State House yard the next day with their arms and equipments :—that all persons who have arms and accouterments which they can not or do not mean to employ in defense of America, are hereby ordered to deliver them to Mr. Robert Towers, who will pay for the same; and that those who are convicted of secreting any arms or accouterments will be severely punished."

On the fourteenth, when advised that General Howe had actually returned to New York, and that the British army was definitely entering winter quarters, he felt the necessity and entertained a plan, for immediate offensive action. He exhausted appeals to Governors and State committees for fresh troops, and resolved to keep his army active while its short term of service held out. His determination, "to face about and meet the enemy" had only been postponed through Lee's disobedience.

On the fourteenth he wrote to Governor Trumbull, " The troops that came down from Ticonderoga with Arnold and Gates, may in conjunction with my present force, and that under General Lee, enable us to attempt a stroke upon the forces of the enemy, who lay a good deal scattered, and to all appearance, in a state of security. A lucky blow in this quarter would be fatal to them, and would most certainly raise the spirits of the people which are quite sunk by our late misfortunes." On the same date he wrote to Gates, " If we can draw our forces together, I trust under the smiles of Providence we may yet effect an important stroke, or at least prevent General Howe from executing his plans. I have wrote to General Arnold to go to the eastward " (Rhode Island) " on account of the intelligence from that quarter."

The closing paragraph carries with it the correction of a statement made in Hughes' History of England, that *Arnold* proposed to Washington the capture of Trenton. Hughes quotes Adolphus, and Adolphus had it " from private information, source unknown."

Washington wrote to Heath on the same day, " If we can collect our force speedily, I should hope we may effect something of importance, or at least give such a turn to our affairs as to make them assume a more pleasing aspect than they now have."

On the twentieth he wrote sternly to Congress, "that ten days more will put an end to the existence of this army. This is not a time to stand upon expense. Our funds are not the only object of consideration. If any good officers offer to raise men upon continental pay and establishment, in this quarter, I shall encourage them to do so, and regiment them when they have done it. If Congress disapprove of the proceeding, they will please signify it, as I mean it for the best. It may be thought I am going a good deal out of the line of my duty to adopt these measures, or to advise thus freely. A character to lose, an estate to forfeit, the inestimable blessing of liberty at stake, and a life devoted, must be my excuse." This letter, which is long and full of important details, seems to start Washington on a career of greater independence of action, and with corresponding advantage to his army and its work. He had already ordered the recruiting of three battalions of artillery : and as Congress was then at Baltimore, more than one hundred and thirty miles distant, he proceeded directly to work, under the Resolution which they adopted before adjournment. Major Sheldon, of Connecticut, who had the only mounted men then with the army, was also commissioned by him as lieutenant-colonel, to complete a battalion of six troops, and was furnished with fourteen thousand dollars for the purpose.

In order to learn the exact disposition of the British forces, a scout was sent out. On the twentieth, Washington settled upon his plans, and directed the three regiments from Ticonderoga to halt at Morristown, where he understood there were already eight hundred militia collected, " in order to inspirit the inhabitants, and as far as possible cover that part of the country." He adds, " I shall send General Maxwell this day to take the command of them, and if it can be done, to harass and annoy the enemy in their quarters, and cut off their convoys."

On the twenty-first, Adjutant-general Reed, then at Bristol, reported, " Pomeroy, whom I sent by your order to go to Amboy, and on through the Jerseys, and round by Princeton to you, returned to Burlington yesterday." After reporting fully as to Pomeroy's visit to Cranberry, Brunswick, Princeton, and elsewhere, he adds, " In Burlington county he found them," the Hessians, " scattered through all the farmers' houses, eight, ten, twelve, and fifteen in a house, and rambling over the whole country.

"Colonel Griffin has advanced up the Jerseys with six hundred men as far as Mount Holly, within seven miles of their headquarters at the Black Horse. The spirits of the militia are high, they are all for supporting him. We can either give him a strong reinforcement, or make a separate attack. . . . Some enterprise must be undertaken in our present circumstances, or we must give up the cause, . . . will it not be possible my Dear General for your troops, or such part of them as can act with advantage, to make a diversion or something more at or about Trenton. . . . If we could possess ourselves again of New Jersey, or any considerable part of it, the effect would be greater than if we had never left it. Delay with us is now equal to a defeat. It is determined to make all possible preparation to-day, and no event happening to change our measures, the main body *here* will cross the river to-morrow morning, and attack their post between this and the Black Horse." Colonel Reed was then with Cadwallader. On the same day the army return was made up showing a total of ten thousand one hundred and six men, and of these, only four thousand seven hundred and seven rank and file were present for duty. To this should be added four regiments which arrived from the northern army, twelve hundred men; also Cadwallader's Pennsylvania militia, eighteen hundred men, and Sullivan's division, late Lee's, three thousand men. The total force, deducting the sick of the added commands, numbered nearly or quite nine thousand men, but this was the entire force for all purposes whatever.

On the following day Washington thus disclosed to the Adjutant-general in confidence, his own matured plans.

"CAMP ABOVE TRENTON FALLS, 23*d December*, 1776.

DEAR SIR:—The bearer is down to know whether your plan was attempted last night, and if not, to inform you that Christmas day at night, one hour before day, is the time fixed upon for our attempt at Trenton. For Heaven's sake keep this to yourself, as the discovery of it may prove fatal to us; our numbers, sorry am I to say, being less than I had any conception of; but necessity, dire necessity, will, nay must, justify my attack. Prepare, and in concert with Griffin, attack as many of the posts as you can with a prospect of success; the more we can attack at the same instant, the more confusion we shall spread, and greater good will result from it. If I had not been fully convinced before of the enemy's design, I have now ample testimony of their intention to attack Philadelphia, as soon as the ice will afford the means of conveyance. As the colonels of the Continental regiments might kick up some dust about command, unless Cadwallader is considered by them in the light of a brigadier, which I wish him to be, I desired General Gates who is unwell, and applied for leave to go to Philadelphia, to endeavor, if his health would permit him, to call and stay two or three days at Bristol on his way. I shall not be particular.

We could not ripen matters for our attack before the time mentioned in the first part of this letter, so much out of sorts, and so much in want of everything are the troops under Sullivan, etc. Let me know by a careful express the plan you are to pursue."

   .   .   .   .

                                " I am dear sir, your obedient servant,

                                          "GEORGE WASHINGTON."

"P. S. I have ordered our men to be furnished with three days' cooked rations, with which and their blankets they are to march ; for if we are successful, which heaven grant, and the circumstances favor, we may push on. I shall direct every ferry and ford to be well guarded, and not a soul suffered to pass without an officer's going down with a permit ; do the same with you."

    " To Joseph Reed, Esqr., or in his absence,

    " To John Cadwallader, Esqr., only, at Bristol."

The countersign for the day written by Washington himself, was " Victory or Death."

The letter of Adjutant-general Reed supplies the gap, which Mr. Sparks refers to, in foot-note of " Writings of Washington, vol. iv— page 242," where he says, " The *plan* mentioned at the beginning of the letter, is not explained."

In a letter of Robert Morris to Congress, written on the twenty-sixth, when he heard of the success of the movement, he writes, " This manœuver of the General had been determined upon several days ago, but he kept it secret as the nature of the service would admit."

Washington was as capable of keeping his own counsels as was Frederick the Great, and there is no responsible authority for crediting any other man with the plan to capture the garrison of Trenton. Others saw the exposed condition of the enemy : but Washington acted upon his own motion. The British troops in New Jersey were so disposed as if no enemy was within striking distance. And yet every effort to cross the Delaware, or even to procure boats for that purpose, was met by the fact that the entire opposite shore for miles, was under vigilant watch. This alertness to anticipate a British advance, carried with it the contingency of incursions from so keen a rear-guard : and Colonel Rahl, the post commander at Trenton, had been one of the most active officers where hard fighting had been experienced, from the twenty-second day of August, when he landed upon Long Island. As the American army controlled all the boats on the river, they had the means of passage at all times ready at hand. From a letter written by General Howe to Lord Germaine it appears that he understood exactly the condition of Washington's army, and that after the first of January it would become a skeleton. This fact exposed one of those military pauses, when a force having capacity to do, must do at once, or never. The obligation upon Washington as a soldier was imperative, and as already seen, he realized the fact. General Howe and the officers of the corps of observation along the Delaware *ignored the American army*, and rested, anticipating an easy march to Philadelphia. It was just when they should have seen that the last week of the year was the most hopeful for Washington and the most critical for their river posts. Already the militia had demonstrated toward Mount Holly and challenged Colonel Donop at Bordentown; but they had positive orders not to be drawn into an engagement, and to retire upon the approach of the Hessians.

Several small stations had been threatened near Trenton itself, and Washington had publicly made known his purpose to measure out the treatment of prisoners, and carry on war, by the gauge which the British general-in-chief should adopt. If the weather allowed the Americans to keep the field, it furnished the more potential reason why the better equipped British army should bring boats from New York, and overwhelm the dissolving ranks of the enemy, by a quick onset.

General Grant, commanding at Brunswick, wrote on the twenty-fourth, " It is perfectly certain there are no more rebel troops in Jersey: they only send over small parties of twenty or thirty men. On the last Sunday Washington told his assembled generals that, " the British are weak at Trenton and Princeton. I wish the Hessians to be on the guard against sudden attack ; but at the same time I give my opinion that nothing of the kind will be undertaken."

The closing paragraph destroyed the benefit of the previous statement, which showed that his military forecast of an exposure to attack was sound, and that he knew that Washington appreciated the opportunity.

NOTE. Compare above with first sentence of General Grant's report of the affair at Trenton, viz., " On the twenty-fifth, in the evening a party of the enemy attacked an outguard from the post of Trenton. . . which party was beaten back. Washington certainly ordered no detail across the river to put the Hessians on their guard and defeat his surprise. Either General Grant took up some confused report and therefrom builds an argument to show that Colonel Rahl had timely warning; or the attack was from some random party, not in force, nor under responsible authority. It is easier to presume General Grant to have been misinformed than to define the occurrence. See Washington's instructions, page 268.

CHAPTER XXXIX.

HESSIANS SURPRISED AT TRENTON. 1776.

ON the twenty-fifth day of December, 1776, the regiments of Anspach, Knyphausen, and Rahl, with fifty chasseurs, and twenty light dragoons, making a total effective force of not quite fifteen hundred and fifty men, constituted the garrison at Trenton. The command had six pieces of artillery, including two in front of Colonel Rahl's quarters ; but contrary to the previous advice of Colonel Donop, there were neither field works nor defense of any kind before the ferry or at any of the approaches to the town. One such work on the summit, at the fork of King and Queen's streets, and one on Front street, would have seriously endangered the American movement, especially under the circumstances of severe weather, which almost disarmed the assailants. It is well known that rumors of an impending offensive return by Washington had reached Colonel Rahl, and that a small picket guard had been stationed on the old Pennington road, half a mile beyond the head of King street, and another was in position, equally advanced upon the river road leading to the next upper, or McConkey's ferry, past the houses of Rutherford and General Dickinson.

It was Christmas day, a holiday in great favor with the troops which composed the garrison. It is profitless for the author's purpose to enter into details of the manner in which that garrison observed that holiday, and spent the night which closed its enjoyment. It is enough to state that military negligence was absolute, and that it cost the commander his life. That negligence lasted through the night, and prevailed up to eight o'clock in the morning. It appears that the usual morning parade-routine had been observed, and the men had returned to their barracks. These barracks, now cleft by a street, were still standing in 1875, and showed that they afforded a good defensive position, if promptly occupied and firmly held. The disposi-

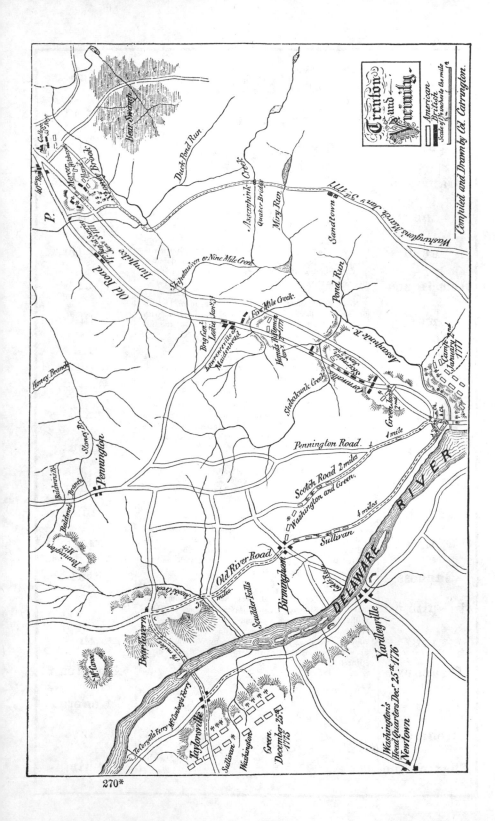

Trenton and Vicinity

American
British
Scale of five-tenths the mile

Compiled and Drawn by Col. Carrington.

Washington's March Jan'y 3, 1777.

Washington's March Jan'y 3, 1777.

Bear Swamp.

Duck Pond Run.

Assanpink Creek.

Quaker Bridge.

Miry Run.

Sandtown.

Pond Run.

Turnpike.

Old Road.

Road of Jan'y 3, 1777.

Little Shabakunk

Maidenhead.

Lawrenceville or

Brytton's Leslie Jan'y 3.

Mercer.

Shabakunk or Nine Mile Creek

Five Mile Creek.

Ward's retreat Jan'y 2, 1777.

Shabakunk Creek.

Assanpink R.

Carrington

Sullivan

Greene.

P.

Honey Branch

Stoney Br.

Baldwin's Br.

Pennington

Baldwin's Branch

Pennington Mills

Pennington Road.

Scotch Road 2 miles

Washington and Green.

1 mile

4 miles

Sullivan

4 miles

DELAWARE

RIVER

McKanes

Bear Tavern

Jacob's Creek

Old River Road

Scudder Falls

Birmingham

2 miles

To Corycll's Ferry or Lamb's Ferry

Taylorsville

Sullivan

Washington

Green.
December 25, 1775

Yardleyville

Washington's
Head Quarters Dec. 25, 1776

Newtown

270*

The

March

which

traversed

and

saved

New Jersey,

was

planned

and

executed,

with

Supreme

Faith

in

Success,

in spite of

the

Treachery

of

General

Charles Lee.

Trenton and Vicinity.

NOTES.

NOTE.—General Charles Lee kept back his division of troops, for selfish ends, although repeatedly ordered to join Washington, and thus crippled his superior officer in his movements.

NOTE 2.—Washington moved from Newtown, December 25th, to Taylorsville, 9 miles above Trenton, with 2,400 men, where he formed his two columns for the surprise of Rahl.

NOTE 3.—General James Ewing was to cross below Newtown with 547 men, to sieze the bridge across the Assinpink and cut off retreat to the South.

NOTE 4.—Col. John Cadwallader was to cross at Bristol, below Bordentown, where Donop's Hessians were stationed, and co-operate with Griffin, already East of the Delaware, who was to occupy Donop's attention from the North.

NOTE 5.—General Putnam was expected to cross at Philadelphia with one thousand men.
Disaffection in that City prevented him.

NOTE 6.—The column of Washington alone effected a timely crossing. Donop abandoned Bordentown after a sharp skirmish with Griffin ; and on the 27th, Cadwallader reached Bordentown with 1,800 men The ice prevented the landing of his artillery on the 26th, and he abandoned the attempt then made.

NOTE 7.—The Map indicates the sub-division and march of Washington's columns ; the advance of Cornwallis from Princeton, January 2d, 1777, when he crowded Hand and Greene back upon Trenton ; also the American march of January 3d, whereby Washington fell upon the rear of the British Army, under Mawhood, at Princeton.

The

great

Soldiers,

Statesmen

and

Writers

of

the

Old

World,

paid

Tribute

to

this

great

Stroke

of

the

American

General

in

Chief.

22

tion of the American army for the attack was eminently bold and judicious. Griffin was expected still to occupy the attention of Donop, as if the demonstrations across the river were but the feverish action of local militia. A small centre column, under General James Ewing, of Pennsylvania, whose brigade reported but five hundred and forty-seven rank and file for duty, was to cross just below Trenton, to occupy the bridge across the Assanpink, and thus sever communication with Donop's corps at Bordentown. Still further down the river, as a constraint upon the possible movement of that corps to the support of Colonel Rahl, the right wing under Colonel John Cadwallader, not yet promoted, was ordered to cross at Bristol, below Bordentown, with view to a direct attack upon Donop from the south, and thus coöperate with the militia in that quarter. General Washington reserved for himself the conduct of the left wing, consisting of twenty-four hundred men, which was to cross nine miles above Trenton, at McConkey's ferry. Learning that Maidenhead was almost without garrison, except a troop of dragoons, it was the purpose of the American commander also to include that sub-post within his raid.

It was also expected that General Putnam would cross from Philadelphia early on the twenty-sixth, with at least a thousand men. The plan embraced the entire deliverance of the left bank of the Delaware.

The right wing landed a portion of its troops; but on account of the ice could not land the artillery, and returned to Bristol. Cadwallader expressed his great regret in his report to Washington, remarking, "I imagine the badness of the night must have prevented you from passing over as you intended."

It was not until four o'clock that Cadwallader succeeded in regaining Bristol; and Moylan, who then started to join Washington, found the storm so violent that he abandoned his purpose, believing that that officer could not possibly effect a crossing. The centre column failed to effect a landing for the same reason.

Reference is made to maps, "Operations in New Jersey," "Operations near Philadelphia," "Trenton and Vicinity," and "Battle of Trenton." The narrative will now adopt official elements without formal detail of the fragments embodied.

The left wing of the army under Washington, accompanied by Greene and Sullivan as division commanders, formed evening parade under cover of the high ground just back of McConkey's Ferry, now known as Taylorville. It was designed to move as soon as darkness set in, so as to complete the crossing at midnight, and enter Trenton as early as five o'clock on the morning of the twenty-sixth.

It was such a night as cost Montgomery and Arnold their fearful experience under the rock of Quebec. It was cold, snowy, and tempestuous. A few days of milder weather had opened the ice ; now it was again rapidly freezing, checking the current and skirting the shore.

The scanty protection of blankets was as nothing to protect men in such a conflict. There were young volunteers from Philadelphia in that command, going forth for the first time to study war. There were nearly ragged and shoeless veterans there, who had faced such storms, and the fiercer storms of war before. Stark, of Breed's Hill, was there. Glover, the man of Marblehead, a hero of the Long Island retreat, and Webb and Scott, and William Washington and James Monroe were there. Brain and courage, nerve and faith were there. Washington's countersign of the twenty-third, " *Victory or Death*," was in the inner chambers of many souls, guarding manhood, quickening conscience and defying nature. This was all because the path of duty was so well defined. The order to embark and cross over, had been given. It was short, and made no allusion to the swift current, the cold or snow. These were almost negative facts, circumstances of delay and discomfort, but could not set aside duty. Those men had been retreating, and had rested on the bank of the Delaware, almost hopeless of better times. They were now faced upon their late pursuers. The " man of retreats," and temporary positions, was in his fighting mood, and men went with him, counting no impediments and sternly in earnest.

"As severe a night as I ever saw," wrote Thomas Rodney ;—" the frost was sharp, the current difficult to stem, the ice increasing, the wind high and at eleven it began to snow."

The landing of the artillery was not effected until three o'clock, but the army did not march until four. Retreat could not be made without discovery, annoyance, and consequent disheartening of his troops, and late as it was, the advance was ordered. The snow ceased, but sleet and hail came fiercely from the northeast, as the march began.

A mile and a quarter from the landing brought them to Bear Tavern, where they reached the direct river road to Trenton. Three miles and a half more brought them to Birmingham. Sullivan here notified Washington by a messenger that the men reported their " arms to be wet." " Tell your General," said Washington, " to use the bayonet and penetrate into the town. The town must be taken. I am resolved to take it."

Here the army divided. Sullivan's division moved at once by the river road, toward Trenton, then only four and a half miles distant. Washington with Greene, took direction to the left, crossed over to the old Scotch road, and entered the Pennington road one mile from town. This route was about equally distant with the other from the points aimed at by the respective divisions. Washington's division, as he says, "arrived at the enemy's advanced post exactly at eight o'clock; and three minutes after, I found from the fire on the lower road, that that division had also got up." The pickets on both roads behaved well, but were quickly swept away by the force which already hastened to its achievement.

Washington moved directly to the junction of King and Queen streets. The flying pickets had already given the alarm, and the Hessians were beginning to rally within sight, as he rode in advance.

Under his direction Colonel Knox placed Forrest's battery of six guns in position so as to command both streets, which there diverged at a very acute angle; Queen street running southward to the Assanpink, and King street inclining east of south, to the crossing of Second and Front streets, by which Sullivan must approach. Colonel Rahl occupied the large frame house of Stacy Potts, near where Perry street joins King street. He promptly put himself at the head of a hastily gathered detachment for the purpose of advancing up King street to its summit, but Captain Forrest's battery of six guns had already opened fire. The regiment of Knyphausen attempted to form in open ground between Queen street and the Assanpink, while a third detachment, completely demoralized, moved rapidly toward the Princeton road to escape in that direction. This last detachment was met by Colonel Hand's rifle battalion which had been deployed to Washington's left, as a guard upon that possible line of retreat, as well as to watch the approaches from Princeton. Scott's and Lawson's Virginia battalions had been thrown still further to the left, thus completely closing the gap between Hand and the Assanpink river.

While Rahl was gathering his own companies as rapidly as possible, the two guns at his headquarters had been partially manned and were ready to deliver fire; when captain Washington, with lieutenant James Monroe and an active party, rushed upon the gunners and brought away the pieces, before a sufficiently strong infantry support could be brought up for their protection. Rahl moved his companies

18

as soon as formed, and joined Knyphausen's regiment, but almost immediately moved back for the cover which the buildings afforded.

Galloway, Stedman, and some other early writers, have alleged that the Hessians returned to load wagons and carry off their accumulated plunder. It is difficult to regard such statements as other than traditional fables. Individuals may have tried to save their effects, but there was very little time to spare for that business, and Colonel Rahl was too strict a soldier to have permitted it at such a moment.

Captain Forrest's guns swept the open ground as well as the streets, and the adjoining orchard was equally untenable, hopelessly exposing the men to a fire which could not be returned. Two of the guns which were afterwards taken, seem to have been cut off from the reach of the Hessians when they were themselves drifted eastward from their magazine and barracks by the American control of both King and Queen streets; and two guns with the Knyphausen regiment were of little service. General Sullivan's division entered the town through Front and Second streets. Colonel Stark who led the column, moved directly to the Assanpink bridge, to cut off retreat toward Bordentown, but the chasseurs, the light horse and a considerable infantry force, at least two hundred men, had already crossed the bridge in retreat upon that post. St. Clair took possession of the foot of Queen street, and as Stark swung round and moved up the Assanpink, the Hessians were literally between two fires, while the additional enfilading fire upon the streets closed their left, and the Assanpink closed their right.

For a short time small parties of Hessians who had been unable to join their companies, kept up a fruitless scattering fire from houses where they had taken refuge; but the fall of Colonel Rahl while urging his men to assault the summit where Washington controlled the action, and the advance of Sullivan's division which shut up all avenues of escape to Bordentown, forced the Hessians out of the town to the open field and orchard, where the whole command surrendered.

The American casualties were two killed and three wounded, captain Washington and Monroe being amone the latter. Several were badly frozen; in two instances resulting fatally. The Hessian casualties were given by General Howe as forty men killed and wounded besides officers; and nine hundred and eighteen prisoners were taken, of whom thirty were officers. Subsequently, a lieutenant-colonel, a deputy-adjutant-general, and scattering members of the Hessian corps were taken, making the total number of prisoners, as reported by Washington on the twenty-eighth of December, at about one thousand." The trophies of war were six bronze guns, four sets of colors, over a thousand stand of arms, twelve drums, many blankets and other garrison supplies. General Howe says, " This misfortune seems to have proceeded from Colonel Rahl's quitting the post and advancing to the attack, instead of defending the village." The fact is overlooked that Washington's position at the head of King and Queen streets with artillery, which commanded both streets, afforded a very poor opportunity for the surprised Hessians. The more men they gathered in those narrow streets, the better it was for American artillery practice. Rahl followed the instincts of a soldier, and as he had not the force to assault the enemy, and dispossess them of their commanding positions, he sought ground where he could form his command and fight as he could get opportunity. The movement of Washington which threw Hand, Scott, and Lawson to the left, together with his superiority in artillery, and the pressure of Sullivan's division from the rear through Second street, forced Colonel Rahl to his fate. His mistakes had been made before the alarm of battle recalled him to duty; and then he did all that time and Washington permitted. The disparity in casualties is accounted for by the facts stated. The American artillery had its play at will beyond musket range and upon higher ground, with little chance for the Hessians to render fire in return. A few skillfully handled guns determined the action. Washington on this occasion evinced the force of individual will applied, under extreme necessity, to a determining issue. The battle occupied less than one hour. Its fruit was like the grain of mustard seed which developed a tree under whose branches a thousand might take shelter. He marched back to Newtown *with prisoners of war*, reaching his headquarters the same night; a new experience for the American army. This countermarch was attended with great hardships and suffering. The entire distance marched by the troops which left Newtown with Washington, was nearly thirty miles, before they again reached their camp, and more than a thousand men were practically disabled for duty through frozen limbs and broken down energies.

General Gates did not participate in the action, having gone to Baltimore to meet Congress of his own volition without invitation, and without advising with Washington. Major Wilkinson of his staff was indeed sent to report the fact to the general-in-chief, and so reported while Washington was superintending the crossing of the troops during the evening of the twenty-fifth. General Putnam made no demonstration, through apprehension that if he left Philadelphia there would be an uprising of royalists in his rear. Colonel Griffin, who had recrossed the Delaware after his first skirmish with Colonel Donop did not return to the Jersey bank to coöperate on the evening of the twenty-fifth, so that the entire attack was limited to the operations of the extreme left wing.

The Hessian troops were marched through the streets of Philadelphia to prove to the people that the dreaded European veterans were no longer invincible, and the effect upon that city and the States of Pennsylvania and New Jersey was of lasting value to the American cause.

Colonel Donop did not wait for an assault upon his post. In his skirmish with Griffin he had employed nearly his whole garrison, consisting of two thousand men, with little advantage; and upon the arrival of the fragments of Rahl's command, he abandoned the post altogether, with the stores, his sick and wounded, and marched with haste to Princeton *via* Crosswick's and Allentown, and started on the next day for South Amboy.

On the twenty-seventh, Cadwallader crossed over from Bristol with eighteen hundred men, and reached Bordentown the next day, not indeed knowing that Washington had recrossed the river. Generals Ewing and Mifflin followed successively with five hundred and eight hundred men, but Mount Holly and Black Horse had already been abandoned by the Hessians.

While the Continental troops who participated in the battle of Trenton rested, Washington perfected his means for further offensive movements. He learned from a letter of Colonel De Hart, written from Morristown on the twenty-seventh, the gratifying news that the three regiments of Greaton, Bond, and Porter, would extend their terms of service two weeks. That officer also reported that only five or six hundred Highlanders remained at Elizabethtown, and that the outposts at Boundbrook and in that vicinity had been withdrawn to Brunswick. Generals McDougall and Maxwell, then at Morristown, were instructed " to collect as large a body of militia as possible, and assure them that nothing is wanting but for them to lend a hand and drive the enemy from the whole province of New Jersey." On the twenty-eighth he wrote to Maxwell, "As I am about to enter the Jerseys with a considerable force immediately, for the purpose of attempting a recovery of that country from the enemy, and as a diversion from your quarter may greatly facilitate this event by distracting and dividing their troops, I must request that you will collect all the force in your power together, and annoy and distress them by every means which prudence can suggest." To General Heath he wrote, " I would have you advance as rapidly as the season will admit with the eastern militia, by the way of the Hackensack, and proceed downwards until you hear from me. I think a fair opportunity is offered of driving the enemy entirely from, or at least to, the extremity of the province of Jersey."

On the thirtieth Washington, having again crossed to Trenton, was able to announce that the continental regiments of the eastern governments had agreed to remain six weeks longer in the service, upon receipt of a bounty of ten dollars; and earnest messages were sent out in all directions, to eminent citizens as well as officers, to make use of the success of Trenton as a stimulus to recruit for the army and hasten the concentration of the militia. The responses were of the most encouraging nature; but the great fact remained, that the ordeal of the conversion of raw material into soldiers would have to be gone through again after a few weeks, and every hour was to be improved to get the largest possible results out of the service of the four thousand of old troops who had consented to remain for that short period. The success on the twenty-fifth aroused great expectations, and Congress shared in the confidence which the people extended to the Commander-in-chief of its armies.

NOTE. Major Wilkinson thus describes the delivery of General Gates' letter to General Washington, at McConkey's Ferry, after dusk, December 26th. I found him alone, with his whip in his hand, prepared to mount his horse. When I presented the letter of General Gates to him, before receiving it, he exclaimed with solemnity, ' What a time is this to hand me letters!! Where is he?' Answer. ' I left him this morning in Philadelphia.' What was he doing there? ' I understood him, that he was on his way to Congress.' He earnestly repeated : ' On his way to Congress,' then broke the seal, and I made my bow and joined General St. Clair, on the bank of the river. This incident is given in connection with another statement of the same officer, that General Gates said it was his intention to propose to Congress that General Washington should retire to the south of the Susquehanna. This explains his failure to join Washington. The success at Trenton was not anticipated by General Gates.

NOTE. Rahl, or Rall. Dr. Frederick Kapp, of Berlin, in a letter to Adjutant-general William Stryker, of Trenton, New Jersey, May, 1776, says, " Rall is correct." In modern usage, the silent h, their only silent letter, is dropped by German scholars. Hence Bancroft adopts Rall. As Washington, Sparks, Irving and general history have retained the h, the name is retained as most familiar at the period of the war. It is immaterial, as the pronunciation, in either case, would be as if the name were spelled in English, Rarl. Dr Bailey Myers, a German scholar of repute, and Professor Green, in his German element in the Rev. War., retain Rahl.

CHAPTER XL.

WHILE the land operations of the British and American armies were thus constant during the latter part of the year 1776, the Americans made considerable progress in the building of the ships of war which had been previously authorized.

The Columbus and Hamden were at Providence nearly ready for sea on the second of November, but were soon shut up with the Warren and some smaller vessels, by the British occupation of Newport. The Alfred had sailed and had already captured several valuable prizes. The New Hampshire, Raleigh, Randolph, Congress, Delaware, Montgomery and several other frigates were nearly finished but needed cannon. Thirteen had been launched, and two ships of the line and five additional frigates were on the stocks by the twenty-first of December. At that date Robert Morris sent to the American Commissioners at Paris a statement of the condition of public affairs, and then apologized for the apparently slow progress made in fitting out vessels to prey upon British commerce, by stating the want of heavy guns. Besides the Alfred, however, the Reprisal, Andrew Doria and Lexington were at sea, as well as the sloops Providence, Hornet, Fly, Independence and Sachem, and the schooners Wasp, Musquito and Georgia-Packet. Privateering however monopolized the chief interest in naval warfare, because it was lucrative ; and it was with difficulty that suitable crews could be obtained, for other vessels of all kinds had captured, according to the official list, three hundred and forty-two, had retaken forty-four and burned five.

In aid of their operations at home the Americans already began to count upon foreign assistance. Correspondence had been opened with agents at Paris looking to the enlistment of France in the war ; and the prizes of the American privateers had found special favor in the

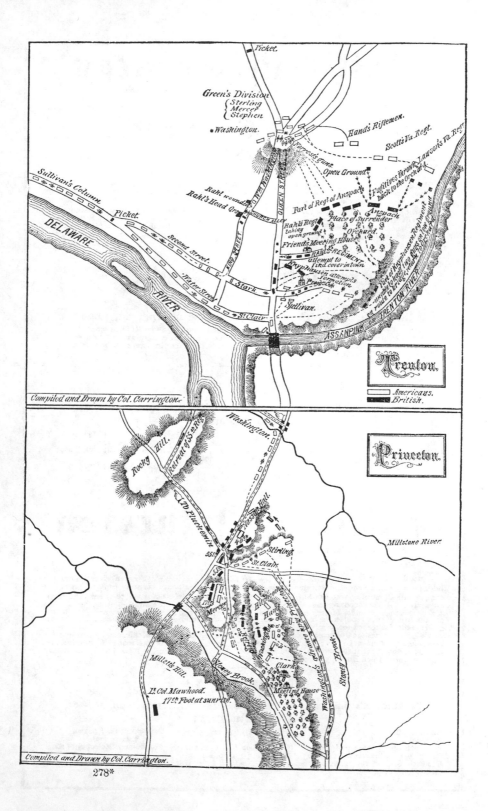

Picket.

Green's Division
Sterling
Mercer
Stephen

• Washington.

Hand's Riflemen.

Forrest's Guns.

Scott's Va. Regt.

Open Ground.

Fugitives thrown
back to the orchard.

Lawson's Va. Regt.

Rahl wounded.
Rahl's Head Quarters.

Part of Regt. of Anspach

Anspach

Rahl's Regt.
taking
open ground.

Place of Surrender

Friends Meeting House

Orchard.

RAHL'S REGIMENT
attempt to
find cover in town.

Part of Knyphausen Regiment
under Rahl forming on open ground.

Knyphausen
attempts
Princeton

Formation

Stark

Sullivan.

St. Clair

ASSANPINK OR TRENTON RIVER

DELAWARE

Sullivan's Column.

Picket.

Second Street.

Water Street.

RIVER

Compiled and Drawn by Col. Carrington.

Trenton.

☐ Americans.
■ British.

Washington.

Rocky Hill.

Retreat of 55 Regt.

L. D. Phuctewith

55th

Nassau Hall.

40th

Stirling

St. Clair

Millstone River.

Mercer.

Hitchcock.

Hall.

Clarks.

Millett's Hill.

L. Col. Mawhood.
17th Foot at sunrise.

Stony Brook.

Meeting House

Washington Road

Stoney Brook.

Compiled and Drawn by Col. Carrington.

Princeton.

Battle of Trenton

DECEMBER 26th, 1776

American Commander

WASHINGTON

Strength, 2,400   Casualties, 2 killed, 3 wounded

MEM.—*Among the wounded were Captain, afterwards Col. Washington, and Lieut. James Monroe, afterwards President Monroe. They were wounded while capturing two guns in front of Rahl's Headquarters, on King's Street.*

NOTE. The two columns, advancing as indicated on previous map, respectively gained the head and foot of King's street, at 8 o'clock in the morning, after a hard march, through hail, sleet and rain, in which many were frost bitten. Several died. The surprise of the Hessians was complete. Hand's riflemen, and the Virginia regiments of Scott and Lawson, prevented the escape of many, along the Assanpink river.

British Commander

RAHL

Strength, 1,400   Casualties, 40   Force surrendered, 1,009

NOTE.—Portions of Anspach and Knyphausen's regiments, serving under Rahl, attempted to rally, east of Queen street, but the lower town and the bridge across the Assanpink, had been seized by Sullivan, Stark and St. Clair, and surrender was inevitable. The American guns at the head of King and Queen streets commanded the situation.

References:

CARRINGTON'S "BATTLES OF THE AMERICAN REVOLUTION," pp. 270-278.

School Histories:

Anderson, ¶ 39 ; p. 76.
Barnes, ¶ 3 ; p. 117.
Berard (Bush), ¶ 68; pp. 154-5.
Goodrich, C.A. (Seaveys), ¶ 9, p. 122.
Goodrich, S. G., ¶ 1-7 ; p. 216.
Hassard, ¶ 8 ; p. 182.

Holmes, ¶ 23 ; p. 121.
Lossing, ¶ 23 ; p. 128.
Quackenbos, ¶ 326; p. 233.
Ridpath, ¶ 26-7 ; p. 198-9.
Sadlier (Excel), ¶ 6 ; p. 188.
Stephens, A. H., ¶ 13 ; p. 195.

Swinton, ¶ 123 ; p. 130.
Scott, ¶ 18 ; p. 173.
Thalheimer (Eclectic), ¶ 259 ;
p. 147.
Venable, ¶ 137 ; p. 104.

Battle of Princeton

JANUARY 3d, 1777

WASHINGTON, then entrenched on the east bank of the Assinpink (Trenton) river, leaving the bridge guarded and camp fires burning, made a forced march to extricate his army from an impending conflict with Cornwallis, who had hurried from Brunswick on the defeat of Rahl, to attack the American army. Col. Mawhood, commanding the British rear-guard, had left Princeton, when he saw the American vanguard under Mercer enter the town. He returned and attacked with vigor. Mercer fell, but the British were repulsed with a loss of 100 in killed and wounded, and 230 prisoners. The American casualties exceeded 100.

Washington restored temporary confusion which occurred on the fall of Mercer, by personal exposure and great bravery. He gained a strong position among the hills, in the rear of Cornwallis, and thereby forced the British army back to New Brunswick and New York. New Jersey was, for the time, delivered from British control.

References:

CARRINGTON'S "BATTLES OF THE AMERICAN REVOLUTION," pp. 284-294.

School Histories:

Anderson, ¶ 43 ; p. 78.
Barnes, ¶ 1 ; p. 118.
Berard (Bush), ¶ 82-3 ; p. 158-9.
Goodrich, C. A.(Seaveys) ¶ 10; p. 123.
Goodrich, S. G., ¶ 1-7 ; p. 217-18.
Hassard, ¶ 11 ; p. 183.

Holmes, ¶ 1 ; p. 123.
Lossing, ¶ 5 ; p. 151.
Quackenbos, ¶ 327 ; p. 234-5.
Ridpath, ¶ 1-4 ; p. 201.
Sadlier (Excel), ¶ 8 ; p. 188.
Stephens, A. H., ¶ 15 ; p. 196.

Swinton, ¶ 124 ; p. 130.
Scott, ¶ 2 ; p. 179.
Thalheimer (Eclectic), ¶ 260 ;
p. 147-8.
Venable, ¶ 137 ; p. 105.

ports of that country and of Spain, by a skillful avoidance of any public act that would offend Great Britain.

The proclamation which General Howe published when his army entered the Jerseys had received its death-blow when Trenton was taken; and Congress silenced the still existing anxiety for some kind of a compromise by an unequivocal course which left no alternative but the issue of battle.

The British army was theoretically in Winter quarters. The garrison of Rhode Island made no demonstrations which corresponded to the force at disposal, and Massachusetts had so far recovered from the alarm incident to its first arrival as to turn her attention to a fresh support of the national army. The middle and southern States were also active in the organization of fresh battalions. New foundries were established, and an attempt was made to secure a complete field outfit for the army, on the new establishment of eighty-eight battalions. One hundred thousand small arms and two hundred bronze cannon were solicited of France, by way of purchase, and, more needed than almost anything else, a gold loan was also earnestly urged. As the certainty of another campaign became apparent, so the mind of Washington was tasked to provide for its support.

The British government found itself compelled to increase its own army and multiply the stores for garrison, siege and field service. Great difficulties attended the second effort to obtain troops from the small German States, the entire number of recruits and reinforcements secured, being only three thousand and six hundred men. The Brunswick and Hanau recruits, and four companies of Hanau Yagers were sent to Canada; but the residue came to General Howe. The reinforcements from Great Britain and Ireland, however, which sailed for America before January 1st, 1777, embraced three thousand two hundred and fifty-two men for New York and nearly eight hundred for Canada. General Howe increased his requisition for troops to twenty thousand men, and declared it as his opinion that it would be impossible to organize the Canadian army so as to reach Albany before August or September of the year 1777. His prediction was subsequently confirmed by experience.

The cabinet contemplated that a very considerable Indian force could be made auxiliary to the regular troops; but neither Howe nor Carleton had confidence in the measure. As a question of military policy, it was ruinous to the supremacy of the crown to employ savages against the colonists.

On the part of the Americans, in anticipation of another northern campaign, large bateaux were built to support a boom and chain at Ticonderoga. Mount Washington was ordered to be fortified, and Fort Stanwix was ordered to be put in thorough order to anticipate Indian aggression in conjunction with an invasion from the north. For the time being it seemed as if the American people would heartily facilitate the organization of the army up to the demands of the crisis.

As early as December seventh a citizen of Pennsylvania publicly proposed a Dictator for that State, to serve for three or six months, and propounded this question, " Has not the want of a suitable person, entrusted with such powers in time of war, ended in the ruin of several of the most flourishing Republics of antiquity ? "

At last Congress realized the condition of the army and the necessity for some controlling master spirit in the conduct of the war, and supplemented its action of the twelfth of December by a more positive declaration on the twenty-seventh, clothing Washington, for the period of six months, with enlarged authority, of which the following extracts indicate the tenor. " Full, ample and complete powers to raise and collect together, in the most speedy and effectual manner, from any and all of the United States, sixteen battalions of infantry in addition to those already voted by Congress ; to appoint officers for the said battalions : to raise officers and equip three thousand light horse, three regiments of artillery and a corps of engineers, and to establish their pay ;—to apply to any of the States for such aid of the militia as he shall judge necessary ; to form such magazines of provisions and in such places as he shall deem proper : to displace and appoint all officers under the rank of Brigadier-general, and to fill up all vacancies in every other department of the American army ; to take, wherever he may be, whatever he may want for the use of the army, if the inhabitants will not sell it, allowing a reasonable price for the same, and to arrest and confine persons who refuse to take the continental currency, or are otherwise disaffected to the American cause."

These large grants of power were made when " affairs were in such a condition that the very existence of civil liberty depended," as Congress stated, " on the right execution of military powers," and when " the vigorous decisive conduct of these being impossible to distant, numerous and deliberative bodies," it was " confident of the wisdom, vigor, and uprightness of General Washington." It was under the burden of this responsibility that Washington rested when he closed the year 1776 in camp near Trenton.

It is a matter of interest to bear in mind a few of the contemporaneous criticisms which the affair at Trenton called forth from British and European authorities.

" All our hopes were blasted by the unhappy affair at Trenton," said Lord Germaine. " It has excited not less astonishment in the British and auxiliary quarters than it has done joy in those of the Americans. The Hessians will be no longer terrible, and the spirits of the Americans will rise amazingly," wrote Gordon, quoting from the Annual Register of Burke. " Thus ended a campaign glorious to the fame of Washington," is the tribute of Hughes. Stedman charges all the fault upon General Howe and his assignment of foreign troops to the posts on the Delaware. " The fact is," wrote Burke, " from the successes of the preceding campaign, and the vast superiority which they perceived in themselves in army actions, the ' Hessians ' had held the Americans in too great contempt, both as men and as soldiers, and were too apt to attribute those advantages to some extraordinary personal virtue and excellence, which were in reality derived from the concurrence of a number of other and very different causes; from military skill, experience and discipline ; from the superior excellence of their small arms, artillery, and other engines, furniture and supplies necessary for war, and still more particularly to a better supply and a more dextrous and effective use of the bayonet."

Walter in his " History of England on Christian Principles," says of the whole campaign : " The same want of energy which prevented Sir William Howe from making the most of the hour of success, also prevented him from maintaining the strict discipline which is necessary to keep a victorious soldiery from insulting and injuring the inhabitants of a country which they regard as their conquest, so that though the prudent care and pains taken by General Clinton and Lord Percy hindered the people of Rhode Island from having any occasion to complain of the conduct of the troops under their command, all the inhabitants of the portion of Jersey and of the districts on which the forces under the immediate management of General Howe were cantoned, soon became bitter enemies to England from exasperation at the injuries inflicted on them, not only by the Hessians, but by the British soldiers ; and that the Americans were inspirited by Trenton with the hope that courage might compensate for their inferiority in the knowledge of the art of war."

Lord Mahon, in his History of England, says, " the posts that were on this occasion the most exposed had been left the weakest manned, and undefended by a single intrenchment or redoubt," and adds, "whoever may have the earliest devised this scheme, the merit of its details and execution belongs entirely to Washington." Knight briefly notices the action, adding, "Washington went back to secure his prisoners, and again crossed the Delaware, the outposts of the British being abandoned without a struggle by panic-stricken fugitives."

A London writer discourses as follows: "As the capture of the Hessians and the manœuvers against the British took place after the surprise of General Lee, we find that Lee is not the only efficient man in the American service. We find also that the mere moving through a province is not subduing it. Perhaps the small scale of our maps deceives us; and as the word America takes up no more room than the word Yorkshire, we seem to think the territory they represent much of the same bigness, though Charleston is as far from Boston as London is from Venice. It is a bad rule to think the fate of America is to be decided by the transient possession of a few villages and hamlets. Our danger increases as we penetrate the country, in proportion to our distance from our fleet and our dispensary."

The Abbé Raynal, writing in his curious little book, "The Revolution in America," published in 1787, thus philosophizes. "The effect of strong passions, and of great dangers, is often to astonish the mind and to throw it into that kind of torpor that deprives it of the use of its powers; by degrees it recovers itself; all its faculties, suspended for a moment, display themselves with redoubled vigor; every spring of action is awakened, and it feels its powers rise at once to a level with the difficulty it has to encounter. In a great multitude there are always some who feel this immediate effect, which rapidly communicates itself to others. Such a revolution took place among the Confederates. It caused armed men to issue from all quarters."

Botta writes at fever heat of that entire winter's campaign. "Thus by an army almost reduced to extremity, Philadelphia was saved, Pennsylvania protected, New Jersey nearly recovered, and a victorious and powerful enemy laid under the necessity of quitting all thoughts of acting offensively in order to defend itself. Achievements so astonishing acquired an immense glory for the Captain General of the United States. All nations shared in the surprise of the Americans. All equally admired and applauded the prudence, the constancy and the noble intrepidity of General Washington. An unanimous voice proclaimed him the savior of his country; all extolled him, as equal to the most celebrated commanders of antiquity.

His name was in the mouth of all.   All proclaimed him the FABIUS of America.   He was celebrated by the pens of the most distinguished writers.   The most illustrious personages of Europe lavished upon him their praises and their congratulations."   Washington thus answered the voice of Congress.   "Instead of thinking myself freed from all *civil* obligations, I shall constantly bear in mind that, as the sword was the last resort for the preservation of our liberty, so it ought to be the first thing laid aside when those liberties are finally established."   "I shall instantly set about making the most necessary reforms in the army."

It was a source of inspiration to the people, an assurance of the wisdom of their chief Captain, and an earnest appeal to the courage and endurance of the army, as well as a comfort to Washington himself, that his first offensive movement had been favored with success : but at midnight of the thirty-first of December, 1776, he realized the solemnity of the hour, when in the face of this single brilliant fact, the peril of his army and of the cause which commanded his "life devotion," were again extreme and oppressive.

CHAPTER XLI.

FROM PRINCETON TO MORRISTOWN. THE ASSANPINK AND
PRINCETON. 1777.

ON the first day of January, 1777, the American General in chief was at Trenton, New Jersey. The Assanpink or Trenton river is a small stream just east of the town. At that time the banks were abrupt, and the adjoining hill was generally thickly wooded, but with occasional clearings and cultivated tracts toward Bordentown. The stream itself, quite inconsiderable in the summer months, was much swollen after rains or melting snow, and a bridge was necessary a little above the point where it emptied into the Delaware river. The road to Bordentown crossed this bridge.

Washington received advices that Lord Cornwallis, who had been on the eve of sailing for England, had resumed the command of a division and was on his route from Brunswick, to attack him at Trenton. Instead of falling back and uniting the forces then at Bordentown and Crosswicks for a march down the Delaware toward Philadelphia, he ordered the troops then under the command of Generals Mifflin and Cadwallader, the latter just promoted, to join him. During the night of the first and the following morning these troops, three thousand six hundred in number, arrived at Trenton, thereby swelling the nominal force of Washington's army to five thousand men.

The main body of this army was established along the east bank of the Assanpink for a space of two miles, in successive lines, so as to give all the concentration of resistance which their numbers and position would warrant. Guards were established at all points which offered facility for fording, and several pieces of artillery were planted at the bridge and supported by some of the steadiest of the continental troops.

An advance guard from General De Fermoy's brigade, was with two pieces of artillery established on rising ground well flanked by woods, a little more than a mile in advance of Trenton. Colonel Hand's riflemen were pushed forward as far as "Five Mile creek," and a small supporting party occupied quite a defensible position at Shebakonk creek, where heavy timber and uneven ground afforded a good position for irregular troops.

The weather had relaxed its severity, as is usual in America at the mid-winter season, and the frozen roads had been partially thawed, so that the movement of troops having artillery and baggage wagons was necessarily slow. The Delaware was filled with floating ice, large masses were banked up in its curves, and retreat to the west bank was impracticable in the face of an advancing enemy. It was also argued by Washington that all that had been gained in the way of moral support to the people of New Jersey would be sacrificed by an attempt to withdraw to the southward. It was not indeed impossible that the British troops would ultimately cross the river and move upon Philadelphia, whatever course he might adopt, and he resolved to do his best to save the army, and leave that city to the contingencies of the campaign.

General Cornwallis left Brunswick with the reserve, which was a part of his old command, the Waldeckers, Colonel Donop's Hessians, and the former garrisons of the adjacent posts, two regiments of Highlanders, and Köhler's heavy artillery, making a total strength of a little over seven thousand men. Cornwallis led the advance in person, followed by the main army, leaving, however, three companies of light dragoons, and the Seventeenth, Fortieth, and Fifty-fifth regiments of foot at Princeton ; and General Leslie with a small brigade as rear guard, was still at Maidenhead when the leading battalions entered Trenton. The advance was met shortly after it left Maidenhead by Colonel Hand's riflemen, who kept up a lively skirmish fire as they slowly fell back, and at Shebakonk this resistance was sufficiently spirited to require Cornwallis to push another regiment with artillery to the front. Upon coming up to the position where the guns had been placed, an additional delay was interposed to his advance by General Greene. He promptly opened fire for the express purpose of keeping the enemy from reaching Trenton in time to make an attack before night.

Washington visited the detachment when Greene took command and then returned to the bridge, to be prepared to cover the troops as they retired to the lines closely pressed by the British column. It was about four o'clock in the afternoon, nearly sunset in America in the latitude of Trenton, but Cornwallis at once threw skirmishing detachments along the river to feel the fords and practicable crossings, and opened fire with artillery, near the bridge and above the town. At all points he found wooded ascents, an active adversary, and the determination to give battle if he should attempt to force a crossing.

He sent a strong column down Queen street, and made three separate efforts to force the bridge-passage, but the fire was so constant and direct that further attempt was abandoned.

The British army had made a trying march, and orders were sent to Princeton to forward the light dragoons as well as the Seventeenth and Fifty-fifth regiments, and General Leslie was ordered up from Maidenhead to be prepared for morning work. The armies were separated less than a mile, and the picket guards were within hail, from side to side. Under existing circumstances Cornwallis wisely declined a night attack; but his reconnoissance should have been so complete that he could have made an attack when the American army commenced its movement. He should have anticipated the possibility of an attack upon his own communications and base. The cannonading was kept up until dark, the camp fires were lighted on both sides of the Assanpink, and the armies awaited the issues of another day.

During the afternoon the hazy weather gave way to a clear sky, and after sunset the night became cold, freezing the ground hard, and making travel more easy. Washington had matured a plan of escape from his hazardous position, whereby he might avoid a battle with superior and well drilled troops, without the loss of prestige and the inevitable disaster which would follow a retreat from his adversary, so soon after the success at Trenton. He was now satisfied that the army of Cornwallis had gathered up its principal columns for the proposed attack. He had learned from reconnoissances ordered during the latter part of December, both the character of the roads and the most expeditious routes to Brunswick. He also sent a small party to learn whether the British troops had any detachments on the old Quaker road, to the east of the Assanpink, and was assured that the path was clear. Colonel Donop afterwards stated that he advised Cornwallis to send a division by the old road east of the creek, which would have accomplished, as against Washington, the very movement which Ewing attempted before the attack upon Trenton; but his advice was not followed.

Washington also assumed from reports of the original force at

Brunswick that its great magazines of stores and supplies must have been left under small guard, and believed that by a quick dash he might capture or destroy them. It was a bold strategic movement, and a fit companion-enterprise to his first return of the offensive at Trenton. A council of war was convened for the consideration of the movement. It was promptly endorsed by the officers consulted, and was speedily carried into effect. No time was lost. The baggage wagons which had been posted in the rear on the Bordentown road, were started for Burlington under a small guard as soon as it was dark. The fires were plied with dry rails from fences and fallen trees, and shortly after one o'clock the army was in motion with all the light artillery that could be taken along. The weather had been so mild for a few days that many of the blankets had been packed in the baggage wagons, when the army first moved across the Assanpink, and the night was sufficiently cold to cause much suffering; but the letters of officers written after arrival at Morristown, show that the march was silent, orderly, and almost entirely without halts. The route was made somewhat longer by following a new trail where the stumps had not been removed, until the old Quaker road was reached, when the advance was made with much more celerity and compactness of movement.

The picket guards who were left on post, had been furnished with ample supplies of fuel for the night, and they kept up their regular round of challenge, replenished their fires, and did not decamp and follow the army until nearly morning. A small working party was also engaged in throwing up light field-works before the bridge, and at one point up the stream, to give greater assurance of watchfulness and preparation for an attack.

Just before leaving camp, Washington sent a messenger to General Putnam, advising him of his movements, and instructing him to send up troops to occupy Crosswicks, and he also thereby secured the safety of his baggage train which had started down the river.

The vanguard of the American army reached Stony Brook about sunrise. Washington there re-formed his columns, sending General Mercer to the left, by the Quaker road, and intended to advance directly to the village itself, by a lower road, under cover of rising ground, and thus expedite his proposed movement upon Brunswick. General Mercer, upon wheeling out of column, passed a thick woods and orchard near the Friends' meeting house, and moved up the creek for the purpose of destroying the bridges and thus delaying pursuit from

Trenton, as well as to cut off fugitives from Princeton. His force was composed of the remnants of Haslett's and Smallwood's regiments, the seventh Virginia and a few volunteers, making a total however of less than four hundred men. He was rapidly approaching the Trenton road, when he found his command suddenly confronted by the seventeenth British foot, which was rapidly crowding for a commanding position directly to his right toward Princeton. This regiment had received the order of Cornwallis to join him, had already crossed the Stony creek bridge by the old road, and had reached the summit of Millett's Hill when Colonel Mawhood first noticed the small command of Mercer as they passed in front of the orchard near the house of William Clark.

The American army however was not in sight and the column of Mercer did not largely exceed Mawhood's own force. Without any hesitation he recrossed Stony Brook and found himself within five hundred yards of their advance guard. General Mercer moved northward toward the same elevated ground which Mawhood recognized as commanding the situation, and having reached it first, then advanced to the cover of a zigzag rail fence which crossed the hill, and delivered fire. The British returned but one volley, and instantly made a steady, impetuous charge with the bayonet. The onset was too solid and the defense too nominal for Mercer's command to withstand the attack. They fell back in confusion and took refuge in Clark's orchard and other high ground near the Friends' meeting house. As soon as the firing began, Washington pushed additional troops to the summit on the left of his advancing column, and this force, although furnished with two guns, was also assailed by Mawhood's with such vigor that several companies gave way, and it appeared as if they were to follow the fate of the troops first engaged.

Captain Neal of the artillery had already fallen, and the British attack was directed to the capture of Captain Moulder's guns, which from their position were beginning to tell upon their column with effect. Washington, as previously at Kipp's bay, spurred his horse through the scattering militia to the front, and maintained his place for a few minutes in a position of extreme personal danger, directly in the line of fire of the opposing troops. The men, inspired by his example, rallied promptly to his support.

As a matter of fact the British troops reached the crest of the hill in the pursuit of Mercer's flying column before it came to the knowledge of Colonel Mawhood that he was entering the lists against the entire American army.   Its extended column was then in full view moving toward the town where the Fortieth and Fifty-fifth were stationed.   The latter regiment had been in readiness to march for Trenton when the action began, and make an effort to support the Seventeenth ; but Colonel Hand had wheeled out of the main column and taken his position with the troops which Washington had first sent to the support of Mercer, and Colonel Hitchcock with equal promptness turned the left of Mawhood and cut him off from Princeton as well as from assistance.   Generals Stirling and St. Clair, and Colonels Poor, Patterson and Reed were also advancing upon the Fifty-fifth, and the only avenue of retreat was toward Trenton.   Abandoning his cannon, the British commander, already receiving the fire of more than four times his own force, threw his men across Stony Creek at all practicable places, mostly by the bridge, and took refuge at Maidenhead, where General Leslie's column still halted.   The Fifty-fifth, closely pressed by weight of numbers, and these constantly augmented, took a position on the high sloping ground immediately south of Nassau Hall, Princeton College, where a ravine separated them from the Americans, and where a small force could make a successful resistance to a much larger force of infantry.   The American artillery was promptly brought to bear upon their ranks.   Several regiments passed clear of the hill and gained the main street in front of the college.   The doors of the building were soon forced and that regiment with the Fortieth attempted to escape to New Brunswick, one by the Kingston and the other by the Rocky Hill route.

The entire action consumed less time than its recital.   The British loss was heavy, exceeding one hundred men in killed and wounded, while two hundred and thirty were taken prisoners, including fourteen officers.   Captain William Leslie, son of the Earl of Levin, was among the killed, and was buried with every becoming token of respect.

The American loss in rank and file was greatly less than the British, but the efforts of the officers to check them at the crisis of the panic cost valuable lives.   General Mercer, who had already gained much credit as an officer, and served with Washington in the old Indian war of 1756–1766, was mortally wounded while endeavoring to rally his men near Clark's house, and Colonels Haslet and Potter, Major Morris, and Captains Fleming, Shippen, and Neil were among the killed.   General Mercer, a native of Scotland, was an assistant surgeon at the battle of Culloden, a physician of high attainment at Fred-

19

ericksburg, Virginia, when the American war called him to arms, and he was held in high estimation by all who knew him, as an officer of great judgment and promise.

A detachment was immediately sent to destroy the bridge over Stony Creek, and the army advanced to Kingston, only about three miles beyond Princeton, on the other side of Millstone river.

Upon reaching that town, Washington hastily consulted his general officers as to further movements. General Greene had started his column up the Millstone, on the supposition that it was of first importance to reach some strong position where a decided resistance could be offered to pursuit. The men were cold, hungry, and nearly worn out. The greater part of the command had been on constant duty from the time they left Bordentown and Crosswicks. Many were barefooted, and no time had been allowed for the distribution of rations since breaking camp opposite Trenton. Before the main column had crossed the Millstone, the sound of renewed firing at Princeton gave warning that the troops at Maidenhead were already in pursuit. The possibility of striking the stores at Brunswick depended therefore upon being able to do it with no delay of resistance, as a defense, however brief, would compel a general action with the approaching British army. The latter had " mounted troops," while the Americans were practically without any. The fugitive detachments of the Fortieth and Fifty-fifth would certainly put the Brunswick garrison on the alert.

Farther pursuit of these troops was therefore abandoned, and the army moved directly and promptly from Kingston, up the east bank of the Millstone, and the next day secured a strong position at Pluckemin, when the troops obtained refreshment and partial rest.

While these events transpired, Cornwallis had realized the consequences of under-estimating the mental resources and executive ability of his adversary. The American lines had been deserted while he was resting for a triumph. The camp fires still burned as day dawned, but there were no pickets on post, and the bridge head was without defenders. The opinion expressed by Sir William Erskine the night before, which is well accredited, that Washington would not abide attack but withdraw his forces, was confirmed, and the report of artillery in the direction of Princeton and Brunswick, showed that while Cornwallis was indeed on the Delaware, his adversary was between him and his base, and his very depot of supplies was in peril. The light dragoons were hurried to the rear, and the whole army followed with all possible expedition. The distance was but ten miles, while Washington had marched very nearly sixteen; and the British vanguard approached the Stony Creek bridge as the American rear guard was completing its destruction. There was nearly an hour's delay at this point before artillery could be placed across the creek; but some of the regiments were forced over, regardless of ice and water, to quicken pursuit. There was additional delay at Kingston, as the bridge over the Millstone had also been destroyed, and the British army apparently unconscious, or neglecting to examine the trail of the Americans' retreat, precipitately hastened to Brunswick, where they found the public stores were in safety, but the army of Washington was not there awaiting capture.

Cornwallis also found upon his arrival at Brunswick late on the same night, that the retreating troops had aroused great terror in the small garrison, and General Matthews had already commanded the removal of baggage and warlike stores. Seventy thousand dollars in gold was at the post for payment of the troops, and this money was promptly returned to New York.

The condition of the American army during a rest of two days at Pluckemin was one of great suffering, and it is difficult to understand how a defense could have been maintained if Cornwallis had immediately made an attack. On the fifth, Washington found time to send a report to Congress, and to make up dispatches to Putnam and Heath. He instructs the former to send on the army baggage, to march to Crosswicks, to "give out your strength to be twice as great as it is, to keep out spies, to put horsemen in the dress of the country, and keep them going backwards and forwards for that purpose, and to act with great circumspection, so as to not meet with a surprise."

He ordered General Heath to collect boats for the contingency of the detail of part of his force into New Jersey, and instructed him that it had been determined in council that he should move down toward New York with a considerable force, as if with a design upon that city.

On the seventh the American army reached Morristown, where log huts were erected and winter quarters were established. His own headquarters during that winter were at the old Freeman Tavern, on the north side of the public square. On the seventh additional orders were sent to General Heath, to General Lincoln, who had arrived at Peekskill with four thousand New England militia, and to other

officers, north and south, in anticipation of ulterior movements. A
single letter to General Heath, which was subsequently written, after
hearing that the latter officer had demanded the surrender of Fort
Independence in very strong language, and followed up his demand
by withdrawing his force, will illustrate the directness with which
Washington began to deal with injudicious subordinates.

General Heath was before Fort Independence on the eighteenth of
January, 1777. General Lincoln advanced by the Hudson river road,
General Scott by White Plains, and Generals Wooster and Parsons
from New Rochelle and East Chester. A few prisoners were taken at
Valentine's Hill, and the garrison of nearly two thousand Hessians
were allowed "twenty minutes in which to surrender or abide the
consequences." After nearly ten days of delay about King's Bridge,
with his half organized militia force, without barracks and under circumstances of peculiar exposure, a sally from the garrison created a
panic in one regiment at an advance post, and the entire army soon
withdrew.

As a demonstration toward New York it undoubtedly had a great
effect upon General Howe's movements, and the plan itself was well
conceived, well initiated. The divisions arrived at King's Bridge with
remarkable concert of time; but there they stopped, and the chief
objective was not realized.

Washington thus wrote, on the third of February: "This letter is
additional to my public one of this date. It is to hint to you, and I
do it with concern, that your conduct is censured (and by men of sense
and judgment who have been with you on the expedition to Fort
Independence) as being fraught with too much caution: by which the
army has been disappointed and in some degree disgraced. Your
summons, as you did not attempt to fulfill your threats, was not only
idle but farcical, and will not fail of turning the laugh exceedingly
upon us."

During the winter and spring, skirmishes were frequent, and often
with marked benefit to the American troops. Washington issued a
counter proclamation to that which General Howe had promulged
during the original retreat through New Jersey, and all offensive
operations on the part of the British forces were suspended.

Mr. Botta thus justly sums up the relations of the contending armies.
" Washington having received a few fresh battalions, and his little
army having recovered from their fatigues, soon entered the field anew
and scoured the whole country as far as the Raritan. He even crossed

this river and penetrated into the county of Essex. made himself master of Newark, of Elizabethtown, and finally of Woodbridge ; so that he commanded the entire coast of New Jersey in front of Staten Island.   He so judiciously selected his positions and fortified them so formidably, that the royalists shrunk from all attempts to dislodge him from any of them.   Thus the British army, after having overrun victoriously the whole of New Jersey quite to the Delaware, and caused even the city of Philadelphia to tremble for its safety, found itself now restricted to the two only posts of Brunswick and Amboy, which moreover could have no communication with New York except by sea. Thus, by an army almost reduced to extremity, Philadelphia was saved, Pennsylvania protected, New Jersey nearly recovered, and a victorious and powerful army laid under the necessity of quitting all thoughts of acting offensively, in order to defend itself."

CHAPTER XLII.

MINOR EVENTS, JANUARY TO JULY, 1777.

THE operations of the year 1777, comprised a second invasion of New Jersey, for the purpose of drawing the American army into a decisive battle, a series of operations in execution of the original purpose of the British cabinet to gain control of Lake Champlain and the Hudson river, and the occupation of Philadelphia.

Spirited skirmishing, brief incursions, and some brilliant feats of minor adventure characterized both armies; but all battles proper are referable to one of the three systems of endeavor above indicated.

A brief outline of minor facts will give clearness to the subsequent battle details.

The headquarters of Washington remained at Morristown until the twenty-fourth of May.

On the twenty-first of January two thousand British troops were withdrawn from Rhode Island to reinforce General Howe at New York. Generals Spencer and Arnold, then in command of about four thousand American troops at Providence, were instructed to prepare a plan for the capture of Newport; but they failed to secure adequate militia support, and it was abandoned. General Parsons, then on recruiting service in Connecticut, was advised by Washington to make a descent upon Long Island during February, but was unable to raise the necessary force until they were needed for general defense. During the same month General Knox was dispatched to Massachusetts to enlist a battalion of artillery, and during this trip advised the selection of Springfield, Massachusetts, as the best place in New England, for the establishment of a laboratory and cannon foundry. General Schuyler was instructed to draw from the *New England States* the entire force required to resist the anticipated advance of Carleton from Canada; because " troops of extreme sections could not be favorably combined." General Maxwell was stationed at Elizabethtown to watch tories and the movements of the British. The exchange of General Lee and his status, whether to be regarded as a prisoner of war, or British deserter, was discussed. Orders were issued repressing the plundering done by the American militia; a protest was sent to General Howe against similar outrages perpetrated by Hessian and British troops, and the usual difficulties of recruiting, equipping, and sustaining the American army were experienced.

During the month of March a ship arrived at Portsmouth, New Hampshire, from France, with twelve thousand fusees, one thousand barrels of powder, blankets and other military stores, and a second ship reached Philadelphia with eleven thousand more of similar arms. Congress assigned five thousand of the new arms to Massachusetts, three thousand to Connecticut, and two thousand to New Hampshire. On the second of the month, Washington sent to Robert Morris the following cast of the British plans: "General Howe can not, by the best intelligence I have been able to get, have less than ten thousand men in New Jersey, and on board of transports at Amboy. Our number does not exceed four thousand. His are well disciplined, well officered, and well supplied; ours, raw militia, badly officered, and under no government."

"His numbers can not be in a short time augmented, ours must be very considerably, and by such troops as we can have some reliance upon, or the game is at an end. His situation with respect to horses and forage is bad, very bad, I believe, but will it be better? No, on the contrary worse, and therefore if no other, to shift quarters. General Howe's informants are too numerous, and too well acquainted with all these circumstances, to suffer him to remain in ignorance of them. With what propriety then can he miss so favorable an opportunity of striking a capital stroke against a city from whence we derive so many advantages, the carrying of which would give such eclat to his arms, and strike such a damp to ours? Nor is his difficulty of moving so great as is imagined. All the heavy baggage of the army, their salt provisions, flour, and stores might go round by water, while their superior numbers would enable them to make a sweep of the horses for many miles around them, not already taken off by us." This letter foreshadows the final action of General Howe, and while it was Washington's opinion that the movement of troops would be overland, its statement, in view of the course finally adopted by General Howe, is given in this connection, and the elaborate documentary matter which affords a detailed index to the passing phases of opinion which preceded the battle of Brandywine, and the capture of Philadelphia, is omitted.

The same month of March developed the fruits of the promotions made by Congress. Stirling, Mifflin, Stephen, St. Clair, and Lincoln were made major-generals, and *Arnold was omitted.* He tendered his resignation, highly offended. Poor, Glover, Patterson, Learned, Varnum, Huntington, George Clinton, Wayne, De Haas, Hand, Reed, Weedon, Muhlenburg, Woodford, Scott, Nash, Conway, and Cadwallader were appointed brigadier-generals. The last named officer had been appointed to that grade by Pennsylvania, just after the battle of Trenton, and declined the appointment of Congress. As most of these officers appear in the subsequent narrative, their names are given. Their order of appointment gave infinite trouble, and their assignment to duty gave additional occasion for jealousy and conflict.

General Wooster had already resigned and was in command of the Connecticut militia. St. Clair acted as adjutant-general after Reed resigned, and on the thirtieth of March, Washington appointed Colonel Timothy Pickering to that office. General George Clinton had been assigned by Congress to the command of the forts in the Highlands. General McDougall succeeded General Heath at Peekskill, and on the twenty-second a British fleet ascended the Hudson, effected a landing, and destroyed the valuable stores at that place. General Sullivan was so sensitive as to the so-called separate commands of other officers, as to call forth the following rebuke from Washington, " Why these unreasonable, these unjustifiable suspicions, which can answer no other end than to poison your own happiness and add vexations to that of others. I know of but one separate command properly so called, and that is the northern department, and General *Sullivan,* General St. Clair, or any other general officer at Ticonderoga will be considered in no other light, while there is a superior officer in the department, than if he were placed at Chatham, Baskenridge or Princeton. I shall quit with an earnest expostulation that you will not suffer yourself to be teased with evils that only exist in the imagination, and with slights that have no existence at all, keeping in mind that if there are several distinct armies to be formed, there are several gentlemen before you in point of rank who have a right to claim preference."

General Greene was sent to lay before Congress the necessities of the army, and the month of March closed with an earnest appeal to the governors, committees of safety, and Congress, to furnish troops and supplies for the impending summer campaign.

On the third of April, General Washington corrected a popular impression as to judging British forces by the number of regiments reported, placing a very correct judgment upon the strength of the Hessian troops, but under-estimating the average of the British regiments. He wrote to Governor Cooke of Rhode Island, "The Hessian regiments, when they came out complete, did not exceed six hundred men each, and the British two hundred and fifty each." The basis upon which the British army was recruited for service in America has been previously stated, as drawn from official sources.

On the twenty-fifth of April two thousand British troops under Governor Tyron landed near Fairfield, Connecticut, and moved upon Danbury, to destroy public stores at that point collected. Generals Silliman and Wooster of the Connecticut militia, and General Arnold, then on his way to visit Congress, distinguished themselves by their gallant conduct. Arnold threw up a breastwork near Ridgefield and fought with great spirit, having two horses shot under him before the British retired. General Wooster was mortally wounded. The stores however, including sixteen hundred tents, were destroyed. Arnold was immediately promoted : but did not obtain the lineal rank which he claimed to belong to him and was still dissatisfied. Early in May, Greene was sent to inspect and put in good order the posts in the Highlands. The troops under Washington's immediate command were at that time organized in five divisions of two brigades each under Major-generals Greene, Stephen, Sullivan, Lincoln and Stirling, and included forty-three regiments from New Jersey, Pennsylvania, Delaware, Maryland and Virginia, commanded by Brigadiers Muhlenburgh, Weedon, Woodford, Scott, Smallwood, Deborre, Wayne, DeHaas, Conway and Maxwell. Colonel Hand was also appointed Brigadier-general. The artillery was still commanded by General Knox. The force for duty was nearly eight thousand men. The New York and Eastern regiments were near Peekskill or at Ticonderoga.

On the twenty-third of May, Colonel Meigs crossed to Long Island from Guilford, Connecticut, and at Sag Harbor, Long Island, effected the destruction of twelve brigs and sloops, one of these carrying twelve guns, and a large quantity of British stores, the troops having been withdrawn to New York two days before. This exploit involved ninety miles of transportation, most of the route in whale boats, and the command safely returned in twenty-five hours. On the twenty-ninth of May, General Washington moved his headquarters to Middlebrook.

On the seventh of June Arnold was placed in command of Philadelphia, to act with General Mifflin in anticipation of General Howe's anticipated movements in that direction, and on the thirtieth General Howe marched from Brunswick toward Princeton. His command included two more regiments, which had joined from Newport, and with the Hessians amounted to the splendid force of nearly seventeen thousand men. Orders had been given for the army to march at eleven o'clock of the evening of the twelfth, thereby hoping to cut off Sullivan's brigade, which was at Princeton. After the march began, Cornwallis with the right column was directed to Hillsborough and De Heister to Middlebrook, turning off from the Princeton road, and the line was definitely prolonged to Somerset court-house, as indicated on the map.

In a subsequent letter of July fifth, addressed by that officer to Lord George Germaine, he says that his "only object was to bring the American army to a general action." The British army rested its left on Millstone river, while its right held fast to Brunswick, having the Raritan in front. Two redoubts were also erected in the horseshoe of the river bend before his centre, and also, near Brunswick. The subsequent controversies between Generals Howe and Clinton do not entirely warrant the criticism by General Clinton of this position, as it was naturally assumed by General Howe that Washington would not rest passively in his trenches while the British army had control of the line of communication with Philadelphia. In "Letters to a Nobleman" General Howe is very severely criticised for moving to Somerset court-house, where an unfordable river parted the armies, and it is claimed that if Howe had moved toward Philadelphia, Washington would have given him battle. It was however then, as ever, inconsistent with Washington's purpose to risk his army for any city whatever.

The New Jersey militia were posted on Lowland Hill, near Flemington, to which place Sullivan had retired from Princeton as soon as he observed the movement of General Howe to cut him off from the main army. Orders were sent to forward from Peekskill all the continental troops, except one thousand effective men, under Generals Parsons, McDougall and Glover, and these troops were to march in three divisions, at one day's interval, the first two columns to bring two pieces of artillery each.

On the twentieth Washington received a message that Burgoyne was approaching St. John's and that a detachment of regular troops, Canadians and Indians were to penetrate by the Mohawk valley. General Putnam was ordered at the same date to hold four Massachusetts regiments, then at Peekskill, in readiness to go up the river at a moment's notice, and to procure sloops from Albany and keep them for that purpose.

Washington and Congress alike erred in their opinion as to the subsequent operations of the British army ; for both alike anticipated that the army of Canada, then more than thirteen thousand strong, would come down to New York by sea, and participate in the advance upon Philadelphia. As a matter of military judgment their views as to the propriety of his march proved to be correct, as the proposed combined movement of Clinton from New York and of Burgoyne from Canada actually failed because inadequate forces were furnished for its execution. Washington wrote to Schuyler on the twentieth, upon receiving intimation of Burgoyne's preparations, expressing his " confidence in the strength of Ticonderoga and the facility with which Putnam's troops could be sent to its support, if threatened," adding, " he certainly will never leave the garrison of Ticonderoga in his rear : and if he invests it to any purpose, he will not have a sufficient number left to send one body to Oswego, and another to cut off the communications between Fort Edward and Fort George." General St. Clair wrote, not to send reinforcements until they were needed, for " they would consume the supplies." Meanwhile Washington strengthened the right wing of his position at Middlebrook by redoubts, ordered Arnold to watch Trenton and the upper ferries, and rested under the belief that Howe would not advance toward the Delaware and attempt a crossing, while his own army was in the rear. He argued thus ; " Had they designed for the Delaware, on the first instance, they would probably have made a secret, rapid march of it, and not halted as they have done, to awaken our attention and give us time to prepare for obstructing them. Instead of this they have only advanced to a position necessary to facilitate an attack upon our right, which is the part they have the greatest likelihood of injuring us in : and added to this consideration they have come out as light as possible, leaving all their baggage, provisions, boats and bridges at Brunswick, which plainly contradicts the idea of pushing for the Delaware."

On the morning of the nineteenth, General Howe suddenly

abandoned his position and retired to Brunswick. Maxwell was at once sent forward to take a position between Brunswick and Amboy, so as to cut off detached parties or baggage, and General Greene was sent with three brigades to follow the river, observe the crossing, and attack their rear as soon as they should leave post. The entire American army was put in readiness to support the movement.

General Howe started on the twenty-second early in the morning. Morgan and Wayne drove the Hessian rear-guard forward upon the main body after a spirited action. It had been Greene's intention to have Maxwell strike the column near Piscataway, while he should hold them under fire. The messenger sent to Maxwell with the order was captured or lost, and he received his orders at last only after the Hessian corps had joined the advanced troops. Stirling then joined Maxwell, and Greene carried the pursuit as far as Piscataway.

Washington promptly advanced the army to Quibbletown, now New Market, upon the counsel of his officers, that the retreat was genuine ; yet not without suspicion that the whole was a skillfully developed *feint* for the purpose of drawing him from his stronghold. General Stirling's command was stationed in advance at Metuchen.

Few events of that war involved more sharp discussion than the advance and sudden retreat of General Howe. The anonymous " Letters to a Nobleman," " Galloway's Reflections," " Howe's Narrative," and other documents of the kind, still have freshness and interest ; but none of them settle the controversy. Howe occupied a position in which he could neither attack nor be attacked. Neither army was in danger from the other. *His forte* was in the field proper, and his purpose was to entice Washington's army into a position where the advantages would be with himself. If he had marched on the north side of the river, Washington would have given him a fight. The chief fact indicated by his course, and that is supported by his own defense, was the appreciation he began to entertain of the character of Washington, and he would not engage at all under risks. He claimed that his force was inferior in numbers to that of Washington ; but his advocates as well as critics are obliged to accept the facts as already recorded.

Stedman, who served in the British general staff under Howe, Clinton and Cornwallis, and whose volumes are among the most interesting which were published at the close of the war, takes occasion, while reviewing the New Jersey campaign of 1777, to pass judgment upon the relative strength of the armies from the commencement of operations on Long Island, up to the first of July, 1777. As that period is under brief notice, his estimate is given for permanent reference.

"BRITISH AND REBEL FORCE IN 1776."

Dates.	British.	Rebels.
August	24,000	. 16,000
November	26,600	. 4,500
December	27,700	. 3,300

IN 1777.

March	27,000	. 4,500
June	30,000	. 8,000

On the twenty-sixth, General Howe put his entire army in motion to resume the offensive, and advanced to Scotch Plains and Westfield.

Cornwallis marched *via* Woodbridge, with the right wing of the army, at seven in the morning, while General Howe in person led the left wing by Metuchen Meeting House, intending to connect with the rear of the right column at that point, and then swing upon the left of the American main army. Cornwallis with the extreme right, was to gain the passes to Middlebrook. A third body of troops with four battalions and six pieces of artillery were sent to Bonhamton, to demonstrate toward the American right wing. Cornwallis had hardly passed through Woodbridge, when he was confronted by Stirling's division. A spirited skirmish ensued, which was to the benefit of Cornwallis, whose artillery were of a more effective caliber ; and he crowded the retiring division as far as Westfield, and the present Plainfield, capturing three brass guns, and inflicting a loss in killed, wounded and prisoners, of nearly two hundred men, with a loss to his own command of not more than seventy.

Maxwell, who had been stationed near the Raritan, on the line of the original retreat of General Howe, retired without loss. Washington quickly comprehended the purpose of his adversary, and recovered the passes to his old post before Cornwallis who had been delayed so long by Stirling could accomplish his purpose, which was to seize them while General Howe should threaten Washington's front. On the afternoon of the twenty-seventh, the division of Cornwallis left Westfield, passed through Sampton unopposed, and joined General Howe, who had effected nothing of value by his movement.

On the thirtieth the British army crossed to Staten Island, and the military career of General Howe in New Jersey ended.

The immediate activity of the shipping at New York now satisfied Washington that a diversion would be made up the Hudson to draw him in that direction, and that operations toward Philadelphia would be made by sea. Letters from General St. Clair stated positively, that Burgoyne had advanced with view to attack Ticonderoga and its dependent posts. Orders were at once sent to Putnam to place Varnum and Parsons' brigades at Peekskill to observe the river, in the place of Nixon's which had been hurried to Albany, and *the expedition from Canada was at last on its march.*

The narrative will follow the order indicated at the opening of the chapter, and take under notice the " Operations of Burgoyne's Campaign."

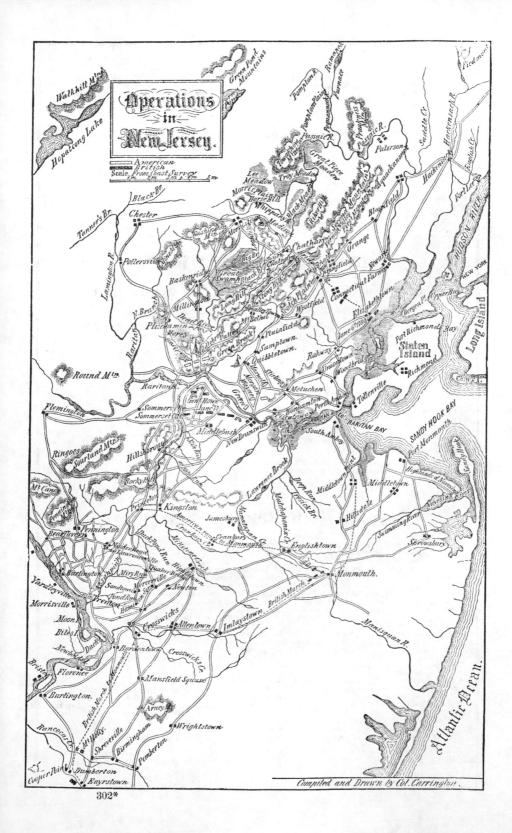

Operations in New Jersey.

American
British
Scale From Coast Survey

Compiled and Drawn by Col. Carrington.

Operations in New Jersey

American Commanders

GREENE   **WASHINGTON**   SULLIVAN

LAFAYETTE, LEE, STIRLING, MAXWELL

MEM.—*New Jersey was the strategic battle-ground of the war, and was more generally overrun by the British army than any other Colony, except South Carolina.*

British Commanders

CLINTON   **HOWE**   CORNWALLIS

KNYPHAUSEN, GRANT, DONOP, RAHL

NOTE.—The following places are identified with military operations:

Fort Lee,	Morristown,	Metuchen,	Westfield,
Hackensack,	Middlebrook,	Newark,	Woodbridge,
New Brunswick,	Mt. Holly,	Piscataway,	Allentown,
Trenton,	Imlaystown,	Quibbletown,	Springfield,
Princeton,	Plainfield,	Samptown,	Scotch Plains,
Bound Brook,	Chatham,	Millington,	Bonhampton,
Cranbury,	Somerset C. H.,	Sandtown,	Middletown,
Bordentown,	Hightstown,	Crosswicks,	Rahway,
Burlington,	Dumbarton,	Monmouth,	South Amboy,
Baskinridge,	Pennington,	Haddenfield,	Perth Amboy,
Kingston,	Elizabeth,	Red Bank,	Billingsport,
Maidenhead,	Hillsborough,	Englishtown,	Middlebrook.
Pluckamen,	Gloucester,	Summerville,	Paulus Hook.

The issue between Washington and Howe was one of careful strategy. This was solved, in 1777, by Howe's failure to entangle Washington in any action which imperilled American liberty. The contest is briefly noticed.

Second New Jersey Campaign

On the 13th of June, 1777, Howe marched from Brunswick to Princeton with 17,000 men. Cornwallis, with the right column, was directed to Hillsborough, and De Heister to Middlebrook, turning off from the Princeton Road, and the line was definitely prolonged to Somerset Court House, as indicated on the map. Howe threatened Philadelphia, hoping that Washington would risk a general engagement in its behalf. The New Jersey militia were posted on Lowland Hill, near Flemington, to which place Sullivan had withdrawn from Princeton.

Washington ordered all the Continental troops, then at Peekskill, except 1,000 men, to join him. He also strengthened the right wing of his position at Middlebrook, by redoubts. He argued, that Howe did not intend to cross the Delaware river because his baggage, boats and bridges had been left at Brunswick. On the 19th Howe found that he could not draw Washington from his strong position, and returned to Brunswick.

Maxwell was at once sent forward to take position between Brunswick and Amboy, to cut off detached parties or baggage, while Greene was sent with three brigades to follow the river and attack their rear, so soon as they should leave the post. Stirling joined Maxwell, and Greene pursued as far as Piscataway. Washington moved his army to Quibbletown, and Stirling was placed in advance, at Metuchen.

On the 26th, Howe resumed the offensive, and advanced to Scotch Plains and Westfield. Cornwallis marched, via Woodbridge, at 7 A. M. with the right wing, and Howe with the left wing, approached Metuchen Meeting House, expecting that Cornwallis would gain the passes to Middlebrook. Four battalions, with six guns, were also sent to Bonhampton to threaten the American right wing. Cornwallis had hardly passed through Woodbridge when he was confronted with Stirling ; but, by superior artillery, crowded him back as far as Westfield and Plainfield, capturing three guns, and inflicting upon Stirling a loss of 200 men, at the cost of not more than 70. Maxwell retired without loss. Washington at once comprehended the whole movement, recovered the passes to his old post, before Cornwallis, who had been delayed by Stirling, could reach them, and Howe, who had threatened his front, in favor of the movement of Cornwallis, was *foiled*.

On the afternoon of the 27th, Cornwallis left Westfield, passed through Sampton, and joined Howe. On the 30th, Howe regained Staten Island, and closed his military career in New Jersey.

CHAPTER XLIII.

BURGOYNE'S CAMPAIGN OPENED. 1777.

ON the twenty-second day of August, 1776, Lord George Germaine handed to Captain Le Maitre, an aid-de-camp of General Carleton, then commanding in Canada, a letter, to be delivered by him to General Carleton upon his arrival at Quebec. The aid-de-camp found it impossible to make the passage on account of ice in the St. Lawrence, and returned the dispatch to Lord Germaine, at the palace of Whitehall, London.

On the twenty-sixth of March, 1777, the letter was again sent, accompanied by the instructions, that it was his Majesty's pleasure that General Carleton should return to Quebec as soon as he should have driven the American's forces from Canada, taking with him such part of his army as in his judgment and discretion appeared sufficient for the defense of the Province ; and that Lieutenant-general Burgoyne or such other suitable officer as General Carleton should think most proper, be detached with the remainder of the troops,—" to proceed with all possible expedition to join General Howe and put himself under his command."

Lord Germaine maintained, that "with a view of quelling the rebellion as soon as possible, it had become highly necessary that the most speedy junction of the two armies should be effected : that the king had designated three thousand men as the force to be left in Canada, and that the remainder of the army should be employed in two expeditions : the one under the command of Lieutenant-general Burgoyne, who was to force his way to Albany ; and the other under Lieutenant-colonel St. Leger, who was to make a diversion on the Mohawk river.

It was explicitly stated, also, that the plan under consideration "could not be advantageously executed without the assistance of

Canadians and Indians." It was "left to the influence of General
Carleton among those bodies of men, to assure a good and sufficient
number, for the purpose in view."

Lieutenant-general Burgoyne was ordered to proceed to Quebec
forthwith, in order to carry out the wishes of the crown with the
utmost dispatch. The instructions above referred to, were so explicit
as to indicate the number of men, and even the particular detachments,
which should be respectively assigned to the enjoined operations.
The statement of the details thus made, will have interest during the
course of the narrative. The force detained for the defense of Canada
was to consist of

"The 8th Regt., deducting 100 for the expedition to the Mohawk . 460 men
  Battalion companies of the 34th; deducting 100 for the expedition
    to the Mohawk . . . . 348 "
  Battalion companies of the 29th and 31st regiments . . . 896 "
  Eleven additional companies from Great Britain . . . 616 "
  Detachments from the two brigades . . . . . . 300 "
  Detachments from the German troops . . . . . 650 "
  Royal Highland emigrants . . . . 500 "
            Total 3770

This assignment of troops for the protection of Canada expressly
and justly presumed, that the operations in progress in different parts
of America would confine the attention of its people to their own
necessities, and that the force thus designated would be ample for
local defense. The assignment of troops to the moving columns was
equally exact.

General Burgoyne's command was thus stated :

The grenadiers and light infantry of the army: (except of the 8th
  regiment and the 24th regiment) : as the advanced corps, under the
  command of Brigadier-general Fraser . . . . . . 1568 men
First brigade : battalion companies of the 9th, 21st, and 47th regiments ;
  deducting a detachment from each corps to remain in Canada . 1194 "
Second brigade : battalion companies of the 20th, 53d, and 62d regiments ; deducting 50 from each corps to remain as above . . 1194 "
All the German troops except the Hanau Chasseurs, and a detachment of 650 . . . . 3217 "
The artillery, except such parts as shall be necessary for Canada
            Total . . . . 7173 "

This command was "to be associated with as many Canadians and
Indians as might be thought necessary for the service," and when so
organized, it was "to proceed with all expedition to Albany, and be

placed under the command of Sir William Howe." The force which
was carefully assigned to the command of Lieutenant-colonel St.
Leger, was *thus* stated :

Detachment from the 8th regiment	100 men
Detachment from the 34th regiment	100 "
Sir John Johnson's regiment of New York	133 "
Hanau Chasseurs	342 "
Total	675 "

To this force, there was also " to be added a sufficient number of
Canadians and Indians " ; the same " to proceed to Albany, and never
to lose view of their intended junction with Sir William Howe as their
principal object."

The foregoing instructions are the voice from Whitehall Palace.
They read like orders from a corps commander, who can judge from
his daily returns, exactly of the force in hand for immediate use.

Lieutenant-general Burgoyne left London, March twenty-seventh,
and reached Quebec on the sixth day of May. He notified General
Sir William Howe immediately of his strict instructions, and expressed a wish that he had sufficient latitude of movement to warrant
a diversion towards Connecticut. From the first inception of the
enterprise, it was declared to be of necessity that Albany should be
the objective of the march, " after the capture of the American posts
which lay upon Lake Champlain." General Carleton entered into the
outfit of the expedition with as much zeal and energy as if it had been
to his individual credit to assure success. Burgoyne afterward testified that " he could not have done more for his brother."

The inherent difficulties of the movement were in many respects
similar to those which affected the American expedition to Canada.
These must be briefly stated in order to secure a fair opinion of the
capacity and wisdom of the lieutenant-general commanding.

The Canadian troops, *estimated for* at two thousand men, could
not be enlisted. Less than two hundred reported for duty. The
pioneers who were to make and repair roads, carry provisions, and do
much of the practical part of the logistics of the march, were not only
greatly deficient in numbers, but still more wanting in willingness to
work, and fitness for the duty required of them. Neither money nor
constraint could secure the requisite numbers of carts and horses for
the outfit. The weather was unpropitious and the roads were almost
impassable. Reference is made to map entitled " Burgoyne's Saratoga
Campaign," as the first of the series designed to illustrate its progress.

The preliminary camp was established on the Boquet river, on the western shore of Lake Champlain, and the troops reached that station as early as the twentieth day of June. The Indians, who had been looked upon as valuable auxiliaries, were yet to be secured. In re sponse to a well circulated appeal, addressed to various tribes, about four hundred Iroquois, Algonquins Abenaquies, and Ottowas, met General Burgoyne in conference on the twenty-first day of June, at his headquarters. In view of the odium which was cast upon this officer by an unwise proclamation at that time issued, it is proper to say, that in his address to the warriors who agreed to take up the hatchet for the king, he expressly stated the "necessity of restraint of their passions, and that they must be under control, in accordance with the religion, laws of warfare, principles and policy which belonged to Great Britain,"—"positively forbidding bloodshed, when not op- posed in arms,"—declaring "aged men, women, children, and prisoners, sacred from the knife, even in the time of conflict," and otherwise instructing the savages, that "the war must not be made as when they went forth alone, but under the absolute will and control of the army of the king."

His proclamation to the Americans, as well as the address to the Indian chiefs, assumed all that could possibly be asserted as to the guilt of rebellion; and while extremely pompous and extravagant in language, preshadowed the extreme vengeance of savage auxiliaries if resistance should be prolonged. It was extremely unprofessional, and more in harmony with the abstract political dogmas of the crown than with Burgoyne's own character. Its much ridiculed assertion of personal title, and of royal prerogative, was quite in harmony with his instructions, and somewhat offensive for its vanity, while it lacked the wisdom which a better knowledge of his opponents soon inculcated. It aroused sensible men to a more stubborn resistance, and was more effective than appeals of Congress, to induce the people of New Eng- land to take up arms for border defense. They knew well from ex- perience just what a war with savages meant, and they were inclined to class the British troops who employed them, in the same list of enemies with the savages themselves.

Washington issued a counter-proclamation. One paragraph is worthy a space in all records of that war: and is peculiarly expressive of the character, consistency and faith of the man, while it affords an index of his firmness in the path of duty. It reads as follows:

" Harassed as we are by unrelenting persecution, obliged by every tie to repel violence by force, urged by self-preservation to exert the strength which Providence has given us to defend our natural rights against the aggressor, we appeal to the hearts of all mankind for the justice of our course ; its event we leave to Him who speaks the fate of nations, in humble confidence, that as His omniscient eye taketh note even of a sparrow that falleth to the ground, so He will not withdraw His countenance from a people who humbly array themselves under His banner, in defense of the noblest principles with which He has adorned humanity."

The army advanced to Crown Point, rested three days, and moved forward on the thirtieth. The British light infantry and grenadiers, with the twenty-fourth British foot, some Canadians and Indians, with ten pieces of artillery, marched down the west shore and took post within four miles of Ticonderoga. The German reserve, Brunswick chasseurs, light infantry and grenadiers followed the east shore ; and General Burgoyne accompanied the fleet.

On the first of July the investment began. General Burgoyne's muster of that date gave his force, rank and file, as follows :

British Regulars	3724 men
German "	3016 "
Artillery "	473 "
	7213 "
Canadians and Provincials about	250 "
Indians about	400 "
Total about	7863 men.

As early as the twenty-eighth of February, one month before he left England, General Burgoyne embodied his views in a letter to Lord George Germaine. The document is a model paper in its anticipation of the contingencies of the proposed service; and while the general ideas of that letter were incorporated into his ultimate instructions, he was not allowed the full regular force which he deemed necessary for the undertaking, and his auxiliaries from Canada and from Indian tribes were too few to be of much practical value, while they burdened him with an element which did more harm than good, at times of real crisis. His proposed diversion into New England was predicated upon support from the troops then at Newport, Rhode Island, and the assurance that there would be adequate and prompt support from the army at New York. He had, on one occasion, advised that the northern movement should be limited to the occupa-

tion and firm possession of the posts on Lake Champlain, and that the
troops which were destined to coöperate with General Howe should go
from Quebec to New York, or Newport, by sea, and thus secure the
earliest possible field service in the campaign of 1777. It has been
shown in another connection that General Howe himself expressed
the opinion, in a letter to Lord Germaine, that a movement from
Canada down the Hudson river could not be supposed to be of practical benefit before Septemper. General Burgoyne encountered the
difficulties which he, alone, anticipated, and many trials which should
have been spared him ; and yet he was face to face with the American
army, within thirty-two miles of Albany, by the middle of August.

He was before Ticonderoga the first of July, with the forces already
indicated.

He was harshly censured for taking with him an alleged excess of
heavy guns. But these were distributed on ships, or placed in the
captured posts, so that the artillery of his moving column did not
average two pieces to a battalion, twenty-six guns in all, and ten of
these were formed into a special park under General Phillips, to be
used wherever needed, so as to secure a greater combined effect, as
with modern batteries. Four howitzers and two light twenty-fours,
constituted his heavy ordnance, and the remainder were light threes
and sixes. This complement of artillery was the lowest which the
regulations of the service admitted ; and there was no reason for him
to doubt that he would be furnished with adequate transportation,
until the failure of Canadian allies and of proper support, had placed
him where there was no remedy for meagre resources but in the desperate conflict of battle against superior numbers.

The advance to Ticonderoga was followed up with vigor. The
old French posts on the heights, north of the fort, had been partially
repaired and strengthened by new intrenchments ; and one block-
house had been erected on a hill which commanded the northern
extremity of Lake George. On the second day of July these works
were abandoned and the wooden defenses were burned by the Americans. General Phillips promptly occupied the hill, giving it the name
of Mount Hope.

On Mount Independence opposite Ticonderoga there was a star
fort, which commanded the water passage, and at the foot of the hill
batteries had been established. These were well supplied with heavy
guns.

General Riedesel encamped just north of this position, and the ships of war were anchored across the lake just within range of the American batteries. At the head of Lake Champlain, South river, so called, ending in Wood creek, and in fact a narrow lake, unites with Lake George ; and the intervening tongue of land, called Sugar Loaf Hill, is seven hundred feet above the line of the lake, and commands Ticonderoga. Its steep ascent had been regarded by the Americans as impracticable of occupation ; but on the fourth of July, Lieutenant Twiss, commanding the British Engineers, reconnoitered the summit and reported that it commanded a direct practicable range of fire upon both Ticonderoga and Mount Independence, at a distance of not more than fifteen hundred yards from the latter, which was the more distant post. It also commanded the bridge of communication which connected the American posts.

This bridge had a double purpose ; one for communication, and the other to prevent the passage of ships into South river. It was supported by twenty-two sunken pieces of large timber at nearly equal distances. Between the piers were separate floats, fifty feet long and twelve feet wide, strongly fastened together by chains and rivets, and well secured to the piers. Before the bridge was a boom, also made of heavy timbers, carefully united by clinched bolts and double chains of inch and a half iron. Upon the report of Lieutenant Twiss, a pioneer corps and a force of sappers were put to work, and by the morning of the fifth a British force crowned the summit of Sugar Loaf Hill, which was promptly dignified by its occupants with the name of " *Fort Defiance.*" A practicable path had been made for the carriage of guns, which were dismounted for the purpose, and the battery was soon in its new position.

While these arrangements had been in progress for the complete isolation and control of Ticonderoga, the garrison of the post was not indifferent to passing events. Its exact condition is worthy of notice, in order to appreciate the erroneous impression which Congress, General Washington and the American people entertained, upon hearing of its evacuation by General St. Clair, without battle. In proportion as its defense was desired and expected, just to that degree did the public judgment impute fault to both the immediate and remote commander ; so that General Schuyler as well as General St. Clair suffered seriously through this inevitable disaster.

The Northern Department, necessarily so isolated from other fields of operation, was habitually a browsing place for aspirants after independent command, and this disposition was strengthened by the natural tendency to repose its defense in the hands of the New England militia who were most intimately related to that defense.

On the twenty-fifth of March, General Schuyler had been relieved from the command by General Gates, but was reinstated in May, after fairly presenting his case before Congress. He returned to his headquarters at Albany on the third of June and at once tendered to General Gates the command of Ticonderoga, as the most exposed and most honorable post within the department. That officer declined the command. It was his purpose to obtain the command of the department itself, and his correspondence is impregnated with the spirit of jealous aspiration. While urging that Albany should not be retained as headquarters, he wrote, " If General Schuyler is solely to possess all powers, all the intelligence, and that particular favorite, the military chest, and constantly reside in Albany, I can not, with any peace of mind, serve at Ticonderoga."

At this period the valley of the Mohawk and its relations to Indian operations, based upon British support through the lake port of Oswego, invested Albany with peculiar value as a centre of control. In determining the wisdom of Schuyler and Burgoyne in their subse-quent career, it must not be forgotten that the St. Leger expedition from Canada, *also* had Albany as its objective, *via* Oswego, Fort Schuyler (Stanwix), and the Mohawk Valley, and that both the Brit-ish armies were to be watched by Schuyler ; while Burgoyne not only had positive orders to make Albany the objective of his march, but he was held to a faithful concert of action with St. Leger, in order that both expeditions should realize their common objective. The drift of such action was to incline Burgoyne to march down the west bank of the Hudson, and it was equally vital to the American cause that the department commander should have ready access to both lines of operation which thus converged upon Albany.

Gates had accomplished nothing of real value in the preparation of the lake posts for defense during the two months he had been in command of the department, and was still at Albany when Schuyler returned. He had made a requisition upon Washington for tents, and when the commander-in-chief replied, " As the northern troops are hutted, the tents must be used for southern troops until a supply can be obtained," he answered, " Refusing this army what you have not in your power is one thing ; but saying that this army has not the same necessities as the southern army is another. I can assure your excellency the service of the northern army requires tents as much

as any service I ever saw." To Mr. Lovell, of the New England
delegation, he wrote, " Either I am exceedingly dull, or unreasonably
jealous, if I do not discover by the style and tenor of the letters from
Morristown, how little I have to expect from thence. Generals are
like parsons, they are all for christening their own child first ; but let
an impartial moderating power decide between us, and do not suffer
southern prejudice to weigh heavier in the balance than the northern."
In connection with this outcropping of an appeal to sectional feeling
which was the exact counterpart of that exhibited by Lee while he was
at New Castle Heights, it is only necessary to say that Washington
used the term *southern* only as comparing the operations of two geographical departments, and not in any personal sense. He stated a
military fact, without argument, and the conduct of Gates is self-
interpreting.

On the ninth of June, Gates took leave of absence and left the
department.

Schuyler ordered all forts to be put in condition for service,
appealed to the States to forward their militia, and on the twentieth
proceeded to inspect the imperiled posts for himself. Generals St.
Clair, De Rochefermoy, Poor and Patterson were then at Ticonderoga. The garrison of that post and of Mount Independence combined amounted to only twenty-five hundred and forty-six continental troops, including artisans, and about nine hundred militia. A
council of general officers concurred in the opinion that the troops
were inadequate to protracted defense, but that the posts should be
maintained, if possible, until the arrival of reinforcements, or until the
stores and troops could be safely withdrawn. It was considered *impracticable* to fortify Sugar Loaf Hill. The troops could not well be
spared, it is true ; but the possibility of its occupation by a hostile
force was not considered a serious question of fact.

During this trip General Schuyler found the condition of the troops
to be beyond his worst apprehensions. The clothing was nearly
worn out, military supplies other than pork and flour had not accumulated as anticipated, the number of bayonets did not exceed a few
hundred, and there was very little to encourage the expectations
which the country entertained as to the ultimate strength of Ticonderoga as a real fortress.

General Schuyler returned to Albany to hasten forward additional
troops. General St. Clair, still hopeful of his ability to resist assault

wrote to him on the last of June, " should the enemy attack us, they will go back faster than they came."

Schuyler's own aid-de-camp, Major Henry B. Livingston, who remained at Ticonderoga sick, when he left, wrote in a similar strain. General Schuyler was less sanguine, and wrote to Colonel Varick on the first of July :

" The insufficiency of the garrison at Ticonderoga, the imperfect state of the fortifications, and the want of discipline in the troops, give me great cause to apprehend that we shall lose that fortress, but as a reinforcement is coming up from Peekskill, with which I shall move up, I am in hopes that the enemy will be prevented from any farther progress."

The departure of General Schuyler from Ticonderoga without effectual provision for the contingency of its abandonment, or waiting to test its capacity for defense, was the subject of grave criticism, and resulted in a Court of Inquiry. That court consisted of Major-general Lincoln, Brigadier-generals Nixon, George Clinton (the only one from Schuyler's State), Wayne and Muhlenburg, and Colonels John Greaton, Francis Johnson, Rufus Putnam, Mordecai Gist, William Russell, William Grayson, Walter Stewart, and R. J. Meigs, with John Lawrens as Judge Advocate ; and found "that Major-general Philip Schuyler was not guilty of neglect of duty, and is acquitted with the highest honor."

The fall of Ticonderoga was peculiarly aggravating to this officer, as he had sent sloops to Peekskill for the troops which, as before noticed, had been ordered by Washington to his aid, and on the fifth he wrote to Congress, " If they do not arrive by to-morrow, I shall go on without them, and do the best I can with the militia." He marched on the seventh with all the militia he could assemble, but the activity of Burgoyne had anticipated the movement, and the British troops were again in possession of all posts on Lake Champlain.

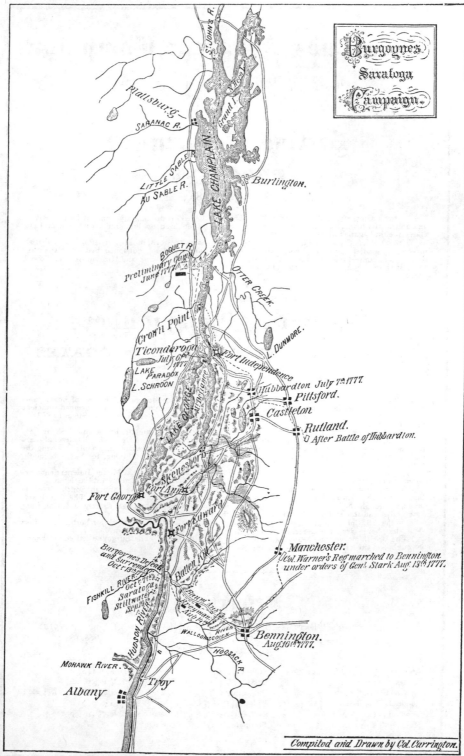

Burgoynes Saratoga Campaign

St. John's R.

Isle of Mott I.

Grand I.

Plattsburg.

SARANAC R.

LITTLE SABLE R.

AU SABLE R.

LAKE CHAMPLAIN

Burlington.

BOQUET R.

Preliminary Camp
June 1777.

OTTER CREEK.

Crown Point

L. DUNMORE.

Ticonderoga
July 6th 1777.

Fort Independence

LAKE PARADOX

L. SCHROON

Hubbardton July 7th 1777.

Pittsford.

Castleton

LAKE GEORGE

Rutland.

After Battle of Hubbardton.

Skenesboro.

Fort Ann

Fort George

Fort Edward

Batten Kill

Manchester.
Col. Warner's Reg. marched to Bennington
under orders of Genl. Stark Aug. 13th 1777.

Burgoyne's Defeat
and Surrender
Oct. 1777.

FISHKILL RIVER
Oct. 7th 1777.
Saratoga
Stillwater
Sept. 19.

Baum's

Breyman's Aid of

Baum Aug. 16

WALLOONSCOICK RIVER

WALLOOMSCOICK

HUDSON RIVER

Bennington.
Aug. 16th 1777.

MOHAWK RIVER.

HOOSACK R.

Troy

Albany

Compiled and Drawn by Col. Carrington.

Burgoyne's Saratoga Campaign

From JUNE 20th to OCT. 19th, 1777

British Commander

BURGOYNE

Strength, 7,863.

NOTES. On the 20th of June, 1777, Burgoyne established his preliminary camp at Boquet River, and on the 21st held a conference with Indian auxiliaries, engaged by him, under direction of Lord Germaine, but against his own judgment.

The army left Crown Point, to which it had advanced on the 30th, in three divisions. The British infantry, grenadiers and 24th Foot, with Canadians, Indians and ten guns, marched down the west shore and encamped four miles from Ticonderoga. The German reserve and Hessian troops followed the east shore. Burgoyne accompanied the fleet.

American Commanders

SCHUYLER   ST. CLAIR   GATES

Strength, 3,446, including Militia.

NOTES. The first British objective was the capture of Ticonderoga. A bridge of boats communicated with Fort Independence. A boom of heavy logs and sunken timbers was deemed sufficient to prevent the passage of ships into South River. The Americans neglected to fortify Sugar Loaf Hill, deeming it inaccessible.

The investment began July 1st. During the night of July 4th, the British occupied Sugar Loaf Hill, south of the fort, commanding it, and named the new position, Fort Defiance. Riedesel also extended his lines, so as nearly to enclose Fort Independence. The fort became untenable. During the night of the 5th of July, the Americans started 220 batteaux, under Col. Long, for Skenesborough, with their surplus supplies and invalid troops.

At 3 A. M., July 6, when the retreat was well begun, a burning house at Mount Independence exposed the movement to the besiegers. General St. Clair had already started toward Castleton. Phillips sent Fraser in pursuit, and joined Burgoyne, who took shipping through South River for Skenesborough. Riedesel put a garrison in Fort Independence and followed Fraser. The British seamen cut through the bridge, and the fleet landed its troops at Skenesborough, shortly after Col. Long had landed and started for Fort Ann, 11 miles to the south.

On the 7th, Col. Long had a sharp engagement with Lieut.-Col. Hill and Major Forbes, near Fort Ann; but, being compelled to retreat, burned the fort and retired to Fort Edward.

The British moved their heavy guns, by water, to Fort George, while Burgoyne halted at Skenesborough, and the left wing under Fraser and Riedesel pursued St. Clair.

References :

CARRINGTON'S "BATTLES OF THE AMERICAN REVOLUTION," pp. 301-312.

School Histories :

Anderson, ¶ 57 ; p. 81.
Barnes, ¶ 1 ; p. 121.
Berard (Bush), ¶ 73 ; p. 156.
Goodrich, C. A.(Seaveys) ¶ 18; p. 126.
Goodrich, S. G., ¶ 4 ; p. 224.
Hassard, ¶ 5 ; p. 191.

Holmes, ¶ 5 ; p. 125.
Lossing, ¶ 18 ; p. 157.
Quackenbos, ¶ 334; p. 240.
Ridpath, ¶ 12 ; p. 202-3.
Sadlier (Excel.), ¶ 9 ; p. 189.
Stephens. A. H., ¶ 21 ; p. 198.

Swinton, ¶ 142 ; p. 134.
Scott, ¶ 12 ; p. 184.
Thalheimer (Eclectic), ¶ 262 ; p. 150.
Venable, ¶ 140 ; p. 106-7.

CHAPTER XLIV.

FROM TICONDEROGA TO FORT EDWARD. 1777.

ON the morning of July fifth, 1777, the British occupation of Sugar Loaf Hill gave warning to the garrison of Ticonderoga that it lay at the mercy of the enemy. Previous to that occupation, the British had been drawn closely about the fort, and the garrison looked forward to an assault, with real courage and hope. It was very evident, however, on the fifth, that the post must fall without the credit of real resistance. A council of war fully considered the condition of affairs, and resolved that " retreat ought to be undertaken as soon as possible, and that we shall be fortunate to effect it." The possibility of maintaining the post on Mount Independence was more than counterbalanced by the certainty that the British would control South river, and cut off all supplies from New England and New York. General Riedesel had already swung his left wing to the rear, and eastward of the latter post, and the south face of Mount Independence alone remained open to American forces.

It was not until after dark that the army was notified of the determination of its officers. The invalids, ammunition, and a large quantity of commissary stores were placed upon two hundred and twenty bateaux, then lying in South river below the bridge, and these were started for Skenesborough under Colonel Long, then post commander of Ticonderoga.

Lights were extinguished at the usual hour, and occasional firing was maintained from the summit of Mount Independence, upon the new works upon Sugar Loaf Hill, to keep up the appearance of the usual garrison habits and activities, and to indicate a purpose to contest the supremacy of the so-called Fort Defiance.

The retreat began at three o'clock of the morning of July sixth, and the arrangements for its execution were eminently judicious.

The heavy guns had been spiked, but the trunnions were not knocked off, lest the click of the sledges should be borne on the night air to the watchful enemy, and give warning of the attempt to escape.   The night was still, and a partial moon dimly lighted the mountain sum- mits, while the shadows deepened under Mount Independence, just where the bridge was waiting to perform its last office for its builders. The British guns made no response to the firing of the Americans, and as soon as Colonel Long's command, with the American flotilla, had started on its way, General St. Clair took up his march for Castleton. No other evidence is required to show the skill with which these troops began their disheartening retreat, than the single fact that the entire garrison safely crossed the bridge.   At this most critical moment, when the last detachment was clear of the fort, and the troops on Mount Independence had descended its southern slope, the house which had been occupied by General De Fermoy (signed De Rochefermoy) was fired in contravention of orders, and the whole scene was illuminated for the information of the besiegers.

The most active measures were at once taken in pursuit.   Day- light was just coming on.   General Phillips pushed General Fraser with a flying column after the retiring Americans, left the Sixty-second British regiment as a garrison, and embarked his own division upon ships to accompany Burgoyne in pursuit of the American shipping. General Riedesel placed the Brunswick regiment of Prince Frederick in garrison on Mount Independence, and followed General Fraser with three battalions to give him support in the pursuit.   Commodore Lutwidge, with a party of seamen, soon cut a passage through the bridge, and Burgoyne, with the Inflexible and Royal George frigates and the swiftest of the gun-boats, was moving up South river before nine o'clock.   This floating column, constituting the right wing of the British army, reached Skenesborough only two hours later than the Americans, and at once began the attack.   A brief resistance was made near the falls where Wood creek enters into South river.   The British destroyed all that the Americans did not burn, including all the supplies which had been saved with so much care.   The Ninth, Twentieth, and Twenty-first British regiments were landed, ascended the mountains, and made a detour to turn a small fort which had been built to command the passage at Wood creek, but it was abandoned by the Americans without resistance.   Mills, storehouses, and other valuable property which had been accumulated at this station were soon destroyed.

By reference to the map, " Burgoyne's Saratoga Campaign," it will be seen that the right wing of the British army had thus gained an advance upon General St. Clair, as Castleton was nearly thirty miles south-east from Ticonderoga, and nearly twelve miles north-east from Skenesborough, so that General Burgoyne followed the base of the triangle of which Castleton was the apex, and made a quick trip by water, while St. Clair made a tedious march over land, through an almost pathless wilderness.

Colonel Long landed his battalion about three o'clock in the after-noon, and upon the approach of the British ships, marched directly to Fort Ann, a distance of eleven miles to the south. Lieutenant Colo-nel Hill and Major Forbes, of the British Ninth regiment, followed and spent the night bivouacked in the woods within three miles of that post. General Schuyler was then at Fort Edward, about thirteen miles further to the south, on the Hudson river.

He promptly sent a reinforcement to Fort Ann, and early in the morning of the seventh Colonel Long advanced to a ravine three miles north of the fort, where Colonel Hill had spent the night, and attacked his command. Major Forbes thus describes the attack, in evidence laid before the House of Commons, page 61 of official documents, relating to Burgoyne's expedition.

" At half past ten in the morning, they attacked us in front wit a heavy and well directed fire. A large body of them passed up the creek to our left and fired from a thick wood across the creek on the left flank of the regiment; then they began to recross the creek and attack us in the rear. We then found it necessary to change our ground to prevent the regiment being surrounded. We took post on the top of a high hill to our right. As soon as we had taken post, the enemy made a very vigorous attack and they certainly would have forced us, had it not been for some Indians that arrived and gave the Indian whoop."

General Powell had been dispatched by General Burgoyne with two regiments, as well as the Indian auxiliaries, to the support of Lieutenant Colonel Hill, and the American troops retreated under the pressure of superior numbers, burned Fort Ann, and then retired to Fort Edward.

General Phillips, who had accompanied the British right wing as far as Skenesborough, returned to Ticonderoga and commenced the removal of artillery, ammunition and provisions to Fort George, with all other heavy baggage which could be more readily moved by water transportation ; while General Burgoyne established his headquarters at Skenesborough to await the movements of the left wing, to rest his troops and organize for a further advance.

The British left wing followed the American line of retreat. Colonel Francis, commanding the American rear-guard, left Mount Independence about four o'clock on the morning of the sixth. St. Clair moved through the forests with such expedition that his advance reached Hubbardton quite early in the afternoon. Leaving Colonel Warner with one hundred and fifty men, to collect stragglers and await the arrival of Colonel Francis, he hastened forward and reached Castleton, six miles further south, the same night.

General Fraser marched seventeen miles on the sixth and halted, General Riedesel being at that time only three miles in his rear. " At the earliest day-light, or a little before," he promptly renewed the pursuit. Colonel Francis had joined Colonel Warner on the previous evening and their entire force, together with the regiment of Colonel Hale, which also came up from the rear, amounted to nearly thirteen hundred men. They resolved to await General Fraser's approach and give battle. The American troops occupied a plateau between Castleton creek and one of its dependent forks which offered an eligible site for defense. General Fraser's command descended a long slope to the creek and were compelled to ascend directly upon the plateau, in order to meet the Americans on equal terms. The latter did not await the attack, but upon the alarm of the pickets met them promptly and with vigor. A sharp skirmish ensued. Colonel Hale, himself an invalid, (subsequently acquitted of the charge of cowardice) with his poorly disciplined regiment, abandoned the field precipitately, and fled in the direction of Castleton ; so that the whole burden of the fight devolved upon Colonels Francis and Warner, who were left with a force of not more than nine hundred men. The command of General Fraser is officially reported at eight hundred and fifty-eight. The Americans, hotly pressed as they were, took prompt advantage of falling timber and all other obstructions which gave effect to individual skill with the rifle, and Stedman thus compliments their good conduct : " The Americans maintained their post with great resolution and bravery. The reinforcements (Riedesel's), did not arrive so soon as expected, and victory was for a long time doubtful."

The advance of Fraser was as spirited as the unexpected resistance was obstinate. He entered the action with the confidence that his supports were close at hand, and very nearly paid the penalty which subsequently fell upon Baum at Bennington. The Earl Balcarras, who was slightly wounded during the engagement, was advanced on the right to occupy the Castleton road and cut off the retreat. The stubborn resistance of the Americans exposed his detachment to be cut off, when at the critical moment, General Riedesel moved over the hill and came on rapidly with three battalions, music playing, and amid loud cheers of his men. This new force prolonged itself upon Fraser's left, ascended the plateau with fixed bayonets, turned the American right, and compelled its immediate retreat. Some fled to Rutland, others over the mountains to Pittsford, and about two hundred were taken prisoners. Colonel Francis was killed. Colonel Warner retired to Rutland with a remnant of his force, and joined General St. Clair two days after with eighty men. The latter officer heard the firing and promptly sent orders to two militia regiments which were between Castleton and Hubbardton to return to that place to support Colonel Warner, but instead of obedience to the order, they only quickened their march to Castleton. St. Clair had previously sent an order to Colonel Warner, that " if he found the enemy pursuing him too hotly and in force, he must join him at Rutland." This place was selected as the rendezvous, having just heard of Burgoyne's occupation of Skenesborough, " because Rutland was at nearly equal distances from both places." This order did not reach Colonel Warner. The defection of Hale had forced him to so close a fight that it ended only in the dispersion of his command. The only alternative was its capture.

The British casualties amounted to one hundred and eighty-three in killed and wounded, including Major Grant, who led the first attack. The Brunswickers lost but twenty-two men, as the action was closed almost as soon as they gained the American right, and their prompt advance carried with it the impression that a still larger force was engaged in the pursuit of the American army. The Americans lost in killed forty officers and men, and the total casualties including wounded and prisoners was about three hundred and sixty. The entire dispersion of the command gave currency to exaggerated estimates of the numbers engaged and of the losses incurred; but the capture of Colonel Hale's regiment during its retreat, swelled the number of prisoners, so that the report of General Burgoyne is reconcilable with the facts, when the entire skirmish near Hubbardton is taken into the account. This fact also reconciles all conflicts which have entered into previous reports of the battle.

On the tenth of July, General Burgoyne issued a general order, beginning as follows: "The rebels evacuated Ticonderoga on the sixth, having been forced into the measure by the pressure of our army. On one side of the lake they ran as far as Skenesborough; on the other side as far as Hubbardton. They left behind all their artillery, provisions, and baggage." (Burgoyne's report of the stores captured at Ticonderoga included 349,760 pounds of flour, and 143,830 pounds of salt provisions.) He also summoned the people of certain designated townships to return to their allegiance, making " Colonel Skene " the representative of the Crown in their behalf, fixing the fifteenth of the month as the day for such submission, " under pain of military execution on failure to pay obedience to such order."

On the thirteenth, General Schuyler, then at Fort Edward, issued a counter proclamation, declaring " all to be traitors who should in any way assist, give comfort to, or hold correspondence with, or take protection from the enemy; commanded all officers, civil and military, to apprehend or cause to be apprehended such offenders, and closed with the demand, that the militia of the townships to which General Burgoyne's circular was addressed, who had not marched, should do so without delay, and join his army or some detachment thereof."

On the tenth, General Schuyler began a systematic effort to obtain control of all live stock and and staple supplies which belonged to the country threatened by Burgoyne, and attempted to make the entire route from Skenesborough to Fort Edward as nearly impassable as human skill could do it. Large trees were felled along all trails or natural roads, creeks were choked with timber and branches, so as to make them overflow and deepen the marshes, all bridges were destroyed, some small streams were diverted in their course so as to impair travel; and such was the success of this laborious undertaking that General Burgoyne found himself compelled to build forty new bridges, besides the repair of old crossings, and in one instance to lay a timber causeway of two miles before he could move his column.

The correspondence of Schuyler with Washington during this period was full of hope, and the confidence was mutual and unabated, notwithstanding the retreat from Ticonderoga was a real disaster, and full of discouragement at the time of its occurrence. Subsequently a Court of Inquiry and Congress itself affirmed the propriety of that retreat.

A single fact is mentioned by Chief Justice Marshall, which deserves a place in this connection, inasmuch as all kinds of political and social gossip about the Generals of the war of 1776–1781, have been made pivot points for judgment of military conduct.   Marshall thus records the fact referred to.   " In this gloomy state of things it is impossible that any officer could have used more diligence or judgment than was displayed by Schuyler."

Chief Justice Kent and Daniel Webster have also left on record the most positive tribute to the unselfish patriotism, wonderful energy and executive ability of this officer; the latter using the following somewhat enthusiastic language : " I was brought up with New England prejudices against him ; but I consider him as second only to Washington in the services he rendered to the country in the war of the Revolution."   These services, however, embraced his wise management as superintendent of the Indian affairs of the north, as well as the more limited sphere of his military duty, which are to be judged by their own merits."

Washington seemed almost to anticipate the affair at Bennington, while all others were disheartened.   On the twenty-second of July, he wrote to Schuyler : " Though our affairs have for some days past worn a dark and gloomy aspect, I yet look forward to a fortunate and happy change.   I trust General Burgoyne's army will meet sooner or later an important check, and as I have suggested before (letter of July 15th) that the success he has had will precipitate his ruin.   From your accounts he appears to be pursuing that line of conduct which of all others is most favorable to us: I mean acting in detachments. This conduct will certainly give room for enterprise on our part and expose his parties to great hazard.   Could we be so happy as to cut one of them off, though it should not exceed four, five or six hundred men, it would inspirit the people and do away much of this present anxiety.   In such an event they would lose sight of past misfortunes ; and, urged at the same time by a regard for their own security, they would fly to arms and afford every aid in their power."

On the thirtieth of July, Burgoyne reached Fort Edward.   General Schuyler had withdrawn the garrison from Fort George, after destroying the fort ; and having first retired to Saratoga, afterwards established his camp at Stillwater, near the mouth of the Mohawk river.   Colonel Warner was at Manchester recruiting his command and watching for an opportunity to assail Burgoyne's rear.   Glover and Nixon had joined with less than a thousand men.   Two thousand militia from Massachusetts, sent to supply the places of others whose term of service had nearly expired, returned home in a body, and the harvest season was so exacting in its demands that it seemed as if no large force could be permanently maintained. Upon Schuyler's urgent request that an active general officer be sent to coöperate in raising troops, Arnold was selected; but the critical condition of the main army, growing out of the uncertainty of General Howe's movements, rendered it impossible for Washington to spare any considerable force for the northern department.

Burgoyne himself had been greatly embarrassed during the last two weeks of July by the increasing burdens under which his small army labored. He urged upon General Carleton that a portion of the three thousand regular troops still in Canada should be detailed as garrison for Ticonderoga, but that officer had no latitude in his instructions from the crown, and did not feel at liberty to accede to the request. General Riedesel, who had made some demonstrations into the New Hampshire Grants, (Vermont), conceived the impression that the people were quite friendly to the British cause, and initiated a plan to procure horses and mount his dragoons, who were still doing infantry duty.

On the twenty-ninth of July, General Phillips succeeded in reaching Fort George with the first consignment of military stores, and the practical difficulties of the great separation of the army from its base began to unfold their lessons.

The small garrison at Castleton and Skenesborough had been withdrawn when General Riedesel joined Burgoyne, so that the only remaining communication with Ticonderoga was through Lake George; and the garrison of the former place was less than the strength of a full battalion. The expedition of St. Leger had reached Oswego, but no definite information had been received as to its progress or prospects.

The detention of General Riedesel at Castleton had been protracted on account of the wounded men who could not be removed from Bennington to Ticonderoga after the battle at the former place.

All efforts to organize a New England battalion of Royalists dragged slowly, and the Indian auxiliaries began to become unmanageable, so that at the end of one month after the occupation of Ticonderoga, the British army was but entering upon the serious duties of the campaign, and the American army was in no suitable condition to resist its progress. The practical success thus far realized, had however inured to the benefit of the royal troops. Both armies watched with solicitude the movements of General Howe. General Schuyler took advantage of the reduced garrison at Ticonderoga to dispatch General Lincoln into New England for the purpose of raising troops to make an attempt to regain that post and cut off Burgoyne's communications with Canada, and then once more reorganized his camp, upon the islands a little below the mouth of the Mohawk river, and continued his importunate requisitions for reinforcements. Such, substantially, was the condition of the northern campaign on the first of August, 1777.

BRITISH EFFECTIVE FORCE.

NOTE. From " Original returns in the British Record Office." Date, June 3d, 1777.

JERSEY.

British Artillery	385
" Cavalry	710
" Infantry	8361
Hessian "	3300
Anspach "	1043
	13,799

NEW YORK.

British Infantry	1513
" Artillery	20
Hessian Infantry	1778
	3,311

STATEN ISLAND.

British Infantry	515
" Artillery	11
Waldeck Infantry	330
	856

RHODE ISLAND.

British Infantry	1064
Hessian "	1496
British Artillery	71
	2631

PAULUS HOOK.

British Infantry	360

Total of the army	20,957

FOREIGN TROOPS IN AMERICA.

Hessian	12,777
Anspach	1,293
Waldeck	679
Total	14,749

21

CHAPTER XLV.

FORT SCHUYLER, ORISKANY AND BENNINGTON. 1777.

THE month of August, 1777, developed and concluded the expedition of Colonel St. Leger to the valley of the Mohawk river, and with equal exactness terminated the operations of Burgoyne on the eastern bank of the Hudson.

St. Leger ascended the River St. Lawrence and Lake Ontario, ascended the Oswego and Oneida rivers to Oneida lake, crossed that lake, and found himself on Fish creek, within a few miles of Fort Stanwix, (Schuyler) near the present city of Rome, on the Mohawk river. It is to be noticed that with the exception of the short portage between Fish creek and the Mohawk, there was water communication for light boats and bateaux from Oswego to Albany. The intervening streams were all subject to the fluctuations of wet and dry seasons, but the burden of military transportation was greatly lightened by the character of the route adopted for the invasion of New York from the west.

The character of the settlers in that region, particularly in Tryon county, had fostered loyal sentiments, and the diversities of interest among the various Indian tribes involved a constant uncertainty as to the integrity of their conduct, no matter what might be the terms of a contract into which they could be enticed by high sounding promises and presents.

Notwithstanding the protracted negotiations and repeated interviews of General Schuyler with the Six Nations, the Oneidas alone remained neutral in the campaign under notice.

Fort Schuyler, at the bend of the Mohawk river from a southerly to an easterly course, was commanded by Colonel Peter Gansevoort, as early as April, 1777. He found that it was actually untenable against any enemy whatever. Although in doubt whether to provide for resistance to artillery, he went to work with such industry,

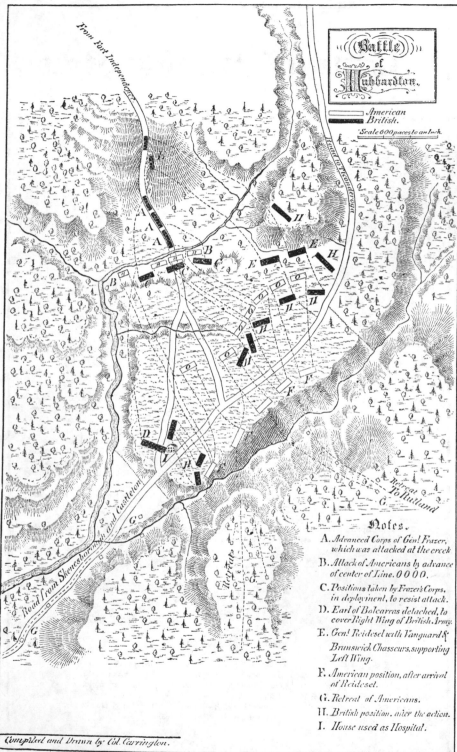

Battle of Hubbardton

JULY 7th, 1776

American Commander

FRANCIS

Strength, 1,300   Casualties, 360

British Commander

FRASER

Strength, 1,400   Casualties, 203

NOTE.—General St. Clair, retreating from Ticonderoga, hastened toward Castleton, which he reached by night, July 6th. He left Col. Seth Warner with 150 men at Hubbardton, to collect stragglers and await the arrival of Col. Francis, who left Mount Independence with the rear guard of the American army at four o'clock in the morning. Col. Francis, being joined at Hubbardton by Col. Hale, and thus having a force of nearly 1,300 men, determined to give battle. He attacked Fraser as soon as his pursuing columns appeared, before they could select their ground, and by use of fallen trees and other cover, made an effective attack. The precipitate retreat of Hale (then an invalid) left Francis and Warner but nine hundred men, just when Riedesel and Earl Balcarras arrived with their battalions, and entered into the action with vigor, band playing, and confident of success.

STEDMAN (*British author*) says: " The Americans maintained their post with great resolution and bravery." The reenforcements did not arrive so soon as expected, and victory was for a long time doubtful.

The wide dispersion of the fugitives in the woods, after Col. Francis fell, when resistance became hopeless, induced an excessive estimate of the American casualties.

References:

CARRINGTON'S " BATTLES OF THE AMERICAN REVOLUTION " pp. 214-242

School Histories :

Anderson, ¶ 58 ; p. 82.
Barnes, ¶ — ; p. —.
Berard (Bush), ¶ 74 ; p. 156.
Goodrich, C. A. (Seaveys), ¶ 19; p. 127.
Goodrich, S. G., ¶ 4 ; p. 224.
Hassard, ¶ 6; p. 191.

Holmes, ¶ —; p. —.
Lossing, ¶ 18 ; p. 157.
Quackenbos, ¶ 334; p. 240.
Ridpath, ¶ 12 ; p. 203.
Sadlier (Excel), ¶ — ; p.—.
Stephens, A. H., ¶ 22 ; p. 198.

Swinton, ¶ — ; p. —.
Scott, ¶ 12 ; p. 184.
Thalheimer (Eclectic), ¶ 5; p. 159.
Venable, ¶ 140 ; p. 107.

that when the test was made, it proved fully adequate to withstand the fire of the light ordnance which accompanied the column of St. Leger in August of that year.

On the twenty-ninth of May, Colonel Marinus Willett was ordered to report with his regiment for duty at the same post, and to aid in putting the fort in a thoroughly defensive condition. He reached Fort Schuyler in July. On the second of August five bateaux arrived with sufficient stores to increase the rations and small-arm ammunition to a supply for six weeks. The garrison then numbered seven hundred and fifty men. Lieutenant Mellon, of Colonel Wesson's Massachusetts regiment, with two hundred men, accompanied the bateaux as their escort, and joined the garrison. On the same day, and within an hour after the landing of this timely invoice of supplies, Lieutenant Bird of the British Eighth regiment approached the fort, and established a position for St. Leger's advanced guard ; and on the third of August his army began the investment.

The advance of St. Leger was conspicuous for its excellent adjustments. This was largely due to the presence of those who had skill in frontier Indian warfare. The entire force was so disposed by single files and the wise distribution of the Indian auxiliaries, as to make a surprise impossible, and afford the best possible opportunity for their peculiar style of skirmishing warfare, in case of an attack. Stone's Life of Brant very clearly represents this movement, and Lossing reproduces it with full details of the antecedent Indian operations in central New York.

Colonel Daniel Clark, son-in-law of Sir William Johnson ; Colonel John Butler, afterward conspicuous at the massacre of Wyoming ; Joseph Brant, a full blooded Mohawk, son of an Onondaga chief ; and Sir John Johnson, a son of Sir William Johnson, who succeeded to the title in 1774, were associated with St. Leger in command of this composite army of regulars, Hessian-chasseurs, Royal-greens, Canadians, axe-men, and non-combatants, who, as well as the Indians, proved an ultimate incumbrance and curse to the expedition. The investment was immediate. A proclamation of St. Leger, was followed by an appeal from General Nicholas Herkimer to the militia of Tryon county, and on the sixth he passed three scouts into the fort, with notice that he was at Oriskany, near the present village of Whitesborough, with eight hundred men advancing to its relief. He also requested that three guns might be fired to give notice of the safe arrival of his couriers. Colonel Willett, as had been suggested by

General Herkimer, promptly sallied forth with two hundred and fifty men, portions of Gansevoort's, and of Wesson's regiments, and one iron three pounder, to make a diversion in favor of the advancing militia. St. Leger had been advised of this movement of the militia, and was so engaged in preparation to attack it in the woods, and had so large a fatigue detail at work upon the intrenchments, as to have entirely ignored the possibility of offensive action on the part of the garrison. The sortie was therefore successful in the capture of much camp plunder, such as blankets, arms, flags, and clothing, a few prisoners, St. Leger's desk and papers, and the destruction of two sections of the intrenchments; but failed to unite with General Herkimer. That officer, overborne in his judgment by the impetuosity of younger officers, who mistook his caution in approaching the Indian camp for cowardice, allowed his march to be crowded too rapidly, and while crossing a ravine near Oriskany creek, he fell into an ambuscade which involved great slaughter. General Herkimer himself was severely wounded, and the total American casualties were not less than one hundred and sixty killed, besides more than two hundred wounded, and some prisoners. The Indian loss in killed and wounded was nearly eighty, including several valuable warriors, and the field was abandoned by the assailants. Colonel St. Leger made no official report of his loss, except that of his Indian allies. The fight continued for several hours, only suspended for a short time by a thunder storm, and stands on record as one of the most fiercely contested conflicts of the war.

On the afternoon of the seventh, St. Leger demanded the surrender of the post, under threat of giving over its garrison to the vengeance of the Indians. A bold defiance was the sole response. He also wrote to Burgoyne on the eleventh, that " he was secure of the fort and would soon join him at Albany." On the tenth Colonel Willett, afterwards active at Monmouth and in subsequent Indian wars, and Lieutenant Stockwell, smuggled themselves through the lines, and reached Fort Dayton (now Herkimer) safely, to arouse the militia to fresh efforts in behalf of the post. General Schuyler had already ordered General Learned's Massachusetts brigade on this duty, designating Fort Dayton as the rendezvous for the relief of Fort Schuyler. Colonel Willett went directly to Albany, and returned in company with Arnold and the first New York regiment ; but while the troops were yet forty miles distant from Fort Dayton, St. Leger, alarmed by reports of Arnold's march and rumors of a disaster to Burgoyne's army, precipitately abandoned his intrenchments and fled to Oswego, leaving a portion of his artillery, baggage and camp equipage on the field. In his official report, dated at Oswego, August twenty-seventh, St. Leger explained his retreat by charges of treachery and exaggerated reports of Arnold's force, closing with the suggestive statement that his own men " are in a most deplorable situation from the plunder of the savages."

Thus ended the British advance upon Albany, by the Mohawk valley. The moral effect of its failure was as encouraging to the American army, as the tidings of its advent, coupled with the successes of Burgoyne, had been depressing ; and the animation of the army was fully shared by the people.

General Washington wrote as follows to General Schuyler, on the twenty-first of August, when advised of the battle of Oriskany and of his detail of General Arnold to the relief of Fort Schuyler : " I am pleased with the account you transmit of the situation of matters upon the Mohawk river. If the militia keep up their spirits after the late severe skirmish, I am confident they will, with the assistance of the reinforcements under General Arnold, be enabled to raise the siege of Fort Schuyler, which will be a most important matter just at this time."

At the time when St. Leger established his camp before Fort Schuyler, General Burgoyne began to realize the difficulties which attended the supply of his army. He had received altogether, a reinforcement of nearly a thousand Indians, but the murder of Miss Jane McCrea and repeated violations of the usages of civilized warfare, as well as the additional mouths to feed, increased the discomfort and embarrassment of his position. The reports of German officers to their sovereigns, abound in descriptions of the horrors of this warfare. One wrote, that " to prevent desertions it was announced in orders that the savages would scalp runaways." Schlöozer states, that " on the third of August, they, the Indians, brought in twenty scalps and as many captives." It is clear that there was no responsibility on the part of Burgoyne for the murder of Miss McCrea, or other personal violence, and a careful sifting of all accessible reports as clearly shows that most of the outrages reported at the time were exaggerations of a style of warfare which was under as good control as possible under any commander. The Indians could not be civilized *instantly*, nor be readily made to acquiesce in the limit of rations which was assigned to regular troops, and all their demands were of the most imperative kind.   Burgoyne thus states his own views upon this subject, " I had been taught to look upon the remote tribes which joined me at Skenesborough, as more warlike :—but, with equal depravity in general principles, their only preëminence consisted in ferocity."   He also experienced difficulty in managing *Indian agents*, and thus expresses a sentiment which will be appreciated by all officers who have engaged in frontier Indian service, where interpreters and intermediate civil agents are employed.   " The interpreters, from the first, regarded with a jealous eye a system which took out of their hands the distribution of Indian necessaries and presents; but when they found the plunder of the country, as well as that of the government, was *controlled*, the profligacy of many was employed to promote dissension, revolt and desertion.   Although I differed totally with St. Luc, "then in general charge of the Indian auxiliaries," in opinion upon the efficiency of these allies, I invariably took his advice in the management of them, even to an indulgence of their most capricious fancies, when they did not involve the dishonor of the King's cause and the disgrace of humanity."   " He certainly knew that the Indians pined after a renewal of their accustomed horrors and that they were become as impatient of *his* control as of any other : though the pride and interest of authority and the affection he bore his old associates induced him to cover the real causes, under various pretenses of discontent with which I was daily tormented."

At a council held August fourth, it appeared that the tribes with which St. Luc was immediately connected and for which he interpreted, were determined to go home.   Burgoyne thus writes to Lord Germaine, " I was convinced that a cordial reconciliation with the Indians was only to be effected by a renunciation of all my former prohibitions and indulgence in blood and rapine."   Many of the Indians did in fact leave the next day, and many others before the expedition to Bennington was planned, so that the loss of valuable scouts and skirmishers was greatly felt during operations in the forests on the line of that march.   An additional statement of General Burgoyne is properly recorded to his permanent credit.

" The Indian principle of war is at once odious and unavailing, and if encouraged, I will venture to pronounce, its consequences will be severely repented by the present age, and universally abhorred by posterity."

This statement was made before the House of Commons, but that it was not an after-thought, is clearly seen from the statement made by Burgoyne to St. Luc, in the presence of the Earl of Harrington : " I would rather lose every Indian, than connive at their enormities." St. Luc was angry because Burgoyne insisted that a British officer should accompany all Indian forays, and take account of their proceedings and their plunder ; and several parties were brought into his camp as prisoners, who affirmed that they had been treated with proper clemency.   It was not until this rule was enforced that St. Luc stirred up the Indians to desertion and outrage.   He is not a competent witness in the case.

The following entry appears upon Burgoyne's record, " August fifth.   Victualling of the army *out* this day, and from difficulties of the roads and transports, no provisions came in this night.   Sixth August.   At ten o'clock this morning, not quite enough provisions for the consumption of two days."

In this emergency advantage was taken of the statement of Philip Skene, whose coöperation brought mischief only to the expedition, and of others supported by scouts sent out by General Riedesel, that a large depot of commissary supplies had been accumulated at Bennington for the American army, and an expedition.was organized for the threefold purpose of securing these supplies, procuring thirteen hundred horses for mounting Riedesel's dragoons and Peter's corps, and two hundred for general army use, and of making a demonstration in the Connecticut river valley.   On the ninth, carefully written instructions were prepared for Lieutenant-colonel Baume, who was intrusted with the command of the expedition, and these were so judiciously framed as to anticipate all possible contingencies of the march.   They took into view the fact that Colonel Warner was still at Manchester, and the possibility that Arnold's main army, at that time suggested for a proposed movement to Burgoyne's rear, might attempt to intercept his return march.   In view of the exceptions taken to the assignment of German troops to this expedition, it is in evidence that even General Fraser, who considered the Germans as *slow*, declined to suggest to General Burgoyne the substitution of other troops, although asked to do so by Adjutant-general Kingston, " if he thought other troops should be detailed," remarking " the Germans are not a very active people, but it may do."   This matter was especially submitted to General Fraser, " because the scouts and guides were attached to his, the advanced corps, and it was thought that he might know more of the nature of the country."   There was no declared difference of opinion among the general officers as to the value and wisdom of the expedition itself. It was to comprehend Arlington, lying between Manchester and Bennington, and as wide a scope of country as would afford opportunity to overawe the people and secure supplies, and was allowed a margin of two weeks time, with adequate instructions in case the main army should advance towards Albany before its return.

Burgoyne thus states the case : " It was soon found that in the situation of the transport-service at that time, the army could barely be victualed from day to day, and that there was no prospect of establishing a magazine in due time for pursuing present advantages. The idea of the expedition to Bennington originated upon this difficulty, combined with the intelligence reported by General Riedesel, and with all I had otherwise received. I knew that Bennington was the great deposit of corn, flour, and store cattle, that it was only guarded by militia, and every day's account tended to confirm the persuasion of the loyalty of one description of inhabitants and the panic of the other. Those who knew the country best were the most sanguine in this persuasion. The German troops employed were of the best I had of that nation. The number of British was small, but it was the select light corps of the army, composed of chosen men from all the regiments, and commanded by Captain Fraser, one of the most distinguished officers in his line of service that I ever met with."

An additional statement is necessary at this stage of the narrative, to show exactly the status of the British army, in the matter of Logistics.

Fort Edward was sixteen miles from Fort George. Only one haul could be made each day. Six miles below Fort Edward were rapids which required a transfer of all stores to boats below; and the unloaded boats had to be hauled back against a strong current. The horses from Canada came by land from St. John's to Ticonderoga, through a country then hardly less than a desert, and the whole number of carts and horses at that time received, was barely enough to keep the army in supplies.

As early as May thirtieth, while at Montreal, an order was issued that blanket-coats, leggings, and all clothing but summer wear should be left behind, and before leaving Skenesborough the officers were ordered to send all their personal baggage to Ticonderoga, except a soldier's common tent and a cloak-bag.

The roads, bridges, quagmires, and rocks were constant causes of delay in hauling stores. Heavy rains set in. Ten and twelve oxen were often required to haul a single bateaux, and only fifty head had been procured for the entire army use. There was no remedy but patience, no honorable retreat, no alternative but to make the most of the present, and press toward Albany and the anticipated union with General Howe and St. Leger.

On the fourteenth of August, a bridge of rafts was thrown across the river at Saratoga, where the vanguard of the British army had been established, to be in position for an advance upon Albany as soon as the supplies should be realized from the expedition then on the move. Lieutenant-colonel Breyman's corps was posted at Batten-kill, to be in readiness to render support to that of Lieutenant-colonel Baume if it became necessary.

Lieutenant-colonel Baume himself marched, on the eleventh, with two hundred dismounted dragoons of the regiment of Riedesel, Captain Fraser's marksmen, Peter's Provincials, the Canadian volunteers, and something over one hundred Indians, making, as stated by Burgoyne, a total strength of about five hundred men.

He halted at Batten-kill to await orders, where General Burgoyne inspected the command ; and he expressed himself satisfied with the force placed at his disposal. In a note from his camp, he adds this postscript: " The *reinforcement of fifty chasseurs* which your excellency was pleased to order, joined me last night at eleven o'clock."

After marching sixteen miles, he reached Cambridge at four o'clock in the afternoon of the thirteenth, and reported a skirmish with forty or fifty rebels who were guarding cattle; and stated that the enemy were reported to be eighteen hundred strong at Bennington. He also stated that " the savages would destroy or drive away all horses for which he did not pay the money," and asked authority to purchase the horses thus taken by the savages, " otherwise they will ruin all they meet with, and neither officers nor interpreters can control them." This express started from Cambridge at four o'clock of the morning of the fourteenth. The letter closed, " Your excellency may depend on hearing how I proceed at Bennington, and of my success there. I will be particularly careful on my approach to that place to be fully informed of their strength and position, and take the precautions necessary to fulfill both the orders and instructions of your excellency." Burgoyne replied, August fourteenth at seven at night, instructing fully as to the items of the dispatch received, adding, " should you find the enemy too strongly posted at Bennington, I wish you to take a post where you can maintain yourself till you receive an answer from me, and I will either support you in force, or withdraw you."

On the fourteenth at nine o'clock, he reported from Sancoick (Van Schaick's Mills) of a skirmish, the capture of flour, salt, etc., that "five prisoners agree that from fifteen to eighteen hundred men are at Bennington, but are supposed to leave on our approach," adding, " I will proceed so far to-day as to fall on the enemy to-morrow early, and make such disposition as I think necessary from the intelligence I receive. People are flocking in hourly, but want to be armed ; the savages can not be controlled. They ruin and take everything they please." *Postscript.* " Beg your excellency to pardon the hurry of this letter, as it is wrote on the head of a barrel."

This was the last dispatch from Baume, and no reinforcements were called for, neither was there intimation that they would be required. Careful examination fails to find the data upon which many historians make the statement. The record of this message made at head-quarters is as follows: " 15th August, express arrived from Sancoick at five o'clock in the morning. *Corps de reserve* ordered to march."

General Burgoyne promptly and wisely started Breyman's force of five hundred men to the support of Baume as soon as advised that the " secret expedition " had been discovered by the enemy, and that the American force was probably greater than he had before anticipated."

Colonel Breyman received his orders at eight o'clock on the morning of the fifteenth, and marched at nine, with one battalion of chasseurs, one of grenadiers, one rifle company and two pieces of cannon. " Each soldier carried forty rounds of ammunition in his pouch, and on account of the scarcity of transportation, two boxes of ammunition were placed upon the artillery carts." This command met with constant disaster. A heavy rain continued during the day, so that the troops made but a half English mile an hour : the guns had to be hauled up hills, alternately ; one artillery cart was overturned ; a timbrel was broken up and its ammunition wasted ; the guide lost his way, and at night the detachment was still seven miles from Cambridge. Lieutenant Hanneman was sent forward to inform Lieutenant-colonel Baume of the approach of reinforcements.

Breyman reached Van Schaick's mill at half past four o'clock in the afternoon, where he met Colonel Skene, who notified him that Baume was two miles in advance. He pushed on to his support with no intimation that any engagement had taken place. " At the bridge, a force of men was met, some in jackets and some in shirts, whom Skene declared to be royalists, but they proved to be rebels, attempting to gain high ground to his left." " A vigorous attack was made, with varying success and lasting until nearly eight o'clock. The ammunition was expended, the horses had been killed, Lieutenant Spangenburg and many others were wounded, and the American forces were constantly adding to their numbers. The guns were abandoned. The troops reached Cambridge at twelve o'clock and regained camp on the morning of the seventeenth." Such is the melancholy summary of Breyman's report, closing, " could I have saved my cannon I would with pleasure have sacrificed my life to have effected it."

General Stark had returned to New Hampshire some time after the battle of Trenton, on a recruiting expedition, and resigned his commission upon hearing that Congress had promoted junior officers over his head. The appeal of his native State was not to be resisted when the invasion of Burgoyne took place ; and he accepted a command, upon condition that he should not be compelled to join the main army.

General Lincoln visited Manchester, where recruits were assembling, with an order from General Schuyler for Stark to report for duty ; but could not induce him to swerve from his purpose. He was at Bennington on the night of the thirtieth, when advised that a body of Indians had reached Cambridge. Colonel Gregg was at once sent with two hundred men to oppose their advance. During the night an express messenger brought word that a large force of British troops was on the march, of which the Indians constituted only the vanguard. He immediately sent to Colonel Warner, then at Manchester, an appeal for aid, aroused the militia, and made preparations to meet the enemy.

On the fourteenth Lieutenant-colonel Baume advanced to within four miles of Bennington. The Americans, unprepared for battle, retired before his advance, and encamped on the Bennington road, (see map). General Burgoyne in his report states that " Lieutenant-colonel Baume sacrificed his command by violation of orders, in continuing his advance when met by superior numbers, and by too widely scattering his force. The embarrassment of Baume was two-fold. His force was not homogeneous ; and his adversary was too strong. He followed orders quite literally in holding his dragoons together and using the Provincials and other irregular troops as pickets, but the latter were a mile from his own position and there was no possibility of concert of action in defense.

He occupied a commanding hill quite thickly wooded at a bend of the Walloomscoick, and at once intrenched his position. On the fifteenth, the rain which retarded the march of Breyman suspended active operations, except skirmishing ; but Colonel Warner made the march from Manchester, and Colonel Symonds arrived at Bennington with a detachment of Berkshire militia, so that on the morning of the sixteenth the force of General Stark amounted to nearly or quite two thousand men. Colonel Warner's regiment halted at Bennington to rest from their march and dry their arms and equipments, while Stark so distributed the regiments of his own brigade and the militia, as to be ready in the morning for the assault, which, after conference with his officers, he had already arranged. Riedesel's dragoons with a part of the rangers occupied the summit already referred to ; while one company advanced down the slope, to cover the chasseurs, who were near the foot of the hill where a small creek enters the Walloomscoick. One company of grenadiers, with a portion of the rangers, occupied a position behind the bridge, on the road to Bennington, and the Canadians with a detachment of Royalist Americans, took possession of houses south of the bridge, and a slight elevation lower down, near the ford, where a trench was hastily dug for partial protection. A second detachment of grenadiers and royalists occupied the extreme British right, in open ground to the northwest, at the foot of the hill near the Saratoga road. A portion of the Indian scouts took position on the opposite side of the road, on their first arrival, but they fled on the fourteenth, as soon as the Americans were found to be in force. The remainder who encamped in the woods to the rear of Baume, broke away between the advancing columns of Nichols and Herrick as soon as the battle began on the sixteenth.

General Stark reserved for himself the direct attack up the steepest part of the hill, and held his men in hand until the other troops took their assigned positions. Nichols struck the British left. Herrick took their extreme right, in the rear. Stickney cut off the detachments at the bridge from union with Baume ; and Hubbard with equal spirit attacked the positions held in advance of the bridge. These attacks were made with great promptness and the utmost vigor. Hubbard drove the American volunteers and Canadians across the river at the first charge, where they were met by Stickney. The Rangers alone retired in good order ; but Herrick and Nichols having completed their flank movement and driven in all opposing detachments, united at the summit and participated with Stark in storming the breastworks where Baume made a persistent stand and offered real fight.   The battle, which began about three o'clock, was soon over, and many of the militia were engaged in collecting the trophies of the action, when Lieutenant-colonel Breyman's command reached the bridge and attempted to regain the heights.   His guns opened fire upon the scattered Americans, and this was the first intimation that they received that the victory was still to be won.   The opportune arrival of Colonel Warner's regiment, fresh and in good order, checked the advancing column, and a vigorous action was maintained until the ammunition of the British artillery gave out, and the day closed.

The American trophies included four brass field pieces, twelve brass drums, two hundred and fifty dragoon swords and several hundred stand of arms.

The British casualties are variously stated.   Dawson in his " Battles of the United States by Sea and Land," which is compiled with remarkable faithfulness and judgment, adopts Gordon's statement and places the number of killed at two hundred and seven, and the prisoners at seven hundred.   Irving states the prisoners at five hundred and fifty-four ; Bancroft at six hundred and ninety-two, and Lossing at nine hundred and thirty-four, including the killed and wounded, and one hundred and fifty tories.   This last element must be fully considered, in view of General Burgoyne's official report that " many armed royalists joined the command on the march."   It is the only way by which to reconcile the disproportion of casualties to the actual British force which was detailed to Lieutenant-colonel Baume's command.

The Americans lost about forty killed and as many wounded. The killed of the British force must have been mainly from the Canadians and royalists who fled and were shot down by eager pursuers, as nearly four hundred Hessians were among the prisoners captured.   Reports of the capture of arms, largely in access of the British force, are predicated upon the idea that these arms were taken with the expedition for distribution to royalists.   The *secret* nature of the expedition at the start, and the fact that it was with great difficulty that arms were obtained for six hundred of these recruits, the maximum ever secured by the army, renders such reports untrustworthy.

Thus this battle added its trophies to the gallant fight of Oriskany and the successful defense of Fort Schuyler.   General Stark was promptly promoted by Congress. These events seemed to be the ripe fruit of Washington's prophetic forecast. The militia began at once to hasten to the camp of Schuyler. That officer had been superseded by General Gates, under the direction of the American Congress; but the latter did not arrive to assume command until August nineteenth, just in time to gather laurels already maturing for any discreet commander of the reviving army of the North. General Schuyler received him with courtesy, permitted no mortification at this sudden removal from command to chill his enthusiastic support and earnest coöperation in securing men and supplies for the prosecution of the campaign; and although not invited by his successor to a council of war which was convened to determine the exact condition of the department, and the necessary measures which its interests demanded, was as loyal to the demands upon his honor and his zeal as if he had been supreme in command, and was about to put on a crown of victory.

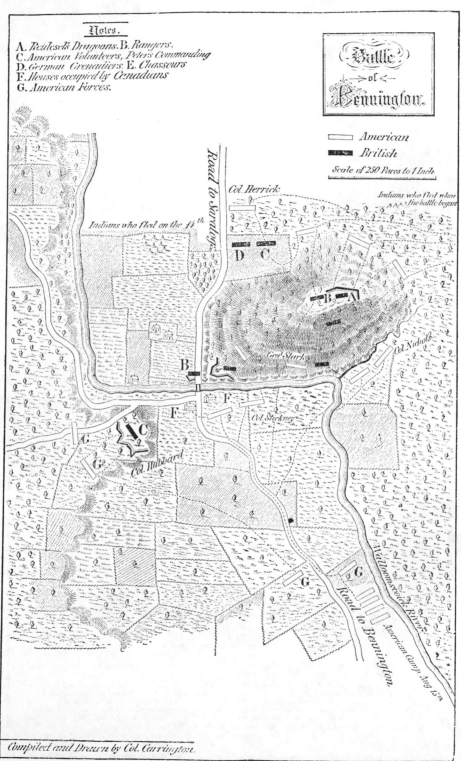

Notes.

A. *Reidesel's Dragoons.* B. *Rangers.*
C. *American Volunteers, Peter's Commanding*
D. *German Grenadiers.* E. *Chasseurs*
F. *Houses occupied by Canadians*
G. *American Forces.*

Battle of Bennington.

☐ *American*
■ *British*

Scale of 250 Paces to 1 Inch.

Road to Saratoga

Col. Herrick

Indians who fled when the battle began

Indians who fled on the 14th

D C

B A

Col. Nichols

Gen. Stark

Col. Stickney

Col. Hubbard

Walloomscoick River

Road to Bennington

American Camp Aug 15th

Compiled and Drawn by Col. Carrington.

Battle of Bennington

AUGUST 16th, 1777

American Commander

STARK

Strength, 1,450   Casualties, 84

British Commander

BAUME

Strength, 550   Casualties, 207.

Americans take 600 prisoners, including Tories

MEM.—(*The battle of Bennington resulted from an attempt made by Burgoyne to secure flour and other supplies, which a loyalist, Major Skene, had reported to be collected at that place. The route from Skenesborough to Fort Edward, on the Hudson river, had been so obstructed by felled timber and broken bridges, by order of Gen. Schuyler, that Burgoyne did not reach that post until July 30th, and his army already experienced a scarcity of provisions.*

NOTES.—On the 11th of August, Lt. Col. Baume was started from Batten Kill, with 550 men to capture the stores. On the 14th he had a skirmish at Van Schaik's mill, where he destroyed some flour, and wrote to Burgoyne that a force of fifteen to eighteen hundred men was reported to be at Bennington. Meanwhile, loyalists, with and without arms, were joining him, to share in the plunder of the expedition. He advanced the same day, within four miles of Bennington; but, upon assurances that the Americans were in force, he entrenched upon a wooded hill at a bend of the Walloomschoick river, placed a detachment of Rangers at the river crossing, and one of Loyalists on a knoll at the forked roads, in front of the crossing, and awaited attack, or reenforcements.

On the 15th, at 8 A. M., Lt. Col. Breyman received orders, and, at 9 o'clock, left Burgoyne's headquarters with reenforcements, viz.: 500 men and two guns. Heavy rain retarded the column, limiting the advance to less than a mile an hour. On the same day Col. Warner left Manchester for Bennington, where he halted one day, to rest the men and dry their arms and equipments. With the arrival of Col. Symonds, the Americans numbered nearly two thousand men.

On the 16th, Stark, without waiting for the entire command to be ready, advanced against the enemy. Stickney cut off the detachment at the bridge. Hubbard dispersed the small force in front of the bridge. Herrick attacked the British Grenadiers, who were posted near the Saratoga road, on the British right, while Nichols turned Baume's left. Stark, himself, ascended the face of the hill and stormed the breastworks. The Indian allies deserted Baume at the first attack, and by four o'clock the battle was over. The British lost in killed, 207, and in prisoners, including loyalists or tories, not far from 600.

Lt. Col. Breyman arrived and opened fire with his guns, while the Americans, widely dispersed, were collecting the trophies of the field. The failure of Breyman's artillery ammunition, and the timely arrival of Col. Warner with his fresh regiment, completed the victory at Bennington.

References:

CARRINGTON'S "BATTLES OF THE AMERICAN REVOLUTION," pp. 327-334.

School Histories:

Anderson, ¶ 62; p. 83.
Barnes, ¶ 2; p. 123.
Berard (Bush), ¶ 76; p. 157.
Goodrich, C. A.(Seaveys),¶ 19; p. 127.
Goodrich, S. G., ¶ 1-7; p. 226.
Hassard, ¶ 12-13; p. 194.

Holmes, ¶ 7; p. 126.
Lossing, ¶ 20: p. 158.
Quackenbos, ¶ 338; p. 242-3.
Ridpath, ¶ 13; p. 203.
Sadlier, (Excel), ¶ 2; p. 191.
Stephens, A.H. ¶ 26; p. 200.

Swinton, ¶ 145; p. 134.
Scott, ¶ 16; p. 186.
Thalheimer (Eclectic), ¶ 264, p. 151;
Venable, ¶ 140; p. 107.

NOTE.—The invasion by Burgoyne had support from a movement into Central New York *via* Oswego, under St. Leger, against Fort Schuyler.

Its object was to reach Albany by the Mohawk Valley, in the rear of the American army. The "Battle of Oriskany" was fought; General Herkimer was wounded and, the American casualties were nearly 400. Col. Marinus Willett held the fort, with success; and the approach of Arnold to its relief induced St. Leger to give up the siege, which he began with assurance of success. General Schuyler planned the relief from this attack, provided for the detail of Learned and Arnold for the purpose, and the result vindicated his own expectations, and those of Washington.

Carrington's "Battles of the American Revolution," pp. 324-5.

CHAPTER XLVI.

BATTLE OF FREEMAN'S FARM.

GENERAL GATES took command of the Northern Department August nineteenth, 1777. Congress clothed him with large powers, and conceded to his demand all for which General Schuyler had in vain made requisitions. His communications were also made direct to Congress, over the head of the commander-in-chief; and to such an extent was this practiced, that his ultimate report of the surrender of General Burgoyne entirely ignored the position of Washington, as if Gates already occupied his place. It is not proposed in this connection or elsewhere, to enter into the details of his systematic efforts to attain the general command ; but, as in the case of General Lee and other officers, to notice occasional military facts and documents which determine the qualifications of officers in respect of subordination, discipline and military conduct.

His accession to command was signalized by an extraordinary letter addressed to General Burgoyne, containing the following paragraph : " The miserable fate of Miss McCrea was peculiarly aggravated by her being dressed to receive her promised husband, but met her murderer *employed by you.*" " Upward of one hundred men, women, and children have perished by the hands of ruffians to whom it is asserted *you have paid the price of blood.*"

Burgoyne replied, " I would not be conscious of the acts you presume to impute to me for the whole continent of America ; though the wealth of worlds was in its bowels, and a paradise upon its surface." The letter of Gates received passing applause. The reply of Burgoyne still honors his name.

The army daily increased in numbers. Congress directed that Morgan's riflemen, then thoroughly organized, should be sent to the Northern Department, and after nearly three weeks of delay, Gates advanced his command from Schuyler's old camp on the islands of the

Mohawk, to a position about four miles north of Stillwater, and twenty-four from Albany, on the west or right bank of the Hudson river.

A narrow meadow skirted the river at the point which Kosciusko, then an engineer in the American service, had selected for the camp. The headquarters were established on the first hill west from the river. The breastworks proper took the general form of a half circle three-quarters of a mile in extent, projected towards the north. Several redoubts were established to command the front and the river meadows; and the old Neilson barn, built of heavy logs, was fortified at the nearest approach of the enemy. Light earthworks also rested upon the meadow itself, covering both the old road and the bridge of boats which established communication with the opposite shore of the Hudson. Still farther to the left on the adjoining hill eastward, additional earthworks were commenced but they were never entirely completed. The position itself was well protected by its elevation and steep face. Bemis' Heights was to the north and west. Freeman's farm-house occupied a cultivated tract of limited extent nearly north of the American left, and between the middle and south ravine, which here cut through from the hills to the river. Mill creek and its branches swept through the forests lying between the American position and that which the British army occupied on the seventeenth day of August. The south ravine was behind and south of the American camp, and the north ravine, which was the deepest, was nearly in front and south of the British position. The middle ravine was between the American camp and Freeman's farm. Reference is made to the maps, " Battle of Freeman's Farm," " Battle of Bemis' Heights," for a general review of the respective positions of the two armies. The two maps alike reproduce the portion of country which was common to the military movements from September seventeenth to the eighth of October.

General Poor's brigade, consisting of the New Hampshire regiments of Cilley, Scammel, and Hale; Van Cortland's and Henry Livingston's New York regiments; Cook's and Latimer's Connecticut militia; Morgan's rifle corps, and Major Dearborn's light infantry composed the left wing under Arnold, resting on the heights nearly a mile from the river. General Learned's brigade, Bailey's, Wesson's, and Jackson's Massachusetts regiments, and James Livingston's New York regiments occupied the adjoining fortified plateau to the left near the Neilson barn. The main body under the immediate command of General Gates, and composed chiefly of Nixon's, Patterson's and Glover's brigades, formed the right wing upon the bluff, reaching across the low ground to the river. General Stark joined with his brigade of militia, but they did not remain long after their short time of service expired. Whipple's, Patterson's, Warner's, Fellows', Bailey's Wolcott's, Brickell's, and Ten Broeck's brigades also joined the army. The works were all well advanced by the fifteenth of September.

On the twentieth of August, Burgoyne wrote to Lord Germaine, that Fort Stanwix held out stubbornly in spite of St. Leger's victory (over Herkimer),—that he had accumulated but about four hundred loyalists, not half of them armed, the rest *trimmers* merely actuated by interest—that he was afraid the expectations of Sir John Johnson as to the rising of the country would fail,—that the great bulk of the people is undoubtedly with the Congress in principle and in zeal, and that " their measures are executed with a secrecy and dispatch that are not to be equaled;" adding, " wherever the king's forces point, militia to the amount of three or four thousand assemble in twenty-four hours, and bring their subsistence with them, and the alarm over, they return to their farms." " The Hampshire Grants, in particular, a country unpeopled and almost unknown in the last war, now abounds in the most active and rebellious men of the continent, and hangs like a gathering storm on my left."

Of his correspondence with Sir William Howe he reports that he " knew that two of his messengers had been hanged, while only one letter had been received ; " that " Sir William Howe informed him that his intention was for Pennsylvania, that Washington had dispatched twenty-five hundred men to Albany, that Putnam was in the Highlands with four thousand men, but that Sir Henry Clinton remained in the neighborhood of New York and would act as circumstances might direct." Almost immediately after this dispatch was sent, he received the news of the retreat of St. Leger and that the American army was relieved from that pressure upon its left flank and rear.

The utmost effort was made to secure supplies ; and by the twelfth of September, provisions had been procured for thirty days' issue. The bridge of rafts had drifted away by a rise of the Hudson ; a new bridge of boats had been built, and on the thirteenth and fourteenth of September the entire army crossed the Hudson and encamped on the plain of Saratoga. It is proper to state in this connection that his crossing of the Hudson river, was not only in the direct line of general instructions, but it had the concurrence of his officers, and was

22

regarded as the only method of meeting the responsibility which devolved upon the army.

On the fifteenth the army moved to Dovegat (now Coveville); on the sixteenth repaired bridges, reconnoitered the country and made a still further advance, and on the seventeenth encamped upon advantageous ground within four miles of the American army, near Snoods' House, as indicated on the map entitled " Battle of Freeman's Farm." On the eighteenth skirmishing was active between the two armies. On the nineteenth, after careful reconnoitering of the great ravine and other avenues of approach to the American lines, the British army advanced to the attack. An approximate idea of the succeeding movements can be secured.

Major-general the Marquis de Chastellux who served under the Count de Rochambeau, revisited America in 1780–81, and 82, and after an entertainment at General Schuyler's mansion, " visited the ground where the actions of the nineteenth of September and of the seventh of October happened." He says, " I avoid the word *field of battle*, for these engagements were in the woods, and on ground so intersected and covered, that it is impossible either to conceive or discover the smallest resemblance between it and the plans given to the public by General Burgoyne."

Whether " the depth of the snow through which he waded," or his " upset in a great heap of snow while traveling in a sledge," had any thing to do with the difficulty in tracing the route of Burgoyne or not, the genial traveler does not indicate. These maps however do set forth with substantial distinctness the general positions of the two armies; and with some modifications and enlargement of detail, are the best guides from which to obtain a fair conception of the engagements referred to. It is not unseldom the case that a single error in the starting point, will even confuse one who participated actively in field operations, if it be only through approaching the position from a contrary direction ; and in reports of nearly all battles, the movements made by different corps must be examined, in order to understand the actual relations of the principal parties engaged.

The advance of General Burgoyne will be taken from his own initiative, sustained by the evidence of officers of his staff and his division commanders; and these will be combined with the report of Adjutant-general Wilkinson, of General Gates' staff, and other American officers, so as to gain as accurate an estimate of the battle referred to as may be gained by such analysis.

Six companies of the Forty-seventh British regiment guarded the bateaux which were at the river bank, in the rear of the camp.   Two companies of this regiment remained behind on Diamond Island, Lake George.   When the army left Fort Edward, " General Fraser's corps, sustained by Lieutenant-colonel Breyman's made a circuit, in order to pass the ravine commodiously without quitting the heights ; and afterwards to cover the march of the line to the right.

The Canadians were in advance and were speedily driven back, but rallied upon Fraser's approach.   The American volunteers and Indians were also employed on the flanks, and to the front.   The British and German grenadiers and the Twenty-fourth regiment moved steadily along the height, until they were required to change direction to the left, which brought them directly in contact with the American troops, who having been repulsed by General Fraser, shortly after engaged the British centre.   General Burgoyne says of this particular movement : " In the meantime the enemy, not acquainted with the combination of the march, had moved in great force out of their intrenchments, with a view of turning the line upon our right, and being checked by the disposition of Brigadier-general Fraser, *countermarched*, in order to direct their great effort to the left of the British." " From the nature of the country, efforts of this sort, however near, may be effected without possibility of their being discovered."

The centre column, led by Burgoyne in person, " passed the ravine in a direct line south, and formed in line of battle as soon as they gained the summit (out of the ravine) at the first opening of the wood to the right, to give time to Fraser's corps to make the desired circuit, and to enable the left wing and artillery, which, under the command of Major-generals Phillips and Riedesel, kept the great road and meadows near the river, and had bridges to repair, to be equally ready to proceed."   The latter corps, upon reaching the position, changed direction and marched nearly due west, to connect with the left of the British centre, which had engaged the enemy before their arrival.   " All columns moved at signal guns, a little after one o'clock in the afternoon.   A few cannon shot soon dislodged the Americans from a house where the Canadians had been attacked," and " Brigadier-general Fraser's corps arrived with such precision in point of time, as to be found upon a very advantageous height on the right of the British centre as soon as the action began."   This position has been already adverted to.   The American troops made their first advance upon General Fraser's corps ; but by three o'clock, or soon after, the whole action concentrated near Freeman's Farm, from which position the British army made a determined advance for the purpose of turn-ing the American left. The Twentieth, Sixty-second, and Twenty-first regiments advanced directly from their original place of formation, leaving the Ninth in reserve. The British grenadiers and the Twenty-fourth were brought to their support after this advance to Freeman's Farm; and the light infantry which had been on Burgoyne's right, also came into action on the left of the grenadiers, thus connecting with the Ninth regiment when it subsequently advanced. Major Forbes of the Ninth, who commanded the pickets, states that "he was attacked with great vigor from behind rail fences and a house, by a body of riflemen and light infantry"; that "the Americans attempted to turn the left of the Sixty-second, when the Twentieth was advanced to its support." The Americans pressed forward also upon the right of the British column, until the advance of the British light infantry, and the movement of the grenadiers of Fraser's command to the left, com-pelled them to fall back and take their final position on good ground, between Freeman's Farm and Chatfield's house. Earl Balcarras, in his evidence upon this part of the battle, says, "The enemy behaved with great obstinacy and courage." The Earl of Harrington says that "the British line was formed with the utmost regularity, that different attempts were made by the General's orders to charge the enemy with bayonets, and all failed but the last, when the British troops finally drove them from the field, and that the action was dis-puted very obstinately by the enemy." During this time the rifle-men and other parts of Breyman's corps were left on the heights to protect the extreme right from being turned.

Major-general Phillips and Major Humphreys, with four pieces of artillery, arrived from the extreme left in advance of General Riedesel, and led the Twentieth again to the front, "restoring the action," (says Burgoyne) "in a point which was critically pressed by a great superi-ority of fire." General Riedesel brought up the Jagers, Specht's com-mand, and his Brunswickers, only in time to engage in the final charge, which was just as night came on, and both armies gave up the contest. The Earl Balcarras occupied Freeman's Farm with the light infantry and fortified the position. Colonel Breyman threw up works to the right and rear, to protect the right wing, and the remainder of the army was prolonged to the river, behind Mill creek, Hanau's corps occupy-ing the meadow near the river bank. The whole line was at once fortified, and five redoubts were established on detached hills having commanding positions. The British regiments of the centre which had been held under fire for the entire afternoon, went into action with eleven hundred men, and lost in killed and wounded more than half their force.

The Twentieth and Sixty-second were almost destroyed. Colonel Anstruther and Major Hamage, and many other officers, were either killed or wounded, and Adjutant-general Kingston states, that "the survivors did not probably exceed fifty, besides four or five officers." Captain Jones, commanding four guns, had thirty-six men killed or wounded, out of a total of forty-eight. The fight over these guns was desperate.

Such is the summary of the British reports of this action; and they clearly vindicate the excellence of the order of battle which Burgoyne adopted and the skill with which his force was handled in the midst of woods and where there were few tracts of open ground for manœuvering troops. Early in the day, upon the advice of Arnold, Gates had directed him to send Morgan's riflemen and Dearborn's light infantry to oppose the advance of the British right. This was the force encountered by Major Forbes and afterwards by Earl Balcarras. Its temporary success was turned into a repulse by the support which Major Forbes received, and Morgan fell back (" counter-marched," says Burgoyne) with the loss of Captain Swearigen and twenty men and with his corps so greatly disorganized that he thought it was " ruined." The regiments of Scammel and Cilley were ordered to Morgan's support, and Arnold pushed a strong column to the attack, from his division. The firm resistance of General Fraser required additional troops. Arnold finally pushed his entire division to the front and then it was that the attack shifted and fell upon the centre, commanded by Burgoyne in person.

Sergeant Lamb says, in his Journal, " Here the conflict was dreadful; for four hours a constant blaze of fire was kept up, and both armies seemed to be determined on death or victory." Arnold finally brought his whole division into action and other reinforcements came up until at least three thousand American troops were engaged.

The American casualties were sixty-five killed, two hundred and eighteen wounded and thirty-eight missing. The British army was unable to resume the fight; and the American army awaited the arrival of ammunition before venturing to advance again upon the enemy. General Gates reported this action to Congress in brief terms, declining "to discriminate in praise of the officers, as they all deserve the honor and applause of Congress." The names of Lieutenant-colonels Colburn and Adams, who were killed, are however specifically mentioned.

To what extent General Arnold accompanied the successive portions of his division which bore the brunt of this day's fight, is not clearly or uniformly defined by historians. That contemporaneous history gave his division credit, is nowhere questioned : and that he was a listless observer or remained in camp regardless of the fact that he was responsible for the entire left wing, which was then assailed, is perfectly inconsistent with his nature and the position he occupied. Wilkinson, Adjutant-general of Gates, and by virtue thereof "*prima facie*" good authority as to the acts of Gates, makes the remarkable statement, that "not a single general officer was on the field of battle, the nineteenth of September until evening," and states the execution of this wonderful military exploit, that "the battle was fought by the general concert and zealous coöperation of the corps engaged, and sustained more by individual courage than military discipline." Bancroft states that "Arnold was not on the field," and adds "so witnesses Wilkinson, whom Marshall knew personally and believed." But Marshall says, "Reinforcements were continually brought up, and, about four o'clock, Arnold, with nine Continental regiments and Morgan's corps, was completely engaged with the whole right wing of the British army. The conflict was extremely severe and only terminated with the day."

Gordon says, "Arnold's division was out in the action, but he himself did not lead them ; he remained in the camp the whole time." This statement is not inconsistent with the fact that Arnold regulated the resistance before his lines, although a curious intimation concerning a man like Arnold. There was little disposition on the part of historians who wrote just after the war, to do Arnold justice for real merit ; but Stedman, equally good authority with Gordon in most respects, says, "The enemy were led to the battle by General Arnold, who distinguished himself in an extraordinary manner." Dawson, who has few superiors in the careful examination of American history, and Lossing, who has devoted his life to this class of specialties, and Tomes, concur with Marshall ; while Colonel Varick, writing immediately from the camp, and Neilson, and Hall and many other writers, give to Arnold not merely the credit of superintending the field operations of his division, but of leading them in person. It is difficult to

understand how the withdrawal of troops from Fraser's front, and
their transfer to the British centre, with the consequent movements
described by General Burgoyne, which required such rapid and exhaustive employment of the whole force wnich he brought into action,
could have taken place undirected, and with no strong will to hold the
troops to the attack and defense.   It is material that other facts be
considered in order to appreciate the value of Wilkinson's statement.
He was a young man about twenty years of age, restless, migratory in
the camp, and like a boy in his eagerness to see everything every·
where.   He exercised his functions as assistant Adjutant-general, as
if he were the duplicate of his chief, and repeatedly gave orders as if
the *two persons* made the general commanding.   The unprofessional
reader of history would take the statement that " General Gates
ordered out Morgan's corps on the morning of the nineteenth," to
mean *just that*.   But when it is understood, as appears from Arnold's
report, that *General Gates ordered Arnold to send out Morgan's corps*,
there is involved a negation of the absence of Arnold during the
attack upon his lines.   Arnold also, in his objections to the transfer
of Morgan from his command, and neither Gates nor Wilkinson dissent from his statement, thus addresses General Gates : " On the 19th
inst., when advice was received that the enemy were approaching, I
took the liberty to give it as my opinion, that we ought to march out
and attack them.   You desired me to send Colonel Morgan and the
light infantry, and support them.   I obeyed your orders, and before
the action was over, I found it necessary to send out the whole of my
division to support the attack."

General Arnold was complaining that " he had been informed that
in the returns transmitted to Congress of the killed and wounded in
the action, the troops were mentioned as a detachment from the army."
He also says : " I observe it is mentioned in the orders of the day,
that Colonel Morgan's corps, not being in any brigade or division of
this army," (just then withdrawn) " are to make returns and reports
only to headquarters, from whence they are alone to receive orders ;
although it is notorious to the whole army, they have been in and
done duty with my division for some time past."   " I have ever supposed that a Major-general's command of four thousand men was a
proper division, and no *detachment*, when composed of whole brigades,
forming one wing of the army ; and that the general and troops, if
guilty of misconduct or cowardly behavior in time of action, were
justly chargeable as a division."   " Had my division behaved ill, the

other divisions of the army would have thought it extremely hard to have been amenable for their conduct."

Wilkinson also says, " *This battle was perfectly accidental*," (see Burgoyne's carefully conceived advance,) that " neither of the generals meditated an attack at the time, and but for Lieutenant-colonel Colburn's report it would not have taken place." .He states that this officer was "sent across the Hudson river to observe the movements of the enemy by climbing forest trees or other practicable means," that on "his making his communications to the General, that the enemy had taken up their camp, he immediately ordered Colonel Morgan," (as if it were a direct personal order) " to advance with his corps." When the firing began, and Major Wilkinson wanted to see what was going on, and General Gates answered, " It is your duty, sir, to await orders," he " made an excuse to visit the picket on the left for intelligence, put spurs to his horse, and, directed by the sound, entered the woods." It would be idle to follow his extraordinary personal experiences through the woods, as related in his memoirs. The most eventful elements of his early career are embodied in data, gathered by him on such unofficial, voluntary excursions.

It is a fact that General Gates did not pass under fire, neither was it necessary for him to do so ; but the whole conduct of that officer, and of his Adjutant-general, savors of the disgust with which in an earlier war, King Saul heard the shouts that " Saul had slain his thousands, but David his tens of thousands." Arnold must stand credited with personal valor and a gallant defense of the left wing of the American army on the nineteenth day of September, 1777.

There is no method of determining the details of his conduct, and the student of history must unite with Sparks and Irving and Marshall in the general sentiment that Morgan only, of American officers, can compete with Arnold for the brightest laurels of the Saratoga campaign.

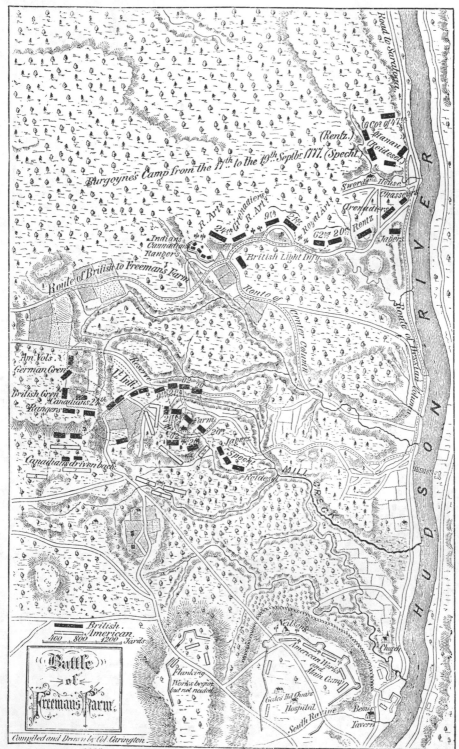

Burgoyne's Camp from the 11th to the 19th Septbr. 1777. (Specht.)

(Rentz.)

G Co. of 47th

Hanau (Reidesel)

Swords House

Chasseurs

Grenadiers

R. Art.   24th   Grenadiers   R. Art.   9th   21st   Royal Art.   62d   20th   Rentz

Indians   Cannadians   Rangers   British Light Infy.   Jägers

Route of British to Freemans Farm

Route of

Route of Center Column

Am. Vols.   German Gren.   Reserve   L. Infy.   62d   21st   British Gren.   Canadians 24th   Rangers   20th   9th   Farm   20th   62d   9th   Jägers   Specht   Reidesel   MILL

Canadians driven back

British.
American.
400   800   1200   Yards

Battle
of
Freemans Farm

Compiled and Drawn by Col. Carington.

Flanking Works begun but not needed.

Vols.

American Works and Main Camp.

Church

Gates' Hd Quars.   Hospital

South Ravine

Bemis Tavern

HUDSON RIVER

Road to Saratoga

314*

Battle of Freeman's Farm

SEPTEMBER 17th, 1777

American Commanders

MORGAN   **GATES**   POOR
LIVINGSTON   LEARNED   ARNOLD   DEARBORNE

Strength, 3,500.   Casualties, 321

AMERICAN POSITION.—Gates succeeded Schuyler, August 19th, 1777, and established his camp, four miles north of Stillwater, and twenty-four above Albany, on the west bank of the Hudson river, at a point selected by Kosciusko, then Engineer in the American service. The position was strong, and adequately armed.

British Commanders

FRASER, RIEDESEL, **BURGOYNE** BALCARRAS, PHILLIPS
HANAU, HUMPHREYS, ANSTRUTHER, HAMAGE
JONES, KINGSTON, FORBES

BRITISH POSITION.—As early as August 14th, a bridge of rafts had been thrown over the river at Saratoga, where Gen. Burgoyne made his headquarters, in preparation for an advance upon Albany. This bridge was carried away by a rise of the Hudson, but was replaced by a bridge of boats, by which, on the 13th and 14th of September, the entire British army crossed. On the 15th, the army moved to Dovegat (Coveville), and on the 17th, encamped within about four miles of the American lines.

NOTES.

NOTE I.—Skirmishing occurred between the two armies on the 18th, and on the 19th Burgoyne advanced, in three columns, to attack the American position. Six companies of the 47th Regiment guarded camp. The *right wing*, under Fraser, with the 9th and 24th Regiments, the British grenadiers, the Rangers and Canadians, moved west, then south, and had a sharp skirmish near the spot where Fraser was killed Oct. 8th. *This wing* then moved east, toward Freeman's Farm, to aid the centre. The *centre*, under Burgoyne, including 62d and 20th Regiments, moved southward, and deployed westward, on the road, and waited for Fraser to complete his longer march and gain the position assigned him on the right, and, also, for the left to gain its designated position. The *left wing*, under Phillips and Riedesel, moved down the river bank, and then westward, to support the centre, but did not arrive until it was hotly engaged.

NOTE II.—The Americans early took the offensive. Upon Arnold's advice, Gates ordered him to send Morgan's Riflemen and Dearborne's Light Infantry from his division, to oppose the British *right*, which attempted to turn the American *left*. The movement was timely and successful. The Canadians were driven back, and both Americans and British, during the conflict, moved eastward, until they took part in the general engagement, which centered about Freeman's Farm, by four o'clock in the afternoon. At this time the whole of Arnold's division was engaged with the British right wing ; and, as the Americans received reenforcements, it required the timely arrival of the Hessian column, with artillery, to resist their impetuous assaults.

The American *left*, at one time, advanced beyond the farm-house, which Earl Balcarras had fortified, and attempted to turn the position of the 62d Regiment. The 9th (reserve) came to its relief. The 20th and 62d Regiments were almost destroyed.

NOTE III.—This action left both parties worn out, for the day. The British *centre*, under Burgoyne, 1,100 men, had half its force killed or wounded through their desperate charges. Jones' battery (four guns) lost 36 out of 48 men. Sergeant Lamb says, in his Journal : "The conflict was dreadful ; for four hours a constant blaze of fire was kept up, and both armies seemed determined on death or victory."

The American casualties were 65 killed, 218 wounded and 38 missing. Morgan's Riflemen were especially active, while the regiments of Cillery, Scammel, Hale, Van Cortland, H. B. Livingston, Cook and Latimer, with Dearborne's Light Infantry, all of Arnold's division, vied with those of Bailey, Wesson, Jackson and James Livingston, in the contest.

References:

CARRINGTON'S "BATTLES OF THE AMERICAN REVOLUTION," pp. 335-346.

School Histories:

Anderson, ¶ 64 ; p. 84.	Holmes, ¶ 9 ; p. 126-7.	Swinton, ¶ 148 ; p. 135.
Barnes, ¶ 2 ; p. 123.	Lossing, ¶ 22 ; p. 159.	Scott, ¶ 18 ; p. 187.
Berard (Bush), ¶ 78 ; p. 157.	Quackenbos, ¶ 342 ; p. 244.	Thalheimer (Eclectic), ¶ 265 ;
Goodrich, C.A. (Seaveys), ¶ 22, p. 128.	Ridpath, ¶ 15 ; p. 204.	p. 152.
Goodrich, S. G., ¶ — ; p. —.	Sadlier (Excel), ¶ 11-12; p. 191.	Venable, ¶ 19 ; p. 108.
Hassard, ¶ 15 ; p. 195.	Stephens, A. H., ¶ 28 · p. 201.	

CHAPTER XLVII.

BEMIS' HEIGHTS. BURGOYNE'S SURRENDER, 1777.

ON the twenty-first of September, a letter from Sir Henry Clinton, written in cypher on the twelfth, advised General Burgoyne of his intention to attack the Hudson river posts in about ten days. No other message was received from New York during the month; and on the third of October the ration-issue was largely reduced. On the seventh, the condition of the army was such as to compel energetic measures for its deliverance. The paramount object of the campaign was kept in view, for it was evident that a sudden retreat would set free the rapidly increasing American army, for operations against Clinton. There was no difference of opinion among the British generals as to the duty of immediate action, and two alternatives were considered; either to make a bold offensive movement and force a passage through, or past, Gates' army; or, to so dislodge and cripple him, as to make a secure retreat practicable. To rest in camp was to starve, or perish by the sword. The troops selected for the proposed movement consisted of fifteen hundred regulars, to be commanded by Burgoyne in person, accompanied by Generals Phillips, Riedesel and Fraser. Generals Hamilton and Specht were ordered to hold the intrenchments and redoubts; and the defense of the river meadow, with the magazine and hospital, was intrusted to General De Gall. Two howitzers, two twelve, and six six-pounder guns were attached to the command.

The column was formed and deployed within three-quarters of a mile of the American left, upon high and quite open ground, surrounded by woods; and Captain Fraser's rangers, the Indians and Provincials, were ordered to make their way through by-paths of the forest, to attempt a demonstration to the rear of the American army. These light troops had hardly started, when a sudden and rapid

attack was made upon the left of the line, already formed for immediate advance.   The British grenadiers under Major Ackland met the
attack with great resolution ; but the increasing numbers of the enemy
gradually bore them back.   Before any portion of the German troops
on the right and to the centre, could be withdrawn to support the
yielding grenadiers, the centre was assailed, and then the right ; so
that the entire line was actively engaged almost as soon as the action
commenced.

The fragments of the Twentieth and the Sixty-second, with a small
body of light infantry, were all that could be brought forward, until
Earl Balcarras was withdrawn from the extreme right, and General
Fraser took a position to cover the impending retreat of the whole
force.   While thus engaged in strengthening the left and securing
some steadiness to the yielding centre, that officer was mortally
wounded.   A general retreat was ordered.   Sir Francis Clarke, who
bore the message, was also fatally wounded.   Six guns were at once
abandoned the horses and most of the men having been killed ; and
as the troops entered their old lines, "the works were stormed with
great fury by the Americans, who rushed on, under a severe fire of
grape shot and small arms."   The intrenchments occupied the night
before and regained by Earl Balcarras, successfully resisted assault ;
but the attacking force swept by them and successfully stormed those
which Lieutenant-colonel Breyman occupied.   He was killed, and his
troops broke in confusion to the rear.   Such is the British history of
the action.

General Gates had detailed Colonel Brooks with three hundred
men to move around the British right and annoy their outposts.
Morgan had already skirmished with a small Canadian force which
threatened the American pickets on the comparatively clear ground
between the middle and north ravine, and an officer was sent to determine the strength and disposition of the British forces which had been
reported as in line of battle threatening the left wing of the American
army.   When the aid-de-camp reached the hill, near Chatfield's house,
he found that the ridge was already held by an advanced detachment
from the British column, and that Mungen's house was occupied by
officers who had been sent forward to reconnoiter the country near
the American lines.

At this time the American army occupied substantially the same
position as on the nineteenth of September.   An altercation between
Arnold and Gates, owing to the removal of a portion of the division

of the latter without giving him notice, and other vexatious questions which had their prime root in the unabated confidence of Arnold in Schuyler, had driven him, in one of his passionate outbursts, to ask leave to go to headquarters and join Washington. Gates readily granted this request, and General Lincoln, who arrived on the twenty-ninth, was at once placed in command of Arnold's division. Arnold, however, quickly repented his passionate outburst and lingered with the army, having the general sympathy of the officers, but still venting his anger in daily imprudence. On the seventh of October as the battle came on, he was like a war-horse gnawing his curb and panting for the fray.

Gates sent Morgan to the left to gain high ground on the British right. Poor's brigade, made up of Scammel's, Hale's, and Cilley's New Hampshire regiments, was ordered to cross the hill by Chatfield's house and attack the British left.

Major Dearborn was placed in readiness to advance to Morgan's right, and the Connecticut regiments of Cook and Latimer, and Van Courtland's and Henry Livingston's New York, were to support Poor. Learned's brigade, recently under Arnold's command, was also placed in readiness to follow immediately; and General Tenbrouck was held in reserve to give support as needed. The formation was made under cover of the woods, and as already indicated by the British report of the action, the counter assault was a practical surprise to the troops assailed. The composition and positions of the British corps are cor rectly indicated on the map, " Battle of Bemis' Heights." The brig- ades of Poor and Learned crossed Mill creek, reserved their fire, and moved up the slope with steadiness and in good order. The first fire delivered by the British troops was aimed too high and did little mis- chief. The Americans without hesitation rushed upon the guns.

Again and again these pieces were alternately controlled by the opposing forces, until at last the British left wing, overwhelmed by numbers, gave way. Major Ackland was wounded, and Major Williams was taken prisoner. Morgan had already gained the right flank, and was actively engaged. Dearborn was in front, and the Connecticut regiments filled the interval still further to the right. The whole line was under the pressure of a wildly impetuous assault. The German troops in the centre broke. The Royal artillery, losing their horses and half their men, abandoned their guns, and the Earl Balcarras with his light infantry became the chief dependence of General Fraser, who was trying to rally the grenadiers and establish behind the left wing a second line, as cover for the general retreat then ordered.

At this stage of the battle, Arnold, no longer under self-control, burst from the camp, and like a meteor rode to the front of Learned's brigade, which had been so recently under his command, and dashed into the fight.   He was cheered as he rode past, and like a whirlwind the regiments went with him upon the broken British lines.   Fraser fell mortally wounded in this assault, and swiftly behind the half crazy volunteer came Tenbroeck, with a force nearly double that of the whole British line.   That line was now in full retreat.   Phillips and Riedesel, as well as Burgoyne, who took command in person, exhibited marvellous courage in an hour so perilous, and withdrew the troops with creditable self-possession and skill, but nothing could stop Arnold.   Wherever he found troops he assumed command; and by the magnetism of his will and passion, he became supreme in daring endeavor.   With a part of the brigades of Patterson and Glover, he assaulted the intrenchments of Earl Balcarras, but was repulsed.   To the right of the Earl Balcarras, the Canadians and Royalists were posted under cover of two stockade redoubts.   Arnold here again met Learned's brigade, took the lead, and with a single charge cleared these works, leaving the left of Breyman's position entirely exposed. Without waiting for the result of the further attack at this point, he rode directly in front of Breyman's intrenchments, under fire, and meeting the regiments of Wesson and Livingston and Morgan's rifle corps, which had made the entire compass of the British right, he ordered them forward, and then riding on with a portion of Brooks' regiment which joined at that moment, he turned the intrenchments of Breyman, entered the sally port and was shot, with his horse, as the victory was achieved.

" It is a curious fact, that an officer who really had no command in the army was the leader of one of the most spirited and important battles of the Revolution."   Thus writes Sparks, adding, " His madness or rashness, whatever it may be called, resulted most fortunately for himself.   The wound he received at the moment of rushing into the arms of danger and of death, added fresh lustre to his military glory, and was a claim to public favor and applause."

Arnold was promptly promoted by Congress for his gallant conduct.   Wilkinson says, " he would not do injustice even to a traitor," and after describing his erratic course, substantially as stated, declaring that he was in the field exercising command, but not by order or permission of General Gates, makes these statements which belong to history, and must go to the credibility of his other testimony, " The

General (Arnold) parted off to another part of the field, soon after this incident, (referring to his striking an officer); finding himself on our right, he dashed to the left through the fire of the lines and escaped unhurt; he then turned to the right of the enemy, just as they gave way, when his leg was broke, and his horse killed under him; but whether by our fire, or that of the enemy, as they fled from us, has never been ascertained." (?)   "It is certain that he neither rendered service nor deserved credit on that day; and the wound alone saved him from being overwhelmed by the torrent of General Gates' good fortune and popularity."   The author gives these extracts, because of their connection with other quotations from this officer's memoirs, and to vindicate history; without claiming the ability to determine, by the accepted rules of evidence at common law, just where the memoirs of Wilkinson divide between history and romance. Inasmuch as many writers state that during this battle Major Wilkinson overtook Arnold, and ordered him to return to camp, it is proper to give the incident its proper place as stated by him.   "When Colonel M. Lewis, on the evening of the 19th of September, reported the indecisive progress of the action, Arnold exclaimed, with an oath, ' I will soon put an end to it,' clapping spurs to his horse, and galloped off at full speed."

This action seems to imply a sense of responsibility for the movement of his division, at the close of its day's work.   "Colonel Lewis observed to General Gates, you had better order him back, the action is going well, he may by some rash act do mischief."   "I was instantly dispatched," says Wilkinson, "overtook, and remanded Arnold to camp."   Up to this time Arnold's open difference with General Gates had not taken place and he was in full command of the exposed wing of the army; and on the previous day he had been especially detailed by General Gates to go with fifteen hundred men and watch the approach of the enemy.   What should induce a deputy Quartermaster-general to interfere, when the officer second in command goes promptly to his division, about which there is such a report as he gave, is not explained.

The battle was over.   The British troops had been overwhelmed as by a torrent, by a force at least three times their number.   Besides Breyman killed, and Fraser mortally wounded, Sir Francis Clarke had fallen.   He was borne to Gates' headquarters and died that night.   He was the nominal guest of General Gates; although his death-bed scene involves a painful altercation with that officer.   Major

Ackland was also wounded and a prisoner of war, and with Major Williams he shared the same hospitality.

Fraser was carried to the house of John Taylor near Wilbur's basin, and died the next morning. The American loss did not exceed one hundred and fifty. The British casualties equaled nearly half the command engaged.

General histories have room for the solemn funeral *orgies* of General Fraser, at sunset of the eighth, within range of the American fire; the devotion of Madames Ackland and Riedesel, and the numberless minor events which give peculiar gravity and character to the termination of this campaign, and intensify its tragic experiences.

At night General Lincoln's division relieved the well-worn troops and advanced to the upper fork of the north ravine.

On the eighth, at nine o'clock in the evening, General Burgoyne abandoned his hospital and needless baggage and retreated, amid heavy rain, toward Saratoga (Schuylersville) across the Fishkill river, and compactly intrenched his camp.

As he approached Saratoga he found an American force engaged in throwing up intrenchments, but they retired upon his advance. The bateaux which contained the meagre amount of remaining supplies were under constant fire from the opposite shore, where General Fellows was stationed with a large force, and the Fishkill was not crossed until the morning of the tenth. Captain Fraser's marksmen, the Forty-seventh regiment and Mackey's Provincials, were then ordered to escort a party of artificers to repair bridges and open a road up the west side of the river toward Fort Edward; but "the provincials ran away; the American army occupied the heights in force, and the detail was withdrawn."

A battery of five guns had also been established at the bridge-head, where the British army had first crossed the river, and this was amply supported by American infantry. Morgan and Dearborn hovered about the skirts of the camp, cutting off foraging parties and all communications with Fort George, and all avenues of retreat were controlled by the American troops. The American army already exceeded thirteen thousand effective men, amply supplied with artillery, which had been received from France. This force patiently and without risk was pressing more and more closely upon the wasting and scantily-fed forces of Lieutenant-general Burgoyne.

October eleventh it became necessary to land the supplies which remained in the bateaux, and to carry them up the hill, as a constant

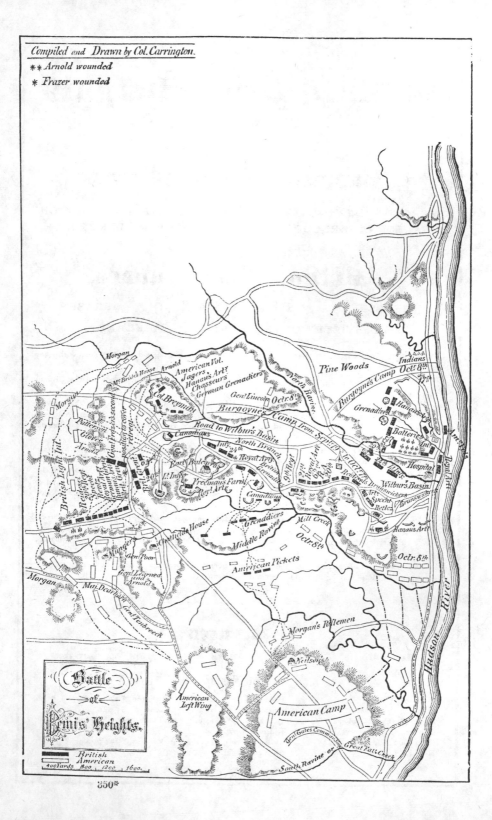

Battle of Bemis' Heights.

British
American
400 Yards   800   1200   1600.

350*

Battle of Bemis Heights

OCTOBER 7th, 1777

American Commanders

MORGAN   LEARNED   **GATES**   POOR   NIXON

DEARBORNE, ARNOLD, (Volunteer,) LIVINGSTON, TENBROECK,

British Commanders

RIEDESEL   **BURGOYNE**   FRASER

DeHEISTER   BALCARRAS   ACKLAND

NOTE I.—Burgoyne, with provisions scarce and army wasting, made a desperate effort, with 1,500 men and ten guns, to turn the American left and gain its rear.

NOTE II.—Gates, equally prompt, started troops, under Col. Brooks, to move around the British right.

NOTE III.—The British line formed on the Heights (see map, for details of formation), was attacked furiously by Morgan, Learned, Poor, Dearbone and Tenbroeck. Arnold, although relieved by Lincoln, who had arrived on the 29th of September, dashed on, with his old command, regardless of

NOTE IV.—The British artillery, which, at first, fired over the assailing column, was speedily overrun by the swift charge. Fraser fell, while rallying the broken line. Patterson and Glover bring up their columns. The British order a general retreat. Balcarras still holds Freeman's Farm ; but the American troops sweep on, and storm the works held by Breyman. He is killed, and Arnold is wounded as he enters the redoubt, from the north. The regiments of Wesson and Livingston were among the most active in the final assault.

NOTE V —The long delayed promotion of Arnold was promptly made by the American Congress.

NOTE VI.—The British casualties exceeded 500. The American casualties were not more than 150. Sir Francis Clark died from wounds received, and Major Ackland, also wounded, became a prisoner, as well as Major Williams.

NOTE VII.—The British army retired to (present) Schuylersville, crossed the Fishkill, and carefully entrenched its camp, leaving their old camp on the 8th, at night.

References:

CARRINGTON'S "BATTLES OF THE AMERICAN REVOLUTION," pp. 345-350.

School Histories:

Anderson, ¶ 65 ; p. 84.	Holmes, ¶ 9 ; p. 126-7.	Swinton, ¶ 149 ; p. 135.
Barnes, ¶ 1 ; p. 124.	Lossing, ¶ 22 ; p. 159.	Scott, ¶ 18 ; p. 187.
Berard (Bush), ¶ 80; p. 158.	Quackenbos, ¶ 344 ; p. 246.	Thalheimer (Eclectic), ¶ 266 ;
Goodrich, C.A. (Seaveys), ¶ 22, p. 128.	Ridpath, ¶ 16 ; p. 204.	p. 152.
Goodrich, S. G., ¶ —; p. —.	Sadlier (Excel), ¶ 11-12; p. 191.	Venable, ¶ 19 ; p. 109.
Hassard, ¶ 18 ; p. 195.	Stephens, A. H., ¶ 29 ; p. 201,	

36

fire was opened upon any approach to the river. Scouts sent across the Hudson at its bend to the westward, reported that the fords were guarded; a camp had been established between Fort Edward and Fort George, and Colonel Cochran was in possession of Fort Edward itself.

The Americans occupied commanding positions through three-fourths of a circle, so that no attack upon any single position would afford hope for escape of the British army. Canadians, Provincials, and Indians had disappeared. Thirty-four hundred men only, remained fit for duty. Rations were reduced to a supply for three days. No message came from Clinton. " By day and night grape shot and rifle shot reached the lines." There had been no cessation of danger, and " the men had become so worn out, and at the same time so accustomed to the incessant firing, that a part slept while others watched," and the army had no interval of real rest. There had been just one half hour's interval of hope.

On the afternoon of the tenth, the American vanguard reached the ridge between Saratoga church and the creek, and General Gates established his own headquarters a mile to the rear. The advance had been made slowly, on account of the heavy rain, and under the impression that the British army was still at Saratoga. On the morning of the eleventh, during a dense fog, and while the British army was fully prepared for an attack, General Gates ordered an immediate advance across Fishkill creek to be made. Without any reconnoissance whatever, he summoned his general officers, and informed them that he had received reliable intelligence that Burgoyne had started for Fort Edward, leaving only a rear-guard in camp. Morgan was pushed over the creek. Nixon's brigade followed. Glover's brigade, succeeded by those of Patterson and Learned, were moving down the bank, when a British deserter fell into Nixon's hands. He gave the information that the entire army was in battle array immediately on the hill. The order was disobeyed, and then countermanded, and Nixon retired, but not without some loss to his own command as well as to Morgan's from the British artillery, which opened fire as soon as the retrograde march commenced. The American army had been placed in imminent peril.

On the twelfth, a council of war proposed a retreat; but the facts already cited and obtained from scouts, terminated the discussion. Information was also received that General Lincoln, before his union with Gates, had made a successful expedition in the vicinity of Ticonderoga, had captured its outposts, several gunboats, nearly four companies of the Fifty-third regiment, and had otherwise impaired every facility for retreat which depended upon the British control of Lake George and Lake Champlain.

On the thirteenth a flag was sent to General Gates, and by the sixteenth, the terms of capitulation had been adjusted, and the following day was assigned for their execution. During that night, Captain Campbell of the British army reached camp with dispatches from Sir Henry Clinton, announcing the capture of Forts Clinton and Montgomery, and that Generals Vaughan and Wallace had started up the river upon an expedition as far as Esopus (Kingston). It was too late to recede from the contract solemnly undertaken, and the surrender took place, under circumstances of honor and courtesy, such as were due to the valor and persistency of the preceding struggle.

The terms are briefly stated,—" The troops to march out with all the honors of war ; to have free passage to Great Britain, upon condition of not again serving during the war ; subject of course to a cartel of exchange ; that the army should march to Boston, be subsisted regularly, and not be delayed when transports should arrive for them ; officers to retain their baggage ; Canadians to be returned home, and all corps of any kind to be placed on the same footing." Minor items are embraced in the details, and for several days there was a critical difference between Gates and Burgoyne, the latter asserting that he would resort to the most desperate resistance rather than accept the degrading terms first offered. The final terms were reasonable and generous.

On the eighth, General Putnam had written to General Gates, giving him a statement as to his trouble in retaining militia and stating the presence of Clinton's army and Sir James Wallace's fleet near by, saying, " I can not flatter you or myself with the hope of preventing the enemy's advancing; *therefore prepare for the worst.*" " The enemy can take a fair wind, and with their flat-bottomed boats which have sails, can go to Albany, or Half-moon," (only sixteen miles below Gates' camp) " with great expedition, and I believe without any opposition." This letter without doubt had its effect on the settlement of the terms of Burgoyne's surrender; as it seemed as if the original plan of the British campaign was at last to be consummated, and Gates could not afford to wait until a fresh enemy should assail his rear.

The total force surrendered was five thousand seven hundred and sixty-three. Philip Skene who had been a burden to the army from his first affectation of influence in New England, who had been lieu-tenant-governor of Ticonderoga, and major, placed his name on the original parole, for the record of history, as if to escape undue notice and responsibility, as " Philip Skene, a poor follower of the British army."   The people changed the name of his old home to Whitehall ; and he left America never to return.

The American force at the time of the surrender, numbered nine thousand and ninety-three continental troops, and General Gates' return of October sixteenth made the total force, including militia, thirteen thousand two hundred and sixteen men present fit for duty.

The sick numbered six hundred and twenty-two present, and seven hundred and thirty-one absent. The detached commands numbered three thousand eight hundred and seventy-five, and on furlough, one hundred and eighty, making the total strength of his command, eighteen thousand six hundred and twenty-four.

General Burgoyne returned to England, and completely vindicated his conduct of the campaign before the House of Commons. He entered parliament, opposed the further prosecution of the war, and upon failure to obtain a military trial or assignment to duty, resigned his commission in the army.

The prisoners were transferred from Cambridge and Rutland to Charlotteville, Virginia, and made the march of seven hundred miles during the winter of 1778. Baroness Riedesel accompanied her hus-band, and her narrative is full of touching experiences.

After frequent changes of location, the larger portion ultimately became settlers, and remained in the country after the war closed. There is no occasion to discuss the differences between the Ameri-can and English authorities which practically reversed the terms of capitulation and prevented the return of the troops to Europe, as the consideration of the campaign is the only legitimate object of this narrative.

General Burgoyne's campaign was characterized by a brave, skillful and persistent effort to execute his orders and reach the objective designated by his superiors.

The evidence is conclusive that the idea of failure on the part of General Howe to support him from New York was never entertained by himself or his officers.

Reinforcements were due in New York, during September, and although they did not arrive until early in October, and after a voyage of three months' duration, he had no occasion to doubt their prompt arrival and proper disposal, under the original plan of the campaign. His maxim was illustrated in his career. " He who obeys at the expense of fortune, comfort, health and life, is a soldier! he who obeys at the expense of honor is a slave." His independence of opinion in matters purely under the rule of his own conscience cost him his commission. He certainly obeyed orders with an unselfish consecration of every energy to his work. The disaster at Bennington was a serious check to his expedition, but the arrival of Stark at Bennington, just at that crisis, was thoroughly unpremeditated and providential for the Americans, so that the memory of Burgoyne unjustly suffered by the disaster.

He certainly followed St. Clair promptly and by the shortest route ; and from Fort Edward to Saratoga and in every leading movement for which he was abused, he was clearly right. Such is the judgment of impartial history. Burgoyne says, with very natural emphasis, I reasoned thus, " The expedition I commanded, was evidently meant, at first, to be hazarded. Circumstances might require that it should be devoted. A critical junction of Mr. Gates with Mr. Washington might possibly decide the fate of the war. The question of my junction with Sir Henry Clinton, or the loss of my retreat to Canada could only be a partial misfortune."

Burgoyne's Saratoga Campaign, which was so redolent of inspiration for the New Republic, must stand to his individual credit as a SOLDIER.

NOTE. General Washington transmitted a Major-general's commission to Benedict Arnold on the 20th of January, 1778, using the following words. " It is my earnest desire to have your services the ensuing campaign. I have set you down in an arrangement, and for a command, which I think will be agreeable to yourself, and of great advantage to the public." On the same date, in writing to General Lincoln who had also been wounded, he thus refers to Arnold. " General Arnold is restored to a violated right, and the restitution, I hope, will be considered by any gentleman, as an act of justice."

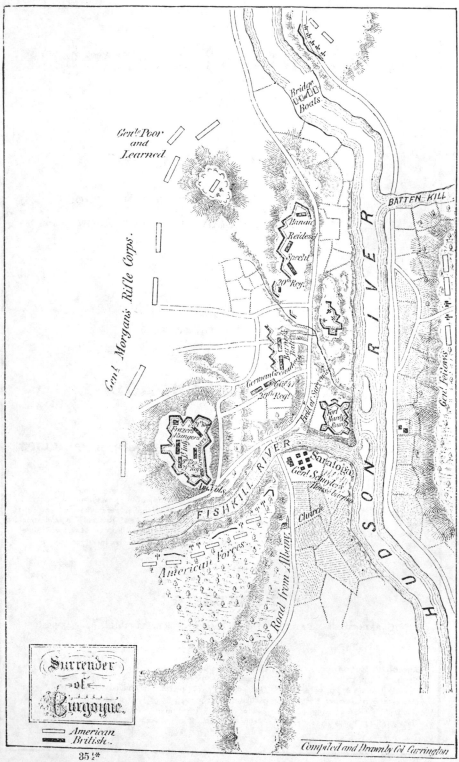

Genls Poor and Learned

Genl Morgan's Rifle Corps.

Bridge of Boats

BATTEN KILL

HUDSON RIVER

Hanau Reidesel Specht 20ᵗʰ Regᵗ

Balcarra Redoubt

German Grenadiers Genl u 9ᵗʰ Regᵗ

Field of Surrender

Fort Hardy Ruin

Genl Fellows

FISHKILL RIVER

Frazer Rangers 47ᵗʰ Regᵗ

Redoubts

Saratoga Genl Schuyler's House burned

Church

American Forces

Road from Albany

Surrender of Burgoyne.

American
British.

351*

Compiled and Drawn by Col Carrington

Surrender of Burgoyne

OCTOBER 17th, 1777

American Commanders

NIXON   MORGAN   **GATES**   LINCOLN   BROOKS

LEARNED,   DEARBORNE,   GLOVER,   PATTERSON,   POOR

Strength,	18,624
Detached,	3,875
Sick	622
Absent,	731
Present Oct. 16th,	13.216
Regulars present,	9,093

British Commanders

BURGOYNE

DeHEISTER,   RIEDESEL,   SPECHT,   BALCARRAS,   PHILLIPS

Force Surrendered, 5,763.

NOTE.—The Americans occupied the east bank of the Hudson in force; established a battery of five guns above the bridge of boats; cut off all retreat northward; supplies were exhausted, and surrender ensued. The prisoners of war were sent to Cambridge, Mass., and Rutland, Vt., and afterward, during the winter of 1778, were marched 700 miles, to Charlottsville, Va. Madame Riedesel accompanied her husband. The descendants of many of these soldiers survive in Virginia.

References :

CARRINGTON'S "BATTLES OF THE AMERICAN REVOLUTION," pp. 345-355.

School Histories :

Anderson, ¶ 66 ; p. 84.
Barnes, ¶ 1 ; p. 125.
Berard (Bush), ¶ 80 ; p. 158.
Goodrich, C. A.(Seaveys) ¶ 23; p. 128.
Goodrich, S. G., ¶ 5 ; p. 230.
Hassard, ¶ 19 ; p. 195.

Holmes, ¶ 9 ; p. 126-7.
Lossing, ¶ 22 ; p. 159.
Quackenbos, ¶ 345 ; p. 248.
Ridpath, ¶ 17 ; p. 204.
Sadlier (Excel.), ¶ — ; p. —.
Stephens, A. H., ¶ 30 ; p. 202.

Swinton, ¶ 150 ; p. 135-6.
Scott, ¶ 19 ; p. 187-8.
Thalheimer (Eclectic), ¶ 266 ; p. 152.
Venable, ¶ 19 ; p. 109.

CHAPTER XLVIII.

CLINTON'S EXPEDITION UP THE HUDSON. CAPTURE OF FORTS
CLINTON AND MONTGOMERY. 1777.

THE operations of Sir Henry Clinton in the Highlands of the
Hudson, are among the concurrent events which properly fill
up the outline of Burgoyne's Saratoga campaign.

Forts Clinton and Montgomery crowned high points of the Highlands on the west bank of the Hudson river, and were separated by a
narrow depression, through which Poplopen's creek found its way from
the mountains to the river. Both were above the range of fire from
ships of war and bomb-ketches; while their height and isolation
afforded peculiar facilities for being made capable of protracted resistance to any ordinary force. Fort Montgomery was a large work, then
unfinished, and at the date of its capture the garrison consisted of one
company of artillery, a few regulars, and some half-armed militia,
hastily assembled from the adjoining counties. A boom and heavy
iron chain extended from the foot of the river-cliff to "Anthony's
Nose," a sharp promontory on the opposite side of the Hudson.
Colonel John Lamb commanded the post.

Fort Clinton was on the south side of the creek, and more compactly and thoroughly built, but much smaller in extent. Its garrison
consisted of a few regulars and raw militia, under the command of
Brigadier-general James Clinton. The surrounding country was
mountainous, almost pathless, and here and there slashed by deep
and impassable defiles.

On the east side of the river, northward nearly seven miles, and
opposite West Point, was Fort Constitution.

Twelve miles southward, and five miles below Fort Clinton was
Fort Independence. General Israel Putnam was in general command
of the Highland range of defenses, with his headquarters near Peeks-

kill, where a depot of supplies had been established. This post was also the general rendezvous for the inter-transit of troops between New England and the Middle States.

The detachment sent from his command to that of Schuyler, afterwards Gates's, had so reduced his force that his chief dependence was on the militia of the immediate vicinity and of Connecticut.

Advices had been received that an expedition had been organized in New York for a demonstration up the Hudson. Governor Clinton promptly ordered a considerable militia force to report to General Putnam, but that officer furloughed the men during fall harvest and seed time, because the New York garrison seemed to rest quietly in their quarters. Governor Clinton promptly changed the programme, allowing one-half of the militia, however, to spend a month on their farms, while the remainder were ordered to assemble at the mouth of Poplopen's creek and Peekskill. Before this modified order, however, could take effect, and while the entire force which had assembled for the defense of Forts Clinton and Montgomery was less than six hundred and fifty men, the expedition from New York was in full activity. Stedman says, that " the enterprise was entirely spontaneous on the part of Sir Henry Clinton,—was conducted with more energy than most of the military operations that took place in America," and that " the ulterior view in the measure (after taking possession of the forts which forbade the passage of our vessels up to Albany) was not so much to create a diversion in favor of General Burgoyne, the necessity of which was not suspected, as to open a communication which might have been important when that commander should have fixed himself at Albany." This statement, while substantially true, is put too unequivocally, in view of the whole history of operations from Canada as a base, as it involves the supposition that Burgoyne's command was considered fully equal to its proposed mission, without any aid from New York. The text of Burgoyne's instructions certainly must be held to mean that his union with General Howe contemplated a union with whoever commanded at New York; and although General Howe felt confidence in the ability of Burgoyne to complete his campaign after the capture of Ticonderoga, he did not, in fact, lose sight of the northern army. His " Narrative," states that he regarded the operations against Philadelphia and the occupation of Washington's army to the fullest extent, as a very substantial diversion in favor of Burgoyne ; and on the thirtieth of July, when " off the Delaware," he wrote as follows to General Clinton, then at

New York, "and having under his command a force of eight thousand five hundred men fit for duty. If you can make any diversion in favor of General Burgoyne's approaching Albany with security to King's Bridge," (which was occasionally threatened by General Putnam), " I need not point out the utility of such a measure." The following dispatch of Lord Germaine, dated the eighteenth of May, 1777, gives the view taken by the British cabinet, although it was not received by General Howe until the sixteenth of August : " Trusting, however, that whatever you may meditate, it will be executed in time for you to coöperate with the army ordered to proceed from Canada, and put itself under your command." As a matter of fact, the movement of General Howe so crippled General Washington, that he could not adequately support General Gates, and the opportune success of the Americans at Bennington and Fort Schuyler proved to be the best ally of the American army of the north. It is not to be overlooked, as intimated in a preliminary chapter, that much of the needless re-crimination that passed between Howe, Clinton, and other British officers, had their foundation in the difficulties of prompt communication and real concert of action, in the great distance which separated their armies, and above all, in the numerical inadequacy of forces sent to the execution of their trust. Without further notice of the intentions of the parties who shared the responsibility of the Saratoga campaign, the expedition will be followed to its end.

On the third of October, eleven hundred British troops were transported from New York to Spuyten Duyvel creek, thence to Tarrytown, where they landed early on the morning of the fourth. A second division, which Commodore Hotham reports at about the same number, marched from King's Bridge to Tarrytown by land, reaching that place the same day. The third division took transports from New York on the fourth under convoy of the Preston frigate, the Mercury and the Tartar, and in the course of the same tide arrived off Tarrytown." On the same night, the wind favoring, and by the use of a large number of flat boats previously collected, the entire command was advanced to Verplanck's Point, where it landed at or about the fifth. The expedition was managed with signal skill. General Putnam's report shows that he was entirely deceived by the manœuvers of Sir Henry Clinton.

His own force he states at twelve hundred continental troops, and three hundred militia. On the afternoon of the fifth, a detachment from the British army embarked on forty flat boats, besides ships and galleys, under convoy of the vessels of Sir James Wallace, and "made every appearance of their intention to land, both at Fort Independence and Peekskill." Governor Clinton was keenly watchful of every movement. He adjourned the legislature, then at Kingston, and hastened to Fort Montgomery to give his personal support to the garrison, and to watch the approaches by the Haverstraw road which passed through the mountains, and with which he was familiar.

Sir Henry Clinton transferred his army from Verplanck's Point to Stony Point, early on the morning of the sixth. The demonstration of Sir James Wallace up the river completely masked the main movement by King's Ferry, and a heavy fog so obscured the view that General Putnam, who discovered a large fire at the ferry on the west side, supposed that a party had landed for the sole purpose of destroying the storehouses at that point.

Reference is made to maps " Attack on Forts Clinton and Montgomery," and " Hudson River Highlands."

Five hundred regulars, consisting of the Fifty-second and Twenty-seventh regiments, and Emerick's chasseurs, with four hundred Provincials commanded by Lieutenant-colonel Campbell, and Colonel Robinson of the Provincials, second in command, marched to occupy the pass of Dunderberg (Thunder Hill). This detachment was ordered " to make the detour of seven miles round this hill and Bear Hill, to the rear of Fort Montgomery." General Vaughan, with twelve hundred men, consisting of grenadiers, light infantry, the Twenty-sixth and Sixty-third regiments, one company of the Seventy-first, and one troop of dismounted dragoons, and the Hessian chasseurs, covering the corps of Lieutenant-colonel Campbell until it should pass Dunderberg, was to halt at the point where that corps took its course around Bear Hill to the left, and upon its approach to Fort Montgomery was to move by the right to storm Fort Clinton from the south. General Tryon with the Seventh regiment, and the Hessian regiment of Trumbach, while coöperating with General Vaughan, was to occupy the pass and preserve communication with the fleet ; and ultimately that officer joined General Vaughan and participated in the final assault upon Fort Clinton.

The approach to Fort Clinton was steep and difficult. Besides an advanced redoubt, large trees had been felled and distributed as *abatis* down the slope, and a heavy stone wall crossed the foot of the hill below the timber, extending from the Hudson to Sissipink pond or lake

On the evening of the fifth, Sunday, Governor Clinton "sent Major Logan, who was well acquainted with the ground, through the mountains to reconnoiter. He returned at nine o'clock on Monday, with the information that a considerable force was between King's Ferry and Dunderberg; but the numbers could not be discovered on account of the fog." Lieutenant Jackson marched out two miles on the Haverstraw road with a small party, but was compelled to retire. Lieutenant-colonel Bruyn with fifty continental troops, and as many militia under Lieutenant-colonel McLaughry, were sent to support Lieutenant Jackson, but they were too late to seize the pass, and fell back slowly, in good order, "disputing the ground inch by inch." Governor Clinton was the life of the defense of both posts. A dispatch was sent to General Putnam asking for reinforcements, and Lieutenant-colonel Lamb was directed to send a six-pounder, the only field-piece at Fort Montgomery, with sixty men and a supporting party of the same strength to check the advance of Lieutenant-colonel Campbell, who was approaching that fort. This detachment fought with great spirit, but was compelled to retire, abandoning the gun after spiking it. A second detachment was hurried to their support, and a twelve-pounder was advanced to cover their retreat, which was accomplished with some loss, including captain Fenno, taken prisoner. This was about two o'clock in the afternoon, as stated in the official report of Governor Clinton. The attack upon the fort was maintained until five o'clock, when a flag was sent, demanding a surrender. This was refused, and the fight continued until dusk, when the works were stormed on all sides, and the garrison made their best efforts to escape.

In Sir Henry Clinton's report he states that "after the advanced parties before Fort Clinton were driven into the works, Trumbach's regiment was posted at the stone wall to cover our retreat in case of misfortune," and "the works were stormed at the point of the bayonet, without a shot being fired."

He reports his "loss as not very considerable, excepting in some respectable officers who were killed in the attack." Lieutenant-colonel Campbell was killed in the assault upon Fort Montgomery. Count Grabowski, aid-de-camp of Clinton, Majors Sill and Grant, and Captain Stewart, were among the killed. Commodore Hotham in his official report, states the British loss at about forty killed, and one hundred and fifty wounded. The American loss was not far from three hundred killed, wounded, and missing. A list of two hundred and thirty-seven who were taken prisoners is given by Eager in his History of Orange county, New York. General James Clinton received a bayonet wound, but escaped to the mountains, as did the larger part of the garrison; and Governor Clinton safely crossed the Hudson in a skiff and joined General Putnam. That officer, only the day before the attack upon the forts, had withdrawn Colonel Malcolm's regiment from the pass of Sydham's bridge, had detailed Major Moffatt with two hundred men from the garrison to supply his place, and transferred sixty more to Anthony's Nose. But for this ill-timed action the American position would have been greatly strengthened.

One hundred cannon, including sixty-seven in the forts and others on vessels, and very considerable quantities of powder, cartridges and shot were trophies of the assault. The boom, chain and *chevaux de frise*, which they protected, were displaced, and the frigates Montgomery and Congress, which had been ordered down the river by General Putnam for defense of the boom, were burned. The former was against the chain, without anchor or wind, and could not be moved. The latter had been ordered up the river by Governor Clinton on the previous day: but being poorly manned, grounded upon the flats. Both were burned, to forestall capture.

General Putnam as already seen, was led to expect an attack upon his own immediate post. He retired to the heights behind Peekskill, and after consultation with General Parsons, " thought it impracticable to quit that position to attack the enemy." A reconnoissance was then made southward. It was just two days too late. His official report states, that on his return with General Parsons, " we were alarmed with a very heavy and hot firing, both of small arms and cannon at Fort Montgomery." " Upon which I immediately detached five hundred men to reinforce the garrison; but before they could possibly cross to their assistance, the enemy, superior in numbers, had possessed themselves of the fort."

As the result of the occupation of these forts, Peekskill was abandoned, then Forts Independence and Constitution; and General Putnam retreated to Fishkill. The expedition of Sir Henry Clinton was a success. Continental village, three miles above Peekskill, was burned by the British troops, and a considerable amount of public stores were taken or destroyed.

General Vaughan, under escort of Sir James Wallace, went up the river as far as Esopus (Kingston) and burned the village. On their return, Forts Clinton and Montgomery were thoroughly ruined and

Sir Henry Clinton retired to New York. General Putnam, reinforced by militia from Connecticut, New Jersey and New York, soon re-occupied Peekskill ; and after the surrender of Burgoyne, additional Continental troops were sent from the northern army.   It is only necessary to add that the presence of an intelligent commanding officer of reasonable military skill, or the absolute control of the posts by Governor Clinton, would have prevented the loss of Forts Clinton and Montgomery.   The patriotism and industry of General Putnam did not supply the elements which the importance of the posts required for their protection ; and the limited demonstrations northward which attended their capture, to that extent confirms the statement of Stedman that the relief of Burgoyne was not a part of the plan of Sir Henry Clinton.   The reasons why full harmony should have been secured between the British commanders in this military movement have been sufficiently indicated.

General Howe himself was now asking for reinforcements, and the third feature of the main operations of 1777, that which made the occupation of Philadelphia its objective, now demands attention.

CHAPTER XLIX.

MOVEMENT ON PHILADELPHIA. FROM NEW YORK TO THE
BRANDYWINE, 1777.

DURING the period occupied by the march of Burgoyne from
Ticonderoga to the place of his surrender, there had been
other operations in progress which had equal significance in determining the general result of the war.

These movements were so co-related, while independent in fact,
that those which are material to our appreciation of the campaign of
General Howe for the acquisition of Philadelphia, must pass under
review. The uncertainty of that officer's design was a determining
element in the plans of General Washington. The following letter in
the handwriting of General Howe, signed by him and directed to
General Burgoyne, came into Washington's hands on the twenty-
fifth of July.

"NEW YORK, *July* 20, 1777.

"DEAR SIR—I received your letter of the 14th of May from Quebec, and shall
fully observe its contents. The expedition to B——n (Boston) will take the place
of that up the North river. If, according to my expectations, we may succeed rapidly
in the possession of B——, the enemy having no force of consequences there, I shall,
without loss of time, proceed to coöperate with you in the defeat of the rebel army
opposed to you. Clinton is sufficiently strong to amuse Washington and Putnam.
I am now making a demonstration southward, which I think will have the full effect
in carrying our plan into execution. Success attend you.

W. HOWE."

The British fleet had already sailed from Sandy Hook, destination
unknown, when the above letter reached Washington for whom it
was intended. It was a transparent device which did not deceive
the American Commander-in-chief. General Howe, however slow to
improve opportunities, rarely misconceived the general scope of a
campaign, and his field operations were carefully planned and scien-

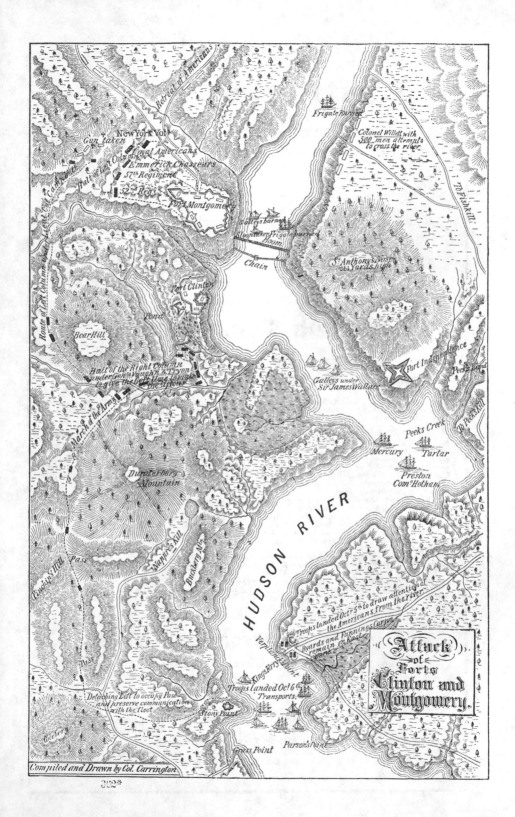

Attack of Forts Clinton and Montgomery

Compiled and Drawn by Col. Carrington

⇒ Capture of Forts ⇐

CLINTON and MONTGOMERY

OCTOBER 6th, 1777

American Commanders

Gen. James Clinton   Gen. George Clinton (Governor)

MEM.—Gen. Putnam in Command at Peekskill.

British Commanders

VAUGHAN   Sir HENRY CLINTON   TRYON

EMERICK   ROBINSON   TRUMBACH   CAMPBELL

NOTE I.—Clinton lands at Verplanck's Point, Oct 5th, and sends ships to Peekskill (see map) to threaten that post and draw attention from the river. A large force, in forty flatboats, also threatened Fort Independence.

NOTE II.—Putnam retires to high ground, to avoid being taken in rear.

NOTE III.—On Oct. 6th, Clinton lands at Stony Point, favored by a heavy fog; leaves a strong rear guard, and sends two divisions, simultaneously to attack Forts Clinton and Montgomery.

NOTE IV.—Vaughan, with 1,200 men, and Tryon, with the 7th Regiment and Trumbach's Hessians, having passed behind Dunderberg Mountain unobserved, halt and take lodgment in a ravine to the right, and near Fort Clinton, to give the advance column of 500 regulars and 400 Provincials, under Campbell and Robinson, full time to make its detour and gain a position before Fort Montgomery.

NOTE V.—Governor Clinton, who superintended the defense of both forts, learned, on the evening of the 5th, that British troops were between King's Ferry and Dunderberg; and two parties, each with a gun, were sent from Fort Montgomery to resist Campbell's advance. A messenger was also sent to advise Putnam of the situation.

NOTE VI.—The detachment, sent out, was too late to seize the pass, and both forts were stormed, after a vigorous defense, which continued from five in the afternoon, until dark.

NOTE VII.—The American casualties were about 300, including 227 prisoners. General James Clinton was wounded by a bayonet, but escaped to the mountains; and General Clinton escaped by crossing the river.

NOTE VIII.—The British casualties were 40 killed and 150 wounded. Lieut.-Col. Campbell was killed in the assault of Fort Montgomery. Count Grabowski, *Aide-de-camp* of Clinton, Majors Sill and Grant, and Capt. Stewart, were also killed.

NOTE IX.—Two frigates were burned to save their capture by the British; the boom across the river was destroyed; Putnam retired to Fishkill; and Esopus (Kingston) was burned by the British, under Vaughan, before Sir Henry Clinton returned to New York, there to learn of Burgoyne's disaster

---

References:

CARRINGTON'S "BATTLES OF THE AMERICAN REVOLUTION," pp. 355-362

School Histories:

Anderson, ¶ 67; p. 84.

Barnes, ¶ —; p. —.

Berard (Bush), ¶ 81; p. 158.

Goodrich, C. A. (Seaveys), ¶ 24; p. 128.

Goodrich, S. G., ¶ 8; p. 230.

Hassard, ¶ ⁻7; p. 195.

Holmes, ¶ —; p. —.

Lossing, ¶ 24; p. 160.

Quackenbos, ¶ —; p. —.

Ridpath, ¶ —; p. —.

Sadlier (Excel), ¶ —; p. —.

Stephens, A. H., ¶ —; p. —.

Swinton, ¶ —; p. —.

Scott, ¶ 20; p. 188.

Thalheimer (Eclectic), ¶ —; p. —.

Venable, ¶ 19; p. 110.

tifically executed. His movement toward Philadelphia, by sea, was subjected to the strain which attends all maritime expeditions, and the change of its destination from the Delaware river to the Chesapeake Bay was an incident clearly beyond his control. He was expected to end the war very summarily ; and as with Burgoyne, after the disaster at Bennington, and with all officers who fail to do impossibilities with inferior resources, he was to be made the scapegoat for the failure of any enterprise which was, theoretically, within his power. He did not overlook New England ; but claimed that " his movement in that direction would draw Washington's army thither, where the population was dense, and the spirit of resistance was animated." " In Connecticut, there was no object for which he could be tempted to risk a general action, and only two or three places upon the coast of the Sound could be kept in the winter." " If his reinforcements had been forthcoming, New England would have had a share in the general operations of the campaign, while the main army acted to the southward." To have moved up the Hudson river, in force, would have imperiled New York, or " sacrificed all other operations to a union with Burgoyne ; who was expected to force his own way to Albany." To enter Pennsylvania, was not only to assail the capital (reference is made to page 53 as to making a capital the objective of a campaign) but it attempted " the surest road to peace, the defeat of the regular rebel army." Such was the reasoning of General Howe, stated in his own words.

The embarkation began early in July, General Clinton having arrived at New York on the fifth ; and on the fifteenth an express from General Burgoyne informed General Howe of the success of that officer at Ticonderoga,—" that his army was in good health ; and that Ticonderoga would be garrisoned from Canada, which would leave his force complete for further operations." It has been seen that Carleton's instructions, construed strictly, disappointed the natural expectations of Burgoyne.

The expedition southward sailed from New York July fifth, from Sandy Hook the twenty-third, and arrived off the Delaware on the thirtieth. It was soon found that the Delaware River had been so obstructed that no landing could be effected above the confluence of the Delaware and Christiana Creek.

On the sixteenth of August the squadron and transports entered Chesapeake Bay. It was at this time that General Howe received the official letter referred to in another connection, which anticipated, that "whatever he might meditate, would be executed in time for him to coöperate with the northern army."

General Howe states the chief difficulties which he encountered, in a single sentence. "Almost every movement of the war in North America was an act of enterprise, clogged with innumerable difficulties. A knowledge of the country, intersected as it everywhere is by woods, mountains, water or morasses, can not be obtained with any degree of precision, necessary to foresee and guard against the obstructions that may occur."

The fleet which appeared off the Delaware was given by Sir Andrew Snope Hammond, in his examination before a committee of the House of Commons, as numbering two hundred and fifty sail.

" The navigation was intricate and hazardous, and large ships could pass certain places, only at particular times of the tide." In the determination of the ultimate course adopted by General Howe, it is necessary to consider this testimony, just as the facts impressed his mind at the time and affected his action.

On the thirteenth of July, Sir Andrew Hammond reported that "Washington had crossed the Delaware, and was marching down to Wilmington from Philadelphia." This officer had been on duty upon the coast of Delaware and Virginia, commanding a detached squadron for a year and a half, short intervals excepted. His report was therefore derived from personal experience, and is thus condensed: "The coast of Delaware from Cape Henlopen to Ready Island, is of marshy low lands, very full of creeks ; from Ready Island to Chester, the channel is so narrow as to require four miles of anchorage for the fleet, and the vessels must lie within cannon shot of the shore, and in many places within musket shot, with a tidal current of between three and four miles an hour to stem ; that the water-guard of the Americans consisted of the Province ship, the Delaware frigate, two xebecks, one brig, two floating batteries, besides two frigates, one partly manned," and added to this protection, there was the " fort on Mud Island, and numerous channel obstructions " ; while the vessels of the fleet, the " Cornwallis galley excepted," were illy adapted to force a passage against the American light craft, and the interposed obstructions and defenses." A rigid cross-examination of this officer only elicited the fact that there was depth of water at Newcastle, and for a short distance, a channel two miles wide ; but that the naval force of three frigates and two gun-ships furnished as convoy, was not adequate to meet all the contingencies which the landing would involve ;

and that the movement up the Chesapeake was a wise and proper measure. This opinion controlled the action of General Howe, whose duty involved no responsibility for the management of the fleet.

It was a grave question, inasmuch as Newcastle was but about seventeen miles from the head of Elk river, by land, while the distance from Cape Henlopen to the head of the Elk by sea, was nearly three hundred and fifty miles. It is, however, certain that the opportunities of Washington for resisting a landing, and his careful reconnoissance of the coast, fully justified the British military and naval commanders in declining to imperil the army by forcing a landing where every advantage was in favor of the American forces. The error lay in failure to provide the necessary vessels of light draught before leaving New York, and in neglect to obtain accurate knowledge of the difficulties to be encountered before entering the Delaware river.

The sudden withdrawal of the fleet from the Delaware, and its long voyage, greatly protracted by contrary winds, completely foiled the calculations of Washington as to its ultimate destination.

On the twenty-first of August, Washington submitted the condition of affairs to a council of war, which rendered the unanimous opinion that General Howe had most probably sailed for Charleston. On the twenty-second, at half past one o'clock in the afternoon, President Hancock sent the following dispatch to Washington: " This moment an express arrived from Maryland, with an account of near two hundred sail of General Howe's fleet being at anchor in the Chesapeake Bay."

The army of Washington had been promptly marched to Philadelphia as soon as he became satisfied that the British fleet departed southward from Sandy Hook. The most active measures possible were resorted to for gathering the militia, and so to occupy the country adjoining the Delaware as to anticipate any attempt to effect a landing. Upon the disappearance of the fleet, his army was removed to Coryell's Ferry, to be ready for a march northward, in case the fleet should return to New York, either for the purpose of ascending the North river, or of making a descent upon New England or New Jersey. Upon notice of Howe's arrival in the Chesapeake, the army marched through Philadelphia, decorated with evergreens, and with all possible display ; thence to Derby, Chester, and Wilmington. General Sullivan also joined the command, having been detained in New Jersey. On the twenty-second of August he had made an unsuccessful attempt upon the British posts of Staten Island, with a portion of Smallwood's and Deborre's brigades, incurring some loss and gaining no credit. The nominal strength of the American army which marched to meet the army of General Howe was fourteen thousand men, but the effective force did not exceed eleven thousand.

On the third of September General Maxwell, with a light infantry corps composed of one hundred men from each brigade, which had been organized after Morgan's riflemen had been sent to the Northern Department, approached Elk river to remove public stores; but found the enemy had anticipated their arrival, and after active skirmishing he retreated to White Clay creek, and then toward the main army.

On the seventh the entire army advanced to Newport and took a position along the east bank of Red Clay creek. On the same day General Howe placed his vanguard within eight miles of Red Clay, and occupied Iron Hill. Maxwell again retreated, after another sharp skirmish with a body of German Yagers at the hill. The landing had been effected on the twenty-fifth; the total force approximating eighteen thousand men.

On the twenty-eighth the main body reached the head of Elk Creek (Elkton) fifty-four miles from Philadelphia, leaving General Knyphausen with three brigades at the landing place,—one brigade to keep open communication, and a detachment to destroy such vessels and stores as could not be removed. General Howe reports, that " on the third the Hessian and Anspach chasseurs and the Second battalion of light infantry who were at the head of Lord Cornwallis' column, fell in with a chosen corps of one thousand men (Maxwell's.) advantageously posted, which they defeated with the loss of only two officers wounded, three men killed and nineteen wounded."

On the sixth General Grant joined the army, and on the eighth the whole marched, at evening, *via* Newark, and encamped at Hokessom, upon the road leading from Newport to Lancaster, at which place Washington had taken post, having his left to Christiana creek and his front covered by Red Clay creek."

The British at once made a demonstration as if to turn Washington's right, crowd him upon the Delaware and thus cut off his communication with Philadelphia. Reference is made to map " Operations near Philadelphia." A council of American officers was summoned and by their unanimous advice the army marched at half past two o'clock on the morning of the ninth, for the Brandywine, and at ten o'clock took a new position, selected by General Greene, upon the east bank, on high ground just behind Chadd's Ford upon the Chester and Philadelphia road.

During the afternoon of the same day Lieutenant-general Knyphausen marched to New Garden and Kennett Square, seven miles in front of Chadd's Ford, where Cornwallis joined him with the right wing, on the morning of the tenth. The right wing was thrown to the left and rear, in the direction of the Lancaster road, while Knyphausen was slightly advanced, preparatory to a direct attack upon the American lines. This division was not entirely composed of Hessians and other European continental troops, but included such regiments as the Fourth, Fifth, Twenty-third, Twenty-eighth, Fortieth, Forty-fourth, Forty-ninth and Fifty-fifth, with Ferguson's rifles, the Queen's rangers and two squadrons of dragoons. Generals Cornwallis, Gray, Matthews and Agnew were accompanied by General Howe, although Cornwallis was the immediate commander of the column. It is a fact, to be noted, that General Howe rarely kept out of action when his army had fighting to do; but placed himself where the example of the General-in-chief would most inspire his troops.

The Brandywine which is formed by the union of two inconsiderable creeks, called the North Branch and the West Branch, flows twenty-two miles southeasterly from their fork, joins Christiana creek near Wilmington, and empties into the Delaware about twenty-five miles below Philadelphia. Its banks, then steep, uneven and bordered by forests, were cut through at such places as furnished convenient fords for public or local travel.

These crossings were quite frequent between Brandywine village and the forks of the river. Pyle's Ford was two miles below Chadd's Ford, and Brinton's was one mile above it. Then followed Jones', at a distance of two miles; and Wistar's (Skunks) a mile further up the river. On the north branch was Buffington's, (now Brinton's), then Jeffries', six miles above Chadd's Ford, and Taylor's, still higher up, at the crossing of the old Lancaster road. On the west branch was Trimble's Ford, more than half a mile west from the fork of the river, and five miles or a little more above Welsh Tavern, near which the British army encamped.

Reference is had to the map "Battle of Brandywine." The centre of the American army lay near Chadd's Ford, and embraced the brigades of Wayne, Weedon and Muhlenberg, with Maxwell's light infantry, Major-general Greene commanding the division. Light earthworks and a redoubt were at once laid out, and Captain Proctor was in command of the artillery thus put in position.

The Pennsylvania militia under General Armstrong constituted the left wing, and extended through rough ground to Pyle's Ford below. The portion of the country was very rugged and little apprehension was entertained that a crossing would be effected in that direction.

In the formation of the right wing, composed of six brigades, in three divisions, the division of Sullivan was on the left, that of Sterling on the right, and that of Stephen in the centre. This was exactly right, inasmuch as Sullivan acted in the light of a modern corps commander and was theoretically detached from his division, so that Stirling, the next senior Major-general, was entitled to the right. The official reports of Sullivan, however, make no mention of a conflict as to position, but give an adequate cause for his tardy participation in the battle.

If his consultation with the other general officers, hereafter noticed, involved a question as to where he should be relatively stationed, in the line, he omits to state it ; neither is it material as he could not bring his division, as such, into any position whatever in good fighting order on that occasion. The discussion of questions of that character, in the absence of sufficient facts to cover the whole battle record, only confuses the narrative, and might drop out of history without loss to history. The American pickets extended beyond Sullivan's grand division well up the river. Colonel Bland crossed at Jones' Ford, and Major Spear was thrown as far to the right as Buffington's Ford.*

Such were the relative positions of the two armies on the night preceding the battle of Brandywine.

* It is somewhat doubtful whether the ford known as Buffington's in 1777, was not *below* the forks of the Brandywine ; but it does not change responsibility for proper reconnoissance toward Jeffries' and Taylor's Fords.

CHAPTER L.

BATTLE OF BRANDYWINE.

A CAREFUL survey of the positions first taken by the opposing armies, as indicated by the map, will aid in the appreciation of their subsequent movements.

It will be found that the brigades of Muhlenberg and Weedon were withdrawn from Chadd's Ford to form a reserve, while Wayne's brigade deployed to the left, in their place, and that a portion of the right wing actually crossed the river at Brinton's Ford, before the general action was precipitated by the flanking movement of General Howe. The American army did not rest on the passive defensive. General Maxwell crossed at Chadd's Ford early on the eleventh, and advanced to Kennett Meeting House, where by resort to trees, fences, and all available obstructions, he maintained an efficient skirmish with the vanguard of Knyphausen, and sustained himself skillfully, until forced back to high ground near the ford, and ultimately to the ford itself by the pressure of greatly superior numbers. Having been reinforced, he regained the heights, and at the same time Porterfield and Waggoner crossed and moved to his left, vigorously attacking Ferguson's rifles, who were engaged, with a portion of the Twenty-eighth British regiment, in throwing up light field-works to put two guns in position on *their* right. These detachments passed up a narrow, well wooded valley, and compelled a company of British troops supported by one hundred men from General Stirn's Hessian brigade, to take cover behind a stone house for protection until additional troops came to their aid. This movement and the pertinacity of Maxwell's attack compelled Knyphausen to bring two brigades and artillery to the front; and a strong column was also sent toward Brinton's Ford, outflanking Maxwell, and compelling him to fall behind the river. At the same time the Queen's Rangers, led by Captain

Wemys, of the British Fortieth regiment, swept the narrow valley on the right, and forced Porterfield and Waggoner to retreat, and recross the river. Lieutenant S. W. Werner, of the Hessian artillery, whose diagram, taken on the field, affords the best data for a right judgment as to those movements, was actively engaged in these skirmishes on the west bank. The American casualties during these minor movements did not exceed sixty, and those of the Hessians and British troops were about one hundred and thirty.

Upon the retreat of General Maxwell, the high ground thus vacated was occupied by Knyphausen in force, and guns were placed in position to command the crossings.

Proctor's artillery responded ; but little damage was inflicted on either side. The demonstrations were simply such as engaged the attention of the American troops, but no attempts were made to force a passage.

Information reached General Washington, that Cornwallis had moved northward from Kennett Square, as if to seek some higher and unprotected crossing, and attempt a movement against his right flank. Knowing that Major Spear had been advanced as far up the river as Buffington's Ford, and depending on General Sullivan for due notice of any such movement against his right flank, he resolved to strike Knyphausen while thus separated from Cornwallis, and make up for inferior numbers by overwhelming the British divisions in detail. It was also known that Knyphausen's column did not make its advance until about nine o'clock. There was good reason to believe that there would be ample time for this offensive movement, since Cornwallis could not double the forks unless by about twelve miles of marching, even if he should cross near Buffington's, where Major Spear was on duty.

During the morning a fog spread over the creek and through the woods ; and while this operated in favor of Maxwell's skirmishing party, it contributed its share to confuse the scouts at the upper fords, in their estimate of the strength of the British column which moved in that direction.

It was between nine and ten o'clock in the morning that Colonel Bland crossed at Jones' Ford with a few light horse, and observed the movement of Cornwallis, who was then approaching Trimble's Ford on the west fork. He immediately notified General Sullivan. A report similar in substance was made by Colonel Hazen. The following dispatch, which is a model for clearness in all details then needed, was sent by Lieutenant-colonel Ross, and was forwarded by General Sullivan to the Commander-in-chief.

> "GREAT VALLEY ROAD, ELEVEN O'CLOCK A. M.
>
> "DEAR GENERAL.—A large body of the enemy, from every account five thousand, with sixteen or eighteen field-pieces, marched along this road just now. This road leads to Taylor's Ferry and Jeffries' Ferry on the Brandywine, and to the Great Valley, at the Sign of the ship, on the Lancaster road to Philadelphia. There is also a road from the Brandywine to Chester, by Dilworthtown. We are close in their rear, with about seventy men. Captain Simpson lay in ambush with twenty men and gave them three rounds within a small distance, in which two of his men were wounded; one mortally. I believe General Howe is with this party, as Joseph Galloway is here known by the inhabitants with whom he spoke, and told them that General Howe was with them.   Yours,
>
> "JAMES ROSS, *Lieutenant-colonel.*"

Washington at once ordered Sullivan to cross the Brandywine and attack this division of the British army, which it was supposed would attempt a crossing at some point below the fork; while the main army was to cross at Chadd's Ford, and make a direct onset upon Knyphausen's division. General Greene was ordered to cross above Chadd's Ford, in order to strike the left flank of the Hessian general. This transpired before twelve o'clock, and the advance guard of General Greene was already across when the following note reached Washington:

> "BRENTON FORD, *September* 11.
>
> "DEAR GENERAL—Since I sent you the message by Major Moore, I saw Major Spear of the militia, who came this morning from a tavern called Martin's, at the fork of the Brandywine. He came from thence to Welsh's Tavern, and heard nothing of the enemy about the fork of the Brandywine, and is confident they are not in that quarter; so that Colonel Hazen's information must be wrong. I have sent to that quarter to know whether there is any foundation for the report, and shall give your excellency the earliest information.   I am, &c.,
>
> "JOHN SULLIVAN."

General Sullivan hastily reached conclusions not warranted by his informant's statements; since the route referred to in the dispatch of Lieutenant-colonel Ross, led to Taylor's and Jeffries' Ferry, as stated, and was nearly a mile west of the fork, so that the truth of Major Spear's statement was no proof that those of Lieutenant-colonel Ross and Colonel Hazen were not also true. One grave fact enters into history, that the question as to where "the large body of the enemy," seen by Lieutenant-colonel Ross, *were,* was not solved, nor was the solution adequately attempted by Major-general Sullivan, until he was compelled to face them hurriedly in battle.

Sergeant Tucker is said to have made a similar report to that of Major Spear; but the fact is immaterial. The orders issued for crossing the river were suspended upon receipt of General Sullivan's note, and General Greene's advanced detachment was withdrawn. The tenor of the dispatch would indicate that the main body of the enemy was within supporting distance of Knyphausen. Washington advanced Colonel Bland to the extreme right. Another dispatch came from General Sullivan, including one from Colonel Bland. They read as follows:

"TWO O'CLOCK P. M.

"DEAR GENERAL,—Colonel Bland has this moment sent me word that the enemy are in the rear of my right, coming down. There are, he says, about two brigades of them. He also says he saw a dust, back in the country, for above an hour.
    I am, &c.,
                                "JOHN SULLIVAN."

The enclosure is as follows:

"A QUARTER PAST ONE O'CLOCK.

"SIR—I have discovered a party of the enemy on the heights, just on the right of the two widow Davis's, (see map) who live close together on the road called the Fork road about half a mile to the right of the Meeting House (Burmingham). There is a higher hill in their front.
                                "THEODORE BLAND.'

The column of Cornwallis which had been seen on the Lancaster road was at last found. In order rightly to estimate the succeeding battle events, some additional facts are to be noticed in connection with this defective reconnoissance.

In a letter to Washington dated October twenty-fourth, General Sullivan says: "Upon my asking whether there were no fords higher up (than Buffington's) I was informed in presence of your excellency, that there was none within twelve miles; to cross at which the enemy must make a long circuit through a very bad road, and that all the light horse in the army were ordered to the right, to watch the enemy's motions in that quarter. I had no orders to take any care above Buffington's Ford, nor had I light horse, or light troops for the purpose. I found four with Major Taylor whom I sent to Brenton's Ford, two of whom I sent off with Colonel Hazen to Jones' Ford; nor did I see any till Major Jameson came to me the day of the battle at nine o'clock. On the day I came to the ford I detached the Delaware regiment to Buffington's: and as soon as I saw Major Jameson, I advised him to send an officer over to the Lancaster road, who returned and said that no enemy had passed that way. Major Jameson said he came from the right of the army, and I might depend, there was no enemy there."

It is evident, if Major Jameson's visit to the Lancaster road was not made quite early in the forenoon, due allowance was not made for the early march of Cornwallis ; and no careful examination of the road could have been made, or he would have confirmed the statement of Lieutenant-colonel Ross, which was substantially exact. When the question afterwards arose as to the responsibility for the unexpected appearance of the British army in force, upon the American right flank, Washington, generously avoiding to reflect upon Sullivan, who was both patriotic and brave, used the following language in reply to a letter from that officer who was then obtaining certificates to use before Congress: "With respect to your other query, whether your being posted on the right was to guard that flank, and if you had neglected it, I can only observe, that the obvious, if not the declared purpose of your being there, implied every necessary precaution for the security of that flank. But it is at the same time to be remarked, that all the fords above Chadd's, from which we were taught to apprehend danger, were guarded by detachments from your division ; and that we were led to believe, by those whom we had reason to think well acquainted with the country, that no ford above our pickets could be passed, without making a very circuitous march." Washington's information, however, was obtained through Sullivan.

It will appear that the movement of General Howe was as brilliantly executed as it was eminently scientific, and peculiar to his military habit. From General Sullivan's communications, afterwards made to Congress, in which he claims that the movement was just what he anticipated, it is difficult to understand his neglect to exhaust reconnoissance and determine for himself, whether there was no ford nearer than twelve miles, and if not, whether *that* ford was not available to an earnest adversary; unless it be borne in mind that after the battle of Long Island, when he had the misfortune to fall under censure for similar neglect of reconnoissance, he anticipated the movements of an enemy in a similar manner, without the power to stop it. Another document has value, in connection with the proposed advance of Washington against Knyphausen. It is clearly seen that such a movement was in the spirit of a true soldier ; and its success, on the basis of a supposed wide separation of the two British armies, would have been brilliant.

It stimulated the enthusiasm of raw troops by offensive action, where terrors like those of a stolid defense are unknown, and carried with it the courage which a sharp offensive return almost invariably inspires. It was one of those rare instances in which Washington assumed great risks, and the sudden suspension of the movement saved the army.

Additional extracts are given from the document already referred to, with the remark that Washington understood that the column of Cornwallis was still on the west bank, and as a matter of course, he would not have attacked Knyphausen if he suspected that two-thirds of the British army, fully equal to his own entire command, was already bearing down upon his right and rear.

EXTRACTS FROM GENERAL SULLIVAN'S STATEMENT.

"It was ever my opinion that the enemy would come round on our right flank. This opinion I often gave to the General. I wrote to him that morning that it was clearly my opinion. I sent him two messages to the same purpose in the forenoon, and the first intelligence I received that they were actually coming that way, I instantly communicated to him; after which the General sent me word to cross the Brandywine and attack the enemy's left," (obviously meaning Cornwallis, *i. e.* the real British left, not the left of the army immediately opposite,) "while the army crossed below me to attack the right. This I was preparing to do, when Major Spear came to me and informed me that he was from the upper country; that he had come in the road where the enemy must have passed to attack our right, and that there was not the least appearance of them in that quarter; and that General Washington had sent him out for the purpose of discovering whether the enemy were in that quarter. The account was confirmed by Sergeant Tucker of the light-horse, sent by me on purpose to make discoveries, and who had passed, as he said, to the Lancaster road."

"This intelligence *did by no means alter my opinion*, which was founded, not upon any knowledge I had of the facts, but upon an apprehension that General Howe would take that advantage which any good officer in his situation would have done. I considered, however, that if my opinion, or the intelligence I had sent the General, should bring him into a plan of attacking the enemy on the advantageous heights of which they were possessed, and a defeat should thence follow, I should be justly censured for withholding from him part of the intelligence I had received, and thereby brought defeat on our army. I therefore sat down and wrote Major Spear's account from his own mouth, and forwarded to his excellency by a light horseman, and ordered the Major to follow himself. *I never made a comment or gave any opinion in the matter.* . . . I beg Congress to see whether I could have been excused for withholding that opinion, merely because my opinion did not coincide with the declaration."

(The opinion of General Sullivan as to the reliability of information received from his scouts, was just what the Commander-in-chief was entitled to.) Colonel Harrison, General Washington's secretary, wrote to President Hancock at five o'clock in the afternoon from Chadd's Ford, that "Sullivan, Stirling, and Stephen with their divisions had gone in pursuit of a detachment of the British army, two or three thousand, or more, which filed off from their left about eleven o'clock, and were supposed to have crossed the Brandywine at Jones' Ford," and adds, that " at half past four the enemy attacked Sullivan at the ford above, that the action was very violent, and a very severe cannonading had begun here (at Chadd's Ford) also." This letter confuses the movement ordered, upon the receipt of the message of Lieutenant-colonel Ross, with the general action which was in progress when the letter was dispatched.

The advance of General Howe began at daybreak, according to his report, and the entire column, after a march of seventeen miles from Kennett Square, crossed Jeffries' Ford by two o'clock, its vanguard having previously reached the vicinity of Osborne's Hill, near Sullivan's right.

Its battle formation was deliberately made in three lines, and was so complete and adequate that the third line was not called into action at all. That formation was as follows: The guards were upon the right, and the First British grenadiers to their left near the centre, supported by the Hessian grenadiers in a second line. To the left of the Second grenadiers who held the centre, were two battalions of light infantry with the Hessian and Anspach chasseurs, supported by the Fourth brigade for a second line. The composition of this brigade is indicated on the map. The Third brigade was held in reserve.

A brief summary of General Howe's report will prepare the way for a better understanding of the movements of the American army. The American position, when the British troops began the attack, was on commanding ground near Birmingham Meeting-house, nearly parallel with Osborne's Hill, behind which the British army so deliberately prepared their advance movement. " Both flanks were covered by very thick woods, and the artillery was advantageously disposed. The light infantry and chasseurs began the attack, the guards and grenadiers instantly advanced from the right, the whole under a heavy train (of fire) of artillery and musketry; but they pushed on with an impetuosity not to be sustained by the enemy, who falling back into the woods in their rear, the king's troops entered with them and pursued closely for nearly two miles. The Americans were dislodged from the second position, within half a mile of Dilworth, and just at dark the infantry, Second grenadiers, and Fourth brigade had a brief action beyond Dilworth, between the two roads which run from Dilworth to Chester." " The Guards, First British grenadiers and Hessian grenadiers who attacked the American left, having in the pursuit got entangled in very thick woods, were no further engaged during the day."

"Lieutenant general Knyphausen, as had been previously concerted, kept the enemy amused during the day with cannon, and the appearance of forcing the ford without intending to pass it, until the attack upon the enemy's right should take place." " When the general action began, the crossing was successfully made under the lead of Major-general Grant, and the American left made a rapid retreat."

As soon as Washington learned of the approach of the British column, General Sullivan was ordered to bring the entire right wing to bear upon its advance. The position at Chadd's Ford was entrusted to Wayne. Greene was placed in command of Muhlenberg's and Weedon's brigades as a reserve, and this force was posted between the extremes of attack. The American formation was quite compact, except on the left where Sullivan dropped his own division, which was in great disorder, and thus "made an interval in the American line of half a mile," until he "rode on to consult with the other general officers and settle upon the location of the troops." He states in his report, that it was "their unanimous opinion that his division should be brought on to join the others, and that the whole should incline further to the right, to prevent our being outflanked;" that "while his division was marching on, and before it was possible for them to form to advantage, the enemy pressed on with rapidity and attacked them, which threw them into some kind of confusion." " He took his own position in the centre, with the artillery, and ordered it to play briskly, to stop the progress of the enemy and give the broken troops time to rally and form in the rear."

" He sent four aid-de-camps for this purpose and went himself, but all in vain ; then left them to be rallied by their own officers and the aids, and returned to the artillery and centre." " Some rallied and others could not by their officers be brought to do anything but fly." The resistance of Stirling and Stephen was such as repeatedly to repulse the British attack. Conway's brigade distinguished itself by its valor. Hazen's, Dayton's and Ogden's regiments alone maintained a resolute position on the left. General Deborre, a French officer of thirty-five years' experience, commanded the right brigade of the entire line, but it gave way early in the action and the chief resistance was made at the centre. (This officer almost immediately resigned, so that he was not dealt with by a military court.) That the retreat of the two divisions of Stirling and Stephen, (except Deborre's brigade) was effected with some steadiness and repeated returns of the offensive, is shown by the fact that they took both artillery and baggage with them ; and there is abundant evidence that General Sullivan exhibited a personal courage which greatly overshadowed his deficiencies as commanding officer of a grand division. There are circumstances associated with the battle which indicate more clearly than the battle itself the difficulties of the day, and make more wonderful the rescue of the American army from entire destruction.

It would be presumed from the order issued to General Sullivan and the position occupied by the American troops, that the three divisions moved, under General Sullivan's directions, directly to the battle-field from their camp on the river bluff; and he has been alternately praised and abused for the position taken. The following is an extract from General Sullivan's personal communication to the American Congress :

" I wish Congress to consider the many disadvantages I labored under in that day. It is necessary in every action that the commanding officer should have a perfect knowledge of the number and situation of the enemy, the route they are pursuing, the ground he is to draw up his troops on, as well as that where the enemy are to be formed, and that he have sufficient time to view and examine the positions of the enemy and to draw up his troops in such a manner as to counteract their design, all of which were wanting."

General Howe did not intend to grant these favors ; and this excellent programme for a sham battle, in experimental practice is not acceptable to those who seek high attainment in the art of war. The paper continues, " We had intelligence of two brigades coming against us; when it was in fact the whole strength of the British army, commanded by General Howe and Lord Cornwallis. They met us unexpectedly, and attacked us before we had time to form, and upon ground we had never before seen. Under these disadvantages, and against those unequal numbers, we maintained our ground an hour and forty minutes; and by giving fresh opposition on every ground that would admit, we kept them at bay from three o'clock until after sunset."

These statements are to be considered in connection with those on page 374, where General Sullivan claims to have expected General Howe's approach from that direction, and necessarily over the ground where the battle was fought. The occasion was one which required exhaustive reconnoissance and thorough anticipation of the contingencies of such an attack. Both were neglected.

It is nowhere recorded in official documents, exactly how the American troops gained the battle-ground. The report of General Sullivan gives his views; but neither those of La Fayette, a volunteer on this occasion, nor Stirling, explain this matter.

General Sullivan, in fact, waited for further orders from Washington, after sending him notice that the enemy was close at hand, as if paralyzed, and the divisions of Stirling and Stephen moved promptly without him, to the nearest good position from which they could resist the advancing British columns.

The author knows full well that this statement, predicated upon examination of documents, regardless in the first instance of all other opinions, does not conform to some narratives, neither has this examination from the first accepted any opinion which was not in harmony with a strictly military review of conditions and data. It is therefore material that additional documentary matter should receive attention. Mr. Sparks, in his Appendix to Vol. V., page 462, states, that " when General Sullivan came up with three divisions of the army, his own, Stephen's and Stirling's, and began to form them into a line about half a mile in front of the enemy, Cornwallis commenced the attack before this manœuver could be completed, and threw Sullivan's troops into confusion, etc."

Washington, writing to General Sullivan under date of October twenty-fourth, 1777, says, " what happened on your march to the field of battle,—your disposition there and behavior during the action, I can say nothing about; no part till the retreat commenced having come under my immediate observation. I can only add, therefore, that the whole tenor of your conduct as far as I have had opportunities of judging has been spirited and active." This letter also contains the following allusion to the information sent by Major Spear, "without comment or opinion." "It was not your fault that the intelligence was eventually found to be erroneous." *And yet when that dispatch was sent, General Sullivan believed it to be erroneous.* In writing from "Camp on Perkiomy, September twenty-seventh, 1777, to President Hancock, General Sullivan thus shows how he reached the battle-field. (The Italics are not so marked in the original.)

"I never yet pretended that my disposition in the late battle was perfect. I knew it was very far from it; but this I will venture to affirm, that it was the best that time would allow me to make. At half-past two I received orders to march with my division to join with and take command of that and two others, to oppose the enemy who were coming down on the right flank of our army. *I neither knew where the enemy were, nor what route the other two divisions were to take, and of course could not determine where I should form a junction with them.*" "I began my march in a few minutes after I received my orders, and had not marched a mile when I met Colonel Hazen with his regiment which had been stationed at a ford three miles above me, who informed me that I might depend that the principal part of the British army was there; although I knew the report sent to headquarters made them but two brigades. As I knew Colonel Hazen to be an old officer and a good judge of numbers, I gave credence to his report in preference to the intelligence before received. While I was conversing with Colonel Hazen, and our troops still on the march, the enemy headed us in the road, (see positions of guards and Hessians on the map 'Battle of Brandywine,') about forty. rods from our advance guard. I then found it necessary to turn off to the right to form, and so got nearer to the other divisions, *which I at that moment discovered, both in the rear and to the right of the place I was then at.* I ordered Colonel Hazen's regiment to pass a hollow way, file off to the right, and face, to cover the artillery. The enemy seeing this, did not press on, but gave me time to form my division on an advantageous height, in a line with the other divisions, about almost half a mile to the left.''

It thus appears that Major-general Sullivan, to whom the command of the entire right wing of the American army from its first establishment on the east bank of the Brandywine had been intrusted, arrived only just in time to take part in the action, and that his personal valor, and that of three regiments, was the sole contribution of his division to the efficiency of the American resistance. If, as appears from some authorities, General Deborre was in Stirling's division, he was in his proper position on the right, and the entangled controversy whether there was a dispute between that officer and General Sullivan as to the command of the extreme right, is settled by the documents already cited, independently of the fact that there was no occasion for a conflict upon such a question, between a general of brigade and the commander-in-chief of the entire right wing. General Sullivan's time was spent in finding the army first, and then in finding a place where he could render service in person, and with such of his own division as he could rescue from panic and flight.

Washington hastened with Greene's division to the support of the right wing; but not in time to save it in position. It had no retreat but toward Dilworth, as the British right wing out flanked it to the left and intervened between it and Chadd's Ford. By a direct march nearly to Dilworth of four miles, effected in fifty minutes, and a wheel to the left for half a mile, he was enabled to occupy a defile and substantial ground from which to open a passage for the retreating battalions and interpose a vigorous resistance. This was temporary, and the retreat was then made under cover of Greene's division. In an orchard beyond Dilworth, three regiments made another vigorous stand, and night separated the conflicting armies.

The militia brigade of General Armstrong, on the extreme left, near Pyle's Ford, was not called into action, but rapidly moved in the direction of Chester; and Generals Wayne and Maxwell, after a vigorous resistance, also took the same direction, losing the guns which were at the ford, and some others.

The American army gained Chester, so that Washington's dispatch from that point to President Hancock was dated at twelve o'clock at night, September 11th, 1777, and the British army remained on the field. There are a few minor items which belong to this record. At the commencement of the action a vigorous skirmish took place in the orchard north of the Birmingham Meeting-house. Special credit is also due to the corps of General Maxwell.

The Marquis de La Fayette, who had been appointed Major-general by way of compliment, as claimed, but not so understood by Washington, served as his voluntary aid-de-camp, distinguished himself by his valor, was wounded in an attempt to rally troops, and joined Washington at Chester.   Captain Louis de Fleury fought with such gallantry that Congress presented him with a horse in place of his own killed in the battle.   The baron St. Ovary, who aided La Fayette in rallying fugitives, was taken prisoner.   The skill of General Howe as a scientific soldier, even amidst woods and thickets, was again demonstrated ; and the wonderful presence of mind, aptitude for emergencies, and extraordinary capacity for making the most of raw troops, was never more thoroughly evinced by Washington in his public career.   With all its mistakes, and the final retreat of the American troops, there was much of real success and real hope as the fruit of the Battle of Brandywine.

CHAPTER LI.

OPERATIONS NEAR PHILADELPHIA. BATTLE OF GERMANTOWN.

1777.

GENERAL WASHINGTON marched from Chester directly to Philadelphia to refit his army, secure ammunition and provisions, and thence to Germantown for one day of rest.

While Congress was making an effort to collect detached Continental troops, and rally the militia, the Commander-in-chief was in motion.

On the thirteenth of September, orders were sent to Monsieur de Coudray to complete the defensive works on the Delaware as rapidly as possible; to General Putnam to send him fifteen hundred Continental troops forthwith; and to General Armstrong to occupy the line of the Schuylkill river, and throw up occasional redoubts near the fords, to be occupied if necessary in crossing that river.

The left wing of the British army had moved from Dilworth toward Goshen, demonstrating toward Reading, as well as toward the Schuylkill and Philadelphia. The right wing under Generals Grant and Cornwallis reached Ashtown on the twelfth, and Chester on the thirteenth. The failure of General Howe to move diagonally toward Crum creek, or Derby, thereby to make a direct route to Philadelphia, shorter than that of Washington's retreat, received severe criticism from his enemies; but important considerations controlled his actions. The wounded of both armies were on his hands, so that he was compelled to procure surgeons from General Washington to assist in their care; and he states that one reason of his occupation of Wilmington, where he captured the Governor and considerable coin, was to provide better for their comfort. Inasmuch as Grant and Cornwallis were in the rear of Washington's army, a march to Philadelphia *via* Germantown afforded a fair opportunity to cut off its retreat, while at the

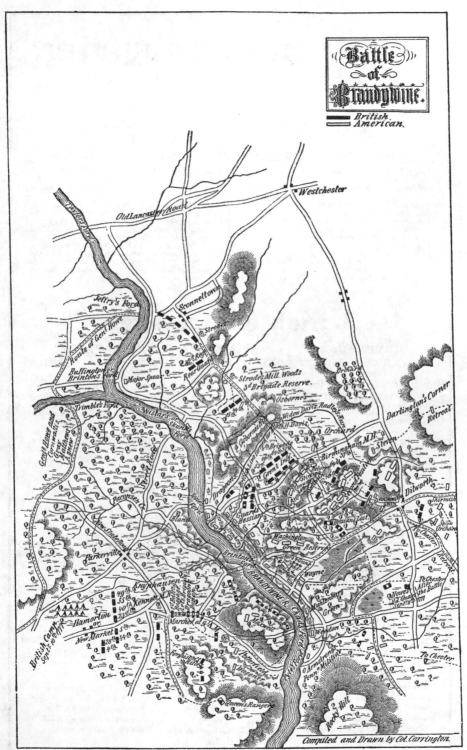

Battle of Brandywine

SEPTEMBER 11th, 1777

American Commanders

SULLIVAN **WASHINGTON** STIRLING

GREENE MUHLENBERG MAXWELL WAYNE STEPHEN

Nominal Strength, 14,000 Effective force, 11,000 Casualties, 780.

AMERICAN DISPOSITIONS. Washington, then in New Jersey, alike watchful of the Hudson, New York City and the large fleet near Staten Island, quickly marched to Pennsylvania, when the fleet sailed southward ; left a sufficient force to observe Clinton, passed Philadelphia, and on the 7th of September took a position at Newport, on the east bank of Clay Creek. (See map 22, p. 49). Maxwell had previously skirmished with the British vanguard at Newark, as they advanced from Elk Creek. Early on the 9th, in order to foil an attempt of Howe to gain his rear and cut him off from Philadelphia, Washington again marched, and took a position selected by Gen. Greene, on the east bank of the Brandywine. The American army formed, from Jones' Ford to Pyle's Ford, from right to left, as follows : Stirling, Stephen, Sullivan (under Sullivan), Wayne, Muhlenberg, Weedon, Armstrong (Greene commanding), and Washington, behind the centre, with a small reserve.

British Commanders

KNYPHAUSEN **HOWE** CORNWALLIS

GRANT MATTHEWS GREY AGNEW STIRN

Strength, 18,000 Casualties, 600.

BRITISH DISPOSITIONS. Howe landed at Head of Elk Creek August 25th, skirmished with Maxwell Sept. 3d, threatened Washington's right on the 8th, and on the 10th reached Kennett Square. Sharp skirmishes occurred on the right, and before Chad's Ford (the centre) with American light troops under Porterfield, Wagner and Maxwell, who had crossed the river for the purpose.

Howe moved at night, and by a detour of 17 miles, crossed the two forks of the Brandywine, repeating the movement made on Long Island, and carefully formed the divisions of Cornwallis, Agnew, Matthews and Grey, in three lines, in rear of the American Army, on and before Osborne's Hill, facing the position, hurriedly taken by Sullivan, when advised of the British advance.

Development of the Action

Washington sent Sullivan, with three divisions, to occupy the hill near Birmingham Meeting House and resist Howe ; put Wayne in command at Chad's Ford to oppose Knyphausen, and formed Muhlenberg and Weedon's brigades, as a reserve, under Greene, with which he took his own position.

Howe and Knyphausen forced the positions they respectively threatened, after much fighting, and the entire army fell back slowly, covered by Washington and Greene, to Dilworth and Chester, without panic or sacrifice, reaching Chester at midnight. Howe remained on the field, in charge of the wounded of both armies. Cornwallis reached Chester on the 13th. Washington refitted his army at Philadelphia, moved up the Schuylkill, crossed at Swedes' Ford and offered Howe battle, at Westchester (September 15th), Storms separated the armies.

Mem. (Among the wounded at Brandywine was Lafayette, who served as a volunteer aid-de-camp, under his commission as Major General, then just conferred by Congress.

References :

CARRINGTON'S "BATTLES OF THE AMERICAN REVOLUTION," pp. 368-381.

School Histories:

Anderson, ¶ 50 ; p. 79.
Barnes, ¶ 3 ; p. 119.
Berard (Bush), ¶ 88-9 ; p. 160-1.
Goodrich, C.A.(Seaveys),¶ 14; p. 125.
Goodrich, S. G., ¶ 3-5 ; p. 221.
Hassard, ¶ 11-12 ; p. 188-9.

Holmes, ¶ 10 ; p. 128.
Lossing, ¶ 13 : p. 154.
Quackenbos, ¶ 346; p. 249.
Ridpath, ¶ 19 ; p. 205.
Sadlier, (Excel), ¶ 14 ; p. 192.
Stephens, A.H. ¶ 31; p. 202.

Swinton, ¶ 135 ; p. 132.
Scott, ¶ 8 ; p. 182.
Thalheimer (Eclectic), ¶ 263 ;
  p. 151 ; *Note* 2, p. 158.
Venable, ¶ 143 ; p. 110.

same time threatening the city. On the fifteenth, Washington was again on the west side of the Schuylkill, having crossed at Swede's Ford, so that the halt of General Howe for a single day on the battle field, rendered it useless for him to make forced marches for that city direct.

Washington moved out on the Lancaster road as far as the Warren Tavern. General Howe, watchful of these movements, advanced beyond Westchester, and both armies prepared for battle. General Howe made a partially successful attempt to turn the American right wing, in order to throw it back upon the Schuylkill; but a heavy storm completely ruined the ammunition of the American army, and was "directly in the faces of the British troops." Washington left Wayne, with fifteen hundred men, in a peculiarly retired and well chosen position near Paoli, to be ready to fall upon the rear of General Howe, and then moved to Yellow Springs, thence to Warwick, on French creek; and after he found that General Howe did not intend a movement toward Reading, crossed the river by Parker's Ford and encamped on the Perkiomy, September seventeenth.

On the twentieth General Wayne was surprised, through the treachery of the people of the country. General Grey advanced from his camp near Trudruffyn at night, using only the bayonet, and inflicted a loss of three hundred in killed, wounded and prisoners, with a mere handful of casualties to his own troops. Wayne saved his artillery and most of his baggage. John Adams thus criticised the crossing of the Schuylkill; and the criticism does more credit to his interest in the war, than to his judgment of military conduct. "It is a very injudicious movement. If he had sent one brigade of his regular troops to have headed the militia, he might have cut to pieces Howe's army in attempting to cross any of the fords. Howe will not attempt it." *He did attempt it!* "He will wait for his fleet in Delaware river. O! Heaven! grant us one great soul! One leading mind would extricate the best cause from that ruin which seems to await it!" But Howe did *not wait for his fleet.* And when Washington crossed the Schuylkill, he knew that Grant and Cornwallis were detached to Chester, so that the movement against one wing of the British army, interrupted by the storm, was soldierly; and the retreat *via* Parker's Ford, was for the purpose of taking the quickest possible offensive and to cover the fords. The disaster of Wayne alone impaired the value of that action. The brigade of Smallwood, which had been left as a support to Wayne, failed to be on time to render such support, although only about a mile from Paoli, and his misfortune drove them to a retreat in partial disorder. The succeeding manœuvers of the armies were respectively affected by the affair at Paoli. The pressure was taken off the rear of Howe's army, and he moved on. Washington says: "They had got so far the start before I received certain intelligence that any considerable number had crossed, that I found it in vain to think of overtaking their rear with troops harassed as ours had been with constant marching since the battle of Brandywine."

"One thousand of his army were bare-footed," and Colonel Hamilton was sent to Philadelphia to force a contribution of shoes from the inhabitants. A small portion of the British left crossed at Gordon's Ford on the twenty-second, and the main body at Flatland Ford, near Valley Forge, on the twenty-third, reaching Germantown on the twenty-fifth. On the twenty-seventh Cornwallis entered Philadelphia. Colonel Sterling, of the British army, was moved across the Delaware to operate against its defenses, including the works at Mud Island and Red Bank, and the fleet of Admiral Howe was already *en route* for the same destination.

There was no rest for either army; and the occupation of Philadelphia was attended by immediate results which showed that the war was nearer its close, through that occupation.

Congress adjourned to Lancaster, and subsequently to York. The powers of Washington were somewhat enlarged, and a peremptory order was sent to Putnam, who was all the time attempting ill-considered attempts upon the British outposts near New York, to send twenty-five hundred troops without delay, to reinforce Washington's army, and that he must "so use militia, that the posts in the Highlands might be perfectly safe." Application was also made to General Gates for the return of Morgan's corps; but they were not sent to the headquarters of the army until after the close of the Northern Campaign.

General Howe had been one month in marching fifty-four miles, from the head of the Elk to Philadelphia. His headquarters were at Germantown.

This village, six miles from Philadelphia, was built upon a single street, the old Skippach road, nearly or quite two miles in length, bearing slightly west of north, as indicated on the map " Battle of Germantown." This map, so far as the positions of the British troops are indicated, is compiled from that of Lieutenant Hill, assisting engineer,

of the British Twenty-third regiment, and while indicating their modified positions shortly after the action began, is accepted as the best.
The additions made afford a fair estimate of the successive stages of
the battle.

The street is not straight ; so that there is at no single point a
complete range for fire throughout its entire extent.   Neither is it on
a uniform or continuous grade so that guns stationed at Mount Airy,
or near the Street Railway station (as occupied in January, 1876,) and
trained down the hill, could have a clear sweep unobstructed by crowning ground.   In other words, troops would be at least twice under cover
in moving through the town.   From the Old School-house lane there
is another gradual rise on the road leading to Philadelphia.   Beyond
Mount Airy, northward, is another declining slope, soon taken up by
the ascent of Chestnut Hill, still further on.   A few small alleys, or
openings, projected east and west for a few rods from the main street,
and several of the old buildings of the era under notice, were in very
well preserved condition at the beginning of 1876, the Centennial year
of American Independence.   In addition to the Skippach road, the
town was approached from the northeast by the Lime-kiln road
which entered the village by the Market House, and by the old York
road which entered the Philadelphia road some distance below.   A
fourth road, called the Manatawney or Ridge road, came from the
upper Schuylkill country, and was located between that river and Wissahickon creek.

The British camp crossed the town on the general line of School-
house lane and the Lime-kiln road, passing the Market-house.

The left was commanded by Lieutenant-general Knyphausen, and
the troops in his camp, until the action came on, consisted of seven
British and three Hessian battalions, and the mounted and dismounted chasseurs.   Generals Stirn, Grey and Agnew were in this
command, although General Stirn seems to have been subsequently
transferred to the right of the road.   This force had General Grant on
the right, where the guards, six battalions of British troops and two
squadrons of dragoons were encamped ; there being no distinct centre,
other than the location of the street crossings, to the south of which,
within half a mile, General Howe had his headquarters and personal
guard.

The chasseurs rested on the Schuylkill, a little advanced, as a
picket guard ; and on the first alarm the two battalions of Minnigerode
were detailed to their support.   The first battalion of light infantry

25

was slightly advanced from the extreme right, and the Queen's rangers were thrown beyond the Old York road to anticipate an attempt to turn the right.

The Forty-ninth British regiment was pushed up Frankford creek after the action began, and some sharp skirmishing ensued near Lucan's Mill, upon Greene's advance. At the head of the street, a mile from the Market-house, the Second battalion of light infantry was posted with advanced pickets, supported by the Fortieth regiment which was on the slope westward, out of the main street, where it commanded a clear view of the country up Wissahickon creek. As the narrative will disclose the fact that the extreme, or rather, the detached wings of the American army failed to touch, or even to approach, the corresponding wings of the British army, it is proper to notice, in this connection, the fact that the British reinforcements sent to the left wing (where the chasseurs were advanced) were withdrawn when the action became general, but did not participate in the battle; and the Hessian grenadiers did not accompany General Grey when he made his subsequent advance movement into the village itself. The Third and Fourth brigades marched obliquely forward to the right, crossing before the regiments of Du Corps and Donop, which had been designated to support the Fourth brigade; but these regiments, General Howe states, did not participate in the action.

General Cornwallis, early apprised of the American attack by the artillery firing near the Chew house, brought up two British battalions, one of Hessian grenadiers "on the run," and one squadron of dragoons, and joined General Grey in pursuit of the column of General Greene after the general action was over.

General Howe on the right, with Generals Grant and Knyphausen to his left, made their advance in a concave order, almost enveloping Generals Sullivan and Greene, who had converged toward the Market-house when the tide of battle turned in British favor.

General Howe states in his Narrative that " he was not surprised:" —that, " the enemy's approach was discovered by our patrols and I had early notice of it. The line was presently under arms, and although it must be admitted that the outposts and light infantry in one quarter, were driven back, it must be equally admitted that they were soon effectually supported, and the enemy was repulsed at the only place where the smallest impression was made."

Sir George Osborne, in his testimony before the Committee of the House of Commons, states, that he " received from General Howe, who was accompanied by his aid-de-camp, only the night before, the order to move on with the grenadiers and light infantry of the guards to Major Simcoe's post, about half a mile in front of the line of infantry, as I might expect.the enemy at daybreak next morning." This officer adds, " The firing of the enemy on the morning of the attack began exactly, or near the time that Sir William Howe acquainted me the night before, it would do."

Washington's camp was near Pennebeck Mill, twenty miles from Philadelphia. Two-thirds of his army participated in the movement upon Germantown. His plan was to occupy the four roads which more or less directly approached General Howe's position, and to make the march in time, first to bring all the divisions into approximate positions, then to give them rest, and make a combined attack at daybreak.

The troops left camp at seven o'clock on the evening of the third, passed Metuchen Hill about nine o'clock, and all the divisions which accompanied Washington reached their halting places, obtained their rest, and made the attack on time.

Sullivan and Wayne, with Conway in advance acting as a flanking corps, were to move directly over Chestnut Hill and enter the town.

Maxwell and Nash, under Major-general Stirling, were to follow this column in reserve.

General Armstrong with the Pennsylvania militia was sent down the Manatawny road to cross the Wissahickon creek, and fall upon the British left wing and rear.

Greene and Stephen, led and flanked by McDougall's brigade, were to move by the lime-kiln road, enter the village at the Market-house, and attack the British right wing.

Generals Smallwood and Forman with the Maryland and New Jersey militia were to follow the Old York road until a convenient opportunity should bring them upon the extreme right flank and rear of the enemy.

Washington accompanied Sullivan's division. A simplification of the subsequent movements, by parts, will aid in reconciling conflicting statements. No attempt to reconcile reports exactly would aid in the matter ; as in all human experience a diversity of statement, according to the standpoint of observation, is invariable, and truth is found in the main features of the combined reports.

General Conway led the way into the town, and attacked the British pickets who were stationed north, and not very far from the Allen

House. This advance picket guard was promptly supported by the British light infantry.

General Sullivan brought up his division next, and crowded the enemy beyond the Allen House.

The Fortieth British regiment, Colonel Musgrave, moved up to the support of the light infantry as indicated on the map; and according to his report, finding that the position was already occupied by American troops in force, he retired down the main street fighting, and took his stand east of the street at the Chew House, a stone building of considerable strength on a crowning site. Up to this time nothing had been heard from the corps of Armstrong or Greene; and the disposition of the centre had to be made independently of their coöperation, and was modified to suit the state of facts.

Conway was thrown out to the right, on the slope west of the town, to protect that flank while Sullivan and Nash could sweep on in a line, also west of the street, towards the Market-house. The extreme advance of Sullivan is noted on the map, to be considered irrespective of intervening incidents in point of time, so as to dispose of the force division by division, and avoid confusion.

Wayne was ordered by Sullivan to take the slope (as Greene did not occupy his designated position there) east from the main street, and his extreme advance is also noted; although he was for a time recalled during the firing at the Chew House. One regiment from Wayne's brigade, and one from Sullivan's division, however, were also placed with Conway to protect the right flank, as the protracted delay of Armstrong endangered the advance. The whole movement through a narrow town was one of peculiar exposure. The troops of Sullivan and Wayne passed on " abreast," according to the report of the former officer. Meanwhile, Musgrave on his retreat, had thrown six companies of the Fortieth regiment into the Chew House, had barricaded the window, refused to surrender on demand, and kept up a vigorous fire upon the American troops near by; while Sullivan says that " his own advance, which had swept past the Chew House, was resisted constantly at every fence, wall, ditch, and hedge." Additional delay occurred from tearing up fences for the passage of horses and artillery.

Maxwell was next brought forward with Colonel Knox, and two guns, to attempt the reduction of the Chew House. Musgrave successfully resisted this attack, and kept them from advance to support the other troops for a full hour or more.

Upon the arrival of Maxwell, Wayne, temporarily recalled as before stated, again moved to the front, making *on the left* a common advance with that of Sullivan which was on the *right* of the town.

More than an hour certainly had passed ; the division commanders differing, as their minds were differently impressed, when *Greene was heard from*.

His division shared the misapprehension which attended the discharge of artillery at the Chew House, as the deepening fog already confused sight and confounded sound. General *Stephen's* division moved out of column, being on the west side of the Lime-kiln road, without waiting for orders from General Greene, followed the noise of battle, and approached the village just south of the Chew House. Here, unfortunately, he struck the rear of Wayne's brigade, and mutual loss was incurred by each mistaking the other for an enemy ; and their part in the action was practically terminated. As *Greene* advanced on the east side of the Lime-kiln road, and bore toward the Market-house, he was obliged to countermarch and take ground to the right, westward, to avoid the extension of the British right wing, which was already advancing to envelop the American troops. He cleared his division, passed inside of the enemy, and with Scott's and Muhlenberg's brigades approached the Market-house. Colonel Matthews, of Virginia, who led the advance, had skirmished all the way from Lucan's Mill, and had taken a detachment of light infantry prisoners. It will be seen by another reference to the map, that Washington, Sullivan, and Greene, were now converging upon the supposed British centre, and that their action was in accordance with the original plan of attack, crippled in its execution by the absence of the columns which should have been at work upon the British flanks and rear, and embarrassed by various incidents which had placed the commands of Maxwell, Stephen, and Wayne out of close communication, and also by the dense fog which left the reserve in utter confusion as to the positions of the troops in advance. It was, however, united in the resistance, when Washington ordered the retreat. Sullivan's division really had extra assignment of duty ; expended all its ammunition, and began to feel the pressure of the British left as it swept along their flank, while also attacking their front. His two aids-de-camp, Majors Sherbourne and White were killed, as well as General Nash, and the column gave back, not a little disturbed in its formation by exaggerated rumors of losses elsewhere. Colonel Matthews also was soon enveloped ; a portion of his men were captured and his prisoners were rescued.   The retreat became general, and the activity of a powerful and almost invisible enemy quickened that retreat.

The artillery was brought off safely and the troops of Wayne and Greene covered the forces as they retired through town and by the Lime-kiln road.

The conduct of General Stephen was submitted to a military court and he was dismissed on the charge of intoxication.   The collision of his division with the brigade of Wayne does not necessarily involve his censure, as Wayne was in an unanticipated position by reason of the delay in the arrival of the left wing.

General Greene's tardiness was incident to the longer route taken, the check at Lucan's Mill, and the nature of the country ; and possibly by the sudden action of Stephen in abruptly leaving his command. General McDougall shared the retreat, but gained no laurels.   General Armstrong states in his letters to General Gates and others, that " we were cannonading from the heights on each side of the Wissa-hickon," " was called to join the General " " we proceeded some three miles, directed by a slow fire of cannon, until we fell in with a superior body of the enemy, with whom we engaged about three-quarters of an hour, but their grape shot and ball soon intimidated and obliged us to retreat, or rather file off," " loss not quite twenty."

The affair at the Chew House was a material issue in the battle, only as it kept troops to the rear ; and a prompt concert of action on the part of all the troops on duty, according to the original order of the day, would probably have realized success, without the aid of Maxwell's command.   It was a diversion, which had its chief importance through the erroneous impressions it gave of the positions of the contending armies.

It is not a correct statement that the whole army halted, to its prejudice, " rather than leave a *fort* in its rear."

Colonel Knox reported that " the action lasted two hours and forty minutes, by his watch ; " and the watch is to be credited with this information.

The British army without doubt was seriously embarrassed, if not partially disordered by the suddenness and persistency of the advance, and was satisfied with the result.

Washington regained Metuchen Hill ; and General Howe returned to Philadelphia.

The British casualties were reported at five hundred and thirty-five, including General Agnew and Lieutenant-colonel Bird.

The American casualties were six hundred and seventy-three, besides prisoners, estimated at four hundred, and many missing, some of whom afterwards regained camp.

Washington's officers had been divided in opinion as to the prudence of this attack until additional troops could be procured ; but there are few operations of the war that show greater skill in design, and the ease with which a victory almost achieved is more readily lost, than the Battle of Germantown.

CHAPTER LII.

OPERATIONS NEAR PHILADELPHIA. MINOR MENTION. CLOSE OF CAMPAIGN, 1777.

THE battle of Germantown which demonstrated the tireless activity and nerve of Washington, incited foolish expectations that he would soon rescue Philadelphia from British control. Whenever the promise of success enlivened the public spirits, there was an instant tendency to over-estimate the value of mere courage as against thorough discipline. Nothing seemed too exacting at such times; and Congress had so much sympathy with clamorous aspirants for office, that the life of Washington is more memorable for his calm faith in ultimate results and the dignity of his contempt for jealousy and intrigue, from whatever source it emanated, than for almost any other quality.

The consciousness of unselfish devotion to duty bore him up, when the spirit of mere ambition would have driven many leaders toward a dictatorship, or treason. The tidings of the surrender of Burgoyne reached him on the eighteenth of October, and no one in America more cordially congratulated General Gates and the Northern army, upon the result. The secondary fruits of the personal honors bestowed upon that officer were however prejudicial to army discipline; for they put the impressive result of that campaign in contrast with the slow, so-called "Fabian policy," of the Commander-in-chief. This spirit of exacting criticism, and laudation of conspicuous deeds, which became so earnest during the winter of 1777–8 began to declare its temper as soon as it was understood that Washington only *almost* defeated Howe at Germantown. The thanks for that which was skillfully devised, soon cooled because the plan failed of complete fruition.

That battle, however, satisfied the British garrison of Philadelphia

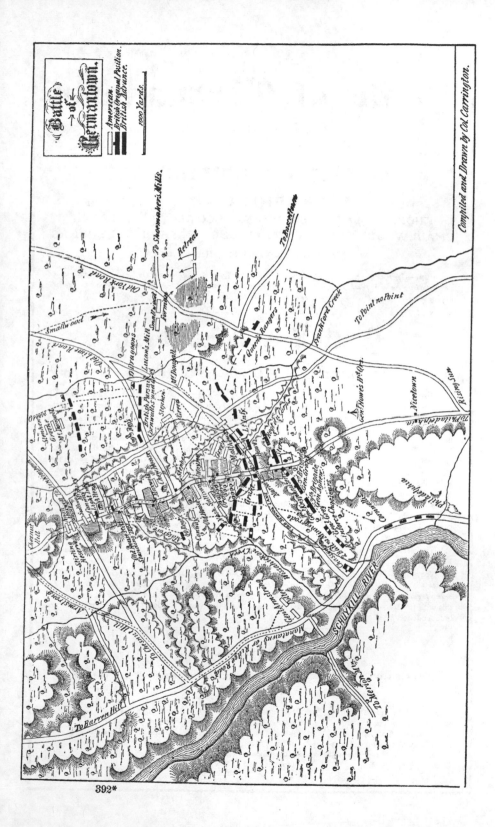

Battle of Germantown.

American.
British Original Position.
British Advance.

1000 Yards.

Compiled and Drawn by Col. Carrington.

392*

Battle of Germantown

OCTOBER 4th, 1777

American Commanders

SULLIVAN **WASHINGTON** GREENE
KNOX, WAYNE, STEPHEN, SCOTT, ARMSTRONG
SMALLWOOD, FORMAN, MAXWELL, NASH, MUHLENBERG

Strength, 7,000 Casualties, 1,073

MEM.—*Germantown, six miles from Philadelphia, and Headquarters of Howe, was then, as now, mainly on one street, not quite straight, which crossed Chestnut Hill, Mt. Airy, and the hill at Chew's House, with gradual descent to the Market House.*

British Commanders

GREY, KNYPHAUSEN **HOWE** AGNEW, STIRN

NOTE I.—In view of the extended distribution of Howe's army, having the left on the Schuylkill and thence deployed nearly parallel with Old School Lane, east and north-east, across the main street, Washington attempted to strike the whole line by a combined movement of his chief divisions. His army was near Pennebecker's Mill, about 20 miles from Philadelphia. Four roads were used. The march began at 7 P. M., Oct. 3d. The plan was for Sullivan, with Wayne and Conway, to lead over Chestnut Hill into the village, supported by Maxwell and Nash, under Stirling; for Armstrong to threaten the British left; for Greene, with Stephen and McDougall, to move by the Limekiln road, and strike the British right near the Market Place, and for Smallwood and Forman to fall into the old York road, and strike the extreme British right, and rear. The advance was prompt, and the surprise promised success. Washington accompanied Sullivan's division. Col. Musgrave, of the 40th **Regiment (British)** threw himself into the **Chew House**, and Knox in vain opened his light guns to dispossess the defenders. At Lucan's Mill a sharp action delayed the left, and a dense fog so commingled the combatants and confused operations, that prisoners taken were retaken, and the army was forced to retreat, but in good order, while **Howe retired to Philadelphia.**

NOTE II.—American casualties were 673, including Gen. Nash and 400 prisoners. **British casualties were 535, including Gen. Agnew.**

NOTE III.—*Count de Vergennes, Minister of Foreign Affairs, Paris, said, "Nothing has struck me so much as Gen. Washington's attacking and giving battle to Gen. Howe's Army. To bring troops, raised within the year, to do this, promises everything."* Louis XVI. promptly coupled this with the Burgoyne campaign, and determined " Not only to acknowledge, but to support American independence."

References :

CARRINGTON'S "BATTLES OF THE AMERICAN REVOLUTION," pp. 302-401.

School Histories :

Anderson, ¶ 52 ; p. 80.
Barnes, ¶ 2 ; p. 120.
Berard (Bush), ¶ 91; p. 162.
Goodrich, C. A. (Seaveys), ¶ 16, p. 125-6.
Goodrich, S. G., ¶ 1-6; p. 234-5.
Hassard, ¶ 14 ; p. 189.

Holmes, ¶ 11 ; p. 129.
Lossing, ¶ 17; p. 156.
Quackenbos, ¶ 348 ; p. 250.
Ridpath, ¶ 21 ; p. 206.
Sadlier (Excel), ¶ 15 ; p. 193.
Stephens, A. H., ¶ 31 ; p. 202.

Swinton, ¶ 137 ; p. 133.
Scott, ¶ 9 ; p. 182-3.
Thalheimer (Eclectic), ¶ 263 ;
p. 151, p. 158, *Note.*
Venable, ¶ 144 ; p. 110.

with immediate field service.   The next matter of importance was to obtain control of the navigable river which ran past the post.   Its channel was obstructed ; and the American authorities regarded those obstructions as substantially complete.

In a necessary notice of the closing events of 1777, the reduction of those posts, and the movements of the army until it went into winter quarters at Valley Forge, follow in natural order.

At Billingsport in New Jersey (Byllinges Point) *chevaux de frise* obstructed the channel of the Delaware.   Just below the mouth of the Schuylkill, and within cannon range, was Mud Island, upon which Fort Mifflin had been built.   Its defenses were chiefly directed toward the approach from the Delaware below ; and the rear was provided with only a stockade and ditch, with two block houses of comparatively little strength.

On the opposite shore, known as Red Bank, Fort Mercer was located ; and this also was mainly designed for river defense.   The southern portion was separated from the northern section by stout palisades, a ditch, and a rampart, so as to have considerable strength ; but the activity of Monseur Duplessis, engineer in charge, had been unequal to the complete protection of the larger area, at the time when the British demonstration was made for its capture.   Chevaux de frise had also been placed in the channel between Red bank and Mud Island; and several galleys and floating batteries, under the direction of Commander Hazlewood, were located in the stream for coöperation in defense.

The acquisition of these posts, and the removal of all obstructions to the navigation of the river, had been resolved upon by General Howe ; and the arrival of Admiral Lord Howe's fleet off New Castle, about the sixth of October, increased the urgency of a movement to secure free communication between that fleet and the city.

Washington was as decided in his purpose to maintain these posts. His position in the country exercised a marked restraint upon supplies for the garrison of Philadelphia, and his control of the river kept up easy communication with New Jersey.

Colonel Christopher Greene, already noticed for courage at Bunker Hill and in Arnold's expedition to Quebec, was assigned to the defense of Fort Mercer, with a detachment of troops from Rhode Island, his native State.   Lieutenant-colonel Smith of Baltimore, with Maryland troops, was stationed at Fort Mifflin.   These garrisons were feeble in numbers, and well worn by extra duty ; but Washington reinforced them with Continental troops, so that each had a complement of four hundred men. A detail from Angell's Rhode Island regiment was sent to Fort Mercer, and a portion of Greene's Virginia regiment joined the garrison of Fort Mifflin.

The land at the mouth of the Schuylkill was marshy, leaving but two points sufficiently solid for batteries ; and these General Howe occupied. Two light redoubts were then thrown up on the northern part of Mud Island, which was low and grown with reeds, as an offset to these batteries.

The first demonstration in force was made against Fort Mercer. The grenadier regiments of Donop, Minnigerode, and Linsing, Winbach's regiment of the line, and the infantry chasseurs, all Hessian, having their own guns, *viz.* eight three pounders and two British howitzers, were detailed to this attack ; while the naval forces of Admiral Howe were relied upon to act in concert with new batteries then being erected on Province Island, opposite Fort Mifflin, on the Pennsylvania shore.

On the first of October, Colonel Sterling crossed the river, and without serious opposition occupied Billingsport ; and the Roebuck frigate broke through the *chevaux de frise* at that point, making a passage wide enough to admit larger ships.

Colonel Donop crossed Cooper's Ferry, at Philadelphia, on the twenty-first of October, was interrupted by skirmishing parties at Timber creek, but early on the following morning suddenly emerged from the woods and demanded of the garrison the immediate surrender of the post.

Upon receiving an unequivocal defiance, he organized two assaulting columns for simultaneous advance against the north and south faces of the fort. The garrison being too few in numbers to oppose his whole force, in the unfinished state of the exterior works, retired to the interior defenses ; occupying also a curtain of the old works, which afforded an enfilading fire upon any storming party who should attempt the stockade. The withdrawal of the garrison was mistaken for want of confidence in resistance ; and the assault was made with spirit and a brilliant dash, as if success were already assured.

That resistance was overwhelming, incessant, and deadly. Colonel Donop fell mortally wounded, and near him Lieutenant-colonel Minnigerode. The casualties of the assailants exceeded four hundred. being one-third of their number. The last attempt was made at the escarpment near the river, which exposed the column to fire from the galleys; and in less than an hour from the first attack, the Hessians were in retreat.

The British ships accomplished nothing. The Augusta 64, and the Merlin, frigate, grounded ; and the following day the former took fire from a hot shot and blew up before her whole crew could escape, while the Merlin was burnt to prevent her capture.

The American casualties were fourteen killed and twenty-one wounded.

Colonel Donop was carefully attended by Major Fleury, a French engineer in the American service, and his burial place at the south end of the old works is ever an object of interest to visitors.

Colonel Greene, Lieutenant-colonel Smith, and Commodore Hazle-wood received testimonials from Congress for " gallant conduct."

During the action, the batteries at the mouth of the Schuylkill directed their fire upon Fort Mifflin ; but with slight result.

On the tenth of November, a deliberate attempt upon that fort resulted in its capture. Four thirty-two pounder guns were withdrawn from the Somerset ; six twenty-four pounders from the Eagle, and these, with one thirteen inch mortar, were added to the works which had been erected on Province Island, to bring a more direct fire upon the fort than could be secured from the batteries at the mouth of the Schuylkill. The following ships, some of which are familiar from their services at Boston, Quebec, and New York, took part in the action, viz., the Somerset, 68, the Isis, 50, the Roebuck, 44, the Pearl, 32, the Liverpool, frigate, the Cornwallis, galley, and several smaller vessels. The Vigilant, 16, and a hulk of light draft, carrying three eighteen pounders, took a position in the channel between Province Island and the fort, and sharp-shooters from their tops picked off the gunners with great precision. Commodore Hazlewood was urged to assail them, but so utterly failed to coöperate with the garrison, as to more than balance his good conduct before Red Bank. Lieutenant-colonel Smith, wounded early in the action, was removed to Fort Mercer. Major Thayer succeeded to the command. Major Fleury, the engineer who planned the works, was also wounded ; and after a loss of two hundred and fifty men, the remnant of the garrison, on the night of the fifteenth, retired to Fort Mercer.

The British loss was thirteen killed and twenty-four wounded. At dawn of the sixteenth, the grenadiers of the Royal Guards occupied the island.

During the movements preparatory to this attack, General Washington ordered General Varnum's brigade to take post at Woodbury, near Red Bank; and General Forman was also directed to collect as many of the New Jersey militia as possible for the same purpose; but no attempt was made by the British to land upon the New Jersey shore.

In Washington's report of this action to Congress, he says, " The defense will always reflect the highest honor upon the officers and men of the garrison. The works were entirely beat down; every piece of cannon was dismounted, and one of the enemy's ships came so near that she threw grenades into the fort and killed men upon the platforms, from her tops, before they quitted the island."

On the eighteenth, General Cornwallis landed at Billingsport in force; but although General Washington sent General Greene to take command of the troops in New Jersey and check his progress, the demonstration was so formidable that the garrison abandoned the works on his approach.

The Americans, unable to save their galleys and other armed vessels, set fire to them near Gloucester Point; and the British forces had at last removed the obstructions of the Delaware.

Reference is made to the map " Philadelphia and Vicinity," and " Operations on the Delaware."

During this movement, the Marquis de La Fayette was intrusted by Greene, with a detachment of troops consisting of ten light horse, one hundred and fifty riflemen and a few militia.

Colonels Armand and Launney and the Chevalier Duplessis and Gimat were also with him. While on a scout toward Red Bank in the rear of the army of Cornwallis, he fell in with a Hessian force of three hundred and fifty men having artillery, and drove them back upon their supports. After several narrow escapes he eluded pursuit, and joined General Greene *via* Haddonfield, with a loss of only one man killed and six wounded. On the first of December he was assigned to the command of the division left vacant by the dismissal of Stephen.

At the same time four general officers of Washington's army, against eleven, voted to take advantage of the absence of General Cornwallis from Philadelphia to attack General Howe.

The American army had remained near Perkiomy creek until late in October, when it advanced to White Marsh. General Varnum's Rhode Island brigade twelve hundred strong, and about a thousand additional troops from Pennsylvania, Maryland, and Virginia had

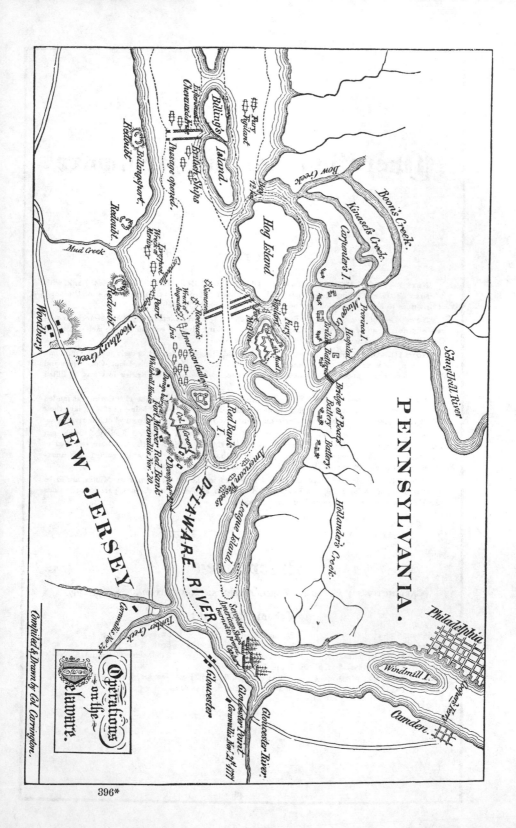

PENNSYLVANIA.

NEW JERSEY.

DELAWARE RIVER

Schuylkill River.

Boon's Creek.

Bow Creek.

Kinsase's Creek.

Carpenter's I.

Mud Creek

Province I.

Hospital

Billing's Island.

Hog Island

Fury
Vigilant

Cheraux de frise
Britist Ships
Passage opened.

Billingsport.
Redoubt.

Redoubt.

Woodbury

Woodbury Creek.

Wreck Liverpool
Merlin

Eberiments
of Roebuck
Wreck
Liverpool
Irist

Cameron's
of Roebuck
Fury
Vigilant

Nine Magon.

Hospital

Bridge of Boats

Battery.
Battery.

American Galley

Col. Green.

Red Bank
I.

American Vessels

League Island.

Seventeen
American Ships
burnt to prevent
being taken to Capture.

Hollander's Creek.

Windmill I.

Philadelphia

Camden.

Gloucester River.

Gloucester Point
Cornwallis Nov. 24th 1777

Gloucester

Timber Creek.

Cornwallis Nov. 24th 1777

Brig Fary & Fort Mercer, Red Bank
Attack Hes Cornwallis Nov. 20.

Operations
on the
Delaware.

Compiled & Drawn by Col. Carrington.

Operations on the Delaware

NOTES.

NOTE I.—**FORT MIFFLIN**, on Mud Island, and **FORT MERCER**, at Red Bank, with *Chevaux de frise* at Billings Island and Mud Island, and a redoubt at Billingsport, were the chief obstructions to British operations on the Delaware River, near Philadelphia.

NOTE II.—Col. Green, brave at Bunker Hill and at Quebec, commanding Fort Mercer, so successfully resisted an assault, Oct. 22d, 1777, that the attacking Hessian column lost 400 men, including Col. Donop, the commander, and Lieut.-Col. Minnigerode.

NOTE III.—On the 10th of November, 1777, Fort Mifflin was defended bravely, until, after a loss of 250 men, the remnant of the garrison retired to Fort Mercer. On the 15th, Lieut.-Col. Smith and Major Fluery, the engineer who planned the works, were wounded. The British loss was 13 killed and 24 wounded.

NOTE IV.—Col. Sterling (British) occupied Billingsport Oct. 1st, and on the 18th Cornwallis landed at the same point. The Americans thereupon abandoned Fort Mercer, and being unable to save their armed vessels, set fire to them, near Gloucester Point, and the British gained control of the river.

NOTE V.—Hon. J. W. Wallace, President of the Pennsylvania Historical Society, brought out clearly, in 1881, the fact that the very man who planted the obstructions in the Delaware, deserted to Lord Howe, and guided his boats in their removal; so that the ships of war which gained such unexpected access to Fort Mifflin, at the time of its capture, secured it by treason.

NOTE VI.—Among the British ships which shared in the attack upon Fort Mifflin, are to be recognized the **SOMERSET**, the **ROEBUCK** and the **PEARL**, which took part in operations near New York in 1776, as appears from maps of same.

References:

CARRINGTON'S "BATTLES OF THE AMERICAN REVOLUTION," pp. 391-397.

School Histories:

Anderson, ¶ 53-4; p. 80-1.	Holmes, ¶ 10; p. 128.	Swinton, ¶ 138; p. 133.
Barnes, ¶ 3; p. 120.	Lossing, ¶ 16; p. 156.	Scott, ¶ 10; p. 183.
Berard (Bush), ¶ 93; p. 162.	Quackenbos, ¶ 349; p. 251.	Thalheimer (Eclectic), ¶ *Note :*
Goodrich, C.A. (Seaveys), ¶ 17, p. 126.	Ridpath, ¶ 22; p. 206.	p. 159.
Goodrich, S. G., ¶ 8; p. 235.	Sadlier (Excel), ¶ 16; p. 193.	Venable, ¶ 144; p. 110.
Hassard, ¶ 15; p. 189.	Stephens, A. H., ¶ 31; p. 203.	

arrived.   Generals Gates and Putnam unadvisedly retained troops for
their semi-independent commands; and the former only grudgingly
sent such as were peremptorily ordered.   He had already taken active
part in movements which reflected upon Washington as Commander-
in-chief, and it required the personal visit of Colonel Hamilton, before
he would dispatch the troops which were absolutely indispensable at
headquarters, and as absolutely useless at Albany.   The history of
the "Conway Cabal" is omitted; but the general fact is noteworthy,
as it furnished to the British commander an element of strength, in
proportion as it weakened the army and influence of Washington.

On the fourth of December General Howe, with a force of fourteen
thousand men and accompanied by Lieutenant-generals Cornwallis
and Knyphausen advanced to Chestnut Hill, within three miles of the
right of the American army, and on the fifth advanced the Second
battalion and part of the First light infantry battalion, under Lieutenant-colonel Abercrombie, to feel the position.   A sharp skirmish
ensued, to the disadvantage of the Americans, resulting in the capture
of General James Irvine, and a small loss to both parties.

On the seventh, the British army left Chestnut Hill and took a
position on Edge Hill, near the American left.   General Morgan,
only just arrived from the Northern department, with his corps, and
the Maryland militia under Colonel Mordecai Gist, had "a sharp conflict with the First battalion of light infantry, and Thirty-third regiment
under General Cornwallis, resulting in a loss to the Americans of forty-
four, and at least an equal loss to the British troops.   Major-general
Grey and the Queen's Rangers, the Hessian chasseurs and one brigade
of British regulars made some impression upon the left wing, inflicting a loss of about fifty men : and both armies prepared for a general
action, the British pickets having been advanced within half a mile of
the American lines.

General Howe says, in his report of December thirteenth, "Upon
the presumption that a forward movement might tempt the enemy,
after receiving such a reinforcement (reported afterwards of four thousand men) to give battle for the recovery of this place (Philadelphia)
or that a vulnerable part might be found to admit of an attack upon
their camp, the army marched out on the night of the fourth inst."

General Washington says, " I sincerely wish that they had made
the attack, as the issue, in all probability, from the disposition of our
troops and the strong position of our camp, would have been fortunate
and happy.   At the same time I must add, that reason, prudence and

every principle of policy, forbade us quitting our post to *attack them*. Nothing but success would have justified the measure ; and this could not be expected from their position."

On the eighth General Howe abandoned his camp and returned to Philadelphia.

The army of Washington, nominally eleven thousand strong, is stated by Baron De Kalb to have had at that time but seven thousand effective men present for duty; so general was the sickness, owing to the extreme cold and the want of suitable clothing and other necessaries of a campaign.

There were not wanting officers, as well as leading civilians, who persistently pressed an immediate attempt to recapture Philadelphia.

Of the officers most officiously antagonistic to Washington, several were placed in high positions by Congress.

On the sixth of November Wilkinson, aid-de-camp of Gates, had been made Brigadier-general; and on the twenty-seventh Gates was made President of the Board of War. Mifflin, withdrawn from his duties as Quartermaster-general, but retaining his rank as Major-general, was also placed on the Board.

On the twenty-eighth of December, Congress appointed Conway Inspector-general and Major-general, and placed him in communication with the Board of War, to act independently of the Commander-in-chief. Lee, then a prisoner at New York, through letters, united with Gates, Mifflin, Wayne and Conway, to oppose Washington's policy and dictate his action; and more than that, there was a strong influence thereby exerted to compel his resignation or removal.

On the nineteenth of December Washington went into winter quarters at Valley Forge, twenty-one miles from Philadelphia. On the same day, a detachment under General Smallwood was sent to Wilmington to occupy the country south of Philadelphia to control supplies for that city, and to be generally useful in that quarter. McDougall was at Peekskill, and Putnam was on the shore of Long Island Sound near New York until nearly the middle of December, when he was ordered back to the Highlands.

The absence of Mifflin from the army and his neglect of his duties as Quartermaster-general, caused the " want of two days' supply of provisions ; and thereby cost," said Washington, "an opportunity scarcely ever offered of taking an advantage of the enemy." Washington reported, December twenty-third, that " two thousand eight hundred and ninety-eight men were unfit for duty, because barefoot and other

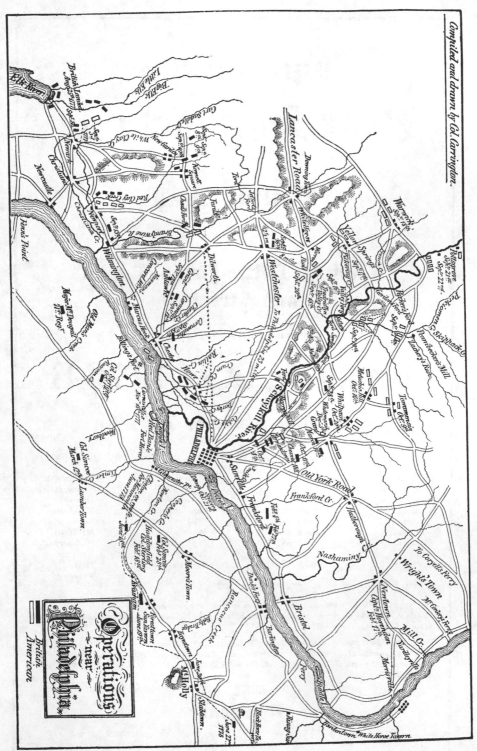

Compiled and drawn by Col. Carrington.

Operations
near
Philadelphia

British
American

398*

Operations Near Philadelphia

BEING AN

Outline Map

OF THE

Country, Battle-Fields, Roads and Streams

WHICH RELATE TO THE

Campaigns of 1776-8

From Elk River to Trenton

INCLUDING :

Philadelphia,	Germantown,	Whitemarsh,	Metuchen Hill,
Pennebecker's Mill,	Pottsgrove,	Warwick,	Yellow Springs,
Valley Forge,	Trudrufflyn,	Westchester,	Dilworth,
Chester,	Chads' Ford,	Kennett Square,	Wilmington,
Newark,	New Castle,	Elk River,	Billingsport,
Red Bank,	Haddonfield,	Moore's Town,	Mt. Holly,
Slabtown,	Yardleyville,	Donk's Ferry,	Hightstown,
Bristol,	Sunville,	Fort Mercer,	Newtown,
Billingsport,	Hillsborough,	Bordentown,	Paoli,
			Wyoming.

NOTE I.—Wayne, with 1,500 men, stationed at Paoli, was surprised, Sept. 20th, 1777, through the treachery of his old neighbors ; and it was his birth-place. He was in camp, near Trudrufflyn, and General Grey made the attack.

NOTE II.—Wyoming is known for an Indian massacre (p. 459—Carrington's Battles), and this massacre was settled (p. 475) by an expedition under Sullivan, James Clinton, Hand, Poor, and Maxwell, who, on the 29th of July, 1779, fought the BATTLE OF CHEMUNG, near the present site of Elmira, New York.

Reference :

CARRINGTON'S "BATTLES OF THE AMERICAN REVOLUTION," p. 398.

wise naked." "The numbers had decreased two thousand, from hardships and exposure in three weeks," (from the fourth of December.) "Only eight thousand two hundred men were present fit for duty," adding, "we have not more than three months in which to prepare a great deal of business. If we let them slip, or waste, we shall be laboring under the same difficulties all next campaign as we have been this, to rectify mistakes and bring things to order. Military arrangements and movements, in consequence, like the mechanism of a clock, will be imperfect and disordered by the want of a part."

To the remonstrances of the Assembly of Pennsylvania and others against his going into winter quarters, he says, " Gentlemen reprobate the going into winter quarters as much as if they thought the soldiers were made of sticks, or stones. I can assure those gentlemen that it is a much easier and less distressing thing to draw remonstrances in a comfortable room, than to occupy a cold bleak hill, and sleep under frost and snow, without clothes or blankets. However, although they seem to have little feeling for the naked and distressed soldiers, I feel superabundantly for them, and from my soul I pity their miseries which it is neither in my power to relieve or prevent."

On the twenty-sixth of December, General Sullivan, who apparently kept aloof from active participation in the movements of intriguing officers, urged Washington to make an attempt upon Philadelphia, and ' risk every consequence in an action."

Nothing moved Washington to depart from his matured plans, and on the thirty-first of December, 1777, his army was still building huts and struggling for life at Valley Forge.

De Kalb had been made Inspector-general the day before, *vice* Conway resigned.

During the year thus closed, the American privateers and vessels had made nearly four hundred captures, and Commodore Nicholas Biddle had gained great credit in handling the Randolph frigate in its disastrous collision with the Yarmouth 64. A brief *résumé* of the disposition of the American ships of war built during the struggle, will be found at the close of the campaign of 1781.

The two events of the campaign of 1777, which made the profoundest impression upon European States, were the surrender of Burgoyne and the battle of Germantown. News of the former occurrence reached London on the second of December. The language of Fox was eminently wise : " If no better terms can be had, I would

treat with them as allies ; nor do I fear the consequence of their independence." With sarcastic wit, he alleged that "the ministry had
mistaken the extent of the colonies, and considered Massachusetts as
including the whole."

It was evident that the seed sown by the employment of European mercenaries, as predicted by the Duke of Richmond (page 172),
would bear unexpected fruit, and that America would find in France
abundant aid. The previous purchase of arms had not been kept
secret, and it was evident that only an occasion was wanting for an
open declaration of sympathy with the United States.

The Duke of Richmond again advocated peace, and on the terms
of " Independence, and such an alliance or federal union as would be
for the mutual interests of both countries." Lord North, already
worn out in his country's service, and Burke, were solemnly impressed
with the conviction that "peace upon any honorable terms was in
justice due to both nations."

The king unwisely adjourned Parliament to the twentieth of
January.

A ship from Boston made a quick passage to France, and the
news from America made a profound sensation at Paris. At an interview of the American Commissioners with Count de Vergennes, Minister of Foreign Affairs, on the twelfth of December, that gentleman
in speaking of the report of the battle of Germantown, just received,
said, " Nothing has struck me so much as General Washington attacking and giving battle to General Howe's army. To bring troops,
raised within the year, to do this, promises everything." Couriers
were sent to Spain to solicit her coöperation, as already, without real
sympathy with America, she had discriminated in favor of American
privateers which took prizes to her ports. Without waiting for reply,
on the seventeenth of December, just when Washington was about
conducting his weary and well worn army to their winter huts, for
partial shelter and rest ; while his own spirit was pained by the small
jealousies which impaired the value of his services, and threatened the
harmony of his command, there was warming up across the ocean a
new ally and friend, and the power and prestige of France were
about to drop into the scales for the vindication and accomplishment
of American liberty. On that day Gerard, one of the secretaries of
Count de Vergennes, informed Franklin and Dean by the king's order,
that " the king in council had determined, not only to acknowledge, *but
to support* American Independence."

CHAPTER LIII.

OPERATIONS NEAR PHILADELPHIA FROM JANUARY TO JUNE, 1778.
VALLEY FORGE. BARREN HILL.

THE American army wintered at Valley Forge, and did not materially change its position until the evacuation of Philadelphia in June ensuing.

The months were full of self-sacrifice and real suffering on the part of the troops; while the British army enjoyed a considerable share of city comfort and social entertainment. One army lived in huts, and depended upon forced contributions from the country people for their scanty food, until Washington shrank from so arbitrary an exercise of necessary authority; while the other army had good quarters, abundant clothing, and such food and fuel as money could purchase in a restricted market. One army was drilling daily under Baron Steuben, to learn the rudiments of military service, so far as shoes and clothing could be provided; while their comrades sat or lay down by burning stumps and logs to escape freezing to death. The other army, according to Stedman and contemporaneous historians, enlivened the dull times with the dance-house, the theatre and "the game of faro.

One of General Howe's inactive intervals had arrived. Philadelphia, resting on a sufficient fleet, was not treated as a *base of operations*, but as snug and agreeable winter quarters. The chief activities of war were suspended. The license which an idle garrison life invariably evokes, began to arouse popular hatred; and the conduct of many commissioned officers was as blameworthy as that of the troops.

The occupation of the city, instead of a camp in the field, actually restricted all valuable field service; because a sufficient garrison had to be retained to ward off attack. The scouting parties from Washington's camp, even at midwinter, gave warning that he was alive and watchful; while their continual success in cutting off supplies from

26

the country as clearly indicated that the military occupation was simply within its picket lines.

General Howe stated, that he " did not attack the intrenched situation at Valley Forge, a strong point during the severe season, although everything was prepared with that intention, judging it imprudent until the season should afford a prospect of reaping the advantages that ought to have resulted from success in that measure, but having good information in the spring that the enemy had strength-ened the camp by additional works, and being certain of moving him from thence, when the campaign should open, he dropped thoughts of an attack."

Reference is made to map " Encampment at Valley Forge," copied substantially from that of Sparks, for an outline of the defensive position of Washington.

After the camp was occupied, it seemed as if the *quasi* antagonism to the Commander-in-chief began to fade out, month by month. It drew no breath from popular sympathy, and in spite of sickness, death, wretchedness and desertion, the soldiers were kept to duty and ac-quired toughness and spirit for future endeavor. A calm reliance upon the future, a strong will, and a straightforward method of deal-ing with men and measures, vindicated Washington's fitness for the supreme command.

During this period a diversion into Canada was proposed with General La Fayette in chief command. That officer accompanied by General the Baron De Kalb, and about twenty French officers, went as far as Albany, to inspect the preparations said to have been made for the expedition.

The army of General Gates had been previously withdrawn, and these officers found that less than a thousand effective men had been concentrated, and that neither clothing, provisions, nor transportation had been furnished. Generals Conway and Stark were also assigned on this duty. To the latter was intrusted the destruction of the British vessels at St. John's, and three thousand troops had been pledged for La Fayette's advance, and reported by General Gates as disposable. Stark could only send back the inquiry, " What am I to do?" "And what troops am I expected to raise?" He had nothing to do with, and this winter enterprise, initiated by the Board of War and approved by Congress, culminated in failure even to organize.

La Fayette was not yet twenty-one years of age, and at first felt some enthusiasm in an attempt to make the conquest of Canada, the

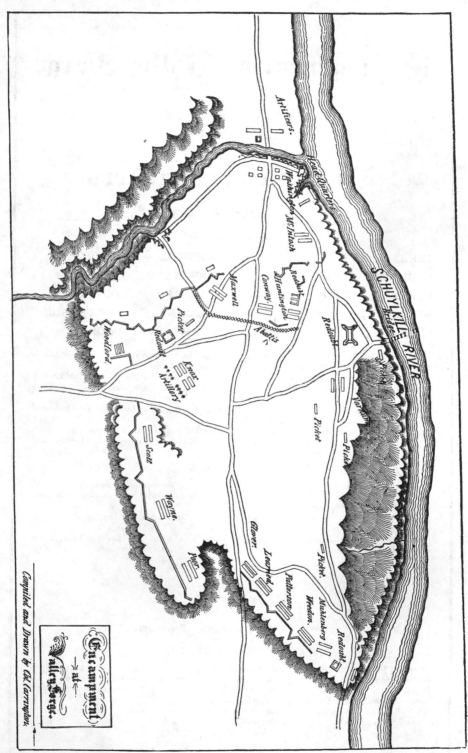

Encampment at Valley Forge.

Compiled and Drawn by Chs. Carrington.

SCHUYLKILL RIVER

402*

Encampment at Valley Forge

WINTER OF 1777-8

American Commanders

WASHINGTON

Commander-in-Chief

GEEENE	WAYNE	MAXWELL	LEARNED
STEUBEN	DeKALB	HUNTINGTON	McINTOSH
CONWAY	LAFAYETTE	VARNUM	SCOTT
WOODFORD	GLOVER	WEEDON	PATTERSON
LIVINGSTON	MUHLENBERG	DUPORTAIL	POOR

NOTES.—The encampment at Valley Forge is memorable for the great suffering which the American army endured, from extreme cold, want of clothing, and insufficient food.

The "Conway Cabal" or scheme for the removal of Washington from supreme command, which for a time had the practical endorsement of Gates and others, spent its force, and Conway returned to France.

During January, 1778, a committee of Congress visited Washington, and upon full examination of the condition of the army, decided to give him full support.

On the 27th of February, Baron Steuben arrived and took charge of tactical instruction.

On the 4th of April, Congress authorized Washington to call upon Pennsylvania, Maryland, and Virginia, for 5,000 militia.

On the 9th, Howe was recalled to England.

On the 10th, Lafayette returned.

On the 7th of May, news of the French alliance was received and solemnly celebrated.

On the 18th, Lafayette was established at Barren Hill, an advance position, midway between Valley Forge and Philadelphia.

On the 19th, Mifflin reported for duty ; and on the 20th, General Charles Lee joined, upon his exchange for Prescott, prisoner of war.

On the 18th of June, Clinton withdrew from Philadelphia, and the encampment at Valley Forge was abandoned for that pursuit of Clinton which resulted in the battle of Monmouth.

References :

CARRINGTON'S "BATTLES OF THE AMERICAN REVOLUTION," pp. 406-414.

School Histories :

Anderson, ¶ 55 ; p. 81.
Barnes, ¶ 3 ; p. 125.
Berard (Bush), ¶ 94 ; p. 163.
Goodrich, C. A. (Seaveys) ¶ 28 ; p. 129.
Goodrich, S. G., ¶ 7-8 ; p. 237.
Hassard, ¶ 1-2 ; p. 196-7.

Holmes, ¶ 13 ; p. 130.
Lossing, ¶ 1-2 ; p. 161-2.
Quackenbos, ¶ 352 ; p. 254.
Ridpath, ¶ 24 ; p. 207.
Sadlier (Excel.), ¶ — ; p. —.
Stephens, A. H., ¶ 32 ; p. 203.

Swinton, ¶ 153 ; p. 136.
Scott, ¶ 1-3 ; p. 189-90.
Thalheimer (Eclectic), ¶ 267 ; p. 152-3.
Venable, ¶ 145 ; p. 111.

former possession of France; but independently of the summary severance of his connection with Washington, which was made without consulting the Commander-in-chief, he soon discovered the folly of the enterprise.

During January a committee from Congress visited Washington at Valley Forge, and obtained some idea of his condition and necessities. On their return they recommended the adoption of his suggestions for the thorough reorganization of the army, both militia and regular, in respect of all elements of enlistment, outfit, and supply. Skirmishing was frequent as well as forays in pursuit of horses; and yet the men themselves did the greater part of hauling logs for huts and fuel, and they were severely tasked to maintain life and love of life.

The arrival of Baron Steuben on the twenty-seventh of February was a new element entirely, and it put the men at such work as stimulated their zeal and enhanced their confidence in their capacity to become soldiers. Officers and men alike were placed under the rigid training of this veteran *martinet*. He was the man for the hour; and the effects of his stern discipline and exacting drill were of permanent value. Although he volunteered his services, he soon received an appointment as Major-general, with this extraordinary *bonus* added, that it was given "without dissent or murmur."

In April Conway resigned, and went to France.

On the fourth, Congress authorized Washington to call upon Pennsylvania, Maryland, and New Jersey, for five thousand militia.

On the ninth, General Howe received his recall to England, and began to arrange for his departure.

On the tenth, La Fayette was again in camp.

On the thirteenth, General McDougall, assisted by Kosciusko, was busy at West Point, to make it the point of resistance to any further movements up the Hudson. General Gates was placed in command at Fishkill on the fifteenth. On the fourteenth, *instead of reinforcements of troops*, Lord North's Conciliatory Bills reached New York, and were published by Governor Tryon the next day. They maddened the British troops, incited mutiny, conciliated nobody and failed to modify the war.

Officers of the American army began to make plans for the ensuing campaign. Various objectives were presented, and opinions greatly differed. It is proper to place them on record, so that other differences with the Commander-in-chief may be more readily left to their individual merits.

Wayne, Patterson and Maxwell recommended Philadelphia; Knox, Poor, Varnum and Muhlenberg advised New York; Greene advised an attack upon New York with four thousand regulars and the Eastern militia, under Washington in person, leaving Lee to command in Pennsylvania, while the main army should remain at Valley Forge; Stirling proposed operations against both cities; while La Fayette, Steuben and Duportail had doubts as to *any* attack until the army should be strengthened, or the British army indicate its plans. This opinion was also that of General Washington.

On the seventh of May the British ascended the Delaware and destroyed public stores at Bordentown.

General Maxwell had been sent to their protection as soon as the expedition was under way, but his movements were retarded by heavy rains, and he failed to be in time to prevent the damage. A force under General Dickinson had been in that vicinity also, but it was too small to oppose the British troops. Several frigates and forty-four vessels, altogether, shared the fate of the stores.

The seventh day of May, 1778, was not entirely a day of gloom for the American army, then encamped at Valley Forge. The breath of spring quickened nature, and the forest began to stir and bud for its next campaign.

So the breath of Heaven bore a French frigate, La Sensible, 36 guns, to Falmouth Harbor (Portland) Maine, and there landed from her deck a herald of France, and he proclaimed an armed alliance between his country and the United States.

On the seventh of May, at nine o'clock, A. M., the American army was on parade. Drums beat and cannon were fired, as if for some victory. It was a day of jubilee, a rare occurrence for the times and place.

The brigades were steady, but not brilliant in their formation. Uniforms were scarce. Many feet were bare. Many had no coats. Some wore coats made of the remnants of their winter blankets. The pomp and circumstance of war was wanting. Strongly marked faces, good muscle, and vigorous action were to be discovered; but there was no such surpassing display of extrinsic splendor as enlivened Philadelphia, only eleven days later.

There was no review by general officers, with a well appointed staff. Few matrons and few maidens looked on. There stood before each brigade its chaplain. God's ambassador was made the voice to explain this occasion of their expenditure of greatly needed powder

The Treaty of Alliance was read, and in solemn silence the American army at Valley Forge united in Thanksgiving to Almighty God that he had given them *one friend on earth.*

One theme was universal: and it flutters yet in the breasts of millions:

" Praise God from whom all blessings flow."

Huzzas for the king of France, for Washington and the Republic, with caps tossed high in air, and a rattling fire through the whole line, terminated the humble pageant.

With the opening spring General Howe found himself constrained to send detachments for supplies and forage, which became scarce in proportion as Washington's army infested the country. Colonel Mawhood and Major Simcoe engaged a militia force under Colonel Holmes, at Quinton's Bridge near Salem, New Jersey, on the eighteenth of March, with little credit and little plunder. On the twenty-first of March another expedition, under Major Simcoe, accompanied by Colonel Mawhood, engaged the militia at Hancock's Bridge, five miles south of Salem, and the incidents, as recorded in Simcoe's own Journal, are not to his credit. On the first of May Lieutenant-colonel Abercrombie, with Major Simcoe, engaged militia under General Lacey, at the Crooked Billet, in Montgomery, Pennsylvania, inflicting some loss, but gathering neither food nor forage.

To cut off and restrict these detachments, Washington, on the eighteenth of May, advanced General La Fayette, with twenty-one hundred chosen troops and five pieces of artillery to Barren Hill, about half the distance toward Philadelphia. His orders gave him command over all outposts and skirmishing detachments, contemplated the contingency of an early evacuation of Philadelphia by the British army, and with caution as to prudence in taking his positions and risking doubtful movements, conferred large authority and discretion in the execution of his instructions.

It was practically a corps of observation, and it was the first really independent command of La Fayette, as a Major-general. The execution of his trust illustrates those peculiar traits of his character which had early attracted the favor of Washington, won his respect, and gradually deepened into an attachment almost paternal in its depth and endurance. The American Commander-in-chief, however reticent of his opinions, rarely failed to read men. He read La Fayette. With singular enthusiasm, great purity of character and purpose, unswerving fidelity to obligation, and thorough contempt for the mean or dishonorable, this young French gentleman, now Major-general, combined a quick sagacity, sound judgment and quick execution.

Reference is made to map " La Fayette at Barren Hill." The site for his camp was well selected. A steep, rocky ledge was on the right toward the Schuylkill as well as to the front where his guns were placed. Captain McLean's light troops and fifty Indian scouts were just below, near the Ridge road, and pickets were still further advanced on the road and in the woods. To the left was a dense forest, and just on its edge there were several stone houses well capable of defense. Six hundred Pennsylvania militia under General Porter were posted on the Whitemarsh road. The sudden retreat of this body without notice or reporting their action, very nearly involved his command in a conflict with more than double its force. At the forks of the two roads there was a stone church in a burying ground which was inclosed by a stone fence ; and La Fayette established his headquarters close by.

General Clinton had already relieved General Howe from the command at Philadelphia. Five thousand British troops were ordered to surprise the American camp at Barren Hill, and Generals Grant and Erskine were associated in the attempt. This command marched early on the morning of May nineteenth by the Lime-kiln and old York roads, and very early the next morning passed Whitemarsh, where it changed direction to the left toward Barren Hill, with the design of cutting off La Fayette's retreat by Swede's Ford. General Grey with two thousand men crossed the Schuylkill and marched along its west bank to a point about three miles below Barren Hill to be in readiness to act in concert with the other detachments. General Clinton with a third division marched by Chestnut Hill, and up the Manatawny road to make enclosure of La Fayette's command within their enveloping forces the more secure. The plan was skillfully conceived. While General La Fayette, as he states, was conversing with a young lady then on her way to Philadelphia, (ostensibly to visit friends, but really to obtain information) he was notified that red uniforms had been seen in the woods, near the road from White-marsh to Swede's Ford, in his rear. One hundred dragoons had been ordered to join him. They had scarlet uniforms and his first impression was that they were close at hand. To assure himself, he immediately sent scouts into the woods and learned the real facts. He changed front immediately, occupied the church, burying ground and all strong points, and then " made a display of false heads of columns," as if preparing to advance promptly upon the enemy.   General Grant halted his advance guard to await the arrival of the whole division, before engaging with the American troops.   The British column then on the Ridge road, also halted, and waited for assurance that the right had really reached La Fayette's rear ; and this was to be determined by an actual attack.

A country road ran from the church directly under Barren Hill to Matson's Ford, which was very little further from Valley Forge than Swede's Ford.   This road was entirely hidden from view by the hill. The British right rested at the crossing of the two principal roads to both fords ; and as will appear from the map, they were nearer to Matson's Ford than La Fayette was; but supposed that they controlled all approaches.

General Poor was ordered to lead the retreat, and La Fayette brought up the rear.   The troops retired in order and so promptly that the main body crossed the ford and occupied high and commanding ground as the British vanguard learned of the movement, and pressed on in pursuit.   As the last troops crossed, a brisk skirmish ensued over the guns, which were the last to follow ; but the retreat was perfected and the guns were saved.

General Washington had a distinct view of the British movement as it advanced, and fired alarm guns to warn La Fayette ; but the wisdom, coolness, and promptness of that officer saved his command. The American loss was nine, and that of the British was reported as three.

La Fayette relates the fact, that " fifty Indian scouts were suddenly confronted by an equal number of British dragoons," and that " the mutual surprise was so great that both fled, with equal speed."

The congratulations of Washington were as cordial on the return of La Fayette as the greeting of the British troops on their return was cool and impassioned.   No doubt had been entertained that the French Marquis would become the guest of the garrison that evening, and this was one of the minor disappointments of this fruitless expedition.

General Howe closed his official connection with the British service on the eleventh of May, but remained in Philadelphia until after the march to Barren Hill.

Extraordinary fetes, parades, salutes, and scenic displays, formed

part of a demonstration in his honor before his departure.   A regatta
on the Delaware, a tournament on land, triumphal arches, decorated
pavilions, mounted maidens in Turkish costumes, slaves in fancy habits,
knights, esquires, heralds, and every brilliant device, made the eigh·
teenth day of May memorable, from daybreak until dark.   Balls,
illuminations, fire-works, wax lights, flowers and fantastic drapery
cheered the night hours, exhibiting, as described by Major Andre, "*a
coup de œil*, beyond description, magnificent."   "Among the fairest
of the ladies was Miss Shippen, the subsequent second wife of Arnold."
At four o'clock on the morning of the nineteenth, the twenty-four
hours of hilarity, adulation and extravagance closed, and the army
hastened to Barren Hill to capture La Fayette.

On the nineteenth, General Mifflin reported at Valley Forge for
duty.

In a letter to Gouverneur Morris, dated May eighteenth, General
Washington expresses his " surprise to find a certain gentleman, who
some time ago, when a heavy cloud of darkness hung over us and our
affairs looked gloomy, was desirous of resigning, to be now stepping
forward in the line of the army," adding, " If he can reconcile such
conduct to his own feelings as an officer, and a man of honor, and
Congress have no objection to his leaving his seat in another department, I have nothing personally to oppose to it.   Yet I must think
that gentleman's stepping in and out, as the sun happens to beam
forth or become obscure, is not *quite* the thing, nor *quite* just, with
respect to those officers who take the bitter with the sweet."

Washington was already advised that the British army was about
to evacuate Philadelphia.   Repeated discussions occurred as to the
future action of the two armies.   The American army began to feel
the throb of hope as they realized that the pressure of a superior
force was to be withdrawn ; and the toil, self-sacrifice and anguish of
a wretched winter was relieved a little by the prospect of entering the
capital, as they entered it in the autumn of 1777.

On the following day a council of war was held, at which Major-
generals Gates, Greene, Stirling, Mifflin, La Fayette, De Kalb, Armstrong and Steuben, and Brigadier-general Knox were present, to hear
a statement of the condition of the two armies.

Washington under-estimated the British forces, as will be seen by
Note.   He estimated the British effective force at Philadelphia as ten
thousand ; that at New York as four thousand ; that at Newport as
two thousand.

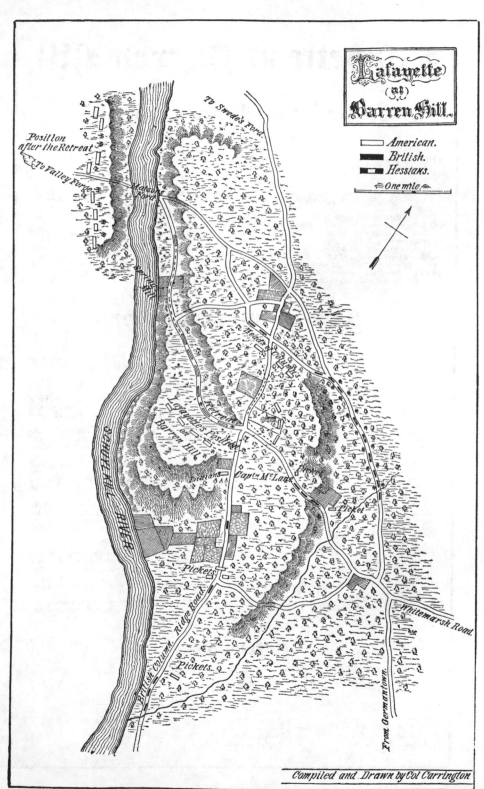

Lafayette
at
Barren Hill.

American.
British.
Hessians.
One mile.

To Swede's Ford.

Position
after the Retreat

To Valley Forge

Matson's Ford

SCHUYLKILL RIVER

Beaver Columns

Ferries

Lafayette's Position
on
Barren Hill

Indians

Capt. McLane

Picket

Picket

Pickets

British Column Ridge Road.

Pickets

Whitemarsh Road.

From Germantown.

Compiled and Drawn by Col Carrington

408*

Lafayette at Barren Hill

American Commanders
LAFAYETTE

POOR   POTTER   McLEAN

Strength, 2,100   Casualties, 9

MEM.—*During the spring of 1778, the repeated incursions out of Philadelphia into the country, to procure supplies for the garrison, induced Washington to establish an advance post at Barren Hill.*

The detachment consisted of 2,100 picked troops, with five pieces of artillery, and was intrusted to Lafayette, being his first independent command.

It was a corps of observation, to watch Philadelphia, and superintend outposts and skirmishing parties between Valley Forge and that city.

American Position.—Lafayette established his headquarters at a Stone Church, which was within a burying-ground and enclosed by a stone fence. A rocky, steep ridge, fell off to the south and toward the Schuylkill. At its foot, southward, the outpost of Captain McLean was established, and a camp of 50 Indian scouts. Another picket detachment was advanced far down the ridge road, and General Potter, with 500 Pennsylvania militia, was posted on the Whitemarsh road.

British Commanders
CLINTON

GRANT   ERSKINE   GREY

Strength, 5,000   Casualties, 3

British Movements.—The end of Howe's administration at Philadelphia was celebrated by a succession of *fetes*, closing after midnight of the 18th of May. At 4 o'clock of the morning of the 19th, Clinton, who had succeeded Howe, took personal command of a column of 5,000 men, and, with Generals Grant and Erskine, made an attempt to capture Lafayette and his command.

General Grey was sent up the west bank of the Schuylkill with 2,000 men to co-operate from that direction. The column which advanced by the Ridge road, was halted, to give time for General Clinton to occupy the road from Germantown to Swede's Ford, and thus cut off the retreat of Lafayette to Valley Forge.

NOTE I.—Potter's militia retired from the picket post without giving notice of the passage of Grant's column, which took a road through the woods, under the ridge, to the east.

NOTE II.—The advance guard of General Grant gained the rear of the American position and halted at the fork of the two roads leading to Matson's and Swede's fords, for the whole division to gain the summit.

NOTE III.—Lafayette was informed that scarlet uniforms had been seen in the woods to the rear. His scouts confirmed the fact that they were British, and not dragoons in similar uniforms, whom he expected from Valley Forge. His action was prompt. He made a strong demonstration of heads of columns, as if in full force, so that Grant declined to attack, until the arrival of his entire force. This delay was fatal to Clinton's entire plan.

NOTE IV.—A country road ran from the church, under Barren Hill, to Matson's Ford. The Indian scouts, confronted by a party of British dragoons, had fallen back in a panic, but the dragoons had retired with equal celerity from so unusual an enemy. Lafayette directed General Poor to withdraw by this road, and to push for Matson's Ford, instead of Swede's Ford, which was nearest to Valley Forge, while he covered the rear.

NOTE V.—The movement was so prompt that the ford was gained and the river crossed with a loss of but nine men; the British losing three.

NOTE VI.—Washington, from high ground, had witnessed the British march, and fired alarm guns; but the wisdom, coolness, and promptness of Lafayette, which saved his command, received the strong endorsement of the commander-in-chief.

References:

CARRINGTON'S "BATTLES OF THE AMERICAN REVOLUTION," pp. 405-409.

School Histories:

Anderson, ¶ —; p. —.	Holmes, ¶ —; p. —.	Swinton, ¶ —; p. —.
Barnes, ¶ —; p. —.	Lossing, ¶ —; p. —.	Scott, ¶ —; p. —.
Berard (Bush), ¶ —; p. —.	Quackenbos, ¶ 355; p. 255.	Thalheimer (Eclectic), ¶ —,
Goodrich, C.A.(Seaveys),¶ —; p. —.	Ridpath, ¶ —; p. —.	p. —;
Goodrich, S. G., ¶ —; p. —.	Sadlier, (Excel), ¶ —; p. —.	Venable, ¶ —; p. —.
Hassard, ¶ —; p. —.	Stephens, A.H. ¶ —; p. —.	

The Continental force at Valley Forge, including the sick and those on command subject to call on emergency, he reported as eleven thousand eight hundred; at Wilmington, fourteen hundred; and on the Hudson, at eighteen hundred.

The opinion was unanimous that the army should remain on the defensive, and await the action of the British commander.

On the twentieth of May, General Charles Lee joined the camp, having been exchanged on the twenty-first of April for Major-general Prescott, who had been very adroitly captured at his headquarters five miles above Newport, Rhode Island, on the night of the twentieth of July, 1777, by Lieutenant-colonel Barton of Providence. General Lee had been placed on parole as early as the twenty-fifth of March, and visited Philadelphia. His parole was extended so that he visited Valley Forge on the fifth of April, and York, where Congress was in session, on the ninth.

It is also to be noticed that on the fifteenth of June, while at Valley Forge, when there was still a doubt as to the ultimate plans of General Clinton after the evacuation of Philadelphia, General Lee addressed a note to General Washington giving his "opinion that the enemy would either go to Newcastle, to draw the American army out and fight it to advantage, or go to Maryland or Delaware or some other independent field where they could control water communications, and act in harmony with frontier Indian aggressions."

A ship of war reached Philadelphia on the seventh with commissioners to represent Lord North's Conciliatory Bills, and this delayed Clinton's movement; but Lee's letter to Washington could not have been more skillfully designed to mislead, if he had at heart the execution by General Howe of the plan he had himself hypothetically suggested while a prisoner of war at New York.

His letter to Washington was in harmony with his advice to General Howe; but the well known French alliance which ripened in January, 1778, made that movement impossible of execution by the British troops, and Lee sought by all means in his power to prevent a pursuit of their retiring army.

A brief retrospect will explain Lee's position.

During the month of February, 1777, he obtained permission from General Howe to send letters to Congress urging that commissioners be sent "to confer with him about confidential matters of vast interest to the national cause." On the twenty-first of February of the same year, Congress declined to send such commissioners "as altogether improper," and " they could not perceive how a compliance with his request would tend to his advantage or the interest of the public." On the nineteenth of March, Lee wrote again. This letter was received on the twenty-eighth ; and on the following day Congress again declined the proposition.

On the fifth of April, 1777, Lee wrote to Washington, " It is a most unfortunate circumstance for myself, and I think not less so for the public, that the Congress have not thought proper to comply with my request. It could not possibly have been attended with any ill consequences, and might have been with good ones. At least it was an indulgence which I thought my situation entitled me to. But I am unfortunate in everything, and this stroke is the severest I have ever experienced. God send you a different fate."

There were not wanting officers at that time, General Greene included, who supposed that the visit of commissioners could do no harm, but the people at large approved the action of Congress. The time had passed for compromise.

On the twenty-ninth, the day that Lee's second application was acted upon by Congress, that officer submitted a paper to the British commissioners which indicated his opinions, wishes and purpose. The original document was brought to light by George H. Moore, an eminent historical scholar, and librarian of the New York Historical Society, in connection with an address before that Society in 1870, and was officially endorsed by the British commission as " *Mr. Lee's plan, 29th March, 1777.*"

A few paragraphs are cited in this connection : " It appears to me that by the continuance of the war, America has no chance of obtaining its ends." " As I am not only persuaded from the high opinion I have of the humanity and good sense of Lord and General Howe, that the terms of accommodation will be as moderate as their powers will admit ; but that their powers are more ample than their successor would be tasked with, I think myself not only justifiable, but bound in conscience in furnishing all the light I can, to enable 'em to bring matters to a conclusion in the most commodious manner."

" I know the most generous use will be made of it in all respects ; their humanity will encline 'em to have consideration for individuals who have acted from principle." Then followed hypothetical data as to the number of troops required, and these sentences: " If the Province of Maryland, or the greater part of it, is reduced or submits, and the people of Virginia are prevented or intimidated from march-

ing aid to the Pennsylvania army, the whole machine is divided, and a
period put to the war ; and if it is adopted in full," (" Lee's plan,") " I
am so confident of success that I would stake my life on the issue."
" Apprehensions from General Carleton's army will, I am confident,
keep the New Englanders at home, or at least confine 'em to the east
side of the river.   I would advise that four thousand men be immediately embarked in transports, one-half of which should proceed up
the Potomac, and take post at Alexandria, the other half up Chesapeake Bay, and possess themselves of Annapolis."   The relations of
various posts to the proposed movement,—the character of the " German population who would be apprehensive of injury to their fine
farms," were also urged in favor of " *his plan* " for terminating the
war on terms " of moderate accommodation."

Washington answered the letter of General Lee, on the day it was
received, written only three days before the evacuation of Philadelphia ; and its contents indicate that he fully appreciated the manner
in which that officer attempted to influence other officers in the regulation of army movements.

" I have received your letter of this date and thank you, as I shall
any officer over whom I shall have the honor to be placed, for their
opinions and advice in matters of importance, especially when they
proceed from the fountain of candor, and not from a captious spirit,
or an itch for criticism, . . . and here let me again assure you
that I shall be always happy in a free communication of your sentiments upon any important subject relative to the service, and only
beg that they may come directly to myself.   The custom which many
officers have of speaking freely of things, and reprobating measures,
which upon investigation may be found to be unavoidable, is never
productive of good, but often of very mischievous consequences."

The encampment at Valley Forge was about to be deserted.
Washington and Lee were ready for the march to Monmouth.

British Effective Force.

NOTE.—From " Original Returns in the British Record Office." Date, March 26th,
1778.

	PHILADELPHIA	NEW YORK	RHODE ISLAND
British	13078	3486	1610
German	5202	3689	2116
Provincial	1250	3281	44
Total	19,530	10,456	3,770

CHAPTER LIV.

FROM PHILADELPHIA TO MONMOUTH. MONMOUTH AND VICINITY, 1778.

THE abandonment of Philadelphia by the British army had become a military necessity, because too remote from the sea coast, unless the Army of Occupation could be so reinforced as to be independent of support from New York. The detail of troops required by General Howe had not been made. The recommendation of General Amherst, military adviser of the king, "that forty thousand men be sent to America immediately," had been disapproved.

It was of vital importance under such circumstances, that Sir Henry Clinton should reach New York with the least delay and the least possible embarrassment from fighting on the march.

The moral effect of the proposed evacuation was in Washington's favor. The purpose of the English Cabinet to transfer all active operations to the Southern States had not been made public ; and when the British army took its departure with twelve miles of baggage train, thoroughly cumulative of all army supplies that could be loaded on wagons, it made a deep impression upon the people.

It indicated that the withdrawal of the army was no temporary diversion, in order to entice Washington from his stronghold to a combat in the field ; but it was a surrender of the field itself to his control. It announced that the royalists would be left to their own resources, and that the British army had not the strength to meet the contingencies of active operations, either in Pennsylvania or New Jersey. The embarkation of nearly three thousand citizens, with their merchandise and personal effects, to accompany the naval squadrons, was equally suggestive.

The coöperation of France in the resistance of the Colonies to British authority had been publicly announced by Congress, and the impending arrival of a French fleet hastened the movement. As a matter of fact, that fleet appeared at the entrance of Delaware Bay almost immediately after Admiral Howe turned Cape May, for New York.

The evacuation of Philadelphia began at three o'clock in the morning, June eighteenth, and the entire army was on the New Jersey shore by ten o'clock.

This movement had not been made so secretly that General Washington had neglected to anticipate its execution. General Maxwell's brigade and the New Jersey militia had been ordered to destroy bridges, to fell trees across the roads, and to so interrupt the march as to give time for his own army to place itself in a favorable position for offensive action. A detachment under General Arnold, whose wound still detained him from field service, entered Philadelphia just as the British rear-guard left.

Reference is made to maps, " Operations in New Jersey " and " Operations near Philadelphia."

General Clinton advanced to Haddonfield the same day. At this point the militia under General Maxwell made a short resistance and retired to Mount Holly Pass. This place was also abandoned as the strong British vanguard arrived ; but the destruction of bridges and other obstructions, combined with the excessive summer heat, made the march of the British army peculiarly painful and exhausting. Clinton, with his usual promptness, crowded so closely upon the Americans that they did not complete the destruction of the bridge at Crosswicks, and the British army passed the creek on the morning of the twenty-fourth.

The column of Lieutenant-general Knyphausen, with the provision train and heavy artillery, went into camp at Imlays' Town, while that of Cornwallis occupied Allentown, and thereby covered the other division from surprise from the north.

According to General Clinton's report, dated at New York, July 5th, 1778, " the column of General Knyphausen consisted of the Seventeenth light dragoons ; Second battalion of light infantry ; Hessian Yagers ; First and Second British brigades ; Stirn's and Loo's brigades of Hessians ; Pennsylvania Loyalists ; West Jersey Volunteers and Maryland Loyalists. The second division consisted of the Sixteenth light dragoons ; First and Second battalions of British grenadiers, the Guards, and Third, Fourth, and Fifth British brigades."

Upon receiving advices that Washington had already crossed the Delaware and that General Gates with the northern army was expected to unite with Washington, thus rendering a direct march to New York more hazardous, General Clinton threw all his baggage under the escort of General Knyphausen, placed it in advance, and occupied the rear with the second division, in light marching order, under his own immediate command; and took the Monmouth route to the sea.

Washington was notified of the movement and took definite action, in pursuit. He had crossed the Delaware, at Coryell's Ferry, nearly forty miles above Philadelphia, without assurance of the real purpose of his adversary. Having detached Colonel Morgan with a select corps of six hundred men to reinforce Maxwell, he marched to Princeton with the main army, and thence to Hopewell township, five miles distant, where he remained until the morning of the twenty-fifth. On the previous day, however, he had sent a second detachment of fifteen hundred chosen troops under Brigadier-general Scott, to reinforce those already in the vicinity of the enemy and more effectually annoy and retard their march.

On the twenty-sixth the army moved to Kingston; and having intelligence that the enemy had been seen moving toward Monmouth Court-House, Washington dispatched a third detachment of one thousand men under General Wayne, together with the Marquis de La Fayette, who was assigned to take command of the entire advanced corps, including Maxwell's brigade and Morgan's light infantry. Orders were given to La Fayette, to "take the first fair opportunity to attack the rear of the enemy."

That officer wrote from "Robin's Tavern, half past four, June 26th," "I have consulted the general officers of the detachment; and the general opinion seems to be that I should march in the night near them, so as to attack the rear-guard on the march. Your excellency knows that by the direct road you are only three miles further from Monmouth than we are in this place. Some prisoners have been made, and deserters come in amazing fast." "I believe a happy blow would have the happiest effect." *Again.* "At five o'clock," "General Forman is firmly of the opinion that we may overtake the enemy. It is highly pleasant to be followed and countenanced by the army; that, if we stop the enemy, and meet with some advantage, they may push it with vigor. I have no doubt but if we overtake them we possess a very happy chance."

Again: "Ice Town, 26th June, 1778, at a quarter after seven." "When I got there," referring to previously expressed purpose to go to Ice Town for provisions, "I was sorry to hear that Mr. Hamilton, who had been riding all the night, had not been able to find anybody who could give him certain intelligence; but by a party who came back, I hear the enemy are in motion, and their rear about one mile off the place they had occupied last night, which is seven or eight miles from here. I immediately put Generals Maxwell's and Wayne's brigades in motion, and I will fall lower down with General Scott's and Jackson's regiment, and some militia. I should be very happy if we could attack them before they halt." "If I can not overtake them, we could lay at some distance and attack them to-morrow morning. . . . If we are at a convenient distance from you, I have nothing to fear in striking a blow, if opportunity is offered." "*If you believe it, or if it is believed necessary or useful to the good of the service and the honor of General Lee, to send him down with a couple of thousand men, or any greater force, I will cheerfully obey and serve him, not only out of duty, but out of what I owe to that gentleman's character.*" The Italics are not so indicated in the original.

The following appeal had been made to General La Fayette by General Lee, when he found that the army was earnestly pressing upon the enemy: "It is my fortune and my honor that I place in your hands; you are too generous to cause the loss of either." La Fayette says in his memoirs, "This tone succeeded better," referring to Lee's change of opinion, and *claim* to the command; and the letter, above cited, contains the generous response.

At evening of the twenty-sixth the whole army advanced from Kingston, leaving their baggage so as to be able to support the advance corps with promptness, and reached Cranbury early in the morning. On the twenty-seventh a heavy rain and intense heat suspended the march for a few hours. Finding that the advance corps was bearing too far to the right to be assured of prompt support from the main body, orders were sent to La Fayette to take ground to the left, toward Englishtown. This movement was also executed early on the morning of the twenty-seventh.

The advance corps was at once strengthened by two additional brigades, as suggested by General La Fayette, and General Lee took command. The whole force thus detailed was about five thousand men.

The main army advanced to within three miles of Englishtown, and within five miles of the British army. The official reports of General Washington show that General Lee positively declined the

command of this advance corps, until its large increase rendered it
certain that it held the post of honor, and would be pushed upon the
enemy. La Fayette was first assigned to the command after a hot
debate in council as to the propriety of attacking Clinton's army at
all; and General Lee used the following language when that assignment was made with his concurrence ; that he " was well pleased to
be freed from all responsibility for a plan which he was sure would
fail." This statement is made important by subsequent events.

Morgan's command was now on the British right flank, and General Dickinson with between seven and eight hundred men, threatened their left. During the subsequent action, Morgan lay with his
corps three miles south of Monmouth at Richmond's Mills (Shuman's)
awaiting orders; only kept from participation in the battle by failure
to receive timely instructions as to his duty in view of the general
movement of the army to the front. It will be seen that he sent for
instructions as soon as he heard the sound of battle.

This battle of Monmouth has less clearness of definition than any
other action of the Revolution. The country had not been reconnoitered, and very loose reports were made, even by officers who were
on the ground, and who afterwards testified before the general court-
martial which tried General Lee.

On the part of the British army it was a bold and successful return
of the offensive, at the very moment when any other policy would
have threatened it with ruin. The pursuit of Clinton by Washington
was fully equal to the opportunity. The limitation of its success was
largely due to the conduct of General Charles Lee. Washington as a
matter of fact made no rash venture, as if in chase of a disappointed
adversary.

He neither underrated nor despised his enemy; but giving credit
for courage and wisdom equal to his own, measured the forces that
were to meet in conflict, and as usual, struck, or struck back as best
he could.

The American army was fully equal to that of the enemy in numbers ; and although fresh from Valley Forge, was not wanting in
energy and nerve. The supply of provisions was scanty, but the army
was eager in the pursuit. It felt the onward spur, when the force
which had so long kept it on the defensive, crossed the Delaware, in
full retreat from the old theater of conflict.

The military issue between Clinton and Washington was in some
elements quite unequal. Clinton *must regain New York.* He had

nothing to hope from a battle, more than a clear path to Sandy Hook. His heavy baggage train restricted his operations to the repulse of an attack, and rendered any protracted pursuit, even of broken columns, a fruitless strain upon his command.

But for Washington to have shrunk back from that retreating army, which he had been prompt to meet upon reasonable terms, would have accredited the British army with that invincibility which Lee affirmed of it; would have sacrificed the impetus which the offensive imparted to his command, and would have made every subsequent issue of the war more hopeless or uncertain. It would have canceled the memory of Trenton. It would have stultified the movement which made Germantown a pledge that the American Commander-in-chief was ready at all times to seize opportunity and do real fighting. Every attempted vindication of the conduct of General Charles Lee has one fatal defect. He knew that he could impair the standing of Washington only by such a limitation of his success as would place himself in the foreground as a wise counselor and commander. He had only to act upon his avowed opinion that American troops could not cope with British troops, and withdraw the former from a test of their mettle. La Fayette dissented from this assumption; but Lee was in command.

While all narratives agree that the advance of subordinate commanders was prompt and orderly, however blindly conducted, and in a direction favorable to success, it is equally clear that General Lee made no adequate effort to concentrate his divisions, promulged no definite orders:—and in the conduct of his own movements and the precipitate retreat, absolutely failed to control his army and keep it in hand. His presence inspired none, discouraged many, and absolutely left the divisions to work their own way out of confusion, as if there were no officer in general command.

A careful examination of the facts seems to exclude the idea that Lee was guilty of any overt act of treason; while it is equally true, that upon the basis of his antecedent opinion, and his expectation of failure, he did not make the proper effort to render that failure the least disastrous possible, and thus fulfill the obligations of high command.

The division which General Lee commanded on the twenty-eighth of June, 1778, according to the evidence of General Wayne, consisted of the following troops, besides the flanking detachments of Dickinson and Morgan. " In front, Colonel Butler with two hundred men; Colonel Jackson with an equal number; Scott's own brigade with a

27

part of Woodford's, six hundred, with two pieces of artillery; General Varnum appeared, about the same number, with two pieces of artillery: My own detachment was about one thousand, with two pieces of artillery; General Scott's detachment fourteen hundred with two pieces of artillery; General Maxwell's was one thousand and two pieces of artillery, in all five thousand, with twelve pieces of artillery, exclusive of the militia." General Lee claimed that this force, so loosely stated by General Wayne, did not exceed four thousand one hundred men; but the force which Grayson took to the front was nearly eight hundred men, and although temporarily detached from Scott's and Varnum's brigades, it must enter the aggregate and be counted as if not detached. The entire force which Lee had at *his disposal* on the evening of the twenty-seventh, considerably exceeded five thousand men, although he took no steps to communicate with Morgan and Dickinson until especially aroused by Washington to action. General La Fayette accompanied General Lee, with his consent, as a volunteer.

Position of the Armies. On the evening of June twenty-seventh, 1778, the British army encamped in a strong position, with their "right extending about a mile and a half beyond the Monmouth Court House, in the parting of the roads leading to Shrewsbury and Middletown, and their left along the road from Allentown to Monmouth, about three miles west of the Court House." This position, well protected on the right and left, and partially in front, by marshy ground and woods, was regarded by Washington as "too strong to be assailed with any prospect of success."

The general direction of the British line while thus encamped and when its march commenced, was south-easterly, exposing their left and centre to an attack from the American troops, whose offensive advance was from the north-west. It therefore became important for General Clinton to change his position and gain the Middletown road to the sea as quickly as possible, especially as a march of only ten or twelve miles would place him upon strong defensive ground beyond danger of successful pursuit. Lieutenant-general Knyphausen was under orders to move at daylight of the following day. The single road which was available for the proposed march, passed almost immediately into a series of bluffs where the baggage train would be greatly exposed to attack from skirmishing parties, and General Clinton undertook the protection of its rear by his own division of selected troops.

The American army was nearly three miles behind Englishtown, and only five miles from the British camp ; while the skirmishing detachments of Morgan and Dickinson were already on the alert for strokes at the British flanks, as the army should break camp.

Monmouth and Vicinity. The reports of Generals Washington, Clinton, and of many other officers who engaged in the battle of Monmouth, are so defective as to localities, that some explanation is necessary to an appreciation of the narrative. The distinctions of " right " and " left " are greatly confused, through the changing positions of the troops ; especially as the right and left of Clinton were reversed when he returned the offensive ; and the statement of officers that " Morgan was on the left " did not become true until they commenced their retreat. Thus, although Dickinson threatened the British left flank on the morning of the twenty-seventh, his demonstration was upon their right during their advance, later in the forenoon.

The Ravines. The terms " ravine," " morass," " first stand," and " last stand," " behind the morass," and " before the morass," are painfully disheartening to one who takes up this battle record, and they will receive notice. Three ravines, or morasses, as they are indiscriminately named, are mentioned by American officers. Clinton mentions only the two which intervened between his advance from the Court House and Washington's main army. The ravine or morass behind which Washington formed the divisions of Greene and Stirling to cover the retreat of the fugitive brigades, is about half a mile southeasterly from the old Meeting House, and about two and a half miles from Englishtown.

The early skirmish which led General Dickinson to believe that the British army had not left Monmouth, but was advancing in force toward the hill, was on high ground just east of this morass, this *west* ravine, and was simply the demonstration of light troops to throw off the American militia, and conceal the withdrawal of their main army. It was on this hill that the hedge-fence, the parsonage, and the orchard, near which the chief fight took place, were located. A second ravine or morass, which will be called the *middle* ravine, crossed the road not quite a mile to the east ; and on the east side of *this*, the British camp rested for a few hours after the battle. This high ground extended still farther eastward, and blended with the so-called " heights of Monmouth," and then dipped toward the low plain, one mile wide, and about three miles long, just east of the Amboy road, which ran from the Court House nearly due north. This narrow plain or valley where Clinton formed his line of attack was also marshy near a small pond, and along a small creek; the latter extending from near the Court House north-easterly, past Briar Hill; and this east ravine is that which Wayne, Varnum, Jackson, Scott, Grayson, and Oswald's artillery crossed and recrossed, and behind which they retired when the British line advanced in force. Just west of the Amboy road, and nearly parallel with it, "so as to cover both roads," is the high wooded ground where Lee proposed to re-form his line, and from which, in fact, the divisions had advanced into the plain without definite orders, or due regard to their mutual dependence and relations.

Water Courses. Wenrock Brook, as indicated upon the State Geological Survey of New Jersey, and recent township surveys, has been erroneously located by most authors. It unites with Geblard's Branch just beyond Englishtown as indicated on map "Operations in New Jersey," and map "Battle of Monmouth," and flows in the opposite course of that indicated by Irving, Sparks, and some others. At the head of the Manisquan, near Monmouth Court House, there was formerly marshy ground, where its small tributaries gathered their waters; and on the north side of Monmouth, Geblard's Branch was bordered by marshy ground. The small stream, or drainage, west of Briar Hill, sometimes called Briar Creek, is not, as sometimes indicated, a branch of Charles River, emptying in to Raritan Bay, but local, and was crossed at the time of the battle by a causeway or bridge. A small fork of the Manalapan brook flowed north-easterly from the Allentown road, and furnished the swampy ground which protected the left of the British camp on the night of the twenty-seventh.

General Features. The low plain below the slope from the Court House and the Amboy road, was quite open for at least a quarter of a mile, with woods well distributed beyond this narrow belt as far north as Briar Hill, to the Middletown road, on the edge of which Colonel Grayson halted his command, nearly parallel with the road upon which the British "column was marching." The summit between the Amboy road and the middle ravine was mostly in woods, with open ground near and just north-west of the Court House, where Butler drove back the Queen's Rangers. To the left of the British line, after it faced west to return the offensive, was another piece of woods out of which the dragoons advanced and from which a strong column emerged for an advance toward the Court House, to turn the American right and cut off Grayson, Scott, Jackson, Maxwell, and Oswald, when they retired behind the east ravine and reached the summit. The causeway and bridges are indicated on the map ; and as late as January, 1876, the middle ravine was still characterized by tangled underbrush and briars, as reported by officers after the battle. The present road from Englishtown runs considerably north of the old road, and there is no trace of two old paths referred to by witnesses on the trial. The fact that all the commanders refer to the *west* ravine, clearly indicates that they made common crossing at its bridge ; and although one division marched to the left from the Meeting House, while other troops took the sharp turn to the right at the forks, the two divisions finally took two routes, for the double purpose of extending their front to prevent flank attacks in a general advance, and to gain room for the movement.

There was difficulty in obtaining guides, and repeated halts ensued on that account. General Maxwell says that he advanced along a morass from the Meeting House, but crossed the hill finally occupied by General Stirling. The small creek emptying into Lules pond fulfills the conditions of his statement. He was informed that there was a second road to the north leading to Englishtown by Craig's Mill, and fears were expressed that the British troops would seek thereby to gain the American rear, but it was not attempted, and the entire retreat was finally made over the causeways at the middle and west ravines.

CHAPTER LV.

PREPARATIONS FOR THE BATTLE OF MONMOUTH, 1778.

GENERAL WASHINGTON, the American Commander-in-chief was in earnest pursuit of the British army under Lieutenant-general Clinton, as it marched from Philadelphia, *en route* for New York. The character of the American people and their reluctance to accept the restraints of strict authority had their effect upon the leader of their armies ; and his orders were sometimes so courteous, in form, that the element—"*do this*," was almost merged in a courteous *request*.

But Charles Lee was a professional soldier, and knew what Washington meant. He knew Washington better, when he took his final orders, on the twenty-eighth day of June, 1778, on the hill by Wenrock Creek, about two miles east of Monmouth Court House. He had been in command of nearly one-half of the American army during that day, and for the thirty-six hours preceding. It was his first active command after his exchange as a prisoner of war; and both at Valley Forge and at Kingston he had opportunity to learn the temper and purposes of his commanding officer. He was not left without more definite instructions after he solicited the command which closed his military career.

Washington's Instructions. The following is a statement of his instructions, as understood by those, (other than General Lee), who were charged with their execution, and it is taken from the record of "Proceedings of a general Court Martial which convened at Brunswick, July fourth, 1778, for the trial of Major-general Lee." Soon after noon, on the twenty-seventh of June, 1778, Washington assembled the senior general officers who belonged to the column, then under marching orders.

GENERAL SCOTT " heard General Washington say, in the presence

of General Lee, the Marquis de La Fayette, General Maxwell and himself, that he intended to have the enemy attacked, the next morning, or words to that effect; and Washington desired General Lee to
call his general officers together that afternoon, to concert some mode
of attack.   General Lee appointed the time, at half past five; but
before the officers met, General Lee had rode out:—fell in with General Lee that evening and told him, that *I had waited on him, and
asked him if he had any orders.*"   " He said he had none; but we
should not be disputing about rank, or what part of the line we should
march in."   " *On cross-examination,*" " understood that Lee was to
proceed on, and whenever he met the enemy, to take the earliest
opportunity to attack them."

General Wayne says;—" General Washington called upon General
Scott, General Maxwell and myself, the twenty-seventh of June, to
come forward to the place he and General Lee were talking, and there
recommended us to fall upon some proper mode of attacking the
enemy, next morning,"—" did not hear General Washington give any
particular orders for the attack; but he recommended that there
should be no dispute in regard to rank, in case of an attack; that as
General Maxwell was the oldest, he of right should have the preference; but as the troops that were under his command were mostly
new levies, and therefore not the troops to bring on the attack, he
therefore wished that the attack might be commenced by one of the
picked corps, as it would probably give a very happy impression."
" General Lee appointed the generals, who were there, to meet at his
quarters about five o'clock in the afternoon, which I understood was
for the purpose of forming a plan of attack on the enemy, agreeable
to the recommendation of General Washington."   " At the hour
appointed met with the Marquis de La Fayette and General Maxwell at General Lee's quarters."   " He said he had nothing further to
recommend, than that there should be no dispute with regard to
rank, in case of an attack, for he might order on, either the right or
the left wing, and he expected they would obey, and if they considered themselves aggrieved, to complain afterwards; that he had
nothing more to say on the subject, but that the troops were to be
held in readiness to move at a moment's warning."   *On cross-
examination :*—" Lee said the position of the army might render any
previous plan invalid, or words to that effect."   " I understood that
we were to attack the enemy on their march, at all events; and that
General Washington would be near us to support us with the main

army;—which, in its consequence, must, if we were pushed, inevitably have brought on a general action."

General Maxwell, "understood by what General Washington said to General Lee, that General Lee was to attack the rear of the British army as soon as he had information that the "front was in motion, or marched off," and he further mentioned that something might be done by giving them a very brisk charge, by some of the best troops. " General Washington mentioned something about my troops—that some of them were new, and in want of cartouch-boxes, and seemed to intimate that there were some troops fitter to make a charge than them." " He further recommended that we should go to General Lee's quarters, at six o'clock." " The orders I got there, were to keep in readiness to march at a moment's warning in case the enemy should march off," " that there should be no differences respecting rank, or which should be called to the front, right or left."

General Lee, in his defense says, "General Washington recommended to me a conference with those gentlemen, relative to any plan of operations to adopt; but as he only *recommended* the conference, I of course thought myself at full liberty on this head." It is to be noticed in this connection that General Lee knew the bold purpose of La Fayette, and that Wayne, Duportail and others had strongly urged the offensive, before the council of war held at Kingston. In his defense he does not state that he was under any obligation to adopt the plans of General La Fayette, or prosecute his policy; nor does he refer to Washington's instructions of the twenty-sixth.

In Washington's immediate answer to the letter written by La Fayette from Icetown, he says, " General Lee's uneasiness on account of yesterday's transaction, rather increasing than abating, and your politeness in wishing to ease him of it, have induced me to detach him from this army, with a part of it, to reinforce or at *least cover the several detachments at present under your command. At the same time that I feel for General Lee's distress of mind, I have an eye to your wishes and the delicacy of your situation; and have therefore obtained a promise from him, that when he gives you notice of his approach and command, he will request you to prosecute any plan you may have already concerted for the purpose of attacking or otherwise annoying the enemy; this is the only expedient I could think of to answer the views of both.* General Lee seemed satisfied with the measure." Washington wrote to the President of Congress on the morning of the twenty-eighth: " I am here (Englishtown) pressing hard to come up with the enemy. We have a strong and select detachment more forward, under command of Major-general Lee, *with orders to attack their rear if possible.*"

The question involved is this : Did General Lee have *no* knowledge of the purpose of Washington in sending more than five thousand men to the front, with the entire army in light marching order, under pledge to support the advance?

Doctor Griffiths stated upon the trial of General Lee, that " about one hour and a half after the action began," General Lee stated, that all was going as he expected ; that his advice had ever been contrary to a general action ; that it had been determined upon in a council of officers not to risk anything by an attack, *notwithstanding that he had that morning received positive orders from Washington to attack.*

Summary of Events. General Lee advanced to Englishtown, but remained inactive until Washington pressed him forward.

General La Fayette called during the evening of the twenty-seventh to know if any disposition of the troops had been made for the next day. " Lee thought it would be better to act according to circumstances, and had no plans." " Between one and two o'clock," as stated by General Lee's aids, " Washington sent an order directing that six or eight hundred men from Scott's and Varnum's commands should be at once sent forward to lie very near the enemy as a party of observation, in case of their moving off, to give the earliest intelligence of it ; to skirmish with them, so as to produce delay and give time for the rest of the troops to come up ; and directing him to write to Morgan to make a similar attack." This order was received as stated, before two o'clock A. M. Dickinson received his notice, and General Lee's aid-de-camp states that he sent a messenger to Morgan, but that officer did not actually receive any instructions until those given by Wayne during the battle to a messenger sent for orders.

"At four o'clock on the morning of the twenty-eighth," says La Fayette, " I went to Lee's quarters to know if there was anything new ; the answer I received was that one brigade was already marching. As I considered myself a volunteer, I asked General Lee what part of the troops I was to be with ; General Lee said, if it was convenient for me, to be with the selected troops. I put myself with them, in full expectation that these troops would act and be opposed to the British grenadiers."

At five o'clock, Dickinson reported to Generals Lee and Washing-

ton that the enemy had commenced their march.   Washington immediately sent orders to General Lee to " move forward and attack the
enemy, unless very powerful reasons prevented," and advised General
Lee that " the entire army had thrown aside their packs and was
advancing to his support."

The following remarkable statement taken from Lee's defense, is
cited in this connection without comment.   " I had no idea that his
excellency was to move from Englishtown, where I was informed he
was posted ; and that situation appeared to me the best calculated to
support my corps, of any I knew of in that country."   In another connection, he says, that on the march he noticed the hill where the final
stand was made to be an excellent position.   The movement of the
troops was very loosely made ; was simply putting them on the march,
and General Lee did not in person superintend that movement.

Colonel Grayson " received orders about three o'clock, to put Scott's and Varnum's brigades in readiness to march and to give notice when they were ready."
" Upon reporting to General Lee at Englishtown ;—was ordered to advance and
halt three miles from the enemy, and send repeated intelligence of their movements.
At the same time a written paper from General Washington to General Lee was
placed in his hands directing General Lee to send out six or eight hundred men as
a corps of observation, to give frequent information of the enemy's movements and
to attack them in case they began their march."

" At a distance of two and a half miles from Englishtown, was ordered to march
slow ; shortly after, to advance."   This brought Grayson to the bridge over the west
ravine ; where the *first skirmish*, hereafter mentioned, took place.

General Scott " had orders about five o'clock to follow Maxwell's brigade ;—
passed Englishtown ; was ordered to halt ; received an order from one of General
Lee's aids to march in the rear of General Wayne's detachment.   About this time
there was a halt of an hour ; marched to the Meeting-house, where there was a
second halt ; advanced a mile and then halted, when several pieces of cannon were
fired, and some small arms, in front of the column.

This brought *Scott* to the west ravine : He continues,—" Soon after I was ordered
on, and soon took a road to the left and then an old road to the right which brought
us into a field to the left of some of our troops that were formed where there was a
pretty brisk firing of cannon on both sides."   This was the location of the *third
skirmish* hereafter mentioned.

General Maxwell; "received orders after five o'clock, to put my brigade in
readiness to march immediately.   Ordered the brigade to be ready to march ; went
and waited on General Lee.   He seemed surprised I was not marched, and that I
must stay until the last, and fall in the rear.   I ordered my brigade to the ground I
understood I was to march by, and found myself to be before General Wayne and
General Scott, and halted my brigade to fall in the rear."

(A temporary diversion made by this brigade under General Lee's order, under apprehension that the enemy were advancing by Craig's Mills, far to the north, was countermanded by one of Washington's aids.)

"Came back to my former position, waited a considerable time before General Wayne and General Scott got past me; then I marched in the rear. There were three pretty large halts before I got up within a mile of the Court House. The Marquis de La Fayette informed me that it was General Lee's wish that we should keep to the woods as much as possible; that as I had a small party of militia horse, he desired I should keep these horse pretty well out upon my right." This light horse, La Fayette handled, as hereafter appears. "It was thereabouts that I heard some firing of cannon and small arms."

This refers to the *third skirmish.*

"The march was pretty rapid from that place, and I followed up General Scott until I got the front of my brigade in the clear ground. General Scott was about one hundred yards in my front." (See map.) "I did expect that General Scott would have moved to the right, as there was a vacancy between him and the other troops, but while I was riding up to him, I saw his troops turn about, and form in column, and General Scott coming to meet me. He told me our troops were retreating on the right and we must get out of that place; that he desired his cannon to go along with me as there was only one place to get over that morass (the east morass) and he would get out of that if he could. I ordered my brigade to march back."

General Wayne: "received orders to prepare and march. Having marched about a mile with a detachment, there was a halt made in front. Half an hour after received a message by one of General Lee's aids, to leave my detachment and come to the front and take command of the troops in front, that it was a post of honor. When I arrived there I found about six hundred rank and file, with two pieces of artillery from Scott's and Woodford's brigades, and General Varnum's brigade drawn up." "Scott's advanced up a morass, the other in rear of it." This was just at the close of the *first skirmish at the west ravine.*

"Upon notice that the enemy were advancing from the Court House, General Lee directed that the troops might be formed so as to cover two roads that were in the woods where the troops had advanced and formed."

"Colonel Butler with his detachment, and Colonel Jackson with his detachment, were ordered to the front. Colonel Butler formed the advance guard and marched on. The troops took up again the line of march and followed him. When we arrived near the edge of some open ground in view of the Court House, we observed a body of the enemy's horse drawn up on the north-west side, between us and the Court House. General Lee ordered the troops to halt, and by wheeling them to the right they were reduced to a proper front to the enemy's horse, though then under cover of the woods. General Lee and myself were advancing to reconnoiter the enemy. In advancing a piece forward, General Lee received some message which stopped him. I went on to a place where I had a fair prospect from my glass of the enemy. Their horse seemed so much advanced from the foot that I could hardly perceive the movement of the foot, which induced me to send for Colonel Butler's detachment, and Colonel Jackson's detachment, in order to drive their horse back.

I then detached part of Butler's people who drove the horse into the village. This was the *second skirmish* hereafter noticed.

"I could perceive the enemy were moving from us in very great disorder and confusion. In about ten or fifteen minutes the enemy made a halt, and appeared to be forming in some order. This intelligence I sent by one of my volunteer aids to General Lee, and requested that the troops might be pushed on. It was General Lee's orders that I should advance with Colonel Butler's detachment and Colonel Jackson's detachment. Upon advancing, the enemy took up their line of march and began to move on. I crossed the (east) morass, about three-quarters of a mile east of the Court House, (north-east) near to the edge of a road leading to Middletown, near the road where the enemy were marching upon.

"The whole of the enemy then in view halted. I advanced a piece (a short distance) in front of the troops, upon a little eminence, to have a view of the position and of their movements. Our troops were advancing and had arrived at the edge of a morass rather east of the Court House. The enemy then advanced their horse, about three hundred, and about two hundred foot to cover them. The horse then made a full charge on Colonel Butler's detachment, and seemed determined upon gaining their right flank, in order to throw themselves in between us and our main body which had halted at the morass. He broke their horse by a well directed fire, which ran "the horse" among their foot, broke them and carried them off likewise. (This was the *third* skirmish.) We had not advanced above two hundred yards, before they began to open three or four pieces of artillery upon us. They inclined first to our right, in order to gain a piece of high ground to the right of where I lay, nearly in front of the Court House. I sent off Major Biles to desire our troops that were in view and in front of the morass to advance. Our artillery began to answer theirs from about a half a mile in the rear of Butler's detachment, when Major Biles returned, and informed me that the troops were ordered to repass the morass, and they were then retiring over it. I galloped up to the Marquis de La Fayette, who was in the rear of Livingston's or Stewart's regiment, who said he was ordered to recross the morass, and form near the Court House, from that to the woods. I again sent to General Lee, asking that troops might be brought up. Major Biles or Major Fishbourne returned, and informed me that the troops had been ordered to retire from the Court House, and that they were then retiring. About the same time one of General Lee's aids told me that it was not General Lee's intention to attack them in front, but he intended to *take them*, and was preparing a detachment to throw upon their left. I then crossed the ravine myself, and went with General Scott to the Court House," but "after viewing the ground about the Court House, sent off one of my aids to General Lee to request him that the troops might again be returned to the place they had left. At this time the enemy did not appear to be above two thousand, about a mile distant in front, moving on to gain the hill before mentioned. A fire was kept up of cannon between us and the enemy at this time. Major Fishbourne returned and informed me that the troops were still retreating, and that General Lee would see me himself. Afterwards I perceived the enemy begin to move rapidly in a column toward the Court House. I again sent Major Lenox and Major Fishbourne to General Lee, requesting him at least to halt the troops to cover General Scott, and that the enemy were advancing, and also sent to order Colonel Butler to fall back, as he was in danger of being surrounded and taken."

" General Lee did not again go to the front, but fell back with the retreating troops, then a mile in the rear."

Colonel Jackson " received orders from Colonel Brooks, acting Adjutant-general of Lee's Division, to fall in the rear of Maxwell's brigade.   There was some misunderstanding between General Scott's detachment and General Maxwell's brigade, by both coming into the road at the same time, and I fell in the rear of General Scott's detachment.   While I was there I received orders to join the advance guard under the command of Colonel Butler.   We marched four or five miles " (from Englishtown) " when we discovered the enemy by Monmouth Court House, a party of horse and a party of infantry.   Colonel Butler was ordered off, and I imagine (correctly) to fall in between that party at the Court House and their main body.   At this time the division under General Lee halted.   Then came orders from General Wayne, for my detachment to immediately join Colonel Butler.   Before that I had orders from General Lee to support Colonel Oswald with his artillery.   Upon these orders coming from General Wayne, General Lee ordered me off immediately to join Colonel Butler."   Colonel Jackson finally gained a position upon the left (see map) and thus describes it.   " I did not like my position at all, as there was a morass in my rear, and a height that commanded the morass.   I asked Lieutenant-colonel Smith if he did not think it best for me to cross the morass and post myself on the height that crowned it.   He asked if I had any orders, I answered no.   He made reply, " for God's sake, don't move without you have orders.   I desired him, or he offered, to go, and see if there was any person to give me orders ; returned in a few minutes and told me there was no person there.   I told him, I'll risk it and cross the morass."

General Forman, " rode forward to discover the number and situation of the enemy, shortly after the enemy's horse had charged Colonel Butler's detachment ; then rode in quest of General Lee, and offered to take a detachment, and by taking a road upon our left, to double their right flank.   General Lee's answer was,—I know my business.   A few minutes afterwards I saw the Marquis de La Fayette direct Colonel Livingston's and Colonel Stewart's regiments to march toward the enemy's left, and I was informed by the Marquis, that he was directed by General Lee to gain the enemy's left flank.   In this time there was a cannonading from both parties, but principally on the part of the enemy.   The Marquis did not gain the enemy's left flank : as I supposed, it was occasioned by a retreat that had been ordered to the village, I presume by General Lee, as he was present and did not contradict it."

This movement, which detached the regiments of Stewart and Livingston from Wayne's brigade was that which is hereafter referred to, under notice of *third* skirmish, which induced the retreat of the entire American left.

Lieutenant-colonel Oswald, "joined Scott's and Varnum's brigades with four pieces of artillery, June sixteenth ; at half an hour after one in the morning of the twenty-eighth, we were assembled in the rear of Englishtown,—marched into Englishtown where we were detained for a guide.   The two brigades under the command of Colonel Grayson, advanced toward Monmouth Court House. When we reached the first morass, just in front of the position afterwards taken by Lord Stirling, we then received intelligence that the enemy were very near us. Colonel Grayson and myself rode up in front upon the hill where we found General Dickinson with a few militia. Colonel Grayson then advanced with his regiment where the militia were engaged and I followed with one piece of artillery. When we got in front of the hedge-row " (afterwards a point of resistance) " we saw no enemy, General Lee, General Wayne and some others rode off to reconnoiter the enemy. I received orders, as I supposed from General Lee, to join Scott and Varnum's brigades upon the hill. At this bridge, (the west ravine) we had crossed and re-crossed two or three times, in consequence of the intelligence we had received being vague and uncertain. Colonels Butler's and Jackson's regiments came up and were advanced in our front, in the road, Scott's and Varnum's brigades following them."

The subsequent movements of Colonel Oswald are embodied in the outline of the third skirmish, after he crossed the east morass.

Lieutenant-colonel Brooks, acting Adjutant-general, " received the order from General Washington to make the detail," already noticed, " about one o'clock in the morning; they began their march about six; about seven, Wayne's and Scott's detachments, Maxwell's brigade and Jackson's corps followed. I rode forward and found General Lee at the Meeting House of Freehold. Intelligence of the most contradictory nature was momently brought General Lee. This occasioned Varnum's brigade and a part of Scott's to pass and repass the bridge " (west ravine) " several times. General Lee now said he would pay no farther regard to intelligence, but would march the whole command and endeavor to find the enemy, and know their condition for himself. For this purpose Jackson's detachment was ordered from the rear to join the advance corps, the command of which was about this time given to General Wayne. Within view of Monmouth Court House, there was a halt for an hour, in which interval General Lee reconnoitered the enemy, who put on the appearance of retiring from the Court House somewhat precipitately, and in disorder. When they had retreated about a mile, on the Middletown road, they halted and formed on high ground. General Lee observed, that if the body now in view were all, or near all, that were left to cover the retreat of the main body, instead of pushing their rear, he would have them all prisoners; he marched his main body to gain the enemy's rear, leaving General Wayne with two or three pieces of artillery to amuse the enemy in front, but not to push them, lest his project should be frustrated. After coming into the plain, about a mile below the Court House, I observed the head of General Lee's column filing to the right, toward the Court House. A cannonading had now taken place between us and the enemy. When I came in the rear of Scott's detachment I perceived a very great interval between that and the front of Maxwell's brigade. Upon General Maxwell seeing me he asked if I had any orders from General Lee. I told him I had not. . . General Scott came up about this time and observed that our troops were going off the field toward the Court House. He asked me whether it was the case. I told him I knew nothing of it, if it was so. During this time all the columns except Maxwell's were moving to the right.   After having seen several battalions pass " (repass) " the ravine I returned to the point where General Maxwell was and found Generals Scott and Maxwell standing together. General Maxwell again asked me if I had any orders.   I told him I had not,"—" I rode toward the ravine to find General Lee, but finding the enemy were pushing that way, thought best to return and came round the ravine and found General Lee about a quarter of a mile this side " (west) " of the Court House. He said, you see our situation ; but I am determined to make the best of a bad bargain. The troops, in a very easy, moderate and regular way continued their march until they had passed the ravine," (middle ravine) " in front of Carr's House. Upon asking several officers who appeared to command the battalions why they left the ground, they said it was by General Lee's and the Marquis de La Fayette's orders."

Immediately after, the battle of Monmouth took place ; General Washington in person commanding.

Captain Stewart, of the artillery, " was on command with the Marquis de La Fayette.   On the road to the left of Monmouth Court House, about a mile, and about half after ten o'clock in the day, I heard the discharge of several pieces of cannon and some musketry in front.   I immediately unlimbered my pieces. . . .   General Lee came up and ordered me to limber, and be ready to march on immediately toward the enemy, toward Monmouth Court House ; at the same time, General Varnum's brigade and the Marquis's detachment obliqued to the right, leaving General Scott's brigade and Colonel Jackson's corps more on the left."

Colonel Stewart of Wayne's brigade asked General Lee " where he should take his men," after the retreat began, and he answered, " take them to any place to save their lives, pointing to an orchard in front."

Captain Mercer, aid-de-camp of General Lee, says, " I was sent by General Lee with an order to General Dickinson, to inform him that he intended to attack the enemy as soon as he was certain of their march for Middletown.   About one o'clock in the morning we were waked up by a letter from General Washington, signed by Colonel Hamilton." . . . " After Colonel Grayson had marched, I was ordered by General Lee to write to the Marquis de La Fayette that he might immediately put himself at the head of Wayne's and Scott's detachments.   I don't conceive that the troops were ready before eight o'clock or half-past eight, at which time General Lee set out from his quarters." . . . " Subsequently," as stated in report of *third skirmish,* " the three regiments in General Wayne's detachment, Colonel Wesson's, Stewart's and Livingston's were ordered to the right." " The enemy were then marching back again to the Court House. General Lee said he believed he was mistaken in their strength, but as they were returning to the Court House, there would be no occasion to push that column further to the left, as they were in the rear already." At this point, the retreat of Grayson, Scott, and Jackson had become a necessity.   " He then ordered me to Scott, with orders for him to halt his column in the wood, and continue there until further orders.   I asked him where I should find General Scott, as I had not been there when the front of the troops filed off. He pointed to the wood over the ravine, and told me I should find them there." I made what speed I could to the ravine, but my horse being very tired I was some time a going. I found great difficulty in passing it as it was very deep and miry. When I got over to the other side, I found Colonel Jackson's regiment retiring over the ravine again.   I took a transient enfilade view of the enemy ; the party nearest us seemed to be a brigade of artillery ; a column of the enemy appeared at a great distance, marching toward the Court House on the right.   I supposed they might be about, not quite, three thousand men ; their horse, very considerable, in my idea."

This officer's testimony is immaterial except as it shows the want of system with which the army was handled.   The testimony of La Fayette, Knox, and twenty-seven officers not cited, simply indicates one fact ; that the division was never concentrated, received no definite orders, and *handled itself*.   The apology for these facts will be found in the record of the battle.

CHAPTER LVI.

THE BATTLE OF MONMOUTH, 1778.

THE Battle of Monmouth was fought during the afternoon of June twenty-ninth, 1778, at Wenrock Creek in Monmouth County, New Jersey; General Washington and General Sir Henry Clinton in person respectively commanding the American and British armies. The original purpose of the American Commander-in-chief has been already stated. The division of General Lee advanced too late in the morning to realize that purpose, and the mismanagement of the troops after they marched, as certainly imperiled the whole army.

The criticisms of the battle of Monmouth do not appreciate that relation of the two columns which gave to five thousand American troops an immense advantage, by striking just where General Washington expected the blow to fall, *viz.*, upon the flank, or rear of a marching column, covering at least four miles of heavy road.

The preliminary movements already adverted to in the evidence cited, will be again noticed for a more definite appreciation of the battle itself.

The first skirmish, was that of Dickinson's reconnoitering party, on the hill just east of the west ravine, between seven and eight o'clock in the morning. Colonel Grayson had advanced with his select detachment, beyond the Freehold Meeting House, half a mile. General Dickinson sent a messenger to Washington and Lee with notice of the British retreat, as early as five o'clock in the morning.

When Colonel Grayson approached the first ravine, he " saw firing, and a party of militia retreating from the enemy."

General Dickinson was then engaged with a small flanking party which had been detached from the British left wing, and which he erroneously supposed to be the advance guard of their returning army. He sent for aid. Colonel Grayson crossed the bridge with one regi-

28

ment and one of Oswald's guns, and just as he ascended the hill, the British retired. General Lee arrived soon after. At this time there was thorough confusion of opinions as to the position and movements of the enemy. General Dickinson claimed that the British were returning from the Court House. Other informants stated that they were retreating towards Middletown. There was some reason for the persistency with which each, "with some heat" pressed their views, as there had been no reconnoissance, in force. General Lee, however, insisted that the British army *had* retreated.

General Clinton states that "Lieutenant-general Knyphausen marched at daylight; and that he descended into the plain at eight o'clock." The statements that the British had left, and that they had not left, were consistent with the facts as known to the different messengers, since General Dickinson referred to the early movement; and the presence of Clinton's division near the Court House and of the flankers with whom he engaged, induced the mistaken opinion that the army itself had returned to take the offensive. As the result of this confusion, the brigades of Scott and Varnum and Colonel Durgee's regiment crossed and recrossed the west ravine several times, as stated by those officers.

The presence of some controlling mind was needed: Troops were rapidly concentrating and halting, until at last General Lee pushed Colonels Butler and Jackson forward, each with two hundred men, and then went in person, to reconnoiter the position. As soon as General La Fayette arrived, the whole division crossed the ravine and advanced toward the Court House. It had been discovered, by this time, after nine o'clock, that the British left wing had entirely left the Allentown road and was marching toward Middletown. The opportunity for striking it on the left flank, while so greatly extended, *had been lost.*

The second skirmish, was with a small rear guard, north-west of the Court House, when Butler, then in advance, acting under the orders of General Wayne drove back the Queen's rangers. La Fayette with a few light horse from Maxwell's brigade, passed beyond the Court House into the plain, to reconnoiter, and the rear guard of the British army was then "a mile in advance." Wayne had taken a position on the left of the road leading to the Court House "having been assigned to the post of honor," as stated by General Lee, with orders to press lightly upon the British rear guard, and to hold it until a movement could be made to cut it off from the main column. As soon as the

Queen's rangers were driven through the village, General Wayne hastened Colonel Butler across the east ravine, and placed his detachment, with two guns, upon a small eminence in the plain, while the other brigades were following the general lead of those in advance, until they formed an irregular line as far as Briar Hill.

The third skirmish took place just after Butler reached the position last referred to, and while the troops were moving from the woods near the Amboy road, to the plain beyond the east ravine, under the general direction of General Wayne. The British light dragoons made a charge upon Colonel Butler which was successfully repulsed. Colonel Grayson was in advance with an orchard to his left; Jackson about a hundred yards in his rear; then Scott somewhat detached, and Maxwell on the edge of the morass. Grayson was informed by a messenger from General Wayne, that he must hold his ground, as the enemy was retiring. He "hallooed to Jackson to come and form upon the hill, (Briar Hill) upon his left." This movement was one which threatened Knyphausen's column, just when it was buried in a long defile, and Clinton was at once aroused to activity to save the baggage train which he supposed the Americans were attempting to attack. Colonel Jackson disregarded the request of Colonel Grayson, because he had no artillery. Scott was then a little to the rear and right of Jackson. Maxwell expected Scott to move to the right, to join on Wayne, close the gap, and let him into the line. Wayne meanwhile held the regiments of Wesson, Stewart, and Livingston to the left of Varnum, to cover Butler with whom he advanced still further into the plain, and also to cover Oswald's artillery, which had drawn two additional guns from Varnum's brigade, and was exchanging shots with the artillery of the enemy. Major Mercer of General Lee's staff told Grayson that his place was in the rear of Wayne, who had no right to order him to the position he held on the left. General Lee states that " he sent Major Mercer, and then a second officer, with express orders to General Scott to hold his position." As a matter of fact, Scott was under Grayson's command, and both were so associated with Wayne, that when he moved toward the Court House, as subsequently ordered, they followed his movements, and received no intimation that they should have done otherwise until the movement was actually made, and the whole army was retreating, by detachments, before the advance of the British army. The American troops had deployed quite at their own discretion. Oswald maintained his guns in position until his ammunition was exhausted, and then retired behind the morass. There he met General Lee, who ordered him, upon obtaining ammunition, to continue firing, and this was done over the heads of Butler's advance detachment, and with great danger, according to the evidence, of doing injury to those troops. At this stage of the conflict, General Lee sent orders to General Wayne to move toward the right, nearer the Court House, where the enemy were threatening a movement. The regiments of Livingston and Stewart began the movement. This, for want of orders to the contrary, was considered by Grayson and Scott as a general retreat, and that opinion was confirmed by the evident pressure of the British left toward the Court House, while their centre and right emerged from the woods into the plain, thus threatening to sever the American line, already weakened in the centre, and cut off the regiments which were on the left toward Briar Hill. The artillery had not returned, and was playing from time to time in the rear of the morass. Grayson, Scott, Jackson, and Varnum recrossed the morass, and with Maxwell entered the wood upon the hill west of the Amboy road. It was not until then, that the messengers from General Lee intimated to General Scott that he was to remain steady on the left. They communicated orders to re-form the line in the woods on the high ground, the right resting on the village. General Lee states that he supposed the houses were of stone, but when he found that the village was open, and the houses were of wood, he fell back before the British advance. General Lee says " the retreat in the first instance was contrary to my intentions, contrary to my orders, contrary to my wishes."

But the entire division was in fact retreating, quickened at this time by his orders ; and the left wing only saved its connection with the main body by a march through the woods, leaving their guns to the charge of Colonel Oswald, who, with his few men, brought off ten pieces, after taking but two into action at first. It was at this period that a messenger from General Morgan, " having in vain sought for General Lee," applied to General Wayne for instructions, and was informed that " he could see the condition of things for himself, and report the facts to General Morgan."

Thus, before eleven o'clock or half-past eleven, the British column, which had been retreating by the Middletown road, had formed an oblique front to the rear, extending, according to the evidence of General Knox and Colonel Hamilton, who saw " *no signs of any plan for the coöperation of the different American brigades in resistance to the movement*," from Briar Hill to the marsh east of and near the Court

House. The British troops appeared in the edge of the woods, hardly a mile distant, and were variously estimated at from fifteen hundred to twenty-five hundred men. The force of Lee then disposable for attack or resistance, if properly in hand, was not less than three thousand men, besides Grayson's detachment. Wayne, during the hour and a half while he was in the plain, sent three times to urge General Lee to advance with the troops, and as he states, refrained from pressing the attack too strongly under instructions, and constantly expecting that General Lee would carry the left wing around the right of the British line to cut it off from the main body.

General Lee's purpose, as understood by General Wayne, and as stated by Lee himself *was* to so swing his left about the British right as to *take them*, and he also states that when he notified General Washington, who sent to learn the progress of the army, that he was confident of success, he supposed the British rear-guard not to exceed fifteen hundred men. His estimate was correct, at the time, as his whole division was then pressing to the front, eager to engage the enemy; but at noon the British army had realized the weakness of the pursuit, and gained time to turn it into a failure. General Lee, in his defense, ridicules the application of General Wayne for support; but *not* in connection with his statement that he placed him at the post of honor, nearest the enemy, and with the largest control which any subordinate officer had over the movements of the picked troops then in front. General Lee admits that he sent no messenger to Washington to advise him of the retreat, and in his appeal to the Court Martial, states that he could appreciate the feelings of Washington when the column rolled back upon him without previous notice of disaster; but that when he met Washington and exchanged words with him, he did not know that the men had thus disorderly fallen back upon the main body.

The retreat. The British army emerged from the woods, and pressed toward the Court House. General La Fayette first reported to General Lee that the right was threatened, having previously been checked in his advance of the American extreme right, by General Lee's personal direction. General La Fayette then consulted General Wayne, and placed the regiments of Livingston and Stewart in position to resist the British advance, which was steady, solid, and in good order.

The details of the retreat of different brigades and regiments are not to be considered. An entirely erroneous opinion prevails as to

their behavior. It is true that there was some confusion, through
want of some authoritative direction of their movements; but it is to
be noticed that there was nothing of the nature of a panic. No commander knew why he retreated, only that such were understood to be
the orders, and that others retreated, and no troops could have rallie l
more promptly than they did, when they felt the presence of Washington. General Lee deserves credit for self-possession, and a real
purpose to bring the men away in safety, when he found he could not
handle the division. The troops had marched and countermarched
under blind guidance, during a day of extreme heat, were falling by
the wayside, fainting with thirst, and worn out, with no stimulus of
hope to hold them up, and the retreat of Monmouth was the victory
of manhood over every possible discouragement that could befall an
earnest army in pursuit of a retiring adversary. Regiment after regiment, brigade after brigade hastened to cross the west ravine, and, to
his credit, Lee came with the last column. At this point the broken
detachments found the main army. Some went to its rear to rest and
rally for a fresh advance in the evening. Some turned about and
fought until their pursuers retired from the field. Colonel Ogden says,
he begged General Maxwell to halt his regiment and face the enemy,
and he did so without difficulty. The division of General Lee was
saved by the self-possession of its officers, and the wonderful endurance of the rank and file.

*The ordeal of Valley Forge saved the army. The arrival of Wash-
ington restored it.*

The Fourth Skirmish, developed the BATTLE OF MONMOUTH. It
was as conspicuous for the promptness of the American troops to respond
to intelligible orders, and for rigidity in position under fire, as their first
exposure to the enemy had been ungoverned and loosely presented.

The cannonading before noon aroused Washington to his full
fighting capacity. The return of his aid-de-camp with the assurance
that General Lee had overtaken the British army, and expected to
cut off their rear-guard, was received as a vindication of his previous
judgment and as an omen of success. The troops dropped every incumbrance and forced the march. Greene took the right at the
Meeting House, and Stirling led the left directly toward the hill where
he subsequently took his strong position. The vanguard under Washington approached the bridge at the west ravine, when repeated interruptions of his progress began to warn him that the battle waited for
the presence of the Commander-in-chief.

First, a mounted countryman, then a frightened fugitive fifer, told his story. " After a few paces, two or three more persons said, that the continentals were retreating." The whole career of Charles Lee was quickly brought to view. Vague and painful suspicions and more painful apprehensions aroused Washington to duty. Harrison and Fitzgerald were dispatched to find out what was the matter. They met Major Ogden. His explanation, strongly expletive, was simply, " They are flying from a shadow." Officer after officer, detachment after detachment, came over the bridge, all alike ambiguous in their replies, or ignorant of the cause of their retreat. Colonels and generals came with broken commands, all knowing that they were retreating, but no one able to say more than that such were the orders, and that " the whole British army was just behind." Washington hastened toward the bridge and met Ramsey and Stewart, Wayne and Varnum, Oswald and Livingston. Upon them he threw the burden of meeting the British columns, and, leading the way, he placed them on the hill. On the left, in the edge of the woods, he established Ramsey and Stewart with two guns, with the solemn assurance that he depended upon them to stop pursuit. On the right, back of an orchard, and covered by a thick hedge fence, he placed Wayne and Varnum, and Livingston ; and Knox and Oswald established four guns there. Maxwell and other generals as they arrived were ordered to the rear to re-form their columns, and La Fayette was intrusted with the formation of the second line, until he could give the halted troops a position which they might hold while he should bring up the main army to their support. It was such an hour as tests great captains and proves soldiers.

Already, with the last retreating column, General Lee had appeared, and finding the troops in line, he addressed himself to a change of their positions and such an arrangement as he deemed best under the circumstances. It had been his purpose, as he states, after he passed Carr's House and after consultation with Wickoff, who knew the country, to place artillery on Comb's Hill, which attracted his attention. Mr. Wickoff showed him that he could take fence rails and make a crossing of the morass and that the British army could not attack him without making a circuit of three or four miles to the south ; but he said there was no time for that, and continued his retreat. While demanding the reason for the existing disposition of the troops on the hill near the west ravine he was informed that Washington had located the troops himself. Regarding this as virtually superseding him in command, he reported to General Washington for orders, and was met by the peremptory demand for " an explanation of the retreat." General Lee seemed to have been overwhelmed by Washington's sternness of manner and replied, " Sir—sir." Upon repetition of the inquiry, he stated that " the contradictory reports as to the enemy's movements brought about a confusion he could not control," and reminded Washington that " the thing was done contrary to his opinion, that he was averse to an attack, or general engagement, and was against it in council,—that while the enemy were so superior in cavalry we could not oppose them." Washington then replied that he " should not have undertaken it unless prepared to carry it through," that, " whatever his opinion might have been, he expected his orders would have been obeyed." General Lee in explanation of this interview, says, " some expressions let fall by the General, conveyed the idea that he had adopted some new sentiments, and that it was his wish to bring on a general engagement. This idea drew forth some sentences such as related by Colonel Tilghman " above quoted :—" that when he set out in the morning it was with the conviction that it was never his intention to hazard or court a general engagement. What his excellency meant by saying that I should not have undertaken what I had no intention of going through with, I confess I did not then, nor do I this day, (August, 1778) understand. The several councils of war held, on the subject of the operations in the Jerseys, reprobated the idea of risking a general engagement, as a measure highly absurd in the *then* circumstances of America (for since the time those councils were held, circumstances are much altered) " and adds, " But whatever may have been the good sense of those councils, I shall readily allow that they ought to have little or no weight with an officer, if subsequent orders from the Commander-in-chief, or even a hint communicated, had been of such a nature as to give reason to think that the idea had been discarded, and that the General had adopted a plan repugnant to those councils." " No letter I received, no conversation I ever held with him, indicated an intention, or wish, to court a general engagement ; if he had I protest solemnly that whatever I might have thought of the wisdom of the plan, I should have turned my thoughts solely to its execution." General Washington closed the interview by asking General Lee if he would take command, while he could form the army in the rear. Lee says, " When Washington asked me whether I would remain in front and retain the command or he should

take it, I answered, that I undoubtedly would, and that he should
see that I myself should be one of the last to leave the field.   Colonel
Hamilton flourishing his sword, immediately exclaimed, " That's right,
my dear General, and I will stay and we will all die here, on the spot."
Lee says:—" the position was not one to risk anything further than
the troops which then halted on it," and ridicules what he styles
Colonel Hamilton's " flustrated manner and phrenzy of valor," and
adds " I answered, I am responsible to the General and to the continent, for the troops I have been entrusted with.   When I have taken
proper measures to get the main body in a good position, I will die
with you, on the spot, if you please."

It is worthy of record that no witness on the trial of General Lee
puts profane words in Washington's mouth, neither does General La
Fayette in his memoirs, but all accounts concur, that his personal
bearing, manner and tone of voice were expressive of that sublime
wrath which followed his conviction that the country and the army
were willfully imperiled by the disobedience of Charles Lee.

Washington placed his army in position ; Greene on the right ;
Stirling on the left, where an admirable disposition of artillery prepared him to withstand the British column, and La Fayette was
placed in command of the second line.   General Greene sent five guns
to Combs' Hill, where they would have enfilading fire upon the British
columns as they advanced against Wayne's line, and the battle of
Monmouth began.

General Clinton " marched at eight o'clock A. M.   Soon after,
some reconnoitering parties appeared on the left flank " (Dickinson's
skirmish).   " The Queen's Rangers fell in with, and dispersed some
detachments among the woods, in the same quarter " (Butler's skirmish).   " The rear-guard having descended from the heights above
Freehold, into a plain, about three miles in length and about one in
breadth, several columns of the enemy appeared likewise descending
into the plain, and about ten o'clock they began cannonading our rear.
Intelligence was at this instant brought me, that the enemy were
discovered marching in force on both our flanks.   I was convinced
that our baggage was their object ; but it being at this juncture
engaged in defiles, which continued for some miles, no means occurred
of parrying the blow, but attacking the corps which harassed our
rear, and pressing it so hard as to oblige the detachments to return
from our flanks to its assistance.   I had good information that
Washington was up with his whole army, estimated at about twenty

thousand; but as I knew there were two defiles between him and the corps at which I meant to strike, I judged that he could not have passed them with a greater force than what Lord Cornwallis' division was well able to engage. The enemy's cavalry, commanded it is said by M. La Fayette, having approached within our reach, they were charged with great spirit by the Queen's light dragoons. They did not wait the shock, but fell back in confusion upon their own infantry. Thinking it possible that the event might draw to a general action, I sent for a brigade of British and the Seventeenth light dragoons from Lieutenant-general Knyphausen's division, and having directed them on the march, to take a position effectually covering our right flank, of which I was most jealous, I made a disposition of attack upon the plain; but before I could advance, the enemy fell back and took a strong position on the heights above Freehold Court House. . . . The British grenadiers, with their left to the village of Freehold, began the attack with so much spirit that the enemy gave way immediately. The second line of the enemy, on the hill east of the west ravine, stood the attack with great obstinacy but were likewise completely routed. They then took a third position, with a marshy hollow in front, over which it would have been scarcely possible to have attacked them. However, part of the second line made a movement to the front, occupied some ground on the enemy's left flank and the light infantry and Queen's rangers turned their left. By this time our men were so overpowered by fatigue that I could press the affair no farther, especially as I was confident the end was gained for which the attack had been made. I ordered the light infantry to join me; but a strong detachment of the enemy" (Wayne) " having possessed themselves of a post which would have annoyed them in their retreat, the Thirty-third regiment made a movement toward the enemy, which with a similar one made by the First grenadiers, immediately dispersed them. I took the position from whence the enemy had been first driven after they had quitted the plain, and having reposed the troops till ten at night to avoid the excessive heat of the day, I took advantage of the *moonlight*,* to rejoin Lieutenant-general Knyphausen, who had advanced to Nut swamp near Middletown."

The attack which was "withstood" with great obstinacy, was at the hedge-row where the Second battalion of British grenadiers suffered extremely, losing their gallant commander Lieutenant-colonel Monckton, whose body fell into the hands of the Americans. Adol-

* No moon, after ten o'clock.

phus states that " relays of grenadiers buried his body, taking turns during the battle, and using bayonets for shovels, mingling tears with the earth they cast upon his body." The grenadiers fell back after the third assault *without* rescuing the body of their leader, and the Americans withdrew behind the ravine. The attempt of General Clinton to cross in force, and turn the American left and right, in turn, was met by Generals Stirling and Greene with promptness; and General Wayne's command, which was directly in front of the bridge, maintained such a galling fire that the regiments referred to by General Clinton were promptly withdrawn.

Upon the retreat of the British army behind the middle ravine, messengers were sent to Englishtown to bring a portion of the troops which had been sent there for re-formation, under the direction of General Steuben, at the time of the first retreat. When the troops retired from the hedge-row, General Lee reported to General Washington, and " requested his excellency's pleasure, how he should dispose of the troops, whether to form in front, along with the main body, or draw them up in the rear." He " was ordered to arrange them in the rear of Englishtown at three miles distance." General Steuben says, " I joined General Lee on horseback before a house, who said he was very glad of my having taken that charge upon me, for he was tired out." " General Maxwell's brigade, a part of General Scott's detachment, were formed behind the creek at Englishtown; then three brigades of the line which arrived with General Patterson, and the second brigade of General Smallwood. The cannonading continued more or less briskly until past five o'clock. Half an hour after it ceased, Colonel Gimat arrived and brought me the order from the Commander-in-chief, that the enemy were retreating in confusion, and that I should bring him a reinforcement. I ordered General Maxwell to take the command of the troops I had placed behind the creek, and to remain there till further orders. I then marched off with the three brigades of the second line. As I passed through Englishtown, I again met General Lee, who asked me ' where I was going;' I imparted to him the order I had received from the Commander-in-chief, which I delivered in the very expressions of Colonel Gimat, that the enemy were retreating in confusion. Upon that word *confusion*, he took me up, and said they were only resting themselves; but said he afterwards, ' I am sure there is some misunderstanding in your being to advance with these troops.' It was not until General Muhlenberg, who led the column, halted, and the precise orders of

General Washington were repeated, that General Lee could understand that the cessation of firing was actually occasioned by the retreat of the British army, and not by the defeat of the army of Washington. 'Then,' said he, 'you are to march,' and General Steuben marched with the troops."

During the evening General Woodford's brigade was advanced on the right, and General Poor's on the left, for the purpose of an early attack upon the British army the following morning. General Clinton having realized every possible benefit from his return of the offensive, skillfully withdrew his army, and the oppressive hot weather prevented pursuit.

The British casualties as reported by General Clinton were as follows : Lieutenant-colonel Monckton, Captain Gore, Lieutenants Vaughan and Kennedy, four sergeants, and fifty-seven rank and file *killed;* three sergeants and fifty-six rank and file died from fatigue ; Colonel Trelawney, Lieutenant-colonel Simcoe, Major Gardner, Captains Cathcart, Bereton, Willis, Leighton, Powell, Bellue and Ditmas, and Lieutenants Kelley, Paumier, Goroffe, Desborough and Gilchrist, seven sergeants. one hundred and forty-eight rank and file *wounded*, and sixty-one rank and file *missing*.

General Washington reported the American casualties as follows : Lieutenant-colonel Bonner, Major Dickinson, three captains, three lieutenants, one sergeant, eight artillery men, and fifty-two rank and file *killed* ; two colonels, nine captains, six lieutenants, one ensign, one adjutant, nine sergeants, eleven artillery men, and one hundred and twenty-two rank and file *wounded* ; five sergeants, one artillery man, and one hundred and twenty-six rank and file *missing*, many of whom who had been overcome by the heat, afterwards came up."

The two reports indicate nearly equal casualties in the two armies. General Washington states that four British officers, and forty privates whose wounds were too dangerous to permit their removal, were left on the field by General Clinton, and that the parties having in charge the burial of the dead, reported the British dead at four officers, including Lieutenant-colonel Monckton, and two hundred and forty-two privates. With due allowance for the usual errors in reports of burying parties, it is evident that the detail of General Clinton's report is defective, as it leaves many men unaccounted for, who were dropped from his subsequent report of the strength of his army.

Lord Mahon says, " On the whole it was a pitched battle."

Adolphus says, " The affair ought to have terminated when Lee was first compelled to retire. There was no hope of making an advantageous assault on the enemy protected by defiles and marshes."

Lamb says, " The conduct of Washington was highly creditable to his military skill."

Stedman states that " It was impossible to attack Washington's front with any prospect of success, that the judicious position which he took probably saved his advanced corps from total ruin."

Gordon says, " Washington animated his forces by his gallant example, and by exposing his person to every danger common to the meanest soldier," and that " the behavior of the American troops in general, after recovering from the first surprise occasioned by the retreat, was mentioned as what could not be surpassed."

A General Court Martial, Major-general Stirling presiding, found General Lee " guilty of disobedience of orders in not attacking the enemy on the 28th of June, agreeable to repeated instructions, of misbehavior before the enemy, by making an unnecessary, and in some few instances a disorderly retreat ; and of disrespect to the Commander-in-chief, in two letters dated the 1st of July (29th June), and the 28th of June (30th June), and sentenced him to be suspended from command for the term of twelve months."

(The error in the date of the first letter was corrected by General Lee on the 30th, when he made another misdate, as above corrected).

The finding of the Court Martial was sustained by Congress, by fifteen affirming and seven dissenting votes. General Lee was not known then as he subsequently made himself known, and he had strong partisan advocates of his cause. If he had been in sympathy with Washington, he would have received no censure. If he had exercised reasonable self-control at the close of the action, he would have saved his commission. He contended indeed with many difficulties. He " knew few of the officers," the country was unknown, the guides were few, and his staff seem to have been inefficient, even in executing his restricted orders ; but he had earnestly solicited the command, and thus fatally closed his military career at Monmouth.

His subsequent death was marked by an atrocious contempt of his Maker, and of religion, so that even in his will he perpetuated that hatred of moral responsibility and true duty which rendered his success while living absolutely impossible. It is but justice to the reader of history, that this element of Charles Lee's character should be perpetuated ; not only for its painful lesson, but as affording an additional key to the motives and conduct of his restless career.

CHAPTER LVII.

FROM MONMOUTH TO NEW YORK. SIEGE OF NEWPORT. CONCURRENT EVENTS.

GENERAL Sir Henry Clinton reached New York the last of June without further detention. At that date the only considerable posts in the Northern States which remained under his control, were those of New York, Staten Island, and Newport, Rhode Island. Sir Augustine Prevost was in command at St. Augustine, Florida. The British Cabinet resolved to renew operations in the Southern States as soon as practicable, and that General Carleton should again occupy the posts on Lake Champlain. This was consistent with the plan suggested by General Lee, who expressed the opinion, in a letter to General Washington, immediately after the battle of Monmouth, claiming immediate trial before a general Court Martial, that "the campaign would close the war."

General Clinton was hardly settled in his headquarters, when the post at Newport was threatened by a large American force, acting in concert with a French fleet. General Washington marched from Monmouth to Brunswick, where he rested his troops; thence to Paramus and Haverstraw Bay, on the Hudson, and finally reestablished his headquarters at White Plains on the twenty-second of July.

On the eighth the Count D'Estaing made the Delaware Capes with the following squadron of twelve ships, and four frigates, viz., Languedoc, 90; Tonnant, 80; Cæsar, 74; Guerriere, 74; Protecteur, 74; Provence, 64; Valliant, 64; Saggitaire, 54; Chiniere, 30; L'Engeante, 26; L'Alemence, 26; L'Arimable, 26. The Chiniere was sent to Philadelphia with Silas Deane, one of the American commissioners just returned from Paris, and Monsieur Conrad A. Gerard, the first French Ambassador to the United States.

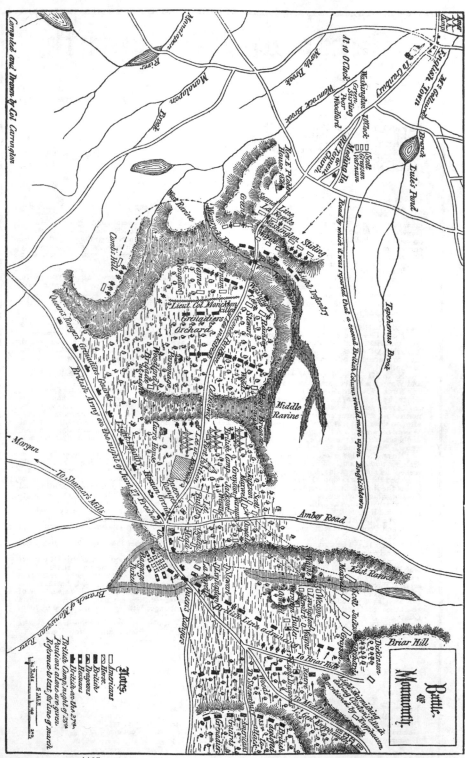

Battle of Monmouth.

Battle of Monmouth

JUNE 29th, 1778

American Commanders	British Commanders
WASHINGTON	**CLINTON**
LAFAYETTE, STIRLING, GREENE	
LEE, WAYNE, POOR, GRAYSON	CORNWALLIS
KNOX, LIVINGSTON, VARNUM	KNYPHAUSEN
MAXWELL, JACKSON, MORGAN,	MONCKTON
WOODFORD, HAMILTON,	SIMCOE
DICKINSON, STEWART.	

Strength, about 12,000 to each Army.

MEM.—*For Clinton's route from Philadelphia, see map, p. 49.*

American Pursuit of Clinton.—Lafayette was entrusted with the advance column, as Lee declined the command, from opposition to the movement. Its gradual reenforcement to nearly 6,000 men, convinced Lee, that if one-half of the army should move upon the enemy, and the senior Major-General be left behind, it would compromise his honor. Lafayette generously yielded the command, on condition that the original plan should be carried out ; and Washington pledged the support of the entire army. That plan, was to strike the British line obliquely, while it was extended for nearly twelve miles with its baggage, and, by the accumulating force of the successive American divisions, to destroy or capture it, in detail.

British Position and Action.—The map indicates the British camp on the night before the battle, with all trains judiciously parked, on the right, so as to lead promptly toward New York, with the main army interposed for its protection. The Policy of Clinton was to gain New York with least delay and loss.

Three subordinate and spirited skirmishes occurred, before the final battle, at which Washington took command in person.

NOTE I.—Clinton started Knyphausen for Middletown with his baggage at daylight, and descended into the plain, beyond the *east ravine*, with the main army, at 8 o'clock.

NOTE II.—The *first skirmish* was between seven and eight o'clock, just east of the *west ravine*, between Dickinson's advance and Clinton's rear guard. Wayne, Jackson and Varnum soon joined. As early as 5 o'clock, Washington had been advised that Clinton was in motion, and sent orders for Lee to pursue, while assuring him that the army had thrown aside its packs and would follow promptly.

NOTE III.—The *second skirmish* was near the Court House, in which Lafayette, as well as Butler and Wayne, actively participated, and forced the Queen's rangers to retreat.

NOTE IV.—The *third skirmish* was that development of the American troops, nearly 6,000 men, which, by its deployment in the plain and its close pressure of Clinton, compelled him to change front to the rear, and give battle. Already the American left wing had so far advanced as to overlap to the northward, and threaten the ravine through which Knyphausen was urging the baggage train. Lafayette, on the right, was hopeful. Varnum and Oswald in the centre, opened their guns with effect, as Wayne advanced, but through a transfer of Livingston and Stewart to the right, breaking the line, and disconnecting the centre and left, and, a want of systematic handling by Lee himself, the whole army fell back, under his orders.

NOTE V.—This retreat, which became confused through conflicting rumors and orders, was general, but not a panic. The troops, disappointed, and over-heated under the blazing sun, hurriedly passed the middle ravine, but were promptly halted by the stern command of Washington as they approached the west ravine. He at once established Livingston, Stewart, Ramsey, Wayne and Varnum across the line of British approach ; while Lafayette placed in position the divisions of Stirling and Greene, which had rapidly followed the commander-in-chief. The repulse of Monckton at the hedgerow, where he fell, was brilliant ; and the artillery of Knox, at the right, and Stirling on the left, of the second line, with Wayne's sharp Infantry fire, checked the effort of Clinton to force a passage.

NOTE VI.—At night, Clinton retired behind the middle ravine, closely followed by Woodford on the right, and Poor on the left, but, before midnight, he abandoned his camp and secured his retreat to New York.

NOTE VII.—The intense heat increased the casualties, and the desertions from the British army were nearly 2,000. The killed and wounded on each side varied little from 300.

NOTE VIII.—Lee opened a disrespectful correspondence with Washington, was tried by court martial, was suspended for a year, and never resumed duty. Monmouth was the only action of the war in which he actively participated. He was sent to Connecticut from Boston in 1776 on recruiting service, thence to New York to help fortify ; thence to South Carolina, where he urged that Moultrie abandon his fort ; thence to the North, where he only embarrassed Washington, until he was out of the way, as a prisoner of war. As a prisoner of war, he betrayed the weak points of the American resistance, to General and Admiral Howe, and, on his exchange, bitterly opposed the pursuit of Clinton.

NOTE IX.—Washington marched from Monmouth to Brunswick, thence to Haverstraw on the Hudson, and on the 22d of July placed his headquarters at White Plains, above New York.

References:

CARRINGTON'S "BATTLES OF THE AMERICAN REVOLUTION," pp. 412-445

School Histories:

Anderson, ¶ 72-4 ; p. 86.
Barnes, ¶ 2 ; p. 127.
Berard (Bush), ¶ 98 ; p. 164.
Goodrich, C.A.(Seaveys), ¶ 32-3; p. 131-2.
Goodrich, S. G., ¶ 4-8 ; p. 238.
Hassard, ¶ 9-12 ; p. 199-200.

Holmes, ¶ 18 ; p. 133.
Lossing, ¶ 4-6 ; p. 162.
Quackenbos, ¶ 5-8; p. 257.
Ridpath. ¶ 6-7 ; p. 210.
Sadlier (Excel), ¶ 9; p. 108.
Stephens, A. H. ¶ 3-6; p. 205-6.

Swinton, ¶ 167 ; p. 138.
Scott, ¶ 6-10 ; p. 191-2.
Thalheimer (Eclectic), ¶ 272 ; p. 155.
Venable, ¶ 146; p. 112-13.

The remainder of the squadron having nearly four thousand troops on board, sailed for Sandy Hook as soon as advised of the evacuation of Philadelphia.

The French fleet sailed from Toulon on the thirteenth of April, but on account of contrary winds, did not pass Gibraltar until the fifteenth of May.

An ordinary voyage would have anticipated the departure of Admiral Howe from the Delaware and have imperiled both his fleet and the army of General Clinton. The British fleet, then at New York, was greatly inferior to that of the French and consisted of only six sixty-fours, three fiftys, two fortys and a few small frigates. Other ships were hastily armed, and extraordinary measures were taken for extreme resistance; but the draught of water on the lower bar would not allow the heaviest of the French ships to enter the harbor, and the chief benefits from the presence of that squadron were derived from the capture of vessels which approached New York without knowledge of their arrival. A fact in this connection illustrates the uncertainty of naval movements.

The British government ordered an additional squadron for America as soon as advised that France designed to coöperate actively with the United States in war with Great Britain. The fleet sailed from Portsmouth on the twentieth of May, but upon a report that the fleet of Count D'Estaing was bound for the West Indies the order was suspended; so that Admiral Byron, who was sent with twenty-two ships to relieve Lord Howe, recalled at his own request, went into Plymouth and did not sail again until the fifth of June. This fleet was greatly scattered by storms. Four ships reached Sandy Hook, separately, soon after the departure of Count D'Estaing, and thereby escaped capture.

The Americans criticised the failure of the Count D'Estaing to engage the British fleet, but without cause. Even Stedman intimates that he " did not seriously intend to make an attempt against the harbor of New York!" A letter to the President of Congress dated the twenty-sixth of August, 1778, contains the following conclusive statement.

" The pilots procured by Colonels Laurens and Hamilton " (of Washington's staff) " destroyed all illusion."

" These experienced persons unanimously declared, that it was impossible to carry us in. I offered, in vain, a reward of fifty thousand crowns to any one who would promise success. All refused, and the particular soundings, which I caused to be taken, myself, too well demonstrated that they were right."

Washington determined to make the capture of Newport the immediate objective of the campaign, while the French fleet remained in American waters.

The condition of the British garrison at New York was such that on the twenty-ninth of July General Clinton wrote to Lord Germaine that he "might be compelled to evacuate the city and return to Halifax." On that day, the Count D'Estaing anchored near Point Judith, Long Island Sound, within five miles of Newport.

Washington directed General Sullivan, then stationed at Providence, to call in the New England militia for a combined movement against Newport and its defenses; assigned Generals Greene and La Fayette to command divisions, and ordered the brigades of Varnum and Glover to join La Fayette's division. These officers served with Greene before Boston, and Varnum was in the original company which marched with Greene, at the outbreak of the war. The proposed coöperation of French troops made the assignment of La Fayette equally judicious.

The American force which assembled at Providence was about ten thousand men. Reference is made to map, " Siege of Newport."

The British garrison consisted of six thousand men under Major-general Pigott, and embraced the following troops;—the Twenty-second, Forty-third, Fifty-fourth and Sixty-third British regiments; Fanning's and Brown's Provincials; the following regiments of Hessian chasseurs, viz., Huyn, Banau, Ditforth, Landgrave, Seaboth and Boit. Two Hessian regiments and Brown's Provincials were stationed on Connanicut Island; but were withdrawn to a strongly intrenched camp in front of Newport, when the French fleet entered the harbor. On the fifth of August, two French ships entered the Narraganset passage, and two frigates passed in through the eastern, or Seaconnet Channel.

The British frigates which had secured the garrison from attack up to that time, were destroyed, to prevent their capture. The Juno, 32; Lark, 32; Orpheus, 32; Cerberus 32; and the King-Fisher, 16, were burned; and the Flora, 32, and the Falcon, 18, were sunk.

It is not to be questioned that General Sullivan unwisely detained the French fleet in the offing, and neglected military courtesies which were no less deserved than proper, while he was maturing his plans for operations by land. The French troops had been nearly five months on ship-board, and their prompt landing would have averted subsequent disaster.

The tenth of August was designated for the attack. The American troops were to cross from Tiverton to Rhode Island at Howland's Ferry, and the French troops were to land on the west side, nearly opposite Byer's Island. On the morning of the twenty-ninth, without giving notice to the French commander, General Sullivan crossed from Tiverton, and occupied the north end of Rhode Island. The French had forced the middle and eastern passages on the eighth, in readiness to land on the tenth. General Sullivan had previously notified Count D'Estaing that he could not move earlier than the tenth, because of the non-arrival of militia and other troops daily expected in camp. Count D'Estaing was a Lieutenant-general of the French army, while General Sullivan was only a Major-general; but the French officer gracefully declined a command, and as gracefully proposed to attach the French troops to the division of General La Fayette. The precipitate landing of the American troops disconcerted the plan of attack, but did not engender a conflict between the American and French commanders, as so often stated at that period, and currently believed.

General Sullivan notified Count D'Estaing that " in consequence of the abandonment of the north end of Rhode Island by the British troops, when the French ships forced a passage into the harbor, he had occupied the position," and " had made a descent upon the island without waiting for the day appointed." Count D'Estaing " had been assured that morning, that not more than two thousand men had landed," and " believing that his (Sullivan's) situation required prompt succor," made a personal visit to General Sullivan. His own statement of the matter is highly honorable to his judgment and candor. In a report to the President of Congress, he says, " Knowing that there are moments which must be eagerly seized in war, I was cautious of blaming any overthrow of plans, which nevertheless astonished me, *and which in fact merits in my own opinion only praise*, although accumulated circumstances might have rendered the consequences very unfortunate."

The Count D'Estaing visited General Sullivan without information that the British fleet at New York had been reinforced, and was on its way to Newport.

On the eighth, General Washington wrote, that he " had received a letter from General Maxwell, dated at nine o'clock the previous

29

morning, near Staten Island, stating that Lord Howe had sailed from
the Hook with his fleet," adding, with peculiar forecast of the future,
" unless the fleet may have received advices of a reinforcement on the
coast, . . . it can only be accounted for on the principle of desperation, stimulated by a hope of finding you divided in your operations against Rhode Island."   The Count D'Estaing visited General
Sullivan with no apprehension that his fleet was in danger. " Two
of the French ships were out of the port in the Sound ; two others
were at the north end of the west channel ; three frigates were in the
east channel, and the eight ships which forced the middle passage
were between Rhode Island, thickly set with batteries, and Connanicut Island.   A large number of his sailors, who were suffering with
the scurvy were on that island ; and when he visited General Sullivan,
he left orders for the troops who were to join in the expedition to
follow."   The dissipation of the morning fog discovered Lord Howe's
fleet approaching the entrance to the port.   He "counted fourteen
vessels with two tiers of guns, and many frigates, thirty-six in all."

It appears that General Pigot promptly notified General Clinton
of the arrival of the French squadron, and the timely arrival of a
portion of Admiral Byron's fleet enabled Admiral Howe to leave New
York on the sixth of August with eight line-of-battle ships, five fiftys,
two forty-fours, several light frigates, three fire ships, two bombs, and
some smaller vessels.   Unfavorable winds delayed their passage.

The scattered fleet of the Count D'Estaing was in peril of being
cut off by detachments.   The wind was from the north east, insuring to
him the weather gauge ; and with due promptness he gathered his
ships and passed the channels to be ready for his adversary.   For
two days the wind remained in the same quarter.   As he retained the
weather gauge, Admiral Howe wisely declined to press up to the
shore against such an advantage in favor of the French fleet.

A storm of unusual severity separated and dispersed both fleets,
just as a partial change of wind had brought them upon nearly equal
terms of conflict.   *Stedman* styles that storm "tremendous."   *Gordon*
says, " a strong gale increased to a violent tempest."   *Marshall* says,
" a furious storm of wind and rain came up from the north-east, which
blew down and almost irreparably ruined all the tents ; rendered the
arms unfit for immediate use, and damaged the ammunition, of which
fifty rounds had just been issued.   The soldiers suffered extremely,
and several perished in the storm, which continued for three days."

Both fleets were seriously damaged, and during their dispersion over fifty miles and more of ocean, there were frequent collisions from the meeting of lost ships and detachments.   On the thirteenth, the Renown, 54, (British) Captain Dawson, fell in with the Languedoc, 84, (flag ship) quite dismantled ; but the vicinity of six other French ships prevented attack.   During the same evening, the Tonnant, 80, lost her mainmast, and would have been attacked by the Preston, 50, Commodore Hotham, but for the presence of other French vessels. On the sixteenth the Isis, 50, (British) Captain Rayner, was nearly stripped, in action with the Cæsar, 74, but the latter vessel was severely handled and drew off to refit.   Admiral Howe himself ran the gaunt-let of a portion of the French fleet and barely made New York.   The British squadron returned to that city, and the French returned to Newport.

The American army, meanwhile, had made such advances toward Newport as the unpropitious circumstances permitted.   The move-ment began on the fifteenth.   Colonel Henry B. Livingston, with a detail of fifty men from each brigade, and certain independent com-panies which had reported for duty during the attempt to regain Rhode Island, formed the advance column.   General Sullivan took position about five miles in advance of the town, at Gibb's Farm ; General Greene at Middletown, on the farm afterwards known as Randolph's ; and General La Fayette at the Boller Garden.   John Hancock, of Massachusetts, came forward as a general officer and commanded the second line.   Colonel West commanded the reserve. General Pigott had industriously perfected the defenses during the delay which occurred after the first arrival of the French fleet.   The neck of land from Coddington's Cove across to Easton's Bay and the pond just above it, was protected by interior and exterior lines, each suitably broken by redoubts.

The interior lines extended, as will appear by reference to the map, and as stated in General Sullivan's report, from the sea to the north end of the island, having a strong redoubt at the head of the pass between Easton's Bay and Pond.   A second redoubt twenty rods north of the first, had a good sweep of fire toward the hill east of the pond.   The first line, a quarter of a mile in advance of this, also presented a strong redoubt eastward ; and from that direction the American approaches were made.   Well arranged abatis crossed the neck from Irish's redoubt, commanding the fork of the east and west roads which extended from that point to the north end of the island. The distance from Castle Hill near the main entrance of the harbor to Butt's Hill, where the Americans made their last resistance, was nearly fifteen miles: Between the fifteenth and the twentieth the Americans had established several batteries and the British were compelled to strengthen their works by redoubts in the manner already stated. On the twenty-third the American army was reported by General Sullivan in a published circular as follows :

"The numbers of our army amount to eight thousand one hundred and seventy-four, rank and file, exclusive of eight hundred artillerymen, the whole exceedingly well officered, and a reinforcement of three thousand men will probably be here in a few days."

On the twentieth the Count D'Estaing returned to port. His fleet was badly crippled by the storm, and some of the ships were cut up by the casualties of action. Generals Greene and La Fayette waited upon him to urge the resumption of the original plan of attack upon the British works ; but he had already decided to sail for Boston, to refit. The instructions of his sovereign were explicit, for any case of severe injury by tempest or in action ; *viz.*, to make the port of Boston. The manifest propriety of these instructions was overlooked by the American officers. He was upon a distant foreign coast, and liable at any time to meet a British fleet. It was a vital matter that his ships should be kept in fighting trim. The Americans urged, that " he could refit at Newport." It is evident that with the siege of Newport on his hands, Newport was wholly unsuited to that purpose. His officers were nearly or quite unanimous in favor of literal compliance with his instructions, and he sailed for Boston on the twenty-second of August, just a month from his departure from Sandy Hook. It has been claimed that the action of his officers originated from jealousy of his assignment to naval command, while a general officer of the army. There is no occasion for that criticism. The French naval officers were fully appreciative of any prospect of success against the British troops ; but no less assured, that their whole future depended upon the condition of their ships.

The Count D'Estaing, in a letter to General Sullivan on the morning of his return, says, " I should be culpable in my duty to America herself if I could for a moment think of not preserving a squadron destined for her defense. I regretted to Colonel Fleury, that you should have landed on the island a day before the time agreed upon between us, and I should be greatly afflicted to know that you are in danger. To decide upon your motives is a wrong which I have not committed. I have refrained from censure ; and the twelve thousand men now under your command will probably prove the correctness of the step, by a success which I desire as a citizen, and as an admirer of your bravery and talents."

A protest was sent to him August twenty-seventh, after he had sailed, signed by John Sullivan, N. Greene, John Hancock, J. Glover, Ezek Cornell, Wm. Whipple, John Tyler, Solomon Lovell, and John Fitzconnel, which overtook and annoyed him, but did not change his purpose; although he gave earnest assurance that he would return as soon as he could do so in fighting condition.

General Sullivan issued an intemperate general order, which he modified two days afterwards; but the following sentence had gone before the people. "The General yet hopes the event will prove America able to procure that by her own arms, which her allies refuse to assist in obtaining."

The departure of the fleet depressed the American army. They dropped from enthusiasm to its opposite extreme, and the militia returned home in large numbers. The public indignation was very bitterly expressed.

At this period of doubt in the American camp, a courier arrived from General Washington with the information that Sir Henry Clinton had left New York with four thousand troops to reinforce the garrison of Newport, and strongly intimated the importance of securing a timely retreat from Rhode Island. Head winds delayed the transports so that General Sullivan had timely notice of the movement. On the twenty-sixth, the heavy baggage and superfluous ordnance were removed in safety. On the twenty-eighth, a council of war decided that the army should fall back to the north end of the island and fortify the position, until a messenger could be sent to Boston to learn if Count D'Estaing was ready to return to Newport. General La Fayette made this trip with remarkable expedition, but failed to move the French General to expose his fleet until it could be thoroughly overhauled. It is certain that if he had responded to the appeal, he would have encountered a superior British force and almost certain destruction. As an index of the spirit in which he received the application, it is only necessary to say, that he offered "to lead his troops in person to Newport, and place himself under General Sullivan's orders." He says, "I was anxious to demonstrate, that my countrymen could not be offended by a sudden expression of feeling, and that he who had the honor of commanding them in America, was and would be at all times, one of the most devoted and zealous servants of the United States."

It must be the judgment of history that he did his duty to France, America, and himself; and under the exasperating character of the abuse which was heaped upon him, he vindicated the confidence of his sovereign in his capacity and wisdom.

By three o'clock on the morning of the twenty-ninth, the American army occupied Quaker Hill and Turkey Hill with their advance guard, and held strong intrenchments across the north end of Rhode Island, and a commanding position on Butt's Hill.

Colonel Henry B. Livingston was pushed forward by the east road, and Colonel John Laurens by the west road, to meet the advance. At a council of war which was held before morning, General Greene urged an attack in force upon the British, so as to cut their detachments off by superior numbers, but his opinion was overruled. The British soon drove the Americans from Turkey and Quaker Hills, but not without loss, and the Americans retired within their lines. General Pigott states that he " did not know of the retreat until the morning, when he made the following disposition of troops : General Prescott and a part of Brown's corps occupied the old works eastward, and moved up the east shore of the island ; Brigadier-general Smith marched the Twenty-second and Forty-third regiments, and the flank companies of the Thirty-eighth and Fifty-fourth by the east road. Major-general Losberg marched with the Hessian chasseurs, and the Anspach regiments of Voit and Seaboth by the west road. As soon as General Smith reported the Americans to be in force on Quaker Hill, the Fifty-fourth British, the Hessian regiment of Huger, and the residue of Brown's Provincial corps were sent to his support. Colonel Fanning's corps of Provincials were sent by the west road to support General Losberg, who encountered a stubborn resistance at Turkey Hill." At Quaker Hill General Glover distinguished himself by a valiant defense, as did Colonels Livingston and Laurens. The American casualties were thirty killed, one hundred and thirty-seven wounded and forty-four missing. The British casualties were thirty-eight killed, two hundred and ten wounded, and a few missing. Just at evening the Americans made an attempt to cut off some chasseurs who were advancing on their right ; but General Pigott states that " the regiments of Fanning and Huger were ordered up to their support, and after a smart engagement, obliged them to retreat to their main body on Windmill Hill."

The Americans pitched a number of tents in front of their lines, and appeared to be diligently at work upon the defenses. A retreat by both Bristol and Howland ferries had been determined upon. The experience and good judgment of General Glover was conspicuous on this occasion, as during the retreat from Long Island in 1776. General La Fayette returned from Boston at eleven o'clock, and devoted himself, as at Brandywine, Barren Hill, and Monmouth, to the care of the rear guard, and "before twelve o'clock," says General Sullivan, "the main army had crossed with the stores and baggage. La Fayette brought off the pickets and other parties which covered the retreat in excellent order; not a man was left behind, nor the smallest article left."

On the morning of the thirtieth, one hundred sail of British vessels appeared in sight, bringing General Clinton's army to the rescue of the garrison. He returned promptly to New York, however, only deterred from a descent upon New London, by contrary winds, which prevented the fleet from entering the harbor. General Grey sailed from Newport, with the transports, to Acushnet river; landed at evening, and within twenty-four hours destroyed seventy vessels. Bedford, Fairhaven and Martha's Vineyard were also visited. These posts were famous for their outfit of privateers, and six armed vessels of from fourteen to sixteen guns, besides warehouses and public stores, were destroyed, and a successful levy was made upon the inhabitants for ten thousand sheep and three hundred oxen. Admiral Howe sailed for Boston, where he arrived September first; but being unable to draw the Count D'Estaing into an engagement, returned to New York.

The popular clamor against the French general had not subsided. On the fifteenth of September, the Chevalier de Saint Sauveur was killed at Boston, while attempting to quiet an affray between the French and disorderly parties at the French bakery. The Massachusetts General Assembly, on the day following, ordered a monument to be erected to his memory, and the judgment of good citizens was fully alive to the disgrace which such disorder and recrimination inflicted on the national cause.

The Count D'Estaing remained at Boston until November third, when he sailed for the West Indies. On the first of November, however, Admiral Byron appeared off the harbor with a large naval force, but was immediately driven off by a severe storm, which so disabled his fleet that he was compelled to go to Newport to refit. This officer *fought the Ocean* during 1778. The passage of his fleet from England was disastrous ; for after the dispersion of his ships on that voyage, he was himself, compelled to make Halifax, before he reached New York.

The first active coöperation of the French navy in support of the United States had resulted in no victories ; but it precipitated the evacuation of Philadelphia, restricted the garrison of New York to operations within reach of the British navy, and was a pledge of practical sympathy in the struggle. To the nations of Europe it was the emphatic declaration that France was ready to maintain, as well as acknowledge, American Independence.

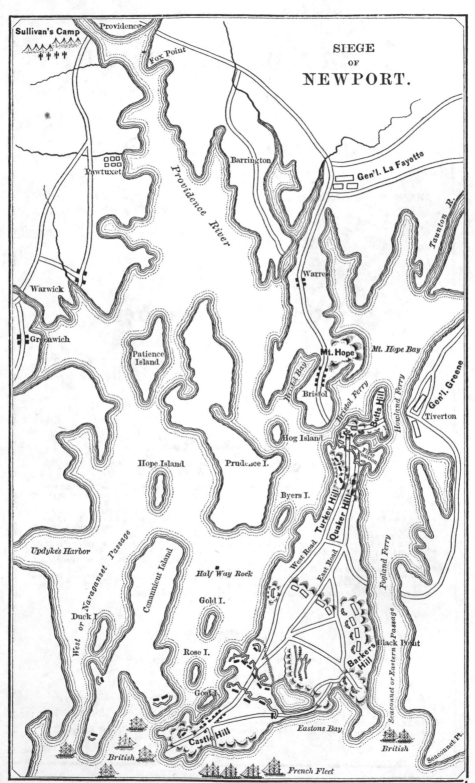

SIEGE
OF
NEWPORT.

Sullivan's Camp

Providence

Fox Point

Barrington

Gen'l. La Fayette

Taunton R.

Pawtuxet

Providence River

Warwick

Warren

Greenwich

Patience Island

Mt. Hope

Mt. Hope Bay

Bristol Basin

Bristol

Gen'l. Greene

Butts Hill

Bristol Ferry

Howland Ferry

Tiverton

Hog Island

Hope Island

Prudence I.

First Position

Byers I.

Turkey Hill

Quaker Hill

West or Naraganset Passage

Updyke's Harbor

West Road

East Road

Fogland Ferry

Duck I.

Conanicut Island

Half Way Rock

Gold I.

Barkers Hill

Black Point

Seaconnet or Eastern Passage

Rose I.

Goat I.

Eastons Bay

Seaconnet Pt.

Castle Hill

British

British

French Fleet

⇒Siege of Newport⇐

AUGUST 1778

American Commanders

SULLIVAN

GREENE, LIVINGSTON, HANCOCK, WEST, LAWSON, HENRY
VARNUM, GLOVER, LAFAYETTE

French Army and Fleet

COUNT D'ESTAING

British Commanders

PIGOT

HUYN, BANAU, DITFORTH, SEABOTH, PRESCOTT,
VOSBERG, SMITH, GREY, BOIT, FANNING

Strength, 6,000.

British Admirals

HOWE   BYRON

PLAN OF ATTACK.—The 10th of August was selected for the attack. The Americans were to cross from Tiverton, at Howland's Ferry, and the French were to land on the west side, opposite Byer's Island.

NOTE I.—Sullivan, without notice to the French Commander, crossed at Tiverton July 29th. The French fleet forced the west and middle passages on the eighth. A heavy storm scattered both French and British fleets, and Count D'Estaing did not regain port until the 20th. Between the 15th and 20th the Americans had established batteries from Parker's Hill across the island.

NOTE II.—The reported movement of Clinton from New York with 4,000 troops, led to a retreat, which began on the 26th of August. On the 29th the Americans still held Quaker Hill and Turkey Hill, as well as Butts' Hill. Livingston, Lawrence and Glover distinguished themselves in the defence, losing 67 men, and inflicting a loss of 248 upon their assailants.

NOTE III.—On the 30th one hundred vessels arrived in sight, with Clinton's division; but the retreat to the main land had been effected, under the personal supervision of Lafayette, "without leaving behind a single man, or the smallest article," as reported by Sullivan.

References:

CARRINGTON'S "BATTLES OF THE AMERICAN REVOLUTION," pp. 448-456.

School Histories:

Anderson, ¶ 75-6 ; p. 87.
Barnes, ¶ 2 ; p. 128.
Berard (Bush), ¶ 100; p. 165.
Goodrich, C.A.(Seaveys), ¶ 36, p. 132.
Goodrich, S. G., ¶ 3-9; p. 242.
Hassard, ¶ 13-14 ; p. 200.

Holmes, ¶ 19 ; p. 134.
Lossing, ¶ 7 ; p. 163.
Quackenbos, ¶ 359 · p. 259.
Ridpath, ¶ 8-10 ; p. 210-11.
Sadlier (Excel), ¶ 10 ; p. 199.
Stephens, A.H. ¶ 8-9; p. 207.

Swinton, ¶ 169-170 ; p. 139.
Scott, ¶ 11-14 ; p. 193-4.
Thalheimer (Eclectic), ¶ 273 ;
p. 155.
Venable, ¶ 147 ; p. 113.

CHAPTER LVIII.

CAMPAIGN OF 1778. JULY TO DECEMBER.

AFTER the failure of operations against Newport, General Sullivan resumed his post at Providence ; General La Fayette occupied Bristol, and afterwards withdrew behind Warren, out of reach of the British shipping, and General Greene, who was still Quartermaster-general, went to Boston to superintend the purchase of supplies for the French squadron.

Washington retained his headquarters at White Plains, until the latter part of September. Upon his first return to this post, after two years' absence, he took occasion to contrast the two periods, thus writing,—" The hand of Providence has been so conspicuous, that he must be worse than an infidel that lacks faith ; and more than wicked, that has not gratitude enough to acknowledge his obligation." It is not too much to say of the American Commander-in-chief, that his wonderful self-control over a passionate natural temper, and his equanimity under exasperating ordeals, owe much of their strength to the sentiment just quoted, so that he could devote his faculties entirely to duty, unhampered by such personal issues as annoyed many of his associates. From White Plains he removed to Fishkill, and on the tenth to Fredericksburg. On the twenty-seventh he announced the disposition of the army for the approaching period of winter-quarters.

It indicates his judgment of the relative value and exposure of different localities and posts. " Nine brigades on the west side of the Hudson River, exclusive of the garrison at West Point ; one of which, the North Carolina brigade, will be near Smith's Clove for the security of that pass, and as a reinforcement to West Point in case of necessity ; another, the Jersey brigade, will be at Elizabethtown, to cover the lower part of New Jersey ; and the other seven, consisting of the Virginia, Maryland, Delaware, and Pennsylvania troops, will be at Middlebrook ; six brigades will be left on the east side of the river, and at West Point ; three of which (of the Massachusetts troops) will be stationed for the immediate defense of the Highlands ; one at West Point, in addition to the garrison already there ; and the other two at Fishkill and Continental village.   The remaining three brigades, composed of the New Hampshire and Connecticut troops and Hazen's regiment, will be posted in the vicinity of Danbury, for the protection of the country lying along the Sound, to cover our magazines lying on Connecticut river, and to aid the Highlands on any serious movement of the enemy that way.   The park of artillery will be at Pluckemin ; the cavalry will be disposed of thus : Bland's regiment at Winchester, Virginia ; Baylis at Frederic, or Hagerstown, Maryland ; and Sheldon's at Durham, Connecticut ; Lee's corps (Colonel Harry Lee) will be with that part of the army which is in the Jerseys, acting on the advanced posts."

General Putnam was assigned to command at Danbury ; General McDougall in the Highlands, and general headquarters were to be near Middlebrook.

The British army.   No extensive field operations took place in the Northern States after the battle of Monmouth.   The time was drawing near when the comparative rest which the Southern States realized after the defense of Fort Moultrie was to be replaced by the pervasive activities of war, and the issues of pitched battles.   The army of General Clinton was largely depleted by order of the British Cabinet. Five thousand men were ordered to the West Indies, and three thousand men to Florida.   Sir Henry Clinton says in a letter of October eighth, addressed to Lord Germaine, " With an army so much diminished at New York, nothing important can be done ; especially as it is also weakened by sending seven hundred men to Halifax, and three hundred to Bermuda."

The retreat from Monmouth involved nearly eight hundred desertions, as authentically verified, and the killed, wounded, and missing, and the contingent casualties of all kinds from the time the evacuation of Philadelphia began, were little less than two thousand men. Many died from exposure to heat, and the waste was not promptly replaced from England.   Several restricted incursions were made which kept the American Commander-in-chief on the watch for the Highland posts ; but these became less frequent, and the year 1778 drew near its close with a material loss of prestige to the British cause, and much of confidence on the part of the United States in final success.

On the twenty-seventh of September, General Grey surprised Colonel Baylor's light horse at Tappan, as completely as he did General Wayne's command at Paoli ; and Lieutenant-colonel Campbell, accompanied by Lieutenant-colonel Simcoe, confirmed their antecedent custom of warfare by forays which brought little plunder and less intrinsic credit.

General Cornwallis, with five thousand men, made an incursion into New Jersey, between the Hudson and the Hackensack, and General Knyphausen, with three thousand men, operated in Westchester county, between the Hudson and the Bronx, but with little acquisition of provisions or other supplies.

On the fifteenth of October, Captain Ferguson of the Seventieth British regiment, with three thousand regulars and the Third New Jersey Volunteers, made a descent upon Little Neck, New Jersey, where many privateers were equipped, surprised a detachment of Count Pulaski's brigade at night, and inflicted a " loss of fifty killed, *none wounded*," including Lieutenant-colonel the Baron de Bose, and Lieutenant de la Borderie. Ferguson says in his official report, " It being a night attack, little quarter could of course be given ; so that there are only five prisoners." Colonel Pulaski vigorously pursued the party, inflicting some loss.

The Indian massacres in the Wyoming Valley, from July first to the fourth, which were to be subsequently avenged, were followed by that of Cherry Valley, November eleventh. These were frontier enterprises, beyond the range of the general campaign ; but they made impressions upon the nation, and multiplied the embarrassments of the prosecution of the war.

On the twenty-seventh of November, Commodore Hyde Parker convoyed a fleet of transports to Savannah, which carried Lieutenant-colonel Campbell, the Seventy-first regiment, two battalions of Hessians, four battalions of Provincial troops, and a detachment of the Royal artillery, making a total force of about three thousand five hundred men. The troops landed at Tybee Island, about fifteen miles from Savannah, and captured the city on the twenty-ninth of December. The American force, under command of General Robert Howe, consisted of about eight hundred men, and with militia did not exceed twelve hundred. (Stedman estimates it at fifteen hundred). Colonel Huger's and Thompson's South Carolina regiments, Colonel

George Walton's Georgia riflemen, one hundred men, and Colonel Elbert's Georgia militia fought well at an advanced position near Tatnal's and Wright's plantations, until resistance was hopeless.

Lieutenant-colonel Campbell, in his official report, states that he was guided by a negro, through a hidden path across a swamp, upon the American right. This movement in force, while only demonstrating in front, insured his success. His report states the capture of thirty-eight officers, four hundred and fifteen non-commissioned officers and privates, and forty-eight pieces of cannon, twenty-three mortars, and ninety-four barrels of powder, besides the shipping in the harbor, and a large quantity of provisions. His loss is given as one officer Captain Peter Campbell, of Skinner's light infantry, two privates killed, and one sergeant, and nine privates wounded, and states that eighty-three American dead and eleven wounded were found on the field.

Thus the Southern campaign of 1779 was inaugurated with the closing days of 1778.

Notwithstanding this, the condition of General Clinton at New York had become critical. The position of the American army restricted his supplies, and compelled him to depend largely upon England ; and on the second day of December, he again wrote despondently to the British Secretary of State :—" I do not complain, but, my lord, do not let any thing be expected of one circumstanced as I am."

The Northern Frontier. The British garrison at Detroit had taken little part in active service after its detachment retired from " the Cedars " in 1776, but the early western settlers were constantly exposed to Indian incursions ; and the defense of Boonesborough, Harrodsburg, and Fort Logan were conspicuous for their valor. Daniel Boone with thirty-seven men had been captured at last by Indians, was taken to Chillicothe, Ohio, and thence to Detroit. He was taken back to Chillicothe and adopted by the Shawnee nation. On the sixteenth of June, 1778, he escaped and reached Boonesborough, one hundred and sixty miles, as he states in his narrative, on the twentieth. Captain Duquesne and eleven other French Canadians from Detroit, acting in the name of Governor Hamilton, and four hundred and fifty Indians, unexpectedly attacked the fort on the twentieth of August but were repulsed.

A small British garrison had been placed at Kaskaskia (Randolph county, Illinois), but this force had been withdrawn to Detroit upon the American invasion of Canada in 1775, and the command of the post was intrusted to a Frenchman by the name of Rocheblave.

Under the patronage of Thomas Jefferson, George Mason and George Wythe, of Virginia, Colonel George Rogers Clark left Williamsburg, Virginia, on the fourth of January, 1778, and on the fourth of July captured Kaskaskia. While descending the Ohio he heard of the alliance with France and from Kaskaskia he moved toward the French settlement at Vincennes (Knox county, Indiana) and there established himself, with the declared purpose of conquering the northwest. Lieutenant Governor Hamilton left Detroit on the seventh of October and recovered Vincennes on the seventeenth of December, postponing operations to recover Illinois until spring. Thus the extreme *west* began to engage in the general war.

Miscellaneous Events. The French alliance had been an impressive sign of the American progress toward recognition among the nations. All efforts to compromise still failed, and the military opinions of General Amherst received no attention.

On the nineteenth of March the constitution had been adopted, to take effect the twenty-ninth of November.

Another expedition to conquer Canada was proposed, to be under the command of La Fayette, associated with the Count D'Estaing. Detroit, Niagara, Oswego, Montreal and Halifax were to be separate objectives of one grand movement; but the wisdom of Washington postponed, and afterwards induced Congress to reject the scheme.

The year 1778 closed; but the American Congress had no money, and the loose union of the States was constantly evoking sectional jealousies. The Commander-in-chief declared that "the States separately were too much engaged in their local concerns, when the great business of a nation, the momentous concerns of an empire, were at stake."

Bancroft thus embodies his sentiment. "He who in the beginning of the revolution used to call Virginia his country, from this time never ceased his efforts, by conversation and correspondence, to train the statesmen of America, especially of his beloved native commonwealth, to the work of consolidating the Union."

Upon visiting Philadelphia at the close of the year, he addressed a letter to Colonel Harrison, Speaker of the Virginia House of Delegates, which solemnly declared his apprehensions for the future. He urged Virginia to "send the best and ablest of her men to Congress," and thus continues: "They must not slumber nor sleep at home in such a time of pressing danger;—content with the enjoyment of places of honor or profit in their own States while the common interests of America are mouldering and sinking into inevitable ruin."

. . . "If I were to draw a picture of the times and men, from what I have seen, heard, and in part know, I should in one word say that idleness, dissipation and extravagance seem to have laid fast hold of most of them; that speculation, peculation and an insatiable thirst for riches seem to have got the better of every other consideration and almost of every order of men; that party disputes and personal quarrels are the great business of the day; . . . while a great and accumulating debt, ruined finances, depreciated money, and want of credit, which in its consequences is the want of every thing, are but secondary considerations, if our affairs wore the most promising aspect; . . . An assembly, a concert, a dinner, a supper, will not only take men off from acting in this business, but even from thinking of it; while a great part of the officers of our army, from absolute necessity, are quitting the service, and the more virtuous few, rather than do this, are sinking by sure degrees into beggary and want."

His convictions were embodied in one sentence. "Our affairs are in a more distressed, ruinous and deplorable condition than they have been since the commencement of the war."

BRITISH EFFECTIVE FORCE.

NOTE.   From "Original Returns in the British Record Office." Date August 15th, 1778

New York	15,886	Long Island	8117
Staten Island	3,244	Rhode Island	5189
Paulus Hook	456	With Lord Howe's Fleet	512
	19,586		14,478

Total 34,064.

This force reduced by detachments sent to the West Indies and Halifax, was taken up November, 1, 1778, as follows:

New York	9508	Paulus Hook	419
Long Island	5630	Providence Island	225
Staten Island	972	Rhode Island	5740
	16,170		

Total, 22,554.

CHAPTER LIX.

JANUARY TO JULY, 1779. POSITION OF THE ARMIES. INCIDENTS
OF THE GENERAL CAMPAIGN.

THE year 1779 opened without offensive actions on the part of either of the armies in the Northern States. The garrison of New York made no demonstration of importance in any direction; and Washington spent the greater part of January in urging Congress to take active measures to recruit the army. It was not until the ninth of March that eighty regular battalions were authorized, and it was found almost impossible to obtain funds, by loan or taxation, to maintain the troops already on duty.

The garrison of Philadelphia was passing through an idle experience, similar to that of the British garrison of the previous year. Congress itself seemed enervated by the temporary suspension of active hostilities. While General Clinton was inactive at New York, General Washington resolved to employ a portion of the army in punishing the Indians who had devastated Wyoming and Cherry Valleys the previous year. New Jersey troops were assigned to this duty, but refused to march until provision was made for the support of their families. The State legislature provided money to pay the officers and men, and order was restored. The immediate elements of the Southern campaign postponed the expedition to Wyoming Valley; but Colonel Schaick, Lieutenant-colonel Willett, and Major Cochran, surprised the towns of the Onondagas, in New York, and on the nineteenth of April destroyed the whole settlement without loss.

The Confederate money soon depreciated so as to be worth but three or four cents on the dollar, and Washington was constrained to offer his own estate for sale to meet his actual necessities. Before fall the issue of two hundred millions of paper money was authorized, and measures were taken to obtain a loan in Europe.

Major-general Benjamin Lincoln had arrived at Charleston on the first of December preceding, superseding Brigadier-general Robert Howe, in command of the American troops. During January, General Prevost captured Sunbury, and Colonel Campbell occupied Augusta.

General Lincoln's command consisted of one thousand one hundred and twenty-one regular troops, and a force of raw militia which made the aggregate three thousand six hundred and thirty-nine. He advanced to Perrysburg on the east bank of the Savannah a few miles north of that city to prevent the crossing into South Carolina of General Prevost's army, then on the opposite bank, and three thousand strong, besides Georgia Provincials. Neither army was inclined to force a passage, but two companies of the Sixtieth, and one company of the Sixteenth British regiments made a diversion toward Beaufort, for the purpose of securing a footing upon Port Royal, a large island seventy-five miles south-west of Charleston.

Colonel William Moultrie was sent to the rescue. He crossed to the island with a force of three hundred militia, one small gun, and nine regulars, including Captain De Trevills, and after a spirited skirmish repulsed the attack.

On the fourteenth, Colonel Andrew Pickens, of South Carolina, and Colonel Dooley, of Georgia, with three hundred men, surprised Colonel Boyd's Provincials on the north side of Kettle Creek, in Wilkes county, Georgia.

On the third of March, General Lincoln sent General Williamson with twelve hundred men up the river to take position opposite Augusta ; General Rutherford with nearly eight hundred men to the Black Swamp; and General Ashe with fifteen hundred North Carolina militia and some Georgia Continental troops, was sent, with orders to cross the river at Augusta (which the British had abandoned), and to move down the west side of the river. This detachment went into camp in the angle of Briar creek and the Savannah, thirteen miles above the British army. The American position was very strong by nature, as Briar creek was deep and broad ; but the right flank was left entirely exposed. General Prevost's report to Lord Germaine states that " while dispositions were made to keep Mr. (General) Lincoln in check, Major McPherson, with the first battalion of the Seventy-first, and some irregulars, with two field pieces, was directed to advance toward Briar creek bridge ; while Lieutenant-colonel Prevost with the second battalion of the Seventy-first regiment, a corps of light infantry commanded by Sir James Baird, and three companies of grenadiers, made a long circuit of fifty miles, surprised the American army and routed it thoroughly."

Seven cannon and a thousand arms were captured, as well as General Elbert, Colonel McIntosh, several other officers, and nearly two hundred men. Nearly an equal number were supposed to have been lost in the action, or in flight through the swamps and the residue, with the exception of four or five hundred men, retired to their homes, and did not rejoin General Lincoln at Charleston. Governor Rutledge had been re-elected governor, and the people assembled at Orangeburg, with a spirit similar to that which had been aroused during 1776.

On the twenty-third of April, General Lincoln again crossed the Savannah river, but after fruitless marching, the American army again retreated to Charleston. General Prevost promptly advanced and demanded the surrender of the city. General Pulaski gained credit in skirmishing before the town, and the vigorous action of Rutledge, Moultrie, Laurens and others, overcame the fears of many citizens who were ready to submit.

On the thirteenth the British withdrew ; and on the twentieth a vigorous attack was made upon a post retained by them at Stono Ferry, which failed for want of full concert in the attack, and prompt support. The British troops retired to Savannah, after establishing a post at Port Royal.

Congress seemed incapable of realizing the impending desolation which must follow a strong invasion of the Southern States, and Washington was powerless to furnish the aid required, so long as General Clinton occupied New York.

General Greene asked permission to go to the Southern States, but his assignment was not authorized by Congress, although approved by the Commander-in-chief. The utmost that could be done was to authorize a portion of the regular troops, which belonged to the Southern Department, to return to that section for service.

La Fayette, finding that active duty was not contemplated, sailed for France in the American frigate Alliance, with the best wishes of the people he had served so intelligently and so well.

At the extreme west, the American forces at Kaskaskia resolved to anticipate the threats of Lieutenant-governor Hamilton, who was still at Vincennes, and had announced his purpose to reduce the Illinois country to submission. Colonel Clark, after great trials and an extraordinary march, captured Vincennes on the twenty-fourth of

30

February; and shortly after, sixty of his men ascended the Wabash river, with armed boats, and captured a large supply of goods *en route* from Detroit. A thousand troops were raised by North Carolina and Virginia to strengthen the frontier, and under the wise support of Thomas Jefferson, then Governor of Virginia, that region was placed in a condition for defense.

The Middle States were not without their experience in that class of warfare which characterized the greater part of the campaign of 1779.

General Matthews left New York with two thousand troops and five hundred marines, late in April, anchored in Hampton Roads on the ninth of May, laid waste Portsmouth and Norfork, destroyed over a hundred vessels, and returned to New York within the month, having taken seventeen prizes, and at least three thousand hogsheads of tobacco.

The first six months of 1779 was a severe test of the endurance of the bankrupt Republic, and an equally severe test of the patriotism of the Southern States, which began to feel the pressure from rapidly augmenting hostile forces, while the general government was powerless to render them adequate aid for defense. Thus far the campaign had been exhaustive, without many critical issues to arouse the people to a passionate resistance.

One single demonstration was made by General Clinton, which seemed to have in view the reduction of the Highland posts, and this confirmed the policy of Washington in retaining his army in such a position that he could quickly reach the Hudson river. On the thirteenth of May General Clinton ascended the river, accompanied by General Vaughan, under convoy of the fleet of Sir George Collier, and took possession of Verplanck's Point and Stony Point. The latter post was being fortified, but by a very small force, entirely inadequate to resist a naval attack. It really had little defensive value; but the two posts taken together formed the lower passage to the Highlands, and their occupation by the British troops would be a standing menace to West Point. The Seventeenth British regiment, the grenadier companies of the Seventy-first, and artillery, under Lieutenant-colonel Webster, were placed at Stony Point; a garrison of equal strength was left at Verplanck's, each covered by the presence of several small frigates and sloops of war, and General Clinton retired with the main body to Yonkers.

The American army was removed from Middlebrook to Smith's

Clove early in the month.   On the twenty-third, Washington removed his headquarters to New Windsor, leaving General Putnam in command.   General Heath was ordered from Boston, and General Wayne was stationed between the Clove and Fort Montgomery, near Dunderberg mountain.

Such were the modified positions of the two armies of the northern zone, at the close of June, 1779.

BRITISH EFFECTIVE FORCE.

NOTE.   From "Original Returns in the British Record Office."   Date, Feb. 15th, 1779.

New York	9100	Nova Scotia	3011
Long Island	5714	Georgia	4330
Staten Island	1619	Bermuda	240
Paulus Hook	387	Providence Island	240
Rhode Island	5642		
			7821
	22,462		

Total, 30,283.

SAME, May 1st, 1779.

New York	9123	Halifax	3677
Long Island	6056	Georgia	4794
Staten Island	1344	West Florida	1703
Paulus Hook	383	Bermuda and Providence Island	470
Hoboken	264		
Rhode Island	5644		10,644
	22,814		

Total, 33, 458.

CHAPTER LX.

AS the first of July perfected the lodgment of British troops at the entrance to the Highlands; so it witnessed renewed activity of their northern army, by detachments. On the second, at eleven o'clock at night, Lieutenant-colonel Banastre Tarleton, from his camp on the river Bronx, made report of his operations during the previous twenty-four hours. With seventy of the Seventeenth light dragoons, a part of the Legion infantry and cavalry, (Tarleton's) Queen's Rangers, Hessians, and some mounted Yagers, two hundred men, he passed North Castle Meeting House, and through Bedford to Pound-Ridge, to surprise Colonel Sheldon, who commanded a force of about ninety cavalry at that point. The British troops pursued the partially surprised Americans nearly to Salem; burned the Presbyterian Meeting House and some dwellings, captured Sheldon's colors which had been accidentally left in their quarters,—some baggage of the officers, and a few arms; but inflicted and received small loss. Lieutenant-colonel Tarleton says, " I proposed to the militia terms; that if they would not fire from buildings, I would not burn. They persisted in firing, till the torch stopped their progress." The retreat was followed up by the militia, availing themselves of fences and other obstructions which shortened the expedition and made it unprofitable.

On the third of July General Tryon left New York with two thousand six hundred men, under convoy of the fleet of Sir George Collier, to invade Connecticut. In the report of the latter officer to Mr. Stephens, Secretary of the Admiralty, he states, that he "first sent the Renown, Thames, Otter, and two armed vessels, to block up New London harbor and the east entrance to the Sound, and proceeded from New York, *via* Hell Gate, with his Majesty's ships Camilla, Scorpion, Halifax (brig) and Hussar (galley) together with the transports, and on the fifth landed the army, in two divisions, at New Haven.

On Sunday, July 4th, the day before General Tryon landed, he issued a proclamation which foreshadowed his purposes. A single extract is given, to illustrate its character: "The ungenerous and wanton insurrections against the sovereignty of Great Britain, into which this colony had been deluded by the artifices of designing men, for private purposes, might well justify in you every fear which conscious guilt could form, respecting the intentions of the present armament. The existence of a single habitation on your defenseless coast ought to be a subject of constant reproof to your ingratitude." The people to whom this was addressed, were preparing, so soon as the Sabbath should pass, to honor the day upon which his proclamation was dated. General Tryon reports, that " the first division, consisting of the Guards, Fusileers, Fifty-fourth regiment, and a detachment of Yagers, with four field pieces, under Brigadier-general Garth, landed about five o'clock ('A. M.) a mile south of West Haven, and began their march, making a circuit of upwards of seven miles, to head off a creek on the western side of the town. Before noon, after the return of the boats, General Tryon, in person, disembarked with the Hessians, Landgraves and " King's American " regiments and two pieces of cannon, on the eastern side of the harbor, and instantly began the march of three miles, to the ferry from New Haven, east to Brentford, "(Branford)." The Rock battery (Fort Hale) was then occupied, and the armed vessels entered the Bay. " General Garth got into the town, not without opposition, loss and fatigue, and reported at half-past one, that he should begin the conflagration which he thought it wanted. In the morning, the first division embarked at the southeast part of the town, crossed the ferry, and joined the other on the East Haven side. In their progress on the preceding day from West Haven they were under continual fire ; but the rebels were every where repulsed. The next morning, as there was not a shot fired to molest the retreat, General Garth changed his design and destroyed only the public stores, some vessels and ordnance, excepting six field-pieces and an armed privateer which were brought off. The troops reëmbarked at Rock-Fort and anchored on the morning of the eighth off the village of Fairfield."

The landing of General Garth was at Savin Rock. At the " West Haven Green," Captain James Hillhouse, with a party of students from Yale College and other young men of the city, made a courageous resistance; throwing the British light troops back upon the main body. The plank had been taken from the bridge where the Milford turnpike crossed West River, and at this point Adjutant Campbell of the guards was killed, and Rev. Naphtalie Daggett, afterwards President of Yale College, was made a prisoner, and suffered much personal violence. The British troops fell back, passed up the western bank of the river, crossed at Thompson's bridge and entered the town on the old Derby road by the way of Hotchkissville, coming into Chapel street from the west, a little before two o'clock in the afternoon. General Tryon landed at Light House Point. After General Garth joined General Tryon in the evening, the troops found that it was impossible to obtain control of the Neck-bridge, and his division remained north of the town without crossing; while General Tryon remained on the East Haven Heights. The American loss is stated in the Connecticut Journal of July 17th, 1779, at twenty-two killed, and seventeen wounded. General Tryon states his own loss at two officers and seven men killed; three officers and thirty-seven men wounded and twenty-five missing.

The pecuniary damage was stated by a committee of the General Assembly of Connecticut, appointed in October, 1779, to have been of the cash value of twenty-four thousand eight hundred and ninety-three pounds, seven shillings and six pence, besides Continental money which was destroyed. Several prominent citizens were taken away by the fleet.

On the eighth and ninth of July, Fairfield was burned, including two meeting-houses, eighty-three dwelling houses and shops, two school-houses, the jail, and the county house; of "the total estimated cash value of £34,559 5s. and 6d. The estimates were based upon the money value of 1774."

The British loss is reported by General Tryon, as nine killed, thirty wounded, and five missing. General Tryon says in his report, " I regret the loss of two places of public worship at Fairfield, which took fire unintentionally from the flakes from the buildings, and I gave strict orders for the preservation of that of Norwalk." Lord Germaine wrote to General Clinton, November fourth, " You will acquaint General Tryon and the officers that were under his care that their conduct has met with his majesty's approbation; but I can not help lamenting with you, that the behavior of the rebels in firing from their houses upon the troops, rendered it necessary to make use of severities that are ever painful to British soldiers to inflict ; but were such as are justified by the general practices of all nations upon such occasions."

Lord Germaine's statement simply indicates how utterly incapable he was of appreciating the character of the war, and of distinguishing a contest between armies, from marauding expeditions against the homes of a civilized people. Green Farms, near by, suffered the loss of the meeting-house, fourteen dwellings, thirteen barns, and a store, " valued in all at £3904 17s."

The fleet crossed the Sound to Huntington, Long Island, for supplies, and on the eleventh returned to the Connecticut shore, and anchored five miles from the bay of Norwalk. A landing was effected that night by General Fraser at the Cow Pasture, " a peninsula on the east side of the harbor, within a mile and a half of the bridge which formed the communication between the east and west parts of the village, nearly equally divided by a salt creek."

The second division under General Garth landed at the " old well," on the west side of the harbor. Sir George Collier sums up the operations briefly : " For the treacherous conduct of the rebels in murdering the troops from windows of houses after safe-guards were granted them, the town of Norwalk was destroyed, with five large vessels, two privateer brigs on the stocks, two saw mills, considerable salt works, several warehouses of stores, merchandise, etc. The small town of Greenfield suffered the same chastisement."

" The rebels firing from the windows and the tops of houses, occasioned the *band of royal refugees* to set several of these on fire, which communicating to others, burned the whole town, and also several whale boats."

General Parsons arrived with two thousand troops, but too late to prevent the destruction of the town.

On the thirteenth the expedition returned to New York. General Washington was engaged on the sixth in inspecting out-posts, and on the seventh first learned that troops had been sent toward Connecticut. An express was sent to Governor Trumbull. Glover's brigade, then at Providence, was ordered to coöperate with the militia, in case the enemy should make a descent ; but the expedition had accomplished its mission before the orders were received.

This incursion has been thus referred to, in order to illustrate the character of that warfare which only incites resistance, embitters the struggle, and makes submission possible, only through extermination and ruin.

The British army was not furnished with the necessary reinforcements to contend in the field; and its activities were expended in forays which barbarized the soldiers and made subsequent *small* reinforcements useless.

The discussions embraced under "Statesmanship in War," and "Civil Wars," afford the key to this mode of warfare. The atrocities committed on either side, originated almost entirely in the employment of European mercenaries, Provincials, Royal refugees, and Indians. The Legionary troops and American partisan corps invariably took large liberties, reciprocated personal violence, and disregarded those principles of war between civilized nations, which as a general rule, were honorably regarded by the British and American regular troops.

The invasion of Connecticut was immediately followed by a strictly military expedition of characteristic boldness and distinguished success. As early as the tenth, Washington organized an expedition against Stony Point, the execution of which was intrusted to General Wayne. The plans finally adopted were substantially those of the Commander-in-chief. The details laid down by him were carefully executed by General Wayne.

The British garrison had been supplied with heavy guns, and strong defenses had been well advanced during the preceding six weeks of British occupation. Breastworks and batteries were built in advance of the fort, and two rows of abatis crossed the slope to the rear. The American right consisted of Colonel Febiger's regiment in front, followed by Colonel Webb's (Lieutenant-colonel Meigs commanding), and a detachment from West Point under Major Hull.

Colonel Butler's regiment, and two companies of North Carolina troops under Major Murphy, formed the left wing. Colonel Lee's light horse formed the reserve, and the brigade of General Muhlenberg, three hundred strong, which had been so manœuvered as not to lead vagrants or spies to anticipate its ultimate destination, formed the covering party, and took post on the opposite side of the swamp.

The troops left Sandy Beach at midnight of the fifteenth and marched by single files, over mountains, through deep morasses and difficult defiles. At eight o'clock on the evening of the sixteenth, the troops were within a mile and a half of the fort; and the columns of attack were rapidly formed, as previously designated in orders. A reconnoissance was made by Wayne, in person, and at half-past eleven the advance was ordered. One hundred and fifty volunteers, with fixed bayonets and unloaded muskets, under Lieutenant-colonel Fleury, led by a forlorn hope of twenty men under Lieutenant Gibbon of the Sixth Pennsylvania, formed the extreme right; and one hundred volunteers under Lieutenant Knox of Ninth Pennsylvania, led by a similar party of twenty, formed the extreme left.

To avoid the possibility of any deserter giving warning to the garrison, the previous purpose of the expedition was not disclosed until the final formation for the attack. The following order had been given, "If any soldier presume to take his musket from his shoulder,—attempt to fire, or begin the battle, till ordered by his proper officer, he shall be instantly put to death by the officer next him."

The full tide made the morass more difficult of passage, and the advance of Major Murphy, in the centre, was somewhat delayed. The right column fell in with an outpost which gave the alarm. Major Murphy's column advanced immediately, as if it were the only attacking party, and received a heavy fire of musketry and grape shot. Each officer and soldier, at the suggestion of Washington, had been directed to fix a piece of white paper to his cap, to distinguish him from an enemy, and a watchword "the fort is ours" had been given for each detachment to *shout aloud*, as they gained the positions they were ordered to attack "thus to prevent confusion and mistakes." The troops had been carefully drafted by Washington himself. A reward of five hundred dollars and immediate promotion, was offered the first man who entered the works; and one hundred dollars to each of the four, next in turn."

General Wayne, in person, led Febiger's solid column, half platoon front, followed by the other troops of the right wing; and Colonel Butler advanced, on his left, with the second division. The abatis were wrenched away by the pioneer corps. Every detachment moved on its course as if crowded by some resistless, unseen power, and the two assaulting columns met in the centre of the works, about the same moment.

General Wayne fell, while passing the abatis, wounded in the head, but not dangerously, by a musket ball; and the total American loss was only fifteen killed and eighty-three wounded.

The British casualties were one officer and nineteen men killed, six officers and sixty-eight men wounded, two officers and fifty-six men missing; twenty-five officers and four hundred and forty-seven men taken prisoners. The stores, valued at 158,640 dollars, were divided among the troops, in proportion to the pay of the officers and men.

The extraordinary and *literal* success of this movement, as planned, is due to Washington's mature preparation, and the no less remarkable faithfulness and skill of Wayne and his entire force. It was distinguished by a courtesy to prisoners and an entire absence of violence, after the surrender, which received high praise from British officials.

General Clinton moved up the river to cover Verplanck's Point from threatened attack, and General Sterling was detailed to attempt the recapture of the post; but it was abandoned by the Americans, as untenable, after removal of the stores, and the British troops resumed possession.

A second expedition, undertaken in July, without the sanction of Washington, was less fortunate. General McLean of the British army commanding at Halifax, established a post of six hundred men, on the site of the present town of Castine, Maine, on Penobscot Bay. The State of Massachusetts organized an expedition to reduce the post. Nineteen armed vessels carrying three hundred guns, and twenty-four transports carrying about a thousand men, entered that bay July twenty-fifth, and landed on the twenty-eighth. It was a failure from that moment. The troops were too few to storm the works; the armed ships were too ignorantly handled by an officer of militia, to make an impression, and the subsequent arrival of Sir George Collier with a sixty-four gun ship and five frigates, insured the dispersion of the American troops.

Twenty-four transports and the following armed vessels were burned. *Brigs:* Active, 16; Defence, 16; Hazard, 16; Diligence, 14;—The Providence (sloop) 14; was blown up. The Nancy, 16; and Rover, 10, (sloops) were captured; and the Spring-Bird, 10, (sloop) was burned.

On the twenty-second of July, Joseph Brandt led a party of Indians and disguised royalists into Orange County, New York, laying waste and destroying as they went, and at Minisink, ten miles west of Goshen, on the Neversink river, burned the church, houses and other property. Count Pulaski had quartered in the vicinity during the previous winter; but when he was ordered south, no troops were ordered to take his place. Application was made to Colonels Hathorn, Tuston, and Major Meeker of the militia for aid. An ill-managed pursuit, an ambuscade, and a massacre followed. Forty-four were killed in the field; and of one hundred and forty-nine who engaged in the enterprise, only thirty returned to tell their story.

In contrast with this expedition, and more like Wayne's assault of Stony Point, was Major Henry Lee's capture of Paulus Hook, directly opposite New York, where Jersey City now stands. The Hook, so called, was an island at high water, and here the British authorities had established an outpost of New York. A detachment from the Sixty-fourth British regiment, and a few Hessians occupied it. The Americans, four hundred in number, crossed the Hackensack, marched down the west bank of the Hudson, and stormed the works, using the bayonet only, not a shot having been fired. The assault was made at half past two o'clock on the morning of August nineteenth. The American loss was twenty, and that of the British fifty, and one hundred and fifty-eight prisoners. The retreat was accomplished with difficulty, but safely; the march having been at least thirty miles, over mountains, through morasses and defiles, with their rear threatened by a considerable force.

A single additional expedition is mentioned, that of General Sullivan against the Seneca Indians. The command was tendered to General Gates on the sixth of March, when the expedition was first authorized by Congress. An enclosed letter tendered the command to General Sullivan, if General Gates declined the command, in which event he was to relieve General Sullivan, then at Providence. General Gates, then at Boston, wrote under date of March 16th: "Last night I had the honor of your excellency's letter. The man who undertakes the Indian service should enjoy youth and strength, requisites I do not possess. It therefore grieves me, that your excellency should offer me command to which I am entirely unequal. In obedience to your command, I have forwarded your letter to General Sullivan, and that he may not be one moment detained, I have desired him to leave the command with General Glover, until I arrive in Providence."

General Sullivan marched from Easton, Pennsylvania, to Wyoming, reaching the valley on the last of July, and Tioga Point, New York, August eighth. General James Clinton commanded the northern division, and joined General Sullivan on the twenty-second of August. The additional brigades of Generals Hand, Poor, and Maxwell, Major Parr's rifle corps, and Proctor's artillery were attached to the command, making a total force of five thousand men. On the twenty-ninth, the battle of Chemung was fought, near the present site of

Elmira.   The American loss was seven killed; that of the enemy, unknown.   The towns of the " Six Nations" were laid waste.   Orchards, gardens, houses, cabins, clothing, provisions, and life, suffered indiscriminately, and the expedition, which returned in September, failed to put an end to Indian aggression, and equally failed to recommend Christian civilization by any contrast of its warfare with that of the enemies it was sent to punish.

The numerous minor operations of the year 1779, thus briefly outlined, have been illustrative of the war which centered in the movements of large armies; and as they fill the gap between pitched battles, are used to illustrate the extent of the war, and the characters whose military record is made up of the minor, as well as more prominent, events of the campaigns.

The year did not close however, without one conspicuous action, and that entailed upon the Southern States a series of struggles which lasted until the close of the war.

Admiral Arbuthnot arrived at New York, August twenty-fifth, with reinforcements, not greatly exceeding three thousand men, and relieved Sir George Collier.   Sir Andrew Hammond arrived with an additional force of fifteen hundred men from Cork, on the twenty-first of September.   The French squadron of Count D'Estaing having captured St. Vincents and Granada, suddenly appeared on the coast of Georgia.

Spain had joined France in war against Great Britain, and the whole line of British posts, from Halifax to St. Augustine, was exposed to such naval attacks as these two powers might attempt, to divert attention from their more direct operations against her West India possessions.   These small British reinforcements did not warrant any attempt upon West Point, which Washington was strengthening with great industry; and Sir Henry Clinton rightly apprehended an attack upon New York itself, by a coöperation of the French fleet with the American army.

General Clinton abandoned Newport, October twenty-fifth, then Stony Point and Verplanck's Point, so that New England and the Hudson river were free from British restraint.

The military operations for the season terminated with the siege of Savannah and the departure of Sir Henry Clinton from New York, to again attempt the capture of Charleston.

CHAPTER LXI.

SIEGE OF SAVANNAH. GENERAL CLINTON SAILS FOR
CHARLESTON, 1779.

GOVERNOR RUTLEDGE, of South Carolina, and General
Lincoln, then stationed at Charleston, were alike convinced
that the recovery of Savannah was the best method of protecting
South Carolina and rescuing the State of Georgia from British control. As early as July twentieth, Governor Wright had returned
from England and resumed office at once. The season was approaching when the West India harbors were liable to hurricanes or sudden
tempest, and the suspension of naval operations in those waters, after
the French capture of Granada, afforded a plausible opportunity for an
appeal to Count D'Estaing to employ his fleet against Savannah.
Monsieur Plombard, the French Consul at Charleston, concurred in
the feasibility of the movement, and messengers were at once sent to
the French commander to urge his coöperation. He thoroughly
approved the plan, and sailed immediately for the American coast.
A division of two ships and three frigates was sent to Charleston to
perfect the details of operations, and the remainder of his squadron,
consisting of twenty ships of the line, two fiftys and eleven frigates,
with six thousand troops, appeared off Tybee Island near Savannah,
on the eighth of September, and on the ninth, anchored off the bar.
The Experiment, 50, (British) Sir James Wallace commanding, and
two store ships were captured near the harbor entrance, and the
Ariel, 24, which had been cruising off Charleston bar, shared the
same fate.

Reference is made to map "Siege of Savannah" which is chiefly
copied from the survey of a British officer of the garrison, and was
engraved for Stedman in 1794.

Several of the ships had been seen off the coast as early as the
fourth, and the detachment which sailed for Charleston had given

still earlier warning, so that a dispatch-vessel had been sent to General Clinton to give notice of their presence on the coast. It does not appear, from the report of General Prevost, then in command at Savannah, that he was confident of their purpose to attack Savannah, until about the eighth; but from the first intimation of the appearance of French ships, he industriously applied himself to strengthening his defenses. The smaller armed vessels then in port were moved up the river, and their guns and seamen were transferred to the city. A horse-shoe battery was at once built on the extreme right of the town and entrusted to the care of sailors. The Fowey, Rose, Keppel and Germaine were kept in service and were so stationed as to defend the harbor passage from a landing by boats, or to retire up the river, as might be deemed necessary. Captain Henry's dispatch to the Admiralty, of November eighth, states that every exertion was then being made to increase the fortifications of the town. The buoys were removed from the harbor entrance, a large number of negroes were impressed and put at work; new redoubts of palmetto logs, inter-filled with sand, were erected; a strong line of palisades was completed, and an inner line of detached, but mutually supporting earth-works, were added to the lines. Reliefs of troops and negroes were assigned to duty, so that the labor was incessant, by night as well as by day. Captain Moncrieff, a distinguished engineer, had charge of the preparations; and every hour of protracted delay in making the investment was earnestly improved by the garrison in preparation to resist an attack.

As the purpose of the enemy unfolded, the guns were removed from the " Rose," already unseaworthy, and it was sunken with the Savannah and other vessels, in the channel. The Germaine retained her armament and was stationed off the horse-shoe redoubt, to flank the lines on the right of the town.

Lieutenant-colonel Conger was then at Sunbury with a small detachment, and Lieutenant-colonel Maitland was at Beaufort with a force of eight hundred excellent troops. Both officers were ordered to report at Savannah, with their commands.

The American authorities at Charleston took hold of the enterprise with great zeal, and sent galleys with other small vessels to assist the French in landing. This fleet of small craft promptly took on board three thousand five hundred and twenty-four French troops and passed up Ossabaw inlet to Bieulien, about twelve miles from Savannah, where they were landed under cover of four armed galleys.

The command marched immediately to Savannah, and on the six-teenth the Count D'Estaing summoned the garrison "to surrender to the arms of the King of France." . . . General Prevost had declined an unconditional surrender and invited terms. A truce of twenty-four hours was granted by Count D'Estaing; and during that period Lieutenant colonel Maitland skillfully conducted his com-mand through "Walls Cut," behind the islands, and joined the garri-son. The surrender was then peremptorily declined. The object of the truce had been realized.

At Charleston all was active. The legislature adjourned:—militia took the place of the regulars in the forts, and on the eighth, after four days' notice of the proposed movement, a considerable force marched for Savannah. General Lincoln left the city on the twelfth.

General Prescott had not neglected the land approaches to Savan-nah, while especially watching the river front; but had destroyed bridges, and otherwise obstructed the roads, so that the Americans did not join the French army until the sixteenth.

A council of war was held; the demand made upon the garrison by the Count D'Estaing, prior to the arrival of General Lincoln, was satisfactorily explained, and on the twenty-third the trenches were commenced. The difficulty of procuring animals of draught for hauling the heavy guns a distance of five miles, occasioned a delay which still further enured to the benefit of the British troops.

On the twenty-fourth, Major Graham made a sally from the in-trenchments without valuable results. On the night of the twenty-seventh, Major McArthur made such a bold and skillful demonstration toward the centre of the allied forces as to occasion a firing between the French and American camps. On the fifth of October, at an early hour, fire was opened from a battery of nine mortars, and thirty-three pieces of heavy artillery, from the land side, and sixteen guns from the river, and was maintained without interruption until the eighth. The works were strengthened and advanced, additional guns were placed in position, and the effect was soon visible in the burning of houses and general damage to the town of Savannah, without serious injury to the defensive works. On the eighth, Major L'Enfant, with five men advanced under fire, screened themselves behind the abatis, and kindled the timber; but the green wood failed to burn, and the attempt, however daring, was a failure.

General Prevost sent out a flag requesting permission to send the women and children out of the city. This was refused by both General Lincoln and Count D'Estaing, and the cannonading continued.

The French fleet had been more than a month on the coast. On his arrival, the Count D'Estaing stated that his time was very limited, and the opinion prevailed among the American officers that his delay before Savannah would not necessarily exceed from ten to sixteen days. Upon this understanding he landed his troops. The French West India Islands had been left suddenly without naval support; and the time already wasted had been sufficient for the British fleet at New York to be advised of the siege, and make the voyage to relieve the garrison. Many seamen and gunners from the French ships were in the trenches, and the fleet itself was seriously exposed. These facts, in connection with the lateness of the season, were urgent reasons for pressing the siege. The French commander, as at Newport, shrank from no conflict, but held that his fleet was his first care, and that his support of America must be consistent with his allegiance to France. The engineers reported that it would require ten days more to complete the trenches. It had therefore become impracticable for him to await the slow process of a regular siege, by systematic approaches, and a council of war resolved to assault the British works without delay. The only alternative was to raise the siege.

The force detailed for the direct assault consisted of three thousand five hundred French troops, six hundred American regulars, including Pulaski's corps, and two hundred and fifty Charleston militia, the whole force divided into two columns. General Dillon, of the Irish brigade in the French service, was to take the extreme left, and pass under and past Spring Hill, with the purpose of attacking the British extreme right near the horse-shoe or sailors' battery.

The Count D'Estaing and General Lincoln were to move with the second division, which was to attack the Spring Hill redoubt itself and its flanking defenses, while the Count Pulaski was ordered to storm the redoubt still farther to the north on their left.

General Huger, of South Carolina, with five hundred men of the First and Second brigades of militia, General Williams' brigade, and the Second battalion of militia, were to make *feint* attacks upon the south and east sides of the town, with orders to improve any fair opportunity to push on and take the garrison in the rear; and the trenches and batteries were to be occupied by American militia, as if the usual cannonading was to be continued.

On the evening of the eighth, General Lincoln ordered the troops to place white paper on their hats for distinction from the enemy, and to be ready to make the assault at four o'clock the next morning, the ninth, which had been designated for the movement.

The march was so delayed that it was daylight when Count D'Estaing, supported by General Lincoln, Colonels Laurens and McIntosh, reached the foot of Spring Hill and commenced the attack. Under a wasting fire the French troops and the American light infantry pressed on, heedless of the fall of men by the score at every step. The picked troops of the garrison had been concentrated to meet the assault. General Dillon pressed so far into the marsh, beyond the main column, as to lose his way, so that he was not disentangled until the battle was over ; and the column of General Huger which waded through rice fields was unable to make any practical advance, and retired after a loss of twenty-eight men. The Sergeant-major of the Charleston grenadiers had deserted during the night, after the order had been promulgated to the troops, and the garrison adapted their defense to the well understood onset which they were to resist.

Count Pulaski promptly took his position, and by the impetus of his attack was carried into the face of superior numbers where he fought without yielding, until he was mortally wounded. The head of the main column not only forced the entrance to the Spring Hill redoubt, but climbed the palisades, and at one moment Lieutenants Bush and Homes, of the Second South Carolina, had planted the South Carolina colors by the side of the French standard, within the redoubt. Both officers fell, and Lieutenant Grey raised the colors only to receive a mortal wound. Sergeant Jasper raised one of them a third time, but received his death wound also. He lived to bring away the colors in safety. For fifty-five minutes the assailing column, crowded within a narrow space, was exposed to a constant fire from troops well under cover, as well as from the British grenadiers and Major Glazier's marines who met them in front.

General Moultrie says, " Our troops were so crowded in the ditch and upon the beam, that they could hardly raise an arm, and while they were in this situation, huddled up together, the British loaded and fired deliberately, without any danger to themselves.

At this time the Germaine and several galleys maintained a deadly enfilading fire across the slope of the hill, until, overwhelmed with the severity of the storm, the troops withdrew to their encampments.

With perhaps the exception of Bunker Hill, there was no action of the war where so great a loss was received in so brief a period.

31

The British casualties were as follows: Captain Tawes, who commanded the Spring Hill redoubt with great gallantry, Captain Simpson, Lieutenant McPherson, Ensign Pollard, and thirty-six non-commissioned officers and privates were killed. The wounded and missing, including two captains and two lieutenants, numbered sixty-three, and the deserters and missing fifty-two.

The American casualties included among the killed, Majors Mott, Wise, and Jones, Captains Beraud, Shepherd, and Donnom, and Lieutenants Hume, Bush, Wickham, and Bailey; among the wounded and missing, General Pulaski (mortally), nine captains and eleven lieutenants; non-commissioned officers, and privates killed and wounded, according to General Lincoln's statement, one hundred and seventy. General Moultrie, in his Memoirs, puts the American casualties at four hundred and fifty-seven, which is undoubtedly the correct number.

General D'Estaing was twice wounded, and the French casualties amounted to fifteen officers and one hundred and sixty-eight subalterns and soldiers killed, and forty-three officers and four hundred and eleven subalterns and soldiers wounded.

Lieutenant-colonel Maitland, of the British army, Major Moncrief, chief engineer, and Captain Henry, who had charge of the naval forces, distinguished themselves; and Colonel Laurens was equally conspicuous for gallantry at the head of the American light infantry. The French withdrew their artillery, and sailed on the twenty-ninth, and the American army retired to Charleston.

General Moultrie says in his Memoirs, "There can not be any doubt, but if the French and Americans had marched into Savannah when they arrived on the seventeenth, they would have carried the town very easily, because at that time they had only the Spring battery completed, and no abatis round the town," and then adds, "after this repulse we were in a much worse situation than before. The Count D'Estaing departed; the unfortunate militia of Georgia, who had taken the British protection could not go back to them again, but were obliged to seek shelter in a strange country, or live in the backwoods of their own. It depressed our spirits, we began to be apprehensive for the safety of these two Southern States; it also depreciated our money so low that it was scarcely worth anything."

The result of the siege of Savannah determined the movements of both the northern armies. The French fleet was dispersed by a storm soon after it left the American coast, and four frigates fell into the hands of the British. A portion of the fleet returned to the West Indies, and the Count D'Estaing returned to France.

On the twenty-sixth of December, Sir Henry Clinton left New York to the command of Lieutenant-general Knyphausen, and embarked with seven thousand five hundred men for Charleston under convoy of five ships of the line and several frigates, Admiral Arbuthnot commanding the squadron. Washington had assembled a large force of New York and Massachusetts militia for the purpose of making an attack upon New York, but these were at once disbanded.

Learning that Sir Henry Clinton was embarking a large force upon transports, and believing that their destination was either Georgia or South Carolina, he ordered the North Carolina brigade to march to Charleston in November, the Virginia line to march in December, and the remainder of the army was placed in winter quarters.

One division under General Heath was stationed in the Highlands, the cavalrymen were sent to Connecticut, and Washington with the main army established his headquarters, for the second time, at Morristown, New Jersey.

BRITISH EFFECTIVE FORCE.

NOTE. From " Original Returns in the British Record Office." Date, December 1st, 1779.

New York and its Dependencies.............	British.......................	13,848
	German.......................	10,836
	Provincial....................	4,072
		28,756
Halifax and Penobscot..		3,460
Georgia...		3,930
West Florida...		1,787
Bermuda and Providence Island.....		636
		9,813

Total, 38,569.

CHAPTER LXII.

JANUARY TO JULY, 1780. CONDITION OF THE ARMIES.

WHILE General Clinton was once more on the ocean, to again attempt the capture of Charleston, the American army was in huts, surrounded by snow to the even depth of two feet, badly drifted in all defiles and undergoing a physical ordeal hardly less trying than that of Valley Forge. In order to induce Congress to make still more urgent efforts to bring the army up to a fair service-standard, Washington prepared a statement of his force as it appeared on the muster rolls of the army. That statement included the total nominal force, (except from South Carolina and Georgia) with all independent organizations; and upon the impossible assumption that every man on the original rolls was still living and in the service, the aggregate was only twenty-seven thousand and ninety-nine men; this included invalids, drummers, fifers, in fact, the entire army.

Two thousand and fifty-one enlistments were to expire December thirty-first. Six thousand four hundred and twenty-six would expire March thirty-first. By the last of April, the total reduction by expiration of term of service would reach eight thousand one hundred and eighty-one; by the last of June, ten thousand one hundred and fifty-eight; by the last of September, ten thousand seven hundred and nine, and during the year, twelve thousand one hundred and fifty-seven.

The total force, enlisted for the war, was but fourteen thousand nine hundred and ninety-eight; and from the numbers already given, there was to be made the necessary allowance for artificers, armorers, wagoners, quartermasters, employees and all the subordinate details which lessen the fighting force of an army; as well as the casualties since the original muster. The several States furnished their quota for different periods and at different times; so that there was a constant addition of raw levies, and the army had no opportu-

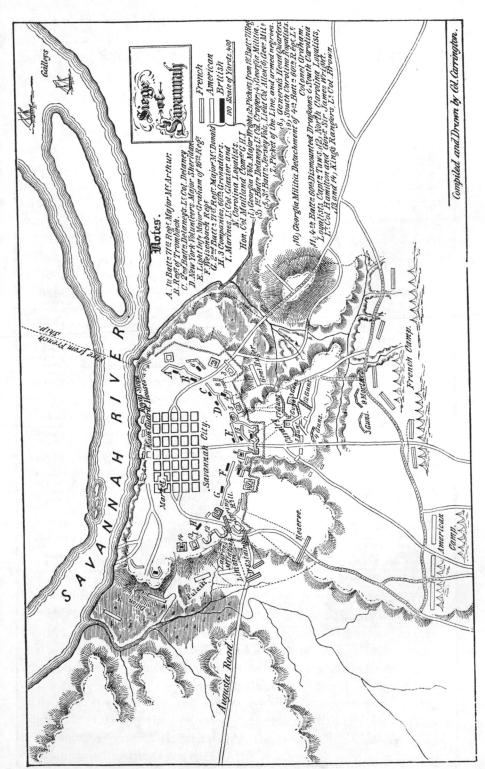

Siege of Savannah

SEPTEMBER 16th to OCTOBER 9th 1780

American Commanders
LINCOLN

LAURENS, McINTOSH, HUGER, DILLON, PULASKI

Strength, 3,600   Casualties, 457

French Commander
Lieut.-Gen. COUNT CHARLES HECTOR D'ESTAING

Strength, 6,000   Casualties, 651

POSITION OF THE ALLIED ARMIES.—The French fleet arrived off Tybee Island September 8th, and anchored near the bar. On the 9th the troops landed twelve miles below Savannah. and on the 16th D'Estaing summoned the garrison to surrender. General Prevost asked and gained a truce of twenty-four hours, during which interval Lt.-Col. Maitland skillfully eluded the American outposts, and joined, with eight hundred excellent troops. Surrender was then declined The American army joined the French on the 16th, and batteries were at once placed in position.

BRITISH POSITION.—At the first intimation that a large French fleet was off the coast, General Prevost removed the buoys from the harbor, and put a large force of negroes at work, to strengthen the post. New redoubts, made of double palmetto logs, interfilled with sand, a strong palisade, and a series of minor detached defences, were pushed forward with energy. Relays of men enabled the work to be carried on at night, as well as by day. Capt. Moncrieff, Engineer-in-charge, has left his notes, which are reproduced, on map. Major Graham made a sally Sept. 24, and Major McArthur another on the 27th, at night, but without valuable results.

NOTES.

NOTE I.—On the 5th of October, a battery of nine mortars, thirty-three heavy guns from the land side, and sixteen from the river, opened fire, and this was kept up until the 8th. Houses were burned, but little damage was done to the defences. It became evident that the siege would be protracted, and the season of the year was so dangerous that the French fleet could not remain longer on the coast. It was necessary to raise the siege, or storm the town.

NOTE II.—The force detailed for that assault consisted of 3,500 French troops; 600 American regulars; Pulaski's corps, and 250 militia; to form two columns.

NOTE III.—General Dillon, of the Irish Brigade, in the French service, was to take the extreme left, and attack the horse-shoe or sailor's battery, at the British right; D'Estaing and Lincoln were to attack Spring Hill, and Pulaski to attack a redoubt beyond, toward the direction of Dillon's advance, while Huger and Williams were to make feint attacks, upon the east side of town, and take advantage of any opportunity to force an entrance.

NOTE IV.—The batteries maintained fire, as if preparatory to an assault in front; but by the desertion of the Sergeant-Major of the Charleston Grenadiers, during the night, the enemy had knowledge of the real plan of attack.

NOTE V.—Dillon got involved in a marsh, and Huger could make little progress through the rice fields, and lost 27 men. Pulaski fell, mortally wounded, in a brave, but unsuccessful attack.

NOTE VI.—The main column, which was also accompanied by Laurens and McIntosh, forced the palisades and the ditch, but were met by the British Grenadiers and Glazier's Marines, whose concentrated fire, for fifty-five minutes, was too heavy to be silenced. Sergeant Jasper received his death wound here. Bush and Holmes, 2d S. C. Regt., planted their colors within the redoubt, and fell in their defence.

NOTE VII.—D'Estaing was twice wounded. The French lost 15 officers killed and 43 wounded; rank and file, 168 killed and 411 wounded.

NOTE VIII.—The siege of Savannah was at an end. Prompt attack, when the troops landed, would have promised success.

References :

CARRINGTON'S "BATTLES OF THE AMERICAN REVOLUTION," pp. 476-483.

School Histories:

Anderson, ¶ 88 ; p. 90.
Barnes, ¶ 2 ; p. 129.
Berard (Bush), ¶ 105-6 ; p. 166-7.
Goodrich, C. A.(Seaveys) ¶ 4; p. 134.
Goodrich, S. G., ¶ 1-6; p. 250.
Hassard, ¶ 6 ; p. 204.

Holmes, ¶ 10 ; p. 141.
Lossing, ¶ 11 ; p. 170-1.
Quackenbos, ¶ 369 ; p. 267.
Ridpath, ¶ 9-10; p. 215.
Sadlier (Excel.), ¶ 14; p. 200-1.
Stephens, A. H., ¶ 23 ; p. 212.

Swinton, ¶ 184-7 ; p. 141.
Scott, ¶ 1-3 ; p. 196-7.
Thalheimer (Eclectic), ¶ 285 ; p. 163.
Venable, ¶ 155 ; p. 118.

nity to become alike disciplined and drilled, in all its parts. Such was the condition of the army of the United States when the second campaign in the Southern States began.

At the time this statement was made, shortly before General Clinton sailed, the British force at New York and. its dependencies consisted of twenty-eight thousand seven hundred and fifty-six effectives.

Three thousand nine hundred and thirty men were in Georgia: one thousand seven hundred and eighty-seven in Florida ; and at Penobscot, Maine, and Halifax, subject to call, there was an additional British force of three thousand four hundred and sixty men, making a total force of nearly thirty-eight thousand men.

General Clinton sailed with seven thousand five hundred and fifty men ; thus increasing the British force in the Southern Department to thirteen thousand two hundred and sixty-seven men, and leaving twenty-one thousand and six in and near New York. Even this garrison was not without apprehensions of an attack from Washington's army. Unprecedented cold froze the bay so that teams and artillery could cross upon the ice.

The British army in New York was almost in a starving and frozen condition. Transports were broken up for fuel and almost all country supplies were cut off by the extremely cold weather and the difficulty of sending out expeditions to hunt for food or wood.

Notwithstanding the severe cold, Lord Stirling crossed to Staten Island with a force of twenty-five hundred men, but failed to surprise the posts, and a channel, which opened quite suddenly through the ice, put the garrison in speedy communication with the city.

A few prisoners were taken, but the men suffered severely. On the twenty-fifth of the same month, Lieutenant-general Knyphausen sent a small command across the ice, at Paulus Hook, which captured a company at Newark; while Lieutenant-colonel Buskirk crossed from Staten Island to the main land and captured the picket guard at Elizabethtown, with two majors, two captains and forty-two privates. In the first instance the academy was burned, and in the other, the town house and the church of Rev. James Caldwell, then Chaplain in Colonel Elias Dayton's regiment.

On the second of February, Lieutenant-colonel Norton with four companies of guards, two of Hessians and one of Yagers, with some cavalry, and two small guns, made a march, using sleighs for the men, against a small American post near White Plains, in Westchester county; burned the house of a man by the name of Young, which was the post headquarters, and captured ninety prisoners, incurring a loss of two killed and twenty-three wounded. Such random incursions comprised the whole active operations of the garrison of New York until spring,

The American army at Morristown fought cold, nakedness and famine. During the "*great freeze*" of January, 1780, the suffering became intense. Washington found that even military constraint was unable to collect food from a region almost depleted of supplies. His transportation was so limited that it was with difficulty that fuel could be hauled for camp fires, and the troops were repeatedly without meat for two or three days. It was at such a time that the people of New Jersey, whose soil was a constant battle-field from the beginning to the end of the war, exhibited their confidence in Washington and their sympathy with his troops. The patriotism of the citizens was of the same temper as that of the people of South Carolina. In each State the royalist element was bold and active. As the capture of Charleston subsequently developed that element and gave it organization and boldness, so the presence of General Clinton's army in New York encouraged the belief that British supremacy would ultimately be restored. The American royalists therefore considered the property of the patriots to be legitimate plunder; and the American soldier who found an enemy in an old neighbor, and regarded him, at best, as only a spy, was quickened to acts of violence which he would not have committed against a British regular.

Quite a large number of those who were disaffected to the new government had joined the British Provincial battalions, and with those of New York of this class, there was carried into General Clinton's returns for December, 1779, a force of four thousand and sixty-four men. Thus organized, and knowing the country thoroughly, they made successful irritating forays, and the State was treated as a free granary for both armies. In Washington's hour of trial, the self-sacrifice of heads of families, past the age of military service, and of the women, was practically extended to his relief. Impressive instances are numerous, and they illustrate one of the redeeming elements of a war of revolution, when surpassing trials develop transcendent virtues.

The Rev. Dr. Joseph F. Tuttle, afterwards President of Wabash College, a son of New Jersey, and for a long time a resident of Morris county, devoted many years to the study of the Revolutionary history of that State, and by personal visits to survivors of the war, at their own homes, accumulated a store of memorial facts which greatly redound to the credit of that people.   Both Mr. Irving and Mr. Bancroft have acknowledged their indebtedness to his valuable manuscripts, and the author cites a few facts kindly furnished, to illustrate the condition of affairs at Morristown, the spirit of the people, and the state of the army at the beginning of 1780.

The camp.   " The paths at the camp near Morristown were marked with blood from the bare-footed soldiers."

Its approaches.   " *The enemy never passed Short Hills.*   The alarm gun, the beacon fires, the express riders, were always ready.   The light kindled at Short Hills, could be seen at Pompton and Baskingridge; and this was answered from Kimball mountain, Rockaway Heights, and Vernon, in Sussex."   " The pass through to Chatham was as a closed gate and secure."

Devotion of women.   " Mrs. Uzal Kitchell, daughter of Daniel Tuttle, with husband, father, and four brothers in the service, declined a British protection, saying, " If the God of battles will not protect us we will fare with the rest."   " As many as twelve soldiers at a time were repeatedly billeted at her house, and as with many others of like spirit, they contributed from slender means for army uses, without asking for vouchers for the articles furnished."

Hunger appeased.   " On one occasion her sister, Mrs. Keturah Flatt, filled a large kettle with meat, placed it over the fire, and started to sift some meal for a hungry party.   They eagerly snatched the uncooked food in her absence, and preferred the unsifted meal, because there was more of it, and it was good enough as it was."

Clothing.   " Stockings, mittens, leggins, blankets, and all kinds of domestic fabric employed these earnest women."

" The Kitchells, Smiths and Greens of Hanover; the Jacksons, Beeches and Winds of Rockaway and Pequannock; the Condits, Fords, Johns, and Hathaways of Morristown; the Carters, Piersons, Sayers, Millers, Thompsons and Browns of Chatham; the Thompsons, Drakes and Carys of Windham, were only a few, who from the beginning of the war counted all things as loss unless independence was won; and the army was made recipients of their bounty."

All this was in keeping with that spirit which comforted the army about Boston in 1776, which saved Virginia and the Carolinas, which worked mightily by firesides, like unseen leaven, to maintain the struggle which Congress well nigh despaired of, and the army seemed too feeble to sustain.

Washington says of New Jersey at that period, that " his requisitions were punctually complied with, and in many counties exceeded."

Irving says : " Exhausted as the State was by repeated drains, yet, when deep snows cut off all distant supplies, Washington's army subsisted by it."

Bancroft says: " Generally throughout the war, the women of America never grew weary of yielding up articles necessary for the comfort of their own households, to relieve the distresses of the soldiers. The women of Philadelphia rallying round the amiable Esther Reed, wife of the President of Pennsylvania, now made a more earnest effort ; they brought together large donations of clothing, and invited the ladies of other States to adopt a like plan.   They thus assisted to keep alive the spirit of patriotism in the army, but their gifts could not meet its ever-recurring wants."

On the eleventh of January, Quartermaster-general Green wrote, " Such weather never did I feel.   For six or eight days it has been so cold that there has been no living abroad ; the snow is also very deep, and much drifted.   We drive over the tops of fences.   We have been alternately out of meat and bread for eight or nine days past, and without either for three or four."

With all this destitution of the army and local waste through New Jersey, the New England States and Pennsylvania were once more without British garrisons ; and the active anxieties of impending danger gave way to a lethargy which seemed almost to ignore like dangers which had only been transferred to other portions of one common country.   There was scarcity of money.   Practically, there was no money.   The soldiers had not been paid for five months ; their families were suffering ; recruiting was almost suspended ; and the burden of the war seemed to rest more depressingly on the Northern States which had respite from its active operations, than upon the Southern States, which, left mostly to themselves, were called to endure afflictions such as New Jersey had experienced during previous campaigns.   The comparative independence of the separate States weakened their essential union, and the jealousy which Congress, representing the States, entertained of central authority, prevented that prompt confidence in the counsels of the Commander-in-chief which had been so reliable after the battle of Trenton, and which was indispensable to general success. These elements had memorable expressions which illustrate this crisis of the war.

Washington thus states the first difficulty : " Certain I am, unless Congress are vested with powers, by the separate States, competent to the great purposes of war, or assume them as a matter of right, and they and the States act with more energy than they have hitherto done, our cause is lost. We can no longer drudge along in the old way. By ill-timing in the adoption of measures; by delays in the execution of them, or by unwarrantable jealousies, we incur enormous expenses and derive no benefit from them. One state will comply with a requisition of Congress; another neglects to do it : a third executes it by halves : and all differ in the manner, the matter, or so much in point of time, that we are always working up hill. While such a system as the present one, or rather want of one prevails, we shall ever be unable to apply our strength or resources to any advantage. . . . I see one head gradually changing into thirteen. I see one army branching into thirteen, which instead of looking up to Congress as the supreme controlling power of the United States, are considering themselves as dependent upon their respective States. . . . Congress have already scarcely a power left but such as concerns foreign transactions ; for as to the army, they are at present little more than the medium through which its wants are conveyed to the States. This body never had, or at least in few instances, ever exercised powers adequate to the purposes of war. . . . In a word, I see the powers of Congress declining too fast for the consideration and respect which are due to them as the great representative body of America, and I am fearful of the consequences."

Unequal pay and bounties continued to aggravate these difficulties, until Washington wrote to the President of Congress on the third of April, so plainly and unequivocally of the mutinous spirit, intense disgust and absolute desperation of his small, famished and depleted command, that a committee of three was appointed, after a hot debate, to consult with him as to measures of relief. Even this advisory committee was reluctantly conceded. M. de La Vergne wrote on the seventeenth of April to Count Vergennes: " It was said that this appointment of a committee, would be putting too much power in a few hands and especially in those of the Commander-in-chief ;— that his influence was already too great ; that even his virtues afforded motives for alarm ; that the enthusiasm of the army, joined to the kind of dictatorship already confided to him, put Congress and the

United States at his mercy ; that it was not expedient to expose a man of the highest virtues to such temptations." General Schuyler, then in Congress, John Matthews and Nathaniel Peabody were appointed the committee.

In a letter to James Duane, dated May fourteenth, Washington says of the appointment of General Schuyler upon this committee, that "no man could be more useful, from his perfect knowledge of the resources of the country, the activity of his temper, his fruitfulness of expedients and his sound military sense."

As a result of this conference and the persistent pressure which the Commander-in-chief brought to bear upon Congress, it was determined that the soldiers' pay should be equalized and more systematic efforts be made to recruit and maintain the army.

The first six months of the year were peculiarly trying because the main army was unable to take part in the active operations of the Southern campaign, during the occupation of New York by a superior force, supported by an adequate fleet. The capture of Charleston, and another invasion of New Jersey, for the purpose of capturing the Morristown fastness, were the chief military events, but there were other incidents which require notice before those actions receive attention.

On the twelfth of February, Congress affirmed the action of a General Court Martial which sentenced Arnold, then commanding at Philadelphia, to be reprimanded for giving passes to disaffected citizens and using public transportation for private uses. The reprimand was mildly administered, but Arnold was angry. His life of ostentatious display, wild extravagance and loose views of moral obligation had aroused public indignation ; and the charges which would have been comparatively unnoticed if he had observed Republican simplicity, were pressed somewhat sternly, because of suspicions that he had repeatedly used his official position for private emolument.

General La Fayette returned from France, reached Morristown on the twelfth of May, was received with enthusiasm, and brought the welcome news that France had detailed the Count de Rochambeau with a large army to aid the United States, and the first division was already on its passage. The extraordinary tact of this officer, not a little aided by the efforts of the beautiful and enthusiastic Marie Antoinette, had achieved this result ; and with wise appreciation of the difficulty of real harmony between French and Anglo-American troops, he succeeded in securing such instructions from Louis XVI.

that a jar of interest or duty between the allies seemed improbable. "The troops were to obey Washington; to admit the precedence of American officers of equal rank; on all formal occasions to yield the right to the American army, and bear in mind that the whole purpose was heartily and efficiently to execute the will of the American Commander-in-chief." The only drawback was found in the entirely unprepared condition of the United States to provide for their support, and to furnish an equivalent army force, so as to make the joint operations more immediately effective.

Long before their arrival the American army had lost in numbers even more than anticipated by Washington, in his report already cited. While the call from South Carolina for aid became more and more imperative he was compelled to groan in spirit and send only words of sympathy, instead of men to fight. On the second of April his whole force, on both sides of the Hudson river, consisted of only ten thousand four hundred rank and file and of these two thousand eight hundred had but four weeks to serve. Lord Rawdon took two thousand five hundred British and Hessians to reinforce General Clinton, but nearly twelve thousand remained behind; and while this warning of the purpose of the British commander to strike with decisive effort at Charleston, aroused the alarm of Washington for the fate of the Southern campaign, he could not leave the Northern States to render substantial aid. The Maryland division, however, the Delaware regiment and the First artillery, with the consent of Congress, were ordered South; and the Baron De Kalb was instructed to lead the troops to Charleston. It is just here that one fact in the struggle for American Independence should have specific notice. From 1776, before Boston, and through the entire war, the states of Maryland and Delaware were represented on nearly every battle-field. Although their troops were few in numbers they were distinguished for valor, so that their failure in an emergency was a sign of great peril, or of some over-mastering superiority, or panic.

But it was not on battle fields, north or south, that the entire interest of the period concentrated. The southern army was numerically weak, and the northern army was hungry. On the twenty-fifth of May two Connecticut regiments mutinied, declaring that they would march home, "or at least gain subsistence by the point of the bayonet." Handbills printed in New York were secretly circulated, urging the soldiers to desert. "This mutiny," says Washington, quite impressively, "has given infinite concern. There was no money but continental paper, and adds, " *it is evidently impracticable, from the immense quantity it would require, to pay them as much as would make up the depreciation.*" " This is a decisive moment, one of the most ; I will go farther and say *the* most important America has seen. The court of France has made a glorious effort for our deliverance, and if we disappoint its intentions by our supineness, we must become contemptible in the eyes of all mankind; nor can we after venture to confide that our allies will persist in an attempt to establish what, it will appear, we want inclination or ability to assist them in."

General Greene, then Quartermaster-general, thus addressed the Colonel of the Morristown militia : " There are no more provisions than to serve one regiment in the magazine. The late terrible storm, the depth of the snow, and the drifts in the roads prevent the little stock from coming forward which is in distant magazines. The roads must be kept open by the inhabitants, or the army can not be subsisted. Unless the good people lend their assistance to forward supplies, the army must disband. The army is stripped naked of teams as possible, to lessen the consumption of forage. Call to your aid the overseers of highways and every other order of men who can give dispatch to this business."

" P. S. Give no copies of this for fear it should get to the enemy."

General Greene resigned his place as Quartermaster-general, but continued to act until August, when Colonel Pickering assumed its duties. He desired to join the southern army.

On the thirteenth of June, Congress, without consulting Washington, appointed General Gates to the command of the Southern Department. He had spent the winter at his home in Virginia, but eagerly accepted this high command. His old confidant and companion in arms, Charles Lee, sententiously forewarned him on his departure ; " Take care that you do not exchange northern laurels for southern willows."

CHAPTER LXIII.

SOUTH CAROLINA AND NEW JERSEY INVADED. SIEGE OF CHARLESTON. BATTLE OF SPRINGFIELD. 1780.

GENERAL CLINTON left New York December twenty-sixth, 1779. Under fair promise, he had a voyage of only ten days before him. He cleared the ice of the harbor without difficulty, and the whole fleet got under way. For a few days the weather proved favorable; the admiral led the van, and kept in shore, but this gleam of fortune was not sufficiently permanent to give a fortunate termination to the voyage. A succession of storms dispersed the fleet. Few ships arrived at Tybee, in Georgia, before the end of January. Some were taken, others separated, one ordnance vessel foundered, most of the artillery, and *all* the cavalry horses perished. Such is Lieutenant-colonel Tarleton's brief record of the voyage. In his " History of the Campaigns of 1780 and 1781," he says, " The richness of the country, its vicinity to Georgia, and its distance from General Washington, pointed out the advantages and facility of its conquest. While it would be an unspeakable loss to the Americans, the possession of it would tend to secure to the crown the southern part of the continent which stretches beyond it."

The British troops made Tybee Island, near Savannah, their first rendezvous, but were unable to leave for South Carolina until the tenth of February, landing on St. John's Island, thirty miles below Charleston, on the following day.

The troops which accompanied General Clinton consisted of the following commands, and were reported at the time, at London, to be of the strength now indicated. The statement is given ; but so many *round numbers* indicate error.

Light Infantry	800	Queen's Rangers	200
Grenadiers	900	Guides and Pioneers	150
Seventh Regiment	400	Fanning's Corps	100

Twenty-third Regiment . . 400	Hessian Grenadiers 1000
Thirty-third " . . . 450	Ferguson's Corps 300
Forty-second " . . . 700	Second Hessian Regiment . . . 800
Sixty-third " . . . 400	Yagers 200
Sixty-fourth " . . . 350	British Artillery 200
British Legion 200	

Total . . . . 7550.

Lieutenant-colonel Tarleton states that transportation was provided for eight thousand five hundred men; and that is the number generally reported as connected with the expedition prior to reinforcements received from Savannah and New York.

Admiral Arbuthnot furnished the convoy, consisting of the Europe, 64; Russel, 74; Robuste, 74; Defiance, 64; Raisonable, 64; Renown, 50; Romulus, 44; Roebuck, 44; Blonde, 32; Perseus, 32; Camilla, 20; Raleigh, 28; Richmond, 32; Virginia, 28.

The British troops were promptly transferred to James Island, then crossed Stono and Ashley rivers, and took position across the narrow neck between the Ashley and Cooper rivers, where they established themselves on the twelfth of March. It will be noticed by reference to map, "Siege of Charleston," that the possession of Wappoo Creek enabled the British troops to use small boats for transferring troops to the Ashley river, without entering the harbor from the sea. Meanwhile, the British fleet had been ordered to silence Fort Moultrie, and force an entrance to the inner bay.

The garrison of the city did not exceed two thousand two hundred regulars and one thousand militia, when General Clinton crossed the Ashley; but he delayed his advance upon the city for two weeks, so that the troops under General Patterson, who had been ordered to join him from Savannah, could arrive and make his force equal to any contingency of stubborn resistance by the American troops. Governor Rutledge had reached Charleston, having discretionary authority from the State to act according to his own will in all matters of essential concern; and General Lincoln was in command of the garrison. It appears, from documentary data, that the retention of the city was principally owing to the demand of the inhabitants, since the neglect to anticipate an attack from the land side had prevented the completion of thoroughly defensive works; and it was clearly an error to retain the town with inadequate forces. Commodore Whipple of the American navy felt strong confidence, not shared by Washington, that he could prevent the British ships from crossing the bar; and too much confidence was reposed in the capacity of Fort Moultrie to maintain its good record, although it had been allowed to become almost worthless from neglect. The few vessels at his (Whipple's) command, consisted of the Briscole, nominally 44, but mounting only 26 guns ; the Providence and Boston, each 32 guns ; the Queen of France, 28 ; L'Aventure and Truite, each 26 guns ; the Ranger and General Lincoln, each 20 guns, and the Notre Dame of 14 guns. These were moored between Sullivan's Island and the middle ground, previously noticed. On the twentieth of March the British squadron safely crossed the bar, and the American fleet retired. With the exception of the Ranger, 20, the American ships were sunk in Cooper River, between the city and Shutes Folly ; and the guns, stores and men were transferred to the city defenses. The Ranger and two galleys were placed in Hog Island channel to keep up communications with the country north of Charleston.

On the seventh of April General Woodford crossed Cooper River, and joined the garrison with seven hundred Virginia troops, having made a forced march of nearly five hundred miles in thirty days. The Americans still retained a post at Monk's Corner ; and the garrison depended wholly upon that section of the State for supplies, after the Neck came into the possession of British troops. General Clinton thoroughly understood his position, but still awaited the arrival of General Patterson.

At one o'clock on the ninth, Admiral Arbuthnot weighed anchor, leading with the Roebuck, followed in order by the Richmond, Romulus, Blonde, Virginia, Raleigh, Sandwich, armed ship, and the Renown, and passed Fort Moultrie with a loss of only twenty-seven men, without stopping for its fire, and came to anchor off Fort Johnson which had been abandoned. "The Aretus ordnance ship grounded and was burned. The Richmond's foretop-mast was shot away ; some damage was done to the masts and rigging of the other vessels, but their hulls suffered but slightly."

General Lincoln had confidently expected that the proclamation of General Rutledge, and the great emergency which threatened the city, would bring a larger force to the defense, but he was disappointed.

General Patterson marched for Charleston about the middle of March with twelve hundred men. He was joined by Lieutenant-colonel Tarleton near Port Royal. This officer had partially remounted his dragoons, and Major Cochran with the legion infantry and Major Ferguson's riflemen, formed an additional force, to make the reinforcement important to General Clinton's success.

Several skirmishes occurred as they approached Charleston, in one of which Colonel William Washington, with Pulaski's corps, Bland's light horse, and a detachment of regular cavalry, gained decided credit, capturing Lieutenant-colonel Hamilton of the North Carolina Provincials and some other prisoners. Tarleton says, " the affair ended with equal loss to both parties." Colonel Washington was then attached to General Huger's command, which consisted of the cavalry already named and some militia, with headquarters at Monk's Corner, thirty miles distant from the city. Lieutenant-colonel Webster with fourteen hundred men, consisting of the Thirty-third and Sixty-fourth British infantry, accompanied by Tarleton's and Ferguson's mounted men, marched on the thirteenth of April, surprised the post, and captured one hundred officers and men, four hundred horses, and fifty wagons loaded with arms, clothing and ammunition.

On the twenty-ninth, Admiral Arbuthnot formed a brigade of five hundred seamen and marines under Captains Hudson, Order and Gambier, which landed at daybreak, at Mount Pleasant. This compelled the Americans to abandon their position at L'Empries Point, with a loss of nearly a hundred men, who were captured by the guard-boats of the fleet, while retiring to Charleston.

On the fourth of May, Captains Hudson, Gambier and Knowles landed before daylight upon Sullivan's Island, with two hundred seamen and marines, and the garrison of Fort Moultrie surrendered.

Ground had been broken on the night of the first of April, at a distance of eight hundred yards from the American lines, and on the tenth a summons was sent to General Lincoln, demanding the surrender of the city. This was promptly refused, and by the nineteenth the second parallel was opened at a distance of only four hundred and fifty yards. The American detachment at Biggins' bridge, over the Cooper River a few miles above Charleston, was also dispersed, and upon the arrival of reinforcements from New York, April the eighteenth, Lieutenant-general Cornwallis took command upon the north bank of that river and closed all communication between the city and the country adjacent.

On the sixth of May the third parallel was occupied and preparations were made for an assault.

By reference to marginal notes upon the map, the relative positions of the American batteries will be understood. Two rows of abatis, a double picketed ditch and several redoubts crossed before the town, connecting the swamps that skirted the city on both rivers, and a canal was still further advanced before these, making a wet ditch. The third British parallel tapped this ditch and it was at once converted into a sure cover for pressing more closely upon the lines of abatis.

There was no longer any hope of successful resistance. The guns were dismounted, the works were in ruins, and on the twelfth of May Major-general Leslie took possession of the city, under honorable terms of surrender.

The British casualties, as reported by General Clinton, May thirteenth, were seventy-six killed and one hundred and eighty-nine wounded. The American casualties were nearly the same. The schedule of prisoners reported by Deputy Adjutant-general *John Andre* made an aggregate of five thousand six hundred and eighteen men, which in fact included all male citizens, as the Continental troops, including five hundred in hospital, did not exceed two thousand men.

The citizens, as well as the militia, were treated as prisoners on parole, and were allowed to return home, while the Continental troops and seamen were retained as prisoners of war, including the Lieutenant Governor and five of the council. Four hundred and five pieces of ordnance, large and small, were among the acquisitions of the capture.

At this time Colonel Buford with three hundred and eighty Virginia regulars and two field pieces was *en route* for Charleston, but upon hearing of its capture he fell back towards North Carolina, joined by Colonel Washington and the few of his cavalry who had escaped from the affair at Monk's Corner. Immediately after the surrender, General Clinton sent Lieutenant Conger up the Saluda to Ninety-six (see map of " Operations in Southern States ") and Lieutenant-colonel Tarleton with one hundred and seventy dragoons, one hundred mounted infantry and a three pounder gun, to pursue Colonel Buford. In a forced march of twenty-four hours he reached Rugely's Mills, beyond Camden, and by three o'clock of the afternoon overtook the Americans on the bank of the Waxhaw. A messenger was sent in advance, exaggerating the pursuing force, and demanding a surrender, which was declined ; and Tarleton pressed on so rapidly that he fell upon the American troops before they were prepared for action, threw them into disorder and committed great havoc. His

3²

report gives the American casualties as one hundred and thirteen killed, one hundred and fifty wounded, *unable to travel*, and fifty-three prisoners. General Clinton's report states the number of killed, at one hundred and seventy-two. The British casualties were two officers and three privates killed, one officer and fourteen privates wounded, eleven horses killed, and nineteen wounded. Colonel Tarleton says, " a report among the cavalry that they had lost their commanding officer (when his horse was shot) stimulated the soldiers to a vindictive asperity, not easily restrained; but the wounded of both parties were collected with all possible dispatch, were treated with equal humanity, were placed at the neighboring plantations and a meeting-house, and surgeons were sent for from Charleston and Camden to assist them."

The inauguration of a bitter partisan warfare at once began ; and on the twentieth of June at Ramsour's Mills, in Lincoln County, North Carolina, a party of Whigs, distinguished by white paper on their hats, and a party of Tories wearing twigs of pine, had a deadly encounter, where acquaintances and old neighbors fought until nearly three hundred were killed or wounded.

On the third of June, two days before his departure, General Clinton issued a proclamation, " requiring the inhabitants of the Province of South Carolina, including prisoners on parole, to return to their allegiance, or be treated as rebels to the government of the king." It was based on the assumption of restored supremacy; it ignored the terms of honorable surrender; it set at naught all sound military policy, and quickened the energies of the people to fresh assertion of independence. Its key is found in the hasty and enthusiastic communication of General Clinton to Lord Germaine, which says, " The inhabitants from every quarter declare their allegiance to the king, and offer their services in arms. There are few men in South Carolina who are not either our prisoners, or in arms with us."

In following General Clinton to New York, it is to be noticed that the mutinous spirit which had been evoked in the American army through actual famine, had been misinterpreted by the British officers at New York, and that on the sixth of June, General Knyphausen with Generals Mathews, Tryon, and Sterling, with five thousand troops, crossed from Staten Island to Elizabethtown Point, for the purpose of coöperating with any movement which might favor the restoration of British supremacy, or afford a prospect of a suc-

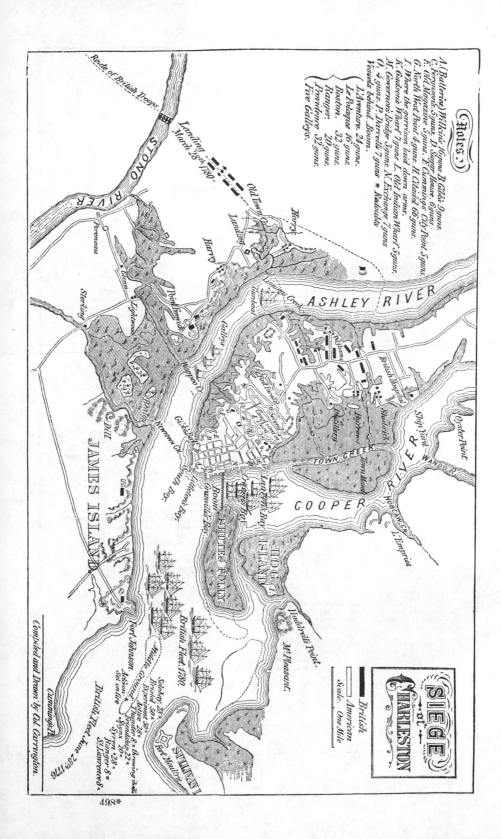

Siege of Charleston

MAY 12th, 1780

American Commanders

WHIPPLE   **LINCOLN**   WOODFORD

Strength, 3,000. Casualties, 276.

MEM. *The schedule of prisoners, which was made up by Major Andre, embraced the names of all male citizens. Total, 5,618.*

AMERICAN POSITION. The garrison embraced 2,200 regulars, and about 1,000 militia, when Clinton crossed the Ashley; but his delay, for Patterson to join him from Savannah allowed Woodford to steal quietly into the city April 7th, with 700 Virginia troops. They had made a march of 500 miles in 30 days. Commodore Whipple withdrew his ships behind a boom, and they rendered no service. Their guns were mounted in the city. He over-estimated the resisting capacity of Fort Moultrie.

British Commander

CLINTON

Strength, 8,500. Casualties, 265.

BRITISH POSITION. Clinton left New York, Dec. 26th, but storms dispersed his fleet. All the cavalry and most of the artillery horses perished. Tybee Island, near Savannah, was the first rendezvous; but it was not until February 11th, that the troops landed on St. John's Island, thirty miles below Charleston.

They were transferred to James Island, crossed Stono and Ashley rivers, and established themselves across the narrow neck above Charleston on the 12th of March.

NOTES.

NOTE. I.—Admiral Arbuthnot weighed anchor March 9th, leading with the Roebuck frigate, and passed Fort Moultrie with a loss of but 27 men. On the 20th he crossed the bar, and on the 29th he landed a brigade of 500 seamen and marines at Mount Pleasant. This compelled the Americans to abandon their outpost at L'Empries Point. On the 4th of May 200 seamen and marines landed on Sullivan Island, and Fort Moultrie was surrendered.

NOTE II.—The British broke ground on the night of April 1st, at 800 yards before the American lines, and on the 10th demanded surrender of the city. April 19th the second parallel was opened at 450 yards, and on the 6th of May, the third parallel was established by converting a canal into a dry ditch.

NOTE III.—The Americans lost by the surrender, 405 pieces of ordnance of various calibre.

NOTE IV.—The map also indicates the position of Admiral Parker's fleet, June 28th, 1776, when Clinton made his first attempt to capture Charleston, and the resistance at Fort Moultrie, endorsed by Governor Rutledge, but opposed by General Charles Lee, defeated the British attempt to capture Charleston.

References:

CARRINGTON'S "BATTLES OF THE AMERICAN REVOLUTION," pp. 492-498.

School Histories:

Anderson, ¶ 89-90 ; p. 91.
Barnes, ¶ 1 ; p. 132-3.
Berard (Bush), ¶ 115; p. 169.
Goodrich,C.A.(Seaveys),¶ 13,p. 137.
Goodrich, S. G., ¶ 5-6; p. 262.
Hassard, ¶ 1-3 ; p. 209-10.

Holmes, ¶ 11 ; p. 142.
Lossing. ¶ 1-6; p. 174-5.
Quackenbos, ¶ 371 ; p. 269.
Ridpath, ¶ 2-3 ; p. 216-17.
Sadlier (Excel), ¶ 15 ; p. 201.
Stephens,A.H. ¶ 1-4; p. 214-15.

Swinton, ¶ 193-5; p. 144.
Scott, ¶ 3-5; p. 201-2.
Thalheimer (Eclectic), ¶ 285 ; p. 163.
Venable, ¶ 158; p. 119

cessful attack upon Morristown itself. General Sterling advanced before daylight toward Elizabethtown, but found that the militia were on the alert. An American sentry fired into the advancing column while it was only dimly distinguishable before daylight, and General Sterling received the shot in his thigh, which ultimately proved fatal. He was carried to the rear, and General Knyphausen took his place at the front. By this time the sun had risen, and the regiment of Colonel Elias Dayton began to assemble, falling back slowly however before the advancing British troops. A squadron of Simcoe's Queen's Rangers followed, leading the British and Hessian infantry. As by magic, the militia appeared. Fences, thickets, orchards, houses, and trees were made available for single riflemen, and the column suffered constant loss. Stedman says, " a mutinous spirit had certainly discovered itself among the soldiers of the American army, but arose from distress, and not from disaffection. The British commander experienced a grievous disappointment. Instead of being received in the Jerseys as friendly, the militia very gallantly turned out to oppose them. During the march from Elizabethtown to Connecticut Farms, a distance of only seven miles, they were annoyed by parties of militia the whole way. When the British troops approached Springfield, a detachment from that army which was represented to be mutinous, was seen drawn up in force on the other side of the river to dispute their passage." As Colonel Dayton fell back, he found that General Maxwell's brigade was ready to support him, and a vigorous skirmish was maintained until the enemy brought artillery to the front as well as additional troops. The village of Connecticut Farms was burned, including the church and parsonage, and the wife of Chaplain Caldwell was killed by a bullet. Irving says, " The tragical fate of Mrs. Caldwell produced almost as much excitement throughout the country as that which had been caused in a preceding year by the massacre of Miss McCrea." Like that event, however sad, it could not be charged to the account of the British commander.

General Knyphausen advanced within half a mile of Springfield, and halted, to determine the wisest plan of action. The whole country seemed aroused. General Maxwell was on the bank of the Rahway. On the short hills in the rear, Washington was posted in force. The smoke of beacon fires spread the progress of the alarm and throughout the country. When night came on, dark and rainy as it was, the fires still blazed with increasing numbers, and the deep boom of the alarm guns on the mountains warned the people far and wide that every man who had a gun was wanted at once. Before morning the Hessian general attempted to regain Staten Island ; but the tide was out, and the whole shore was covered with deep mud, which the cavalry could not cross. Stedman says, that " It was determined for the credit of the British arms to remain some days longer in New Jersey, lest their precipitate retreat should be represented as a flight." Such considerations could hardly have controlled the actions of a veteran soldier like Lieutenant-general Knyphausen. As early as the first of June he had learned of the capture of Charleston, and that General Clinton was to return to New York, which was a good base for an advance upon Morristown. He therefore strengthened his position and awaited the arrival of his superior officer.

Washington wrote on the tenth that " their movements were mysterious, and the design of the movement not easily penetrated." As a matter of fact, there were few movements during the war which bore so directly upon the safety of the American army and the general cause, as the operations of the British army before Springfield during June, 1779 : and the conduct of both sides indicated some appreciation of its importance.

Sir Henry Clinton reached Staten Island on the seventeenth, and a plan was at once matured to strike the camp and magazines of Washington at Morristown. Troops were embarked upon transports, and all suitable demonstrations were made as if an expedition against West Point was intended. Washington deliberately, but actively, put his army in motion, and advanced eleven miles toward Pompton, on the twenty-second, *en route* to the Hudson, when he discovered the purpose of his adversary.

General Greene had been left in command near Springfield on the twenty-first of June, with Maxwell's and Stark's brigades, Lee's cavalry corps, and the militia.

The British advance was made in two columns, at five o'clock on‍ the morning of June twenty-third ; one by the Vauxhall, and the other by the Springfield road, the whole force consisting of five thousand infantry, besides cavalry and eighteen pieces of artillery. The British pressure was quite deliberate, but earnest, upon the left, on the Springfield road, as if it were the main attack. The column formed near the Matthews house, on a small eminence where artillery could gain a commanding position, because just at the left of the bridge, Colonel Angell's Rhode Island regiment with one gun, was holding an orchard which commanded the bridge over the Rahway and afforded some cover.   The British guns were aimed too high at first, and did little execution ; but by fording the stream, not more than twelve yards wide, the command turned the American position, and crowded Colonel Angell back to the second bridge, over a branch of the Rahway, where Colonel Shreve resisted with equal obstinacy.   Colonel Angell lost one-fourth of his men and was compelled to fall back with Colonel Shreve upon the brigades of Maxwell and Stark.

Colonel Dayton's regiment contributed to their resistance, and "none," says Irving, " showed more ardor in the fight than Caldwell the chaplain, who distributed Watts' psalms and hymn books among the soldiers when they were in want of wadding, with the shout ' put Watts into them, boys.' "

The other British column had a still more important objective in view, being no other than to gain the pass leading to Chatham and Morristown.   Major Lee's cavalry and a picket under Captain Walker were posted at Little's Bridge, on the Vauxhall road, and Colonel Ogden's regiment covered them.   General Greene soon found that he could not afford to hold so extended a front, and concentrated his force at other positions eminently strong and capable of defense. Reference is made to map " Battle of Springfield."   The remainder of General Maxwell's and Stark's brigades took high ground by the mill, with the militia force of General Dickinson on the flanks.   The Vauxhall bridge was contested as hotly as that at Springfield.   General Greene ultimately took post on the first range of hills, in the rear of Byram's tavern, where the roads were brought so near that succor might be readily given from one to the other, " and he was thus enabled to detach Colonel Webb's regiment, Lieutenant-colonel Huntington commanding, and Colonel Jackson's regiment with one piece of artillery, which entirely checked the advance of the enemy on the American left, and secured that pass."   Reference is also made to map—" Operations in New Jersey."   The map previously referred to designates the various British and Hessian corps engaged in the action.

General Clinton's army withdrew, after burning Springfield, and at midnight crossed to Staten Island, removing their bridge of boats after the passage.

The American casualties were one officer and twelve non-commissioned officers and privates killed, Captain Davis' detachment and the militia not reporting, five officers and fifty-six privates wounded and nine privates missing. The British loss was not officially stated but was estimated by contemporary journalists as about one hundred and fifty. General Clinton says, " I could not think of keeping the field in New Jersey," and wished " to land the troops and give a camp of rest to an army of which many corps had had an uninterrupted campaign of fourteen months." It appears from this report that General Clinton had no immediate designs upon the Hudson River posts, but his operations were so conducted as to keep the American army on constant duty.

New Jersey had been a scene of constant warfare for five years; and it was at last relieved from the pressure.

Washington was still imploring the States to fill their quota under new assignments, and the first six months of 1780 closed their battle record.

BRITISH EFFECTIVE FORCE.

NOTE.—From "Original Returns in the British Record Office." Date May 1st, 1780.

	NEW YORK	SOUTH CAROLINA	NOVA SCOTIA	EAST FLORIDA
British	7711	7041	2298	536
German	7451	3018	572	
Provincials	2162	2788	638	
	17,324	12,847	3,508	

	WEST FLORIDA	GEORGIA	BERMUDAS	PROVIDENCE ISLAND
British	590	—	—	—
German	547	862	—	—
Provincials	316	1016	326	130
	1453	1878		

Total, 38,002.

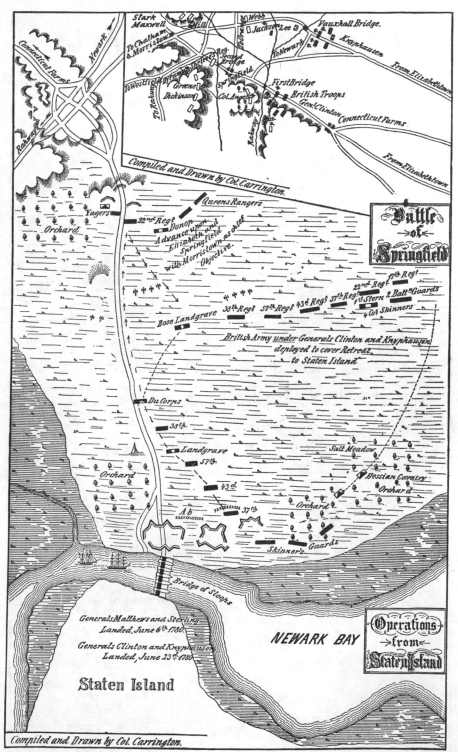

Battle of Springfield

Operations from Staten Island

Compiled and Drawn by Col. Carrington.

Generals Matthews and Sterling Landed, June 6th 1780.

Generals Clinton and Knyphausen Landed, June 23d 1780.

Staten Island

NEWARK BAY

British Army under Generals Clinton and Knyphausen deployed to cover Retreat to Staten Island.

Compiled and Drawn by Col. Carrington.

502*

Battle of Springfield

AND

Operations from Staten Island

DURING JUNE, 1780

American Commanders	British Commanders
GREENE	
Maxwell, Stark, Angell, Jackson, Lee	CLINTON KNYPHAUSEN
Webb, Dickinson, Dayton, Shreve	Sterling, Matthews, Simcoe, Stirn, Tryon
Estimated Strength Available 7,800	Strength, 5,000

AMERICAN POSITION. Washington held firm hold of his well protected camp near Morristown, carefully guarded the pass at Chatham, and so disposed his advance posts as to be fully advised of British activity. (*A reference to map 11, p. 26-7, will indicate the relations of Staten Island to the operations referred to*).

BRITISH MOVEMENTS. Lieut. Gen. Knyphausen, commanding at New York, during Clinton's operations against Charleston, determined to draw Washington into a general engagement and seize his camp. On the 6th of June, with Matthews, Tryon, Sterling, and 5,000 excellent troops, he crossed from Staten Island, by a bridge of boats, to Elizabethtown Point.

The mutinous conduct of the American army, after a winter of great severity, and the suffering incident to scant food, clothing, fuel, medicines and all necessaries, had inspired the opinion that a prompt invasion would induce many to return to British allegiance.

Sterling advanced toward Elizabethtown at daylight, but the militia were on the alert. He was mortally wounded by an American sentry, and Knyphausen took his place at the front. When the sun had risen, the British army not only discovered that orchards, houses and single trees were sheltering keen marksmen, but that the regiment of Col. Elias Dayton was rapidly forming to resist their march. The Queen's Rangers (Simcoe's) led the Hessian column; but instead of any friendly indications, there was opposition at every step. Connecticut Farms, seven miles beyond Elizabethtown, was burned, with its church and parsonage, and the wife of Chaplain Caldwell was killed by a bullet.

When within half a mile of Springfield, it was found, that, as Dayton fell back, he was amply supported by Maxwell on the bank of the Rahway, and that Washington was fully prepared for the issue.

A stormy night, enlivened by watch fires, which blazed on every hill, warned Knyphausen that he was surrounded by vigilant adversaries, and he retired to Staten Island.

Clinton, returning from Charleston, reached Staten Island on the 17th of June, and he also resolved to strike the camp and magazines of Washington, at Morristown. Troops were embarked, ostensibly, to ascend the Hudson and attack West Point. Washington left Greene to command, behind Springfield, with Maxwell, Stark and Col. Lee, and marched on the 22d eleven miles toward the Hudson; but upon appreciating the *feint* of Clinton, regained his post.

The Battle of Springfield followed

NOTE I.—The British advanced in two columns, at 5 o'clock A. M. June 23d, with 5,000 infantry, cavalry and 18 guns; one column (Clinton's), by the Connecticut Farms' Road, and the other (Knyphausen's), by the Vauxhall road.

NOTE II.—At the first bridge over the Rahway, Clinton found that Col. Angell, with a Rhode Island regiment and one gun, occupied an orchard on a hill, and practically commanded the bridge. He at once gained high ground for his own guns, but finding their effect to be inconsiderable, forded the stream; turned Angell's position and forced him back to the second bridge, where Colonel Shreve disputed the advance. This officer lost one-fourth of his men; but found himself promptly supported by the brigades of Maxwell and Stark. They took a position at a mill which afforded strength, and Greene so disposed of Dickinson's militia as to check the British ardor.

NOTE III.—Knyphausen's column attempted to seize the Chatham pass, in the rear, and thus gain the avenue to the Morristown camp. At Little's bridge, on the Vauxhall road, he was met by Lee's cavalry, well supported by Col. Ogden's regiment, and a brisk struggle took place for its possession. Greene promptly moved the regiments of Webb and Jackson, with one gun, to the Chatham pass, and the object of the expedition was foiled.

NOTE IV.—Clinton burned Springfield, returned to Staten Island, removed his bridge of boats, and the last New Jersey campaign closed.

NOTE V.—The American militia made no return of their losses. The regular troops had 13 killed and 61 wounded. The British loss was not officially stated, but was estimated at 150, including missing.

References:

CARRINGTON'S "BATTLES OF THE AMERICAN REVOLUTION," pp. 498–502.

School Histories:

Anderson, ¶ —; p. 102.	Holmes, ¶ —; p. —.	Swinton, ¶ —; p. —.
Barnes, ¶ —; p. —.	Lossing, ¶ 13: p. 178-9.	Scott, ¶ 11; p. 205.
Berard (Bush), ¶ 123; p. 174.	Quackenbos, ¶ —; p. —.	Thalheimer (Eclectic), ¶ —,
Goodrich, C.A.(Seaveys), ¶ —; p. —.	Ridpath, ¶ —; p. —.	p. —;
Goodrich, S. G., ¶ 5, p. 265.	Sadlier, (Excel), ¶ —; p. —.	Venable, ¶ —; p. —.
Hassard, ¶ 2; p. 214.	Stephens, A.H. ¶ —; p. —.	

CHAPTER LXIV.

FRENCH AUXILIARIES. ARNOLD'S TREASON. SOUTHERN SKIRMISHES, 1780.

LIEUTENANT-general the Count de Rochambeau, arrived at Newport, Rhode Island, July tenth, 1780, with nearly six thousand French troops, constituting the first division of a corps of twelve thousand men, which Louis XVI. had designated as aid to the United States in their war for national independence. Major-general the Marquis de Chastellux, a relative of La Fayette, accompanied the command. The Chevalier de Ternay commanded the convoy, which consisted of seven heavy ships, *viz.*, two 80s, one 74, four 64s, two 40s, a cutter, 20; hospital ship, pierced for 64 guns, a bomb ship and thirty-two transports.

It was the purpose of Washington to make the capture of New York his immediate objective; and a plan of operations was submitted to the French commander soon after his arrival at Newport; but on the thirteenth of July, Admiral Graves arrived at New York with six ships of the line, which gave the British naval forces a superiority of ships and metal; and the enterprise was postponed until the French second division should arrive.

Sir Henry Clinton, in turn, proposed an expedition to Rhode Island, and eight thousand troops were advanced as far as Huntington, Long Island, but a prompt movement of Washington with his army, and advices of the strength and position of Rochambeau, gave such assurance that he would meet a superior force, that the project was converted into a simple naval demonstration, with the double purpose of blockading the French squadron and cutting off the expected second French division when it should enter the American waters.

The Count de Rochambeau, with a soldier's exactness, at once comprehended the situation, and in his dispatch of July sixteenth, to Count de Vergennes, thus epitomizes the condition of American affairs:

"Upon our arrival here, the country was in consternation, the paper money had fallen to sixty for one. . . I spoke to the principal persons of the place, and told them, as I write to General Washington, that this was merely the advanced guard of a greater force, and that the king was determined to support them with his whole power. In twenty-four hours their spirits rose, and last night all the streets, houses and steeples were illuminated, in the midst of fire-works and the greatest rejoicings. . . You see, sir, how important it is to act with vigor. . . Send us troops, ships and money; but do not depend upon these people, nor upon their means; they have neither money nor credit; their means of resistance are only momentary, and called forth when they are attacked in their homes. They then assemble for the moment of immediate danger and defend themselves. Washington commands sometimes fifteen thousand, sometimes three thousand men."

The above letter would fairly represent a condensed statement of Washington's experience during the greater part of the entire war. The entire campaign of 1780, is interwoven with reports of deficiency in men, food, clothing and money; and the numerous entreaties, protests and demands, heretofore cited, are but feeble expressions of the patience as well as agony of spirit which characterized both the official and unofficial correspondence of the American Commander-in-chief.

The last six months of 1780 was without active field operations in the Northern States. The French fleet was blockaded at Newport by a superior British naval force, and repeated consultations between General Washington and the Count de Rochambeau, resulted in the postponement of a proposed attack upon New York.

A proclamation was published over the signature of La Fayette, with the sanction of Washington, announcing to the Canadians that the French troops would assist in expelling the British from Canada. The object of this paper was to divert the attention of the garrison of New York from the proposed attack upon that city. General Clinton, under date of August thirty-first, forwarded a copy to Lord Germaine, calling his attention to its purport; but, as a matter of fact, the expedition was never seriously proposed. During the discussion of the project to attack New York, General Arnold was advised by Washington that he would be tendered a command. Still pleading his old wounds as an excuse from active service, he expressed a prefer-

ence for a *post-command*, and after repeated solicitations of himself
and friends, he was granted his choice, and on the third of August,
was assigned to the command of " West Point and *its dependencies*, in
which *all* are included, from Fishkill to King's Ferry."

A protracted clandestine and confidential correspondence had long
been carried on between himself and Sir Henry Clinton through Major
Andre, under the assumed names of Gustavus and John Anderson,
and this was so disguised by commercial forms as to be intelligible
only to the parties holding the secret.   By this means General Clinton was frequently advised of the condition, movements and resources
of the American army, and was undoubtedly greatly restrained in his
military movements by the possession of the secret and a corresponding dependence upon Arnold to instruct him as to times and modes
of action.   Arnold's pretended preference for post duty was deliberately treasonable and base.

On the twenty-fifth of August, General Clinton wrote to Lord
Germaine officially as follows : " At this new epoch of the war, when a
foreign force has already landed, and an addition to it is expected,
I owe it to my country, and I must in justice say to my own fame, to
declare to your lordship that I become every day more sensible of the
utter impossibility of prosecuting the war in this country without
reinforcements.   .   .   .   We are, by some thousands, too weak to
subdue this rebellion."

Lord George Germaine wrote in reply, under date of September
twenty-seventh : " Next to the destruction of Washington's army,
the gaining over officers of influence and reputation among the troops
would be the speediest means of subduing the rebellion and restoring
the tranquillity of America.   Your commission authorizes you to avail
yourself of such opportunities, and there can be no doubt that the
expenses will be cheerfully submitted to."

It is impossible to determine how far Lord Germaine's confidence
in the ability of Arnold to execute his plan dissuaded him from sending troops to the United States; and yet such would be the natural
effect of substituting the use of gold for the force of arms in the prosecution of a costly and protracted war.   The archives, then secret,
show that he was kept advised of the entire scheme.

On the thirtieth of August, Arnold solicited an interview *with
some responsible party* in order definitely to settle upon the price of his
honor.   On the eighteenth of September he wrote, advising that
Andre be sent up the river to the Vulture, sloop of war, then at

anchor in Haverstraw Bay, promising " to send a person on board with a boat and a flag of truce. General Clinton received the letter the following day ; troops were embarked under the pretense of an expedition into the Chesapeake, and Andre reached the Vulture on the twentieth.

On the twenty-first, about midnight, Andre landed, met Arnold, and accompanied him first to the Clove, and then to the house of Joshua Helt Smith, see map " Highlands of the Hudson." Subsequent examinations failed to convict Smith of any knowledge of the details of the conspiracy. His antecedents were favorable to sympathy with the British army; but the secret was too valuable to be intrusted to a convenient tool. The terms of purchase were soon settled, simply "*gold* and a brigadier-general's commission."

Andre crossed the Hudson, to return to New York by land, was captured on the twenty-third, and on the second of October was executed as a spy.

America grieved over this painful necessity, but there was no alternative except an exchange for Arnold, who escaped by taking refuge on the Vulture, the twenty-fourth, and this exchange was declined by General Clinton.

General Clinton wrote to Lord Germaine, " Thus ended this proposed plan, from which I had conceived such great hopes and imagined such great consequences."

General Greene was at once assigned to the command made vacant by the treason of Arnold. The garrison was changed ; the works were modified and strengthened, and Washington took post with his main army at Prakeness, near Passaic Falls, in New Jersey. (See map, " Operations in New Jersey.")

During these months of uncertain plans, depreciated credit, and exposed treason at the north, the south was the theatre of active war. For a short time there had been a superficial peace in South Carolina and Georgia, and Lord Cornwallis, then at Charleston, undertook to reduce North Carolina to submission. Lord Rawdon was placed in command at Camden. A considerable royalist militia force was enrolled, but the effort to force paroled citizens and prisoners to render service to the crown, gradually destroyed all confidence in official pledges, and developed a partisan warfare of most persistent daring and bitterness. The cane-brakes, rice swamps, and evergreen forests were hiding places and natural strongholds which an army could not penetrate without guides, and to which small detachments, unable to take the field against regular troops, could retreat when closely pressed, with little danger from pursuit.

A few of the principal skirmishes are briefly stated, in order to illustrate the style of warfare which the Southern campaign evoked, and which properly enter into the minor operations of war.

On the twelfth of July, Captain Christian Houk, who, with thirty-five dragoons, twenty New York volunteers, and sixty royalist militia, was detached from the garrison at Rocky Mountain, " to collect the royal militia and push the rebels as far as he deemed convenient," " was surprised and destroyed," as Colonel Tarleton states, through placing his party carelessly, without pickets, or sending out patrols at Williamson's Plantation. " This," says Justice Johnson, " was the first check the British regular troops had received from the militia since the fall of Charleston." Among the Americans who participated were the brothers Adair, one of them the subsequently well known General John Adair. This expedition first went to the house of a Mrs. McClure, found her sons James and Edward in the act of converting her tea-pots into bullets, and took them off, as they said, to hang them. The plantations of Colonel Bratton and James Williamson, who afterwards took part in the skirmish, were ravaged. Mrs. McClure reported the facts at Sumter's camp, where Colonel Bratton, Captain McClure and five of the Williamsons were on duty. With seventy-five men, they stole upon Houk's party, separated them from the picketed horses and then punished them. Captain Houk was among the killed. These facts illustrate the character of many skirmishes which the passing weeks developed.

On the thirteenth of- July, Sumter made an unsuccessful attack upon the British post at Rocky Mount, on the west side of the Catawba, thirty miles northwest from Camden, and eleven miles from Hanging Rock, then commanded by Lieutenant-colonel Turnbull. This post consisted of two log-houses, perforated for small arms, and a small redoubt surrounded by a ditch and abatis. Three assaults were made and repulsed. The American casualties included Colonel Reed and thirteen men killed or wounded. Tarleton gives the British casualties at one officer *killed*, one wounded, and about ten men killed or wounded, and says " at the last assault, the Americans penetrated the abatis, but were finally repulsed."

On the first of August, Colonel Elijah Clark, of Wilkes County, Georgia, was followed by a Mrs. Dillard, who had just fed his command, and informed that Major Ferguson was in close pursuit. She was just in time to prevent a surprise, and in the two skirmishes that followed nearly sixty men were killed or wounded, the dragoons leaving twenty-eight dead on the field, and the Americans losing Major Smith, and four men killed, and Colonels Clark and Robinson, Major Clark and twenty-three others wounded.

The character of the warfare, coupled with the ill-advised policy of General Clinton, produced absolute disregard of the formal obligations of surrender and parole.

On the sixth of August, Colonel Tarleton reported to General Cornwallis, " that Lieutenant-colonel Lisle, who had been paroled, and had exchanged his parole for a certificate of a good subject, carried off a whole battalion of men which he raised in the districts of the Ennoree and Tyger, as soon as they received arms and ammunition, to join Colonel Sumter," adding " *This treachery ruined all confidence between the regulars and militia.*"

" This reinforcement," says Colonel Tarleton, " added to his former numbers, inspired Colonel Sumter with a desire of signalizing himself by attacking some of the British posts upon the frontier." On the sixth of August, at seven o'clock in the evening, he approached the flank of the post " of Hanging Rock," which was entrusted to the North Carolina refugees, under the orders of Colonel Bryan. They fled. " The legion charged twice with fixed bayonets to save their three pounder." " Colonel Sumter still persevered in his attack, and very probably would have succeeded, if a stratagem employed by Captains Stewart and McDonald of the British Legion had not disconcerted his operations." This was the simple detachment of a small force of buglers to the flanks, who gave such signals as to indicate the approach of additional troops. It was repeatedly practiced during the war. Colonel Tarleton omits to state that the American success at one time was so promising, that, as at Bennington, they allowed themselves to fall into disorder by plunder of commissary and other supplies, and thus greatly imperiled the success achieved at the first onset. The conditions of the battle, for it was more than a skirmish, changed repeatedly during nearly four hours of conflict. Gordon says, " The Prince of Wales regiment which defended the place was nearly annihilated, and the arms and ammunition taken from the British who fell in the beginning, were turned against their associates ; that Colonel Sumter's party had not more than ten bullets to a man when the action commenced." The British loss was two hundred and sixty-nine, killed, wounded and taken prisoners.

The American loss was severe, but not officially reported. Colonel Tarleton states that "about one hundred dead and wounded Americans were left on the field of battle, adding significantly, " The repulses he (Colonel Sumter) received, did not discourage him, or injure his cause. The loss of men was easily supplied, and his reputation for activity and courage was fully sustained by his late enterprising conduct." Irving says—" among the partisans who were present in this fight, an orphan boy of Scotch-Irish descent, was Andrew Jackson." That boy became a successor of Washington, as President of the United States.

During these desultory operations, of which a few only are stated, the condition of the American army proper is to be noticed. On the sixth of July, the Baron De Kalb was at Buffalo Ford and Deep River. He left Morristown, New Jersey, on the sixteenth of April, with nearly fourteen hundred men, embarked at the head of Elk river on the third day of May, reached Petersburg early in June, entered North Carolina on the twentieth of June, halted at Hillsborough to rest his troops and secure supplies, and then advanced. General Gates reached De Kalb's camp on the twenty-fifth of July. He had previously written to General De Kalb, from Hillsborough, " Enough has already been lost in a vain defense of Charleston ; if more is sacrificed, the Southern States are undone ; and this may go nearly to undo the rest."

General Caswell's North Carolina militia had already crossed the Peedee on the route for Camden in *defiance of the wishes* and orders of General De Kalb. There was some jealousy of foreign officers, and General Caswell made a mistake in not reporting directly to General De Kalb. That officer felt the slight, and wrote on the seventh of July to his wife, " Officers of European experience alone, do not know what it is to contend against difficulties and vexations. My present condition makes me doubly anxious to return to you." It had been his purpose to advance by Salisbury and Charlotte, through a fertile country where supplies would be ready at hand. Adjutant-general Williams urged the movement ; but General Gates decided differently, upon his arrival, and to the amazement of his officers ordered the troops to be ready to start at a moment's warning, and " on the twenty-seventh," says Irving, " put what he called the Grand Army on its march, by the shortest route to Camden, through a barren country which could offer no food but lean cattle, fruit and unripe maize." Marion was detached and sent to the interior of South Carolina to watch the British troops and make a report.

On the third of August, the army crossed the Peedee and united with the command of Lieutenant-colonel Porterfield, who had been dispatched to the relief of Charleston, but who with superior enterprise and judgment had operated on the border, after hearing of the capture of that city. Neither prisoners nor medicines could be had. The army ate peaches for bread. Dysentery broke out in the camp; many could hardly walk. "On the fourth of August, General Gates issued a proclamation." A portion is copied from Colonel Tarleton's official reports, with Italics, as given by that officer, "*inviting the patriotic citizens of Carolina to assemble under his auspices, to vindicate the rights of America; holding out an amnesty to all who had subscribed paroles imposed upon them by the ruffian band of conquest; and excepting only those who in the hour of devastation, had exercised acts of barbarism and depredation upon the persons and property of their fellow citizens.*"

Colonel Tarleton's troubles with American militia had not ended with the desertion of Lieutenant-colonel Lisle. As General Gates moved toward Camden, Major McArthur collected boats on the Peedee, upon which he placed one hundred sick, many of whom were from the Seventy-first British regulars, which had suffered greatly from the climate." "Colonel Mills, who commanded the militia of the Cheraw district, though a very good man," says Tarleton, in his report of August sixth, "had not complied with my instructions in forming his corps, and attended more to oaths and professions, and attended less to the former conduct of those whom he admitted. The instant that the militia found that Major McArthur had left his post, and were assured that Gates would come there the next day, they seized their own officers, and the hundred sick, and carried them all prisoners into North Carolina." Colonel Mills escaped.

On the seventh, Gates effected a union with Caswell's North Carolina militia, and the half-famished army advanced to Lynch's Creek. The British withdrew their post from Cheraw's Hill, and fell back to Camden. If the American column had marched by the route suggested and urged by Baron De Kalb, it would have reached Camden in the rear of Cheraw Hill before Lord Rawdon could have gained that post, and would have secured ample supplies.

Colonel Tarleton says, "The American commander had not sufficient penetration to conceive that by a forced march up the creek, he could have pushed Lord Rawdon's flank, and reached Camden;

which would have been an easy conquest, and a fatal blow to the British." This was a fact which may have given to Cornwallis more confidence in his subsequent attack upon Gates at Sander's Creek. He was too good a soldier not to notice such mistakes and profit by them.

General Gates halted two days, and on the thirteenth encamped at Rugely's Mills, twelve miles above Camden. On the fourteenth, General Stevens joined the army with seven hundred Virginia militia.

"On the night between the thirteenth and fourteenth," Lord Cornwallis reached Camden, having left Charleston on the tenth. The Twenty-third, Thirty-third, and Seventy-first British regiments, the Volunteers of Ireland, and Lieutenant-colonel Hamilton's corps had also been collected at that post. Four companies of light infantry from Ninety-six joined the same day. Colonel Tarleton himself having just recovered from a fever, crossed the Santee River on the sixth, then Black River, joined Lord Rawdon on the tenth, and with him, fell back to Camden.

Meanwhile a train of clothing, ammunition, and other supplies had left Charleston for the use of the British troops. Colonel Sumter made application to General Gates on the fourteenth for a detachment of four hundred regulars and volunteers to join his command of an equal number, for the purpose of capturing that train. A detail was made by General Gates upon hastily formed impressions that his own force was seven thousand men, and consisted of one hundred Maryland regulars, under Lieutenant-colonel Woodford, three hundred North Carolina militia, some artillerymen, and two brass guns.

Colonel Sumter met the train as it slowly traveled up the west bank of the Wateree, and was about to cross the river within a mile of Camden. The surprise was complete, but the roar of cannon soon advised him that there was severe fighting on the other side of the river. During the next day he was informed by a messenger from Major Davis of the defeat of Gates at Sander's Creek, and at once hastened toward Charlotte, North Carolina, as ordered.

On the night of the seventeenth, his command, oppressed by the heat, worn out by marching, and encumbered by more than one hundred prisoners, went into camp on the north side of Fishing creek, about two miles above its junction with the Catawba.

Colonel Tarleton had already crossed the Catawba in pursuit, and was resting his men at Fishing creek. On the morning of the eigh-

teenth, he dashed in upon the surprised Americans, cutting them off
from their color line where the arms were stacked, inflicted a loss of
one hundred in killed and wounded, captured three hundred prisoners,
besides the rescue of his own men, and the train they had lost, took
one thousand stand of arms and two cannon, and dispersed the entire
command as with the suddenness and success of a whirlwind.

BRITISH EFFECTIVE FORCE.

NOTE.—From "Original Returns in the British Record Office." Date, August 1st, 1780.

REGULAR TROOPS ONLY.

New York	19,115	West Florida	1,261
South Carolina	6,589	Nova Scotia	3,524
Georgia	1,756	Bermuda	204
East Florida	453	Providence Island	118
	27,913		5,107

Total, 33,020.

December, 1st 1780.

New York	17,729	West Florida	1,261
On an Expedition	2274	Nova Scotia	3,167
South Carolina	7384	Bermuda	387
Georgia	968	Providence Island	143
East Florida	453		
	28,808		4,958

Total, 33,766.

Provincial forces at close of year... 8,954

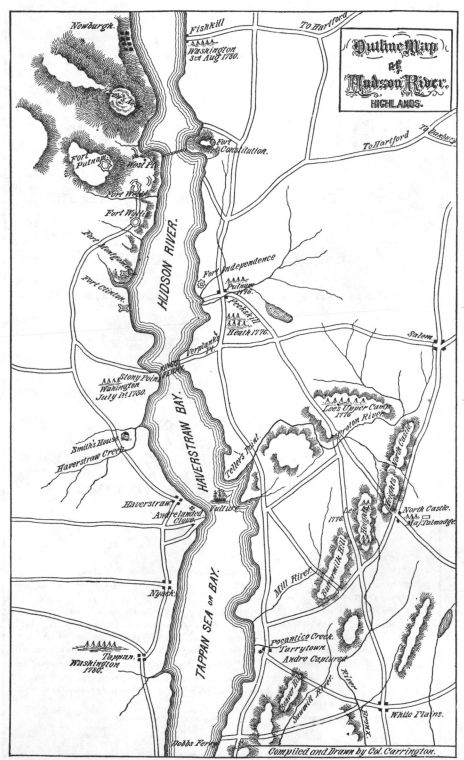

Outline Map of Hudson River. HIGHLANDS.

Newburgh.

Fishkill.

To Hartford

Washington Sept. Aug. 1780.

Fort Constitution.

To Hartford

To Roxbury

Fort Putnam.

West Pt.

Fort Webb.

Fort Wylls

HUDSON RIVER.

Fort Montgomery.

Fort Clinton.

Fort Independence

Putnam 1776.

Peekskill

Heath 1776.

Salem

Verplanks Pt.

Lee's Upper Camp 1776

Croton River.

Stony Point

Wakington July 1st 1780.

North Castle

HAVERSTRAW BAY.

Teller's Point.

Lee's 1776

Heights

North Castle.

Maj. Talmadge.

Smith's House

Haverstraw Creek.

Haverstraw.

Andre landed Cloves.

Vulture

Buttermilk Hill.

Mill River.

HUDSON RIVER.

TAPPAN SEA OR BAY.

Nyack.

Beaver Dam

River

Sawmill River.

White Plains.

Bronx.

Tappan.

Washington 1780.

Pocantico Creek.

Tarrytown

Andre Captured.

Dobbs Ferry.

Compiled and Drawn by Col. Carrington.

512*

Outline Map

OF THE

⇀ Hudson River ↽

FROM

Dobbs Ferry to Fishkill and Newburgh

INCLUDING

Tappan and Tarrytown

HAVERSTRAW, where Andre landed, from British Sloop, Vulture;

PEEKSKILL, NORTH CASTLE & WHITE PLAINS

ALSO

Stony Point

FORT INDEPENDENCE

FORT CLINTON   FORT MONTGOMERY

FORT PUTNAM and WEST POINT

NOTE.—**Stony Point** is memorable, as follows:

It was stormed under direction of Washington, by Wayne, Febiger, Webb, Meigs, Butler, Lee, Muhlenburg, Fleury, Knox, and Gibbon. July 16, 1779. (*Carrington's "Battles," pp.* 472-474).

It was abandoned (same, p. 474).

It was re-occupied by Clinton; but abandoned (Oct. 25, 1779). *Carrington's "Battles,"* p. 476.

MEM. *As the Hudson River separated New England from the central colonies, and its control was contended for, by both armies, it is to be noted, that Governor Tryon, both in 1777 and 1779, made incursions into Connecticut, in vain attempting to divert Washington from his general plans. April 25, 1777, when Fairfield and Danbury were visited, he was bravely resisted by Arnold, at Ridgefield. General David Wooster was fatally wounded. July 4, 1779, Tryon visited New Haven, and on the 8th and 9th burned Fairfield, including 2 churches, 83 houses and shops, 2 school-houses, jail and County-House.*

British expeditions, out of New York, into Westchester County, were frequent.

CHAPTER LXV.

BATTLE OF CAMDEN. KING'S MOUNTAIN. POSITION OF SOUTHERN ARMIES.

THE battle of Camden, or Sander's Creek, was one of the most suggestive of the war. The force of discipline, exact appreciation of the adversary, quick seizure of opportunity, and the delivery of incessant blows upon every exposed point in turn, were illustrated in the conduct of Lord Cornwallis. Webster, Rawdon and Tarleton recognized the controlling will of the general commanding, and obeyed orders implicitly, confidently, and at all hazards. The British regulars only did their duty as usual. It was characteristic of their general conduct during the whole war.

Lord Cornwallis hesitated, as he states, whether to risk an action against the American army, or to retire to Charleston. His scouts were constantly on the alert, and he formed so correct an estimate of the character of General Gates, and the composition and disposition of the American army, as to risk an attack, although he knew that it was superior in numbers to his own, and occupying a good position at Rugely's Mills. General Gates was thoroughly " sure of victory, and of the dispersion of the British army." It has been seen that he participated actively in no part of the operations near Saratoga until the morning of August eleventh, 1777. Confiding in numbers, and neglecting reconnoissance, he then imperiled his army by forcing several brigades across Fishkill creek, while remaining in the rear himself.

He brought his worn-out, sick and hungry army to Rugely's Mills despite of advice and prudence, and intended at once to attack a strong post and veteran troops, as if the prestige of the Burgoyne campaign was a formidable part of his aggressive force, instead of an element to incite Cornwallis to a more determined resistance. He

33

had about fourteen hundred good troops well officered. The remainder were raw militia just collected, many of whom had never been in action, and had only just received bayonets, without instruction in their use. They had no idea of tactical formations and movements, and no provision was made for a rallying point in case of disaster. General Gates seems to have been limited in capacity to the simple issue of an order, and to take the consequences of its mode of execution as "one of the uncertainties of war." He did not know that Cornwallis had reached Camden when he advanced, nor the weakness of his own force until he ordered the battle; then assumed that a general should never retreat under whatever circumstances, and lacked the wisdom to consult with other officers when uncertain as to the proper line of duty.

General Gates placed in the hands of Adjutant-general Williams an elaborate general order, dated "Camp Clermont, 15th of August," directing the "Grand army to march promptly at ten o'clock that night." It was evident from its tenor that the general commanding did not even know the strength of the force that was to be handled. Adjutant-general Williams at once called upon the general officers, of whom thirteen were with the army, for exact returns of their commands. The abstract was placed before General Gates, "as he came from a council of officers." It showed that the total, nominal strength, was only three thousand and fifty-two men. Turning to his chief of staff, he simply said, "Sir, the numbers are certainly below the estimate made this morning. There was no dissenting voice in the council where the orders have just been read; there are enough for our purpose." The orders were then published in the army, without deliberation or consultation with anybody.

Through the coincidence of each army attempting to surprise the other, they left their respective camps at the same hour, ten o'clock, so as to gain time to strike the adversary before daylight on the following morning.

Colonel Armand with his cavalry, only sixty men, led the advance, although he remonstrated at the detail of mounted men as a pioneer corps for night service, since the profoundest silence was enjoined in orders. Colonel Porterfield's light infantry were ordered to march upon his right flank and Major Armstrong on the left flank, each in single file, two hundred yards from the road.

Colonel Armand's orders were, "being thus supported, in case of an attack by the enemy's cavalry, in front, not only to support the shock of the enemy's horse, but to *rout* them; and to consider the order, to stand the attacks of the enemy's cavalry, be their numbers what they may, as positive." Between two and three o'clock in the morning the advance guard of the British army, consisting of twenty Legion cavalry and as many mounted infantry, confronted, hotly attacked and routed Armand's detachment. Colonel Porterfield faithfully executed his orders and was mortally wounded in the skirmish; but the prompt arrival of the light infantry, the Twenty-third and Thirty-third British regiments in support of their advance guard, compelled him to retire. The retreat of Armand's cavalry threw the First Maryland brigade into confusion; and both armies, well satisfied with their experience of a night attack, awaited the morning and formed their lines for action. It was still within the power of General Gates to fall back to a strong position; but he lacked nerve and decision for such an hour. A prisoner who fell into the hands of the Americans reported the British force to be three thousand strong, under the immediate command of Lord Cornwallis. This fact was reported to General Gates. Adjutant-general Williams says, " General Gates called the general officers together in the rear, asking— " what is to be done. " All were mute for a few moments, when the gallant Stevens exclaimed," " Gentlemen, is it not too late *now* to do anything but fight." " When the Adjutant-general went to call the Baron De Kalb to council, he said, " and has the General given you orders to retreat the army," thus indicating his opinion of the proper action required. " The Baron did not however oppose the suggestion of General Stevens; and every measure that ensued was preparatory for action." Adjutant-general Williams says " that the General seemed disposed to await events—*he gave no orders.*" " Upon his suggesting a brisk attack by Stevens' brigade upon the British right, he answered, " Sir, that's right; let it be done." " This was the last order the deputy Adjutant-general received." Reference is made to map " Battle of Camden." This battle, as far as it was a battle, on the part of the Americans, and not a rout, was confined to the right wing where the gallant De Kalb fought his small command admirably. He did not know that the rest of the army had fled, until, surrounded by overwhelming numbers, he learned the fate of the day.

The British army had passed Sander's creek and entered upon a narrow belt of solid land, bordered on each side by an impassable swamp. The American army was flanked by the same swamps; but the interval rapidly widened in the direction of Rugely's Mills, so that their flanks, the left especially, became exposed in case the engagement was pressed and they failed to hold their original ground. The artillery was then placed in the centre of the front line; and Major Armstrong's light infantry, which had retreated at the first encounter, was ordered to cover a small interval between the left wing and the swamp in that quarter. Frequent skirmishes during the night disclosed the relative positions of the armies; and the British army advanced at dawn of day.

"Lieutenant-colonel Webster commanded the right wing, consisting of three companies of light infantry, the Twenty-third and Thirty-third British regiments. Lord Rawdon commanded the left, consisting of the volunteers of Ireland, the Legion Infantry, Hamilton's corps and Bryan's refugees. Two six pounders and two three pounders, were to the left of the road, under Lieutenant McLeod. The two battalions of the Seventy-first regiment, with two six pounders, formed the second line. The Legion cavalry remained in column, on account of the thickness of the woods to the right of the main road, close to the first battalion of the Seventy-first regiment, with orders to act as opportunity offered, or necessity required."

The Second Maryland brigade, General Gist commanding, with the Delaware troops under Baron De Kalb, formed the American right; the North Carolina militia formed the centre, under General Caswell; and the equally untried Virginia militia, under Stevens, were on the left. The First Maryland brigade formed the second line, and the artillery under the direction of Captain Singleton, was so posted as to command the road.

The morning was calm and hazy; and the smoke settled so near the earth, that "it was difficult," says Cornwallis, "to see the effect of a very heavy and well supported fire on both sides." He says, "Observing a movement on the American left which I supposed to be with an intention to make some alterations in their order, I directed Lieutenant-colonel Webster to begin the attack." The movement referred to, was an attempt on the part of Adjutant-general Williams to force the brigade of Stevens to charge upon the British right wing before it could fully deploy; and to give time for their advance, he threw a small party of skirmishers forward, with orders "to take to single trees and thus annoy the enemy as much as possible." The British right wing however was too quick and spirited for this movement of untried militia, who did not know how to use the bayonet just received. They came on with a steady front and loud cheers, instantly carrying everything before them.

The Virginia militia threw down their loaded arms and fled. The North Carolina militia, with the exception of a small detachment under General Gregory who made a short pause, and of a part of Dixon's regiment who were next in line to the second Maryland brigade, fled also. The power of example is illustrated by Dixon's conduct in view of his position. "At least two-thirds of the army," according to Adjutant-general Williams, "fled without firing a shot." The First Maryland brigade two hundred yards in the rear, repeatedly resisted the attack upon their left, until the British right wing overwhelmed them by numbers and forced them to retire. It was just then that the British legion, which had pursued the militia until they were started to the rear, joined Lieutenant-colonel Webster, and made the decisive charge upon the First Maryland brigade. The Second Maryland brigade did not flinch; but after repulsing Lord Rawdon twice, charged bayonet under Baron De Kalb, broke through the British left, wheeled upon its centre, and fought alone until the whole British army enveloped them in fire. Baron De Kalb fell, wounded in eleven places, and could hardly be convinced that the Americans were not the victors, so faithfully had he executed his orders, in the assurance of equal good conduct on the part of the other divisions. The rout was utter. General Gates was carried away with the militia, which he calls "a torrent," and knew nothing of the resistance so stubbornly maintained by the right wing of his army.

Adjutant-general Williams says, "If in this affair the militia fled too soon, the regulars may be thought as blamable for remaining too long on the field; especially after all hope of victory must have been despaired of." General Gates hurried with General Caswell to Charlotte, sixty miles from the field of battle, and by the twentieth safely reached Hillsborough, one hundred and eighty miles from Camden, without gathering a sufficient force of the fugitives to form even an escort.

The North Carolina militia fled to their homes, or wherever they could find refuge. General Stevens followed the Virginians to Hillsborough, and back over the route they came, to attempt to rally them, but their term of service was short and he soon discharged them.

General Cornwallis reports his force at two thousand two hundred and thirty-nine men, and his casualties sixty-eight *killed*; two hundred and fifty-six wounded and missing. General Gates subsequently reported the loss of General De Kalb and five officers killed, and thirty-four officers wounded, including Lieutenant-colonels Woodford, Vaughan, Porterfield, and Du Buson, most of whom had been taken prisoners; and that by the twenty-ninth seven hundred non-commissioned officers and soldiers of the Maryland division had rejoined the army. This is a remarkable statement, greatly to the credit of those troops. The Delaware regiment had been almost literally destroyed. The Maryland troops lost between three and four hundred in killed, wounded and prisoners, and the original force was hardly fourteen hundred strong.

General Gates undoubtedly, as stated by him, made all the effort within his power to check the flight; but he had *no power* in action, and there is not a redeeming fact during his connection with the Southern army to show his fitness to command troops. Generals Smallwood and Gist secured their escape, as did the greater portion of Armand's cavalry. The British came into the possession of seven pieces of artillery, two thousand muskets, the entire baggage train, and prisoners to the number of nearly one thousand, according to the report of Cornwallis, including Generals De Kalb, Gregory, and Rutherford.

Congress had assigned General Gates to the command of the Southern Department at a time when the Commander-in-chief had selected General Greene for the detail; and the battle of Camden was an impressive commentary upon their action. It is not to be lost sight of that the expedition of Colonel Sumter took four hundred men from the army at a critical hour, and that a reasonable resistance on the part of the militia who were clumsily posted in the most exposed part of the field would have given increased value to the good conduct of the American right.

On the day of Sumter's misfortunes at Fishing creek, a skirmish occurred at Musgrove's Mills, South Carolina, on the Ennoree River, in which the Americans successfully surprised Colonel Ennis, who was in command of a mixed force of regulars and royalists.

On the twenty-first a skirmish occurred at Wahab's plantation. The house was burned, but the Americans under Colonel Davis secured ninety-six horses, and one hundred and twenty stand of arms, inflicted a loss upon the legion, who quartered there, of sixty men, losing about thirty.

Early in September, Brigadier-general Patterson retired from Charleston on sick leave, and Lieutenant-colonel Balfour succeeded to the command of that post.

Lieutenant-colonel Brown was stationed at Augusta, Lieutenant-colonel Conger at Ninety-six, and Lieutenant-colonel Turnbull at Camden. General Cornwallis advanced on the twenty-second with the Seventh, Twenty-third, Thirty-third and Seventy-first regiments of infantry, the Volunteers of Ireland, Hamilton's corps, Bryan's Refugees, four pieces of cannon, and a detachment of cavalry, toward Charlotte, *via* Hanging Rock. In a skirmish near the Court House on the twenty-sixth, while entering the town, the British advance was actively resisted, being fired upon from behind stone fences and buildings. Colonel Tarleton reports "about thirty of the enemy were killed and taken; the king's troops did not come out of this skirmish unhurt. Major Huger and Captains Campbell and McDonald were wounded, and twelve non-commissioned officers and men were killed and wounded. The American report states their loss as "Colonel Francis Locke, (who fought at Ramsour's Mills) *killed*, Major Graham and twelve men wounded."

It was now the purpose of General Cornwallis to take active measures for the invasion of North Carolina; but the whole region, drained by the Pacolet, Tyger, Ennoree, and Saluda Rivers was a troublesome one to leave in his rear. Of the people of Mecklenburg County, around Charlotte, Colonel Tarleton thus gives his opinion, " It was evident that the counties of Mecklenburg and Rohan were more hostile to England than any others in America. The vigilance and animosity of these districts checked the exertions of the well-affected, and totally destroyed all communications between the king's troops and the loyalists in the other parts of the province. No British commander could obtain any information; the foraging parties were every day harassed by the inhabitants, who did not remain at home to receive payment for the products of their plantations, but generally fired from covert places to annoy the British detachments. Individuals, with expresses, were frequently murdered. Notwithstanding their checks and losses, they continued their hostilities with unwearied perseverance, and the British troops were so effectually blockaded, that very few out of a great number of messengers could reach Charlotte, in the beginning of October, to give intelligence of Ferguson's situation." These statements clearly indicate the fact that the British policy was developing an increased antagonism among the people, and that the conquest did not extend beyond garrison limits. This irregular warfare was bearing fruit.

Colonel Clark threatened Augusta, and in two days inflicted considerable loss upon the garrison, but was repulsed, Lieutenant-colonel Brown, the post commander, being wounded, and Captain Johnson killed. Colonel Tarleton says that the British loss fell principally upon their Indian auxiliaries. General Cornwallis states that the Indians pursued and scalped many of the Americans.

On the eighth of October the battle of King's Mountain entered into the operations of the campaign and did very much to offset the British victory at Camden. Tarleton and Ferguson operated along parallel belts separated by the Catawba and Broad Rivers as circumstances of pursuit or scouting determined, and the latter officer who had hoped to cut off Colonel Clark's detachment and other border partisan corps, before winter, found himself compelled to take refuge on King's Mountain on the sixth of October, closely pursued by a superior force. Colonel Isaac Shelby with a force from Sullivan County (now in Tennessee); Colonel William Campbell, with men from Washington County, Virginia; Colonel Benjamin Cleveland with men from Wilkes and Surrey Counties; Colonel Charles McDowell, with men from Wilkes and Rutherford Counties, North Carolina; Colonel John Sevier with men from Sullivan, reached the Cowpens, on Broad River on the sixth of October, and were joined the same evening by Colonel James Williams of South Carolina with a small force, the total command numbering nearly or quite sixteen hundred men, who had been selected for the purpose. It was an impromptu, unpaid army of volunteers, hastily combined for the purpose of ridding the country of Ferguson's corps.

King's Mountain, about a mile long and about a hundred feet above the surrounding country, is one of a series of rocky summits extending from the south-east to the north-west, and is just within the boundary line of North Carolina, as indicated on the map " Operations in Southern States."

Nine hundred men were selected to storm the hill in front and on the flanks. The detachment of the Seventy-first British regulars, fought with such spirit that in three bayonet charges they crowded their assailants to the foot of the hill. Major Ferguson was killed and the command devolved upon Captain Abraham De Peister, of the King's American regiment. After an hour of desperate struggle the command surrendered.

The American casualties were Colonel Williams, Major Chromile, Captain Mattocks, two lieutenants, four ensigns and nineteen men killed; one major, three captains, three lieutenants and fifty-three privates wounded.

The British casualties are characterized by a report which is so similar to those of Tarleton respecting "the wounded unable to march," that it confirms the generally accepted opinion that a deliberate slaughter was made of the so-called Tory troops. The casualties are reported as, "Two colonels, three captains and two hundred and one privates killed, one hundred and twenty-seven privates wounded, and *being unable to march*, left on the field; one colonel, twelve captains and with other officers and men, six hundred and forty-eight prisoners. The regulars lost, besides Major Ferguson, one captain, two lieutenants and fifteen privates killed; thirty-five wounded but *unable to march* and left on the ground; two captains and sixty-eight taken prisoners."

Fifteen hundred muskets and other arms, with the baggage, were captured. Tarleton thus briefly sums up his statement: "The action was disputed with great bravery near an hour, when the death of the gallant Ferguson threw his whole corps into total confusion. No effort was, made after this event, to resist the enemy's barbarity or revenge the fall of their leader."

Lossing and Dawson justly regard this action as one of the most obstinate of the war, and the associated skirmishes already briefly noticed, are but indicative of the intensely personal and destructive character of the campaign.

"It was now evident," says Tarleton, "beyond contradiction, that the British general had not adopted the most eligible plan for the invasion of North Carolina. Winnsborough was selected for the winter quarters of the army, and the sick were placed at Camden, where "redoubts were built, to make up for the badness of the position." Works were also erected at Nelson's Ferry, to secure the communications with Charleston, and also at Ninety-six.

"The success of the Americans at King's Mountain," says Tarleton, "and the distance of Cornwallis's army, prompted many of the disaffected inhabitants of South Carolina to break their parole, and to unite under a leader, 'Marion,' in the eastern part of the province." Sumter still operated on the banks of Broad River, cutting off foraging parties, and endangering the post at Ninety-six. Major Wemyss of the Sixty-third British regiment, and some cavalry of the legion, attempted to surprise him at Fish Dam Ford, on the ninth of November, lost twenty-five men as prisoners, and failed in the attempt. Later in the month, Colonel Sumter, strongly reinforced by Colonels

Thomas and Bratton, and Majors McCall and Hammond, of South Carolina, marched toward Ninety-six to attempt its capture, but was pursued by Colonel Tarleton, and a skirmish ensued, November twentieth, at Blackstock's plantations, on the Tiger River, which left Colonel Sumter in possession of the field.

The skirmish is given in order to indicate the extraordinary conflict in reports of this partisan warfare. American statement of their own loss, three killed, four wounded, among the latter General Sumter; of the enemy, ninety-two killed and one hundred wounded. Tarleton's statement, Americans killed and wounded, upwards of one hundred, and fifty made prisoners. British loss, Lieutenants Gibson and Cope killed, four officers and forty-five non-commissioned officers and men killed and wounded.

Stedman " takes the whole account of the action from Mackenzie's strictures on Tarleton's campaign," very justly reviewing inconsistencies in Tarleton's report, which disprove his statement of casualties and adds, " The wounded of the British detachment were left to the mercy of the enemy; and it is but justice to General Sumter to declare that the strictest humanity took place upon the present occasion; they were supplied with every comfort in his power. Although Tarleton was repulsed at Blackstock's Hill, the immediate effects were nearly the same as a victory. General Sumter being disabled by his wound from keeping the field, his followers dispersed, after conveying him to a place of safety."

The summer and fall campaign in the Southern States had been one of constant activity, and as the year 1780 drew to its close there was no cessation of demands upon the vigilance of either army. The remnants of General Gates' army were being reorganized as rapidly as possible, and before the departure of that officer to answer before a Court of Inquiry ordered by Congress, as to the disaster at Camden, he had collected a nominal force of two thousand three hundred and seven men, more than half of whom were militia, and as afterwards stated by General Greene, " but eight hundred in the whole force were properly clothed and equipped."

The post commander at Charleston, Lieutenant-colonel Balfour, was taking extreme measures to terrify and intimidate the people; Marion had increased his partisan detachment to the strength of an efficient corps, and with no severity of climate such as impaired operations at the north, the campaign of 1781 practically began when General Nathaniel Greene arrived to take command of the Southern Department on the third of December, 1780.

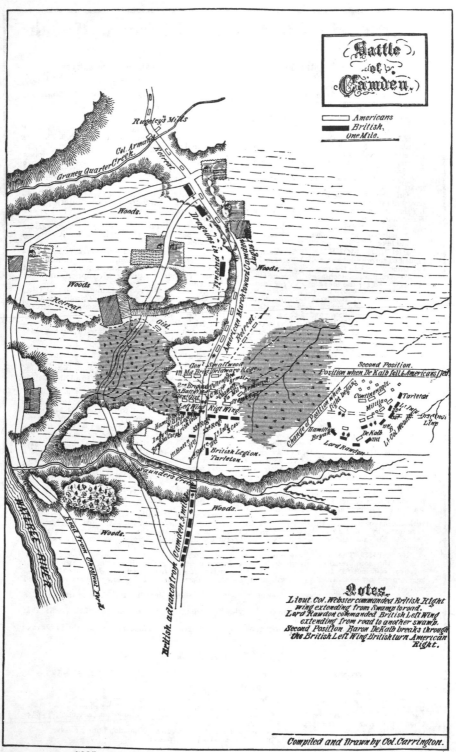

Battle of Camden.

Americans
Brittish.
One Mile.

Rugeley's Mills

Col. Armand

Graney Quarter Creek.

Retreat

Woods.

Dragoons in ruin

Woods

Retreat

American March toward Camden

Retreat

Gent Smallwood
1st Md Brig Delaware Reg.
2nd Brigade Gist Armstrong
1st Brig.
Left Wing   Rigt Wing

Change of Position when fight began

British Legion.
Tarleton.

Saunders Creek

Road from Cherford Ford

Woods.

Woods.

Woods

WATEREE RIVER

British advance from Camden 5 miles

Second Position.
Position when De Kalb fell & Americans fled

Continentals.
Militia
De Kalb

Hamilton
Bryan
Lord Rawdon

Tarleton
Lt. Inffy Second
Line

Lt. Col. Webster

Notes.
Lieut. Col. Webster commanded British Right
wing extending from Swamp to road.
Lord Rawdon commanded British Left Wing
extending from road to another swamp.
Second Position Baron De Kalb breaks through
the British Left Wing British turn American
Right.

Compiled and Drawn by Col. Carrington.

522*

Battle of Camden or Sander's Creek

AUGUST 16th, 1780

American Commanders

GATES

Porterfield, Armstrong, Williams, Gist, DeKalb, Caswell, Singleton, Stevens, Marquis Armand, Rutherford, Gregory

Strength, 3,052 Casualties, 971, beside missing

British Commanders

CORNWALLIS

Rawdon, Tarleton, Webster, Hamilton, Bryan, McLeod

Strength, 2,239 Casualties, 324

AMERICAN MOVEMENTS.—The army of Gates, strengthened by that of DeKalb, left Hillsborough, N. C., July 27th, crossed Deep River at Buffalo Ford, and by the 3d of August, 1780, gained the Peedee River, and united with Porterfield's command. On the 7th, the North Carolina militia, under Caswell, joined, and on the 13th, Gates encamped at Rugely's Mills, twelve miles above Camden. On the 14th, Stevens joined, with 700 Virginia militia. The troops of De Kalb, 1,400 men, Maryland and Delaware troops, accompanied him from Morristown, New Jersey, having left headquarters, April 16th.

On the 15th of August, Gates ordered the army to march, at ten o'clock that night, to attack Camden, and insisted upon the order, after Adjutant-General Williams exhibited the daily Returns, showing that the real force was less than half his estimate. He did not know that Cornwallis had joined Rawdon at Camden.

Marquis Armand, with his squadron of 60 dragoons, led the advance, in spite of his protest against using mounted men for pioneer night service, as it required perfect silence. Porterfield and Armstrong were to take the woods, on his flank, and give him full support.

BRITISH MOVEMENTS.—Cornwallis, advised of Gates' force and his advance, alike intended to surprise his enemy. Upon reaching Sander's Creek, five miles from Camden, between two and three o'clock in the morning, the advance guard of 40 cavalry, and mounted infantry, met and routed Armand's detachment. Porterfield was mortally wounded in giving his support, and both armies waited for the break of day for further developments.

Note I.—The American *first line* was formed as follows: Right Wing, under General Gist, with the Delaware troops of DeKalb; Centre, under General Caswell, with North Carolina militia; Left Wing, under General Stevens, with raw Virginia militia. Singleton's guns occupied the road. General Smallwood commanded the *second line* with the First Maryland brigade.

Note II.—The British *first line* was as follows: Right Wing, Webster, with 23d and 33d regiments, and three companies of light infantry. Lord Rawdon commanded the left wing, viz.: Volunteers of Ireland, the Legion Infantry, Hamilton's Corps, and Bryan's Refugees, and five guns under McLeod. The two battalions of the 71st regiment, with two guns, formed the second line. Tarleton's dragoons remained in column, on account of the thickness of the wood, to act as required.

Note III.—Upon crossing Sander's Creek, the British army entered upon a narrow belt of land, bordered on each side by an impassable swamp, while the American line, also between the swamps, on a widening area, would become exposed to any flank movement, unless they firmly held their original ground.

Note IV.—Before the action, Gates had learned from a prisoner, taken in the night skirmish, that Cornwallis was in command; but hesitated so long as to what was to be done, that he lost the opportunity for retreat to Rugely's Mills. Stevens pronounced it to be anything but right, and in the silence of Gates as to orders, gallantly followed the suggestion of Adjutant-General Williams, to attack the British right wing as it advanced, before it could gain room for full deployment. Skirmishers were ordered to take single trees for cover, and aid the movement.

Note V.—"It was calm and hazy, so that the smoke settled, until it was difficult," says Cornwallis, "to see the effect of a heavy and well-directed fire on both sides." He observed a movement on the American left, which he supposed to indicate some change in their order of battle. He at once precipitated Webster's regiments upon the Virginia militia, before they could gain the position they sought. They threw down their loaded arms, and fled. The North Carolina militia, except a small force under Gregory, also fled.

Note VI.—The British right wing, having then broken through, next attacked the 1st Maryland brigade, where it met firm resistance, until Tarleton's dragoons came to their support, when, overwhelmed with numbers, they retired.

Note VII.—The British left wing was firmly received by DeKalb. He bore down upon them with the bayonet, broke through their ranks, wheeled to the left, and fought, until his force was enveloped by the British right wing, which turned back to charge this, suddenly, adverse tide of battle. DeKalb fell, wounded in five places, still confident that victory was certainly with the Americans.

Note VIII.—The rout of the militia was utter. Gates hurried to Charlotteville, sixty miles, and by the 20th, reached Hillsborough, one hundred and eighty miles from Camden, without fugitives sufficient for an escort. The Delaware regiment was almost destroyed, while the Maryland troops lost more than 300 in killed, wounded, and prisoners. Forty-one officers were killed or wounded.

Note IX.—The gallantry of DeKalb's conduct is shown by the British casualties, which Cornwallis admitted to be 324.

Note X.—Of the missing from the Maryland division, it is to be noted, to their credit, that by the 29th, 700 had rejoined the army.

Note XI.—The British captured 7 guns, 1,000 prisoners, 2,000 muskets, and all the baggage of the American army.

References:

CARRINGTON'S "BATTLES OF THE AMERICAN REVOLUTION," pp. 513-523.

School Histories:

Anderson, ¶ 93; p. 92.
Barnes, ¶ 2; p. 133.
Berard (Bush), ¶ 119; p. 170.
Goodrich, C. A.(Seaveys) ¶ 15; p. 138.
Goodrich, S. G., ¶ 4-8; p. 264.
Hassard, ¶ 8; p. 212.

Holmes, ¶ 13; p. 143.
Lossing, ¶ 9; p. 177.
Quackenbos, ¶ 277; p. 274-5.
Ridpath, ¶ 7; p. 218.
Sadlier (Excel.), ¶ 17; p. 201-2.
Stephens, A. H., ¶ 6-7; p. 217.

Swinton, ¶ 4; p. 157.
Scott, ¶ 7; p. 203.
Thalheimer (Eclectic), ¶ 288; p. 165.
Venable, ¶ 161; p. 121.

CHAPTER LXVI.

THE year 1780 closed with the promise of still more active operations in the Southern Department; but there were many
hindrances to prevent prompt support from the North. The defeat
of the American army at Camden was not known by General Washington until September, and it was impossible to spare from the
Northern army a sufficient force to cope with that of Lord Cornwallis.

The second division of French troops, so long looked for, and
reported as blockaded in the port of Brest, did not arrive. The
blockade of Newport compelled the French army to remain almost
idle, as a support to the fleet, and the American army rapidly diminished in numbers as winter drew near.

Occasional demonstrations were made as if to attack New York,
but chiefly to prevent the detachment of any portion of its garrison to
the South. A serious attack upon the city was impracticable, until
reinforcements should arrive from France.

During the month of October, however, La Fayette elaborated a
plan, which was so far advanced that boats were built and placed
upon wagons, thereby to unite the advantages of attack both by
land and water. This plan included Fort Washington, the city of
New York and Staten Island, as objectives of simultaneous attack,
and proposed to make the blow as sudden as that upon Trenton in
1776. It was abandoned for want of boats. There were few periods
during the war when more diverse and widely separated interests
required the attention of the American Commander-in-chief.

Major Carleton, with a force of eight hundred troops, regulars,
Canadians and Indians, captured Forts George and Ann in October.
Fort Edward was saved through the sagacity of Colonel Livingston,

who having a garrison of only seventy-nine men, averted attack, by sending a letter to the commanding officer of Fort George (to be intercepted by the enemy) exaggerating his own strength and declaring his purpose to go to the rescue of that post. The British troops however, actually advanced to the vicinity of Saratoga, burned some houses, and then returned to Lake Champlain.

An incursion from Fort Niagara into the Mohawk Valley brought another brief struggle with Sir John Johnson, Joseph Brandt and the Indians. The Oneidas, friendly to the United States, were expelled from their homes, the Schoharie region was desolated, and much wheat was destroyed.

On the sixth of November, General Washington confided to General Schuyler the fact, that some leaders in Vermont were corresponding with British officials in Canada, and directed him to concert measures with General Clinton to detect and thwart their plans. The prompt response of General Schuyler was characteristic of his entire career during the war : and it is but justice to say, that garbled documents, and sneers at his high social position and culture, have in some instances usurped the place of history and dishonored records otherwise reputable for general accuracy of statement. These movements required three additional regiments to be sent to Albany, and constant uneasiness prevailed along the whole northern and northwestern frontiers.

On the seventh of November it was known to Washington that the American army was "experiencing almost daily want ;" while the " British army in New York was deriving ample supplies from a trade with New York, New Jersey and Connecticut, which had, by degrees, become so common that it was hardly thought a crime."

General Sullivan having left the army, took his seat in Congress, September eleventh. In a letter of November twentieth, Washington uses the following urgent and laconic terms, in writing to him : " Congress will deceive themselves, if they imagine that the army, or a State that is the theater of war, can rub through a second campaign, as the last. It would be as unreasonable to suppose that because a man had rolled a snowball till it had acquired the size of a horse, he might do it until it was the size of a house. Matters may be pushed to a certain point, beyond which we can not move them. Ten months' pay is now due to the army. Every department of it is so much indebted that we have not credit for a single expense, and some of the States are harassed and oppressed to a degree beyond bearing. . . To depend, under these circumstances, upon the resources of the country, unassisted by foreign bravery, will, I am confident, be to lean upon a broken reed."

General Sullivan had advised that the French fleet should force its way from Newport to Boston, and the French army report at headquarters. This proposition had been urged at a conference held with the Count de Rochambeau, at Hartford, Connecticut, but it was not adopted. As early as October sixteenth, General Leslie left New York with nearly three thousand troops and landed at Portsmouth, Virginia ; but afterwards re-embarked, and landed at Charleston, late in December. Colonel Rochambeau, son of Count de Rochambeau, left Newport on the twenty-eighth of October, ran the gauntlet of the British fleet during a gale, and safely reached France, with a formal application for additional aid of men, arms and money. The Chevalier de Ternay died at Newport, on the fifteenth of December, and was succeeded in command of the fleet, by Chevalier Destouches. Some ineffectual negotiations took place looking to a union of Spanish and French ships in a common movement on the American coast ; but no practical results were realized, more than to hold the British ships fast before Newport, and thus prevent their operations down the Atlantic coast. Colonel Fleury, who had been distinguished at Fort Mifflin and Stony Point, joined the French army under Rochambeau.

On the twentieth of December, General Washington wrote to Benjamin Franklin, Minister at the Court of Versailles, stating that "the campaign had been thus inactive, after a flattering prospect at the opening of it and vigorous struggles to make it a decisive one, through failure of the expected naval superiority which was the pivot upon which everything turned," and added : "The movements of Lord Cornwallis during the past month or two have been *retrograde*. What turn the late reinforcements, which have been sent to him, may give to his affairs, remains to be known. I have reinforced our Southern army, principally with horse ; but the length of the march is so much opposed to the measure that every corps is in a greater or less degree ruined. I am happy, however, in assuring you that a better disposition never prevailed in the legislatures of the several States, than at this time. The folly of temporary expedients is seen into and exploded, and vigorous efforts will be used to obtain a permanent army and carry on the war systematically, if the obstinacy of Great Britain shall compel us to continue it. We want nothing but the aid of a loan to enable us to put our finances into a tolerable train. The country does not want resources, but we want the means of drawing them forth."

It appears from this letter that Washington had reached a point where he felt that ultimate success was not far distant. The reconstruction of the army to which he refers, was a plan then pending for the consolidation of battalions, reducing their numbers and thereby settling upon something like a permanent army establishment.

The new army was to consist of fifty regiments of foot, including Hazen's, specially reserved—four regiments of artillery, and one of artificers, with the two partisan corps under Armand and Lee, and four other legionary corps, two-thirds horse and one-third foot. All new enlistments were to be for the war. The total force upon the reëstablished company basis would amount to thirty-six thousand men. Not more than half that number were ever in the field at the same time, and the full complement was never recruited. Hazen's regiment, and the corps of Armand and Lee were recruited at large. The other regiments were assigned as follows: to Massachusetts and Virginia, eleven regiments each; Pennsylvania, nine; Connecticut, six; Maryland, five; North Carolina, four; New York, three; New Hampshire, New Jersey and South Carolina, two each; Rhode Island, Delaware and Georgia, one each.

This reorganization was attended with difficulties. There were many who had taken commissions with the purpose of devoting their life to military attainment. Their entire life, (as a soldier would understand the expression) was involved in their military service. The consolidation involved sacrifices, and there was a strong party in Congress, " led by Samuel Adams," which as Hildreth concisely states the fact, " was very jealous of military power, and of everything which tended to give a permanent character to the army." The retirement of officers on partial pay was bitterly opposed by this party; and the jealousy of a regular army, the value of which was in Washington's estimation, and in fact, one of the great lessons of the war, was the perpetual cause of waste, disaster, and the postponement of success.

Colonel Robert H. Harrison, former secretary to the Commander-in-chief had become Chief Justice of Maryland, and was succeeded in the staff by Jonathan Trumbull, Jr. Hand was appointed Adjutant-general, vice Scammel resigned. Smallwood succeeded to command of a division, vice De Kalb, killed in battle. Morgan was promoted as Brigadier-general, and sent to the Southern Department, together with General Steuben and Lee's corps, three hundred and fifty strong, together with Kosciusko as engineer, vice Du Portail captured at Charleston.

A specie tax of six millions was imposed, and in spite of countless minor embarrassments the sixth annual campaign of the war drew near its close.

On the twenty-eighth of November, Washington designated the winter quarters for the army, his own being established at New Windsor. The Pennsylvania line were established near Morristown ; the Jersey line at Pompton ; the Maryland regiment of horse at Lancaster, Pennsylvania ; and Sheldon's horse at Colchester, Connecticut ; one New York regiment at Fort Schuyler, one at Saratoga, and the remainder of the line at Albany, Schenectady, and other exposed posts.

In the location of troops in southern New England, where the French army was quartered, there was much local apprehension lest forage would be inadequate to the demand ; and some local feeling was aroused in Connecticut against the assignments made. In a letter to Governor Trumbull, of December seventeenth, Washington plainly asserted his prerogative as Commander-in-chief to direct the movements of the army, asserting that any local interference intrenched upon his prerogative and endangered the national cause. Governor Trumbull, as always, fully supported Washington.

The condition of Great Britain at this period of the struggle was one of supreme trial. Her insular position was suggestive of independence ; but her maritime superiority was a source of universal jealousy and envy. Whatever may have been her errors of policy or her failure to compromise issues with foreign states, the close of 1780 found her in practical conflict with Europe, and under apprehensions of invasion from France. Spain and France were united in open war, and their combined fleets threatened her West India possessions. Spain was pressing the siege of Gibraltar. Denmark and Sweden had already united with Catharine of Russia to adopt the famous system of " Armed Neutrality," declaring that " free ships make free goods," and that neutrals might carry any goods or supplies wherever they pleased with complete immunity from search or capture. This was a blow at British commerce. Even in the East Indies her crown was one of thorns. Hyder Ali swept through the province of Madras, and Warren Hastings was contending, as for life, to save British supremacy from overthrow.

France sent aid to Hyder Ali as well as to America, and thereby was limited in her contributions to the army of Washington.

Early in September a correspondence had been well advanced between the United States and Holland, looking to a commercial treaty between the two nations. Laurens was sent as a commissioner to Holland, was taken prisoner, carried to England, and confined in the Tower on a charge of high treason. His papers were captured, and as the result of a brief correspondence between the British Cabinet and the States-General of Holland, the British government declared war against that state on the second day of December. Instructions had been previously sent to her fleets, and immediate blows were struck at the Dutch colonies and Dutch commerce.

Domestic excitements added their burden to the great external pressure which seemed to threaten the Island Empire. Eighty thousand volunteers had been enrolled in Ireland, in view of apprehended invasion from France. The agitations for parliamentary reform became earnest, and the independence of the Irish Parliament was said to be in peril. Meanwhile the British advocates of "peace with America at the price of recognized independence" became more earnest, and the crisis rendered the detachment of any considerable body of troops to increase the armies at New York and Charleston, absolutely impossible. The period was one which vindicated the claim of Great Britain to the admiration of the world for her wonderful capacity to withstand external force, and no less emphatically disclosed the equally wonderful resources at her control. It was in exact keeping with the struggle which made the American Colonies unconquerable by force of arms. Thus England and France alike were restrained from strengthening the contending armies of the New World.

General Greene accepted the southern command with eagerness, supported by the confidence of Washington. General La Fayette desired to accompany him; but in view of his intimate relations to the French alliance, his services were deemed essential to successful operations at the north.

General Greene started for the south. There was breadth of territory sufficient to satisfy any reasonable ambition; but he needed an army. He resolved to develop an army, in accordance with the peculiar kind of service which would be required, and his suggestion was approved by Washington when he first submitted his plan on the eighth of November, 1780. He would have that army a "flying army," lightly equipped, mobile, and as familiar as possible with the country in which operations were to be prosecuted. The Commander-in-chief addressed letters to Governor Thomas S. Lee of Maryland, to Governor Abner Nash of North Carolina, and to Governor Thomas Jefferson of Virginia, invoking their cordial coöperation in the work of the new Department commander.

The southern army, as Greene wrote to General Knox, "is shadow rather than substance, having only an imaginary existence." Congress could not supply troops; but by the adding of Maryland and Delaware to his department, he secured the control of militia, additional to that which he was to draw from the actual field of operations. He was also clothed with the same powers which General Gates had been empowered to exercise, such as authority to draw upon the Southern States for troops or money and to impress subsistence or transportation, whenever unavoidable necessity should require it.

On the twenty-third of November he began his journey, attended by General the Baron Steuben and his aids Colonel Morris and Major Burnet. At each State capital he urged the necessity of immediate action. To Governor Rodney of Delaware, he wrote:—"Do not suffer those States, now struggling with the enemy, to sink under their oppression, for want of a reasonable support." To Governor Lee, of Maryland:—"Unless they are soon succored and countenanced by a good regular force, their distresses will inevitably break their spirits, and they will be compelled to reconcile themselves to their misfortunes. There is no alternative but base submission, or an effectual prosecution of the war." Generals Gist and Smallwood were at once employed by these two States, upon recruiting service. General Greene's order of November twentieth, thus gives clearness to his will,—"You will please to make all your applications in writing, that they may appear hereafter for our justification; that we left nothing unessayed to promote the public service. Let your applications be as pressing as our necessities are urgent; after which, if the northern States are lost, we shall stand justified. The greatest consequences depend upon your activity and zeal in the business."

Upon reaching Virginia, he found that the State was necessarily absorbed in its own defense. General Leslie had taken possession of Norfolk and Portsmouth, and fortified both. Generals Muhlenberg and Weedon, had been sent by Washington to organize the militia, and upon General Greene's arrival they were organizing their

34

forces to oppose any advance of General Leslie beyond the immediate limits of the two posts which his army garrisoned. The consolidation of regiments and the reduction of their number, left several valuable officers out of service; but nearly all of these, as well as Generals Muhlenberg and Weedon, had served under General Greene at the north. Among the officers thus left without commands was Colonel Edward Carrington. The first thing General Greene determined upon was " to select depots, and laboratories,—posts of rest and communication, and to provide transportation for hospital and other army stores."

Justice Johnson states that "he fixed his eye upon Colonel Carrington as eminently qualified to undertake the task of combining and conducting the means at the Quartermaster-general's department; that he obeyed the call to the office and discharged it with unequaled zeal and fidelity." Chief-justice Marshall confirms the statement. The principal depot of stores and arms was established at Prince Edward Court House, and General the Baron Steuben was charged with maintaining the supply of powder from the manufactories, and of lead from the mines in Fincastle County. He was also placed in command of the District of Virginia, with a special charge "to collect, organize, discipline and expedite the recruits for the Southern army."

Before his departure for the field General Greene wrote to Governor Jefferson, urging the immediate completion of the regiments, under the reduced standard, to their maximum; and makes the following points emphatic: "It is perfectly consistent, in all cases, to carry on war *abroad,* rather than *at home*, as well in matters of expense, as in humanity to the inhabitants. But this policy is rendered doubly necessary to Virginia, from the ease with which the enemy can penetrate through North Carolina and possess themselves of all the low country of Virginia. . . It must be the extreme of folly to hazard our liberties upon so precarious a dependence," referring to the militia. "They are the bulwark of civil liberty if they are not depended upon, as a principal, but employed as an auxiliary." " *Officers are the very soul of an army,* and you may as well attempt to animate a dead body into action, as to expect to employ an army to advantage, when the officers are not perfectly easy in their circumstances, and happy in the service."

In the sphere of Logistics which so materially affects all military operations, General Greene had peculiar experience, and he evinced great discrimination and practical judgment. In this letter to Governor Jefferson, he says: "The late distressing accounts from the Southern army claim the immediate attention of government, both with respect to provisions and clothing. It is impossible for men to remain long in the field unless they are well furnished with both these articles; and to expose them to the want of either, will soon transfer them from the field to the hospital, or lay them under the necessity of deserting." . . . "Great pains should be taken to fix upon some place for feeding the army with live stock, and I think of none unless it be putting up a large quantity of beeves to stall-feed." . . . "The distress and suffering of the people of North and South Carolina deserve the most speedy support to keep alive that spirit of enterprise which has prevailed among them lately, so much to their honor. It is much easier to oppose the enemy while the tide of sentiment runs in our favor, than it will be to secure Virginia after they are overrun."

Orders were issued to Colonel Carrington "to explore the Dan, Yadkin and Catawba, and make himself thoroughly acquainted with the streams into which they discharged themselves." This order was executed with great exactness, and the casual reader of general history who has regarded the subsequent movements of General Greene as accidental, will see that a previous knowledge of the country in which he was to operate was one element of his military success. Colonel Carrington accompanied General Greene to Richmond after the organization of his department. General Stevens executed the survey of the Yadkin. Kosciusko, Greene's engineer-in-chief, examined the Catawba, and other officers visited the Dan. The result of this forethought materially affected the subsequent campaign.

On the second of December, General Greene reached Charlotte, and immediately relieved General Gates of the command, under circumstances which redounded to the credit of both officers. Mutual courtesies were exchanged, and General Gates went to his farm. The condition of his army was General Greene's first care. He found that everything was needed, and in a letter to Governor Jefferson, states quite clearly the facts. A few paragraphs are given: "I find the troops in a most wretched condition, destitute of everything necessary either for comfort or convenience, and may literally be said to be naked." "It will answer no good purpose to send men here in such a condition." "There must be either pride, or principle, to make a soldier. No man will think himself bound to fight the battles of a state that leaves him to perish for want of clothing, nor can you inspire a soldier with the sentiment of pride while his situation renders him more an object of pity than of envy.   The life of a soldier in the best estate, is liable to innumerable hardships ; but where these are aggravated by the want of provisions and clothing, his condition becomes intolerable; nor can men long contend with such complicated difficulties and distress.   Death, desertion, and the hospital must soon swallow up an army under such circumstances, and if it were possible for men to maintain such a wretched existence, they would have no spirit to face their enemies, and would inevitably disgrace themselves and their commander.   It is impossible to presume discipline when troops are in want of everything ; to attempt severity will only thin the ranks by a more hasty desertion."

For two months General Greene remained in camp. He anticipated the necessity for axes, and even nails, and fabricated cheap substitutes for articles that could not be readily secured otherwise.

On the twentieth of December, having been delayed four days by rains, the huts at Charlotte were abandoned, the main army reaching Hicks creek, a branch of the Peedee, near Cheraw Hill, on the twenty-sixth. General Morgan was detached, however, on the sixteenth, with three hundred and twenty from the Maryland line, two hundred Virginia militia, and Colonel Washington's horse, less than a hundred strong, to cross the Catawba, and "take command in that quarter, to act offensively or defensively, to protect the country, spirit up the people, annoy the enemy, collect provisions and forage, form magazines, prevent plundering, etc." .   .   .

Marion at once placed himself in communication with General Greene. In a letter to that officer, responsive to one addressed to General Gates, he says, "Your letter of the 22d last month to General Gates is before me. I am fully sensible your service is hard and sufferings great ; but how great the prize for which we contend. I like your plan of frequently shifting your ground. It frequently prevents a surprise, and perhaps the total loss of your party. Until a more permanent army can be collected than is in the field at present, we must endeavor to keep up a partisan war, and preserve the tide of sentiment among the people in our favor as much as possible. Spies are the *eyes of an army*, and without them a general is always groping in the dark."

Marion was then on Black River, but soon returned to his camp in the forks of Pedee and Lynch Rivers, and on the twenty-seventh of

December reported to General Greene the arrival of General Leslie at Charleston, his march to Camden, and the establishment of Colonel Watson at Nelson's Ferry with two hundred men. From that time forward the campaign was fairly in motion. With Morgan on the west and Marion in the eastern districts, the new commanding officer had carefully prepared his way to contend with the British forces in a manner of warfare which should suit itself to the character of his troops, and the country in which the war was to be carried on. It is very clear from the unofficial letters of General Greene to La Fayette and other officers, that he realized the grave responsibilities of his position and endeavored to anticipate the contingencies of the campaign. A reference to chapter thirty-six will show that at that early period of the war, he understood the importance of preparing *in advance* for an army movement; and as already indicated, much of his success at the south was secured by the tedious system of reconnoitring which he inaugurated before he marched from Virginia.

Other troops followed slowly. The patience of Baron Steuben was severely tasked. On the fifteenth of December Colonel Lee marched with his corps, three hundred strong, and Colonel Christopher Greene accompanied him with four hundred men, but they did not reach the Peedee until the twelfth of January.

The closing active campaign of the war for American Independence thus opened, and its principal military events will be considered in detail.

CHAPTER LXVII.

CONDITION OF SOUTHERN AFFAIRS. MUTINY AT THE NORTH. OPERATIONS OF GENERALS GREENE AND CORNWALLIS. BATTLE OF COWPENS, 1781.

THE campaign of 1781 was the last of the American war, but in some respects it was less earnestly supported than were those of previous years. The American army could not be recruited up to the new standard, and the British received no considerable reinforcements from abroad. The American people seemed to consider the presence of the French troops as equivalent, rather than as an encouragement, to extra exertion ; and a corresponding impression of the English crown that the south was almost conquered and would quite generally rally to the royal standard, had its tendency, equally to quiet the English authorities and prevent the shipment of troops.

The addition of Holland to the enemies of England had its effect also, since it compelled England to leave American affairs almost entirely to the care of officers then on duty in the United States ; and on the other hand, the Americans could not fail to see that any large addition to the British army, from abroad, was impossible. In addition to these considerations, there was a sense of fatigue which affected the people on both sides of the Atlantic, as if there had been sufficient fighting over an issue which could have but one possible result, *separation*. The English whigs remonstrated against its continuance, and the Cabinet itself began to realize the fact that the war was crippling all efforts in other directions ; while the Americans themselves, outside of the Southern States, largely entertained the conviction that the war would soon end, and therefore failed to make the necessary exertions to end it summarily, by supplying the necessary force, at once. Money, food and clothing, were as scarce as at any previous period, and protracted sacrifice, uncompensated labor and unpaid services, began to wear out both soldiers and people.

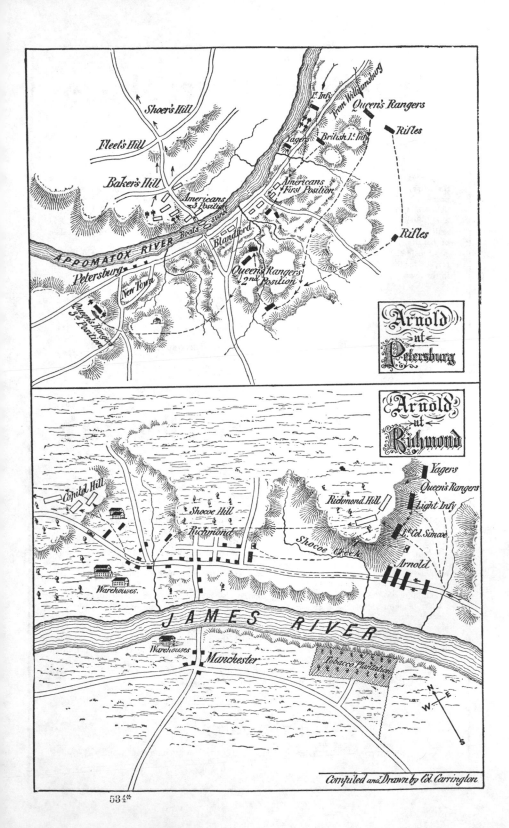

Arnold at Petersburg

Shoer's Hill
Fleet's Hill
Baker's Hill
L.t Inf.y
from Williamsburg
Queen's Rangers
Rifles
Yagers
British L.t Inf.y
Americans First Position
Americans 3 Position
swamp
Appomatox River
Boats
Blandford
Petersburg
New Town
Queens Rangers 2.nd Position
Queens Rangers 3.d Position
Rifles

Arnold at Richmond

Capitol Hill
Shocoe Hill
Richmond
Yagers
Queen's Rangers
Light Inf.y
Richmond Hill
L.t Col. Simcoe
Shocoe Creek
Arnold
Warehouses
James River
Warehouses
Manchester
Tobacco Plantation

N E W S

Compiled and Drawn by Col. Carrington.

534*

Arnold at Petersburg

APRIL 25th, 1781

NOTES.—Benedict Arnold, having a force of 1,553 men, sailed to City Point (see map page), and on the 25th marched to Petersburg, arriving at 10 o'clock. Generals Steuben and Muhlenberg were at the post with about 1,000 militia. They advanced to a strong position before Brandon (Bradford) which compelled the Queen's Rangers and Rifles to make a long detour to cut off their retreat and gain Petersburg. Steuben fell back to cover Petersburg; but being unable to meet the opposing superior force, in action, recrossed the Appomattox River, with a loss of only twenty men. A third position was taken on Baker's Hill, which Arnold did not venture to assail.

Arnold claims that " he did not pursue because the enemy took up the bridge," and that he destroyed four thousand hogsheads of tobacco, one ship and a number of small vessels on the stocks and in the river.

References:

CARRINGTON'S "BATTLES OF THE AMERICAN REVOLUTION," pp. 589–590.

Arnold at Richmond

JANUARY 5th, 1780

NOTES.—BENEDICT ARNOLD, appointed Brigadier General in the British army, as pay for treason, left New York December 19, 1780, with sixteen hundred men for Virginia. Lieut. Col. Simcoe (Queen's Rangers), and Lieut. Col. Dundas, 18th Regiment (Scotch), belonged to his command.

A gale separated the ships ; but on the 31st he transferred 1,200 men to small vessels and moved up James River. On the 3d of January, at night, Simcoe landed at Hood's Point, to spike a small battery, and on the 4th the expedition landed at Westover, nearly twenty-five miles below Richmond, and marched immediately to that city.

On the 5th, Arnold entered Richmond ; Simcoe dislodged a small force of two hundred militia which Col. John Nichols had assembled on Richmond Hill ; and some mounted men on Shoer's Hill quickly retired. A foundry, laboratory and some shops were burned at Westham, nearly seven miles above Richmond, as well as some public records which had been taken there for safety. A proposition sent to Governor Jefferson, dictating terms upon which the buildings might be saved, for the privilege of quietly taking away the tobacco, was rejected ; and, burning as many houses as time permitted, Arnold retired without loss.

Five brass guns, three hundred stand of arms found in the loft of the capitol, and in a wagon, with a few quartermaster's stores, constituted the chief articles of capture.

References:

CARRINGTON'S "BATTLES OF THE AMERICAN REVOLUTION," pp. 548-9

Hostilities were too inactive to arouse the north to united action: and the English forces at the south were too superior in numbers to encourage the southern people to combine for resistance, unaided by regular troops. It was just the time when the British Cabinet could have made a strong reinforcement very impressive ; provided it could command English sympathy ; and it was just the time that the American people needed the pressure of some permanent danger to arouse them to the offensive.

The French army in America sustained an important relation to this period. It prevented General Clinton from risking the offensive, and to the same extent lessened the zeal of the New England people in the preparations for troops for the new campaign, because the urgency of their employment did not appear immediate and absolute.

The active operations of the year eventually transferred La Fayette, and then Washington and Rochambeau, to the Southern department, where Greene had been established in December, 1780.

On the part of the British army, Cornwallis held the chief place of responsible command. Phillips and Arnold made a diversion into Virginia to strengthen his second invasion of North Carolina, and Arnold ultimately made an incursion into Connecticut to suspend the transfer of northern American troops to the south. This latter incursion, however, was entirely ignored by Washington, who had a fixed objective of pursuit, and that was, to capture New York *or* to capture Cornwallis.

It has been asserted that General Clinton was out of favor with the Crown and that on the contrary Cornwallis was a favorite ; that he obtained reinforcements which were refused to Clinton. A profitless controversy subsequently took place between those officers, and the general facts will appear in their proper connection. A single statement will do much to explain the positions of these officers and dispose of frivolous accusations to their discredit.

The attitude of the British Cabinet was based upon the invincibility and sufficiency of the forces sent to suppress the revolution. Allusion has been twice made to the neglect of the military counsels of General Amherst. Demands for reinforcements, strong assurances that the forces were insufficient, repeated unsuccessful campaigns, each expected to close the war, the French intervention, and the accumulating enemies who were determined to cripple the British empire, compelled the Cabinet, by natural logic, to trust those who were mostly in harmony with its opinions and policy.

The positive assurances of General Clinton and of Cornwallis, which were continued until after the battle at Guilford Court House,—that British supremacy in the Southern States had been restored, and that the people were in arms for the Crown, were enough to check reinforcements and contrast the condition of General Clinton, at New York, who was in fear of losing that post, and had no confidence in ultimate success, unless largely strengthened both in army and fleet.

The entire history of the war, and therefore the career of the British commanders, is to be interpreted by similar considerations, which controlled their action, shaped issues, and determined campaigns. It is sufficient for the present purpose to state the matter thus briefly.

The campaign of 1781 will be taken up in detail, in order that its military value and relations may be more distinctly separated from general history. It was the culminating campaign of a long war, a campaign where the forces on both sides were inferior to the forces previously engaged, and where the success of either party, analyzed separately, in view of all the circumstances, seemed impossible; and yet a campaign, where the success of either party seemed positively certain, in case of a thorough, concentrated effort.

This campaign will be considered as follows:

I. Mutiny of the American Army. Its history and effects.

II. The operations of General Greene at the South.

III. Arnold's operations in Virginia.

IV. La Fayette's operations in Virginia.

V. Arnold's raid into Connecticut.

VI. Washington on the Offensive.

These operations substantially ended hostilities, and include the battles of Cowpens, Guilford, and Hobkirk's Hill (near Camden), the sieges of Ninety-six and Augusta, the battles of Eutaw Springs and the siege of Yorktown, as well as the minor operations before Jamestown, Petersburg, Richmond, and New London.

I. Mutiny of the American Army.

The war which now entered upon its seventh year, was a different war from that which Great Britain or the American people anticipated when the struggle began. The contract which George III. made with soldiers was considered a favor to the enlisted men, and the terms, "*three years or during the war*," were regarded as better than a regular enlistment for five, seven, or more years. The term of three years, according to military usage, was a short term.

A similar enlistment of American troops was made under the supposition that the three years was the *maximum*, and that the term " *during the war*," was simply an assurance of earlier discharge, and they hoped the war would not last for the full three years.

As the year 1781 opened and the prospect of a new year of struggle became certain, and the invasion of the Southern States began to indicate the prospect of a southern campaign, which was at all times unpopular with northern troops, a disaffection was developed which at last broke forth in open mutiny, and a peremptory demand for discharge.   This irritation was aggravated by hunger, cold, and poverty.

Marshall says: " The winter brought not much relaxation from toil, and none from suffering.   The soldiers were perpetually on the point of starvation, were often entirely without food, were exposed without proper clothing, to the rigors of winter ; and had now served almost twelve months without pay."

" This situation was common to the whole army ; and had been of such long continuance, that scarcely the hope of a change could be realized."   " It was not easy to persuade the military that their brethren in civil life were unable to make greater exertions in support of the war, or that its burdens ought not to be more equally borne."

On the first of January the Pennsylvania line revolted ; Captain Billings was killed in an attempt to suppress the mutiny ; General Wayne was powerless to restore order, and thirteen hundred men, with six guns, started to Princeton, with the declared purpose to march to Philadelphia, and obtain redress.   They demanded clothing, the residue of their bounty, and full arrears of pay.   A committee from Congress and the State authorities of Pennsylvania, at once entered into negotiations with the troops for terms of compromise.

The American Commander-in-chief was then at New Windsor. A messenger from General Wayne informed him on the third of January of the revolt, and the terms demanded.   It appears from Washington's letters that it was his impulse, at the first intimation of the trouble, to go in person and attempt its control.   His second impression was to reserve his influence and authority until all other means were exhausted.   The complaint of the mutineers was but a statement of the condition of all the army, so far as the soldiers had served three years ; and the suffering and failure to receive pay were absolutely universal.   Leaving the preliminary discussion with the civil authorities who were responsible for much of the trouble, the Commander-in-chief appealed to the Governors of the northern States, for a force of militia to meet any attacks from New York, and declined to interfere until he found that the passion had passed and he could find troops who would at all hazards execute his will. It was one of the most difficult passages in the war, and was so handled that the Commander-in-chief retained his prestige and regained control of the army.

There was a double phase to this mutiny, and General Clinton watched its development with interest. Eager to avail himself of the disaffection which communicated itself to the Jersey troops, and to invade New Jersey itself, he seems to have remembered the unfortunate march to Springfield in 1780, and remained in New York, watching the conduct of Washington.

In a letter to Lord Germaine he says, " General Washington has not moved a man from his army, (near West Point) as yet ; and as it is probable their demands are nearly the same with the Pennsylvania line, it is not thought likely he will. I am, however, in a situation to avail myself of favorable events, but to stir before they offer might mar all."

General Clinton received information of the revolt as early as Washington, on the morning of the twenty-third, and sent messengers to the American army with propositions, looking to their return to British allegiance. He entirely misconceived the nature of the disaffection, and his agents were retained in custody.

It is sufficient to say that a portion of the troops were discharged without critical examination of their enlistments, on their own oath ; that many promptly reënlisted, that as soon as Washington found that he had troops who did not share in the open mutiny, he used force and suppressed the disaffection, and that the soldiers themselves hung several agents who brought propositions from General Clinton which invited them to abandon their flag and join his command. The mutiny of the American army at the opening of the campaign of 1781, was a natural outbreak which human nature could not resist, and whatever of discredit may attach to the revolt, it will never be unassociated with the fact that while the emergency was one that overwhelmed every military obligation by its pressure, it did not affect the fealty of the soldiers to the cause for which they took up arms. It impaired discipline, and disregarded authority ; but it also had in its manifestations, many of the elements of lawful revolution, *the state itself having failed in duty to its defenders.*

La Fayette thus wrote to his wife, " Human patience has its limits. No European army would suffer the tenth part of what the

Americans suffer. It takes *citizens* to support hunger, nakedness, toil, and the total want of pay, which constitute the condition of our soldiers, the hardiest and most patient that are to be found in the world."

An appeal was at once made to the Northern States for money, and enough was secured to bring up three months of the arrears of pay. The States of Massachusetts and New Hampshire also gave twenty-four dollars extra, in specie, to each soldier enlisted from the respective States. Colonel Laurens was appointed as special agent to visit France and secure a loan, which during the year was increased by two other loans, as hereafter noticed. This dependence upon France, however, was calculated to lessen a sense of responsibility at home ; and Count de Vergennes, under date of February fifteenth, when advised of the mission of Colonel Laurens, used the following language : " Congress relies too much on France for subsidies to maintain their army. They must absolutely refrain from such exorbitant demands. The great expenses of the war render it impossible for France to meet these demands if persisted in."

The chief difficulty, however, grew out of the individuality of the States, and the fact that Congress was rather advisory than authoritative in its jurisdiction. A partial relief came with the adoption of Articles of Confederation, which took effect on the second of March, 1781, when Congress assembled under the new powers conceded by that instrument. Maryland yielded her assent on the preceding day, and the long period of four years and four months had transpired from their first adoption by Congress and their submission to the States for acceptance.

During these events which were threatening the very existence of the American army, the blockade of the French fleet was still maintained with vigor. The British squadron occupied Gardiner's Bay, Long Island, for winter anchorage, and was thus enabled to keep a close watch upon all vessels entering or departing from the Sound.

During the latter part of January, it temporarily lost its numerical superiority through a violent storm which sunk the Culloden, 74, dismasted the Bedford, and drove the America out to sea. The interval was improved to dispatch several ships to the Chesapeake, to coöperate with an expedition against Arnold, which will be noticed in its connection.

The American army had become so reduced as hardly to exceed five thousand men for duty, and the French troops were not disposable for general service, so long as the fleet was confined to port.

Under these discouraging circumstances, the European States did not lose their confidence in the ability and resources of the American Commander-in-chief. It would not be an unwarrantable assertion to say that this confidence grew out of their habitual recognition of personal governments at home, and that they quite naturally gave him a corresponding credit for powers which were beyond his prerogative and the jurisdiction of Congress itself. His reputation as a wise commander was well established.

Mrs. Bache, daughter of Franklin, thus cites a letter from her father, which is suggestive of the estimation in which he was held in France : " My father says, if you see General Washington, assure him of my very great and sincere respect, and tell him that *all the old generals here amuse themselves in studying the accounts of his operations, and approve highly of his conduct.*" It is equally certain that no extravagant estimate can be placed upon the services of General La Fayette, whose letters urged the supply of men and money, with the most pointed assurance that the American States would realize success, and be amply able to refund all advances which might be made by the King.

The influence of Adams, Franklin and Jay at Holland, France and Spain was strongly marked, and characteristic of the American temper.

The single intimation of Colonel Laurens, upon his arrival at Paris, that money was indispensable, and that France would do well to hold the American nation up, rather than have it left to join its resources with England against France, was another incident of the opening year which strongly persuaded the French minister to render pecuniary aid to meet the emergency. This cursory reference to the condition of the United States, during the early part of 1781, will indicate the circumstances under which the mutiny at the north took place and the campaign at the south opened.

General Greene's Southern Campaign. Reference is made to map "Operations in Southern States."

It has already been stated that General Greene sent Morgan to the Catawba district, with three hundred and ninety continental troops under Lieutenant-colonel Howard, Colonel Washington's horse, and two companies of Virginia militia. These companies, commanded by Captains Triplett and Tait were not ordinary militia ; but consisted for the most part of old soldiers who had served their terms and reënlisted as substitutes for other militia. Upon reaching

Broad River, General Morgan was joined by General Davidson and Colonel Pickens, and Majors McDowell and Cunningham, with nearly seven hundred volunteers and militia from Georgia and the Carolinas. General Greene's immediate command was not far from two thousand men, mostly militia; and his station was nearly seventy miles east, a little north, from Winnsborough, then the headquarters of Cornwallis. Morgan was on the Pacolet, a branch of Broad River, about fifty miles north-west of Winnsborough, having established his camp on the twenty-fifth of December, 1780. His position threatened not only Ninety-six, but the entire line of small posts in the rear of the British army.

A British invasion of North Carolina was clearly inadmissible while the American troops were thus on both flanks; and Lord Cornwallis determined to strike Morgan and Greene, in turn, before their forces should be further increased from the militia, or the north. Lieutenant-colonel Tarleton was detached on the first of January, with the Legion and a portion of the First battalion of the Seventy-first British regiment, and two pieces of artillery, with orders to pursue Morgan and drive him across Broad River.

On the twenty-seventh of December, General Greene detached Washington's cavalry and McCall's mounted militia, in all two hundred and fifty men, to surprise a party of loyalists twenty miles south of his camp. They were pursued, overtaken and for the most part killed. Justice Johnson says, "the killed and wounded were reported at one hundred and fifty, and the prisoners at forty," and adds, " such were the bloody sacrifices at that time offered up at the shrine of civil discord." A detachment was also sent to surprise Williams, (see map), a small stockade fort; but the garrison retired without resistance.

Lord Cornwallis marched up the west bank of the Catawba, leaving orders to General Leslie, then on the march from Charleston, to follow. Heavy rains delayed the march of the main army, encumbered as it was with a considerable baggage train, while Tarleton, not apprehensive that it would fail to support his advance, pushed forward rapidly, crowded Morgan over the Pacolet, and by crossing at an upper ford drove him still further back to the Cowpens, in the immediate vicinity of Broad River itself.

Colonel Tarleton states that he originally " started with the Legion, five hundred and fifty men, (Cornwallis puts the number at six hundred,) the first battalion of the Seventy-first regiment, consisting of two hundred men, and two three-pounders; but had not proceeded above twenty miles from Brierly Ferry, before he had undoubted proof that the report which occasioned the order for the light troops to march was erroneous, and that Ninety-six was secure." Upon application to Cornwallis, his baggage was forwarded under the escort of two hundred men from the Seventh British regiment, and fifty dragoons, designed as a reinforcement for Ninety-six. These troops were added to Tarleton's command, making the whole detachment one thousand strong, besides a few loyalists. He commenced his advance on the twelfth. The Ennoree and Tiger were crossed on the fourteenth, and advices from Cornwallis indicated that he would move up the east bank of Broad River so as to cut off Morgan's retreat. Cornwallis reached Turkey Creek, (see map) on the evening of the sixteenth, and there waited for General Leslie, whose force consisted of thirteen hundred and fifty men.

That officer marched from Charleston directly for Camden, and was so delayed by swamps, high water, and other difficulties of the way, that the success of the whole movement devolved upon the action of Tarleton alone. Cornwallis himself was nearly twenty-five miles from Tarleton when the battle of Cowpens was fought, and according to Tarleton, had plenty of time to have reached Ramsour's Mills, which would have effectually cut off Morgan's retreat. The delay of General Leslie at Camden, according to Lord Cornwallis' statement, was, "that General Greene might be kept in suspense as long as possible as to the proposed movements."

The battle of Cowpens was fought near Broad River, about two miles south of the North Carolina boundary line, on ground used especially for pasture, which gave name to the locality.

The field of battle itself was open woodland, sloping to the front, and well adapted for skirmishing, while sufficiently clear of undergrowth for the movements of mounted men. Tarleton says, "there could be no better." "Broad River wound around Morgan's left within six miles, and ran parallel with his rear," so that there was no possibility of escape, in case of defeat. Morgan occupied the summit, which was nearly a quarter of a mile from the level ground, and formed his regular troops at the highest point. The Maryland battalion, nearly three hundred strong, were on the left, and the companies of Virginia militia under Triplett and Tate were next in order, with Beaties' Georgians, about one hundred and fifty men, on the extreme right. Lieutenant-colonel Howard commanded this

line. See map " Battle of Cowpens."   One hundred and fifty yards
to the front, a force of two hundred and seventy militia were posted
under Colonel Pickens, in open order.   Major Cunningham, of
Georgia, and Major McDowell, of South Carolina, with one hundred
and fifty picked men, were stationed still further in advance, about an
equal distance, as skirmishers, with orders to take to trees—not to fire
until the enemy were within fifty yards ; and then to fall back, *firing
at will*, as they could find cover.

Colonel Pickens had orders in like manner to reserve fire until the
enemy came within fifty yards, and after two volleys to retire to the
left of the regulars ; but if charged by cavalry, only one man in three
was to fire, while the others must withhold fire until a charge was
made, or the troopers should turn back.   The regulars were advised
of these instructions and cautioned, in case of being forced from their
own position, to retire in good order to the next hill, and be prepared
at any time to face about and attack.   In the rear of the high ground
was a second small elevation behind which Washington's cavalry and
Colonel McCall's mounted men were out of cannon range, and in
reserve for timely use.   Morgan has thus apologized for his choice of
ground : " I would not have had a swamp in view of my militia on
any consideration ; they would have made for it, and nothing could
have detained them from it.   And as to covering my wings, I knew
my adversary, and was perfectly sure I should have nothing but
downright fighting.   As to retreat, it was the very thing I wished to
cut off all hope of.   I would have thanked Tarleton had he surrounded
me with his cavalry.   It would have been better than placing my own
men in the rear to shoot down those who broke from the ranks.
When men are forced to fight, they will sell their lives dearly ; and
I knew that the dread of Tarleton's cavalry would give due weight
to the protection of my bayonets, and keep my troops from breaking
as Buford's regiment did.   Had I crossed the river, one-half of the
militia would immediately have abandoned me."

The British advance was made as early as seven o'clock in the
morning, January seventh.   The troops had marched from early dawn
and were well worn down ; but Tarleton had intimations that additional militia were on the march to join Morgan, and he prepared to
risk the action with equal numbers, trusting to the discipline and
superiority of his troops for the decision of the battle.   His formation
is detailed upon the map.   His advance was prompt and spirited.
The American skirmishers fired effectively, and fell back into the first

line, and the militia after one steady, deadly fire, fell back also and began to move across the front of the second line to take position on their left as ordered.

The British troops taking the whole movement as assurance of easy victory advanced rapidly, with shouts, only to find themselves confronted by the main body, which received them without flinching. The British guns were then moved to the front, and fifty dragoons from each British extremity followed the retreating militia when the first line broke. But upon the resistance of the main body, the Seventy-first British regiment, which had been in reserve, and Tarleton, with two hundred dragoons advanced to the charge. As the British left ascended the hill to turn the American right, the militia there stationed were ordered by Morgan to swing back, thus making a crotchet to the rear, and to hold the position until Colonel Pickens could bring up the militia who were already forming for that purpose, while the American cavalry spurred around the left of the regulars and attacked the British right which had thus far followed the retreating militia. Lieutenant-colonel Howard mistaking this change of position in his right for the contingent movement to the rear, ordered the regulars also to retreat. The British had lost many officers and they pressed on in some disorder. The issue of the day was at its crisis; when Morgan ordered the troops to face about, deliver fire and charge with the bayonet. The British were within thirty yards. The effect was immediate and conclusive at that part of the field. Washington was just then engaged with the artillery endeavoring to capture the guns, and the British infantry and cavalry fled or surrendered. Nearly every gunner was killed or wounded while faithfully fighting by his gun. The Seventy-first regiment with Tarleton's horse were still on the American right wing, until Pickens' militia came up vigorously attacking their flank. Being now under cross fire they also threw down their arms and surrendered. Tarleton escaped with forty horse; after a vain dash to save the guns and restore order. Tarleton and Washington here met face to face, the former received a cut on his hand and the latter a pistol shot in his knee.

He thus states the facts. " The militia, after a short contest were dislodged, and the British approached the continentals. The fire on both sides was well supported and produced much slaughter. The cavalry on the right charged the enemy's left with great gallantry but were driven back by the fire of the reserve and by a charge of Colonel Washington's cavalry. As the contest in the front line seemed equally balanced, he thought the advance of the Seventy-first into line and a movement of the cavalry in reserve, to threaten the enemy's left flank, would put a victorious period to the action. No time was lost. The cavalry were ordered to incline to the left and to form a line which would embrace the whole of the enemy's right flank. Upon the advance of the Seventy-first, all the infantry again moved on. The continentals and backwoodsmen gave ground. The British rushed forward. An order was given to the cavalry to charge. An unexpected fire from the Americans who came about as they were retreating, stopped the British and threw them into confusion. Exertions to make them advance were useless. The cavalry which had not been engaged fell into disorder and an unaccountable panic extended itself along the whole line. Neither promises nor threats could avail."

The British casualties were stated by General Cornwallis at ten officers and ninety men killed, twenty-nine officers and five hundred men captured. He omits the number wounded. Morgan accounts for six hundred prisoners turned over to the commissary officer. The British army returns of February first, reports diminution from last return, January fifteenth, as seven hundred and eighty-four men; which closely approximates the total loss. The American casualties were twelve killed, and sixty wounded.

Two standards, thirty-five wagons, one hundred horses, eight hundred muskets and two cannon were among the trophies of the victory. Lossing states that these guns alternately changed owners, at Saratoga, Camden, Cowpens, and Guilford.

Tarleton severely criticises Lord Cornwallis for neglect to advise him as to his movements, and says, with some bitterness, that "as Ferguson's disaster made the first invasion of North Carolina, so the battle of Cowpens would probably make the second equally disastrous."

He rejoined the army on the following day, and insists that a prompt movement made at that time, might have rescued the prisoners. General Morgan carried out his plan of battle with almost entire success. Leaving his severely wounded under a flag of truce, and his cavalry to cover his retreat, he crossed Broad River that night with his infantry and prisoners, and forded the Catawba on the twenty-fourth. On the same night Cornwallis reached Ramsour's Mills, at the junction of the road from Cowpens with that upon which his army marched. Here he halted two days to burn surplus

35

baggage and wagons, and by this delay lost his opportunity to overtake Morgan. The American command was only twenty miles in advance, and the Catawba was fordable until heavy rains on the twenty-seventh and twenty-eighth raised the waters, and on the twenty-ninth, when Cornwallis reached its bank, it could not be crossed. Morgan started his prisoners for Virginia on the twenty-fifth, and made every possible effort to rally militia and cover his retreat until General Greene could come to his assistance. It has been generally stated that Cornwallis pursued so closely upon Morgan that a sudden flood alone saved the latter. Morgan's letter to Greene dated the twenty-fifth, at his camp on the east side of the Catawba, settles the question of the date of his crossing the river.

As General Leslie joined Cornwallis on the eighteenth and nineteenth, there was ample time to have redeemed Cowpens; but a somewhat characteristic hesitation at a critical hour, and indecision under pressure, lost him the precious opportunity.

General Morgan remained but a few weeks in the service. Severe rheumatism settled in his limbs, and his active days soon ended. From Bunker Hill to Quebec, through Burgoyne's campaign, and wherever he was entrusted with command, he had proved his courage and his fertility in resources during periods of great danger; and Congress vied with States and citizens, in honorable testimonials to his valor, as the victor at Cowpens.

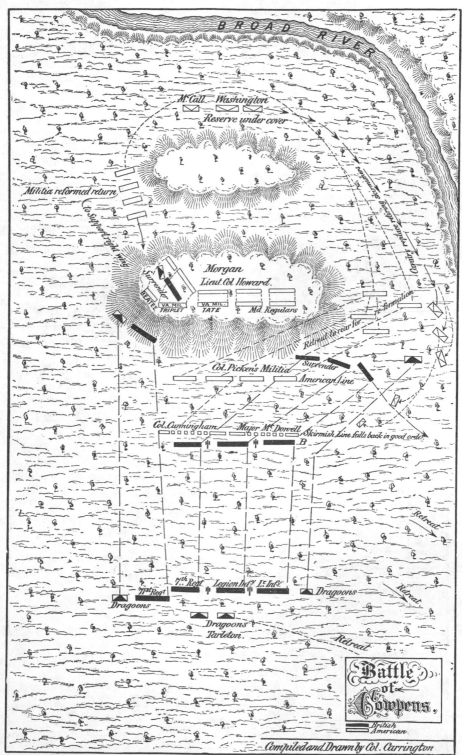

BROAD RIVER

M⁥Call Washington
Reserve under cover

Militia reformed return

to support right wing

Morgan
Lieut. Col. Howard

Surrender
BEATE

VA. MIL.
TRIPLET

VA. MIL.
TATE

M⁥. Regulars

reformation

covering British surplus Cavalry

Retreat to rear for re-formation

Col. Picken's Militia

Surrender

American Line

Col. Cunningham   Major M⁥. Dowell

B

Skirmish Line falls back in good order

Retreat

7th Reg⁥.
71st Reg⁥.   Legion Inf⁥. Lᵗ. Inf⁥.   Dragoons

Retreat

Dragoons

Dragoons
Tarleton.

Retreat

Battle of Cowpens.

British
American

Compiled and Drawn by Col. Carrington

546*

➤ Battle of Cowpens ➤

JANUARY 7th, 1781

American Commanders

MORGAN

COL. WASHINGTON.   HOWARD.   McDOWELL.   PICKENS.

CUNNINGHAM.   BEATTY.   TRIPLETT.   McCALL.

Strength, 1,250   Casualties, 72.

AMERICAN FORMATION. The battle was fought near Broad River, about two miles south of the North Carolina boundary line, on ground used for pasture, and familiarly known as Cow Pens, Broad River wound around Morgan's left, and was parallel with his rear, and the position was selected by him, to prevent retreat and compel his men to fight. An open woodland sloped to the front, which Tarleton said " could be no better for mounted men."

Morgan occupied the summit with the regular troops. Beatty's Georgians,150 men, held the right, Triplett's and Tate's Virginians held the centre. The Maryland battalion, 300 men, held the left. Lieut. Col. Howard commanded this line. Pickens held a line of 270 men, in open order, about 150 yards in advance of the hill, while Major Cunningham, of Georgia, and Major McDowell, of South Carolina, were posted at an equal farther advance, with 150 picked sharp-shooters, under orders to take the cover of trees, fire only at short range, and fall back, firing, as they could still find cover.

Pickens was ordered to reserve fire until the enemy came within fifty yards, and after two volleys, to retire to the left of the regulars; but, if charged by cavalry, only one man in three must take part in the volley, while the rest should reserve their fire until the actual charge, or the troopers should turn back.

The regulars were advised of these orders, and instructed, if they were forced from their first position, to re-form on the next hill, and be prepared to face about and renew the attack. Col. Washington's cavalry and Col. McCall's mounted men were out of sight, in the rear of the hill.

BRITISH FORMATION. Tarleton made his advance at seven o'clock in the morning, with force well worn from hard marching, but under advices that a large force of militia was on the way to join Morgan. Dragoons on each flank, and in rear, supported the infantry, as designated on the map, and two guns opened fire from the intervals between battalions. The 71st Regiment formed, slightly in the rear, as a reserve.

NOTE I.—The sharp-shooters closely obeyed orders, and finally retreated around the American left for re-formation in the rear and to the right. One detachment of dragoons pursued them, as if they were fugitives.

NOTE II.—The British guns are moved to the front, but the resistance of the main line is so obstinate that, Tarleton, with the 71st and two hundred dragoons, takes part in the charge. Howard throws back his right wing, and this is at first taken for an order to retreat. Morgan promptly orders the troops to face about, deliver fire, and charge with the bayonet. The British were within thirty yards.

NOTE III.—Meanwhile the American cavalry move around by the left of the hill and attack the flank and rear of the troops which had pursued the retiring militia. The latter gain their assigned position, and are already ascending the hill to assist Morgan. (See map).

NOTE IV.—Nearly every British gunner had been killed or wounded at his gun. Pickens' militia attack the 71st Regiment by the flank, as they ascend the hill, and the whole force is at the mercy of the cross-fire of the American detachments

NOTE V.—Tarleton escaped with forty troopers; received a sword cut from Washington, who was also wounded in the knee, and the rest of the command surrendered.

NOTE VI.—Two standards, thirty-five wagons, one hundred horses, eight hundred muskets, two cannon and six hundred prisoners, were trophies of the action.

The British lost in killed and wounded, 129 officers and men.

References :

CARRINGTON'S "BATTLES OF THE AMERICAN REVOLUTION," pp. 540-547.

School Histories:

Anderson, ¶ 104; p. 95.
Barnes, ¶ 1; p. 137.
Berard (Bush), ¶ 129; p. 173.
Goodrich, C.A.(Seaveys), ¶ 24; p. 141.
Goodrich, S. G., ¶ 4-5; p. 272.
Hassard, ¶ 10; p. 219-20.

Holmes, ¶ 6; p. 153.
Lossing, ¶ 4; p. 182.
Quackenbos, ¶ 388; p. 284-5.
Ridpath, ¶ 6; p. 223.
Sadlier, (Excel), ¶ 18; p. 203.
Stephens, A.H. ¶ 6-7; p. 223-4.

Swinton, ¶ 7; p. 158.
Scott, ¶ 5; p. 210-11.
Thalheimer (Eclectic), ¶ 289, p. 165;
Venable, ¶ 166; p. 105.

CHAPTER LXVIII.

FROM COWPENS TO GUILFORD COURT HOUSE. MANŒUVERS OF THE ARMIES. 1781.

A MESSENGER from General Morgan reached General Greene, at his camp on Hick's Creek, a fork of the Great Republic, January twenty-fifth, 1781, and informed him of the battle of Cowpens, that a large number of prisoners were to be provided for, and that the army of Cornwallis was in pursuit. The completeness of the success reported made the contrast of his inability to improve it, very tantalizing and painful.

The army, including Morgan's corps, numbered only one thousand four hundred and twenty-six infantry, forty-seven artillerists and two hundred and thirty cavalry. The militia numbered four hundred. These numbers fluctuated greatly, since the Southern militia were quite like the minute men of 1775–6, who volunteered for pressing duty, and then returned to the ordinary pursuits of life. There was no money, little clothing, and constant hardship. A single extract from a letter written by General Greene to General Sumter, two days before the battle of Cowpens, contains this paragraph: "More than half our members are in a manner naked; so much so that we can not put them on the least kind of duty. Indeed there is a great number that have not a rag of clothes on them except a little piece of blanket, in the Indian form, around their waists."

It was under such circumstances that this commander was summoned to save the fruits of Morgan's victory, to expel the British army from the Carolinas, and to vindicate the supremacy and power of the United States. For three days he devoted his time to putting this nominal army in preparation for taking the field; and on the twenty-eighth, accompanied by one aid, a guide and a sergeant's party of cavalry, he started for Morgan's command. On the night of the thirteenth, after a ride of over one hundred and twenty-five miles, he was with Morgan.   His letters to Varnum, then in Congress, to Gist, Smallwood, Rutledge, Washington and others, are full of urgent appeals for at least five thousand infantry and six or eight hundred horse.

It was an extraordinary state of affairs, when a victory seemed but the first step toward disaster, and when even the Commander-in-chief was constrained to write, " I wish I had it in my power to congratulate you on the brilliant and important victory of General Morgan, without the alloy which the distresses of the department you command, and apprehensions of posterior events, intermix.   I lament that you will find it so difficult to avoid a general action ; for our misfortunes can only be completed by the dispersion of your little army, which will be the most probable consequence of such an event."

It must be borne in mind that Arnold landed in Virginia on the fourth day of January, with sixteen hundred regular troops, so that General Steuben's local responsibilities were as pressing as when General Greene passed through Virginia on his way to the Southern Department.

A brief diversion from the immediate narrative is necessary, in order to indicate the exact circumstances which controlled both Generals Greene and Cornwallis, in their subsequent movements, and to correct the impression that the campaign consisted simply of a swift pursuit and successful retreat, and, one where ravines and floods alone determined the result.   The spring campaign of 1781 was one of *operations*, and there was no retreat of General Greene which did not constitute a manœuver, having in view an ultimate engagement, with the recovery of the South as the chief objective.

A statement of Arnold's position and operations up to the first of February, is an essential element to be taken into view.   He left New York on the nineteenth of December, 1780, with sixteen hundred men.   It appears from General Clinton's letters that he did not rely upon that officer's discretion, and attached Lieutenant-colonels Simcoe and Dundas to the command, " two officers of tried ability and experience, and possessing the entire confidence of their commander."   The Queen's Rangers, and the Eighteenth British regiment (Scotch), respectively commanded by the officers named, formed the larger portion of Arnold's division.   The characteristic accompaniment of the naval movements of the period, a gale, separated the fleet on the twenty-sixth and twenty-seventh of December ; but on the thirty-first, without waiting for other transports still at sea, twelve hundred men were transferred to small vessels and moved up the James River. On the night of January third, Lieutenant-colonel Simcoe landed at Hood's Point with one hundred and thirty of the Queen's Rangers and the light infantry and grenadiers of the Eighteenth regiment, spiked the guns of a battery, which was abandoned by the small detachment of fifty men who occupied it, and on the fourth the expedition landed at Westover, nearly twenty-five miles below Richmond, and marched immediately to that city. On the afternoon of the fifth, Arnold entered Richmond. Lieutenant-colonel Simcoe quickly dislodged a force of two hundred irregulars, militia which Colonel John Nichols had assembled on Richmond Hill, and a few mounted men who were on Shrove Hill also retired as the British troops advanced. The Rangers, light infantry and grenadiers, proceeded promptly to West-ham, nearly seven miles above Richmond, and destroyed a foundry, laboratory and some shops, as well as the auditor's records which had been withdrawn from Richmond for safety, and returned to the city in the evening. Arnold sent to Governor Jefferson a proposal to compromise the terms of his incursion, and to save the buildings if vessels might come up the river and remove tobacco and other plunder. Upon its rejection, he burned so much of the city as time permitted, and returned to Westover on the sixth, without loss to his command. The expedition was a surprise, but the loss, except to private property and the capture of the books and papers of the coun-cil, was very inconsiderable. Five brass guns, three hundred stand of arms, found in the loft of the capitol and in a wagon, and some quartermaster stores, constituted the chief articles captured. Even the workshops and warehouses were not wholly consumed. Reference is had to maps "Operations in Southern States," and "Arnold at Richmond."

On the eighth, Lieutenant-colonel Simcoe visited Charles City Court House, and, according to Tarleton's narrative, killed or wounded twenty militia, with a loss of one man killed and three wounded.

General Steuben had in vain attempted to equip a sufficient force to anticipate the movement. Of six hundred men at Chesterfield Court House, he had clothing for only one hundred and fifty. The appearance of some militia at Manchester, however, and information that General Steuben was at Petersburg, led Arnold to hasten back to save his line of retreat, and he proceeded at once to Portsmouth to put it in a defensive condition.

At this time General Leslie also received advices that General

Phillips was preparing to leave New York with additional troops for Virginia, so that the difficulties in the way of receiving reinforcements from the north increased daily, and the whole Southern army was in pursuit of Morgan.

As the mind reverts to the contentions for high command which characterized the first years of the war, and one officer after another, then so ambitious, disappears from battle record, it looks as if the man who sat by Morgan on the banks of the Catawba on the thirtieth of January, 1781, must have felt as if a new generation had taken the place of old comrades, and that he was only waiting to pass away also.

The hazard of delay aroused him to action. Lee was ordered to hasten back and join Morgan without delay. The commissary of supplies was ordered to remove everything from the sea coast to the interior. The commissaries at Hillsborough and Salisbury were placed in readiness to move the prisoners into the upper counties of Virginia. Colonel Carrington, Quartermaster-general, was ordered to collect magazines on the Roanoke. Letters were written to General Steuben to hasten on his recruits; to the governors of North Carolina and Virginia, to fill up their quotas of regulars and to call into the field all the militia they could arm; to Shelby, Campbell and the other participants in the battle of King's Mountain, to bid them come out once more, to repel the threatened invasion; to General Huger, " to march to Guilford Court House direct instead of to Salisbury," adding, "from Cornwallis' pressing disposition and the contempt he has for our army, we may precipitate him into some capital misfortune."

Just then, the tidings came that a garrison had been landed at Wilmington, almost in the rear of the small army which he left at Hick's Creek. The terms of service of the Virginia militia brigade was about expiring and according to precedent they were to be discharged at the place where they organized. Availing himself of this opportunity he placed General Stevens in command, consigned to him the escort of the prisoners then in depot at Hillsborough and thereby saved a detail from his other troops. General Stevens discharged the duty and reported back promptly to meet the responsibilities of the campaign.

The condition of Cornwallis requires passing notice. He affirms that "his second invasion of North Carolina was approved by General Clinton:" "that the defense of the frontier of South Carolina, even against an inferior army, would be, from its extent, the nature of the climate and the disposition of the inhabitants, utterly impracticable, while the enemy, could draw supplies from North Carolina and Virginia." Of the affair at Cowpens he says, "the disaster of the seventeenth of January can not be imputed to any defect in my conduct, as the detachment sent, was certainly superior to the force against which it was sent, and, put under the command of an officer of experience and tried abilities." "The public faith was pledged to our friends in North Carolina, and I believed my remaining force to be superior to that under the command of General Greene," but, "our hopes of success were not founded only upon the efforts of the corps under my immediate command, which did not much exceed three thousand men; but principally upon the most positive assurances, given by apparently credible deputies and emissaries, that upon the approach of a British army in North Carolina, a great body of the inhabitants were ready to join and to coöperate with it, in endeavoring to restore his Majesty's government." "All inducements in my power were made use of without material effect; and every man in the army must have been convinced that the accounts of our emissaries had greatly exaggerated the number of those who professed friendship for us:—a very inconsiderable number could be prevailed upon to remain with us, or to exert themselves in any form whatever."

It will hereafter appear that Cornwallis' movement lost sight of a possible dependence upon support from the British army in Virginia, and that his selection of the Salisbury route, for his invasion, contemplated the control of the river sources, so as to force Greene eastward and make his destruction or capture more certain.

When Greene took command on the Catawba, on the thirty-first of January, the army of Cornwallis was only eighteen miles below, unable to cross the river by reason of high water. Greene summoned the neighboring militia to turn out and guard the fords as the water fell. Beatie's Ford, where the army encamped, is about six miles above McCowan's Ford and nearer to Salisbury. On the evening of January thirty-first, Morgan was sent forward toward Salisbury while General Greene remained to bring off the militia. The river fell rapidly and Colonels Webster and Tarleton crossed at Beatie's Ford shortly after it was abandoned. General Davidson, with three hundred men, met the division of Cornwallis toward morning, February first, and while resisting their crossing at McCowan's Ford, was killed, and his men were scattered. A few rendezvoused at Tarrant's Farm ten miles on the road to Salisbury, but were there attacked and cut to

pieces by Tarleton.   By the third, Morgan had crossed the Yadkin.
Cornwallis burned most of his remaining baggage and wagons,
doubled teams, mounted a portion of his infantry and sent a strong
corps under General O'Hara in pursuit.   It rained all day on the
first of February.   Greene knew that within two days the water
from the mountains would fill the Yadkin.   As yet it was not so deep
but that his cavalry crossed safely, and his forethought in having
boats provided, enabled him to secure all his command.   Many inhabitants followed the army, retiring in dread of Tarleton, and the
vanguard of the British force only captured the rearmost wagons.
A useless cannonade was maintained during the day.   Cornwallis
remained at Salisbury four days, and passed the Yadkin on the eighth.
Greene marched on the fourth, after one day's halt, and united his
command at Guilford Court House.

A council of war was held which advised not to offer battle.   The
re-united army only numbered two thousand and thirty-six men, including fourteen hundred and twenty-six regulars.   Some course of action
was to be immediately decided upon.   Colonel Carrington joined the
command, with the report, that boats had been secured, and secreted
along the Dan, so as to be collected on a few hours' warning.   The
British army was at Salem, only twenty-five miles from Guilford.
This was on the tenth of February.   Preparatory to the march,
General Greene organized a light corps of seven hundred picked
troops under Colonels Williams, Carrington, Howard, Washington
and Lee, to cover his rear.

Kosciusko had joined Greene, and was sent forward to throw up
a breastwork to cover the landing of the boats, and the army commenced its march.

Cornwallis bore to the left to cross above Greene.   He had no
idea that Greene could effect a crossing at the few ferries which lay
below the possible fording places, while by cutting him off from the
fords above, he could follow down the river and strike his small command as well as the army marching from the camp on the Peedee.
But that army had already joined Greene.   In a letter to Lord Germaine, of March nineteenth, he says, " I was informed that the
American commander could not collect many flats at any of the
ferries on the River Dan."   Colonel Carrington, however, had been
specially charged with this duty by General Greene, with the aid of
Captain Smith, of the Maryland line; had anticipated almost any
contingency which should require the passage of the river; and so

provided boats at Boyd's and Irwin's ferries, which were neighboring ferries, that on the fourteenth of February the whole division safely crossed the river, secured their boats, and were beyond reach of the enemy. Tarleton thus reports this affair: "The light army (Williams) which was the last in crossing, was so closely pursued, that scarcely had its rear landed when the British advance appeared on the opposite bank; and in the last twenty-four hours it is said to have marched forty miles. The hardships suffered by the British troops for want of their tents and usual baggage, in this long and rapid pursuit through a wild and unsettled country, were uncommonly great; yet such was their ardor in the service that they submitted to them, without a blow, to the American army, before it crossed the Roanoke."[1] Tarleton adds, "That the American army escaped without suffering any material injury, seems more owing to a train of fortunate incidents, judiciously improved by their commander, than to any want of enterprise or activity in the army that pursued. Yet the operations of Lord Cornwallis, during the pursuit, would probably have been more efficacious, had not the unfortunate affair at the Cowpens deprived him of almost the whole of his light troops."

Lord Cornwallis returned to Hillsborough and issued a proclamation, "but," says Tarleton, "the misfortunes consequent on premature risings had considerably thinned out the loyalists, originally more numerous in North Carolina than in any of the other colonies. Their spirits may be said to have been broken by repeated persecutions. Still, the zeal of some was not repressed; and considerable numbers were preparing to assemble, when General Greene, reinforced with six hundred Virginia militia under General Stevens, took the resolution of again crossing the Dan, and re-entering North Carolina." Lieutenant-colonel Lee, with his legion, was detached across the river on the twenty-first of February, and the next day General Greene passed it with the rest of the army.

Meanwhile General Greene posted a portion of his army at Halifax Court House, and made every exertion to prepare an offensive return. On the seventeenth, his whole force in camp consisted of one thousand and seventy-eight regular infantry—sixty-four artillery, and one hundred and seventy-six cavalry, with one hundred and twelve legionary infantry, so many troops had been detached in

[1] "The upper Roanoke is known as the Dan; the upper Peedee as the Yadkin; the upper west branch of the Santee, first as the Congaree, and then as Broad; the upper east branch, first as the Wateree, and then as Catawba."

charge of prisoners, the baggage, and the sick. The Delaware troops under Kirkwood, so terribly cut up at Camden, did not exceed eighty men for duty. On the nineteenth, Stevens was ordered by Greene to engage volunteers for the service, and he joined within three days, with nearly eight hundred men.

By the twenty-third the whole army was demonstrating towards Guilford, and Lee and Pickens hovered near the outposts of Cornwallis.

At this time the loyalists were organizing a corps under Colonel Pyle upon the marshes of the Haw, and Tarleton was sent to assist and protect them. More than four hundred had collected a little north of the old Hillsborough and Salisbury road, two miles from the Allamance River, in Orange County, Virginia. Lee and Pickens fell in with this party, having been advised of their movements by two men whom they picked up while hunting for Tarleton. Tarleton says, " the loyalists were proceeding to Tarleton's encampment, unapprehensive of danger, when they were met in a lane, by Lee with his legion. Unfortunately, mistaking the American cavalry for Tarleton's dragoons they allowed themselves to be surrounded; no quarter was granted; between two and three hundred were inhumanly butchered. Humanity shudders at the recital, but cold and unfeeling policy aroused it, as the most effective means of intimidating the friends of royal government."

There is no doubt that the loyalists commenced the firing as soon as they recognized the Maryland troops in the rear of Lee, and that Lee himself had hoped to pass and strike at Tarleton himself; but after the firing began, it was continued, until the whole party were killed, wounded, or driven into the woods.

Cornwallis withdrew from Hillsborough on the following day, even before the expiration of the time designated in his proclamation for the people to report to him for duty. Stedman, then his commissary, intimates that the army could not be supported at that point. On the twenty-seventh he crossed the Haw and fixed his camp near Allamance Creek, one of its tributaries. Greene adopted a line of march nearly parallel to that of his adversary, and advanced to the heights between Reedy Fork and Troublesome Creek, having his divided headquarters near the Speedwell iron works and Boyd's Mill, on two streams. Greene had gained the choice of position entirely, reversing the old relations of the armies. He could give battle, retire as he advanced, or move into Virginia by the upper fords which Cornwallis had so eagerly controlled a few weeks before. It will be noticed that the camp of Cornwallis, between the Haw and Deep rivers, was where the roads from Salisbury, Guilford and Hillsborough unite, and thus controlled the direct road to Wilmington, his depot of clothing and supplies, of which his army was already in great need. The light troops of both armies were actively employed, daily, and on the sixth of March, a skirmish at Wetzell's Mills, which was skillfully anticipated and supported by the whole British army, put in peril the whole column of Williams and Lee.

On the eighth, commissioners finally settled upon a plan of exchange of prisoners, the British having exacted paroles of the militia wherever they went, while charging them to the account as if captured in battle. Colonel Carrington and Frederick Cornwallis made an adjustment so that General Greene obtained some officers who would have otherwise been idle during the campaign, but the arrangement had no immediate value as to private soldiers and militia.

In the midst of these anxieties troops began to arrive, and on the twelfth Greene determined to offer battle. On the thirteenth orders were issued for all detachments to report at Guilford Court House, and on the fourteenth of March, General Greene was in readiness for the struggle.

CHAPTER LXIX.

BATTLE OF GUILFORD COURT HOUSE. 1781.

THE American army which was formed for battle near Guilford Court House, March fifteenth, 1781, consisted of four thousand four hundred and four men; including one thousand four hundred and ninety regular infantry, and one hundred and sixty-one cavalry. Lieutenant-colonels Lee and Campbell were sent, early in the morning, to feel the enemy and skirmish with its advance column.

Cornwallis accepted the challenge, sent his baggage back to Bell's Mill, on Deep River, and marched toward Guilford. The cavalry, the light infantry of the guards, and the Yagers, composed his advance guard. "A sharp conflict," says Tarleton, "ensued between the advanced parties of the two armies. In the onset, the fire of the Americans was heavy, and the charge of their cavalry was spirited. Notwithstanding their numbers and opposition, the gallantry of the light infantry of the guards, assisted by the legion, made impression upon their centre before the Twenty-third regiment arrived to give support to the advanced troops. Captain Goodricks, of the guards, fell in this contest; and between twenty and thirty of the guards, dragoons, and Yagers were killed and wounded. The king's troops moved on until they arrived in sight of the American army." Reference is made to map "Battle of Guilford;" and the narrative will follow the movements of the attacking force. The American first line was formed in the edge of woods, behind open ground, and under cover of fences. From this point the surface gradually ascended to the Court House, and was quite thickly wooded. Other hills were on either side, and the Court House itself stood upon a still more abrupt ascent. The first line consisted of North Carolina militia under Generals Butler and Eaton, one thousand and sixty men, besides officers. Captain Singleton occupied the road, with two pieces of artillery. The right was covered by Lynch's riflemen, two hundred men; Kirk-

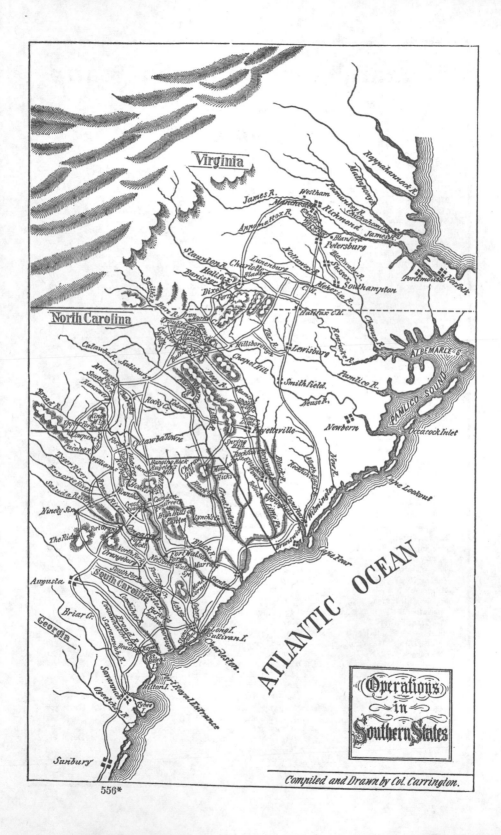

Virginia

James R. Westham
Manchester Richmond *James R.*
Appomattox R. Petersburg Blansford
Steunton R. Charlotte Lunenbury Blacks Nottoway R. Blackwater R. Sussex R.
Halifax Barister's Southampton Portsmouth Norfolk
Smith R. Dan R. Dixon Meherrin R.
North Carolina Iron Works C.H. Halifax C.H.
Catawba R. Salisbury Deep R. Hillsborough Lewisbury Roanoke R. Chowan R. ALBEMARLE S.
McGowan South Fork Ransom's Rocky C. Deep R. Chapel Hill Tar R. Pamlico R. PAMLICO SOUND
Broad R. Upper Fords Kings Wompen Jacob's Catawba Towne Haw R. Smithfield Neuse R. Newbern Peacock Inlet
Tyger River Enoree River Saluda River William Hanging Rock Ragelet's Hills Chapel Hill Monk's Hicks Black R. Fayetteville Cape Lookout
Ninety Six Weber Crossroads Camden Creek Great Pedee Spring Hill Rockfish Little R. Wilmington
The Ridge Fort Granby Fort Motte High Hills of Santee Lynch's Wacket's Brunswick
North Fort Watson Ford Murrays Cape Fear
Augusta Orangeburg Nelson's Salt Savannah R. South Fork South Carolina Beaufort Corners Sinter Charleston
Georgia Briar C. Cambahee Parkers Long I. Sullivan I. ATLANTIC OCEAN
Savannah R. Combahee R. Beaufort Hilton I. Royal Entrance
Ogeechee R. Tybee
Sunbury

Operations in Southern States

Compiled and Drawn by Col. Carrington.

556*

Operations in Southern States

Battles

Sieges

Minor Operations

wood's Delawares, not exceeding eighty men, and a detachment of cavalry under Colonel Washington. The left was covered by Campbell's riflemen and the legion infantry, about two hundred and fifty men, and Lee's horse.

The American second line, about three hundred yards in the rear, consisted of the Virginia militia under Generals Stevens and Lawson, eleven hundred and twenty-three men, rank and file, posted in woods and on both sides of the road. Behind this line Stevens had placed a few veterans to keep the militia up to duty. The American third line was more than three hundred yards further in the rear, upon high ground, with the *left slightly refused;* and was composed entirely of regulars. Kirkwood had been detached from the right, as already noticed, to take a position on the corresponding flank of the first line. General Huger was in command of the right wing, consisting of Virginia troops, and Colonel Williams commanded the left wing, composed of Maryland troops. As this division of regulars would very naturally be regarded as a veteran corps, it is but proper to state that the Second Maryland regiment, Lieutenant-colonel Ford commanding, consisted of the new levies, most of whom had never been in action or under fire at all; and that fully one-half of the Virginia brigade was made up of similar troops. Colonel Gunby's command, which had been handled by Lieutenant-colonel Howard at Cowpens, was the only regular infantry which could be called veteran. A portion of the North Carolina militia had been forced into the service, under suspicion of disloyalty, as a punishment, and with here and there a few substitutes, and with good officers, it was a feeble force to resist any persistent attack of British troops. Its flanks were so well covered, however, that General Greene must have had faith in their ability to make some resistance, when thus well supported and so admirably disposed. General Stevens posted some of his old soldiers in the rear of his line to anticipate any disorder, as many of the Virginia militia also, were raw troops, then for the first time brought to the field. In thus carefully stating the battle formation of the American army, it is proper to notice a characteristic letter from General Morgan to General Greene, under date of February twentieth, which seems to have suggested to General Greene his plan of battle. "I expect Lord Cornwallis will push you until you are obliged to fight him, on which much will depend. You'll have, from what I see, a great number of militia. If they fight, you'll beat Cornwallis; if not, he will beat you, and perhaps cut your regulars to pieces. I am informed that among the militia will be a number of old soldiers. I think it would be advisable to select them from the militia, and put them in the midst of the regulars. *Select the riflemen also and fight them on the flanks, under enterprising officers who are acquainted with that kind of fighting, and put the remainder of the militia in the centre with some picked troops in their rear, with orders to shoot down the first man that runs.* If anything will succeed, a disposition of this kind will. I hope you will not look upon this, as dictating; but as my opinion, in a matter that I am much concerned in."

It is also to be borne in mind that at least six hundred of the militia were enrolled for six weeks only, including the march to the field and the return march for discharge, so that General Greene had little time to lose. The formation of the army for battle has been severely criticised, on the ground that the regulars were so far in the rear; but the flanking bodies in the first line were fully equal in number to the small veteran corps of the reserve, and they were men who had tested their mettle thoroughly on other fields. The disposition of the troops seems to have so equalized the commands as to impart strength to all parts, and to leave the militia *alone*, at *no* point. If Kirkwood's command had covered Singleton's guns in the centre, possibly it would have strengthened the line; but might have sacrificed him, with the militia; and the supports were near enough, if there had been any resistance at all.

The British right wing consisted of the regiment of Bose (Hessian) and the Seventy-first British. General Leslie commanding, with the First battalion of guards in reserve, under Lieutenant-colonel Norton; and the left wing consisted of the Twenty-third and Thirty-third British, Lieutenant-colonel Webster commanding, with the grenadiers and Second battalion of the guards in reserve, under General O'Hara. The light infantry and Yagers were to the left and rear of the artillery, which occupied the road and exchanged fire with Singleton's guns while the British line was forming. The American line, it will be observed, considerably overlapped the British, thereby endangering its flanks in case of a direct advance. The British army had marched through a defile, to their position, and had not sufficient room for deployment until they passed beyond a small creek which crossed the Salisbury road. It will be at once seen that the American first line, with Stevens and Lawson behind its immediate centre, was a strong line, when it is considered that the entire British force was but little if any over two thousand strong, after deduction of the baggage guard sent to Bell's Mills. The tabular statement at close of this chapter indicates the condition of the army of General Cornwallis at different dates.

Tarleton's dragoons were kept in column, on the road, in the rear, to act as opportunity should be furnished by the events of the day, and to cover the artillery which could advance only by the road. It will be seen by reference to the map, that Lord Cornwallis appreciated the danger that threatened his flanks, upon a simple advance against the centre, and as soon as the militia gave way, so that he felt the sharp fire of the flanking parties, the Twenty-third and Thirty-third regiments changed direction to the left, to let in their reserves on the right, while the light infantry and Yagers marched obliquely to the very left extreme. The right wing also took up *its* reserves, so that the combined line became co-extensive with the entire American front. Lieutenant O'Hara was killed at his guns, during the artillery firing which was maintained quite steadily during the last twenty minutes, before the British army entered the open ground to charge the militia. The advance was steady and in good order. When within about one hundred and forty yards of the fence the North Carolina militia delivered a partial volley and fled, abandoning every-thing. Singleton's guns necessarily retreated up the road as soon as left without support. A considerable portion of Eaton's brigade dashed behind Campbell's riflemen and took refuge in thick woods, on a hill (see map) and the remainder of the division fell back upon the second line, which opened its files for them to pass through, and promptly resumed a steady front toward the enemy. The British left wing was severely galled by the fire of Kirkwood, Lynch and Washington; but finally forced them back to a corresponding posi-tion on the right of the second line. The British right wing was equally annoyed by the riflemen of Campbell, the legionary infan-try and Lee. The British centre had swept on at a bayonet charge againt the second line, and the first battalion of guards, with the regi-ment of Bose, wheeled to the right, to clear their flanks of these assail-ants. The woods were so thick, and so filled with underbrush that their bayonets were of little practical value. As the riflemen fell back the pursuit was continued up the hill so far, that these regiments were absolutely detached from the army and engaged in a separate battle until the principal action was practically ended. While the British army lost numbers by their absence, it is not probable that

Campbell and Lee, after their gallant conduct in the morning, would have let slip an opportunity to attack the British in the rear, if the guards and Hessians had adhered to the originial order of battle. The manner in which this flanking detachment sustained itself will be hereafter noticed.

Meanwhile the British centre and left wing moved directly upon the Virginia militia, which resisted for awhile with great spirit, but was finally compelled to give way and seek cover behind the continental troops, or in the woods. Kirkwood and Washington hastened to their original positions on the right of the reserve line as soon as the second line gave way.

The British centre was embarrassed by the woods, and its advance became unequal. The Seventy-first dropped behind, greatly impeded by ravines, and, possibly and very naturally, to be ready, if needed to support the two regiments which had broken off from its right, and were actively engaged at the time. Cornwallis says, " they advanced upon hearing active firing upon their left and front."

The Thirty-third, the light infantry, and Yagers pressed after Kirkwood and Lynch whom they had opposed from the beginning of the action, dropping the Twenty-third behind, and this regiment, like the Seventy-first of the right wing was again dropped, when the Second battalion of the guards and the grenadiers advanced toward the American third line.

Lieutenant-colonel Webster advanced directly upon the American regulars, and made two successive charges, which were repulsed. Colonel Gunby with the First Maryland regiment, supported by the left wing of General Huger's command, delivered a well directed fire, resorted to the bayonet and compelled the assailing column to cross a deep ravine and take refuge upon a hill to its rear. Tarleton says, " At this period the event of the action was doubtful, and victory alternately presided over either army. Webster, however, gained an excellent position till he could hear of the progress of the king's troops on his right."

The Americans had thus repulsed and detached the British left, and the extreme British right was engaged with Campbell and Lee at a disadvantage, more than a mile to the right and rear. The Second battalion of the guards and the grenadiers were continuing their march, and without waiting for support, made an impetuous attack upon the left of the American reserve near the Court House. The Second Maryland regiment gave way almost instantly, losing the guns which had been withdrawn to this line. The advance of the guards had not been perceived by Colonel Williams on account of an intervening clump of trees (see map) until they made their charge. Its effect was to threaten the entire line, take it in the rear, and force it towards Webster. The First Maryland wheeled to the left and used the bayonet. Colonel Gunby was almost immediately dismounted, and Lieutenant-colonel Howard took command. Tarleton and Cornwallis confirm the statement of the gallant conduct of this regiment. Tarleton says, " The Maryland brigade, followed by Washington's cavalry, moving upon them before they could receive assistance, retook the cannon and repulsed the guards with great slaughter, the ground being open. Colonel Washington's dragoons killed Colonel Stewart and several of his men, and pursued the remainder into the woods. General O'Hara, though wounded, rallied the remainder of the Second battalion of the guards to the Twenty-third and Seventy-first, who had inclined from the right and left, and were now approaching open ground."

To cover their advance, Lieutenant McLeod was placed with two guns upon a small knoll near the road, which should have been held by Singleton, and checked the American advance, until the arrival of the two British regiments last referred to exposed the Maryland regiment to the attack of a largely superior force. The American onset was so persistent and the moment was so critical that General Cornwallis commenced this artillery fire before the guards were disengaged, and while they were actually exposed to its effect. When the First Maryland regiment wheeled upon the guards, it uncovered the Virginia line, and Lieutenant-colonel Webster availed himself of the opportunity to recross the ravine and join the main body. Tarleton's dragoons had just returned from the support of the regiment of Bose, and was immediately followed by the First battalion of the guards. The force now concentrated near the Court House could not be resisted, and General Greene ordered a retreat. This retreat was made under cover of Colonel Greene's regiment, which from its situation had been held fast to watch the movements of Webster after he occupied the hill nearly opposite, and had taken no active part in the operations to its left.

The Twenty-third and Seventy-first regiments followed a short distance in pursuit; but Tarleton says, " Earl Cornwallis did not think it advisable for the British cavalry to charge the enemy, who were retreating in good order."

36

The contest between Campbell and the Legion light infantry, supported by a few militia who rallied in the woods, had in the meantime been so spirited, that the British regiments "found men behind trees on all sides of them," and Tarleton says, that "when he made his charge, he found officers and men of both corps in the possession of the enemy." He had been sent in that direction on account of the continuous firing which had been noticed by Cornwallis; and at the time he was so detached, there was no opportunity to handle his cavalry to advantage at the centre. The American riflemen had their choice of ground, and their mode of fighting was destructive to the guards and Hessians, with little loss to themselves. His arrival was opportune, and the Americans retreated to the woods. Fortunately for Tarleton, Colonel Lee had abandoned the hope of resistance, more than to check pursuit, and had made a detour for the purpose of joining the main army at the Court House before that officer appeared.

He lost a great opportunity, and in fact failed to reach the main army until the next morning. He states that if General Greene had known the condition of the British army, a retreat would have been unnecessary, and the victory certain. He did not reach Greene, however, and did not so advise him. His arrival at that moment would have settled the issue.

Tarleton gives it as his opinion that "if the American artillery had pre-occupied the small hill by the road-side, the Twenty-third and Seventy-first regiments could not have united with the guards; and the result would have been fatal to the army of Cornwallis." He says, that "one-third of the British army was killed or wounded during the two hours of battle." The casualties are stated as given in the official Returns, made up immediately after the battle, and the numerous conjectures which have exaggerated the losses on both sides, are of little value, when the acknowledged facts and the admitted valor of the troops, who did any fighting, on either side, sufficiently indicate the desperate character of the action.

British casualties—Royal Artillery, Lieutenant O'Hara, and one man killed; four wounded. *Guards*—Lieutenant-colonel Stewart, eight sergeants, twenty-eight rank and file killed; Captains Schmultz, Maynard, and Goodrick died of wounds; Captains Lord Douglas, Smeaton, and Maitland, Ensign Stewart, Adjutant Colquhoun, two sergeants, and one hundred and forty three rank and file wounded, and twenty-two missing. *Twenty-third* regiment: Lieutenant Robinson and twelve men killed; Captain Peter, one sergeant, and forty-three wounded. *Thirty-third* regiment: Lieutenant-colonel Webster died of wounds; Ensign Talbot, and ten men killed; Lieutenants Salvin and Wyngand, Ensigns Kelly, Gore, and Hughes, Adjutant Fox, and fifty-six men, wounded; *Seventy-first:* Ensign Grant and twelve men killed, fifty-six men wounded. *Regiment of Bose:* Captain Wilmousky and Ensign De Trott, died of wounds; ten men killed; Lieutenants Schnœner and Graise, and sixty-two men killed; three missing. *British Legion* — Lieutenant-colonel Tarleton and thirteen men wounded; three men killed. Total casualties reported: Five hundred and forty-four. General Howard who volunteered to accompany Cornwallis, was also wounded.

Sergeant Lamb relates that he saw Lord Cornwallis crossing clear ground, where the guards suffered so severely, riding upon a dragoon horse, (his own having been shot,) and that he was carried directly toward the Americans. The trooper's saddle-bags were underneath the horse, embarrassing his control of the creature. Lamb "seized the bridle, turned the horse's head, and ran by the side until the Twenty-third regiment was gained." Cornwallis and Leslie were the only general officers of the British army who were not wounded.

American Casualties. Virginia Regulars—One captain, two subalterns, and twenty-six men killed: four sergeants and thirty-five men wounded, and thirty-nine men missing. *Maryland Regulars:* One major, one subaltern, and thirteen killed; five captains, one sergeant, and thirty-six men wounded; ninety-seven missing. *Delaware Battalion* —seven killed; thirteen wounded, fifteen missing. *Washington's* detachment of First and Third cavalry, three killed; two captains, two subalterns, and four wounded (prisoners,) three missing. *Lee's Corps,* three killed; one captain, eight men wounded (prisoners); seven missing. Total casualties of regulars, three hundred and twenty-nine. General Huger was also wounded. *Stevens' Brigade*—Two captains and nine men killed. Brigadier-general Stevens, one captain, four subalterns, and thirty men wounded. One major, three subalterns, and one hundred and thirty-six men missing. *Lawson's Brigade*—One killed. One major, two subalterns, and thirteen men wounded. One subaltern, eighty-six men missing. *Campbell's* and *Lynch's Rifle Regiments*—Two captains and one man killed; one captain, one subaltern, and fourteen men wounded; one captain, seven subalterns, and eighty-six missing. Total casualties of Virginia militia, four hundred and eight. *North Carolina militia*, six killed; one captain, one subaltern, and three men wounded; two captains, nine subalterns, and five hundred and fifty-two missing. Total casualties of brigade, five hundred and seventy-four. Total American casualties, thirteen hundred and eleven. The large number of missing are accounted for by both British and American authorities, as having fled to their homes. Two days afterward the returns of the Virginia Regulars showed seven hundred and fifty-two men present, and of the Maryland Brigade, five hundred and fifty, which reduced their loss, reported on the seventeenth as two hundred and sixty-one men, to one hundred and eighty-eight.

General Greene retreated nearly twelve miles to the iron works on Troublesome Creek. Although the American army had thus fallen back to the rendezvous which had been selected in case of defeat, it was not disheartened. On the morning of the sixteenth, preparations were made for battle, on the conviction that Cornwallis would pursue. The resistance which had been made, aroused the remnants of the militia to a sense of responsibility for previous failure ; and the example of the First Maryland encouraged them to seek an opportunity to redeem their credit. Surgeons were sent to Guilford, where they found that all possible care had been taken of their wounded by the British officers.

Greene, writing on the same day, says, "the enemy gained his cause, but is ruined by the success of it." Tarleton regarded "the victory as the pledge of ultimate defeat." "The British had the name ; the Americans the good consequences of victory," wrote Ramsey.

"Another such victory would ruin the British army," said Fox in the House of Commons.

Pitt and other political leaders in Great Britain, regarded it as the "precursor of ruin to British supremacy in the south"; and the correspondence of Cornwallis, official and unofficial, breathes but one sentiment as to the repugnance of the southern people at large to respect British authority.

After providing for the badly wounded to the best of his ability, and leaving those who could not march to the protection of a flag of truce, he issued a formal proclamation of victory and a rallying call to the people, and immediately crossed Deep River, as if on the march to Salisbury. Recrossing it lower down, he moved to Ramsey's Mills. General Greene gathered such troops as had a reasonable time of service before them, and marched to Buffalo Ford, when he ordered an inspection of his command with view to a spirited pursuit and the contingency of another battle.   It became necessary to send back to his train for additional ammunition, lead and bullet moulds, so that he did not reach Ramsey's Mills until the twenty-eighth, one day after Cornwallis had bridged the river and moved on toward Cross Creek (Fayetteville) on the direct Wilmington road.

The British army was almost destitute of clothing and other needed supplies.   The destruction of their train during the winter had been a constant source of trouble, and the loss had not been compensated by results.   Messengers were sent to Lord Rawdon, then at Camden, warning him that Greene would probably invade South Carolina, and the army, reduced to " not quite fifteen hundred men (1435) through sickness, desertion, and losses in battle," marched to Wilmington, reaching that town on the seventh of April.   The messengers failed to reach Lord Rawdon, and General Greene entered upon his South Carolina campaign.

NOTE.—State of the troops that marched with the army under the command of Lieutenant-General Earl Cornwallis.   (Official.)

RANK AND FILE PRESENT AND FIT FOR DUTY.

DATES.	British.								German.		Provincials.		
	Brigade of guards.	7th Regiment.	16th Regiment 3 companies.	23d Regiment.	33d Regiment.	71st Regiment 1st Battalion.	71st Regiment 2nd Battalion.	71st Regiment Light comp'y.	Regiment of Bose.	Yagers.	British legion.	N. Carolina volunteers.	Total.
January 15, 1781.	690	167	41	286	328	249	237	69	347	103	451	256	3224
February 1, 1781.	690	..	..	279	334	..	234	..	345	97	174	287	2440
March 1, 1781...	605	..	..	258	322	..	212	..	313	97	174	232	2213
April 1, 1781....	411	..	..	182	229	..	161	..	245	97	174	224	1723

The force ultimately able to march to Virginia, has already been stated at 1435 men.

CHAPTER LXX.

GENERAL GREENE resolved to move directly against the military posts of South Carolina, irrespective of the action of Lord Cornwallis. He did not believe that pursuit would be attempted. Even in that case, he would at least relieve North Carolina from danger, and would occupy such a position as to be able to attack either Rawdon, or Cornwallis, without their possible coöperation against him. He moved so rapidly that he reached Rugely's Mills before Cornwallis knew that he had left Deep River; and it was then too late to intercept his march to the south. That officer had already determined that the most hopeful method of reducing the Southern States, was by occupation of Virginia, and by control of Chesapeake Bay and its contributory water courses. This plan involved a separation of the south from the north, so that neither could aid the other. He resolved to march to Virginia, by the shortest route, and to effect a junction with General Phillips, who arrived in Chesapeake Bay on the twenty-sixth of March, with two thousand troops from New York, and with instructions to report to Lord Cornwallis and act under his orders.

The narrative would be incomplete without some further reference to this sudden abandonment of a campaign which had been so entangled and eventful, especially as the military policy of the British Cabinet and of General Clinton are involved in the movement.

General Cornwallis, in his answer to General Clinton's " Narrative," thus states the case: " I could not remain at Wilmington, lest General Greene should succeed against Lord Rawdon, and, by returning to North Carolina, have it in his power to cut off every means of saving my small corps, except that disgraceful one of an embarkation, with the loss of the cavalry, and every horse in the

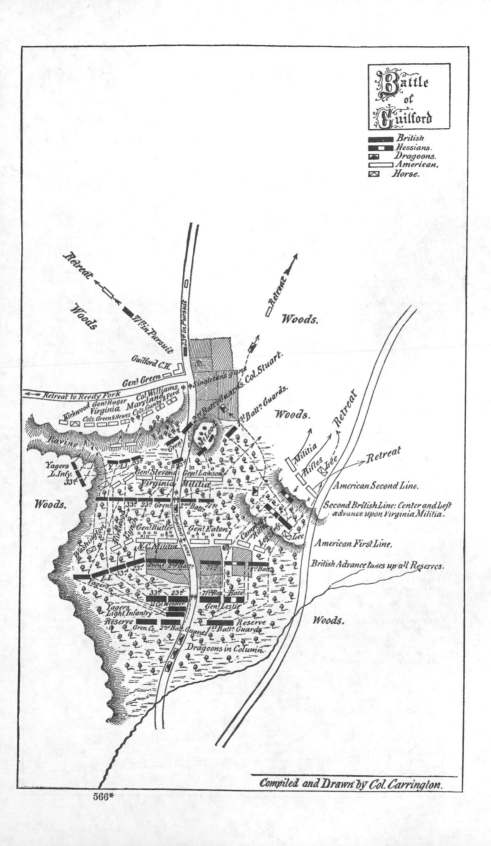

Battle of Guilford

British
Hessians.
Dragoons.
American.
Horse.

Retreat

Woods

Woods.

Retreat

W. in Pursuit

23rd in Pursuit

Guilford C.H.

Gen! Green

Kingston's Place

Brit. Brig Guards, Col. Stuart.

Retreat to Reedy Fork

Col. Williams

1st Batt! Guards.

Kirkwood Gen! Huger Virginia Maryland

Woods.

Cols. Green & Hewes Cols. Gunby & Ford

Ravine

Retreat

Yagers L. Infy. 33d

Y. L.I.

Gen! Stevens Gen! Lawson

Militia

Rifles

Lee

Retreat

Woods.

Virginia Militia

American Second Line.

33d 23d Gren. 2nd Batt. 71st

Second British Line: Center and Left advance upon Virginia Militia.

Washington

Gen! Butler

Gen! Eaton

Camp. Rifles

Lee

American First Line.

Militia

British Advance takes up all Reserves.

L.I. Yagers

33d 23d

33d 23d

7th Reg. Bose

Lt. Col. Webster

Gen! Leslie

Woods.

Yagers Light Infantry Reserve

Gren. Co. 2nd Batt. Guards

1st Batt. Guards

Reserve

Dragoons in Column.

Compiled and Drawn by Col. Carrington.

566*

Battle of Guilford Court House

MARCH 15th, 1781

American Commanders	British Commanders
GREENE	CORNWALLIS
Butler, Eaton, Ford, Col. Washington, Gunby, Kirkwood, Singleton, Williams, Huger, Stevens, Lee, Lynch, Hewes	Webster, O'Hara, Leslie, Norton, Tarleton McLeod, Howard
Strength, 4,404 Casualties, 1,311	Strength, 1,800 Casualties, 554

MEM.—*The movements of the two armies had been such, that Greene selected Guilford Court House, for an issue with Cornwallis; and Cornwallis, as deliberately, resolved to attack the American army, whenever it offered battle.*

AMERICAN FORMATION.—The *first line*, 1,060 men (see map), was formed in the edge of woods, behind open ground, under cover of fences. From this point, the surface, quite thickly wooded, gradually ascended to the Court House, with hills on either side. Singleton placed his two guns on the road. Lynch's Rifles (200 men), Kirkwood's Delawares (80 men), and Washington's Dragoons, held the extreme *right*, to threaten the British *left;* while Lee's horse and the infantry of the Legion, with Campbell's Rifles, held the *left*, to threaten the British *right*.

The *second line*, 1,123 men (see map), was posted, 300 yards in the rear, with a few veterans, behind the line, to keep them up to duty.

The *third line*, 1,400 regulars, near the Court House, well posted, included Gunby's veteran regiment; but that of Ford, on the extreme left, was of new levies.

The map gives the divisions, by brigades.

BRITISH FORMATION.—*Right wing.* Bose (Hessian), and 71st regiment, with Leslie, commanding; 1st Guards (Norton) in reserve. *Left wing.* 23d and 33d regiments, under Webster; 2d Guards (General O'Hara) and Grenadiers in reserve. The Yagers and Light Infantry, to the left of the road, supported McLeod's guns. Tarleton's dragoons were in column, on the road, at the rear, to act as ordered.

Preliminary Skirmish.—Lee and Campbell were sent out by Greene, early in the morning, to feel the advancing enemy. In this skirmish, Captain Goodrick, of the British Guards, was killed, and nearly thirty of the Yagers and Dragoons were killed, or wounded. The Americans lost as many.

Development of the Battle

NOTE I.—As appears from the map, the American *first*, or advance line, over-lapped and attempted to flank, the British line.

NOTE II.—Cornwallis urged the troops forward, in order to give full effect to their discipline ; and rapidly combined the whole force in one line, which thereby equalled the American front. Lieut. O'Hara was killed at his guns, and the American wings delivered a hot fire; but the militia, in the *center*, gave way, in confusion, and Singleton took his guns to the rear, in their flight.

NOTE III.—The American *left* gains a wooded hill and holds the pursuing British *right* wing, to a separate, sharp engagement. The American right falls back in good order to the second line.

NOTE IV.—The *second* American line, resists bravely, but yields to pressure, and is put to flight, while Washington and Kirkwood, fall back in good order, to the reserves.

NOTE V.—At this stage of the action, the British assume, that success is no longer in doubt, and, that their entire progress, is to be unresisted. While the 71st regiment halts in the woods, to await a report from the rest of the right wing, which is engaged on the wooded hill, with Lee and Campbell, the 23d regiment halts, also. The extreme left wing was pushed directly for the American reserves, while the 2d Guards and Grenadiers, in like manner, moved impetuously to the front, without waiting for other support.

NOTE VI.—Gunby, and the left wing of Huger's brigade, meet the British left wing, with the bayonet, and drive them over a ravine to the west, where they remain, for a while, out of action.

NOTE VII.—The attack of the 2d Guards and Grenadiers was a surprise to Colonel Williams, of the American left wing, and both guns, which had been withdrawn to this point, were captured. Gunby, and, after his fall, Lt. Col. Howard, wheels the 1st Maryland, applies the bayonet, regains the guns, and repulses the attack. Washington's dragoons charge upon the disordered Guards. Stewart is killed, Gen. O'Hara is wounded, but rallies the Guards, and brings the 23d and 71st regiments into action. To cover their advance, the guns of McLeod are placed upon a knoll, near the wood, *which Singleton should have occupied in his retreat*, and Cornwallis pours fire into the American line, at risk to his own troops, which are not wholly disengaged from the American assault.

NOTE VIII.—When Gunby wheeled upon the Guards, the British left, under Webster, re-crossed the ravine and joined the main body.

NOTE IX.—Tarleton had dispersed Lee's horse, and with Bose's regiment and the 1st Guards, takes part in the action. The American left wing is overwhelmed, and Greene withdraws his army in good order, to Troublesome Creek, under cover of Colonel Green's regiment, which had remained nearly intact during the action. Cornwallis retired to Wilmington, N. C.

MEM.—*Tarleton says : "If the American artillery had pre-occupied the small hill by the road-side, the 23d and 71st could not have united with the Guards ; and the result would have been fatal to the army of Cornwallis."*

References :

CARRINGTON'S "BATTLES OF THE AMERICAN REVOLUTION," pp. 556-565.

School Histories :

Anderson, ¶ 107 ; p. 95.
Barnes, ¶ 2 ; p. 138.
Berard (Bush), ¶ 131; p. 174.
Goodrich, C. A.(Seaveys) ¶ 26; p. 142.
Goodrich, S. G., ¶ 8 ; p. 273.
Hassard, ¶ 14 ; p. 221.

Holmes, ¶ 8 ; p. 154-5.
Lossing, ¶ 6 ; p. 183-4.
Quackenbos, ¶ 390 ; p. 286-7.
Ridpath, ¶ 10 ; p. 223-4.
Sadlier (Excel.), ¶ 21; p. 205.
Stephens, A. H., ¶ 10 ; p. 225.

Swinton, ¶ 9 ; p. 158.
Scott, ¶ 7 ; p. 212.
Thalheimer (Eclectic), ¶ 291 ; p. 166.
Venable, ¶ 166 ; p. 127.

army." . . " I was most firmly persuaded, that until Virginia was reduced, we could not hold the more southern provinces; and that, after its reduction, they would fall, without much difficulty." On the eighteenth of April he advised Lord Germaine, that " the great reinforcements sent by Virginia to General Greene, whilst General Arnold was in the Chesapeake, are convincing proofs that small expeditions do not frighten that powerful province."

General Cornwallis wrote to General Clinton on the tenth of April:—" I can not help expressing my wishes that the Chesapeake may become the seat of war, even (if necessary) at the expense of abandoning New York. Until Virginia is in a measure subdued, our hold of the Carolinas must be difficult, if not precarious." The following appreciation of the theatre of operations is included in the same letter. " The rivers of Virginia are advantageous to an invading army; but North Carolina is, of all the provinces in America, the most difficult to attack, (unless material assistance could be got from the inhabitants, the contrary of which I have sufficiently experienced) on account of its great extent, of the numberless rivers and creeks, and the total want of interior navigation." In reply, General Clinton, under date of May twenty-ninth, says, " Had it been possible for your Lordship, in your letter to me of the 10th ult., to have intimated the probability of your intention to form a junction with General Phillips, I should certainly have endeavored to have stopped you, as I did then, and do now, consider such a move as likely to be dangerous to our interests in the southern colonies." In a dispatch to General Phillips, of April thirteenth, marked " *secret and most private*," and which Lord Cornwallis found at Petersburg after the death of General Phillips, General Clinton says, " His Lordship tells me he wants reinforcements. I would ask—how can that be possible? And, if it is, what hopes can I have, of a force sufficient to undertake any solid operation? As my invitation to Lord Cornwallis to come to the Chesapeake, was upon a supposition that everything would be settled in the Carolinas, I do not think he will come." . . . " If Lord Cornwallis proposes anything necessary for his operations, you of course must adopt it, if you can; *letting me know your thoughts thereon.*"

A dispatch which he received from Whitehall Palace says, " Lord George Germaine strongly recommends to General Clinton, either to remain in good humor, in full confidence to be supported as much as the nature of the service will admit of, or avail himself of the leave of coming home, as no good can arise, if there is not full confidence between the general and the minister," and, on the sixth of June, Lord Germaine wrote to General Clinton, " Lord Cornwallis' opinion entirely coincides with mine, of the great importance of pushing the war on the side of Virginia, with all the force that can be spared."

It is impracticable more than to notice these leading facts, in the examination of voluminous correspondence and dispatches, which illustrate the relations of these officers, and the policy of the crown. General Clinton had suggested to General Phillips, a movement up the Delaware, with the contingency of an attack upon Philadelphia, to be supported by a movement on his part, from New York; and he was at the same time having difficulty with Admiral Arbuthnot, of whom he said: " He is more impracticable than ever, swearing to me (Clinton) that he knows nothing of his recall; to others, he says he is going home immediately." Rumors of a French naval reinforcement prevailed, and the situation of General Clinton was doubly embarrassing, by the contrast of the condition of the South with that which he guaranteed when Charleston was captured and Cornwallis was left in command. He very properly declared "a naval supremacy to be the first essential element to success in Virginia," and at the same time realized the uncertainty of securing that supremacy, so long as the fleets of Spain and France were operating in the West Indies, within striking distance of the American coast. Differences of opinion between the naval, as well as the military commanders, ultimately proved fatal to the campaign; and at this time, the Cabinet was almost equally divided between an assurance of easy victory at the South, and apprehensions of the possible fruits of the European coalition against Great Britain.

General Cornwallis wrote to General Clinton, April twenty-third, " My present undertaking sits heavy on my mind. I have experienced the distresses and dangers of marching some hundreds of miles, in a country chiefly hostile, without one active or useful friend —without intelligence and without communication with any part of the country. The situation in which I leave South Carolina, adds much to my anxiety; yet I am under the necessity of adopting this hazardous enterprise, hastily, and with the appearance of precipitation, as I find there is no prospect of speedy reinforcements from Europe; and that the return of General Greene to North Carolina, either with or without success, would put a junction with General Phillips out of my power."

Lord Cornwallis began his march from Wilmington on the twenty-fifth of April, having "remained eighteen days at that post, to refresh and refit his army." He sent orders to General Phillips to march and meet him at Petersburg, then took a direct route, *via* Smithfield, Lewisburg, and Halifax Court House, as indicated on map "Outline of Atlantic Coast," and reached the designated rendezvous without serious interruption, on the twentieth of May. Meanwhile, General Phillips reached Petersburg on the eighth, died of sudden illness on the thirteenth, and was succeeded in command by General Arnold, pending the arrival of Lord Cornwallis. The operations of the Middle Department will be considered in connection with General La Fayette's Virginia campaign.

The movements of General Greene will be first followed to the close of active operations at the South.

During the march to Rugely's Mills, on the sixth of April, he had detached Colonel Lee with orders to join Marion, and break Lord Rawdon's communications with Charleston. Sumter, already recovered from his wound and restored to duty, was located between Camden and Ninety-six; and General Pickering, with militia, was instructed to operate between Ninety-six and Augusta.

On the twenty-third of April, Lee and Marion captured Fort Watson, a post on the Santee River, on the Charleston road, directly in the rear of Camden. This capture was attended by incidents which illustrate the minor operations of war. The fort was a simple stockade, upon an Indian mound forty feet high, near the Santee, and at the upper end of Scott's Lake. The garrison consisted of eighty regulars and forty royalists. The stockade was surrounded by fallen trees, doing service as abatis, but not firmly embedded in the ground. The supply of water for the garrison was from the lake. This was cut off. Then a trench was dug to the level of the river-bed, and the garrison became independent of lake and river. The assailants had no artillery, and the range of fire was over the heads of the garrison. To meet this emergency the ingenious device of a log crib, filled with sand, was resorted to. From its summit, the skilled riflemen picked off the garrison, and the fort surrendered.

The fall of Fort Watson, and the immediate seizure of the passes through the hills, cut off Lord Rawdon's supply-route on the north side of the Santee. Colonel Watson, then *en route* to Camden with five hundred men to reinforce its garrison, was compelled to retrace his steps and march up the west bank

The advance of Lee and Marion against Fort Watson had been made as early as the fifteenth; and application was made to General Greene for one piece of artillery. The guns lost at Guilford had been partly replaced by two which were brought down from Oliphant's Mills, at the head of the Catawba, and Colonel Harrison was then on his march with two other pieces from the general depot at Prince Edward Court House. A gun could not be sent directly to Marion without passing through Camden, and there was no wagon road across Pine Tree Creek. Upon a report that Colonel Webster was approaching Camden, Colonel Carrington was ordered to take the artillery and baggage back to Rugely's Mills, and Captain Findley was to start from that point down the Black River road to join Marion with one gun, so that he might meet Watson in the field, if he found opportunity to do so. Greene sent his cavalry to the east bank of Pine Tree Creek, to anticipate any movement to cut off the escort which accompanied the gun, and advanced on the nineteenth to Log Town, within half a mile of Camden, where he made demonstrations to the east and south-east of the town, but failed to draw Lord Rawdon from the post. His own force was too weak to venture an assault. On the twenty-fourth General Greene withdrew to Hobkirk Hill, and sent orders to Colonel Carrington to return with the artillery and supplies for the troops. That officer had moved the guns and baggage to Lynch's Creek, nearly eight miles beyond Rugely's Mills, so that he was unable to execute the order of recall until after nine o'clock of the morning of the twenty-fifth. Rations were at once distributed and the troops were at breakfast, when the subsequent attack was made upon their position by Lord Rawdon. These facts are given as explanation of the reported negligence and surprise of the American camp. On the previous day the following order had been issued:

"CAMP BEFORE CAMDEN, NORTH QUARTER, *Tuesday, April 24th.*

" *The general orders respecting passes are punctually to be observed. None are to be granted but by commandants of corps. The rolls are to be called at least three times a day, and all absentees reported and punished. Officers of every rank are to confine themselves to their respective duties. And every part of the army must be in readiness to stand at arms at a moment's warning.*"

The battle of Hobkirk's Hill, sometimes and quite correctly called the battle of Camden, occurred on the following day. General Greene had sent orders to Marion to join him as soon as he should reduce

Fort Watson, and that officer started for the main army on the evening of the twenty-third. Lord Rawdon was advised of this movement, and resolved to attack his adversary before he could be thus reinforced. He had also learned from a deserter that Colonel Carrington had been sent to Rugely's Mills with the artillery, but had not been advised of his return. Reference is made to maps, " Battle of Hobkirk Hill," and " Operations in Southern States."

Hobkirk's Hill is described as a narrow sand ridge of very little elevation, which separates the head springs of two small branches, the one running into the Wateree, the other into Pine Tree Creek. It was quite thickly wooded, quite abrupt toward Camden, sloping more gradually, eastward, and protected from approach on the east and north-east by impassable swamps.

The country between the hill and Log Town was also covered by trees and thick shrubbery; from Log Town to Camden the woods had been cut down, to prevent their being used to cover an advancing enemy. When Lord Rawdon understood General Greene's position, he placed the post in charge of convalescents from the general hospital, and by a detour to the east, attempted to surprise the American camp. Lord Rawdon had already been advised by Colonel Balfour, that the Commander-in-chief had directed the abandonment of Camden; but the operations of Greene, Marion, Lee and Sumter, had rendered such a movement impracticable. On that account he had directed Colonel Watson to join him. His protracted delay, through the movements of the American partisan corps, left the post greatly exposed. Several skirmishes had already taken place near Camden, and Tarleton states that " Lord Rawdon had learned from prisoners, that " Greene's army was not by any means so numerous as he had apprehended, but that considerable reinforcements were expected. To balance this he received the unfavorable intelligence that Marion had already taken such a position as rendered it impracticable for Colonel Watson to join him."

The command, consisting of about nine hundred men, with fifty dragoons, marched at ten o'clock, and by filing close to the swamp on their right, gained the woods unperceived. This route of march also carried the British column to the left of the American front, which had less natural strength, and brought on an immediate skirmish with the pickets, nearly a mile from the camp. These were commanded by Captains Benson and Morgan, of Virginia, besides Kirkwood's small detachment of Delaware troops. The resistance was so efficient as to delay the advance until the American line was formed.

The Sixty-third British regiment formed the right, the New York volunteers the centre, and the king's Americans the left, of the first line. The Volunteers of Ireland on the right, and Captain Robertson's detachment, formed a supporting line; and the South Carolina regiment and the dragoons were still in reserve. The front was too narrow, and the plan of General Greene was well designed to envelop and crush it. The secondary diagram on the map indicates that plan. The American right wing consisted of General Huger's brigade, with the regiments of Lieutenant-colonels Campbell and Hawes; and the left wing, under Colonel Gunby and Lieutenant-colonel Ford, Colonel Williams commanding. It was quite similar to the formation of the reserve line at the battle of Guilford. The North Carolina militia, consisting of about two hundred and fifty men under Colonel Reade, formed the reserve, but took no part in the action. The artillery, three guns, under Colonel Harrison, just arrived, was masked in the centre, and orders were given for the regiments on the right and left of the guns to open for their fire; and then to " charge the enemy with the bayonet, withholding their own fire until the British line was broken." The regiments on the right and left of the line, were to left and right oblique, upon the respective flanks of the advancing enemy. Much confidence was felt in the assurance that Lord Rawdon was unadvised of the return of the artillery, and implicit reliance was placed upon the regiments at the centre. Colonel Washington was sent to double the right flank and take them in the rear."

Lord Rawdon quickly perceived that his front was too contracted, and as at Guilford, the reserves were brought up to equal the front of the enemy. Lieutenant-colonel Campbell with the Sixty-third British regiment and the king's Americans pressed on firmly, notwithstanding the fire of the artillery, while Campbell on the right, and Ford on the left of the American line, were descending the hill with spirit, in accordance with the plan of battle. Both of the British wings, brought up so hurriedly to the support of the original column, began to give way under pressure. Ford fell, severely wounded, and his men hesitated in their advance. Captain Beatty on the right of Colonel Gunby's regiment, was mortally wounded. His own company on the right of the regiment, began a hasty firing, and almost immediately after, fell back in disorder. It was the critical moment of the battle. The interval thus made, was filled by the British advance, and Colonel Gunby made the grand mistake of retiring the other companies, to re-form the regiment. This movement, says Greene, "gave the whole regiment an idea of a retreat, which soon spread through the Second regiment, which fell back accordingly. They both rallied afterwards, but it was too late. The enemy had gained the eminence, silenced the artillery, and obliged us to haul it off."

Greene himself pulled at the drag ropes to encourage his men, and, "the guns were simply hauled into the bushes at the rear of the hill ; and overlooked by the British troops in their brief pursuit."

Tarleton says, "They pursued three miles ; but the enemy's cavalry being superior to the British, their dragoons could not risk much ; and Lord Rawdon would not suffer the infantry to break their order for any benefit that might be expected from a pursuit of the fugitives."

Meanwhile Colonel Washington had made a complete circuit as far as Log Town, capturing or parolling as he went; but the defeat of the American centre spoiled General Greene's well arranged plan of battle. Tarleton says, "a part of the enemy's cavalry, under Colonel Washington, either by design, or through ignorance of the state of the action, came round to the rear, and exacted paroles from some of the British officers who lay wounded in the field ; they likewise carried off several wounded men." The design of General Greene was based upon confidence in his best troops.

Great discrepancies occur in the statements as to General Greene's force. These statements seem to have a simple solution. The returns of April twenty-sixth, the day after the action, show present for duty, eleven hundred and eighty-four men ; but contain no column of total numbers. The addition of the casualties makes that total fourteen hundred and forty-six men, which is very near Lossing's figures. Chief-Justice Marshall states the number of Continental troops engaged in the action to have rather exceeded twelve hundred. Ramsey and Gordon, and those who adopted their figures, *omit the casualties of the day.*

The American loss included Captain Beatty, one sergeant and eighteen men *killed,* Lieutenant-colonels Ford and· Campbell, Captain J. Smith, 1st Maryland, Captain Dunholm, Virginia, Captain (Lieutenant) Bruff, Maryland, Lieutenant Galloway, Maryland, Lieutenant Ball, Virginia, and one hundred and eight men, *wounded,* three sergeants and one hundred and thirty-three men *missing*. Of the last number, some were killed, and forty-seven were known to be wounded, and prisoners. Total casualties, two hundred and seventy-one.

The British loss was one officer and thirty-eight men *killed*, twelve officers and two hundred and seven men *wounded* and *missing*. Total casualties, two hundred and fifty-eight.

General Greene retired to Rugely's Mills, and Lord Rawdon fell back to Camden.

" The victory at Hobkirk's Hill," says Stedman, " like that at Guilford Court House . . . . produced no consequence beneficial to the British interest." " Even in Charleston itself, many of the inhabitants, although awed and restrained by the presence of the garrison, gave signs of evident dissatisfaction. Sumter on the northwest frontier, and Marion on the north-east, had kept alive the embers of revolt; but they now burst forth in a flame, as soon as intelligence was received that General Greene had entered the province."

On the seventh of May, Colonel Watson joined Lord Rawdon, and General Greene declined to be drawn into battle.

On the ninth of May, such stores as could not be removed were destroyed, and on the tenth, Lord Rawdon evacuated Camden and retired to Monk's Corner.

Fort Mott surrendered to Lee and Marion on the twelfth. This fort was a stockade defense, built around a private mansion. Mrs. Rebecca Mott, the owner, furnished General Marion with an East India bow and arrows, with which combustible missiles were shot upon the roof, to fire the building.

On the eleventh of May, General Sumter occupied Orangeburg.

On the fifteenth, Lee reduced Granby.

On the fifth of June, Augusta surrendered, having been under observation, and practically under siege, from the sixteenth of April, when the Georgia militia under Colonels Williams, Baker and Hammond first established their camp within gun-shot of the defenses. Pickens, Lee and Clark afterward participated in the siege. As in the case of Fort Watson a log crib, filled with sand, called " a Mayham tower," from Lieutenant-colonel Mayham who devised it, in the first instance, during the siege of Fort Watson, was a prominent element in securing command of the defenses. The garrison was largely made up of Indian auxiliaries.

General Greene was before Ninety-six, as early as the twenty-first of May. Kosciusko planned the approaches.

On the seventh of June, Lord Rawdon left Charleston with the flank companies of three regiments which had just arrived, and on the twenty-first the siege was raised, after the condition of the garrison had become critical. General Greene retired northward, was followed by Lord Rawdon as far as the Ennoree, and eventually retired behind the Tyger and Broad Rivers. Upon learning that Lord Rawdon had abandoned Ninety-six and divided his forces, to cover the outposts of Charleston, General Greene ordered his hospital and baggage, then at Winnsborough to be transferred to Camden, and marched his army to the High Hills of Santee, for rest, during the extreme summer heat. While operations at the extreme south were gradually losing magnitude and the operations could hardly be regarded as the movements of armies, the partisan skirmishes were constant, and bitterly conducted.

At Quinby Bridge, July seventeenth, at Monk's Corner, at Dorchester on Cooper River, almost to the Charleston picket lines, and through the entire region so recently occupied by the British troops, the activities and antagonisms of local warfare were uninterrupted by the summer's heat, and the short repose of the main armies.

Little quarter was given in contests between *Americans*, and the adventures of Sumter, Lee, Marion, and Wade Hampton, Horry, and royalist partisan leaders, would fill volumes. They definitely illustrate the misguided policy which attended the prosecution of the war. The British army was numerically unequal to the demands upon its service ; and the substitution of proclamations, confiscations, and hanging, only multiplied enemies, without securing respect or obedience. Colonel Balfour, the post commander at Charleston, was an energetic commander; but the lawless execution of Colonel Haynes without a trial, and other deeds of extreme severity, tarnished his name, and the acquiescence of Lord Rawdon in his action in that single case, called forth from the Duke of Richmond and other leading statesmen unqualified reprobation.

The British army could not protect. The American army could not rescue. The frightful elements of civil war penetrated all neighborhoods. There was no such place as home. Too often in the extremity of the struggle there was no such thing as family. The bitterest foes were those within the household. *The waste of war was slowly wearing out the war itself.*

BRITISH EFFECTIVE FORCE IN AMERICA.

NOTE. From "Original Returns in the British Record Office. Date May 1st, 1781.

New York..............................	12,257
On an Expedition......................	1,782
" " " under General Leslie.....	2,278
" " " " " Arnold....	1,553
" " " " " Phillips....	2,116
South Carolina........................	7,254
	27,240

East Florida................	438
West Florida................	1,185
Nova Scotia	3,130
Bermuda....................	366
Providence Island...........	128
Georgia....................	887
	6,134

Total..............33,374.

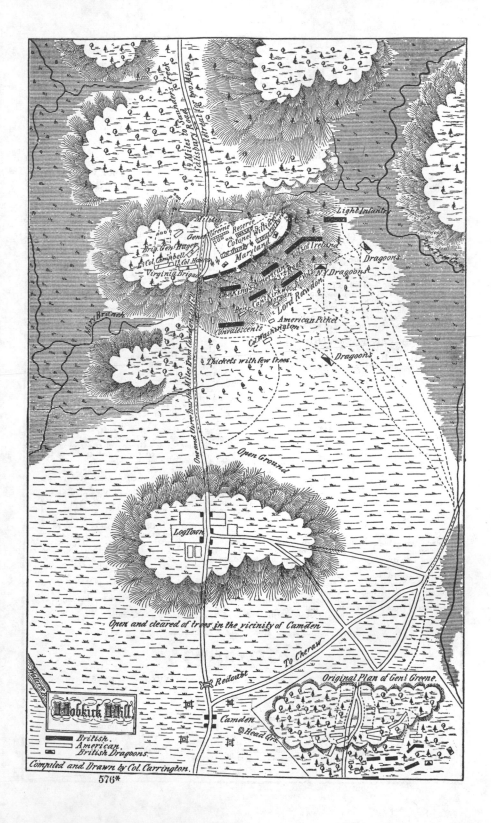

Light Infantry

Militia
General Greene Reserve
Colonel Williams
Brig. Gen. Hager
Lt. Col. Campbell   Lt. Col. Howard
Virginia Brigade   Maryland

Dragoons

1st King's American Regt.   N.Y. Dragoons
Col. Kirkwood   Scovel
Regt.   Morgan
Lord Rawdon

4 Miles to Treadway's Creek
Salisbury Road
Miles to Salisbury Road

Convalescents   American Picket
Col. Washington

Branch   Thickets with few trees.

Dragoons

Open Ground

Open and cleared three four miles Mien Post Salute

LogTown

Open and cleared of trees in the vicinity of Camden

Redoubt   To Cheraw   Original Plan of Gen.l Greene

Camden
Head Qrs.

Hobkirk Hill

━━━ British.
▭▭ American.
◺ British Dragoons.

Compiled and Drawn by Col. Carrington.

576*

Battle of Hobkirk Hill

APRIL 25th, 1781

American Commanders	British Commanders
GREENE	LORD FRANCIS RAWDON
Col. Washington, Williams, Campbell, Gunby, Ford, Hewes, Reade, Kirkwood, Benson, Morgan, Harrison, Beattie	Campbell Robertson
Strength, 1,446 Casualties, 271	Strength, 950 Casualties, 258

AMERICAN POSITION.—General Greene advanced to Log Town, within a short distance of Camden, April 19th, for the purpose of enticing Rawdon to an action ; but failing in this, and being too feeble to attack the post, he withdrew to Hobkirk Hill on the 24th. Upon a previous rumor, that Lieut.-Colonel Webster was on his way to reenforce Lord Rawdon, he had sent Colonel Carrington, with the artillery and baggage, back to Rugely's Mills. That officer had marched eight miles, when recalled, but did not regain camp until after 9 o'clock of the 25th. Greene had sent orders for Marion to join him ; but Rawdon, having learned from a deserter, of this order, and that the artillery had been sent to the rear, resolved to surprise the camp, without delay.

Hobkirk Hill is a narrow sand ridge, separating the head springs of small streams which flow to the Wateree and Pine Tree Creek. It was then thickly wooded, and abrupt, toward Camden. Woods also extended as far as Log Town, from which place, to Camden, the timber had been cleared, to prevent its use as cover for an approach to the post.

The American troops were at breakfast, when the alarm was given, of the approach of the British troops.

AMERICAN FORMATION.—The detachments of regular troops, then with Greene, had proved good soldiers, and he depended upon them fully. Huger took the right, with the regiments of Campbell and Hewes. The left wing, under Williams, consisted of the regiments of Gunby and Ford. The three guns, on their arrival, were masked in the centre, with orders for the supporting regiments to open their ranks after one discharge, then charge bayonet, and reserve their own fire until the ranks of the enemy were broken. The North Carolina militia, 250 men, under Colonel Reade, formed the reserve. In the belief that the assault would be made directly in front, orders were also given for the wings to wheel toward the advancing column, and thus concentrate a destructive cross-fire. Colonel Washington was to move toward Log Town at a gallop, and take Rawdon's forces in the rear. A small picket was also advanced a mile beyond the foot of the hill, under Kirkwood, Benson and Morgan.

BRITISH MOVEMENTS.—Rawdon placed the post in charge of convalescents, and so closely followed the line of swamp, to the eastward, in his march, that he gained the woods, unperceived by the Americans, until he met their pickets. A lively skirmish, first warned Greene of the movement, and led to the formation adopted. This route of march, however, carried the British troops to the left of the American lines, where the approach was easier, and the position less defensible.

The British troops formed, with the Sixty-third Regiment, the New York Volunteers and the King's Americans, as a first line, supported by the volunteers of Ireland and Captain Robertson's regiment, with the South Carolina regiment and fifty dragoons, as a reserve.

Lord Rawdon increased his front by the supports and reserves, as he advanced, to prevent the threatened movement upon his flank, and the action became general. The British line, thus hastily formed, as it advanced, began to give way under the pressure of the Americans, who began to descend the hill, as had been directed, in the plan of the battle.

Lieut.-Colonel Ford fell, severely wounded, and his men halted. Captain Beattie, on the right of Gunby's regiment, was mortally wounded. As the British pressed into the gap, Colonel Gunby made the grave mistake, of retiring the other companies, to reform the regiment. This gave the impression of retreat, and the Second Maryland Regiment fell back. Both rallied ; but it was too late. The British troops gained the summit, silenced the guns, and the retreat became general.

Meanwhile Colonel Washington had made his detour, taken paroles from wounded officers in the woods, gained some prisoners, and returned, to find the battle at an end.

The Americans saved their guns, which the British overlooked in their brief pursuit. Lord Rawdon states, that "the enemy's cavalry being superior to the British, their dragoons could not risk much," "and he would not suffer the infantry to break their order, for any benefit, that might be expected from a pursuit of the fugitives."

General Greene retired to Rugely's Mills,   Lord Rawdon fell back to Camden.

References:

CARRINGTON'S "BATTLES OF THE AMERICAN REVOLUTION," pp. 566–576.

School Histories:

Anderson, ¶ 108 ; p. 96.
Barnes, ¶ — ; p. —.
Berard (Bush), ¶ 132; p. 174-5.
Goodrich, C.A.(Seaveys),¶ 27, p. 143.
Goodrich, S. G., ¶ 5; p. 273.
Hassard, ¶ 17 ; p. 222.

Holmes, ¶ 9 ; p. 155.
Lossing, ¶ 7 ; p. 184.
Quackenbos, ¶ 395 ; p. 289.
Ridpath, ¶ 11 ; p. 224.
Sadlier (Excel), ¶ — ; p. —.
Stephens, A.H. ¶ 11; p. 225-6.

Swinton, ¶ 10 ; p. 158.
Scott, ¶ 7 ; p. 212.
Thalheimer (Eclectic), ¶ — ; p. —.
Venable, ¶ 166; p. 127.

CHAPTER LXXI.

BATTLE OF EUTAW SPRINGS. CLOSING EVENTS OF THE CAMPAIGN. 1781.

LORD RAWDON sailed homeward to recruit his health, but was taken prisoner by Count de Grasse, and carried to Chesapeake Bay, where Cornwallis soon shared his fortunes. Lieutenant-colonel Stewart succeeded to the command of the British army in the Southern Department, with headquarters at Orangeburg, South Carolina. General Greene, who had been resting his army at the High Hills of the Santee, had been reinforced by seven hundred continental troops from North Carolina under General Jethro Sumner, and marched with very nearly two thousand six hundred men, on the twenty-second of August, to engage the British army. Orders had been sent to Lee, Marion, and Pickens to join his command. Colonel Stewart fell back forty miles, and established his camp at Eutaw Springs. See map "Battle of Eutaw Springs." This movement was not made under fear of attack, but to secure supplies for his army. He states the matter squarely, in his official report to Earl Cornwallis, as follows, " The army under my command being much in want of necessaries, and there being at the same time a convoy of provisions on the march from Charleston, which would have necessarily obliged me to make a detachment of at least four hundred men (which at the time I could ill afford, the army being much weakened by sickness) to meet the convoy at Martin's, fifty-six miles from camp, I therefore thought it advisable to retire by slow marches to the Eutaws, where I might have an opportunity of receiving my supplies, and disencumber myself from the sick, without risking my escorts, or suffer myself to be attacked to disadvantage, should the enemy have crossed the Congaree."

On the seventh of September, General Greene encamped at Burdell's plantation, on the Santee River, seven miles from Eutaw Springs.

37

On the eighth of September, the battle of Eutaw Springs was fought. It was the last battle of the last Southern campaign of the war, and its conditions and results are therefore material elements to complete this narrative. Colonel Stewart learned of the position of General Greene's camp, as he states in his official report, from two deserters, about six o'clock in the morning.

Stedman says, " Unfortunately, their report was neither credited nor inquired into; but they themselves were sent to prison." Stedman was not present, and Colonel Stewart's report credits the deserters with information upon which, in part, he acted. Major Coffin had, however, been previously dispatched with one hundred and forty infantry and fifty cavalry, in order to gain intelligence of the enemy; and he reported that they appeared in force in front, then about four miles from camp. Colonel Stewart adds, " Finding the enemy in force so near me, I determined to fight them; as, from their numerous cavalry, it seemed to be attended with dangerous consequences, I immediately formed the line of battle, with the right of the army to Eutaw Branch, and its left crossing the road leading to Roche's plantation, leaving a corps on a commanding situation to cover the Charleston road, and to act as a reserve."

The line was in the woods, in advance of the camp, and the tents were left standing. Major Majoribanks was on the extreme right, in a close thicket, nearly covered from sight. The Third British, known as the " Irish Buffs," which landed on the third of June, constituted the right wing proper, with the American Royalists under Lieutenant-colonel Cruger at the centre; and the Sixty-third and Sixty-fourth British took position on the left. A small reserve of infantry with Captain Coffin's detachment, constituted the remainder of the British force, which did not exceed two thousand men, all told. " Major Sheridan with a detachment of New York volunteers took post in a house, to check the enemy should they attempt to pass it." This brick house and its garden fence, (palisaded,) proved as efficient a *point of resistance*, as did the Chew house, at the battle of Brandywine.

General Greene advanced early in the morning, leaving his camp a little after four o'clock of the eighth of September. " The front was composed," according to his official report, " of four small battalions of militia, two of North, and two of South Carolina." General Marion commanded the right wing, and General Pickens the left wing. Colonel Malmady commanded the centre, which was composed of North

Carolina militia, with a small artillery detachment under Lieutenant Gaines, and two three-pounders, which rested on the road. "The second line consisted of three small brigades of continental troops, one of North Carolina, one of Virginia, and one of Maryland,"— respectively under the command of General Sumner, Colonel Campbell, and Colonel Williams. Two six-pounders under Captain Brown were on the road. Lieutenant-colonel Washington, with his cavalry, and the Delaware troops (Kirkwood's) formed the body of the reserve. Lieutenant-colonel Lee with his legion covered the right flank, and Lieutenant-colonel Henderson, with the State troops, the left. The American force slightly exceeded twenty-three hundred men. Such were the relative tactical positions of the armies; but the fighting was less systematic than the artificial formations. Some matter-of-fact elements, much less formal, preceded the struggle. A portion of the British army had been sent out to dig sweet potatoes, which were just ripe, and were much liked by the soldiers. Colonel Stewart says, nearly at the close of his report, " I omitted to inform your lordship, in its proper place, of the armies having for some time been much in want of bread, there being no old corn, or mills, near me. I was, therefore, under the necessity of sending out *rooting parties*, from each corps, under an officer, to collect potatoes every morning at daybreak; and unfortunately, that of the flank battalions and " Buffs " having gone too far, in front, fell into the enemy's hands before the action began, which not only weakened my line, but increased their number of prisoners."

The rooting party thus found the vanguard of General Greene's army, which they were not seeking, and left the sweet potatoes which they were seeking, with all possible energy; and the pursuit of the rooting party, unarmed as they were, imparted vigor to the American advance, and increased the number of prisoners afterwards reported. Captain Coffin, who had been sent to the front, also had a short skirmish three miles before the British camp; and left forty of his men in the hands of the Americans. Some of his party were killed.

As nearly all critical events in human history have their minor determining issues, so this final battle of the Southern campaign of the war under notice, is easily brought to plain solution.

The American army was superior in numbers, and was well-officered. The preliminary skirmish with Coffin, and the surprise of the rooting party, imparted zest to their advance. It was nearly nine o'clock when the opposing forces met in battle, and the artillery fire on either side, was limited to the range of the road. The "distribution of the British artillery through their line," referred to by several historians, was simply the location of three guns in the centre of a small front of a few hundred yards; and both armies fought under the shade of forest trees, where the American army had every advantage of position, and where individual merit had its best opportunity.

This battle illustrates the fair average of military transactions, when stripped of the poetical adornments which deceive youthful aspirants for glory, and enthuse the people with frenzied excitement over victories won.

Fighting is hard work. The beautiful formation of parade vanishes in the field. The word "*steady*," means *just that;* but the idea of perfect self-possession, so that depleted regiments unite again as fast as men fall, and the aggregate loss is *simply a diminution of a promptly closed-up front*, is theoretical and impossible. The *morale*, or inertia of an army, gives it physical power; and this is made up of elements which must come out of fixed conditions. These conditions are, either an exact and patient training, or the impulsion which comes from some overwhelming passion. Concord, Lexington, and Bunker Hill illustrate the latter; and both the British and Hessian troops almost invariably demonstrated the value of the first condition. The American continental army, so far as permanent, acquired like discipline, and their battalions suffer very little discount, when engaged under equal circumstances with their opponents.

The battle of Eutaw Springs was well fought, until the battle, like that of Bennington, promised a short march to easy victory, and then license supplanted discipline, and vanquished victory.

The action began between the artillery detachments, and their fire was maintained with much vigor, until one of the British and two of the American pieces were dismounted. The British left wing, "by an unknown mistake," says Colonel Stewart, "advanced and drove the militia and North Carolinians before them; but unexpectedly finding the Virginia and Maryland line ready formed, and at the same time receiving a heavy fire, occasioned some confusion." The North Carolina militia, however, fired seventeen rounds before their retreat, and Sumner so promptly pushed the battalions of Ashe, Armstrong and Blount into the gap, that the first line was restored, and the British in turn retreated. The reserve then came to their support. The American second line was promptly brought up, at a bayonet charge, and the British left wing in turn gave way.

Colonel Henderson was wounded early in the action, and Lieutenant-colonel Wade Hampton succeeded to the command of the cavalry on the left flank. Washington, with Kirkwood, advanced toward the position occupied by Majoribanks, and Lee threatened the British left. The bayonet charge led by Colonel Williams shattered the British left wing. The troops broke into disorder and fled through their camp to the cover of the house already occupied by Major Sheridan. While the British officers were rallying their men and forming the line anew, and obliquely to the left, across the open ground behind their camp, a portion of the American troops were plundering the tents, drinking rum, and sacrificing the partial success already attained.

The position of Major Majoribanks was such as to endanger the American left wing. Colonel Washington attempting in vain to dislodge him, was wounded and taken prisoner, together with nearly forty of his men. The thicket was too dense for the movement of cavalry, and the men were taken, one by one, without opportunity to resist. Kirkwood and Hampton made a similar attempt with persistent valor, but Majoribanks only retired to a still stronger position, and eventually behind the palisades of the garden.

General Greene made every possible effort to restore his line, but no troops could withstand the hot fire to which they were exposed. The artillerymen were in open ground, and nearly every one fell upon the field. The house which Sheridan occupied, had windows in the roof, and was practically, as General Greene reports it, a *three story house*. Finding its capture impossible, and that his men were exposed to absolute slaughter, he abandoned the guns and retired to Burdell's plantation. The battle was one of great activity on both sides. The unarmed rooting party of course carried back with them an element of disorder. The British left, made up of the veteran Sixty-third and Sixty-fourth, had served during the war from their landing on Staten Island in 1779 (see page 200). They made an unauthorized plunge upon the American centre to capture its guns, at the beginning of the fight, and lost confidence by the repulse which attended the advance of Sumner. The bayonet charge of Williams and Campbell which followed, was efficient and determining. The conduct of Majoribanks was equally opportune, on the British right. The occupation of the brick house and garden, and the plunder of the British camp, taken together, saved Colonel Stewart's army.

The American casualties are given by General Greene, as one

lieutenant-colonel, six captains, five subalterns, four sergeants, and ninety-eight rank and file, killed ; two lieutenant-colonels, seven captains, twenty lieutenants, twenty-four sergeants, and two hundred and nine rank and file wounded. Total casualties four hundred and eight.

The British casualties are given by Colonel Stewart as three commissioned officers, six sergeants, and seventy-six men, killed ; sixteen commissioned officers, twenty sergeants, and two hundred and thirty-two men missing. Total casualties, six hundred and ninety-three.

On the night of the ninth, Colonel Stewart retired to Monk's Corner, having broken up and abandoned one thousand stand of arms which he threw into the river, and left seventy wounded men to the care of the Americans.

Stedman says, " both armies had suffered so much that for some time afterwards neither of them was in a situation to undertake anything against the other," and adds, " Indeed this was the last action of any consequence that happened in South Carolina between the king's troops and the Americans. The former, from this time chiefly confined themselves to Charleston Neck and some posts in its neighborhood, the security of the town appearing to be their principal object ; and General Greene, either was not or did not think himself in sufficient force to attempt to reduce it."

Tarleton says, " It is impossible to do justice to the spirit, patience and invincible fortitude displayed by the commanders, officers and soldiers during these dreadful campaigns in the two Carolinas. They had not only to contend with men, and these by no means deficient in bravery and enterprise, but they encountered and surmounted difficulties and fatigues from the climate and the country, which would appear insuperable in theory, and almost incredible in the relations." . . . " During the greater part of the time they were totally destitute of bread, and the country afforded no vegetables for a substitute. Salt at length failed, and their only resources were water and the wild cattle which they found in the woods. In the last expedition fifty men perished through mere fatigue." . . " We must not, however, confine the praise entirely to the British troops ; as a detachment of Hessians which had been lent upon the occasion by General De Bose, deservedly came in for their proper share. The same justice requires that the Americans should not be deprived of their share of this fatal glory. They had the same difficulties to encounter, joined to a fortune on the field generally adverse ; yet on

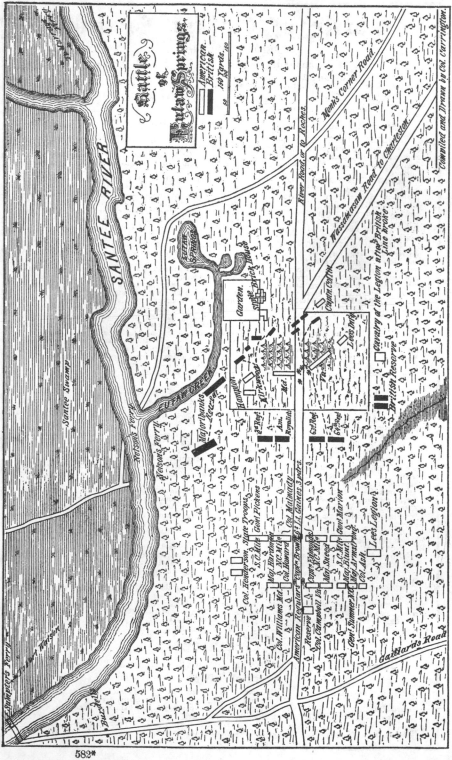

Battle of Eutaw Springs

American ▭
British ▬

150 Yards

SANTEE RIVER

Santee Swamp

Nelson's Ferry

Sumpter's Ferry

Burkan's Ferry

Lieut. Marson

EUTAW SPRINGS

EUTAW CREEK

Garden

Stone Brick House

Majoribanks Recess

Hamilton

Kirkwood

3 Reg

Am.
Royalists

Crqum. Cn Tm

River Road to Roches.

Wassamsaw Road to Charleston.

Nonk's Corner Road

Leo's Inft.

Lee

British Reserve

Cavalry of the Legion after British Line broke

Col. Henderson State Troops

2 S.C. Mili. Genl Pickens

Col. Malmedy

62 Reg

6 Reg

Col. Armstrong

J.L. Gaines 3 yd rs.

Col Howard

Maj. Hardman

2 N.C. Mili.

Col. Williams Mili.

J.C. Mili

Capt. Kyrwood

Maj. Sneed

Genl Marion

Lees Legion

Col. Ash

American Regulars Engr Brown

S.C. Mili

Maj. Blunt

Maj. Armstrong

Reserve

Lol. Clarewell Va

Genl Sumner N.C.

Gaillards Road

Compiled and Drawn by Col. Carrington.

➤Battle of Eutaw Springs◄

SEPTEMBER 8th, 1781

American Commanders
GREENE
Sumner, Lee, Col. Washington, Henderson
Marion, Kirkwood, Hampton, Ash,
Campbell, Armstrong, Pickens, Blount
Sweet, Williams, Malmady, Brown

Strength, 2,400   Casualties, 408

British Commanders
STUART
Coffin.   Majoribanks,   Cruger,   Sheridan

Strength, 2,000   Casualties, 693

AMERICAN SITUATION.—General Greene rested his army at the High Hills of the Santee (see map. p. 72-3), was joined by General Sumner, with 700 Continental troops from North Carolina, and on Sept. 7th, encamped at Burdell's Plantation, on the Santee River, seven miles from Eutaw Springs. At 4 o'clock, A. M., September 8th, Greene marched to attack the British force at Eutaw Springs.

AMERICAN FORMATION.—"Front line, of four small battalions of militia, two of North, and two of South Carolina." Marion commanded the *right* wing, Pickens, the *left* wing, Colonel Malmady, the centre, with North Carolina militia, and two 3-pounders under Lieutenant Gaines. The *second* line consisted of three small brigades of Continental troops, of North Carolina, Virginia, and Maryland respectively, commanded by General Sumner, Colonel Campbell, and Colonel Williams. Captain Brown served two 6-pounders, on the road. Kirkwood's Delaware troops formed the reserve. Lieut.-Colonel Lee covered the right flank with his Legion horse, and Colonel Henderson, with the State troops, covered the left.

BRITISH SITUATION.— Stuart succeeded Rawdon in command at the South, with Head-quarters at Orangeburg, but fell back 40 miles, to Eutaw Springs, upon information that Lee, Marion, and Pickens, were concentrating their forces, under Greene. At 6 o'clock, A. M., September 8th, two deserters reported the situation of the American camp. The report was not credited. Major Coffin had been previously sent forward, with 150 men, to reconnoitre. A detachment from the British "Buffs," and their flanking battalions, had been sent out very early, as usual, to dig sweet potatoes, as they were plentiful, and bread was scarce, and no mills were near for grinding corn.

BRITISH FORMATION.— Stuart formed his line in advance of his tents, and with the purpose to offset, by position, the American superiority in mounted men. The *right* was toward Eutaw Creek, with Major Majoribanks, in a close thicket, nearly covered from sight. The 3d regiment "Irish Buffs," which only landed June 3d, constituted the right wing proper, with the American Royalists, under Lieut.-Colonel Cruger at the centre, and the 63d and 64th regiments on the *left*.

A small infantry detachment, with that of Captain Coffin, constituted a small reserve, covering the left flank of the camp, and the Charleston road ; while Major Sheridan, with some New York Volunteers, occupied a brick house, within a palisaded garden, which ultimately proved nearly as serviceable as did the Chew House at the battle of Germantown. Three guns "were distributed through the line." The field, occupied by both armies, was well wooded.

NOTES.

NOTE I.—Coffin met the American advance guard, nearly four miles from camp, and was driven in with a loss of 40 men. The "rooting parties," unarmed as they were, came in, much demoralized, leaving many prisoners in the hands of the Americans.

NOTE II.—Artillery firing began at 9 o'clock, with vigor, until one British piece and two American pieces were dismounted.

NOTE III.—"The British left wing," says Stuart, "by some unknown mistake, *advanced*, and drove the North Carolina militia before them, but unexpectedly finding the Virginia and Maryland line ready formed, and at the same time receiving a heavy fire, occasioned some confusion."

NOTE IV.—The North Carolina militia had fired seventeen rounds before retiring ; and Sumner sent his brigade so promptly to their support, that the British yielded. They renewed the attack, when supported by the reserve ; but the American reserve was pushed forward by Greene, and a bayonet charge, by Williams, broke the line.

NOTE V.—A sharp skirmish occurred at the right, where Majoribanks was posted. Colonel Henderson was wounded, and Lieut.-Colonel Wade Hampton succeeded to command of the cavalry on the American left. Washington and Kirkwood united in the attack. The thicket was so dense that Washington and 40 men were taken prisoners, and Majoribanks retired to the palisades of the garden.

NOTE VI.—Lee entered the British camp from its left, and   British fell back, to reform, obliquely, before the house.

NOTE VII.—Many American troops began to plunder the tents.

NOTE VIII.—Greene brought up his artillery, and attempted to restore order, and break the palisade defences ; but his gunners were shot down by fire from the windows (a house of three stories, as Greene reports), and leaving his guns, rather that sacrifice the men, he retired to Burdell's Plantation.

NOTE IX.—The 63d and 64th British, had served during the war, from the landing on Staten Island, in 1779.

NOTE X.—On the night of the 9th, Stuart retired to Monk's Corner, broke up, and threw in the river, 1,000 stand of arms, and left 70 wounded men to the care of the Americans.

MEM.—*This was the last formal engagement at the South.*

References:

CARRINGTON'S "BATTLES OF THE AMERICAN REVOLUTION," pp. 577-584.

School Histories:

Anderson, ¶ 109 ; p. 96.
Barnes, ¶ 2 ; p. 138.
Berard (Bush), ¶ — ; p. —.
Goodrich, C.A.(Seaveys), ¶ 28; p. 143.
Goodrich, S. G., ¶ 11 ; p. 274.
Hassard, ¶ 18 ; p. 222.

Holmes, ¶ 11 ; p. 156.
Lossing, ¶ 11 : p. 185-6.
Quackenbos, ¶ 399; p. 292-3.
Ridpath, ¶ 14 ; p. 224.
Sadlier, (Excel), ¶ 22 · p. 205.
Stephens, A.H. ¶ 14; p. 226-7.

Swinton, ¶ 12 ; p. 158.
Scott, ¶ 11 ; p. 214.
Thalheimer (Eclectic), ¶ 291 ; p. 166 ;
Venable, ¶ 166 ; p. 127.

the whole the campaign terminated in their favor, General **Greene** having recovered the far greater part of Georgia and the two Carolinas."

On the twelfth, General Greene crossed the Santee at Nelson's Ferry, and on the fifteenth was at his old camp at the High Hills. Pickens, Marion and Hampton resumed their partisan operations, and Greene's army was soon reduced to less than a thousand effective men, with nearly six hundred wounded men from the two armies in his charge.

One Hector O'Neal with a party of royalists captured Hillsborough, and made Governor Burke and the council prisoners, but was killed, during his retreat to Wilmington, by a party of militia.

On the ninth of November, General Greene's camp was enlivened by official information of the surrender of Cornwallis.

On the eighteenth the High Hills were again abandoned, and numerous minor operations concluded the Southern campaign of 1781.

It was a constant struggle to secure troops, food, medicines and ammunition, while the garrison of Charleston had been increased to an effective force of nearly six thousand men; *but the armies did not again meet in the field.*

CHAPTER LXXII.

LA FAYETTE'S VIRGINIA CAMPAIGN. CONDITION OF THE TWO ARMIES.

ON the twentieth of February, 1781, Congress resolved that a portion of the Pennsylvania line, then near Lancaster, and which had been engaged in the previous mutiny, should be ordered to the south, to constitute a part of the southern army. This was predicated upon the landing of a British force at Wilmington, on the Cape Fear River. That force, however, had been magnified beyond its real importance ; and the ultimate increase of the British army in Virginia gradually modified the disposition of the detachment referred to.

On the same day, General La Fayette was assigned to the command of troops then assembled at Peekskill, having, as his specific objective of operations, a rapid march to Virginia, to *capture Benedict Arnold*. Owing to the temporary reduction of the British fleet at Newport, Rhode Island, by the storm of January twenty-second, before noticed, M. Destouches, then commanding, *vice* Admiral Ternay, deceased, agreed to send one ship of the line and two frigates to Chesapeake Bay, to prevent Arnold's escape. The letters of Count de Rochambeau show that he consented to send a detachment of French troops also ; but this he states, " was thought to be unnecessary and inexpedient as the movement was intended to be rapid ;—it being presumed that the continental troops and militia, in Virginia, were sufficient to operate against Arnold by land." This small naval detachment, commanded by M. De Tully, sailed from Newport on the ninth of February, and captured the British frigate Romulus, 44, in Lynn Haven Bay, as well as two privateers, and eight other prizes ; but the L'Eveille, 64, drew too much water to ascend the Elizabeth River where Arnold had withdrawn his few light frigates :— the Surveillante grounded, and the vessels returned to Newport, on the twenty-fourth. It appears that the entire French fleet would have joined the movement, with a land force added, if Count de Rochambeau had received letters from General Washington in time; but M. De Tully had sailed when the proposition reached the French headquarters.

The division of La Fayette consisted of twelve hundred light infantry, made up of New England and New Jersey troops. He started immediately for his new command, reaching Pompton on the twenty-third of February, Philadelphia on the second, and Head of Elk on the third of March. The troops went to Annapolis by water. La Fayette first went in an open canoe to Elizabethtown, to accelerate preparations for the attack upon Arnold. During this preliminary examination he visited Baron Steuben, then at Yorktown, who entertained the idea that he would rally at least five thousand militia, and then visited General Muhlenberg, at Suffolk, and actually made a reconnoissance of Arnold's defenses at Portsmouth. The return of the French ships to Newport compelled him to return to Annapolis and await further instructions from Washington.

The expedition was immediately reorganized. General Washington visited Newport on the sixth, and held a conference with Count de Rochambeau, on the Admiral's ship. Pursuant to previous correspondence with Count de Rochambeau, he found that eleven hundred and forty men, under Baron de Viomenil, had already embarked, but a delay in the repair of one frigate had prevented earlier sailing. The squadron, consisting of eight ships of the line and four frigates, sailed on the eighth. On the tenth, Admiral Arbuthnot, then at Gardiner's Bay, on the north side and east end of Long Island, wrote to General Clinton to warn Arnold of the expedition, and at once sailed with an equal force, in pursuit of the French ships. On the sixteenth a short naval engagement occurred between the two fleets, off Chesapeake Bay, with well balanced results; but the object of the expedition having been thwarted by the presence of the British squadron, M. Destouches returned to Newport on the twenty-sixth, after an absence of only eighteen days.

A material modification of the plan of campaign was involved in these failures of the French fleet to control the Chesapeake. Under the original order, La Fayette was instructed "to return to the main army, in case Arnold quitted Virginia, or the French lost superiority of naval force." Washington wrote to La Fayette on the fifth of April, as follows: " While we lament the miscarriage of an enterprise which bid so fair for success, we must console ourselves in the thought of having done everything practicable to accomplish it. I am certain that the Chevalier Destouches exerted himself to the utmost to gain the Chesapeake. The point upon which the whole turned, the action with Admiral Arbuthnot, reflects honor upon the chevalier and upon the marine of France. As matters have turned out, it is to be wished that you had not gone out of the Elk; *but I never judge of the propriety of measures by after events.*" La Fayette was also instructed to return to Philadelphia. On the sixth, he was ordered to join General Greene; but when Washington learned of the landing of General Phillips in Virginia, with reinforcements to the British army, he countermanded the order and assigned La Fayette to command in Virginia under General Greene, to whom, as well as to Washington, he made his reports. General Greene thus expressed his views of this detail of General La Fayette, in a letter written "Ten miles from Guilford Court House, March eighteenth": "I am happy to hear the Marquis de La Fayette is coming to Virginia, though I am afraid from a hint in one of Baron Steuben's letters, that he will think himself injured in being superseded in the command. Could the Marquis join us at this moment, we should have a most glorious campaign. It would put Lord Cornwallis and his whole army into our hands." The Baron Steuben as usual, accepted Washington's orders as final; and by a different plan than anticipated by General Greene, the *Virginia operations of La Fayette directly led to the final environment and capture of Lord Cornwallis.*

Many embarrassments attended the opening of this campaign. The troops themselves disliked their transfer to a warmer climate, especially when they were ordered to march to the extreme south; and some dissatisfaction was expressed at the assignment of Colonel Gimat and Major Galvan, both excellent officers, to commands in the corps. Desertions were frequent and the spirit of the army was almost mutinous. One deserter was hung, and then La Fayette changed his policy, and *forgave and dismissed the second offender.* An order was issued declaring that "*he was setting out for a difficult and dangerous expedition; but that he hoped the soldiers would not abandon him; but that whoever wished to go away might do so instantly.*" "From that hour," he states in his memoirs, "all desertions ceased, and not one man would leave." It has already been seen that Washington could send no adequate reinforcements to General Greene, and it is well to notice the condition of the northern army from which La Fayette had withdrawn twelve hundred men.

Condition of the American army. It will be remembered that the new army establishment was fixed at thirty-seven thousand men, and the purpose was to realize this force by the first of January, 1781. The requisitions had been delayed. Marshall says, " The regular force drawn from Pennsylvania to Georgia inclusive, at no time during this active and interesting campaign, amounted to three thousand effective men. Of the northern troops, twelve hundred had been detached under the Marquis de La Fayette to the aid of Virginia. Including these in the estimate, the States from New Jersey to New Hampshire inclusive, so late as the ninth of April, had furnished only five thousand effectives. The cavalry and artillery at no time exceeded one thousand." " During May, the total force reached seven thousand men, of whom rather more than four thousand might have been relied on for action ; but even these had been brought into camp too late to acquire that discipline which is so essential to military service."

Washington thus embodies the gloomy condition of affairs in his diary, commencing the first of May : " Instead of having magazines filled with provisions, we have a scanty pittance scattered here and there in the different States. Instead of having our arsenals well supplied with military stores, they are poorly provided, and the workmen are leaving them. Instead of having the various articles of field equipage in readiness to deliver, the quartermaster-general is but even now applying to the States (as the dernier resort) to provide these things for their troops respectively. Instead of having a regular system of transportation upon credit, or funds in the quartermaster's hands to defray the contingent expenses, we have neither the one nor the other ; and in all that business, or a great part of it, being done by military impressment, we are daily and hourly oppressing the people, souring their tempers and alienating their affections. Instead of having the regiments completed under the new establishment, and which ought to have been so by the ——— of ——— agreeable to the requisitions of Congress, scarce any State in the service has at this time an eighth part of its quota in the field ; and there is little prospect that I can see of ever getting more than half. In a word, instead of having everything in readiness to take the field, we have nothing. And instead of having the prospect of a glorious offensive campaign before us, we have a bewildered and gloomy prospect of a defensive one ; unless we should receive a powerful aid of ships, land troops and money from our generous allies, and these at present are too contingent to build upon." " Chimney-corner patriots," abounded, and it

would be difficult to find a period of modern history where " venality,'
"corruption," "prostitution of office for selfish ends," "abuse of
trust," "perversion of funds from a national to a personal use," and
" speculations upon the necessities of the times," had been more wide-
spread and offensive than as described in unequivocal terms by Washington during the war under notice. Every battle and every campaign was affected by such elements, and the *diffusion of political
responsibility* still made the *United States* only a loose partnership of
scattered and differently related partners.

On the twentieth of February, when the Virginia campaign was
initiated, General Washington urged General Schuyler to accept the
head of the War Department, using these words, "Our affairs are
brought to an awful crisis. Nothing will recover them but the vigorous exertion of men of abilities who know our wants, and the best
means of supplying them. These qualifications, sir, without a compliment, I think you possess. Why then, the department being
necessary, should you shrink from the duties of it? The greater the
chaos, the greater will be your merit in bringing forth order." General Schuyler replied on the twenty-fifth of February, and declared
his intention never to hold any office under Congress unless accompanied with a restoration of military rank, and that "such inconveni-
ences would result to themselves (Congress) from such a restoration, as
would necessarily give umbrage to many officers."

Generals Greene, Gates and Sullivan were considered candidates,
but the matter was dropped, until General Lincoln received the
appointment, October twenty-fifth, 1781. Robert Morris, whose
wealth and energies during the entire war were devoted to the cause,
so that he commanded credit when Congress had none, took charge
of the Financial Bureau, and General McDougall was elected Secretary of Marine.

The foregoing considerations have value in the present connection; and further reference to the condition of the American northern army will be deferred to its association with operations against
Yorktown and New York, after General Washington assumed personal command of all the armies in the field.

Situation of the British army. On the fifth of April, after La
Fayette had reached Head of Elk, General Clinton thus wrote to
Lord Germaine: "I am preparing for every exertion within the compass of my very reduced force, which after the several large detachments sent to the southward, amounts to no more than 6275 auxiliary

troops, 4527 British and 906 Provincials ready for the field." (Reference is made to note at end of chapter.) A letter of General Cornwallis to General Clinton dated April tenth, was noticed in chapter LXX. On the eleventh of April, General Clinton wrote to General Phillips: "The security of the Carolinas is of the greatest moment; but the best consequences may be expected from an operation up the Chesapeake. Let the same experiment be tried there which has been so *unsuccessful* in the south." (Italics not in the original, but suggestive of General Clinton's anxiety, and doubt as to the general campaign.) He continues,—"Virginia has been looked upon as universally hostile, Maryland less so, but has not been tried; but in Pennsylvania, on both sides of the Susquehanna, and between the Chesapeake and Delaware, the friends of the king's interests are said to be numerous. Support should be rendered to them, and means of proving their fidelity put into their hands. If Lord Cornwallis can spare such part of his forces as to effect this movement, it is greatly to be desired." It will be seen that the war was taking the direction which General Charles Lee had recommended to the British commissioners at an early period, and that the views of Lord Cornwallis, based upon the inadequacy of the army to the conquest of the South, so long as Virginia was unsubdued, were beginning to affect General Clinton himself.

The official report of British troops for duty, in Virginia, made up on the first of May, 1778 gives: under Arnold, fifteen hundred and fifty-three men, and under Phillips, two thousand one hundred and sixteen men. The army of Lord Cornwallis increased this force to a little over five thousand men, on the twentieth of May. Colonel Tarleton had received some recruits and mounted the legion upon blooded horses, which were quite uniformly kept by gentlemen in that part of Virginia. Colonel Hamilton's North Carolina Royalists also joined the command. In the meantime General Phillips had completed the fortifications which Arnold began at Portsmouth; and on the eighteenth of April he embarked his troops, sailed up the James River as far as Burwell's Ferry, and marched to Williamsburg. The militia fled. Colonel Simcoe pursued, and it was proposed to occupy Yorktown; but the plan was abandoned for want of the necessary force, both to hold the post and to meet La Fayette, who was advancing toward Richmond. "A small party passed up the Chickahominy in boats, and destroyed," according to Arnold's official report, "several armed ships, the State ship-yards, warehouses, etc., etc." "On the twenty-fourth, the army sailed to City Point, and on the twenty-fifth marched for Petersburg, at ten o'clock in the morning." See map "Arnold at Petersburg." Generals Steuben and Muhlenberg were then at that post with about one thousand militia. A strong position was taken up on a hill east of Brandon, on the Appomatox River, which compelled the British army to make a long detour, with view of intercepting the American retreat. Baron Steuben promptly foiled this intention by falling back to Brandon, and finally re-crossed the river with a loss of but twenty in killed and wounded. A judicious disposition of his artillery on Baker's Hill covered his retreat. Arnold says, "the enemy were soon obliged to retire on the bridge, with the loss of one hundred men killed and wounded as we have since been informed ; our loss was only one killed, and ten wounded. The enemy took up the bridge, which prevented our pursuing them." He says, " four thousand hogsheads of tobacco, one ship, and a number of small vessels on the stocks and in the river were destroyed."

On the twenty-seventh, " General Phillips marched to Chesterfield Court House, burned barracks for two thousand men, three hundred barrels of flour, etc." On the same day Arnold marched to Osborne's, thirteen miles from Richmond, and " destroyed," says La Fayette in his report to General Greene, " some vessels that had been collected there." These vessels had been prepared for an expedition against Portsmouth. General La Fayette was then at Hanover Court House. Arnold's report states that " two ships, five brigantines, five sloops and one schooner, loaded with tobacco, cordage, flour, etc., fell into our hands ; four ships, five brigantines, and a number of small vessels were sunk and burnt. On board of the whole fleet (none of which escaped) were taken and destroyed about two thousand hogsheads of tobacco," " want of boats and the wind blowing hard prevented our capturing many of the seamen, who took to their boats and escaped to shore. On the thirtieth the British army marched to Manchester and destroyed twelve hundred hogsheads of tobacco. The Marquis de La Fayette having arrived with his army at Richmond, opposite to Manchester, the day before, and being joined by the militia drove from Petersburg and Williamsburg ; they were spectators of the conflagration, without attempting to molest us." General La·Fayette says, " Our regular force consisted of nine hundred men, rank and file ; that of the enemy of twenty-three hundred at the lowest estimate. The command of the water, and such a superiority of regular troops gave them possession of our shore. There was no crossing for us but under a circuit of fifteen miles, and from the number and size of their boats, their passage over the river was six times quicker than ours. Richmond being their main object, I determined to defend this capital, where a quantity of public stores and tobacco was contained." (At this time Generals Steuben and Muhlenberg were further up the river, not having effected a crossing.) " Six hundred men ventured on this side, but were timely recalled, and being charged by a few dragoons of Major Nelson, flew into the boats with precipitation. The enemy have lost some men, killed, prisoners, and deserters. Since the British army landed at City Point (some flour excepted at the Court House) no public property has been destroyed." The foregoing is from a letter addressed to General Greene, dated, " camp on Pamunky River, May 3d, 1781."

On the first of May the British troops marched to Osborne's, embarked on the second, reached Westover on the third, and on the seventh, when near Hog Island, received instructions from Lord Cornwallis to meet him at Petersburg, and reached that place on the ninth. Several American officers were captured by their sudden return.

Movements of La Fayette. It has been seen that he reached Head of Elk on the third of March. " The shortest calculation was for the sixth." No operation of the war more clearly demonstrates the value of good logistics, and the facts demand notice in connection with this Virginia campaign. Messengers were sent in advance to arouse the people, and the citizens of New Jersey cheerfully aided the progress of his army.

" Notwithstanding the depth of the mud and the extreme badness of the roads, this march," says La Fayette, writing to Washington, March 2d, 1781, " which I call rapid, (as for example they came in two days from Morristown to Princeton) has been performed with such ardor and alacrity, that agreeably to the report, only two men have been left behind ; and yet these two men have embarked at Trenton with some remains of baggage. At every place where the detachment have halted, they have found covering and wood ready for them, and there has not been the least complaint made to me by the inhabitants. Every third day they have drawn their provisions; the clothing has also been distributed, and having embarked yesterday at Trenton, they passed this city (Philadelphia) about two o'clock with a wind which was extremely favorable. The artillery consisted of one 24, six 18s, two brass 12s, one eight-inch howitzer, two eight-inch mortars, in all, twelve heavy pieces; four six-pounders, and two small howitzers, with a sufficient quantity of ammunition will be at the head of the Elk this day and to-morrow, so that by the 4th I hope we shall be ready to sail. A quantity of medicines and instruments, and fifteen hundred pairs of shoes will be at the head of Elk before we embark." " I am also assured that we will have a sufficient quantity of boats to land the detachment, and two heavy ones will be added for the artillery, and some of the private armed vessels in the bay have been ordered to the head of the Elk. Two dispatch boats are there, and four more have been asked for. As a further security to our subsistence, I have got the Minister's permission to dispose of the French flour and salt meat along the bay in case of necessity." The troops were promptly forwarded to Annapolis; and at Baltimore, besides an advance by the merchants of two thousand guineas, the ladies undertook the work of furnishing his command with suitable clothing for summer wear. The disappointments incident to the failure of the French naval forces to convoy and cover his division compelled his return to the Elk, and by the time the order came to move to the extreme south, the dissatisfaction of his troops already adverted to had taken place, and had been substantially settled. He had also armed several vessels, and proposed to make a miniature fleet for his own convoy, but "some vessels were run off to avoid him," and the adventure against Portsmouth·to capture Arnold came to an end. He "visited the Hermione frigate, however, and obtained a pledge from M. Delatouch, that on his return to Newport, M. Destouches would make an offer of the ship *L'Éveille* and the four frigates, to convoy twelve hundred men to any part of the continent which Washington might think proper." In this connection he adds, " These ships are too strong to be afraid of frigates, and too fast to be in the least concerned by the fear of a squadron."

The plan of La Fayette after the failure of the design upon Portsmouth was, " to take these fast vessels and go by sea to Wilmington or Georgetown, and take Cornwallis in his rear, or in the neighborhood of General Greene." The plan was eminently practicable and wise. La Fayette also confidentially advised General Washington that "two millions and a half had been given to Franklin," adding, " Marquis de Castries and Count de Vergennes are trying to obtain a sum more adequate to our wants; this, however, the minister of finance has requested me not to mention, as it was as yet an uncertainty, and would perhaps give ill-grounded hopes' destructive of the internal efforts we ought to make." On the thirteenth of April, having received notice from General Greene that "he expected that Cornwallis would fall back to Wilmington, and that his own project was to carry the war into South Carolina," La Fayette renewed the suggestion that a corps of light infantry be embarked at Philadelphia, on board of a light squadron, which might have been upon the seat of war in a very short passage." On the twenty-eighth of April, he wrote from Hanover Court House to General Greene: "Having received intelligence that General Phillips' army were preparing for offensive operations, I left at Baltimore everything that would impede our march—to follow us under a proper escort, and with about a thousand men, officers included, hastened toward Richmond, two hundred miles, which I apprehended would be a principal object with the enemy." This outline brings La Fayette up to the date when he reported his arrival near Richmond and the retreat of Generals Phillips and Arnold the day following.

La Fayette had marched with great celerity, leaving his artillery behind, which he said "might appear a strange whim; but it saved Richmond," and adds, "General Phillips had given the signal for attack when he learned of his (La Fayette's) unexpected arrival." A chain of expresses was at once established to Point Comfort. A detachment was sent to Williamsburg to annoy the enemy, and if possible prevent their establishing a permanent post. On the eighth of May he writes: "There is no fighting here unless you have a naval superiority, or an army mounted on race horses. Phillips' plan against Richmond has been defeated. He was going toward Portsmouth; *now* it appears I have business to transact with two armies, and this is rather too much." La Fayette had just learned of the march of Lord Cornwallis northward, and was making an effort to reach Halifax and cut him off from union with Phillips. The sudden return of General Phillips to Brandon on the eighth, defeated that enterprise; but did not divert him from his recognition of the claims of General Greene to be supported. He says, "Each of these armies is more than double the superior of me. We have no boats, few militia, and less arms. I will try to do for the best. Nothing can attract my sight from the supplies and reinforcements destined to General Greene's army. While I am going (marching) to get beaten by both armies (Phillips' and Cornwallis') or each of them separately, the Baron remains at Richmond, where he hurries the collection

38

of recruits and every other requisite. I have forbidden every department to give me anything that may be thought useful to General
Greene, and should a battle be expected (an event which I will try
to keep off,) no consideration will prevent our sending to Carolina
eight hundred recruits, who I hope may be equipped in a fortnight.
When General Greene becomes equal to offensive operations, this
quarter will be relieved. I have written to Wayne to hasten his
march ; but unless I am very hard pushed, shall request him to proceed to the southward. General Greene was on the twenty-sixth
before Camden, but did not think himself equal to the storming the
works." General Washington thus replied : " Your determination to
avoid an engagement with your present force, is certainly judicious. I
hope the Pennsylvanians have begun their march before this . . .
General Wayne has been pressed both by Congress and the Board of
War to make as much expedition as possible, and extraordinary
powers are given him to enable him to procure provisions."

On the eighteenth of May orders were received from General
Greene, directing General La Fayette to take command in Virginia
and to send all reports to the Commander-in-chief. It is worthy of
record, that while General Greene was almost the only one of the
general officers of 1776, who served actively through the war, under
the direct orders of the Commander-in-chief, both of them, alike, and
without disappointment reposed entire confidence in General La Fayette. The foregoing extracts from his papers, indicate the occasion
for that confidence.

When La Fayette assumed command, May eighteenth, he " took
a position, between the Pamunky and Chickahominy Rivers, which
equally covered Richmond and other interesting points of the State,
and sent General Nelson with militia toward Williamsburg."

Upon the return of General Phillips to Petersburg, May ninth, he
took position at Wilton, ten miles below Richmond. Upon application from North Carolina for ammunition, General Muhlenberg was
sent with five hundred men, to escort twenty thousand cartridges over
the Appomatox ; and to divert the enemy's attention, Colonel Gimat,
with his battalion and four pieces of artillery, assumed their position
so that the absence of the troops was not discovered. To Colonel
Hamilton he wrote, on the twenty-third, thus laconically : " Both
armies have formed their junction. Their infantry is near five to one,
their cavalry ten to one. We have no continentals. Is it not strange
that General Wayne's detachment " (the seven hundred Pennsyl-

vanians) "can not be heard of?   They are to go to Carolina; but should I have them for a few days, I am at liberty to keep them. This permission I will improve, so far as to receive one blow; that being beat, I may be beat with some decency.   The command of the waters, the superiority in cavalry and the great disproportion of our force gave the enemy such advantages that I durst not venture out and listen to my fondness for enterprise; to speak truth, I was afraid of myself, as much as of the enemy.   Independence has rendered me the more cautious, as I know my own warmth; but if the Pennsylvanians come, Lord Cornwallis shall pay something for his victory."

From this time, forward, the operations of the two armies were characterized by constant activity, each officer sustaining his reputation; and the wearisome marchings and counter-marchings ended as unfortunately for Lord Cornwallis, as did his pursuit of General Greene, without detracting from his skill as a soldier.

On the twenty-sixth of May Lord Cornwallis acknowledged the arrival of reinforcements under General Leslie, this force being carried into official returns, as two thousand two hundred and seventy-eight men, and informed General Clinton, that he "should proceed to dislodge La Fayette from Richmond."   On the same day he wrote a second letter, as follows, " I have consented to the request of Brigadier-general Arnold, to go to New York; he conceives that your excellency wishes him to attend you, and his present indisposition renders him unequal to the fatigue of service.   He will represent the horrid enormities which are committed by our privateers in Chesapeake Bay; and I must join my earnest wish that some remedy may be applied to an evil which is so very prejudicial to his Majesty's service."

It will be noticed that the operations of Arnold while in Virginia, as elsewhere, consisted of raids upon property, and involved no collision with Americans in force.   It was known to General Clinton and publicly, that Washington's instructions to La Fayette expressly forbade any terms with Arnold which should exempt him from punishment for desertion and treason.   Anxiety for the safety of Arnold is referred to by General Clinton in several dispatches, but on April 11th he apologetically explained that the words used during the pendency of the French attack, meant "the security of him, (Arnold) the troops under his orders and the posts on the Elizabeth river, as the principal objects of your (Phillips') expedition, and *no more* than relieving them of their supposed danger."   This dispatch was opened by Lord Cornwallis after the death of General Phillips. A letter of March twenty-fourth closed thus: "P. S. Pray send Brigadier-general Arnold here by the first opportunity, if you should not have particular occasion for his services." This was received by Lord Cornwallis May twentieth. The position of Generals Phillips and Arnold, in view of the relations of the two officers during the Saratoga campaign, had been such as forbade *friendship;* but the obligation of General Clinton to protect Arnold was peremptory.

Upon the death of Phillips, Arnold wrote to General La Fayette, who declined personal correspondence with him. Arnold threatened to send his prisoners of war to the West Indies, but as already indicated, his retirement to New York followed the arrival of General Cornwallis.

On the thirty-first of May, General Washington wrote to La Fayette, "Your conduct upon every occasion meets my approbation, but in none more than in your refusing to hold a correspondence with Arnold."

It appears that an attempt had been made at first to conceal from La Fayette the fact of General Phillips' decease; and some direct correspondence of Arnold with London officials had disturbed General Clinton. When General Cornwallis reached Petersburg, he found that General Clinton had conceived plans for a broader range of operations than the mere conquest of Virginia, and thus wrote : " In regard to taking possession of Philadelphia, (proposed by General Clinton) by an incursion (even if practicable) without an intention of keeping or burning it, (neither of which appear to be practicable) I should apprehend it would do more harm than good to the cause of Britain. If offensive war is intended, Virginia appears to me to be the only province in which there is a stake. But to reduce this province and keep possession of the country, a considerable army would be necessary, for with a small force, the business would probably terminate unfavorably, though the beginning might be successful. *In case it is thought expedient and a proper army for the attempt can be found, I hope your Excellency will do me the justice to believe that I neither wish nor expect to have the command of it, leaving you at New York on the defensive. Such sentiments are so far from my heart that I can with great truth assure you that few things could give me greater pleasure than being relieved by your presence from a situation of so much anxiety and responsibility.*"

(Italics not in original manuscript, but so placed in justice to Lord

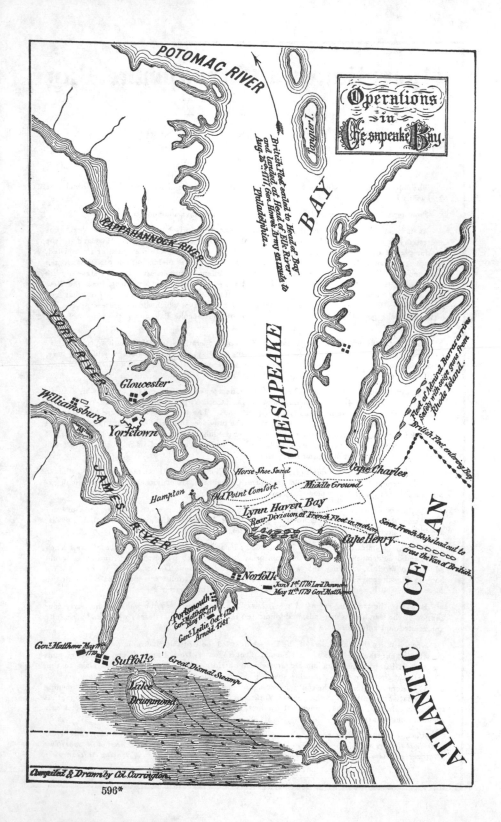

POTOMAC RIVER

Tangier I.

Operations in Chesapeake Bay

British Fleet sailed to Head of Bay and landed at Head of Elk River, Aug. 25th 1777, Gen. Howe having en route to Philadelphia.

RAPPAHANNOCK RIVER

CHESAPEAKE BAY

Fleet of Admiral Barras arrives Society with siege guns from Rhode Island.

British Fleet entering Bay.

YORK RIVER

Gloucester

Williamsburg

Yorktown

JAMES RIVER

Horse Shoe Sand

Hampton

Old Point Comfort.

Middle Ground

Cape Charles

Lynn Haven Bay

Rear Division of French Fleet in motion

Seven French Ships lead out to cross the Van of British.

Cape Henry

Norfolk

Jan. 1st 1776 Lord Dunmore May 11th 1779 Gen. Matthews

Portsmouth Gen. Matthews May 11th 1779

Gen. Leslie Oct. 1780 Arnold. 1781

ATLANTIC OCEAN

Gen. Matthews May 11th 1779

Suffolk

Great Dismal Swamp

Lake Drummond

Compiled & Drawn by Col. Carrington.

596*

Operations in Chesapeake Bay

THEIR SIGNIFICANCE

The effort to isolate the South, from the central colonies, came to an end with the surrender of Cornwallis in 1781.

From 1776, Virginia had been the scene of almost constant invasion and depredation.

As early as March 29th, 1777, General Charles Lee, then prisoner of war, in New York, thus addressed Admiral Howe and his brother, General Howe. " If the Province of Maryland, or the greater part of it, is reduced, or submits, and the people of Virginia are prevented or intimidated, from marching aid to the Pennsylvania army, the whole machine is divided, and a period put to the war; and if it (this plan,) is adopted in full, I am so confident of success that I would stake my life on the issue. Apprehensions from General Carleton's army will, I am confident, keep the New Englanders at home, or at least confine 'em to the east side of the river. I would advise that four thousand men be immediately embarked in transports, one-half of which should proceed up the Potomac, and take post at Alexandria; the other half up Chesaapeake Bay, and possess themselves of Annapolis."

Earl Cornwallis, when urging the transfer of his own operations from the Southern colonies, explicitly recognized the military importance of Chesapeake Bay, and that Virginia was the only base, subordinate to New York, from which to subjugate the South. He thus wrote to General Clinton, April 10th, 1781.

"I cannot help expressing my wishes that the Chesapeake may become the seat of war, even (if necessary) at the expense of abandoning New York. Until Virginia is, in a measure, subdued, our hold of the Carolinas must be difficult, if not precarious. The rivers of Virginia are advantageous to an invading army; but North Carolina is, of all the provinces in North America, the most difficult to attack (unless material assistance could be got from the inhabitants of the country, the contrary of which I have sufficiently experienced)—on account of its great extent, of its numberless rivers and creeks, and the total want of interior navigation."

On the 13th of April, he wrote to Lord Germaine : " The great reenforcements sent by Virginia to General Greene, whilst General Arnold was in the Chesapeake, are convincing proofs that small expeditions do not frighten that powerful province."

On the 21st of August, 1781, Washington, writing from Head Quarters, Kings Ferry, to Governor Livingston, thus confidentially disclosed his plans. (See Mag. Am. Hist., Feb. 1881, vol. IV, p. 141, and "Carrington's Battles," 4th Edition, p. 616, note).

Washington states therein, that " He intended to march in person, with the whole of the French army, and a detachment from the American army, with as much despatch as circumstances would admit, into Virginia, believing, that with the arrival of the Count De Grasse and his fleet, with a body of French troops on board, this would be the fairest opportunity to reduce the whole British force in the South, and ruin their boasted expectations in that quarter."

It was in the maturing events of 1781, that Washington disclosed the value of his early conception of the war, and its demands, and vindicated the wisdom of that strategy which he had so fully appreciated and enforced.

NOTE.—When the manœuvers of the French fleet led the British squadron into the offing, thereto give battle, but thereby allowed the French fleet to enter from Rhode Island with siege guns for the land batteries, and then join De Grasse, and obtain absolute supremacy, it was plain that no adequate aid could come to Cornwallis, by sea; and the allied operations about New York, had assured Sir Henry Clinton that he could never again successfully invade New Jersey. The crowning military fact which attaches to the siege of Yorktown itself, is to be derived from the knowledge, that it was the culmination of that strategetical conduct, by which Washington attested his character as a soldier throughout the war.

Mem.—Among the interesting facts to be associated with Chesapeake Bay, is this, that before Admiral Graves sailed for New York in 1781, the heaviest naval armament known to maritime warfare, viz: seventy-two hostile line-of-battle ships and heavy frigates, was floating on its surface.

Cornwallis, as indicating an error on the part of General Clinton, who afterwards declared that "Lord Cornwallis tried to *dupe* him into a resignation of the general command.")

Upon the departure of Arnold the Virginia campaign became the theatre of more active operations between the Marquis de La Fayette and Earl Cornwallis.

CHAPTER LXXIII.

EARL CORNWALLIS, still further reinforced from New York, commanded seven thousand efficient British troops, and began his campaign in Virginia with hope and vigor. He controlled the water-courses and inlets which exposed Virginia to naval attack, and his adversary lay within a day's march, with an army of less than twenty-eight hundred infantry, including militia, and with less than one hundred disciplined cavalry. The topographical features of the country peculiarly embarrassed the operations of the American troops as well as hindered the concentration of State militia. Many navigable rivers ran so nearly parallel that a small naval force could quickly shift an assailing army from section to section, and the local militia wherever concentrated, could not be transferred with equal celerity to resist incursions or meet organized troops.

General Cornwallis appreciated his position, and endeavored to so avail himself of his superior force, as to strike other organized forces at advantage, and at the same time annihilate depots and prevent the accumulation of supplies, which were vital to General Greene's army at the south, as well as to successful operations against the British army in Virginia itself. The State authorities were not wanting in vigor, but the pressure was as universal as the exposure.

The time was at hand when the war determined toward one field of operations, and that was occupied by La Fayette and Cornwallis. A British ascendency there would make the severance of the south from the north complete; and would leave to General Greene a barren triumph in the Carolinas. The time was at hand when one exhaustive effort was called for on the part of the American Congress and the Commander-in-chief of its armies. The statesmen of Virginia realized the emergency, and all alike looked to Washington for relief; but while Richard Henry Lee and other earnest men urged that dictatorial powers should be granted to the Commander-in-chief, as after the battle of Trenton, Governor Jefferson and another class, equally earnest, deprecated any concentration of authority which would assimilate the ruling element to the royal prerogative of European princes. All classes urged Washington to animate the struggle by his personal presence. Congress was destitute of authority and resources equal to the issue; but when that issue finally ripened, Washington seized the opportunity and achieved its mastery.

General history is full of the civil measures, so feeble and uncertain, which wrought in vain for an adequate increase of the army; and the long war was hastening to its end, through the earnest alliance of France and the wise military conduct of Washington on the one hand, and a marvellous want of concentrated effort on the part of Great Britain.

Washington knew how and when to disregard all exposed localities and seize determining opportunity in view of the whole theatre of war. Clinton failed on the other hand, in strategy, while self-possessed and brave in battle, and was confused by the extent of operations requiring attention. The British Cabinet did not appreciate the real danger which threatened the royal cause in America; and the protection of their numerous colonies as well as the vindication of their honor at sea, had become matters of superior moment.

La Fayette and Cornwallis realized the magnitude of the campaign which they had undertaken; and its details redound to their honor. Finding that he could not hold Richmond, General La Fayette removed the most valuable stores, and marched northward toward the Rappahannock to secure the speediest union with the Pennsylvania line under General Wayne, and then sought by all possible means to avoid a general engagement, while daily harassing the right flank and the rear of the British forces. The assembly of Virginia, quickened to fresh activity by the urgency of the peril, retired to Charlottesville, May twenty-fourth, and put forth all the proper energy within its power.

Fifteen millions of Bills of Credit, realizing a nominal value of one dollar to forty, the declaration of martial law within twenty miles of an army headquarters, and appeals to the militia, were resorted to as extraordinary measures; but this interposition of paper appeals and resolutions could not stop Cornwallis. Charlottesville had been the depot for the prisoners captured at Saratoga, and their rescue had been one of the objectives of the occupation of the upper Dan by that officer in the previous year; thwarted indeed by General Greene's well-considered movement down the Roanoke or lower Dan. These prisoners were now passed over the mountains to Winchester.

Meanwhile, and by the twenty-fifth of May, General Cornwallis was on the march. The James River was crossed at Westover and his headquarters were established at Bird's plantation. By the use of boats, previously constructed by Arnold, and by "swimming all the horses but the best, the entire army, infantry, cavalry and artillery, completed the passage," as Tarleton states, "in less than three days."

On the twenty-seventh the army encamped near White Oak Swamp. At this point information was obtained that General La Fayette had abandoned Richmond and crossed the Chickahominy. The army moved toward Bottom Bridge on that river, and the Americans crossed the Pamunky River. "A few days afterwards," says Tarleton, "an American patrol was captured and among other papers from the Marquis de La Fayette, to General Greene, Steuben, etc., one letter, addressed to Mr. Jefferson, the Governor of Virginia, was particularly striking. After exhorting that gentleman to turn out the militia, he *prophetically declared* that the British success in Virginia resembled the French invasion and possession of Hanover in the preceding war, and was likely to have similar consequences, if the government and the country would exert themselves at the present juncture." Tarleton himself was never more thoroughly in his favorite element. His legion was splendidly mounted with the best stock of the country; at the simple cost of bridles and saddles, when others were not found in gentlemen's stables. With two hundred and fifty men, all but seventy his own dragoons, he was dispatched in the beginning of June toward Charlottesville. Governor Jefferson and the Virginia Assembly were the objectives of pursuit. Lieutenant-colonel Simcoe, with the Yagers, and the infantry and hussars of the Rangers, was at the same time sent to Point of Fork, where Baron Steuben was then stationed in charge of the arsenal and laboratory previously established at that place. See map, "La Fayette in Virginia."

Tarleton marched between the South Anna and North Anna rivers at high speed, notwithstanding the summer heat, "halted at noon," on the third, "just long enough to refresh men and horses, pressed forward again in the afternoon, halted at eleven, near Louisa Court House, and remained on a plentiful plantation till two o'clock in the morning, at which time he again resumed his march." " Before dawn, he fell in with twelve wagons that were on their journey, under a small guard, from the upper parts of Virginia and Maryland, with arms and clothing for the continental troops in South Carolina." These were burned, " to save time and avoid a detail for their escort." Several captures were made at private mansions, including Colonel John Simms, (a member of the Assembly) and two brothers of General Nelson, and after a short halt near the residence of Dr. Walker, the march was resumed. Tarleton says he " imagined that a march of seventy miles in twenty-four hours, with the caution he had used, might perhaps give him the advantage of a surprise. He therefore approached the Rivianna, which river lies at the foot of the hill on which the town is situated, with all possible expedition. The cavalry charged through the water with very little loss and routed the detachment posted at that place." Seven members of the Legislature were secured. Brigadier-general Scott and a few other officers were captured. The casualties were trifling. "One thousand arms were broken up, four hundred barrels of powder and several hogsheads of tobacco were destroyed."

A detachment of dragoons under Captain McLeod visited Monticello, the country seat of Jefferson, three miles from Charlottesville, but their approach was discovered and the Governor escaped. The speaker of the Assembly also escaped and that body at once assembled at Staunton, beyond the mountains. The books, papers and furniture of Governor Jefferson were not disturbed; but his wines were freely used, or wasted, without the authority of the commanding officer.

On the twelfth of June, General Nelson was elected Governor, vice Mr. Jefferson, who had declined re-election in order that the executive office should be held by a man of military knowledge and experience.

On the day of his arrival, toward evening, Tarleton started down the Rivianna toward Point of Fork, to coöperate with Simcoe's expedition. This expedition was quite differently conducted from that of Tarleton. Colonel Simcoe is often underrated, because of frequent ferocity in shortening fights. He killed an enemy as fast as he could, up to the last point of resistance; but he was shrewd and cool, and managed his operations with much deliberation, even when heated by the ardor of battle. He approached the Baron Steuben's position so as to make the most plausible display of his forces, and made the impression, as Cornwallis designed, that the main army was near. General Steuben, having advices of his approach, removed a portion of the public stores, although, as the river was deep, he might have held the defensive with success if he had known the strength opposed. He retired from his position, however, and all public property that remained at the depot was destroyed or disposed of. The small arms were old and undergoing repair; but some valuable stores besides cannon and mortars were among the spoils.

The position of the armies, thus early in June, 1781, is a material fact in the consideration of the future operations of the war.

So far as related to the British army in Virginia, Cornwallis was equal to the position. He had the support of his government and an adequate force in hand. He shaped his plans upon the presumption that army headquarters at New York would hold its own, and would occupy the attention of the army of Washington and Rochambeau, which, combined as it was, did not equal the troops at General Clinton's disposal.

It is not out of place to again refer to the military principles already defined, which compel wise commanders to regard the destruction of opposing armies as more important than any ordinary guard duty over towns and cities.

Cornwallis based his movements, therefore, upon the assurance that his army was at his own disposal for the conquest of Virginia. There can be no doubt of this. He followed Tarleton and Simcoe to Elk Hill, a plantation of Jefferson, near Byrd Creek, in the heart of Virginia, and thus re-united his forces.

His march had not been made regardless of the operations of La Fayette, but a detachment had been sent toward Raccoon Ford as if his own purpose was to follow in force. It was still his plan to employ cavalry to break up depots of supplies, by rapid movements, and to march with the main army against organized troops. As an indication of his discreet military policy, an order issued to Colonel Tarleton on the ninth of June, dated "camp at Jefferson's," is quoted— "destroy all the enemy's stores and tobacco, between James River and the Dan; and if there should be a quantity of provisions or corn collected at a private house, I would have you destroy it, even although there should be no proof of its being intended for the public service, *leaving enough for the support of the family; as there is the greatest reason to apprehend that such provisions will be ultimately appropriated by the enemy to the use of General Greene's army, which from the present state of the Carolinas, must depend on this province for supplies."* (Italics not in original order, but so indicated as to place these instructions in association with those of Washington to General Greene, fully as stern, on page 243.)

Before further notice of this campaign, it should be borne in mind that far away at Wethersfield, Connecticut, on the twenty-first of May, the day after the arrival of Cornwallis at Petersburg, Washington and Rochambeau were in conference ; and that they deliberately discussed the propriety of an attack upon New York. This fact must be kept in mind, in order to appreciate the resulting embarrassments which followed the operations of Lord Cornwallis, under the demands of Clinton for help at headquarters.

During the march of Lord Cornwallis to Byrd Creek, La Fayette effected a junction with General Wayne, near Raccoon Ford on the Rapidan. This was on the seventh. By reference to the map it will be seen that La Fayette was nearly north from the camp of Cornwallis. By a prompt march to Charlottesville he could effect a union with Baron Steuben, who was not far distant southward, and then move eastward toward the British army, reserving to himself a retreat at will, while still threatening their rear. Tarleton thus states the movement : "The Marquis de La Fayette, who had previously practiced defensive manœuvers with skill and security, being now reinforced by General Wayne and about eight hundred continentals, and some detachments of militia, followed the British as they proceeded down James River. This design being judiciously arranged and executed with extreme caution, allowed opportunity for the junction of Baron Steuben, confined the small detachments of the king's troops, and both saved the property and animated the drooping spirits of the Virginians."

On the thirteenth, Tarleton reported to Cornwallis his own movements. This letter was intercepted by La Fayette's scouts, and as promptly published for warning to the people. On the fourteenth, Cornwallis notified Tarleton that he proposed to move the next day to Westham, near Richmond. Tarleton says: "While the royal army marched, the rear and left flank were covered by the British Legion and the Seventy-sixth regiment on horseback; and on its arrival at Richmond, Lieutenant-colonel Simcoe with his corps was posted at Westham, and his own (Tarleton's) corps at Meadow Bridge. During these operations the Marquis de La Fayette continued to advance his light troops to harass the patrols. On the eighteenth, he (Tarleton) made a forced march to intercept General Muhlenberg's detachment, who evaded the blow by an early retreat, and the British Legion returned to the royal army."

La Fayette thus reports this occurrence to General Greene, from "Mr. Tyre's plantation, twenty miles from Williamsburg, June twenty-seventh, 1781:" "On the eighteenth, the British army moved toward us with a design, as I apprehend, to strike at a detached corps commanded by General Muhlenberg. Upon this, the light infantry and Pennsylvanians marched, under General Wayne, when the enemy returned into town. The day following I was joined by General Steuben's corps, and on the night of the twentieth, Richmond was evacuated." Cornwallis thus left Richmond on the twentieth, and directed his course by Bottom Bridge and New Kent Court House for Williamsburg. "At the time the royal army quitted New Kent, the main body of the Americans approached within twelve miles of that place," says Tarleton, "which circumstance nearly occasioned Earl Cornwallis to countermarch; but upon reflection, he pursued his design of moving to Williamsburg, where he arrived on the fifteenth of June."

Within six miles of Williamsburg the next morning, a sharp skirmish ensued. The Queen's Rangers (Simcoe) had marched down the Chickahominy, guarding the British rear and right flank. They were closely pressed by the American advance guard under Colonel Butler, supported by Wayne. La Fayette says, "the whole British army came out to save Simcoe." Tarleton had marched to Burwell's Ferry on the James River, and says, "Before the horses were unbridled, the sound of musketry and cannon announced the commencement of an action at the outpost, and Lord Chewton soon afterwards delivered Earl Cornwallis' orders for the cavalry and mounted infantry to repair with expedition to the army, who were already moving to the relief of Lieutenant-colonel Simcoe. The loss in this affair was nearly equal, upwards of thirty being killed and wounded on each side. The Americans retreated to their army at Tyre's plantation, and the king's troops returned in the evening to Williamsburg, where they found some recruits for the guards who had arrived during their absence." This last paragraph shows that La Fayette correctly supposed that the main army turned to meet his attack, and he thus closes his report: "The post they now occupy is strong, under the protection of their shipping, *but upwards of one hundred miles from the Point of York.*" Under date of June 30th, Lord Cornwallis reports his loss at three officers and thirty privates killed and wounded, and that "three American officers and twenty-eight privates were taken prisoners." But a new element had entered into the campaign. On the twenty-sixth, Ensign Amiel placed in his hands dispatches from General Clinton, the first dated June 11th, already fifteen days old. Besides an estimate that "the continentals under La Fayette could not exceed one thousand, and that the Pennsylvania line under Wayne were so disconcerted that their officers were afraid to trust them with ammunition," (this however may have since altered), he says, "The detachments I have made from this army into the Chesapeake, since General Leslie's expedition in October last, inclusive, have amounted to seven thousand seven hundred and seventy-four effectives; and at the time your lordship made the junction with the corps there were under Major-general Phillips' orders five thousand three hundred and four; a force I should have hoped would be sufficient of itself to have carried on operations in any of the southern provinces of America; where, as appears from intercepted letters of Washington and La Fayette, they are in no situation to stand even against *a division* of that army. . . . By the intercepted letters enclosed to your lordship, you will observe that I am threatened with a siege of this post. My present effective force is only ten thousand nine hundred and thirty-one. It is probable that the enemy may collect for such an object, at least twenty thousand, besides reinforcements to the French, (which from pretty good authority I have reason to expect), and the numerous militia of the five neighboring provinces. Thus circumstanced, I am persuaded your lordship will be of opinion that the sooner I concentrate my forces the better."

The following corps were therefore to be forwarded to New York in succession as they could be spared, "two battalions of light infantry, Forty-third regiment, Seventy-sixth or Eightieth regiment, two battalions of Anspach, Queen's Rangers, cavalry and infantry, the remains of the Seventeenth light dragoons, and such proportion of the artillery as could be spared, particularly men." A second dispatch by the same messenger, dated June 15th, says, "I request you will immediately embark a part of the troops stated in the letter inclosed, beginning with the light infantry, and send them to me with all possible dispatch. . . . I do not think it advisable to leave more troops in that unhealthy climate at this season of the year than what are absolutely wanted for a defensive, and desultory water excursions."

Lord Cornwallis was thus assured that coöperation from New York, *via* Philadelphia, as previously proposed, or otherwise, was improbable, and with the proposed reduction of his army the conquest of Virginia became impossible. The question of retaining any army at all in Virginia was at once a practical one. On the thirtieth, he replied from Williamsburg, " Your excellency being charged with the weight of the whole American war, your opinions of course are less partial, and are directed to all parts; upon viewing York, I was clearly of opinion that it far exceeds our power, consistent with your plans, to make safe defensive posts there and at Gloucester, both of which would be necessary for the protection of shipping. . . . As magazines, etc., may be destroyed by occasional expeditions from New York, and there is little chance of establishing a post capable of giving effectual protection to ships of war, I submit to your excellency's consideration, whether it is worth while to hold a sickly defensive post (Portsmouth) in this Bay, which will always be exposed to a sudden French attack, and which experience makes no diversion in favor of the southern army." While these dispatches were being exchanged, a cipher dispatch from General Clinton of June twenty-eighth, received by Lord Cornwallis July eighth, again avowed a purpose of making a rapid movement to seize the stores, etc., collected at Philadelphia, and afterward to use the force so employed to reinforce New York, urging embarkation of the troops before mentioned, and offering to " return whatever may have been too great a proportion of, the moment the expedition is over." On the date of receipt, Lord Cornwallis replied, that " the troops were ready to embark, and deprecated the detention of *defensive* posts in the country, which can not have the slightest influence on the war in Carolina, and which gives us some acres of an unhealthy swamp, and forever liable to become a prey to a foreign enemy with a temporary superiority at sea. . . . Desultory expeditions in the Chesapeake may be undertaken from New York with as much ease and more safety, whenever there is reason to suppose that our naval force is likely to be superior for two or three months." The letter cited, also describes the attack of La Fayette at Jamestown which will be noticed.

The position assumed by Cornwallis in his correspondence was verified by his ultimate capture. He desired to have the Virginia army equal to a conquest of the State, and able to support itself, or as the alternative, to abandon the passive occupation of posts which could draw no adequate resources from the country around, and could be assured of no security by sea. Sufficient has been said to indicate the uncertainty of his future operations and the embarrassments which followed them. These continued until reinforcements, three thousand men, although not one-third of the number expected, arrived at New York and General Clinton as late as July eleventh, (not received until the twentieth,) " authorized him to disembark the troops then at Portsmouth and ready to sail for New York." Meanwhile the condition of things changed. He had been compelled to act upon the supposition that the depletion of his command would end the Virginia campaign. The embarkation of troops was to be made from Portsmouth.

During this time the American army had followed closely upon the retiring army of Lord Cornwallis.

La Fayette thus wrote to Washington on the twenty-eighth of June: " The enemy have been so kind as to retire before us. Twice I gave them a chance of fighting (taking care not to engage them farther than I pleased) but they continued their retrograde motions. Our numbers are. I think, exaggerated to them, and our seeming boldness confirms the opinion. I thought at first, Lord Cornwallis wanted to get me as low down as possible, and use his cavalry to advantage. His lordship had (exclusive of the reinforcements from Portsmouth, said to be six hundred) four thousand men, eight hundred of whom were dragoons, or mounted "infantry." Our force is almost his, but only one thousand five hundred regulars, and fifty dragoons. One little action more particularly marks the retreat of the enemy. From the place whence he first began to retire to Williamsburg, is upwards of one hundred miles. The old arms at the Point of Fork have been taken out of the water. The cannon was thrown into the river undamaged, when they marched back to Richmond; so that his lordship did us no harm, of consequence, but lost an immense part of his former conquests and did not make any in this State. General Greene only demanded of me, to hold my ground in Virginia. I don't know but what we shall, in our turn, become the pursuing enemy."

The movement of Lord Cornwallis to Portsmouth, nominally begun on the fourth of July, was delayed until the ninth, the fourth and fifth being occupied in the removal of the heavy baggage. General La Fayette advanced to Green Spring, within a few miles of Jamestown, and sent light parties in advance, to attack the British rear guard. The Queen's Rangers crossed James River on the fourth, but the main army still remained on the north side. The British position had natural strength. The right was covered by ponds and swamps, and before the centre and left, the ground was so low and miry, that it could be crossed only by narrow causeways. Tarleton says, "he hired a negro and a dragoon, and charged them to feign desertion, and give false intelligence, and to represent, that the body of the king's troops had crossed James River; and he supposed it "most probable that La Fayette acted upon this false intelligence, rather than through too *great ardor*," adding, "*for it is the only instance of this officer's committing himself during a very difficult campaign.*"

Tarleton's opinion is correct, with this qualification, that in view of the narrow and difficult approaches to the British camp, the American advance pressed on too hotly, while the admirable reticence of the British troops induced the supporting parties also to cross the causeways, only to find themselves confronted by at least thrice their numbers. Some discredit has been cast upon General Wayne for this exposure of the American army, but the force of the enemy was simply underestimated. His self-possession and daring were never more conspicuous, and the Pennsylvania troops under his command fought on equal terms with the best troops of Cornwallis. The American army, except the militia under Baron Steuben; left camp about three o'clock, and reached the British front about five, on the afternoon of the sixth. A few dragoons and the rifle detachments of Majors Call and Willis crossed the causeway first, and took cover in a wood near the Williamsburg road. Armand's and Mercer's cavalry, with McPherson followed. Captain Savage with two guns and two battalions of light infantry under Major Galvan and Major Willis, (of Connecticut,) came next, and these troops were supported by General Wayne's Pennsylvania brigade. The pickets were attacked vigorously and driven in, although promptly supported by the Yagers. The two guns and the battalions of Willis and Galvan came to their support. Lieutenant-colonel Mercer and Major McPherson, respectively, took command of the riflemen on the right and left, while the cavalry advanced upon the British horse which formed in a field to the rear of the picket. Tarleton, then acting under the immediate orders of Cornwallis, says, "the British cavalry supported the pickets on the left, in order to contain the enemy within the woods and to prevent their seeing the main army. Upon the first cannon-shot from the enemy the British army formed and advanced, when the dragoons fell through the intervals made for them by the infantry."

The British right consisted of the Twenty-third, Thirty-third, and Seventy-first regiments, (Yorke's brigade *vice* Webster, killed at Guilford,) the Guards, Hessians, two battalions of light infantry and three guns, commanded by Lieutenant-colonel Yorke, and were opposite the position of Major McPherson. The British left consisted of the Forty-third, Twenty-sixth and Eightieth regiments, with light companies, supported for a second line, by Tarleton's legion and two guns, all under Lieutenant-colonel Dundas, and confronted Mercer, whose riflemen were partially covered by an opportune ditch and a rail fence. supported by the two small battalions of continentals.

After brief opposition the first line gave way. The American left had already retired. Wayne anticipated the advancing columns by a bold bayonet charge, immediately supported by La Fayette, who had finally crossed the causeway; and such was the vigor of the conflict that the American army extricated its front, and retired unpursued to its camp. La Fayette had his horse shot and was conspicuous for personal daring, in the thickest of the fight.

The American casualties so far as reported, were one hundred and eighteen men killed, wounded and missing. The British casualties were seventy-five.

La Fayette withdrew to Malvern Hill to rest his troops, and Cornwallis hastened his departure for Suffolk and Portsmouth. Tarleton claims that Cornwallis could have destroyed La Fayette's army by a vigorous pursuit that night, or the following morning; but he fails to harmonize such a project with obedience to General Clinton's orders, and does not strengthen his reflection upon his commanding officer by stating the fact that the troops did not go to New York, at last. Lord Cornwallis obeyed orders; and could not read the future as Lieutenant-colonel Tarleton interpreted the *past*.

The following order received July twelfth by the Orpheus frigate, certainly must have convinced Lord Cornwallis that he would have committed a fatal error if he had followed the advice of Tarleton:

"NEW YORK, *July 1st*, 1781.

"MY LORD: For reasons which I think it unnecessary to mention to you by this opportunity, I request that whatever troops, etc. your Lordship may have embarked for this place, may sail forty-eight hours after the departure from the Chesapeake of the frigate which carries this letter; and which has orders to return whenever your Lordship signifies to the captain of her, that the troops, etc. are all on board and ready to proceed on the intended service.

"I have the honor to be, etc.,

"H. CLINTON."

This order needs no comment.

On the ninth of July, Lieutenant-colonel Tarleton left Cobham with orders to ravage the country as far as New Haven, in Bedford county, to destroy a depot of supplies supposed to be at Prince Edward Court House, to intercept any British prisoners or American light troops, returning to the northward from Greene's army; and then to retire at his leisure to Suffolk. This expedition was gone fifteen days, marched four hundred miles, and is thus described by Tarleton: "The stores destroyed, either of a public or private nature, were not in quantity or value, equivalent to the damage sustained in the skirmishes on the route, and the loss of men and horses by the excessive heat of the climate. The stores which were the principal object of the expedition had been conveyed from Prince Edward Court House and all that quarter of the country, to Hillsborough and General Greene's army, upwards of a month before the British light troops began their movement." Reference is again made to map, which is compiled from a recent military map of Virginia, prepared by the United States Engineer Corps, and that which accompanies Tarleton's narrative.

During this incursion, Cornwallis, having forwarded to Portsmouth such troops as were designed for New York, awaited the return of Tarleton at Suffolk.

On the twentieth of July, at one o'clock A. M., Brigadier-major Bowers placed in the hands of General Cornwallis a dispatch in cipher from Sir Henry Clinton, dated July 11th, 1781. The following is an extract : " If you have not already passed the James River, you will continue on the Williamsburg neck until the frigate arrives with my dispatches by Captain Stapleton. If you have passed and find it expedient to recover that station you will please do it, and keep possession until you hear from me. Whatever troops may have been embarked by you for this place are likewise to remain until further orders ; and if they should have been sailed, and within your call, you will be pleased to stop them." This dispatch is cited to show authority for detention of the troops. The entire files of dispatches between Generals Clinton and Cornwallis support the movement actually made by Lord Cornwallis to Yorktown, and it was absolutely his only policy, in view of the fact that General Clinton refused to entertain his proposition to abandon Virginia wholly, so long as it was not to be held in force aggressively. In justice to both, it is not too much to say in homely phrase that each had his hands full of responsibility, while there was but one hand full of resources to meet the demand. New York or Yorktown, Clinton or Cornwallis had to suffer. Cornwallis the man of field duty, exposure and trial, was the victim of these inadequate resources. In this the final disaster, he lost no honor, and in his fate, England, then struggling with the civilized world, lost no glory.

On the first of August, Cornwallis proceeded by water to Yorktown, the main body of the army following, and executing the movement by the fourth. On the sixth, Tarleton sailed to Hampton, threw his horses into deep water near shore, landed without loss, and joined Cornwallis on the seventh. General O'Hara's division remained at Portsmouth to destroy the works, and on the twenty-second the British army was concentrated at Yorktown and Gloucester Point, just across the river.

On the thirteenth of August, General La Fayette established his headquarters in the forks of the Pamunky and Mattaponey rivers, from which place he detached light troops to the rear of Gloucester to anticipate any attempt of his adversary to march north, and General Wayne was sent across the James River, demonstrating beyond Suffolk and near Portsmouth, for the purpose of anticipating an attempt of Cornwallis to retreat into North Carolina. He gives as an additional reason for this policy, the belief, that in case the promised fleet of Count de Grasse should arrive, he would thus be able to coöperate more promptly, and if not, that he would be so situated as to occupy Portsmouth, and prevent the escape of Cornwallis by sea in case that officer should attempt to return to that post and embark for New York.

Repeated skirmishes took place. While the British army was fortifying the two posts, Simcoe was actively engaged with La Fayette's light troops in front of Gloucester, and Tarleton made repeated excursions toward Williamsburg, where the American advance guard was established.

These movements were made with extreme caution. On the eighth of August, La Fayette wrote to Washington, " We shall act agreeably to circumstances, but avoid drawing ourselves into a false movement, which, if cavalry had the command of the rivers, would give the enemy the advantage of us. His lordship plays so well, that no blunder can be hoped from him, to recover a bad step of ours. . . . Should a fleet come in at this moment our affairs would take a very happy turn."

On the twenty-first he again wrote, " We have hitherto occupied the forks of York River, thereby looking both ways. Some militia have prevented the enemy's parties from remaining any time at or near Williamsburg, and false accounts have given them some alarm. Another body of militia under Colonel Ennis has kept them pretty close in Gloucester town and foraged in their vicinity. . . . In the present state of affairs, my dear general, *I hope you will come yourself to Virginia.* Lord Cornwallis must be attacked with pretty great apparatus ; but when a French fleet takes possession of the bay and rivers, and we form a land force superior to his, that army must sooner or later be forced to surrender, as we may get what reinforcements we please. I heartily thank you for having ordered me to remain in Virginia ; it is to your goodness that I am indebted for the most beautiful prospect which I may ever behold."

On the thirtieth, the Count de Grasse arrived in Chesapeake Bay with twenty-six ships of the line, besides frigates and transports. The British frigate Guadaloupe, 28, which had started with dispatches for New York, was forced to return to Yorktown, and the Loyalist, 20, stationed in the bay, was captured.

On the third of September the Count de St. Simon landed at Jamestown Island with three thousand two hundred French troops and was joined by La Fayette at Green Spring on the same day. On the fifth the allies occupied Williamsburg, about fifteen miles from Yorktown.

The Count de Grasse had a limited period for operations on the American coast, and united with Count de St. Simon in urging an immediate attack upon Yorktown while its defenses were incomplete, the latter waiving seniority and proposing to serve under La Fayette. This officer, writing to Washington, on the arrival of the fleet, which had been met by one of his officers upon making Cape Henry, says, " I am not so hasty as the Count de Grasse, and think that having so sure a game to play, it would be madness, by the risk of an attack, to give anything to chance. Unless matters are very different from what I think they are, my opinion is, that we ought to be contented with preventing the enemy's forages, with militia, without committing our regulars. Whatever readiness the Marquis de St. Simon has been pleased to express to Colonel Gimat respecting his being under me, I shall do nothing without paying that deference which is due to age, talents and experience ; but would rather incline to the cautious line of conduct I have of late adopted." " I hope you will find we have taken the best precautions to lessen his lordship's (Cornwallis') escape. I hardly believe he will make the attempt. If he does, he must give up ships, artillery, baggage, part of the horses, all the negroes; must be certain to lose the third of his army, and run the greatest risk to lose the whole, without gaining that glory which he may derive from a brilliant defense." *Again*, "September eighth," "If you knew how slowly things go on in this country ! ! The governor does what he can ; the wheels of government are so rusty that no governor whatever will be able to set them free again. Time will prove that Mr. Jefferson has been too severely charged." . . . "We will try, if not dangerous, upon a large scale, to form a good idea of the works; but unless I am greatly deceived, there will be madness in attacking them now, with our force. Marquis de St. Simon, Count de Grasse and General Du Portail agree with me in opinion; but should Lord Cornwallis come out against such a position as we have, everybody thinks that he can not but repent of it ; and should he beat us, he must soon prepare for another battle."

During this period Lord Cornwallis had seriously entertained a purpose of attacking the allied army and made a careful reconnoissance to ascertain its position and force. Lieutenant-colonel Tarleton in his narrative, more than once intimates that Lord Cornwallis had no right to depend upon the assurances contained in the dispatches of General Clinton, as being positive promises to furnish aid, and says, "England must lament the inactivity of the king's troops, whether it proceeded from the noble Earl's misconception, or from the suggestions of confidential attendants, who construed the Commander-in-chief's letters into a definite promise of relief." The dispatches quoted on pages 623 and 631 are the basis for the opinion of Lord Cornwallis and for the intimations of Lieutenant-colonel Tarleton. He also argues that "Lord Cornwallis must have known the superiority of the French naval force, which General Clinton could not have known, when he wrote his dispatches." This position ignores the fact that the aggregate British naval force on the American coast was supposed to be superior to that of France, although divided, and unfortunate circumstances combined to prevent its concert of action. This was beyond the control of both Generals Clinton and Cornwallis. The letters of General La Fayette, already cited, show that he was conducting the campaign with reference to just such a movement as Lieutenant-colonel Tarleton advised, and that its promise of success was small.

It is no injustice to Tarleton or Clinton, to state, that their entire correspondence and discussion upon the events of the war, partakes of the nature of personal controversy, and the conclusions are very often unjust to others, rarely to themselves.

The time was at hand for the arrival of Washington himself. Before entering upon that portion of the narrative, a brief statement of the naval movements which involved such confusion of British opinion and realized such determining consequences, is properly in place.

Just after the arrival of reinforcements for General Clinton, already noticed, the Count de Barras, under date of May eleventh, informed Washington that the Count de Grasse, then in the West Indies, expected to leave Cape Francois for the Chesapeake, with from twenty-five to twenty-nine sail of the line, and three thousand two hundred soldiers; but that such were his engagements with land and naval forces of Spain, then in the West Indies, that he must return by the middle of October. These facts materially changed the plan of campaign. New York had been the objective of attack, according to the original purpose of General Washington, although not favored by General Rochambeau or the French government. There were too many contingencies which rendered any permanent French naval superiority at New York uncertain, if not impossible.

Washington promptly notified La Fayette, by letter of August fifteenth, of the change of plan, and explained to that officer the importance of controlling all avenues of escape, so that a concentrated movement could be made against Lord Cornwallis. It has been seen that General La Fayette was of full accord in opinion, and equal to the duty. The Count de Barras, commanding the French squadron at the north, consisting of seven ships of the line, was the senior of Count de Grasse, and had discretionary authority from the Marshal de Castries, French Minister of Marine, to cruise for British ships off the Banks of Newfoundland; but he waived rank and independent command, and by this prompt exposure of his small fleet and a well-planned voyage, contributed greatly to the final result. Admiral Rodney commanding the British naval force in the West Indies, learned of the proposed movement of Count de Grasse, and detached Sir Samuel Hood with fourteen ships of the line to intercept him. The French force sent to the American coast was greater than under the existing circumstances he could have anticipated. Admiral Rodney presented the facts fully, during November and December, 1781, before the House of Commons, but the discussion is immaterial, although he had Burke as his censor. The defense of Admiral Graves, who succeeded Admiral Arbuthnot at New York, equally discloses one simple fact, which is the *material* fact, that the French fleet was equal to cope with any which it might meet, and Count de Grasse was wise in thus increasing his squadron. The British fleet, so detached from the West India squadron, anticipated that it had only to supplement the New York and Newport fleets, and was not equal to the demand. Failure in concert of action brought additional disappointment.

Admiral Hood sailed for America, crossed the mouth of Chesapeake Bay just before the arrival of Count de Grasse, without entering it; looked into Delaware Bay and sailed for New York, where he arrived August twenty-eighth, and reported to Admiral Graves. That officer had but five ships of the line ready for sea; but upon advices that Count de Barras had certainly started from Newport for the Chesapeake, he took command of the entire squadron, and promptly sailed with nineteen ships of the line, on the last of August. On the fifth of September he passed within the capes without knowledge of the presence of a superior adversary force. The French fleet was weakened by the absence of seventeen hundred seamen who were up James River, and upon first intimation that a squadron was in the offing, Count de Grasse supposed it to be the squadron of Count de Barras. The right wing, however, moved promptly out of the bay *southward*, followed from Lynn Bay by the remaining ships as they could slip anchor and make headway. The fleets manœuvered for five days without coming to a general action, but with several sharp encounters. The French casualties were two hundred and twenty killed and wounded, and the English were three hundred and thirty-six. Several ships suffered considerable damage. Meanwhile, see map "Operations in Chesapeake Bay," Admiral Barras entered the bay from the north with seven ships of the line, fourteen transports and a supply of siege guns, which were of vital importance to the allied army. Admiral Graves again entered the bay; but being advised of the arrival of Count de Barras and apprehending danger to his fleet from the lateness of the season, with no fair prospect of an engagement on equal, or even fair terms, he sailed for New York.

Such was the condition of affairs when Washington reached La Fayette's headquarters. The French fleet numbered thirty-five ships of the line, and no hostile squadron was in sight.

It is a fact to be noticed, that during the war of 1775–1781, these naval operations in Chesapeake Bay brought together one of the heaviest naval armaments known to maritime warfare, the opposing squadrons numbering fifty-two ships of the line when Admiral Graves sailed for New York.

La Fayette in Virginia.

American Forces
British.

Compiled and Drawn by Col. Carrington.

616*

Lafayette in Virginia

American Commanders
LAFAYETTE

WAYNE   MUHLENBERG   STEUBEN

On the 18th of March, 1781, General Greene wrote thus, to Washington: "Could the Marquis (Lafayette) join us at this moment, we should have a glorious campaign. It would put Lord Cornwallis and his whole army into our hands."

On the 25th of April, Cornwallis left Wilmington, for Virginia, and Lafayette, who had reached Richmond, on the 29th, by a forced march from Baltimore, made plans, if reenforced in time, to anticipate the march of Cornwallis, and cut him off from union with Phillips. The reenforcements, seven hundred veterans, under Wayne, had been started southward by Washington, but were delayed in their march. On the 18th of May, Greene assigned Lafayette to the command in Virginia, but to "send all reports to the commander-in-chief" On the 25th of May, Cornwallis was joined by Gen. eral Leslie, with 2,278 fresh troops, which increased his force to 7,000 men, and he wrote to General Clinton, that "he should proceed to dislodge Lafayette from Richmond."

British Commanders
CORNWALLIS

O'HARA   SIMCOE   TARLETON

PARALLEL NOTES

NOTE I.—The General Assembly adjourned to Charlottesville May 24th, and Cornwallis crossed James River at Westover, on the 25th, encamping his whole army at White Oak Swamp on the 27th, in order to take Richmond in rear. Lafayette, with a force less than one-third that of his adversary left the city northward, leading the British more than twenty miles.

NOTE II.—Cornwallis crossed the Chickahominy (see map), passed Hanover C. H., crossed the Pamunkey, then the North Anna, above New Found Creek, to head off the American column; but on the 29th, Lafayette still held the lead, crossed the North Anna, and was on his march to Spottsylvania Court House, in the supposed direction of Wayne's approach.

NOTE III.—Cornwallis dropped the pursuit, sent Tarleton to Charlottesville, to attempt a capture of the General Assembly, and marched to Byrd Creek, where he joined Simcoe, and also Tarleton, upon return of the latter from Charlottesville. The army, reunited, after forcing Steuben from his supply camp, at Elk Island, marched eastward, toward Richmond. Lafayette had been joined by Wayne, turned southward along Southwest Mountains, and by the 19th of June, when Steuben joined him, was marching parallel with the British army, the *pursued* having become the *pursuers*.

NOTE IV.—On the 23d of June, the American army had increased, by militia additions, to nearly 6,000 men, including 1,500 regulars. The British had abandoned Richmond on the 20th, and on the 25th, Lafayette so hotly pressed their columns at Williamsburg, that the entire British army moved out to protect its rear. Each army lost 30 men in the engagement.

On the 4th of July, the "Battle of Jamestown" was fought, the British losing 75, and the Americans 118; but Cornwallis crossed the James River, and Lafayette marched to Williamsburg and shut up the peninsula.

NOTE V.—On the 9th of July, Tarleton made a fruitless raid (see map) to New London, Bedford County, and then joined Cornwallis, who took post at Yorktown, August 4th. By the 22d, the entire British army had concentrated at Yorktown and Gloucester. Lafayette sent Wayne to cut off retreat, southward, and in urging Washington to come in person, and take command, concludes: "the British army must be forced to surrender. I heartily thank you for having ordered me to remain in Virginia. It is to your goodness that I am indebted for the most beautiful prospect I may ever behold."

MEM.—*The forced march to Richmond, skirmish at Williamsburg, the Battle of Jamestown and the weeks of rapid manœuvre, which wore out and shut up the army of Cornwallis, vindicate the confidence which Washington and Greene reposed in Lafayette; and the campaign, which Tarleton complimented in high terms, will stand, in history, as one of the most brilliant of the war.*

References:

CARRINGTON'S "BATTLES OF THE AMERICAN REVOLUTION," pp. 584–598.

School Histories:

Anderson, ¶ 110; p. 96.
Barnes, ¶ 2; p. 139.
Berard (Bush), ¶ —; p. —.
Goodrich, C.A. (Seaveys), ¶ 30, p. 141.
Goodrich, S. G., ¶ 1-2; p. 276.
Hassard, ¶ 9; p. 226.

Holmes, ¶ 12; p. 157.
Lossing, ¶ 13; p. 186.
Quackenbos, ¶ 400; p. 294.
Ridpath, ¶ 17; p. 226.
Sadlier (Excel), ¶ 23; p. 206.
Stephens, A.H. ¶ 15; p. 227-8.

Swinton, ¶ —; p. —.
Scott, ¶ —; p. —.
Thalheimer (Eclectic), ¶ —; p. —.
Venable, ¶ 167; p. 128.

CHAPTER LXXIV.

WASHINGTON AND ROCHAMBEAU. ARNOLD AT NEW LONDON.
FROM THE HUDSON TO YORKTOWN.

THE campaign of 1781 illustrated wise strategy, prompt logistics, and successful tactics, under circumstances of great difficulty. These can be appreciated only by constant reference to the whole theatre of war. The extent of coast, and the nature of the country behind that coast, are physical facts which enhance the value of the successes realized, and indicate the substantial aid which the United States received through the support of France. The British operations were predicated upon the control of American waters. New York was still the general base, and through the movements made in the middle and southern zones, which were carried on from Portsmouth and Charleston, the struggle was gradually coming to a simple issue with Lord Cornwallis, who had in turn commanded in each zone. La Fayette and Greene held nominal relations of mutual support; but neither could receive early information of the movements of the other, so as to act in full accord, and the information which was from time to time received, was so differently interpreted, that it was for a long time uncertain what were the real fruits of Camden, Cowpens and Guilford. The march of Lord Cornwallis into Virginia was the first emphatic fact which enabled General Washington to plan an efficient offensive. The repeated detachment of troops from New York so sensibly lessened the capacity of its garrison for extensive field service at the north, that the American Commander-in-chief determined to attack that post, and as a secondary purpose, thereby to divert General Clinton from giving further aid to troops in the Southern States. As a matter of fact, the prudent conduct of the Virginia campaign eventually rallied to the support of General La Fayette an army, including militia, nearly as large as that of Washington, and the nominal strength of the allied army near Yorktown, early in September was nearly or quite as great as that of Lord Cornwallis.

There were other elements which, as in previous campaigns, hampered operations at the north. The Indians were still troublesome in Western New York, and the Canadian frontier continued to demand attention. The American navy had practically disappeared. The scarcity of money and a powerless recruiting service, increased the difficulties of carrying on the war in a manner that would use to the best advantage the troops of France.

On the twenty-first of May, a military conference was held at Wethersfield, Connecticut, four miles south from Hartford, at which Generals Rochambeau and Chastellux on the part of the French army, met Washington for the purpose of determining a plan for the ensuing campaign. As the result of the interview, the Count de Rochambeau wrote to Count de Grasse, requesting him to send his fleet to act in coöperation with Count de Barras, and to close the port of New York. It has already been noticed that the Count de Grasse indicated his purpose to sail for the Chesapeake, but to return to the West Indies by the middle of October, and that the French government did not deem a movement upon New York as practicable. It is to be made prominent in this connection, as the key to the policy of France, that her navy was upon a foreign coast, that it was spared with difficulty from the West Indies, and that the burden of such an expedition would almost entirely rest upon her shoulders. With the exception of the Crimean war in 1854, if that indeed be an exception, there is hardly to be found in military annals a more cordial coöperation than that which characterized the navy and army of Louis XVI. in aid of the United States during the war of 1775–1781. The *immediate junction* of the two armies was first determined upon at Wethersfield, so as to be prepared for any good opportunity to begin operations. The American army, which exhibited an effective strength of less than forty-six hundred men, was ordered to Peekskill on the Hudson. The Count de Rochambeau with the Duke de Lauzun, marched from Newport, across the State of Connecticut and took post at Ridgebury. This was a small village near Salem, on the road to Danbury, about fifteen miles back from Long Island Sound. The *first* offensive design was to attack Morrisania, where Colonel Delancey's Refugees had their headquarters. This corps, both mounted and foot, was the terror of the region, and Westchester County became the field of their operations, as at its first organization in 1776. During one foray as far as the Croton River, a detachment had surprised a small post commanded by Colonel Christopher Green, already noticed for good conduct at Bunker Hill, Quebec and Red Bank, and he had been mistreated, with a severity which aroused the indignation of Washington and demanded punishment.

A *second* design to be concurrently attempted, was to seize the British posts at the north end of New York Island. Sheldon's dragoons and some continental troops were to coöperate with a French division under the Duke de Lauzun in the former enterprise, while General Lincoln was assigned to the command of a detachment of troops from the American army to prosecute the latter. This force was to descend the Hudson by boats, and the third of July was designated for both attacks. Governor Clinton of New York was advised of Washington's plan, so that he could concentrate the New York militia in case of success, and signal guns and fires had been prearranged, to give him notice of a favorable result. Washington, as a matter of fact, looked beyond the ostensible purpose of these orders, and hoped that a surprise of these posts would induce General Clinton to attempt their recapture, and thus bring on a general action between the armies. The reported detachment of a considerable foraging force from New York garrison into New Jersey also induced the belief that the English commander entertained no fears as to the safety of these detached posts, and that they would be but indifferently guarded.

General Lincoln left Peekskill with eight hundred men on the first of June, proceeded to Teller's Point, then took boats, and with muffled oars rowed down Tappan Sea at night. On the morning of the second, by hugging the eastern shore, he reached Dobb's Ferry without being discovered by the British. Washington moved at daylight, (about three o'clock in that latitude) without baggage, leaving his tents standing, passed through Tarrytown, and reached Valentine's Hill, four miles above Kings'Bridge, by sunrise of the third. He was thus in a good position to support and coöperate with either expedition.

General Lincoln crossed the Hudson in a small boat and landed at old Fort Lee, to reconnoitre the country opposite. He at once observed a British ship of war lying near the shore and that a large British camp had been established on the extreme north end of New York Island. A surprise of Fort Washington, or the outposts further up the island, was of course impossible. The troops previously sent to New Jersey had returned and reoccupied the British advance lines to the northward. General Lincoln left Peekskill with alternate orders, expressly providing for this emergency, and he at once recrossed the river, landed his troops just above Spuyten Duyvel Creek, near Old Fort Independence, and then occupied high ground near King's Bridge, so as to act in concert with the Duke de Lauzun, and cut off any detachment which might attempt to cross the Harlem to support Delancey. The Duke de Lauzun in the meanwhile had only reached East Chester. His troops had been wearied by a hot march over rough country and were several hours later than the time designated for the attack. The troops of General Lincoln were discovered by a foraging party of nearly fourteen hundred men, and a sharp skirmish ensued. The Duke de Lauzun heard the firing and marched to its relief. Washington had already marched, and upon his approach the British retired to New York Island. Washington reconnoitred the position during the afternoon, then fell back to Valentine's Hill, and on the next day to Dobb's Ferry, where Count de Rochambeau joined him on the sixth.

On the eighth, Sir Henry Clinton enclosed some intercepted letters of Washington to Cornwallis—stated that he was "threatened with a siege," and asked for "two thousand troops," adding, "the sooner they come the better."

Meanwhile the American camp had been established with its right on the Hudson, covered by earthworks, and its left across Saw Mill river. For locality, see map "Hudson River Highlands." The French army occupied the hills still further eastward, as far as the river Bronx.

General Washington, Count de Rochambeau, and Generals de Boville and Du Portail crossed to the Jersey Heights, and with a small escort of one hundred and fifty New Jersey troops, made examination of the New York Island outposts. This was immediately followed by a *reconnoissance in force*, of the entire British front, from King's Bridge down the Hudson River and along Hell Gate channel. The command consisted of five thousand men, in two divisions, respectively led by the Count de Chastellux and General Lincoln. The troops marched during the evening of July twenty-first, reached King's Bridge at daylight, and formed on the hills back of Fort Independence. Lauzun's Lancers and Sheldon's light infantry scoured the vicinity of Morrisania, and Sheldon's dragoons went as far as Throg's Neck. The Refugees fled to islands, to vessels, and to the woods. A few were captured, but Delancey himself having succeeded Major André as Adjutant-general, no longer remained at the headquarters of his old corps and was not exposed to capture. Generals Washington and Rochambeau, attended by a squadron of dragoons, then made a careful, ostentatious examination of all the British advance works, and the line of the Harlem, passing repeatedly under fire from vessels and pickets. By midnight of the twenty-third they returned to their encampment. Mr. Irving says, " The immediate effect of this threatening movement appears in a letter of Sir Henry Clinton to Cornwallis, dated July 26th," requesting him to order three regiments to New York from Carolina, writing, " I shall probably want them, as well as the troops you may be able to spare me from the Chesapeake, for such offensive or defensive operations as may offer in this quarter." Cornwallis had already ordered two of the European regiments, which could be spared during the inactive summer months, from Carolina to New York, and was " requested to renew the order." It has been seen in a previous chapter that Clinton had peremptorily and repeatedly ordered troops from Yorktown before the reconnoissance above referred to. Clinton's dispatches of June 8th, 11th, 13th, 19th and 28th, as well as of July 1st, are of this general character. In that of the 8th he thus suggestively limits the previous semi-independent command of Cornwallis. (That officer had directly consulted the Home War Office and had been supported in his suggestions.) " As your lordship is now so near, it will be unnecessary for you to send your dispatches immediately to the Minister ; you will therefore be so good as to send them to me in the future."

The position of the American Commander-in-chief at this time was one of peculiar personal mortification. Appeals to State authorities failed to fill up his army. Three thousand Hessian reinforcements had landed at New York, and the government as well as himself would be compromised before the whole world, by failure to meet the just demands which the French auxiliaries had a right to press upon his attention. Relief came most opportunely. The frigate Concorde arrived at Newport, and a reiteration of the purpose of Count de Grasse to leave St. Domingo on the third of August, for the Chesapeake direct, was announced by a special messenger.

The possibilities of the future at once quickened him to immediate action. With a reticence so close, that the army could not fathom his plans, he re-organized his forces for a *false demonstration* against New York and a *real movement* upon Yorktown. The excellent Logistics of La Fayette's march in February, were to be equaled by the energy and favoring circumstances which attended the progress of the allied

armies under the personal direction of Washington.   Letters to the
Governors of northern States called for aid as if to capture New York.
Letters to La Fayette and the Count de Grasse embodied such intimations of his plans as would induce proper caution to prevent the
escape of Lord Cornwallis, and secure transportation at Head of Elk.
Other letters to authorities in New Jersey and Philadelphia, expressly
defining a plan of operations against New York *via* Staten Island,
with the assurance of ample naval support, were exposed to intercep-
tion and fell into the hands of General Clinton.

As late as the nineteenth, the roads leading to King's Bridge were
cleared of obstructions, and the army was put in readiness to advance
against New York Island.   On the same day the New Jersey regiment and that of Colonel Hazen crossed the Hudson at Dobb's Ferry,
to threaten Staten Island, and ostensibly to cover some bake-houses
which were being erected for the purpose of giving color to the show
of operations against New York.   The plan of a large encampment
had been prepared, which embraced Springfield and the Chatham
Pass to Morristown, and this was allowed to find its way to Clinton's
headquarters.   General Heath was assigned to command of the Hud-
son-river posts, with two regiments from New Hampshire, ten from
Massachusetts, five from Connecticut, the Third artillery, Sheldon's
dragoons, the invalid corps, all local companies, and the militia.

The following forces were selected to accompany the Commander-
in-chief, viz., the light infantry under Colonel Scammel, four light companies from New York and Connecticut, the Rhode Island regiment,
under the new army establishment, two New York regiments, that of
New Jersey and Hazen's regiment, (the last two already across the
Hudson) and Lamb's artillery, in all about two thousand men.

The American troops crossed on the twenty-first, at King's Ferry,
and encamped near Haverstraw.   The French army followed, and
the army was united on the twenty-fifth.   During the delay in the
passage of the troops, Count de Rochambeau accompanied General
Washington to a final inspection of West Point ; and the headquarters at New Windsor, between that post and Newburgh, were substantially abandoned.

The American army marched promptly toward Springfield on the
Rahway, and the French army for Whippany, toward Trenton.   The
American train was accompanied by bateaux on wheels, as if to cross
more promptly to Staten Island, and Washington thus states his object : " That much trouble was taken, and finesse used, to misguide

and bewilder Sir Henry Clinton in regard to the real object, by ficti-
tious communications as well as by making a deceptive provision of
ovens, forage and boats in his neighborhood, is certain. Nor were
less pains taken to deceive our own army, for I had always conceived
when the imposition does not completely take place at home, it would
never sufficiently succeed abroad."

General Washington and suite reached Philadelphia about noon,
August thirtieth. The army had already realized the fact that they
were destined southward. Some dissatisfaction was manifested; but
Count de Rochambeau advanced twenty thousand dollars in gold
upon the pledge of Robert Morris that he would refund the sum by
the first of October, and the effect upon the troops, who had long
been without *any* pay, was inspiring. The arrival of Colonel John
Laurens from France, (reaching Boston on the twenty-fifth,) was a
source of still deeper satisfaction. He brought clothing, ammunition,
and half a million of dollars in cash, as a part of six millions of livres,
$1,111,111, generously furnished by Louis XVI. Additional sums
were pledged. Dr. Franklin had secured a loan of four millions of
livres, $740,740 to cover American drafts, before the arrival of Colonel
Laurens, and Count de Vergennes had agreed to guarantee a loan in
Holland for ten million livres, $1,851,851 more.

On the second of September the American army made its third
glad entry into Philadelphia, and was received with enthusiasm. On
the next day the French army, after a brief halt to clean uniforms
and accoutrements, made its brilliant passage through the American
capital. Their rich foreign uniforms contrasted with the faded clothing of the column that had passed the day before. The whole population again mingled all tokens of congratulation and joy; but there
was no time for protracted honors. The plainly equipped detachment
of Washington's veterans, however, lost no credit, according to the
French authorities, in the steadiness of their march and their fitness
for battle.

Dispatches here received from General La Fayette, dated on the
twenty-first of August, informed General Washington that "the
British troops were fortifying Gloucester"—that "a small garrison
still remained at Portsmouth"—that he "had written to the Governor to collect six hundred militia upon Blackwater"—"to General
Gregory near Portsmouth, that he had an account that the enemy
intended to push a detachment to Carolina,"—to General Wayne "to
move to the southward and be ready to cross the James at West-

over," and that "the army would soon assemble again upon the waters of the Chickahominy." This letter has been previously noticed, for other extracts. He had advised General Washington of the occupation of Yorktown, in a letter dated August eighth. Up to this time no further intelligence had been received of the movements of the Count de Grasse.

On the second of September, while the American army was marching through Philadelphia, Sir Henry Clinton sent a courier vessel to Yorktown, with the following dispatch: (*Clinton* to *Cornwallis*) "September second, 1781." (In cypher.) Received fifteenth September. "Mr. Washington is moving an army to the southward with an appearance of haste, and gives out that he expects the coöperation of a considerable French armament. Your lordship, however, may be assured, that if this should be the case, I shall either endeavor to reinforce the army under your command by all the means within the compass of my power, or make every possible diversion in your favor."

" P. S. Washington, it is said, was to be at Trenton this day, and means to go in vessels to Christiana Creek, and from thence, by Head of Elk, down Chesapeake, in vessels also. . . . Washington has about four thousand French and two thousand rebel troops with him."

On the fifth of September, General Washington started for Head of Elk. He had just passed Chester when a courier met him with dispatches which announced the arrival of the Count de Grasse. He returned to Chester to advise Count de Rochambeau of the news, and moved directly on, reaching Head of Elk the next morning. This dispatch reached Philadelphia during a banquet given by the French officers to the Chevalier de Luzerne, accompanied by the additional announcement of the landing of Count de St. Simon, and his junction with La Fayette. The day had closed with a review of the French army, which had been attended by the President of Congress; and the city was thrilled with fresh pride and hope, as these successive excitements came in to brighten the national life. On the day that Washington arrived at Head of Elk, Sir Henry Clinton sent the following dispatch to Lord Cornwallis:

" *Clinton* to *Cornwallis*, Sept. sixth, at noon. (In cypher.) (Received sixteenth September):

"As I find by your letters that De Grasse has got into the Chesapeake, and I have no doubt that Washington is moving with, at least six thousand French and rebel troops against you, I think the best way to relieve you, is to join you, as soon as possible, with all the force that can be spared from here, which is about four thousand men. *They are already embarked*, (Italics not in the original), and will proceed the instant I receive information from the admiral that we may venture ; or that from other intelligence the commodore and I should judge sufficient to move upon. By accounts from Europe we have every reason to expect Admiral Digby hourly on the coast."

(This sixth day of September was La Fayette's twenty-fourth birthday.)

On the same day a British force from New York landed in New England.

As soon as General Clinton found that Washington had moved against Cornwallis, he attempted to check his march by an invasion of Connecticut ; and this was intrusted to the command of General Benedict Arnold. It was his native State, and he had become an object of as intense hatred as he had formerly commanded homage. No possible selection could have been more injudicious, as a matter of military policy, not excepting that of Tarleton or Simcoe ; and no man was better prepared by his antecedents to move wherever he could safely destroy life and property, regardless of restraint. The man whom Phillips and Cornwallis could not associate with, except officially, and whom Clinton endured under the pressure of past fraternity in his treason, was just the man whom Washington could safely leave to the care of the citizens and militia of New England. Any temporary success would only insure his destruction. A wild animal could commit ravage, but an aroused people would master him at last. So with Arnold. It was a very grave error to presume that he, of all men, could affect the movements of Washington and Rochambeau. If Clinton had taken the garrison of New York, or half of it, into the field, he would have aided, possibly have saved, Cornwallis.

The expedition of Arnold consisting of the Thirty-eighth, one hundred Yagers, the Third battalion of New Jersey volunteers, the loyal Americans, American Refugees and artillerists, and three six pounders and one howitzer, left New York September fourth, and landed on both sides of New London harbor early on the sixth. Captain Beasley's report to the admiral states that it was about half past six when the vessels entered the harbor ; and according to Arnold's report the landing was effected about nine o'clock. Reference is made to map " Benedict Arnold at New London." This expedition was for pur-

40

poses of plunder and desolation, without anticipation of battle. Arnold landed on the west side, so as to enter the town. " An unfinished mere breastwork or water battery," as Hampstead styles it, called Fort Trumbull, almost open, landward, was the only defensive work, except a small redoubt on higher ground in the rear, called Fort Folly or Fort Nonsense. Fort Trumbull was occupied by Captain Adam Shopley's detachment of State troops, less than thirty strong, usually stated at twenty-three or four men besides himself. Arnold detached Captain Willett with four companies of the Thirty-eighth to occupy Fort Trumbull, and advanced directly upon the town. Captain Willett's force was joined by one hundred and twenty American Refugees, under Captain Frink, who had been sent by Lieutenant-colonel Upham from Fort Franklin, a stockade fort at Lloyd's Neck, Simcoe's old headquarters on Long Island, nearly opposite New London. " During the previous year, 1780, there had been organized on Long Island a *Board of Associated Loyalists*, including such persons as would aid the king, but declined a regular military service. It provoked frightful collisions with citizens of opposite sentiments, and some of the more barbarous minor operations of civil war. During July, 1781, Admiral Barras sent a detachment of troops from Newport, with three frigates, to reduce Fort William, then garrisoned by nearly eight hundred Refugees, but abandoned the enterprise after the capture of some British marines at Huntington Bay. Lossing states that the association was dissolved late in 1781, because of the manifest mischief it was working to the royal cause."

Captain Shopley's men delivered one volley, disabling four or five of the assailants, and abandoned the fort, taking boats for Fort Griswold. One boat was shattered by a nine pounder ball, but about twenty of his men safely joined the other garrison. Arnold met with only a nominal resistance from hastily armed citizens, there being no considerable military force in the vicinity.

The right wing, under Lieutenant-colonel Eyer, landed back of Pine Island, and marched in two divisions, the Fifty-fourth and Fortieth regiments respectively leading each. The New Jersey Volunteers and artillery who landed last, were in the rear, and fell behind, while making the circuit of some swampy ground, so that they did not reach the summit of the hill upon which Fort Griswold rested until after the storming party gained possession of the rampart. As soon as Arnold secured possession of Fort Trumbull, he noticed that " the shipping in the harbor was actively engaged in preparations to retire up the Norwich River " (Norwich, only thirteen miles distant, was Arnold's birth-place), and thus states the case in his report: " I found the enemy's ships would escape, unless we could possess ourselves of Fort Griswold. From information I received, before and after my landing, I had reason to believe that Fort Griswold, on Groton side, was very incomplete; and I was assured by friends to government, after my landing, that there were only twenty or thirty men in the fort, the inhabitants in general being on board the ships and busy in saving their property. I therefore dispatched an officer to Lieutenant-colonel Eyer, with the intelligence I had received, and requested him to make an attack on the fort as soon as possible; at which time I expected the howitzer was up, and would have been made use of. On my gaining a height of ground in the rear of New London from which I had a good prospect of Fort Griswold, I found it much more formidable than I expected, or I had formed an idea of from the information I had before received. I observed at the same time that the men who had escaped from Fort Trumbull had crossed in boats and had thrown themselves into Fort Griswold, and a favorable wind springing up about this time, the enemy's ships were escaping up the river, notwithstanding the fire from Fort Trumbull and a six-pounder I had brought with me. I immediately dispatched a boat, with an officer, to Lieutenant-colonel Eyer to countermand my first order; but the officer arrived a few minutes too late. After a most obstinate defense of near forty minutes, the fort was carried by the superior bravery and perseverance of the assailants."

The character of Arnold's incursion is indicated by his confidence that he was to meet with no serious opposition and courted none. While he was watching Fort Griswold, the Fortieth and Fifty-fourth were storming its works. The outline of this work, with a small advanced redoubt, connected with a covered way, is correctly given on the map, and any visitor, as late as 1876, could trace the steep parapet, to the south, the bastions, the deep ditch, and even examine the old well, and the triangular breastwork which guarded the entrance. A small knoll near by, Avery's Hill or Ledge, was the rendezvous for the assailants, who did not wait for their artillery, but with eager confidence, after gathering their forces, were ready to advance to the assault. The position was strong; but its defenders were few. The small reinforcement from Fort Trumbull did not make the garrison more than one hundred and sixty all told. It was a severe test for the handful of men who saw the approaching regulars, who knew that the opposite shore was already in British possession and that their lives were to be imperiled, seemingly, for honor's sake. But a successful defense might reverse the whole issue. New London had then not been fired. The only possible point of resistance was Fort Griswold. Success would drive the British right wing to their ships.

According to Arnold's report, when his messenger reached Lieutenant-colonel Eyer, " he had already sent Captain Beckwith with a flag to demand a surrender." Captain Shopley received the flag, according to the statements contained in Lieutenant Stephen Hamstead's narrative and the equally interesting work of Miss Caulkins, compiled from the statements of survivors of the assault. *At first,* " a council of war unanimously voted that the garrison was *unable* to defend themselves against so superior a force." "Colonel Nathan Gallup of the Groton militia, who was present, insisted however, that he could procure a reinforcement of two or three hundred militia, *in fifteen minutes,* if the garrison would hold out; and Lieutenant-colonel Ledyard was unfortunately misled by these assurances, and returned, through Captain Shopley, an answer, declining to comply with the order. Unfortunately the Colonel failed to meet with that success which he expected—his men *offered to meet the enemy in the field, but peremptorily declining to enter the fort to fight against such great odds with no chance to escape.*"

As a *fair, unsuccessful* resistance involved, ordinarily, only a fair surrender, and as only such men as could be readily rallied could participate in the defense, it is evident that the quotation made can not be precisely historical. Militia would have preferred the fort to the exposure of Groton Hill. Barber, in his Historical Collections, states that " on the advance of the enemy Colonel Ledyard, having but one hundred and fifty men with him in the fort, sent out an officer to get assistance, as there were a number of hundreds of people collected in the vicinity; this officer by drinking too much, became intoxicated, and no reinforcement was obtained."

The defense of Fort Griswold during the afternoon of September sixth, 1781, was correctly characterized by Arnold as "most obstinate." His officially reported loss, viz., "one major, one captain, one lieutenant, two ensigns, two sergeants and forty rank and file killed; and one lieutenant-colonel, two captains, one lieutenant, one ensign, eight sergeants, two drummers and one hundred and twenty-seven rank and file wounded, total of casualties one hundred and sixty-three," and exceeding the number of the garrison, indicates the character of the resistance.

The battle was short, and is briefly stated. The storming parties on the south and south-east were compelled to pass a deep ditch and climb an embankment at least twelve feet in height. The storming party from the east eventually pressed through three embrasures or deep cuts in the rampart flanking the salient angle, for which there were, so far as known, no guns. The first repulse was complete and with great slaughter. The second assault crowned the parapet, and from the moment the troops leaped into the small area of the parade, there was indiscriminate butchery. All that the American militia did at King's Mountain, and all that Tarleton did to avenge his defeat at Cowpens, was summed up in the punishment of the garrison of Fort Griswold for their obstinate defense. There is no redeeming feature which history can recognize. The larger portion of the British casualties occurred outside of the fort, when they were on the trying advance, and they could not, and no troops could, inflict great loss upon active opponents firing from the cover of short pickets, supermounting the parapet. The authorities are conclusive that the American loss was insignificant until the British troops occupied the works and the garrison had practically yielded the contest.

Arnold says "eighty-five men were found dead in Fort Griswold, and sixty wounded, most of them mortally." He adds, "I believe we have about seventy prisoners besides the wounded, who are paroled." This included both sides of the river. He says "their (the American) loss on the other side (the New London side) must have been considerable; but can not be ascertained."

"Lieutenant-colonel Eyer and three other officers of the Fifty-fourth were wounded. Major Montgomery was killed by a spear in entering the enemy's works, and Major Broomfield succeeded to the command."

The gate of the fort was opened by order of Lieutenant-colonel Ledyard; and Lieutenant-colonel Buskirk, of the New Jersey Volunteers, arrived in time to participate in the closing scene, so that the wanton slaughter of Ledyard after he surrendered his sword is to be charged to the memory of an American loyalist, and *not to a British regular officer*. When once this work began, the wounded were not spared and the tragedy was complete.

Meanwhile Arnold was actively engaged in less dangerous work. He says "ten or twelve ships were burned, and one loaded with naval stores, among the former, the cargo of the Hannah, Captain Watson, from London, lately captured by the enemy. The whole of which was burned with the stores, which proved to contain a large quantity of powder unknown to us. The explosion of the powder and the change of wind soon after the stores were fired, communicated the flames to part of the town, which was, notwithstanding effort to prevent it, unfortunately destroyed." Sixty-five dwellings, thirty-one stores and warehouses, eighty ships, twenty barns, a meeting-house, court-house, jail, the market and custom-house were among the trophies which ended the military achievements of Benedict Arnold, and passed him over to the care of universal history.

His daring spirit was indeed fretted by repeated injustice, but his ungovernable temper almost invariably induced the occasion for his many disappointments. With the vindication of his valor at Saratoga, there must be as freely perpetuated, the inevitable doom which awaits a traitor.

From this episode of an important campaign the attention is at once diverted to operations which it did not embarrass.

While the allied army was waiting for additional transportation at Head of Elk, General Washington, accompanied by Count de Rochambeau, visited Baltimore, where they were received with illuminations and civil honors. On the ninth, accompanied by one staff officer, he visited, for the first time during six years, his home at Mount Vernon. On the tenth his own suite and Count de Rochambeau and suite became his guests. On the eleventh General Chastellux and aids-de-camp were added to the company. On the twelfth the hospitalities of the mansion yielded their claim to the behests of duty, and on the fourteenth day of September, 1781, the American Commander-in-chief reached the headquarters of General La Fayette at Williamsburg.

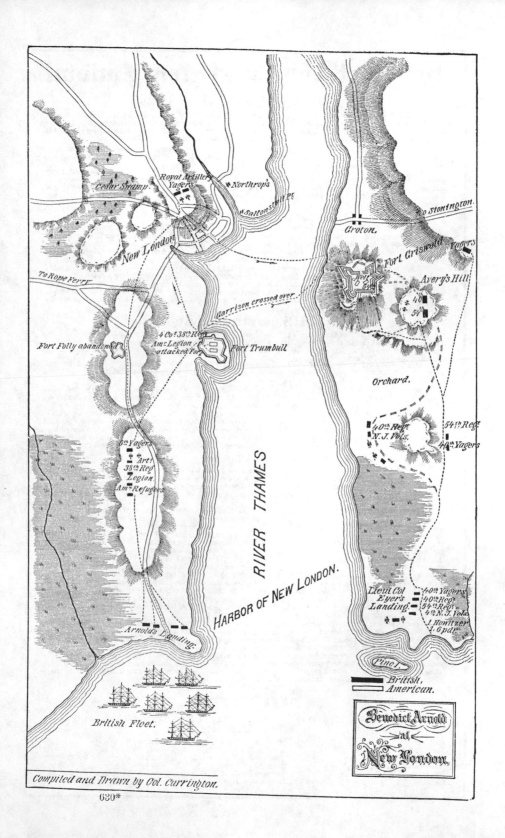

Cedar Swamp.

Royal Artillery Yagers.

Northrop's

New London.

Saltonstall Pt.

To Stonington.

Groton.

To Rope Ferry.

Fort Griswold. Yagers

Avery's Hill.

40 54

Garrison crossed over.

Fort Folly abandoned.

4 Cos 38th Regt. Ams Legion attacked Fort

Fort Trumbull.

Orchard.

40th Regt N.J. Vols.

54th Regt.

44th Yagers.

6th Yagers.
Artt.
38th Regt.
Legion.
Ams Refugees.

RIVER THAMES

HARBOR OF NEW LONDON.

Lieut Col Eyre's Landing.

40th Yagers
40th Regt.
54th Regt.
4 N.J. Vols.
1 Howitzer
1 6 pdr.

Arnold's Landing.

Pine I.

British.
American.

British Fleet.

Benedict Arnold at New London.

Compiled and Drawn by Col. Carrington.

630*

Benedict Arnold at New London

SEPTEMBER 6th, 1781

On the 6th day of September, 1781, the twenty-fourth birthday of Lafayette, and while Washington and Rochambeau were hastening to join the Army of Virginia, and consummate plans for the rescue of that Colony and the capture of Cornwallis, it was left to General Clinton to express his chagrin at thorough out-generalship, by a raid into Connecticut, under the traitor Arnold.

The expedition left New York, September 4th, and entered the harbor of New London, at half-past six in the morning, two days later. According to Arnold's Official Report, the landing was effected on both sides of the harbor, about nine o'clock, September 6th.

As a diversion, to annoy Washington, it was trifling; if so intended. He never swerved from general plans, for small local issues. As a military movement, it contemplated no battle, no substantial resistance ; and, while it might plunder and destroy, it could only intensify opposition to Great Britain As a matter or military policy, it was wretched, since Arnold, the traitor, was sent to lay waste his own birthplace.

New London Defences

FORT TRUMBULL, on the New London bank of the Thames River, was a mere breastwork, or water battery, almost open, landward. Just west of this, on high ground, a small redoubt had been established, but it bore the name, "Fort Folly," or "Fort Nonsense, and had no defenders, Fort Trumbull, itself, was occupied by not more than thirty men, State troops, under Captain Adam Shapley.

FORT GRISWOLD, which crowned the height on the east shore, was a well conceived redoubt, with parapet, bastions, a covered entrance, a well of water, and was supplemented by a small advanced redoubt, slightly down the hill, and this connected by a close passage with the main work. The garrison was less than 160 men, under Lieut. Colonel Ledyard. A small knoll, or ledge, called Avery's Hill, was to the northeast, but while not commanding the works, was a place for the lodgment of assailants. and was finally occupied by the invaders.

British Movements

ARNOLD conducted the left wing, or column, which burned the town. It consisted of 4 companies of the 38th regiment, under Captain Millett ; a detachment of Yagers, with two 6-pounder guns, a portion of the Legion of Loyal Americans, and 120 "American Refugees," under Captain Frink, from Long Island.

NOTE I.—Millett advanced upon Fort Trumbull, and received a volley which disabled several men; but the small command of Shapley, took boats for Fort Griswold, losing several men, in one boat, which was shattered by a ball, but joining its garrison.

NOTE II.—When Arnold reached New London, and saw the escape of Shapley, and the defensive condition of Fort Griswold, he sent orders to Lieut. Colonel Eyre, countermanding the movement on the east side; but too late, as the advance had been made. His own movements were confined to the unresisted destruction of property. He burned ten or twelve ships, with their stores, one of which, the Hannah, from London, recently captured as a prize by the Americans, contained powder. Arnold claimed that the fire which burned 65 dwellings, 35 stores and warehouses, 80 ships, 20 barns, a meeting-house, court-house, jail, market-house, and custom-house, was the result of the explosion of powder, and a change of wind, which "unfortunately destroyed, notwithstanding efforts to prevent it."

The Right Wing or Column

LIEUT. COL. EYRE landed, back of Pine Island, and advanced in two divisions, the 54th and 40th regiments, respectively, leading each. One gun and one howitzer accompanied the command. The right division was supported by a detachment of Yagers, and the left division, by New Jersey Volunteers ; but the last named fell behind, while making the circuit of swampy ground, and did not rejoin, until the storming party mounted the rampart.

CAPT. BECKWITH, who bore from Eyre to Ledyard, a demand for surrender of the fort, received, through Captain Shapley, the prompt rejection of terms. The prompt reenforcement of the fort by militia, who were available, and partially depended upon, in the debate as to the demand for surrender, might have assured a final repulse. Better defences than at Breed's Hill, in 1775, covered the defenders; but although Colonel Nathan Gallup, of the Groton militia, had faith in his ability to fill the fort with men, they would not consent to be enclosed by works, with no avenue for escape. The real battle was quickly fought. The storming parties on the south and southeast, were compelled to pass a deep ditch, and climb an embankment of twelve feet. Those from the east, entered through three embrasures in the rampart, flanking the salient angle. The Yagers passed around, nearly to the gate. The first repulse inflicted a slaughter of the assailants, greater than the number of the garrison. The *second assault* crowned the parapet. Eyre and three other officers had been wounded, and Major Montgomery was killed by a spear, so that Major Broomfield, a New Jersey Loyalist, took command in the final charge with bayonets. Lieut. Colonel Buskirk, of the New Jersey Volunteers, came up tardily, but participated in the assault.

Lieut. Colonel Ledyard ordered the gate opened, and, fairly surrendered the fort ; but nothing would satisfy the tory allies of the British troops, but wholesale slaughter of the brave defenders. Eighty-five men were found dead, and sixty were dangerously wounded. The American loss, up to the moment of a fair surrender, had been trifling.

The British loss was severe, having been officially reported as "one Major," one Captain, one Lieutenant, two Ensigns, two Sergeants, and forty rank and file killed ; and one Lieut. Colonel, two Captains, one Lieutenant, one Ensign, eight Sergeants, two drummers, and one hundred and twenty-seven wounded ; making total casualties, one hundred and sixty-three.

References:

CARRINGTON'S "BATTLES OF THE AMERICAN REVOLUTION," pp. 625-630

School Histories :

Anderson, ¶ 113 ; p. 97.	Holmes, ¶ 15 ; p. 158.	Swinton, ¶ —; p. —.
Barnes, ¶ *Note ;* p. 140.	Lossing, ¶ 15 ; p. 187.	Scott, ¶ 15 ; p. 215.
Berard (Bush), ¶ 137 ; p. 176.	Quackenbos, ¶ 400; p. 294.	Thalheimer (Eclectic), ¶ 295;
Goodrich, C.A.(Seaveys),¶ —; p. —.	Ridpath ¶ 5 ; p. 212.	p. 171-2.
Goodrich, S. G., ¶ 6 ; p. 271.	Sadlier (Excel),¶ —; p. —.	Venable, ¶ —; p. —.
Hassard, ¶ 7 ; p. 225.	Stephens, A.H.¶ —; p. —.	

CHAPTER LXXV.

SIEGE OF YORKTOWN. SURRENDER OF CORNWALLIS. CLOSE OF CAMPAIGN. 1781.

GOOD strategy before New York isolated Clinton; and equal strategy in Virginia and the Chesapeake isolated Cornwallis. The former, outgeneraled, could not overtake the American army by land,—could not divert its commanding general from the crowning objective of his campaign,—could not resolve to hazard something at his own post and throw the bulk of his army upon Philadelphia and the American rear; while to relieve Yorktown by sea required immediate action and the support of an adequate fleet. The following dispatch indicates the position of Lord Cornwallis:

(*Cornwallis* to *Clinton.*) "York, 16th September, 1781. In cypher. Dispatches of 2d and 6th (already noticed) acknowledged. The enemy's fleet has returned. Two line of battle ships, and one frigate, lie at the mouth of this river; and three or four line of battle ships, several frigates and transports, went up the bay on 12th and 14th. I hear Washington arrived at Williamsburg on the 14th. Some of his troops embarked at Head of Elk, and the others arrived at Baltimore on the 12th. If I had no hopes of relief, I would rather risk an action than defend my half finished works; but as you say Digby is hourly expected, and promise every exertion to assist me, I do not think myself justified in putting the fate of the war on so desperate an attempt. By examining the transports with care, and turning out useless mouths, my provisions will last six weeks from this day, if we can preserve them from accidents. The cavalry must, I fear, be all lost. I am of opinion, that you can do me no effectual service, but by coming directly to this place. Lieutenant Conway of this command is just exchanged. He assures me that since the Rhode Island squadron has joined they have thirty-six sail of the line. This place is in no state of defense. If you can not relieve me very soon, you must be prepared to hear the worst.

I have the honor to be, etc.,

CORNWALLIS."

The following dispatches are cited in this connection :

(*Clinton* to *Cornwallis*.) " New York, Sept. 24th, 1781. In cypher. (Received Sept. 29th, 1781). Foregoing dispatch acknowledged. At a meeting of the general and flag officers held this day, it was determined that above five thousand men rank and file, shall be embarked on board the king's ships, and the joint exertions of the army and navy made in a few days to relieve you, and afterwards to coöperate with you. The fleet consists of twenty-three sail of the line, three of which are three-deckers. There is every reason to hope we start from hence the 5th of October.

" P. S. Admiral Digby is this moment arrived at the Hook, with three sail of the line. As a venture, not knowing whether they can be seen by us, I request that if all is well, upon hearing a considerable firing towards the entrance of the Chesapeake, three large separate smokes may be made parallel to it, and if you possess the post of Gloucester, *four*. I shall send another runner soon."

The following dispatch was sent in reply :

" York, 10 P. M., Sept. 29th, 1781. In cypher. I have ventured these last two days to look General Washington's whole force in the face in their position on the outside of my works, and I have the pleasure to assure your excellency that there was but one wish throughout the whole army, which was that the enemy would advance. I have this evening received your letter of the 24th which has given me the greatest satisfaction. I shall retire this night within the works, and have no doubt if relief arrives in any reasonable time, York and Gloucester will be both in possession of His Majesty's troops. I believe your excellency must depend more on the sound of our cannon than the signal of smokes for information ; however, I will attempt it on the Gloucester side ; medicines are wanted."

(*Clinton* to *Cornwallis*.) " New York, Sept. 25th, 1781, (duplicate) in cypher, received October 2d. My Lord :—My letter of yesterday will have informed your lordship of the number of ships and troops we can bring with us. It is supposed the necessary repairs of the fleet will detain us here to the fifth of October and your lordship must be sensible that unforeseen accidents may lengthen it out a day or two longer; I therefore entreat you to lose no time in letting me know your real situation, and your opinion how upon our arrival we can best act to form a junction with you, together with the exact strength of the enemy's fleet, and what part of the Chesapeake they appear to be most jealous of. I have the honor to be, etc.,

H. CLINTON."

"P. S. As your lordship must have better intelligence than we possibly can have, I request you will send a trusty person to each of the capes about the seventh of next month, with every information respecting the force and situation of the enemy you may judge necessary, and directions to continue there until our arrival, when small vessels will be sent to bring off any person they may find there."

The following reply brings the correspondence of these officers up to the practical operations of the siege:

(*Cornwallis* to *Clinton*.) "Yorktown, Virginia, October 3d, 1781, in cypher. Sir:—I received your letter of the twenty-fifth September, last night. The enemy are encamped about two miles from us. On the night of the 30th of September they broke ground, and made two redoubts about eleven hundred yards from our works, which, with some works that had been constructed to secure our exterior position, occupy a gorge between two creeks which nearly embrace this post. They have finished these redoubts, and I expect they will go on with their works this night. From the time that the enemy have given us, and the uncommon exertions of the troops, our works are in a better state of defense than we had reason to hope. I can see no means of forming a junction with us but by York River; and I do not think that any diversion would be of any use to us. Our accounts of the strength of the French fleet have in general been, that they were thirty-five or six sail of the line; they have frequently changed their position; two ships of the line and one frigate lie at the mouth of this river, and our last accounts were, that the body of the fleet lay between the tail of the Horse-shoe and York-spit. And it is likewise said that four line of battle ships lay a few days ago in Hampton Road. I see little chance of my being able to send persons to wait for you at the capes, but I will if possible. I have the honor to be, etc.,

CORNWALLIS."

British Position. York or Yorktown, ten miles up York River, is situated upon the south or *right* bank (which was then quite a bluff,)

between two small creeks, which according to Cornwallis " nearly embraced the post." The British right rested on a swamp which bordered the creek, west of the town. Batteries one, two and three,
see map " Siege of Yorktown," covered this approach; and a large
redoubt, completely fraized and fronted by abatis, had been built upon
the bluff beyond this creek, westward, between the Williamsburg road
and the river. This redoubt was occupied by the Fusileers; and the
Guadaloupe, 28, frigate, lay at anchor off the mouth of the creek.
The east branch of this creek flowed through a deep ravine, or
"gorge," as Cornwallis styles it. It will be seen that any approach
to the town from the west or the front, was hardly practicable, and a
retreat of the garrison, by the same route, would be as difficult. To
the south-east, following the course of the river, was a large space of
solid surface cut into ravines, under cover of one of which the besiegers ultimately moved toward their second parallel, thus shortening
the zig-zag approaches. On the high ground in front of the great
ravine or gorge, the British had located several redoubts. It has
been seen that Lord Cornwallis abandoned them upon receipt of
Clinton's dispatch of the twenty-fourth. Tarleton severely criticises
the movement; but his opinion is to be associated with his other
opinion which favored an attack upon the American camp. He
entirely omits important considerations. To have retained the redoubts until they were assaulted would have demanded successful
resistance, since their defenders could not re-cross that ravine under
pressure. Cornwallis saved the garrisons by abandoning the works.
Their consequent occupation by the French was of value to the besiegers, because it brought them within easy range of fire, and the
ravine in turn protected them from any sally from the garrison. In
view of the whole situation, the natural approaches were from the
north-east, hence the redoubts five, six, seven and eight received
more care. Houses had been leveled, and a second line of trenches
had been placed in their rear, as a last defense. Two redoubts had
also been advanced into the open ground in front. The allied armies
made their regular siege approaches entirely upon this front.

Gloucester Point, across the river, a mile distant, had been first fortified. With swamps flanking both the retiring shores, there was
solid surface in front, and then for more than a mile the ground was
clear of woods.

American Position. On the day after General Washington's arrival at Williamsburg, he notified Count de Grasse that " such of the

American troops as found insufficient transportation at Head of Elk, were marching to Baltimore, to be put on board of transports that might be collected there, and requested assistance in this respect. In a postscript he remarks that "his wishes had been anticipated." Admiral Barras, who arrived on the tenth, had already sent ten transports from the squadron, two frigates captured in the recent naval action, and some other prize vessels, to move the troops. They embarked at Annapolis for James River.

On the seventeenth, General Washington, the Count de Rochambeau, General Knox, and General Du Portail embarked on the Queen Charlotte, and visited Count de Grasse on his flag-ship, the Ville de Paris, arriving on the eighteenth. They were received with appropriate honors, and confirmed their plans for conducting the siege. By reason of severe and contrary winds they did not regain Williamsburg until the twenty-second. The American Commander-in-chief was at once confronted with a question which threatened to destroy his well-laid plans. The arrival of Admiral Digby at New York with three ships of the line, reported at six, inclined Count de Grasse to re-unite his entire fleet, leave two vessels at the mouth of York, four frigates and some corvettes in the James, and then sail toward New York to intercept or engage the British fleet—*then* "to act in concert; but each on his side." An earnest appeal by La Fayette in person, persuaded the Count de Grasse to change his purpose and accept the judgment of the generals commanding the land forces. On the twenty-fifth, the remaining troops reached Williamsburg, making a total force of twelve thousand regular troops, besides militia, which exceeded four thousand men.

On the twenty-eighth, the entire army advanced and took a position within about two miles of the British advanced works, and on the twenty-ninth, after a thorough reconnoissance, the movement began for encircling the town and closing in upon its defenders. On the thirtieth it was found that Lord Cornwallis had withdrawn his troops from the front, and the allied lines were established in the general form of a semi-circle, with each extreme resting on the York River. During the skirmishing incident to reconnoitering service Colonel Scammel, whose services had greatly endeared him to the Commander-in-chief and to the army, was mortally wounded, taken prisoner, and carried into Yorktown. He was removed to Williamsburg by consent of Lord Cornwallis, but died on the sixth of October.

General Lincoln occupied the banks of Wormley's Creek, near

Moore's house, and the general arrangement of the other troops, before the active operations of the siege began, is indicated on the map.

On the Gloucester side, the Neck was occupied by the Duke de Lauzun with his legion of cavalry, and a body of Virginia militia under General Weedon. Eight hundred marines from the squadron of Count de Grasse landed on the first of October to reinforce the detachment. General de Cloisy was in command, and although repeated skirmishes ensued, no persistent efforts were made to break through the American lines, and the offensive action of the allies 'was limited to the confinement of the British troops to its defenses and the area in front of the works. On one occasion, while covering a foraging party, Colonel Tarleton was unhorsed. The British lost one officer and eleven men and the French Hussars lost two officers and fourteen men. The contradictory opinions expressed as to the merits of this skirmish are settled by Tarleton's own report of it, where he says: "A dragoon's horse of the British legion, plunged, on being struck with a spear, and overthrew Lieutenant-colonel Tarleton and his horse. This circumstance happening to occur so much nearer to the body of the French than the British cavalry, excited an apprehension in the latter for the safety of their commanding officer. Impelled by this idea the whole of the English rear set out in full speed from its distant situation, and arrived in such disorder that its charge was unable to make any impression upon the Duke de Lauzun's Hussars. Meanwhile Tarleton escaped the enemy and obtained another horse, when, perceiving the broken state of his cavalry, occasioned by their anxiety for his safety, he ordered a retreat, to afford them an opportunity of recovering from their confusion."

Colonel Tarleton's closing adventure of the war, which did not lessen his reputation as a dashing cavalry officer, failed, as did his whole career, in establishing him any fame as a scientific soldier.

It was not until the sixth that the heavy guns were brought up, and then the utmost vigor was used to push the siege. The Count de Grasse consented to stay on the coast until the first of November, notwithstanding the detention would be greater than he at first anticipated, since it was well understood that Sir Henry Clinton would attempt to relieve the post as soon as he could procure a squadron sufficiently strong to risk a conflict with the French fleet.

Washington reported to the President of Congress, under date of October twelfth, "that the first parallel had been opened on the sixth, at night, within six hundred yards of the enemy, and under the direction of General Lincoln, both French and American troops participating in the movement. One French officer wounded, and sixteen privates killed and wounded comprised the casualties."

"On the seventh and eighth, work was advanced upon this parallel; several redoubts were established and the French mounted heavy guns at the redoubts which the British abandoned on the twenty-ninth." "On the ninth, at five o'clock in the afternoon, the American battery on the right opened with six eighteen and twenty-four pounders, two mortars and two howitzers; the French having opened fire on the left, at three o'clock, with four twelve pounders and six howitzers. This fire was directed against the embrasures, dismounting guns, destroying the hastily constructed earthworks and preparing the way for the next advance.

"On the tenth, two French batteries, one of two eighteen and twenty-four pounders and six mortars and howitzers, and the other of four eighteen pounders, opened fire, and two American batteries, one of four eighteen pounders and one of two mortars, joined in the cannonade.

"During the evening a hot shot from one of the French batteries set the frigate Charon, 44, on fire and in the morning two transports shared the same fate. The Guadaloupe and other vessels were transferred to the Gloucester shore to escape injury from shot and shell which passed over the city.

"On the eleventh, the second parallel was established within three hundred yards of the British works, with the loss of but one man killed and two or three wounded."

The condition of affairs within these works is very clearly indicated by the official reports of Lord Cornwallis, and he, of all men, was better situated to estimate the results thus far realized by the besieging forces. On the tenth he received a dispatch from Sir Henry Clinton by the hands of Major Cochran, dated " New York, September 30th," (duplicate), in cypher, which reads as follows, " I am doing everything in my power to relieve you by a direct move, and I have every reason to hope, from the assurance given me this day by Admiral Graves, that we may pass the bar by the 12th of October, if the winds permit and no unfortunate accident happens. Answer."

(*Cornwallis* to *Clinton*.) " October 11th, 1781, 12 M. In cypher. Cochran arrived yesterday. I have only to report that nothing but a direct move to York River, which includes a successful naval action, can save me. The enemy made their first parallel on the night of the sixth, at the distance of six hundred yards, and have perfected it, and constructed places of arms and batteries with great regularity and caution. On the evening of the ninth their batteries opened and have since continued firing without intermission, with about forty cannon, mostly heavy, and sixteen mortars, from eight to sixteen inches. We have lost about seventy men, and many of our works are considerably damaged; and in such works, on disadvantageous ground, against so powerful an attack, one can not hope to make a very long resistance." " P. S. October 11th, 5 P. M. Since my letter was written we have lost thirty men."

" October 12th, 7 P. M. Last night the enemy made their second parallel at the distance of three hundred yards. We continue to lose men very fast."

On the thirteenth and fourteenth the allies maintained fire from mortars, but occupied the time, chiefly, in completing the second parallel. The line of redoubts and batteries marked F. (French) had been completed, but it was essential to the completion of this parallel that the two advanced redoubts on the British left should be reduced and taken into the lines. Such had been the effect of the fire, so far as could be ascertained, that it was decided to take those by assault, and details of troops were made for the purpose.

The American light infantry, under the direction of General La Fayette, were assigned to the assault of the redoubt nearest the river, and the force was organized as follows :—Colonel Gimat's battalion led the van, followed by that of Colonel Hamilton who took command, then Colonel Laurens with eighty men, to take the redoubt in flank, and Colonel Barber's battalion, as a supporting column.

The French column, under the direction of Baron de Viomenil, was led by the German Grenadier regiment of Count William Fosbach de Deux Ponts, supported by the grenadiers of the regiment of Gatinais. This regiment had been formed out of that of Auvergne, once commanded by De Rochambeau, and once known as the *Regiment D'Auvergne sans tache*, " Auvergne, without a stain." The grenadiers were drawn up to receive their instructions and De Rochambeau, in person, pledged himself to ask of Louis XVI. the restoration of their old name if they did their duty. (The king subsequently redeemed this pledge.)

The attacks were made simultaneously, upon rocket signals, according to agreement. The redoubt nearest the river was defended by a detachment of less than sixty men. Colonel Hamilton led the men rapidly forward with unloaded muskets, climbing over abatis as best possible, and in a very short time he was over the parapet. Laurens entered from the rear, and the occupation of the work was secured in a few minutes. Colonel Gimat and Colonel Barber who came up with his reserve promptly and followed the advance, were both wounded. The American loss was one sergeant and eight privates killed, seven officers and twenty-five non-commissioned officers and privates wounded. The British loss was but eight killed, (the resistance having ceased as soon as the American troops commanded the position) and seventeen prisoners, including Major Campbell, who commanded the redoubt.

The redoubt which was assailed by the French was defended by more than a hundred men. The French sappers removed the abatis deliberately, under fire, and when a path was cleared, a steady vigorous charge with the bayonet effected the result. Count de Dumas, the Chevalier de Lameth, Adjutant-general of La Fayette, and the Count de Deux Ponts were wounded. Before the signal had been given some light words passed between the Baron de Viomenil and General La Fayette, as to the superiority of the French grenadiers for these attacks, and as soon as the Americans achieved their success, La Fayette, with prompt pleasantry, sent Major Barber to tender any needed assistance. The redoubts were taken into the second parallel before morning.

The following dispatch, in cypher, dated October 15th, 1781, is the announcement which Lord Cornwallis made to Sir Henry Clinton of this disaster:

"Sir: Last evening the enemy carried my two advanced redoubts by storm, and during the night have included these in their second parallel, which they are at present busy in perfecting. My situation has now become very critical. We dare not show a gun to their old batteries, and I expect that their new ones will open to-morrow morning, so that we shall soon be exposed to an assault in ruined works, in a bad position, and with weakened numbers. The safety of the place is therefore so precarious that I can not recommend that the fleet and army should run great risk in endeavoring to save us."

The same officer wrote on the twentieth, giving an account of a sortie made from the post, and of his attempt to rescue the chief portion of his army; and the narrative will adopt his description as more personal and impressive than that of the American officers.

(*Cornwallis* to *Clinton.*) October 20th. "A little before day broke, on the morning of the sixteenth, I ordered a sortie of about three hundred and fifty men under Lieutenant-colonel Abercrombie, to attack two batteries which appeared to be in the greatest forwardness and to spike the guns. A detachment of guards with the eightieth company of grenadiers under the command of Lieutenant-colonel Lake, attacked the one, and one of light infantry under the command of Major Armstrong commanded the other, and both succeeded in forcing the redoubts that covered them, spiking eleven guns, and killing or wounding about one hundred French troops, which had the guard of that part of the trenches, and with little loss on our side. This action proved of little public advantage, for the cannon having been spiked in a hurry, were soon rendered fit for service again, and before dark the whole parallel and batteries appeared to be nearly complete. At this time we knew that there was no part of the whole front attacked on which we could show a single gun, and our shells were nearly expended. I therefore had only to choose between preparing to surrender next day, or endeavoring to get off with the greatest part of the troops, and I determined to attempt the latter. . . . It might at least delay the enemy in the prosecution of further enterprises. Sixteen large boats were ordered to be in readiness to receive troops precisely at ten o'clock. With these I hoped to pass the infantry during the night, abandoning our baggage, and leaving a detachment to capitulate for the towns-people, and the sick and wounded, on which subject a letter was ready to be delivered to General Washington. . . . With the utmost secrecy the light infantry, greater part of the guards, and part of the Twenty-third regiment landed at Gloucester ; but at this critical moment, the weather, from being moderate and calm, changed to a most violent storm of wind and rain, and drove all of the boats, some of which had troops on board, down the river. . . . In this situation with my little force divided, the enemy's batteries opened at daybreak ; the passage between this place and Gloucester was much exposed ; but the boats being now returned, they were ordered to bring back the troops, and they joined us in the forenoon without much loss. Our works were in the meantime going to ruin. We at that time could not fire a single gun, only one eight-inch and a little more than one hundred cohorn shells remained. . . . I therefore proposed to capitulate."

At about ten o'clock of the morning of the seventeenth of October and almost at the hour when Sir Henry Clinton, with a land force of seven thousand choice troops under convoy of twenty-five ships of the line, two fifties and eight frigates were sailing down the Bay of New York to go to the relief of the worn-out garrison, a flag was sent to the American headquarters with the following note:

" Earl Cornwallis to General Washington.

" YORK, 17th October, 1781.

" SIR : I propose a cessation of hostilities for twenty-four hours and that two officers be appointed by each side, to meet at Mr. Moore's house, to settle terms for the surrender of the posts of York and Gloucester.

" I have the honor to be, etc.,

" CORNWALLIS."

General Washington to Earl Cornwallis (Reply):

" MY LORD : I have had the honor of receiving your lordship's letter of this date.

" An ardent desire to spare the further effusion of blood will readily incline me to listen to such terms for the surrender of your posts of York and Gloucester as are admissible.

" I wish, previously to the meeting of commissioners, that your lordship's proposals in writing may be sent to the American lines, for which purpose a suspension of hostilities during two hours from the delivery of this letter, will be granted.

" I have the honor to be, etc.,

" GEORGE WASHINGTON."

In accordance with this condition Earl Cornwallis submitted a proposition at half-past four in the afternoon; but its terms being too general, commissioners were appointed: the Viscount de Noailles and Lieutenant-colonel Laurens on the part of the allies, and Colonel Dundas and Major Ross on the part of the British, to define the conditions more explicitly. On the eighteenth, the articles were completed ; on the nineteenth they were signed by Cornwallis and Thomas Symonds at Yorktown, and by George Washington, Le Compte de Rochambeau and Le Compte de Barras, for himself and Compte de Grasse, " in the trenches before Yorktown, in Virginia."

At twelve o'clock, the two redoubts on the left flank of York were delivered over, one to American infantry and the other to French grenadiers.

41

At one o'clock, two works on the Gloucester side were delivered respectively to French and American troops. At two o'clock, the garrison of York marched out to the appointed place in front of the post, with shouldered arms, colors cased, drums beating a British march, grounded their arms and returned to their encampments to remain until dispatched to their several destinations in Virginia, Maryland, and Pennsylvania. At three o'clock, the garrison of Gloucester marched out, the cavalry with drawn swords, trumpets sounding and the infantry as prescribed for the garrison of York.

The land forces became prisoners to the United States, and the marine forces to the naval army of France.

The general conditions of the surrender were the same as those observed when General Lincoln surrendered Charleston during 1780.

The British troops marched to the field of ceremony with their usual steadiness, and the whole army having received an issue of new clothing, their appearance was as soldierly as if on garrison parade. When General O'Hara approached General Washington and apologized for the absence of General Cornwallis, on account of indisposition, he was referred to General Lincoln. That officer received, and as promptly returned his sword, and the troops having deposited their arms returned to the post. The absence of Earl Cornwallis has been often criticised, as if his excuse was but a sham. He was too good a soldier to dodge disagreeable duty, and the ungenerous critics might recall the months of strain to which he had been subjected, before passing censure upon one who had passed through so severe an ordeal. The subsequent courtesies which passed between himself and Washington are matters of history; and the military sagacity of Lord Cornwallis was equal to his good taste, when, in response to a toast given by General Washington, " *The British Army*," Earl Cornwallis turning to his host, thus closed—" And when the illustrious part that your Excellency has borne in this long and laborious contest becomes matter of history, fame will gather your brightest laurels rather from the banks of the Delaware than from those of the Chesapeake."

It was on the nineteenth of October, while the surrender was in progress, that Sir Henry Clinton left Sandy Hook. He made the Capes on the twenty-fourth, but returned on the twenty-ninth, when assured that the fate of the campaign was settled.

" The general return of officers and privates surrendered at Yorktown, as taken from the original muster rolls, is stated by the commissary of prisoners to have been as follows:—General and staff, 79;

artillery, 23; guards, 527; light infantry, 671; 17th regt., 245; 23d regt., 233; 33d regt., 260; 43d regt., 359; 71st regt., 300; 76th regt., 715; 80th regt., 689; two battalions of Anspach, 1077, (these two battalions alone had colonels present) Prince Hereditary, 484; Regiment of de Bose, 349; Yagers, 74; British legion, 241; Queen's Rangers, 320; North Carolina vols., 142; Pioneers, 44; Engineers, 23: Total, including commissary department and 80 followers of the army, 7,247 men: Total of officers and men, alone, 7,073; seamen and from shipping, about 900 officers and men." Other authorities increase this number to over 8,000. It is evident from this report that the record office return of August 15th, cited on page 462 and as intimated elsewhere, over-estimates the really effective force. The return of June 1st, 1782, for example, carries the "late garrison of Yorktown" into the record as 8,806 men.

Seventy-five brass guns, 69 iron guns, 18 German and six British regimental standards, were among the trophies captured.

The military chest contained £2,113 6s. sterling. The Guadaloupe, 28; the *old* Fowey, the Benetta (sloop), 24, and Vulcan, fire ship, 24; thirty transports, fifteen galleys, and many smaller vessels, with nearly nine hundred officers and seamen, were surrendered to the French.

The Benetta was placed at the disposal of Earl Cornwallis as a dispatch vessel, to be returned, or accounted for to the Count de Grasse.

The American casualties during the siege, up to the sixteenth, as recorded in Washington's Diary, were twenty-three killed, sixty-five wounded; the French, fifty-two killed, one hundred and thirty-four wounded. The British casualties were one hundred and fifty-six killed, three hundred and twenty-six wounded, and seventy missing. Major Cochran, acting aid-de-camp to Earl Cornwallis, was the only British field officer who fell during the siege.

In the letter of Earl Cornwallis of the twentieth of October there occurs the following expression as to his treatment after the surrender.

"The treatment, in general, that we have received from the enemy since our surrender, has been perfectly good and proper; but the kindness and attention that has been shown us by the French officers in particular, their delicate sensibility of our situation, their generous and pressing offer of money, both public and private, to any amount, has really gone beyond what I can possibly describe, and will, I hope, make an impression on the breast of every British officer, whenever the fortune of war should put any of them into our power."

This testimonial of Earl Cornwallis is worthy of lasting mention and is in harmony with his own generous character and conduct.

It is in this place proper to place him with Burgoyne, who, with like misfortunes, achieved a record unsurpassed, if equaled, by any other British General, for untiring, unselfish and skillful conduct under circumstances of protracted trial which no misfortune could tarnish.

From Long Island to Yorktown, even in spite of the early errors of military policy which attach to this kind of war and which were maintained by the British Cabinet, he showed himself the rival of Howe in strategic skill, of Clinton in courage, and superior to both in appreciation of the opportunities and demands of the protracted struggle. The narrative has sufficiently illustrated the difficulties of his service ; and the criticisms of Tarleton and Clinton, after the war closed, do not disclose facts to show that he had alternatives of action, in the Southern or Virginia campaigns, which afforded him any better military opportunities than those which he in each case improved to the full extent of the troops and resources at his command.

It would be unjust to General Clinton to take his own correspondence or even his own defense as explanatory of his intercourse with General Cornwallis during the Carolina and Virginia campaigns. In his vindication, which really lies in circumstances beyond his control, he rests too much upon the assumption that one of the two officers must bear the responsibility of the failures, overlooking too often the fact, that adequate support was not furnished. He had, however, in his extreme assurance of success, encouraged the British ministry, in a direction exactly in harmony with its bias and wishes, and his repeated claims for more troops induced a conviction of inefficiency. He was brave, as a soldier, but timid and uncertain in policy, and his excellence lay in execution, when the work was before him and action was the only alternative. Too much was expected of the British Generals, with the resources at their disposal, and the entire series of paper controversy seems like so many attempts to save one at another's expense, *because* there had to be a scape-goat for every unexpected military disaster.

On the date last referred to, October twentieth, 1781, General Washington closed an order of congratulation to the allied army in the following words :

" Divine service is to be performed to-morrow in the several brigades and divisions. The Commander-in-chief earnestly recommends that the troops, not on duty, should universally attend, with that seriousness of deportment and gratitude of heart which the recognition of such reiterated and astonishing interpositions of Providence demand of us."

In closing the career of these two men who have filled prominent places in the Battle narrative, so near its close, there remains only to add the single statement, that the correspondence embodied in the text is to be accepted as written in good faith by both parties, and each suffered. *The French fleet was in their way.*

Washington paid his respects in person to Count de Grasse, and various enterprises were suggested for the vigorous prosecution of the advantage already gained. The most prominent was one against Charleston. A second proposed the transportation of La Fayette to Wilmington with a mixed command of French and American troops. The inevitable delays, the lateness of the season, the heavy draught of the ships, the augmentation of the British naval forces on the North American Station, and the urgent demand for his presence in the West Indies, were among the causes which deterred the Count de Grasse from such movements and eventually suspended further propositions. On the fourth of November he left the coast, having received from Washington, Congress, and the American people, repeated acknowledgments of the services of himself and his fleet. A stand of colors and a piece of ordnance were voted to himself and Count de Rochambeau, and it "was *decreed*, that there should be a marble monument erected at Yorktown to commemorate the alliance between France and the United States and the victory achieved by their associated arms."

The Marquis de St. Simon embarked his troops October thirty-first, and sailed for the West Indies. Count de Rochambeau remained in Virginia, with headquarters at Williamsburg, until the summer, holding his command subject to orders for any required detail. He afterward returned through Philadelphia to the Hudson; thence to New England in the fall, and sailed from Boston for the West Indies early in December, 1782. His army, whether in camp or on the march, was the theme of general praise for its admirable discipline and good deportment.

General Lincoln conducted the main army to winter quarters in New Jersey and on the Hudson, and soon assumed his duties as Secretary of War; St. Clair and Wayne went south to the reinforcement of Greene, and the army was thus widely distributed at the close of this last active campaign. La Fayette seeing no prospect of active service, returned to France, bearing with him the affection of the American people, next to that with which they honored Washington. The usual relaxation of military obligation took place, increased greatly by the conviction that peace was not far distant, and the usual routine of embarrassment followed the efforts to maintain an army.

Sir Guy Carleton succeeded Sir Henry Clinton early in May, 1782, and on the seventh, he advised Washington that he had been associated with Admiral Digby in a commission to consider the terms of permanent peace.

The moderate party in England received fresh strength; the ministry succumbed to the force of the last blow. France was as eager as other nations to stop the cost and waste of war, and the siege of Yorktown eventually wrought out for the people of the United States their National Independence.

BRITISH EFFECTIVE FORCE.

NOTE.—From "Original Returns in the British Record Office." Date September 1st, 1781.

	NEW YORK	VIRGINIA	SOUTH CAROLINA
British	5932	5544	5024
German	8629	2204	1596
Provincials	2140	1137	3155
Total	16,701	8885	9775

	GEORGIA	EAST FLORIDA	WEST FLORIDA
British	—	546	374
German	486	—	558
Provincials	598	—	211
	1084	546	1143

	NOVA SCOTIA	PROVIDENCE ISLAND	BERMUDAS
British	1745	135	354
German	562	—	—
Provincials	1145	—	—
	3452	135	354

Total..................... 42,075.

TROOPS UNDER CORNWALLIS IN VIRGINIA.

NOTE. From "Original Returns in the British Record Office." Date August 1st, 1781.

British	5541	Provincials	1137
German	2148	On Detachments	607
	7689		1744

Total, 9,433.

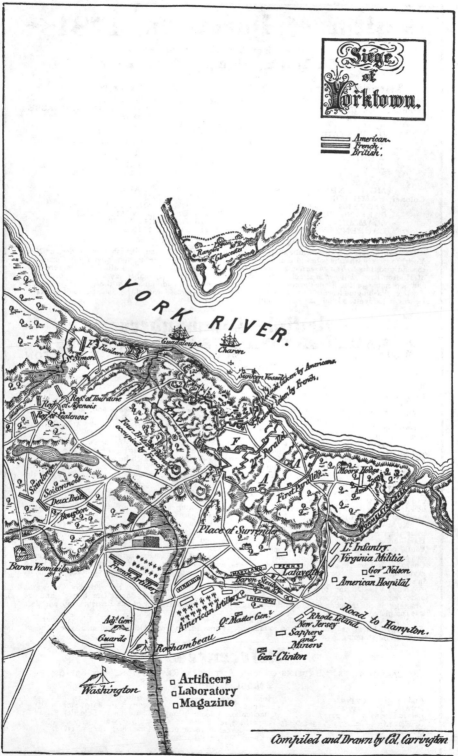

⇢Siege of Yorktown, 1781⇠

Strength of Allied Forces, 16,400
GEORGE WASHINGTON
Commander-in-Chief

American Forces	French Forces
MARQUIS DE LAFAYETTE	Lieut.-Gen. COUNT DE ROCHAMBEAU
General LINCOLN	" and Admiral COUNT DE GRASSE
" WAYNE	Admiral COUNT DE BARRAS
" KNOX	General DE BEVILLE
" DU PORTAIL	" BARON DE VIOMENIL
" BARON STEUBEN	" MARQUIS DE CHASTELLUX
" NELSON	" M. DE CHOISY
" WEEDON	Chevalier Colonel DE LAMETH
" CLINTON	Colonel COUNT DE DUMAS
" ST. CLAIR	" COUNT DE DEUX PONTS
" LAWSON	" GIMAT
" MUHLENBERG	General DUKE DE LAUZUN
Colonel HAMILTON	" DE ST. SIMON
" STEVENS LAMB	MARQUIS DE LA ROUERIE
" CARRINGTON	MARQUIS DE L. MONTMORENCI
" SCAMMEL	MARQUIS DE SAINT MAIME
" LAURENS	MARQUIS DE CUSTINE

INTRODUCTORY NOTE

Washington and Rochambeau pressed Lieut. General Clinton, British commander, at New York, so closely, that he believed that their *feints* were real movements. and called upon Cornwallis to send troops to *resist a threatened siege* of New York. August 25th. The allied armies were west of Hudson River, but *not* to attack Staten Island or New York. September 2d, the American army, and September 3d, the French army, swept swiftly through Philadelphia. On the 5th, while passing Chester, Washington learned from a courier, that Count de Grasse was off the coast.; and on the 14th, he was at Lafayette's headquarters, at Williamsburg, Va.

British Commanders
EARL CORNWALLIS, Lieut.-General
O'HARA   **SIMCOE**   **TARLETON**

Strength, 8,525

NOTE I.—Washington, asking on the 15th. for transportation for his troops, from head of Elk River, found, that Admiral de Barras had already sent ships for that purpose. On the 18th, with Rochambeau, Knox, and Du Portail, he visited De Grasse, upon his flagship, "La Ville de Paris."

NOTE II.—September 25th, the army (12,400 regulars, and 4,000 militia) concentrated, at Williamsburg; took position, within two miles of British advanced works, on the 28th and, after reconnoisance in force, on the 29th environed Yorktown. Colonel Scammel was mortally wounded; **British out-works were abandoned**. Lincoln occupied the banks of Wormley Creek, near the Moore House. (See map, for location of besieging forces).

NOTE III.—On the Gloucester side, Duke de Lauzun, with his cavalry; Weedon's Virginia militia, and 800 French marines, all under General de Choisy, held the Neck, cutting off retreat northward. **Tarleton's last exploit, was in a collision with Lauzun's dragoons, in which he was unhorsed.**

NOTE IV.—October 6th, heavy guns were brought up, and the first parallel was opened, 600 yards from the lines, under Lincoln. On the 7th and 8th, guns were mounted on the works, which the British had previously abandoned.

At 5 P. M., October 9th, the Americans, on the right, opened fire, with six 18 and 24-pounders, two mortars, two howitzers; and the French opened fire, on the left, with four 12-pounders, and six howitzers. On the 10th, two French. and two American batteries, opened fire from ten 18 and 24-pounders, and eight mortars, One hot shot burned the frigate Charon (44).

NOTE V.—October 11th, the second parallel was begun, within 300 yards. October 14th, it became necessary to silence two redoubts, next the river. A column, organized by Lafayette, with Hamilton as immediate commander, and one organized by Baron de Viomenil, with Count Deux Ponts, as immediate commander. stormed the redoubts, at one rocket signal, at night, with perfect success. Laurens supported Hamilton. and in the assault, Colonels Gimat, Barber, Count de Dumas, Chevalier de Lameth, and Count de Deux Ponts, were wounded. At left of parallel, marked F, a ravine answered for a covered approach. (It was also utilized by Colonel Poe, United States Engineer, in 1862.)

NOTE VI.—**On the 19th of October**, pursuant to articles, signed, on the 18th, by Cornwallis and Symonds, at Yorktown; and by Washington, Rochambeau, and De Barras (for himself and De Grasse), "in the trenches, before Yorktown, in Virginia." **the surrender of the British army and post was completed.**

NOTE VII.—*American* casualties, 33 killed, 65 wounded; *French*, 52 killed, 134 wounded. *British*, 156 killed, 326 wounded, and 70 missing. Force surrendered, Officers and men, 7,073, and of seamen and shipping, 900.

References:

CARRINGTON'S "BATTLES OF THE AMERICAN REVOLUTION," pp. 631–647.

School Histories:

Anderson, ¶ 114; p. 97.
Barnes, ¶ 3; p. 139-40.
Berard (Bush), ¶ 140; p. 177.
Goodrich, C. A. (Seaveys), ¶ 13-4, p. 145.
Goodrich, S. G., ¶ 4-9; p. 277-8.
Hassard, ¶ 13; p. 227.

Holmes, ¶ 13; p. 227.
Lossing. ¶ 16; p. 187-8.
Quackenbos, ¶ 400-2; p. 293-5.
Ridpath, ¶ 18; p. 226.
Sadlier (Excel), ¶ 16-18; p. 214.
Stephens, A. H. ¶ 18; p. 229.

Swinton, ¶ 4; p. 158.
Scott, ¶ 16-18; p. 216.
Thalheimer (Eclectic), ¶ 303-6; p. 175-6.
Venable, ¶ 167; p. 128-9.

CHAPTER LXXVI.

CONCLUSION.

IN the consideration of the battles and some of the associated minor operations of the war of 1775–1781, in connection with established principles which must interpret the relations and value of military facts and military conduct, there are found some incidents of the history which are very properly retouched, at the close of the narrative. While partly involved in the general notice of the " Revolutionary Epoch" and more directly suggested by the discussion of " Wars between Nations" and " Military Principles Defined," they are worthy of re-statement, as the legitimate effects of permanent causes.

General Features of the Struggle. This conflict, in the governing resistance of its authorized advocates, was Revolutionary ; and neither an Insurrection nor a simple Rebellion. It necessarily partook of elements which characterize Civil War (Chapter VI), and these elements were multiplied, exactly in proportion as the armies were too small, or too detached, to strike decisive blows in the field. Some of the partisan corps, on both sides, as with the guerilla parties during the Peninsula war in Portugal and Spain, the wars of Vendée, and at certain stages of the American civil war of 1861–5, were numerous, active and unsparing, just as they were at the time beyond the influence and control of organized troops. While skirmishing and scouting parties, which form the light troops of a regular army, are called upon to sever communications, seize and destroy depots of supplies, or otherwise disable an adversary, thereby to reduce his means of offensive action, it is however no more certain now, than it was during the period under notice, that violence to non-resisting soldiers, or citizens, and the infliction of suffering upon the defenseless people of the country where war prevails, is fatal to the best success. It is no less a violation of the rights and obligations of war itself, and repugnant to the spirit of that Christianity which admits of no war, whatever, unless to subserve righteousness and enforce peace.

The causes which, from the very inception of the conflict, seemed to force a wrong " Military Policy " upon the British Cabinet, were considered in the preliminary discussions ; and the perpetuation of that policy was interwoven with the progress of every campaign. The adoption of the views of the moderate party in England, as late as the close of Burgoyne's campaign, even at the cost of American Independence, would have secured to Great Britain a natural ally, and one well located to afford material aid to her operations in the West Indies. It might also have averted the European Coalition which drew inspiration, if not its existence, from the prolonged struggle in America. The progress of all attempts at reconciliation was attended by the assumption, that an unprincipled and groundless rebellion, impelled by an original purpose to obtain national independence, was the kind of opposition which was to be reduced to terms. This failure to appreciate the real character of the issue between Great Britain and the Colonies, involved, at the very outset, a failure to furnish adequate means for the prosecution of the war ; and the error grew more and more glaring, as the pressure from other adversaries made it impossible to supplement the defect. This error was recip- rocated by the American people. Their conduct of the war during each successive campaign is clearly indicative of a failure to adopt an energetic Military Policy, which alone promised early success. Its neglect involved nearly seven years of struggle and more than eight years of unrest and waste. The pressure of an emergency would indeed, now and then, arouse a feverish, popular response ; but when the danger passed by, relaxation ensued ; and then—a series of uncertainties, fluctuations and disasters, just at times, when exhaustive measures were vital to success. That multiplication of miseries, which were often related to mere hunger, cold, or want of money, had its germ in this lack of conscious obligation to devote *all available appliances to the quickest possible destruction of the Brit-ish army*.

There were natural causes for this state of affairs. The jealousy of central authority which individualized states, extended its enfee- bling influence to communities even smaller than states. Local and sectional prejudices were hardly less destructive, through their para- lyzing force, than British armies were in the operations of the field.

The letters of General Greene, embodied in a statement of the true conditions to permanent success, as cited on page 85, are expressive of the true military policy which belonged to the colonies at the beginning of the war.

It is impossible to examine the narrative, condensed as it is, without the conviction that a thorough coöperation of the colonies in the effort to raise a national army, irrespective of local dangers, would have lessened those dangers and would have diminished the cost and shortened the duration of the war. From the many documents, muster-rolls and official statements which have been cited, it appears that there were several occasions when the prompt support of the American army would have achieved victory; and it is equally true that the British army repeatedly had as good assurance of success, but for its over-estimate of the American forces in the field. And yet in proportion as the British forces diminished, or withheld the offensive, so did their opponents seem impatient of further sacrifice; and the constant fluctuations of the American army, together with great scarcity of army supplies, as well as of money, made the opening and close of every campaign to appear as if a single bold stroke of the British troops must end the struggle.

Even when the fall of Yorktown drew near, the effective strength of Washington's army at the north was less than that of the combined French armies of Rochambeau and St. Simon, and was not superior to the army of Cornwallis itself in respect of numbers.

The apprehensions of La Fayette and of the French Minister of Finance, that the Americans would depend too implicitly upon external aid, and would fail to meet a corresponding responsibility, were partially confirmed; and the occasional complaint that the French army and navy did no more, was largely based upon a consciousness of inadequate home effort, and the fatigue experienced under the pressure of protracted struggle.

The reluctance of States to waive leadership and recognize one permanent responsibility, which impaired the efficiency of military action early in the war, was followed by extreme jealousy of a well organized and highly disciplined army. Because Bunker Hill expressed the capacity of true valor to resist efficiently, under favoring opportunity, it did not follow that the fresh regiments of Stark, Chester, Prescott, or Christopher Greene were, man for man, in open field, the fighting peers of the British Fifth, Thirty-eighth, and Forty-second regiments which withered under their fire. The warnings, appeals and protests of Washington were even more earnest for disciplined men than for food or clothing. He knew well that money and supplies would follow success ; and he knew just as well that the people would have confidence in an army only in the proportion that strict discipline, exact accountability, and fitness to sustain the struggle would give the pledge of an earnest purpose to finish the war. The patriotism which endured starvation and exposure at Valley Forge and Morristown had its strength in the discipline attained ; because a conscious fitness for duty inspired pride and courage, while the true patriot was willing to undergo the proper training which would give to his energies the best capacity to achieve.

With this brief resume of the errors and shortcomings of both Great Britain and the American Republic in the direction of Military Policy, there is involved another class of considerations which inspire awe, and unmistakably declare the true Philosophy of the American struggle for National Independence.

The *former* regarded the effectual resistance of the colonies to be just as impossible as King Pharaoh of Egypt believed the persistent demands of the greatest patriotic leader of ancient times to be absurd, and innocent of danger to his ancestral rights and royal prerogative.

The *latter*, in their long protracted importunity for satisfaction, equality and peace, besought, then resisted, struggled on, and still resisted, until the purpose to be emancipated became a part of the inner life. It was at the hearth-stone as well as in the skirmish. It was before the domestic altar, as well as in the tent or barracks. The hands of women wrought in silence and in tears, while their husbands fought the battle amid tumult and carnage. It was with all childish sports until mimic war gave precocious vigor to youth, and boys took part in a conflict with men. But as from year to year, deliverance ever beckoned forward, only to recede, campaign after campaign, and still there was hope, and with it progress ; the American people did not even then anticipate the great duration of that wearisome struggle, any more than the Hebrew militia forecast their forty years of tiresome marchings in pursuit of independence and peace. It was well they did not. Great Britain was blind to operations of the laws which gave her *her* liberty. America was blind to the cost of rescuing *imperiled* liberty. The blindness of the one withheld the force. The blindness of the other supplied the faith.

The Chariot of the Ruler of the Universe rode through and over the theatre of war. *These* on the one side were stayed, and *these* on the other side were encouraged. The weakness of physical might and power in a moral struggle, was made to exalt the emotional and the spiritual, and to vindicate man, by the interposition of his Maker.

Bad Military Policy, as a matter of human science, made the war of 1775–1781 long and costly. Infinite wisdom ordained for both parties an independent prosperity, a higher mission among the nations.

Thus while " Military Science is the key to military history," there is an inner realm of unseen cause which the key of Providence alone controls, and that nation which has the sublimer faith will gather the fruit of peace, while others languish in the pursuit through the endless issues of controversy and blood.

There is still another lesson to be drawn from this narrative, and one which the very weakness of the American army at that period has made impressive for all time, and that is, the ultimate dependence of all nations upon moral convictions, for the vindication of either personal or national liberty. Under the " Apology for the Art of War," the necessity for standing armies was made manifest. Under the review of the American Revolution, the capacity of a people led by a small army has been demonstrated. It is a confirmation of the general principles with which the narrative opened ; and an encouragement to all nations that there is to be a time when the administration of civil law alone will require physical force ; and when the superior obligation of equal justice will alike end armaments and armies.

With this inevitable side drift which carries military policy into all the responsibilities of a national life, there is a necessary recurrence to other elements of the war under notice.

The *Strategy of the war of* 1775–81 is best appreciated by examination and application of the principles heretofore stated. Their repetition is not required. That the location of the American headquarters in New Jersey and on the Hudson, admitted of *all possible strategic combinations* and contingencies which were involved in movements of British troops from Canada, New York, or by the Chesapeake, is evident from the readiness with which such enterprises were met and foiled ; and it is equally evident that the so-called Fabian policy of Washington was based upon the conviction that a true strategic policy would be adopted on the part of the British Cabinet, and *that was* to destroy his army, and let cities, districts, and provinces fall through the want of compact, sufficient and disciplined defenders. The narrative affords the facts by which to judge of the skill employed in the direction of strategy. The example cited suggests the direction of inquiry.

The Logistics of the American army were embarrassed by the great extent of the country, its forests and mountains, its river courses, and marshes, and its widely diffused population. These elements did not alone delay the transportation and concentration of troops, but the productive lands were unequally worked, and in some sections there would be no surplus, and no ready means of accumulating supplies from other sections more densely peopled or under more general culture.

The British troops availed themselves of the advantages which the control of the navigable waters and an organized commissariat supplied, backed by the power of a great empire. But the waste in handling supplies and the misconduct of officials were not exclusively confined to the Americans, who were inexperienced, and therefore improvident. Similar complaints were made of British officials. That class of supplies which was taken by partisan corps on either side was seldom carefully accounted for: but this neglect is largely incident to that kind of military service. The repeated statements of General Washington as to the prevalence of venality, corruption, and malfeasance in office, were applied more directly to the general condition of the country, and largely to the operations of detached state, and other public agencies, and very seldom to the army which had become disciplined and reorganized under responsible control. The opportunities for fraud in the department of logistics, were then, as always, more numerous than in any other, and charges of misconduct in the matter of contracts, for example, were as frequent then as in later times. General Greene was well abused while quartermaster-general, but his vindication was complete.

In Grand Tactics, as well as in other subdivisions of the Art of War, the introductory chapters specified leading illustrations, which are afterwards more fully drawn out in detail. While the American regulars and all really experienced militia displayed steadiness as well as courage, equal to that of their adversaries, the war illustrated a fact which has been a reflection upon its conduct, but is common to all wars, that no troops are exempt from a liability to panic and sudden disaster. At Hobkirk's Hill, an American regiment which had distinguished itself at the Cowpens, lost the battle by perfectly unnecessary misconduct; and at Eutaw Springs the British Sixty-third and Sixty-fourth, veterans, after a too hasty advance, meeting unexpected resistance, gave way in equal disorder. Washington, even at the risk of his life, could not halt the flying regiments of Parsons' brigade (page 226,) during the retreat from New York; but saved his army at Monmouth, by turning fugitives immediately upon their pursuers. This instance illustrates nearly all similar fights. Discipline *tends to avert* panic; but when self-possession is lost, it is the *invisible* and undetermined danger which takes away the breath, and then a shadow or a fancy, will whirl away the very men who would face any foe they could see and measure. The great defect of the American continental system was the constantly changing army basis, and this was the cause of nearly all tactical failures which were not incident to the ordinary operations of every war.

Reference is particularly made to Chapters IX–XIII. inclusive, for the laws by which the conduct of the war of 1775–1781, no less than of all wars, is to be tested.

Strength of Armies. The official records already cited show that the British force never exceeded about forty thousand men at any period, and this included the troops in Canada and Florida, as well as at the Bahama Islands, and was not until 1782. The *American* army, after 1776, never equaled thirty-eight thousand regulars at a single time. It is customary to give a great excess of force to the latter. The people at large constituted a nominal militia of the nature of a *posse comitatus*—minute men—coming at call, and dissolving as quickly. They were not a proper army. They did indeed check forays, and afford temporary garrisons; but the smaller the army, and the greater the number of these isolated, transient detachments, the longer was the struggle, and the more wearing, as well as more unsatisfactory was every local result.

The usual tabular statement of the forces of the United States which served at different periods during the war, is to be considered as a total of recorded years of enlistment, and not as the total of the men who served. Hence a man who served from April nineteenth, 1775, until the formal cessation of hostilities, April nineteenth, 1783, *counted as eight*, in the aggregate.

The following table gives the contributions of the various States to the Continental service, on the basis stated:

New Hampshire	12,497	Delaware	2,386
Massachusetts	69,907	Maryland	13,912
Rhode Island	5,908	Virginia	26,678
Connecticut	31,939	North Carolina	7,263
New York	17,781	South Carolina	6,417
New Jersey	10,726	Georgia	2,679
Pennsylvania	25,678		
		Total,	233,771

The British and American armies were alike limited in their ability to concentrate their forces. A reference to the map "Outlines of Atlantic Coast," furnishes a key to this difficulty.

Washington controlled an interior line while at Middlebrook and Morristown, which nearly doubled both his offensive and defensive capacity; and the British fleets would have been compensated for the American line of land-march through Virginia and the Carolinas, if the uncertainties of the sea and the inadequate garrison at New York had not cost them nearly as much delay as embarrassed the Americans in crossing the rivers and rough country of the States referred to.

Naval Co-operation. Under the head of " Providence in war illustrated," the contingencies of maritime movements were adverted to, and the narrative has shown that a fleet of transports rarely ventured even from New York to Newport without a delay which defeated the enterprise on foot. The British owed their chief success at the south to their control of the sea ; and Yorktown fell as soon as the remarkably successful voyage of the Count de Grasse snatched away that supremacy in the Chesapeake. The American navy had been organized with fair promise. The names and armaments of the principal ships, either built or authorized to be built under the sanction of Congress, have been given in their order as they were authorized. That they accomplished very little as a navy is involved in the general statement of a British naval blockade and an almost undisputed naval superiority. At Newport, New Bedford, Philadelphia, Charleston, Savannah and other ports, most of these vessels were burned or sunk, almost before they had spread canvas. At the outset of the war, seamen and good ship-builders abounded ; but heavy guns were not ready when the ships were, and the success of privateering, which gave to vessels of speed and light draught the best chance for prize money, soon reduced the number of men from whom to make good sailors. The protracted blockade of Newport, the expeditions along the coast, and the incursions which threatened the homes of seafaring men had a similar tendency.

The Randolph, 32, Captain Biddle, one of the first vessels put in commission, blew up at sea during a night action, but her commander escaped. The adventures of Captains Biddle, John Paul Jones, Hopkins, Barry, and others, are creditable to their memory; but the main fact remains, that while the American army, in 1781, was less than half its force during the early years of the war, the navy had but two really efficient ships, that survived the casualties of the contest.

(Reference is made to note on page 144, close of Chapter XXII., for the career of the American navy.)

Foreign Officers. During the early efforts to interest France in behalf of the American cause, Mr. Silas Deane had induced many European officers to visit America under promise of commissions. The jealousy of this movement was so great that even General Greene at one time tendered his resignation, and was sharply rebuked by Congress for interference with its prerogative. Many failed to realize the purpose of their visit—others failed to merit the appointments received, and still others, of those whose names have appeared in this narrative, were an honor to the service. The names of Steuben, De Kalb, Kosciusko, Pulaski, Duplessis, Du Portail, Armand, Fleury, Gimat and others, are associated with honorable mention, while the extraordinary career of the youthful La Fayette is so suggestive of the success of the French alliance, that if his earnest promptings had not sent him early to America, it does not appear how that alliance could have been so completely and successfully maintained under circumstances which repeatedly threatened its rupture.

Military Changes. Generals Gage, Howe and Clinton, in successive general command, Generals Burgoyne, Rawdon and Cornwallis, each in turn made prisoners of war, have been remembered, and their record, with that of Burgoyne, Knyphausen, Donop, Rahl, and scores of others, has been inspired by the motto with which these pages invited notice, " *Justitia et præterea nil.*"

If few traditions of the camp, or field, have enlivened this history neither has the intrusion of social gossip been needlessly interposed to impair the value of the acts of soldiers. The changes which the war wrought among the British characters who represented the prowess and glory of England, were shared by the leaders of the armies of the United States. Few of the early commanders took part in the closing scenes of the war. Schuyler, Sullivan, Varnum, Spencer and others were in the halls of legislation. The earnest and patriotic Putnam, who had so persistently labored to have a second fight, on Bunker Hill, on the memorable 17th of June, 1775, had retired from the service. Wayne and St. Clair joined Greene in the Southern department immediately after the surrender of Cornwallis. Muhlenberg, promoted Major-general, retired to his farm in Pennsylvania. Lincoln, as elsewhere stated, became Secretary of War. Knox, also promoted, who had followed the fortunes of Washington from Boston in 1775, to Yorktown in 1781, afterward succeeded Lincoln as

Secretary of War, and on the twenty-fifth of August, 1783, received from Sir Guy Carleton, the successor of Sir Henry Clinton, the surrender of New York. Joseph Reed, first Colonel, then aid-de-camp, then tendered promotion, and then Adjutant-general, had resigned his commission as early as 1777, but as a member of Congress, or as Governor of Pennsylvania, he made his military association with Washington to enure to the well-being of the army. Of Governors Nelson and Clinton, and others, who combined high social position with great military zeal, and of subordinate officers throughout the north and south, there is allowed no further mention than that already afforded.

This battle record has drawn to its support many interpreting facts which invite, yet exclude, a departure into the field of general history. Individuals only take their place, as links in a necessary chain, and their biography is so clipped as simply to fill the space which defines the principal battles of the war.

If this venture shall inspire fresh interest in the "*principles which underlie national defense*," in the spirit of its dedication, and shall command respect for the valor which applied the Science of War to the Battles of the American Revolution, it will have accomplished its purpose.

Great Britain and the United States, politically separated by that war, have so developed their national life through the arts of peace, that the ocean is no serious restriction upon their intercourse, and America, once the child, then the servant, then of mature age, now competes in honorable emulation, for an equal place among the nations.

There were foreflashings of the future, even during the years of struggle; and few gathered the rays with more prophetic skill than Governor Pownall. In the year 1757 he had been the royal Governor of the Colony of Massachusetts. Its industries and its resources, its warfares, privations and sacrifices, its marvellous endurance under the strain of cold, famine and Indian incursions, and its elasticity where opportunity gave play to its real powers, had wrought into his very soul a recognition of the straight and narrow path by which such a people must rise to power. In writing of the New World, during January, 1780, he thus unfolds his views:

" Nature hath removed her (America) far from the Old World and all its embroiling interests and wrangling politics; without an enemy or a rival, or the entanglement of alliances. This new system has taken its equal station with the nations upon earth. Negotiations are of no consequence either to the right or the fact. The Independence of America is fixed as fate. . . . The government of the new empire of America is liable indeed to many disorders; but it is young and strong, and will struggle, by the vigor of internal, healing principles of life, against those evils, and surmount them. In North America the civilizing activity of the human race forms the growth of the State; we see all the inhabitants not only free, but allowing our universal naturalization to all who wish to be so. In a country like this, where every man has the full and free exertion of his powers, an unabated application and a perpetual struggle sharpens the wits and gives constant training to the mind. . . . In agriculture and in mechanic handicrafts, the New World hath been led to many improvements of implements, tools and machines—leading experience by the hand to many a new invention. This spirit of thus analyzing the mechanic powers hath established a kind of instauration of science in their hands. The settlers find fragments of time in which they make most of the articles of personal wear and household use, for home consumption. *Here,* no laws frame conditions on which a man is to exercise this or that trade. *Here,* no laws lock him up in that trade; and many a real philosopher, a politician, a warrior, emerges out of this wilderness, as the seed rises out of the ground where it hath lain buried for its season."

With a peculiar forecast as to the necessary unity of the new States, then held together by so weak a band, this writer proceeds: "*The nature of the coast and of the winds, render navigation a perpetually moving intercourse of communication; and the waters of the rivers render inland navigation but a further process of that communication:* all which becomes, as it were, one vital principle of life, extending through one organized being—*one nation.* Will that most enterprising spirit be stopped at Cape Horn; or, not pass beyond the Cape of Good Hope? Before long they will be found trading in the South Sea, in Spice Islands, and in China. Commerce will open the door to emigration. By constant inter-communication America will every day approach nearer and nearer to Europe."

"North America has become a new primary planet, which, while it takes its own course in its own orbit, must shift the common centre of gravity."

If such were the anticipations of good for America and the world from the separate nationality of Great Britain and the United States, when seen only through the eye of faith, during a critical period of the war of 1775–81, there is infinitely more of hope for the nations in the assurance that all the progress then foreshadowed has strengthened the kindly relations of America and the mother country, and the lessons of the war may be gladly recalled as so many fresh incentives to a perpetual peace.

The war of 1775–1781, however, did not end without a similar aspiration for the future, as a part of that official act by which the American Commander-in-chief announced its approaching close; and at Meridian, July 4th, in the year of our Lord one thousand eight hundred and seventy-six, while all civilized nations are represented as the guests of America, to honor her industry, and rejoice in her liberty; thus in the fraternity of that intercourse to relax all bonds but those of concord, and thus to renew their obligations to Righteousness, which alone exalteth a nation; and while the hall which a century ago was the birthplace of the Republic, only a century later has become the scene of august ceremonies, in which the nations bear part, to exchange greetings and pledge fellowship for the welfare of man, in the spirit of a broad humanity, it is not ill-suited, that the closing sentiment of a memorial record of that struggle should adopt the last military order of the struggle itself.

" HEADQUARTERS, April 18, 1783.

"The Commander-in-chief orders the cessation of hostilities between the United States of America and the King of Great Britain to be publicly proclaimed to-morrow at twelve at the New Building: and that the proclamation, which will be communicated herewith, be read to-morrow morning at the head of every regiment and corps of the army: after which, the Chaplains with the several brigades, will render thanks to Almighty God for all his mercies, particularly for his overruling the wrath of man to His own glory, and causing the rage of war to cease among the nations.

On such a happy day which is the harbinger of peace, a day which completes the eighth year of the war, it would be ingratitude not to rejoice, it would be insensibility not to participate, in the general felicity.

HAPPY, THRICE HAPPY, *shall they be pronounced hereafter, who have contributed anything, who have performed the meanest office in erecting this stupendous fabric of freedom and empire on the broad basis of independency, who have assisted in protecting the rights of human nature, and establishing an asylum for the poor and oppressed of all nations and religions."*

BIBLIOGRAPHICAL TABLE.

I N stating the principal authorities consulted, it is agreeable to acknowl-
edge facilities furnished by gentlemen in charge of *private* libraries
abroad, especially Thomas Hughes, Q. C.; J. C. Webster, Esq., Secretary
Athenæum Club; Colonel Charles C. Chesney, R. E; Secretary Captain
Douglass Galton, British Sci. Asso.; Secretary H. W. Bates, Esq., R. Geog.
Socy.; Sir T. Duffus Hardy, Colonel H. W. Deedes, A. D. C., and William
Blackmore, Esq. of London; Professors Rolleston and Smith, of Oxford;
Professor Archer, of Edinburgh; Sir William Thompson and Professors
Young and Thompson, of Glasgow; Vice President Andrews, of Queens
College, Belfast; Professor Leslie and Steward Hingston, of Trinity College,
Dublin.

The courtesies of the Athenæum, Athenæum Junior, United Service,
United Service Junior, the Army and Navy and other London clubs opened
valuable libraries and are gratefully remembered.

The cordial aid of Adjutant-general William Stryker, of New Jersey, in
the settlement of facts and names in connection with the war history of that
State has been appreciated.

(Quotations cited are given as written by the Authors referred to.)

REFERENCES.

[English Titles are retained for French or German reprints.]

A.

ADAMS ; Life and Works of John Adams.
Adolphus' Hist. of Great Britain and Geo. III.
Allen's (Ira) Vermont.
Allen's (Ethan) Narrative.
Almon's Remembrancer.
American Archives.
"   Orderly Books.
Andrews' History of the Wars of England, 1775—1783.
"   History of the War with America. 4 vols. London. 1785.
Annual Register, 1774—1784.
Army Returns, American.
"   "   British.
Auburey's Travels.

B.

BAILEY'S Records of Patriotism.
Bancroft's History of the United States.
Barber's and Hoover's Historical Collections New York.
"   Historical Collections, Mass.
"   "   "   Conn.
"   History of New Haven.
Bartlett's History of America.
Barstow's History of New Hampshire.
Bradford's Massachusetts.
Belknap's New Hampshire.
Bell's (Andrew), Journal, (Monmouth).
Benton's Herkimer County.
Bolton's History of Westchester County.
Botta's (M.) American Revolution.
Boone's Narrative.
Butler's History of the United States.
"   "   "   Kentucky.
Burgoyne's Letters.
"   Narrative and Documents.

C.

CALDWELL'S Greene.
Camp Fires of the Revolution.
Campbell's Annals of Tryon County, N. Y.
"   Border Warfare.
"   Virginia.
Campaign of the Naval Army under Count De Grasse.
Cassell's illustrated History of England.
Chapman's Wyoming.
Chastellux, Count de, Visit to America.
Clark's (Joseph) Diary.
"   (John) Narrative of Battle of Bunker Hill.
Clark's Naval History.
Caulkin's (Miss) History of New London.
Cleveland's Greenwood.
Collins' Sketches of Kentucky.
"   New Jersey Gazette.
Civil War in America.
Cooper's Naval History.
"   Chronicles of Cooperstown.
Connecticut Gazette.
Cornwallis' Answer to Clinton.

D.

DAWSON'S Battles of the United States by Sea and Land.
Day's Historical Collections of Pennsylvania.
De Bermere's Narrative.
De Haas' American Revolution.
Duer's Lord Stirling.
Dufour's Principles of Grand Strategy and Tactics.
Dunlap's New York.

E.

EAGER'S History of Orange County, N. Y.

Ellet's (Mrs.) Domestic History of American Revolution.
Ellet's (Mrs.) Women of the Revolution.
Encyclopedias, Biog. and general.

F.

FARMER and Moore's Historical Collections of New Hampshire.
Franklin's Life and Writings.
Filson's Kentucky.
Felton's (John) Reflections, or History of Battle of Bunker Hill.
Force's American Archives.
Forrest's Sketches of Norfolk and Vicinity.
Frothingham's Siege of Boston.

G.

GAGE'S (General) Official Returns.
Gaines' New York Gazette and Mercury.
Galloway's Letters to a Nobleman.
    "   Reflections on the American Revolution.
Galloway's Reply to William Howe's Observations.
Gardiner's Anecdotes of the Revolution.
Gentleman's Magazine.
Graham's Life of Morgan.
    "   History of America, Vol. IV.
Graydon's Memoirs.
Girardine's Virginia.
Green's (G. W.) German Element in the Revolutionary War.
Green's Life of Greene.
Gordon's History of New Jersey.
    "   "   " American Independence.

H.

HALLECK's International Law.
Hall's (Lieut.) Civil War.
Hamilton's Works, by Hamilton.
Hamley's (Colonel) Operations of War.
Hazard's Register of Pennsylvania.
Headley's Washington and his Generals.
Heath's Memoirs.
Hempstead's (Lieut.) Narrative.
Hildreth's History of the United States.
Hinman's Connecticut in the Revolution.
Hinton's History of the United States.
History of the Civil War.
Hollister's Connecticut.
Holmes' Annals.
Holt's New York Gazette.
Homan's History of Boston.
Howe's (Sir William) Narrative.
    "   Historical Collections of Virginia.
House of Commons, Proceedings.

Howland (John), Life and Recollections of.
Habley's History of the American Revolution.
Hughes' History of England.
Hutchinson's Massachusetts.
Humphreys' Putnam.

I.

IMPARTIAL History of the American War (Dublin.) (Anonymous.)
Irving's Life of Washington.

J.

Johnson's Life of Greene.
    "   Traditions of the Revolution.
    "   History of Salem, N. J.
Jomini's Art of War.
    "   Life of Napoleon.
    "   Grand Military Campaigns.

K.

KNIGHT's History of England.

L.

LA FAYETTE's Memoirs and Correspondence.
Lamb, (General) Leaks' Life of.
    "   (Sergeant), Journal of Occurrences.
Lee's Memoirs of the War.
Lee (Charles), Memoirs and Correspondence.
    "   Proceedings of General Court Martial.
    "   (Lieut.-Col.) Memoirs of.
    "   (Genl. H.)   "   "
Lee's Campaign of 1778.
Lodges' Portraits of illustrious personages, vol 8.
Lossing's Field Book of the Revolution.
    "   Washington and the Republic.
    "   Life of Schuyler.
    "   Centennial History of America.

M.

MAHAN's (Lord) History of England.
Manuscript Letters and Reports at London and Paris.
Marshall's Washington.
    "   Kentucky.
Martin's North Carolina.
Massachusetts, Committee of Safety Documents.
Maxwell's (Virginia) Historical Register.
Memoirs of New York Historical Society.
Mills' Statistics.
Memoirs of the Court of George III., Dukes of Buckingham and Chandos.
Miner's Wyoming.
Morris' (Robert) Diary
Moore's (George H.) Treason of General Lee.

Moore's Diary of the American Revolution.
Moultrie's Memoirs.
Muhlenberg, Life of.
Murray's Elizabethtown.
" (Rev. James), History of the War.
Murray's Impartial History of the War in America. 2 vols. Newcastle. 1782.
Maps of Authors Consulted.
" " British Museum, London.
" " " Officers and Engineers.
" " Bibliothèque Nationale, Paris.
" " Congressional Library, Washington.
" " U. S. Coast Survey.
" " U. S. Engineer Corps.
" " New York Historical Society, N. Y.
" " Pennsylvania Historical Society, Philadelphia.
" " Public Record Office, London.
" " Royal Ethnological Society, London.
" " Royal Geographical Society, London.
" " National Geographical Society Paris.
" " Washington's Head Quarters, Morristown, N. J.

N.

NEILSON's Campaign of Burgoyne.
New York, Documentary History of.
New Jersey, Revolutionary Correspondence.
New Hampshire, Historical Society Collections.
North American Pilot.

O.

ONDERDONK's Kings County.
" Queens "
" Suffolk "
Orations of Webster, Everett, King and others in honor of men and battles.

P.

PARLIAMENTARY Register.
Palmer's History of Lake Champlain.
Paris Gazette, 1780, Survey of Procceedings. Summary of Operations.
Pennsylvania Archives.
" Ledger.
" Packet.
Peterson's Rhode Island.
Peck's Wyoming.
Pictorial History of George III.
Provincial Convention of New York, Minutes of.
Proceedings of New Jersey Historical Society.
Putnam (General), Life of.
Public Record Office, London, Official Papers.

R.

RAMSEY's American Revolution.
" Revolution of South Carolina.
" Life of Washington.
Randall's Jefferson.
Rankin's History of France.
Raynal (Abbé) American Revolution.
" " Letters upon North American Affairs.
Reed's (Wm. B.) Life of Joseph Reed.
Riedesel's (Baron) Military Memoirs.
" (Baroness) Memoirs.
Ripley's Fight at Concord.
Rivington's Royal Gazette, N. Y.

S.

SAFFEL's Records of the Revolutionary War.
Sparks" Biographies.
" Life and Treason of Arnold.
" Washington.
" Writings of Washington.
" Life and Writings of Franklin.
Scott's Military Dictionary.
Shattock's Concord.
St. Clair's Narrative.
Stedman's American War.
Sedgwick's Life of Livingston.
St. Leger's Account of Occurrences.
Simcoe's Journal of the Operations of the Queen's Rangers.
Simms' Diary.
" South Carolina.
" Schoharie County, N. Y
Stone's Life of Brandt.
" Tryon County.
" Wyoming.

T.

TARBOX's (J. N.) Life of General Putnam.
Tarleton's Narrative and Campaign of 1780–1781.
Transactions of Historical Societies of N.Y., N. J., Penn. and other States—so far as published.
Thatcher's Military Journal.
Tome's Battles by Land and Sea.
Thompson's Long Island.
Trumbull's Autobiography.
" History of Connecticut.

V.

VAN CAMPEN (Major), Life of.

W.

WALTER's History of England and Sketches of New Jersey.

Warren's (Mrs.) American Revolution.
Ward's (S.) Battles of Long Island.
Washington's Diary.
Wheaton's International Law.
Wheeler's North Carolina.
Weems' Washington.
    "   and Horry's Marion.
Whitehead's Early History and Sketches of New Jersey.
Whiteley's Revolutionary History of Delaware.
White's Historical Collections of Georgia.
Wither's Chronicles of the Border.

Wilkinson's Memoirs.
Willett's Narrative.
Williams' Vermont.
    "   (Colonel Otho) Narrative.
White's Statistics of Georgia.
Woolsey's International Law.
Williamson's History of Maine.
Wraxhall's Historical Memoirs.
Writings of Thomas Jefferson.

Y.

Younge's History of the British Navy.

CHRONOLOGICAL AND GENERAL INDEX.

———— ◆·◆ ————

I N furnishing a Reference Index, the birth, *b*, and death, *d*, of some of the characters
referred to in the Narrative, have been indicated, as suggestive of their age at the date
of particular service, or opinion.

The subsequent verdict of contemporaries has also been indicated in some instances ; as
Cornwallis, *sub* Govr. Genl. of India ; Monroe, *sub*, Pres. U. S. A.

Am. (American), *Br.* (British), *Fr.* (French), *H.* (Hessian), distinguish officers of similar
name and rank.

The omission of names, sometimes associated with service in leading battles, is in accordance with official reports or real fact. Thus Lord Percy is not named by General Clinton
in his very minute report, as associated with the attack upon Fort Clinton ; and Colonel
Haslet (Delaware) was member of a Court Martial at New York, while his regiment was in
battle on Long Island. Brigades were often commanded by Colonels, so that *personal*
brigades, (as Hitchcock's Brigade) do not indicate the rank. On the other hand, personal
regiments participated in action during the absence of their colonel, who commanded a
brigade or division. The rule in the British army is given on page 171. There is a frequent use of titles, which were those of militia rank. The historical identity of the men is
thus preserved, although they were not in the Continental service proper.

Christian names are given, when required to distinguish two of similar name.

Many names are given, in order to maintain due harmony with general history, and
because they interlink family associations which are cherished on both sides of the ocean.
The skeleton of battle operations would be barren without these associations, even although
the battles themselves were shaped by others, of more prominent responsibility.

Abbreviations, *k.* (killed), *w.* (wounded), *pris.* (taken prisoner), *com.* commissioner.

P.

NOTE.

RUTLEDGE, JOHN, was nominated, but not confirmed, by the United States Senate, a Chief Justice of the United States Supreme Court.

In Memoriam.

CHESNEY, CHARLES C. (Br.), Royal Engineers, deceased after the Biographical Table went to press. His reputation deserves permanent honor.